D1234345

Lyman C Draper

KING'S MOUNTAIN

AND

ITS HEROES:

HISTORY OF THE

BATTLE OF KING'S MOUNTAIN,

OCTOBER 7TH, 1780,

AND THE

EVENTS WHICH LED TO IT,

BY

LYMAN C. DRAPER, LL. D.,

Secretary of the State Historical Society of Wisconsin, and member of various Historical and Antiquarian Societies of the Country.

WITH STEEL PORTRAITS, MAPS, AND PLANS.

GENEALOGICAL PUBLISHING CO., INC.
BALTIMORE   1974

Originally Published
Cincinnati, 1881

Reprinted
Genealogical Publishing Co., Inc.
Baltimore, 1967

Reissued
Baltimore, 1971

Baltimore, 1974

Library of Congress Catalogue Card Number 67-28623
International Standard Book Number 0-8063-0097-3

Made in the United States of America

INTRODUCTION.

WITH the siege and fall of Charleston, early in 1780, the rude shocks of war were transferred from the Northern and Middle States to the Carolinas and Georgia. Gates, the victor of Saratoga, was sent to command the Southern army; but his lucky star failed him, and he was disastrously routed near Camden, and the gallant Sumter shortly after surprised at Fishing Creek. Gloom and dismay overspread the whole Southern country. Detachments from the victorious British army were scattered throughout the settlements; and the rebellious Colonies of the Carolinas and Georgia were reported to the Home Government as completely humiliated and subdued. Ferguson, one of the ablest of the Royal commanders, was operating on the western borders of the Carolinas, enticing the younger men to his standard, and drilling them for the Royal service.

At this gloomy period, when the cause of Liberty seemed prostrate and hopeless in the South, the Whig border leaders, Campbell, Shelby, Sevier, Cleveland, Lacey, Williams, McDowell, Winston, Hambright, Hawthorn, Brandon, Chronicle, Hammond, and their compeers, marshalled their clans, united their forces, overwhelming Ferguson and his motley followers, crushing out all Tory opposition, and making the name of *King's Mountain* famous in our country's history. This remarkable and fortunate battle deserves a full and faithful record. The story of its heroes has in it much to remind us of an epic or a romance. They were a remarkable race of men, and played no inconsiderable a part in the long and sanguinary struggle for American Independence. Reared on the outskirts of civilization, they were early inured to privations and hardships, and when they went upon the "warpath," they often obtained their commissaries' supplies from the wild woods and mountain streams of the region where they carried on their successful operations.

As early as 1839, the collection of materials was commenced for this work. Three of the lingering survivors of King's Mountain were visited by the writer of this volume, and their varied recollections noted down—James Sevier, of Tennessee, John Spelts and Silas McBee, of Mississippi ; and Benjamin Sharp, of Missouri, and William Snodgrass, of Tennessee, were reached by correspondence.

The gathering at King's Mountain in 1815, to collect and re-inter the scattered remains of those who fell in the conflict was limited in attendance. In 1855, the seventy-fifth anniversary was appropriately celebrated, with Gen. John S. Preston, and Hon. George Bancroft as the speakers. But it remained for October seventh, 1880, to eclipse the others, in a Centennial celebration, when thousands of people assembled, making a memorable civic and military display, with an address by Hon. John W. Daniel, and poems by Paul H. Hayne and Mrs. Clara Dargan McLean. Then followed the unvailing of a massive granite monument having a base of eighteen feet square, and altogether a height of twenty-eight feet. It slopes from the upper die to the top, which is about two and half feet square, capable of further addition, or to be crowned with a suitable statue. Inscriptions are cut on marble slabs, imbedded two inches in the granite masonry.

This worthy King's Mountain Centennial very naturally excited much interest in the minds of the public regarding the battle itself, and its heroic actors, and prompted the writer to set about the preparation of his long-promised work. Beside the materials collected in former years—in ante bellum days—more than a thousand letters were written, seeking documents, traditions, description of historic localities, and the elucidation of obscure statements. Old newspaper files of the Library of Congress, Philadelphia Library Company, and of the Maryland and the Wisconsin Historical Societies, have been carefully consulted, and information sought from every possible source in this country, England and the British Colonies. Truth alone has been the writer's aim, and conclusions reached without prejudice, fear or favor.

The following deceased persons, who were either related to, or had personal intercourse with, King's Mountain men, kindly contributed in years agone, valuable materials for this work :

THE NEW MONUMENT, KING'S MOUNTAIN.

Ex-Gov. David Campbell, of Virginia; Hon. Hugh L. White, Col. Wm. Martin, Ex. Gov. Wm. B. Campbell, Col. George Wilson, Col. George Christian, Maj. John Sevier, Jr., Col. Geo. W. Sevier, and Mrs. Eliza W. Warfield, of Tennessee; Hon. Jos. J. McDowell, of Ohio; Maj. Thos. H. Shelby, of Kentucky; Hon. Elijah Callaway, Dr. James Callaway, Hugh M. Stokes, Shadrack Franklin, Silas McDowell, Adam and James J. Hampton, of North Carolina; Hon. Wm. C. Preston, Gen. John S. Preston, Dr. M. A. Moore, D. G. Stinson, Jeremiah Cleveland, Mrs. Sallie Rector, Dr. A. L. Hammond, and Abraham Hardin, of South Carolina; Gen. Ben. Cleveland, of Georgia; and Dr. Alexander Q. Bradley, of Alabama.

Special acknowledgements are due to the following persons.

Tennessee:—Dr. J. G. M. Ramsey, Rev. Dr. D. C. Kelley, Hon. J. M. Lea, Anson Nelson, Hon. W. B. Carter, Col. H. L. Claiborne, Mrs. Mary A. Trigg, John F. Watkins Thos. A. Rogers, and Col. H. A. Brown.

Virginia:—R. A. Brock, Hon. A. S. Fulton, W. G. G. Lowry, John L. Cochran, and Col. T. L. Preston.

North Carolina:—Dr. C. L. Hunter, Col. J. R. Logan, W. L. Twitty, Dr. R. F Hackett, Col. Wm. Johnston, Hon. W. P. Bynum, Dr. W. J. T. Miller, Mrs. Mary A. Chambers, Hon. S. McDowell Tate, Col. W. W. Lenoir, Mrs. R. M. Pearson, W. M. Reinhardt, Hon. J. C. Harper, Hon. C. A. Cilly, Miss A. E. Henderson, Dr. G. W. Michal, Wm. A. McCall, Rev. W. S. Fontaine, W. S. Pearson, T. A. Bouchelle, John Banner, J. L. Worth, Dr. T. B. Twitty, M. O. Dickerson, A. D. K. Wallace, John Gilkey, A. B. Long, Dr. J. H. Gilkey, Hon. J. M. Cloud, Rev. W. S. Bynum, J. C. Whitson, Geo. F. Davidson, Mrs. R. C. Whitson, Miss N. M. McDowell, Miss A. M. Woodfin, James E. Reynolds, Lewis Johnson, G. W. Crawford, W. H. Allis, Thos. D. Vance, Dr. J. C. Newland, W. M. McDowell, Rev. E. F. Rockwell, D. Burgin, A. Burgin, Wylie Franklin, James Gwyn, Jesse Yates, Dr. L. Harrill, John H. Roberts, Mrs. M. V. Adams, Mrs. P. E. Callaway, Dr. B. F. Dixon, and Mrs. M. M. Thruston.

South Carolina:—Rev. James H. Saye, Ex-Gov. B. F. Perry, Hon. Simpson Bobo, N. F. Walker, A. H. Twichell, Mrs. Edward Roach, Gen. A. C. Garlington, D. K. Crawford, Hon. John B. Cleveland, Elijah Keese, James Seaborn, and J. T. Pool.

Georgia:—Dr. J. H. Logan, Gen. W. S. Wofford, W. T Hackett, and A. N. Simpson.

Alabama:—Rev. Z. H. Gordon, Col. J. H. Witherspoon, and Mrs. Lewis E. Parsons.

Mississippi:—J. R. Hill.

Arkansas:—Gen. D. H. Hill.

Missouri:—Dr. A. N. Kincannon.

Kentucky:—Isaac Shelby, Jr., and Col. H. H. McDowell.

Illinois:—Sprague White.

Ohio:—Mrs. Jennie McDowell Stockton.

Wisconsin:—Hon. John A. Bentley.

Pennsylvania:—G. R. Hildeburn.

New York:—Gen. J. Watts DePeyster, and Geo. H. Moore, LL. D.

Maryland:—Miss Josephine Seaton.

Washington:—Col. J. H. Wheeler, and Hon. D. R. Goodloe.

England:—Viscount Holmesdale, Col. Geo. A. Ferguson, and Alfred Kingston.

New Brunswick:—J. De Lancey Robinson.

Nova Scotia:—George Taylor.

Ontario:—Rev. Dr. E. Ryerson.

While in the long years past the materials for this work have been collected, ample facts and documents have also been gathered for a continuation of similar volumes, of which this is the commencement—to be called, perhaps, the BORDER SERIES, embracing, in their sweep, the whole frontier from New York and Canada to the gulf of Mexico— *Sumter and his Men—Pickens and the Battle of Cowpens—Life and Campaigns of Gen. George Rogers Clark—Boone and the Pioneers of Kentucky—Kenton and his Adventures—Brady and his Scouts— Mecklenburg and its Actors—Tecumseh, the Shawanoe Leader—Brant, the Mohawk Chief*—and a volume on *Border Forays and Adventures.* If there is a demand for these works, they will be forthcoming.

Should *King's Mountain and its Heroes* be received with favor, and regarded as shedding new light on an interesting portion of our revolutionary history, not a little of the credit is deservedly due to the enterprising publisher, PETER G. THOMSON, who warmly encouraged the undertaking, and has spared no pains in bringing it before the public in a style at once tasteful and attractive.

Madison, Wis., September 1, 1881.

TABLE OF CONTENTS.

CHAPTER I.

1765 to May, 1780.

CHAPTER II.

May, 1780.

CHAPTER III.

1741 to May, 1780.

CHAPTER IV.

1780—May—July.

CHAPTER VIII.

August, 1780—March, 1781.

CHAPTER IX.

July—October, 1780.

CHAPTER X.

September—October, 1780.

CHAPTER XI.

October, 1780.

CHAPTER XII.

King's Mountain Battle, October 7th, 1780.

CHAPTER XIII.

The Battle—October 7th, 1780.

CHAPTER XIV.

October, 1780.

CHAPTER XV.

October—November, 1780.

CHAPTER XVI.

October—December, 1780.

CHAPTER XVII.

Gen. William Campbell.

CHAPTER XVIII.

Cols. Shelby and Sevier, and their Officers.

CHAPTER XIX.

Col. Ben. Cleveland, Maj. Joseph Winston and their Officers.

CHAPTER XX.

Lacey and Other Whigs.—British and Tory Leaders.

APPENDIX.

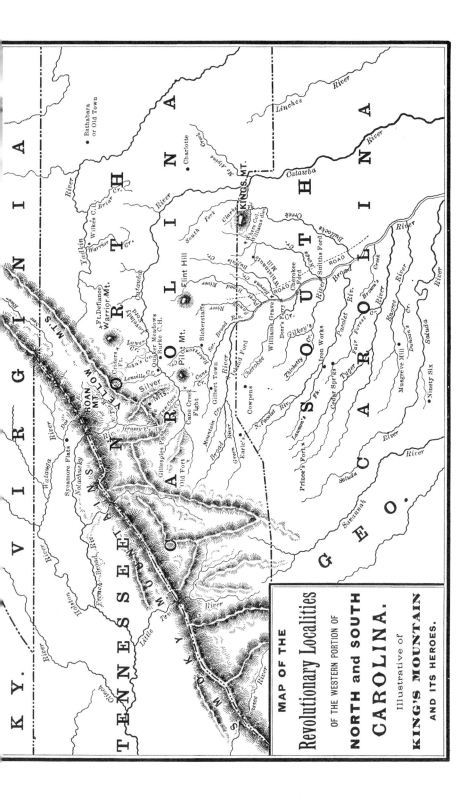

MAP OF THE
Revolutionary Localities
OF THE WESTERN PORTION OF
NORTH and SOUTH
CAROLINA.
Illustrative of
KING'S MOUNTAIN
AND ITS HEROES.

CHAPTER I.

Causes of the Revolution—Alternate Successes and Disasters of the Early Campaigns of the War—Siege and Reduction of Charleston.

For ten years before the outbreak of the American Revolution, the great question of *taxation without representation* agitated the minds of the American people. They rejected the stamps, because they implied a tax; they destroyed the tea, because it imposed a forced levy upon them without their consent, to gratify the insatiate demands of their trans-Atlantic sovereign, and his tyrannical Ministry and Parliament. Should they basely yield one of their dearest rights, they well judged they might be required, little by little, to yield all. They, therefore, manfully resisted these invasions as unbecoming a free people.

When, in 1775, Great Britain determined to enforce her obnoxious laws, the people, under their chosen leaders, seized their arms, forsook their homes and families, and boldly asserted their God-given rights. A long and embittered contest was commenced, involving mighty interests. Freedom was threatened—an empire was at stake. Sturdy blows were given and received, with various results. The first year of the war, the Americans beat back the British from Lexington and Concord, and captured Crown Point, but were worsted at Bunker Hill; they captured Chambly and St. Johns, and repulsed the enemy near Longueil, but the intrepid Montgomery failed to take Quebec, losing his life in the effort.

The second year of the contest, which brought forth the immortal Declaration of Independence, proved varying in its fortunes. The Scotch Tories in North Carolina were signally defeated at Moore's Creek, and the British, long cooped up in Boston, were compelled to evacuate the place; and were subsequently repulsed at Sullivan's Island, near Charleston; while the Americans, on the other hand, were defeated at the Cedars, and were driven from Montreal, Chambly and St. Johns, worsted at Long Island and White Plains, and lost Fort Washington, on the Hudson. Meanwhile the frontier men of Virginia, the Carolinas, East Tennessee, and Georgia, carried on successful expeditions against the troublesome Cherokees, whom British emissaries had inveigled into hostilities against their white neighbors.

Yet the year closed with gloomy prospects—despair sat on many a brow, and saddened many a heart—the main army was greatly reduced, and the British occupied New York, and the neighboring Province of New Jersey. Washington made a desperate venture, crossing the Delaware amid floating ice in December, attacking and defeating the unsuspecting enemy at Trenton; and, pushing his good fortune, commenced the third year of the war, 1777, by securing a victory at Princeton. While the enemy were, for a while, held at bay at the Red Bank, yet the results of the contests at Brandywine and Germantown were not encouraging to the American arms, and the British gained a firm foot-hold in Philadelphia. And subsequently they captured Forts Clinton and Montgomery, on the Hudson.

Farther north, better success attended the American arms. St. Leger, with a strong British and Indian force, laid siege to Fort Stanwix, on the Mohawk; but after repelling a relieving party under Gen. Herkimer, he was at length compelled to relinquish his investiture, on learning of the approach of a second army of relief, retiring precipitately from the country; while the more formidable invading force under Burgoyne met with successive reverses at Bennington, Stillwater, and Saratoga, eventuating in its total surrender to the victorious Americans.

In June, 1778, the fourth year of the war, the British evacuated Philadelphia, when Washington pursued their retreating forces, overtaking and vigorously attacking them at Monmouth. A large Tory and Indian party defeated the settlers, and laid waste the Wyoming settlements. As the result of Burgoyne's signal discomfiture, a treaty of alliance between the new Republic and France brought troops and fleets to the aid of the struggling Americans, and produced some indecisive fighting on Rhode Island.

The adventurous expedition under George Rogers Clark, from the valleys of Virginia and West Pennsylvania, down the Monongahela and Ohio, and into the country of the Illinois, a distance of well nigh fifteen hundred miles, with limited means, destitute of military stores, pack-horses and supplies—with only their brave hearts and trusty rifles, was a remarkable enterprise. Yet with all these obstacles, and less than two hundred men, Clark fearlessly penetrated the western wilderness, killing his game by the way, and conquered those distant settlements. Though regarded at the time as a herculean undertaking, and a most successful adventure, yet none foresaw the mighty influence it was destined to exert on the subsequent progress and extension of the Republic.

Varied fortunes attended the military operations of 1779, the fifth year of the strife. The gallant Clark and his intrepid followers, marched in winter season, from Kaskaskia across the submerged lands of the Wabash, sometimes wading up to their arm-pits in water, and breaking the ice before them, surprised the garrison at Vincennes, and succeeded in its capture. The British force in Georgia, having defeated General Ashe at Brier creek, projected an expedition against Charleston, and progressed as far as Stono, whence they were driven back to Savannah, where the combined French and Americans were subsequently repulsed, losing, among others, the chivalrous Count Pulaski. At the North, Stony Point was captured at the point of the bayonet, and Paulus

Hook surprised; while General Sullivan's well-appointed
army over-ran the beautiful country of the Six Nations,
destroying their villages, and devastating their fields, as a
retributive chastisement for their repeated invasions of the
Mohawk and Minisin settlements, and laying waste the
lovely vale of Wyoming.

The war had now dragged its slow length along for five
successive campaigns, and the British had gained but few
permanent foot-holds in the revolted Colonies. Instead of
the prompt and easy conquest they had promised themselves,
they had encountered determined opposition wherever they
had shown the red cross of St. George, or displayed their
red-coated soldiery. Repeated defeats on the part of the
Americans had served to inure them to the hardships of
war, and learned them how to profit by their experiences and
disasters.

New efforts were demanded on the part of the British
Government to subdue their rebellious subjects; and South
Carolina was chosen as the next field of extensive operations. Sir Henry Clinton, who had met so signal a repulse
at Charleston in 1776, and in whose breast still rankled the
mortifying recollections of that memorable failure, resolved
to head in person the new expedition against the Palmetto
Colony, and retrieve, if possible, the honor so conspicuously tarnished there on his previous unfortunate enterprise.

Having enjoyed the Christmas holiday of 1779 in New
York harbor, Sir Henry, accompanied by Lord Cornwallis,
sailed from Sandy Hook the next day with the fleet under
Admiral Arbuthnot, transporting an army of over seven
thousand five hundred men. Some of the vessels, however,
were lost by the way, having encountered stormy weather
in the gulf-stream—one bark, carrying Hessian troops, was
dismasted and driven across the ocean, an ordnance vessel
was foundered, while several transports were captured by
bold and adventurous American privateers, and most of the
horses for the expedition perished. The place of rendez-

vous was at Tybee Bay, near the entrance to Savannah river, whence Clinton, on his way towards Charleston, was joined by the troops in Georgia, making his force nine thousand strong, besides the sailors in the fleet; but to render his numbers invincible beyond all peradventure, he at once ordered from New York Lord Rawdon's brigade, amounting to about two thousand five hundred more.

Charleston, against which this formidable British force was destined, was an opulent city of some fifteen thousand people, white and black, and was garrisoned by less than four thousand men—not near enough to properly man the extended works of defence, of nearly three miles in circumference, as they demanded. Governor Rutledge, a man of unquestioned patriotism, had conferred upon him by the Legislature, in anticipation of this threatened attack, dictatorial powers, with the admonition, 'to do every thing necessary for the public good; " but he was, nevertheless, practically powerless. He had few or none of the sinews of war; and so depreciated had become the currency of South Carolina, that it required seven hundred dollars to purchase a pair of shoes for one of her needy soldiers. The defeat of the combined French and American force at Savannah the preceding autumn, in which the South Carolinians largely participated, had greatly dispirited the people; and the Governor's appeal to the militia produced very little effect. The six old South Carolina regiments had been so depleted by sickness and the casualties of war as to scarcely number eight hundred, all told; and the defence of the city was committed to these brave men, the local militia, and a few regiments of Continental troops—the latter reluctantly spared by Washington from the main army, and which, he thought, was "putting much to nazard" in an attempt to defend the city, and the result proved his military foresight.

It would have been wiser for General Lincoln and his troops to have retired from the place, and engaged in a Fabian warfare, harassing the enemy's marches by ambuscades, and cutting off his foraging parties; but the leading citizens of Charleston, relying on their former success, urged every argument in their power that the city should be defended to the last extremity. Yet no experienced Engineer regarded the place as tenable.

On the eleventh of February, 1780, the British forces landed on St. John's Island, within thirty miles of Charleston, subsequently forming a depot, and building fortifications, at Wappoo, on James' Island; and, on the twenty-sixth of that month, they gained a distant view of the place and harbor. The dreaded day of danger approached nearer and nearer; and on the twenty-seventh, the officers of the Continental squadron, which carried one hundred and fifty guns, reported their inability to guard the harbor at the bar, where the best defence could be made; and "then," as Washington expressed it, "the attempt to defend the town ought to have been relinquished." But no such thought was entertained. Every thing was done, that could be done, to strengthen and extend the lines of defence, dig ditches, erect redoubts and plant abatis, with a strong citadel in the center.*

Preparations, too, were steadily progressing on the part of the enemy. On the twenty-fourth of March, Lord Cornwallis and a Hessian officer were seen with their spyglasses making observations; and on the twenty-ninth, the British passed Ashley river, breaking ground, on the first of April, at a distance of eleven hundred yards from the American lines. At successive periods they erected five batteries on Charleston Neck.

Late in the evening of March thirtieth, General Charles

---

* There was published, first in a Williamsburgh, Va., paper of April 8th, 1780, copied into Dunlap's *Pennsylvania Packet* of April 18th, and into the New York *Royal Gazette* of same date, an account of a Colonel Hamilton Ballendine having made drawings of Charleston and its fortifications, was directing his course to the enemy, when an American picket guard sent out to Stono, captured him; he, thereupon, exhibited his drafts, supposing that the party belonged to the British army. They soon disabused him of his error, carried him to General Lincoln, who ordered him for execution, and he was accordingly hanged on the 5th of March. As none of the South Carolina historians, nor any of the Charleston diarists or letter-writers during the siege, make the slightest reference to any such person or circumstance, there could have been no foundation for the story.

Scott, commanding one of the Virginia Continental brigade, arrived, accompanied by his staff, and some other officers. "The next morning," says Major Croghan, "I accompanied Generals Lincoln and Scott to view the batteries and works around town; found those on the Cooper river side in pretty good order, and chiefly manned by sailors; but the greater part of the remainder not complete, and stood in need of a great deal of work. General Scott was very particular in inquiring of General Lincoln as to the quantity of provisions in the garrison, when the General informed him there were several months' supply, by a return he had received from the Commissary. General Scott urged the necessity of having officers to examine it, and, as he expressed it, *for them to lay their hands on it.*"[*]

A sortie was planned on the fourth of April, to be commanded by General Scott—one battalion led by Colonel Clarke and Major Hogg, of North Carolina; another by Colonel Parker and Major Croghan, of Virginia, and the light infantry by Lieutenant-Colonel Laurens; but the wind proved unfavorable, which prevented the shipping from going up Town creek, to fire on the enemy, and give the sallying party such assistance as they might be able to render, and thus it failed of execution. General Woodford's Virginia brigade of Continentals arrived on the sixth, and some North Carolina militia under the command of Colonel Harrington. They were greeted by the firing of a *feu de joie*, and the ringing of the bells all night.[†]

Admiral Arbuthnot's near approach to the bar, on the seventh of April, induced Commodore Whipple, who commanded the American naval force, to retire without firing a gun, first to Fort Moultrie, and afterward to Charleston; and the British fleet passed the fort without stopping to engage it—the passage having been made, says the New Jersey

---

[*] MS. Journal of Major William Croghan, of the Virginia Line. Siege of Charleston, 123.

[†] Croghan's MS. Journal.

Gazette,* while a severe thunder storm was raging, which caused the ships to be "invisible near half the time of their passing." Colonel Charles C. Pinckney, who commanded there, with three hundred men, kept up a heavy cannonade on the British ships during their passage, which was returned by each of the vessels as they passed—the enemy losing fourteen men killed, and fifteen wounded, while not a man was hurt in the garrison.† One ship had its foretopmast shot away, and others sustained damage. The Acteus transport ran aground near Haddrell's Point, when Captain Thomas Gadsden, a brother of Colonel Gadsden, who was detached with two field pieces for the purpose, fired into her with such effect, that the crew set her on fire, and retreated in boats to the other vessels. The Royal fleet, in about two hours, came to anchor within long shot of the American batteries.

By the tenth of April, the enemy had completed their first parallel, when Clinton and Arbuthnot summoned the town to surrender. Lincoln answered: "From duty and inclination I shall support the town to the last extremity." A severe skirmish had previously taken place between Lieutenant-Colonel John Laurens and the advance guard of the enemy, in which the Americans lost Captain Bowman killed, and Major Hyrne and seven privates wounded. On the twelfth, the batteries on both sides were opened, keeping up an almost incessant fire. The British had the decided advantage in the number and strength of their mortars and royals, having twenty-one, while the Americans possessed only two ;‡ and the lines of the latter soon began to crumble under the powerful and constant cannonade maintained against them. On the thirteenth, Governor Rutledge was

---

* May 12th, 1780.

† Croghan's MS. Journal.

‡ Such is the statement of Dr. Ramsay, who was present during the siege. The British official returns show nine mortars, ranging from four to ten-inch caliber, and one eight-inch howitzer, surrendered at Charleston, and a ten-inch mortar taken at Fort Moultrie; but probably the most of these were either unfit for use, or more likely, the limited quantity of shells enabled the defenders to make use of only two of this class of ordnance.

persuaded to withdraw from the garrison, while exit was yet attainable, leaving Lieutenant-Governor Gadsden with five members of the Council.

On the same day, General Lincoln, in a council of war, revealed to its members his want of resources, and suggested an evacuation. "In such circumstances," said General Mc-Intosh, "we should lose not an hour in attempting to get the Continental troops, at least, over Cooper river; for on their safety, depends the salvation of the State." But Lincoln only wished them to give the matter mature consideration, and he would consult them further about it. Before he met them again, the American cavalry at Monk's Corner, which had been relied on to keep open the communication between the city and the country, were surprised and dispersed on the fourteenth; and five days later, the expected British reinforcements of two thousand five hundred men arrived from New York, when Clinton was enabled more completely to environ the devoted city, and cut off all chance of escape.

A stormy council was held on the nineteenth, when the heads of the several military departments reported their respective conditions—of course, anything but flattering in their character. Several of the members still inclined to an evacuation, notwithstanding the increased difficulties of effecting it since it was first suggested. In the midst of the conference, Lieutenant-Governor Gadsden happened to come in—whether by accident, or design, was not known—and General Lincoln courteously proposed that he be allowed to take part in the council. He appeared surprised and displeased that a thought had been entertained of either evacuation or capitulation, and acknowledged himself entirely ignorant of the state of the provisions, etc., but would consult his Council in regard to the proposals suggested.

In the evening, an adjourned meeting was held, when Colonel Laumoy, of the engineer department, reported the insufficiency of the fortifications, the improbability of holding out many days longer, and the impracticability of making a retreat; and closed by suggesting that terms of honorable capitulation be sought from the enemy. Lieutenant-Governor Gadsden, with four of his Councilors, coming in shortly after, treated the military gentlemen very rudely, the Lieutenant-Governor declaring that he would protest against their proceedings; that the militia were willing to live upon rice alone, rather than give up the town on any terms; and that even the old women had become so accustomed to the enemy's shot, that they traveled the streets without fear or dread; but if the council were determined to capitulate, he had his terms ready in his pocket.

Mr. Thomas Ferguson, one of the Councilors, declared that the inhabitants of the city had observed the boats collected to carry off the Continental troops; and that they would keep a good watch upon the army, and should any attempt at evacuation ever be made, he would be among the first to open the gates for the admission of the enemy, and assist them in attacking the retiring troops   Colonel C. C. Pinckney soon after came in abruptly—probably having been apprised by the Lieutenant-Governor of the subject under discussion—and, forgetting his usual politeness, addressed General Lincoln with great warmth, and in much the same strain as General Gadsden, adding that those who were for business needed no council, and that he came over on purpose from Fort Moultrie, to prevent any terms being offered to the enemy, or any evacuation of the garrison attempted; and particularly charged Colonel Laumoy and his department with being the sole authors and promoters of such proposals.*

It is very certain, that these suggestions of evacuation or capitulation, occasioned at the time great discontent among both the regulars and militia, who wished to defend the city

---

* The details of this military council are taken from Major Croghan's MS. Journal; and from General Mc'ntosh's Journal, published entire in the *Magnolia* Magazine, Dec. 1842, and cited in Simms' *South Carolina in the Revolution*, 127-129, both of which are, in this case, identical in language.

to the last extremity ; and who resolved, in view of continuing the defence, that they would be content, if necessary,
with only half rations daily.* All these good people had
their wishes gratified—the siege was procrastinated, and
many an additional death, suffering, sorrow, and anguish,
were the consequence.

General Lincoln must have felt hurt, if not sorely nettled,
by these repeated insults—as General McIntosh acknowledges that he did. When matters of great public concern
result disastrously, scape-goats are always sought, and all
participants are apt to feel more or less unamiable and
fault-finding on such occasions. Or, as Washington expressed it, referring to another affair, "mutual reproaches
too often follow the failure of enterprises depending upon the
coöperation of troops of different grades." Looking at these
bickerings in the light of history, a century after their occurrence, one is struck with General Lincoln's magnanimous
forbearance, when he confessedly made great sacrifices in
defending the place so long against his better judgment, in
deference to the wishes of the people, who, we may well
conclude, were very unfit judges of military affairs.

At another council of officers, held on the twentieth and
twenty-first, the important subject of an evacuation was again
under deliberation ; and the conclusion reached was, "that it
was unadvisable, because of the opposition made to it by
the civil authority and the inhabitants, and because, even if
they should succeed in defeating a large body of the enemy
posted in their way, they had not a sufficiency of boats to
cross the Santee before they might be overtaken by the
whole British army."† It was then proposed to give Sir

---

* MS. letter of John Lewis Gervais, cited in Simms, 129.

† The enemy were constantly on the watch for any attempted evacuation on the part
of the Americans. Capt. J. R. Rousselet, of Tarleton's cavalry, has left this MS. note,
written on the margin of a copy of Steadman's *American War,* referring to the closing
period of the siege: "Some small vessels, taken from the Americans, were armed, manned
with troops, and stationed off Town Creek, to prevent the escape of the garrison should
they attempt to evacuate the town by that channel. Capt. Rousselet commanded an
armed sloop, with his company on board, under Capt. Salisbury, Royal Navy."

Henry Clinton quiet possession of the city, with its fortifications and dependencies, on condition that the security of
the inhabitants, and a safe, unmolested retreat for the garrison, with baggage and field pieces, to the north-east of
Charleston should be granted. These terms were instantly
rejected. On searching every house in town, it was found
that the private supplies of provisions were as nearly exhausted as were the public magazines.

On the twenty-fourth, at daybreak, Lieutenant-Colonel
Henderson sallied out with two hundred men, chiefly from
Generals Woodford's and Scott's brigades, surprising and
vigorously attacking the advance flanking party of the
enemy, bayoneting fifteen of them in their trenches, and
capturing a dozen prisoners, of whom seven were wounded,
losing in the brilliant affair, the brave Captain Thomas Gadsden and one or two privates. A considerable body of the
enemy, under Major Hall, of the seventy-fourth regiment,
attempted to support the party in the trenches; but were
obliged to retire on receiving a shower of grape from the
American batteries.* A successful enterprise of this kind
proved only a momentary advantage, having no perceptible
influence on the final result.

It is said Colonel C. C. Pinckney, and Lieutenant-Colonel
Laurens, assured General Lincoln they could supply the garrison with plenty of beef from Lempriere's Point, if they were
permitted to remain on that side of Cooper river with the force
then under their command; upon which the Commissary was
ordered to issue a full allowance again. But unfortunately
the first and only cattle butchered at Lempriere's for the use
of the garrison were altogether spoiled through neglect or
mismanagement before they came over. These gentlemen,
are said, also, to have promised that the communication on
the Cooper side could, and would, be kept open. Being inhabitants of Charleston, and knowing the country well, perhaps the General, with some reason, might be inclined to the

---

*Croghan's MS. Journal.

same opinion ; and besides furnishing the garrison with beef, they were to send a sufficient number of negroes over to town for the military works, who were much wanted. But Colonel Pinckney with the greater part, or almost the whole of his first South Carolina regiment, and Lieutenant-Colonel Laurens with the light infantry were recalled from Fort Moultrie and Lempriere's *—and thus ended this spasmodic hope. Probably this failure caused a strict search to be made, about this time, in the houses of the citizens for provisions ; " some was found," says Major Croghan, " but a much less quantity than was supposed."

The Americans were not slow in perceiving the utter hopelessness of their situation. On the twenty-sixth, General DuPortail, an able French officer and Engineer-in-Chief of the American army, arrived from Philadelphia, having been sent by Washington to supervise the engineer department. He frankly informed General Lincoln that there was no prospect of getting any reinforcements very soon from the grand army—that Congress had proposed to General Washington to send the Maryland Line to their relief.†   As soon as General DuPortail came into the garrison, examined the military works, and observed the enemy, he declared the defences were not tenable—that they were only field lines ; and that the British might have taken the place ten days ago. " I found the town," wrote DuPortail to Washington, " in a desperate state."‡ He wished to leave the garrison immediately, while it was possible ; but General Lincoln would not allow him to do so, as it would dispirit the troops. On learning General DuPortail's opinion, a council was called the same day, and a proposition made for the Continental troops to make a night retreat ; and when the citizens were informed of the subject under deliberation, some of them came into the council, warmly declaring to General Lincoln, that if he attempted to withdraw the troops and abandon the citizens,

* Croghan's MS. Journal ; and McIntosh's Diary.
† Croghan's MS. Journal.
‡ Letters to Washington, ii, 450.

they would cut up his boats, and open the gates to the enemy. This put an end to all further thoughts of an evacuation.*

As late as the twenty-eighth, a supernumerary officer left town to join the forces in the country ; but the next day the small party remaining at Lempriere's Point was recalled, the enemy at once occupying it with a large force ; and thus the last avenue between the city and country was closed. General Lincoln informed the general officers, privately, this day, that he intended the horn work as a place of retreat for the whole army in case they were driven from the lines. General McIntosh observing to him the impossibility of those then stationed at South Bay and Ashley river, in such a contingency, being able to retreat there, he replied that they might secure themselves as best they could. And on the thirtieth, in some way, Governor Rutledge managed to convey a letter to General Lincoln, upon which the General congratulated the army, in general orders, on *hearing* of a large reinforcement, which *may* again open the communication with the country.† It was the old story of drowning men catching at straws.

It is unnecessary to dwell upon the daily details of the protracted siege. Some of the more unusual occurrences only need be briefly noticed, so that we may hasten on to the melancholy catastrophe. Eleven vessels were sunk in the channel to prevent the Royal fleet from passing up Cooper river, and enfilading the American lines on that side of the place ; while a frigate and two galleys were placed above the sunken obstructions, to coöperate with the shore batteries in thwarting any attempt on the part of the enemy for their removal.

But the work of destruction went steadily on. Cannon balls by day and by night went streaking through the air, and crashing through the houses. One morning, a shell burst very near Colonel Parker, a large piece of which fell

---

* Moultrie's *Memoirs*, i, 80.
† Croghan's MS. Journal.

harmless at his feet, when he said, with much composure, "a miss is as good as a mile;"* and, that very evening, while the gallant Colonel was looking over the parapet, he was shot dead. Shells, fire-balls, and carcasses, ingeniously packed with combustibles, loaded pistol barrels, and other destructive missiles, were thrown into the city, setting many buildings on fire, and maiming and destroying not a few of the citizens and soldiery. On one occasion, when a pastor and a few worshipers, mostly women and invalids, were gathered in a church, supplicating the mercies of heaven on themselves and suffering people, a bomb-shell fell in the chuch-yard, when all quickly dispersed, retiring to their several places of abode.

Some of the cases of fatality were quite uncommon. Meyer Moses' young child was killed while in the arms of its nurse, and the house burned down. A man and his wife were killed at the same time, and in the same bed. A soldier who had been relieved from serving at his post in the defence of the city, entered his humble domicil, and while in the act of embracing his anxious wife, with tears of gladness, a cannon ball passed through the house, killing them both instantly. Many sought safety in their cellars; but even when protected for the moment from the constantly falling missiles of death and destruction, they began to suffer for want of food, since all the avenues to the city for country supplies, had been cut off.

General Moultrie has left us a vivid picture of this period of the siege : " Mr. Lord and Mr. Basquin, two volunteers, were sleeping upon the mattress together, in the advanced redoubt, when Mr. Lord was killed by a shell falling upon him, and Mr. Basquin at the same time had the hair of his head burnt, and did not awake until he was aroused from his slumbers by his fellow soldiers. The fatigue in that advanced redoubt was so great for want of sleep, that many faces were so swelled they could scarcely see out of their eyes. I was obliged to re-

---

* *Virginia Gazette*, May 16, 1780.

lieve Major Mitchell, the commanding officer. They were constantly on the lookout for the shells that were continually falling among them. It was by far the most dangerous post on the lines. On my visit to the battery, not having been there for a day or two, I took the usual way of going in, which was a bridge that crossed our ditch, quite exposed to the enemy, who, in the meantime, had advanced their works within seventy or eighty yards of the bridge, which I did not know. As soon as I had stepped upon the bridge, an uncommon number of bullets whistled about me; and on looking to my right, I could just see the heads of about twelve or fifteen men firing upon me from behind a breast-work—I moved on, and got in. When Major Mitchell saw me, he asked me which way I came in? I told him over the bridge. He was astonished, and said, ' Sir, it is a thousand to one that you were not killed,' and told me that he had a covered way through which to pass, by which he conducted me on my return. I staid in this battery about a quarter of an hour, giving the necessary orders, during which we were constantly skipping about to get out of the way of the shells thrown from their howitzers. They were not more than one hundred yards from our works, and were throwing their shells in bushels on our front and left flank."*

Under date of the second of May, Major Croghan records in his Journal, which is corroborated by General McIntosh's Diary, that the enemy threw shells charged with rice and sugar. Simms tells us, that tradition has it, that it was not rice and sugar with which the shells of the British were thus ironically charged, but wheat flour and molasses—with an inscription addressed: '' To the Yankee officers in Charleston,'' courteously informing them that it contained a supply of the commodities of which they were supposed to stand most in need. But the garrison could still jest amid suffering, volcanoes and death. Having ascertained that the shell was sent them from a battery manned exclusively

---

*Moultrie's *Memoirs*, i, 83.

by a Scottish force, they emptied the shell of its contents; and filling it with lard and sulphur, to cure them of the itch, and sent it back to their courteous assailants, with the same inscription which originally accompanied it. "It was understood," says Garden, "after the siege, that the note was received, but not with that good humor that might have been expected, had it been considered as a *jeu d'esprit*, resulting from justifiable retaliation."

"Provisions," as we learn from Johnson's *Traditions*, "now failed among the besieged. A sufficiency had been provided for the occasion; but the beef and pork had become tainted and unfit for food." But the British "were misinformed," says Moultrie, "if they supposed us in want of rice and sugar." Of the latter article, at least during the earlier stages of the siege, such was its plentifulness that it was a favorite amusement to pursue the spent hot shot of the enemy, in order, by flinging sugar upon the balls, to convert it into candy. But towards the close of the siege, the supply of sugar must have become limited. "On the fourth of May," says Major Croghan, "we received from the Commissary, with our usual allowance of rice, six ounces of extremely bad meat, and *a little* coffee and sugar. It has been very disagreeable to the northern officers and soldiers to be under the necessity of living without wheat or Indian bread, which has been the case during the whole siege." So that the Scotch jokers who sent their shot, laden with either rice and sugar, or flour and molasses, ironically hinting at the deficiencies of the beleaguered garrison, did not, after all, hit very wide of the mark.

Clinton, on the sixth of May, renewed his former terms for the surrender of the garrison. With the limited store of provisions on hand, with no prospects of receiving further supplies or reinforcements, and with the admission on the part of the Engineers that the lines could not be maintained ten days longer, and were liable to be carried by assault at any time, General Lincoln was disposed to accept the terms tendered ; but he was opposed by the citizens, as they were required by Clinton to be prisoners on parole, when they wished to be regarded as non-combatants, and not subject to the rigorous laws of war, It was only putting off the evil day for a brief period ; and again the twenty-four and thirty-two pound carronades, the mortars and howitzers, belched forth their shot, shell and carcasses upon the devoted town and garrison, setting many buildings on fire, and keeping up the most intense excitement. So near were now the opposing parties, that they could speak words of bravado to each other ; and the rifles of the Hessian Ya-gers were so unerring, that a defender could no longer show himself above the lines with safety ; and even a hat raised upon a ramrod, was instantly riddled with bullets.

Captain Hudson, of the British Navy, on the fifth of May, summoned Fort Moultrie, on Sullivan's Island to surrender ; the larger portion of its garrison having previously retired to Charleston. Lieutenant-Colonel William Scott,* who com-manded, sent for answer a rollicking reply : "Tol, lol, de rol, lol—Fort Moultrie will be defended to the last extremity." The next day, Hudson repeated his demand, threatening that if he did not receive an answer in fifteen minutes, he would storm the fort, and put every man to the sword. Scott, it would seem, was at first disposed to resort to bravado of the "last extremity" character ; but recalled the officer bearing it, saying on further reflection the garrison thought better of it—the disparity of force was far too great—and begging for a cessation of hostilities, proposed terms of sur-render, which were granted by Captain Hudson. The sur-render formally took place on the seventh.† Thus the historic

---

* Scott was a brave, experienced officer. He served as a Captain during the attack on Charleston, in 1776 and died in that city in June, 1807.

† Gordon's *History of the Revolution*, iii, 354 ; Moultrie's *Memoirs*, ii, 84 ; Ramsay's *Revolution in South Carolina*, ii, 56. Bancroft, x, 305, and others, give May 6th as the date of surrender, but that the 7th was the true date of this occurrence may be seen by com-paring Tarleton's *Campaign*, 53-55 ; Botta's *Revolution*, New Haven edition, 1842, ii 249 ; Johnson's *Traditions*, 259 ; Simms' *South Carolina in the Revolution*, 146 ; and *Siege of Charleston*, Munsell, 1867, p. 167.

Fort Moultrie, which four years before had signally repulsed a powerful British fleet under Admiral Sir Hyde Parker, now surrendered to the enemy without firing a gun.

The seventh of May was further noted by an unfortunate disaster—the partial destruction of the principal magazine of the garrison, by the bursting of a shell. General Moultrie had most of the powder—ten thousand pounds—removed to the north-east corner of the exchange, where it was carefully bricked up, and remained undiscovered by the British during the two years and seven months they occupied the city. Another summons was sent in by Clinton on the eighth—a truce was granted till the next day ; when Lincoln endeavored to secure the militia from being considered as prisoners of war, and the protection of the citizens of South Carolina in their lives and property, with twelve months allowance of time in which to determine whether to remain under British rule, or dispose of their effects and remove elsewhere. These articles were promptly rejected, with the announcement on the part of Clinton that hostilities would be re-commenced at eight o'clock that evening.

"After receiving his letter," says Moultrie, "we remained near an hour silent, all calm and ready, each waiting for the other to begin. At length, we fired the first gun, and immediately followed a tremendous cannonade—about one hundred and eighty, or two hundred pieces of heavy cannon were discharged at the same moment. The mortars from both sides threw out an immense number of shells. It was a glorious sight to see them, like meteors, crossing each other, and bursting in the air. It appeared as if the stars were tumbling down. The fire was incessant almost the whole night, cannon balls whizzing, and shells hissing, continually among us, ammunition chests and temporary magazines blowing up, great guns bursting, and wounded men groaning along the lines. It was a dreadful night ! It was our last great effort, but it availed us nothing. After it, our military ardor was much abated, and we began to cool."

When, on the eleventh of May, the British had crossed the wet ditch by sap, and were within twenty-five yards of the American lines, all farther defense was hopeless. The militia refused to do duty.* It was no longer a question of expediency ; but stern necessity demanded a speedy surrender, and the stoppage of farther carnage and suffering. General Lincoln had proved himself brave, judicious and unwearied in his exertions for three anxious months in baffling the greatly superior force of Sir Henry Clinton and Admiral Arbuthnot. Hitherto the civil authorities, and citizens of Charleston, had stoutly contended that the city should be defended to the last extremity ; but now, when all hope was lost, a large majority of the inhabitants, and of the militia, petitioned General Lincoln to accede to the terms offered by the enemy. The next day articles of capitulation were signed.

The loss of the Americans during the siege was ninety-eight officers and soldiers killed, and one hundred and forty-six wounded ; and about twenty of the citizens were killed by the random shots of the enemy. Upward of thirty houses were burned, and many others greatly damaged. Besides the Continental troops, less than two thousand, of whom five hundred were in hospitals, and a considerable number of sailors, Sir Henry Clinton managed to enumerate among the prisoners surrendered, all the free male adults of Charleston, including the aged, the infirm, and even the Loyalists, so as to swell the number of his formidable conquest. In this way, his report was made to boast of over five thousand six hundred prisoners, when the Loyalist portion but a few days afterwards offered their congratulations on the reduction of South Carolina. The regular troops and sailors became prisoners of war until exchanged ; the militia from the country were permitted to return home on parole, and to be secured in their property so long as their parole should be observed.

---

* Du Portail to Washington, May 17th, 1780.

CHAPTER II.

May, 1780.

Further Incidents Connected with the Siege.—Tyranny of the British Leaders.—Subjugation of South Carolina.

A sad accident occurred shortly after the surrender. The arms taken from the troops and inhabitants, amounting to some five thousand, were lodged in a laboratory, near a large quantity of cartridges and loose powder. A number of the British officers desiring some of the handsome mounted swords and pistols, went to the place of deposit to select such as pleased their fancy, when through carelessness in snapping the guns and pistols, the loose powder was ignited, which communicated to the cartridges, blew up the building, and, in an instant, guards, officers, arms, colors, drums and fifes were sent high into the air—the mangled bodies of the victims were dashed by the violent explosion against the neighboring houses, and, in one instance, against the steeple of a contiguous church edifice. The work-house, jail, and old barracks were destroyed. Captain Collins, Lieutenants Gordon and McLeod, together with some fifty of the British guard, and upward of fifty of the citizens, lost their lives by this unhappy occurrence.*

It is a singular fact, that at least during a portion of the siege, Major John André, Deputy Adjutant-General of the British army, managed in some way to get into the city, and made his home with Edward Shrewsberry, on the east side of East Bay street. William Johnson, a prominent Whig, and others, saw the young man at Shrewsberry's dressed in plain homespun; and were told that he was a

---

* Ramsay's *Revolution*, ii. 62–63 ; Moultrie's *Memoirs* ii, 109–112 ; *Pennsylvania Journal,* July 5th, 1780; Simms' *South Carolina in the Revolution,* 156–157; Mackenzie's *Strictures,* 24.

back countryman, connected with the Virginia troops, and had brought down cattle for the garrison. By this cattle-drover *ruse*, he probably gained access to the city. He was, of course, there for a purpose—to make observations, and gain intelligence, and in some secret way, communicate the result to Sir Henry Clinton The historian, Ramsay, who was present during the siege, admits that there were secret friends of the Royal Government in the city, foment-ing disaffection, and working on the fears of the timid ; and Moultrie, another eye-witness, tells us that when the British marched in, to take possession of the city, Captain Roch-fort said to him, " Sir, you have made a gallant defence ; but you had a great many rascals among you, (and men-tioned names,) who came out every night and gave us in-formation of what was passing in your garrison."*

Stephen Shrewsberry becoming sick, stopped with his brother Edward awhile, and repeatedly saw André there—of course, bearing some assumed name ; and after his re-covery, and the surrender of the city, he was introduced to the same person at his brother's as Major André. Stephen Shrewsberry mentioned this singular circumstance to his brother Edward, who frankly acknowledged that he was the same person ; but asserted his own ignorance of it at the time of his brother's illness. Marion's men subsequently sought the life of Edward Shrewsberry, charging him with treachery to the American cause ; but he survived the war, leaving a daughter, a very amiable lady, who lived till 1844, dying childless.

Certain it is, that André was the devoted friend and pro-tegé of Sir Henry Clinton, who made him his Aid, and pro-moted him to the position of Deputy Adjutant-General of the British army in America ; and it is equally certain, as shown by Beatson's *Memoirs*, that "Adjutant-General, Ma-jor John André " was with the " force that embarked at New York under Clinton and Arbuthnot." Tarleton shows

* Ramsay's *Revolution*, ii, 58 ; Moultrie's *Memoirs*, ii, 108.

that André was performing service in front of Charleston
prior to Arbuthnot's passage of Fort Moultrie early in April ;
a letter of André's is in print, dated at " Headquarters, before Charleston," on the thirteenth of April, 1780, while
the schedule of Charleston prisoners, in May, was reported
by him in his official capacity—all going to show, beyond a
question, that he was at or near Charleston during the whole
period of its investment. It was far less dangerous for him
to pass to and from the city during the siege, than it was to
visit West Point on his subsequent mission to tempt the
Judas of the American Revolution.

However fascinating his talents and deportment, he was
not entitled to the commiseration of the American people as
an honorable but unfortunate foe. Twice he acted the part
of an insidious spy, corrupting and deceiving with falsehoods
and mean dissimulation; and he was twice, at least, guilty of
theft—once while stationed in Philadelphia, plundering from
the library of the University of Pennsylvania, a complete
set of that valuable work, *L'Encyclopedia*, received as a
present from the French Academy of Science by the hands
of Dr. Franklin ; on the other occasion, taking from Dr.
Franklin's residence, which he occupied a while, a portrait
of the philosopher.*

An incident connected with the siege and surrender of
Charleston, serving to illustrate the peculiarities and perils
of the times, will very appropriately find a place here. Rev.
Dr. Percy resided on a plantation not very far from Monk's
Corner, with Mrs. Thomas Legaré for a near neighbor.
One day—probably the thirteenth of May—while Mrs. Le-
garé was present, Mrs. Gibson, a poor woman, was an-
nounced while the family and their visitor was at their meal.
As she was usually the bearer of ill news, her visit very natur-

---

* Johnson's *Life of Greene.* i, note 208–209 ; Johnson's *Traditions of the Revolution,*
255–257 ; Sargent's *Life of Andre,* 225–228 ; Almon's *Remembrancer,* x, 76–77 ; Dawson's
Battles of the United States, i, 578 ; Carrington's *Battles of the Revolution,* 497 ; Tarleton's
Campaigns, 12, 64 ; Beatson's *Naval and Military Memoirs,* vi, 203–204 ; Moore's *Diary
of the Revolution.* ii, 484 ; and Lossing's *Field Book of the Revolution,* ii, 104.

ally excited the anxiety of all. She exclaimed, " Good morning people ; have you heard the news? Charleston has fallen,
and the devilish British soldiers have cut to pieces all the
men, all the cats, all the dogs, and now they are coming to
kill all the women and children." Terrified by her excited
and incoherent statement, the ladies looked ready to faint;
and Dr. Percy cried out, "For shame, Mrs. Gibson ; do you
not know that Mrs. Legaré's husband and son are in
Charleston, and you will frighten her to death by your wild
talk." " Bless you, good woman," replied Mrs. Gibson,
turning to Mrs. Legaré, " I have a husband and four sons
there, too, and God only knows if any of them live." In
the course of a few days, Mrs. Gibson received the sad intelligence that her husband and four sons had all been killed
during the siege.* Such are some of the vicissitudes of
war.

It may well be asked, why did such military men as
Lincoln, Moultrie, McIntosh, Scott, Woodford and others,
suffer themselves, with a body of brave troops, to be cooped
up in a city which they were not capable of successfully defending ? At first they relied on the promises of Congress
and the Executive authorities of North and South Carolina of
sending near ten thousand men, one-half of whom should
be regulars, for the defence of the place.† In the latter
part of February, it was reported that General Hogan was
advancing with troops from North Carolina ; that General
Moultrie was forming a camp at Bacon's Bridge, which was
subsequently transferred to the command of General Huger ;
that a thousand men were expected from General Williamson's brigade in the region of Ninety Six ; and that the
veteran General Richardson, and Colonel Kershaw, were
embodying the militia of the Camden region.‡ General
Richardson sickened and died ; General Moultrie from ill-

---

* Howe's *Hist. Presb. Ch. of South Carolina*, 471.

† Ramsay's *Revolution*, ii, 59; Gordon's *American War*, iii, 348; Marshall's *Washington*, iv, 141–42;

‡ Colonel Laurens, in *Almon*, x, 53 ; Moore's *Materials for History*, 175.

ness had to return to the city. Colonel Sumter at that time had no command, and Marion was hiding away for the recovery of a broken limb. To enthuse the militia, and expedite their movements, Governor Rutledge, the Patrick Henry of South Carolina, and a part of his Councilors, left the beleaguered city in April; but they met with little success. The people relied too much upon succors from the North; besides, they were almost destitute of ammunition.

Hogan's party finally reached the city; and about that time another North Carolina contingent under General Lillington, whose term of enlistment expired, mostly availed themselves of their privilege and retired before the serious part of the siege had commenced; and less than two hundred of the South Carolina militia, probably mostly from the Charleston region, shared in the defence of the place. Congress and the States were alike crippled in resources, and everything moved tardily. General De Kalb had started, past the middle of April, with fourteen hundred Continentals from head quarters in New Jersey; Colonel Armand's corps, and Major Nelson's horse, were on the way; and, as late as the second of May, General Caswell, of North Carolina, had reached Lanneau's Ferry, on the Santee, with eight or nine hundred Continentals and militia; some militia were being gathered at Orangeburg; and Colonel Buford's and Lieutenant-Colonel Porterfield's Virginia detachments, were within the borders of the State. General Huger, with Colonel Horry's cavalry, and the remnants of Colonel White's and Colonel Washington's dragoons, were scattered somewhere about the country. There was no concert or unity of action, and probably not sufficient supplies to admit of their concentration. But all these hopes of succor to the suffering garrison were as illusive in the end as the *ignis-fatuus* to the benighted traveler.

General Lincoln was not altogether destitute of military supplies; for he had four hundred pieces of ordnance of various caliber, for the defence of the city and the neighboring works; but the mortars were few, and of shell there would seem to have been a very limited supply. Powder was so plenty that there were fifty thousand pounds at the surrender, besides ten thousand pounds more bricked up at the Exchange. But even with the aid of six hundred negroes, the defensive works, from their great extent, were totally inadequate to the purpose; and had there been force enough to have properly manned them—of which there was a sad deficiency—the scanty supply of provisions would have been all the sooner exhausted. Food supplies had been stored, in large quantities, to the north eastward of Charleston; but from the little value of the depreciated paper currency, the want of carriages and horses, together with the bad condition of the roads, they could not be transported to town before the investiture was completed. With all these disappointments and discouragements, and the powerful army and navy, with all the appliances of war, confronting them for nearly three months, it is not a little surprising that General Lincoln and his brave garrison were able to hold out so long.

Nor were the whites the only sufferers. As in Prevost's invasion of 1779, so in Clinton's of 1780, the negro servants flocked in large numbers to the British army, and were employed in throwing up their defences and other laborious operations. Crowded together, they were visited by the camp fever; and the small-pox, which had not been in the Province for seventeen years, broke out among them, and spread rapidly. From these two diseases, and the impossibility of their being provided with proper accommodations and attendance in the British encampments, they were left to die in great numbers in the woods, where they remained unburied. A few instances occurred, in which infants were found in unfrequented retreats, drawing the breasts of their deceased mothers some time after life had expired.*

The reduction of Charleston struck the people with pro-

* Ramsay's *Revolution*, ii, 67.

found amazement, coupled with something akin to despair. The futile attempts of the British against the city in 1776, and again in 1779, had inspired nearly all classes with a fatal confidence that their capital city would again escape the snares of the enemy—to be accomplished in some Providential way, of which they had no very clear conception. But in matters of war, as of peace, God helps those who help themselves. Had the people of South Carolina repaired in large numbers to their capital, with proper supplies for a long siege; or had they, while their fellows were cooped up within the devoted city, embodied under such men as Sumter, Williamson, Pickens, Kershaw, Williams and other popular leaders, harassed the besieging army, cut off its foraging parties, kept the communication open, and encouraged the beleaguered garrison to make sorties, and perhaps capture supplies from their enemies, the approaches of the British might have been retarded, and the siege prolonged till, perhaps, the arrival of DeKalb and other forces from the North.

Could the enemy have thus been retarded, they would soon have encountered a yet more dangerous foe in the rapidly approaching hot season, when camp life and exposure in that malarial climate, would have rapidly decimated their forces. And there was, perhaps, still another end to be gained by prolonging the siege On the second of May, a large French fleet, under the Chevalier de Ternay, transporting an army of nearly six thousand of the choicest troops of France, commanded by the Count de Rochambeau, had sailed from Brest, destined to aid the young Republic in its struggle for independence. On the twentieth of June, they encountered a British fleet, in latitude 30°, a little south of the Bermuda Islands, when some distant exchanging of shots occurred between them. Several days before this event, the French fleet had captured a British cutter conveying several British officers from Charleston to the Bermudas, by whom they learned of the siege and capture of

Charleston ; and, soon after taking another vessel, one of Admiral Arbuthnot's fleet, on its return to New York, they learned by its papers and passengers a full confirmation of the fall of the devoted city.*

According to Moultrie, it was the plan of Ternay and Rochambeau to have attempted the relief of Charleston, had they not have learned of its capture. Their intention was, to have entered Ball's Bay, landed the troops at Sevee's Bay, then marched down to Haddrell's Point, crossing thence over to Charleston ; " which," says Moultrie, " they could very easily have done, and would have effectually raised the siege, and taken the British fleet in Charleston harbor and in Stono Inlet, and, in all probability, their whole army.' Had the news of this approaching fleet been known in time by General Lincoln, and the people of the surrounding country, the defence of the city might have been prolonged, and, perhaps, the mortification of surrender averted—and the salvation of Charleston been celebrated in history as one of the grandest achievements of the Revolution.†

But all this misadventure was not without its compensations ; for Rochambeau's fine army landed safely at Newport, and, in time, joined Washington, giving new life and hope to the American cause, and sharing in the capture of Cornwallis the following year. It was a knowledge of the fitting out of Ternay's fleet, and its probable American destination, that prompted Sir Henry Clinton to hasten the capture of Charleston,‡ and then to expedite the larger part of his forces to the northward, lest New York should be attacked and taken by the combined French and American

---

* Rochambeau's *Memoirs*, Paris, 1824, i, 241–243 ; Almon's *Remembrancer*, x, 273

† Moultrie's *Memoirs*, ii, 202–203 ; Johnson's *Traditions*, 262.

‡ The British Government had kept a close watch on this large French fleet during the long period of its fitting out at Brest ; and, no doubt, apprised Sir Henry Clinton of the approaching danger. The *Virginia Gazette* of May 31st, 1780 has a Philadelphia item under date of May 9th, saying a gentleman from New York stated, that it was reported in that city that a French and Spanish fleet was expected upon the American coast, and that the enterprise against Charleston was to be abandoned.

troops and navy; and thus were the Southern Colonies left with Cornwallis' crippled army, rendering possible the noble services of Greene, Sumter, and Marion.

Taking advantage of the calm, British detachments were sent out in all directions to plant the Royal standard, over-awe the people, and require them to take protection. Conspicuously observable was the greediness of the conquerors for plunder. The value of the spoil, which was distributed by English and Hessian Commissaries of captures, amounted to about three hundred thousand pounds sterling; the dividend of a Major-General exceeded over four thousand guineas—or twenty thousand dollars. There was no restraint upon private rapine; the silver plate of the planters was carried off; all negroes that had belonged to Rebels were seized, even though they had themselves sought an asylum within the British lines; and, at a single embarkation, two thousand were shipped to a market in the West Indies. British and German officers thought more of amassing fortunes than of re-uniting the empire. The patriots were not allowed to appoint attorneys to manage or sell their estates. A sentence of confiscation hung over the whole land, and British protection was granted only in return for the unconditional promise of loyalty.*

The dashing Colonel Tarleton had been dispatched with his cavalry in pursuit of Colonel Buford's regiment, which had arrived too late to join the Charleston garrison; and which were overtaken near the Waxhaw settlement, and many of them cut to pieces with savage cruelty. One hundred and thirteen of Buford's men were cut down and killed outright; a hundred and fifty too badly hacked to be removed, while only fifty-three could be brought as prisoners to Camden. If anything at this time could have added to the general depression so prevalent among all classes of people, it was just such a barbarous butchery as this of

*Ramsay's *Revolution*, ii, 66–67; Gordon's *American War*, iii, 382; Bancroft's *History United States*, x, 305–6.

Tarleton's. The highest encomiums were bestowed by Cornwallis upon the hero of this sickening massacre.

On the twenty-second day of May, it was proclaimed that all who should thereafter oppose the King in arms, or hinder any one from joining his forces, should have his property confiscated, and be otherwise severely punished ; and, on the first of June, Clinton and Arbuthnot, as Royal Commissioners, offered by proclamation, pardon to the penitent, on condition of their immediate return to allegiance ; and to the loyal, the pledge of their former political immunities, including freedom from taxation, save by their own chosen Legislature. On the third of that month, another proclamation by Clinton, required all the inhabitants of the Province, " who were now prisoners on parole" to take an active part in maintaining the Royal Government; and they were assured, that "should they neglect to return to their allegiance, they will be treated as rebels to the Government of the King."

Thus tyrannical measures were advanced step by step till the poor paroled people could no longer be protected, as they had been promised, by remaining quietly at home ; but must take up arms in defence of the Government they abhorred, and which was forging chains for their perpetual enslavement. On the eve of his departure for New York, leaving the Southern command under Lord Cornwallis, Clinton reported to his Royal masters in England : " The inhabitants from every quarter declare their allegiance to the King, and offer their services in arms. There are few men in South Carolina who are not either our prisoners or in arms with us."

A few weeks later, when two prominent men, one who had filled a high position, and both prominently concerned in the rebellion, went to Cornwallis to surrender themselves under the provisions of Clinton and Arbuthnot's proclamation, the noble Earl could only answer that he had no knowledge of its existence. And thus his Lordship commenced his career as Commander-in-Chief of the Southern department, ignoring all ideas and promises of a policy of moderation. He sowed the wind, and in the end reaped the whirlwind.

The people of South Carolina, as we have seen, were not sufficiently aroused to a sense of their danger, until it was too late to avert it—if, indeed, they, alone and single-handed, could by any possibility have warded off the great public calamity. When they learned the appalling news of the surrender of Charleston, they had little heart to make any further show of opposition to the power of the British Government. Many of the country leaders, when detachments of the conquering troops were sent among them, unresistingly gave up their arms, and took Royal protection —among whom were General Andrew Williamson, General Isaac Huger, Colonel Andrew Pickens, Colonel Peter Horry, Colonel James Mayson, Colonel LeRoy Hammond, Colonel John Thomas, Sr., Colonel Isaac Hayne, Major John Postell, Major John Purvis, and many others. Sumter braved the popular tide for submission, retired alone before the advancing foe, leaving his home to the torch of the enemy, and his helpless family without a roof to cover their defenceless heads, or a morsel of food for their sustenance ; while Marion, who was accidently injured at Charleston, was conveyed from the city before its final environment, and was quietly recuperating in some sequestered place in the swamps of the lower part of the country. And, so far as South Carolina was concerned,

<blockquote>" Hope for a season bade the world farewell."</blockquote>

CHAPTER III.

1741 to May, 1780.

Early Life of Patrick Ferguson.—Brandywine Battle—Refrains from Shooting Washington—Wounded.—Conducts Little Egg Harbor Expedition.—Nearly Killed by an Accidental Attack by his own Friends. —Biggin Bridge and Monk's Corner Affair.—Resents Insults to Ladies.—Siege of Charleston.

No man, perhaps, of his rank and years, ever attained more military distinction in his day than Patrick Ferguson. As his name will hereafter figure so prominently in this narrative, it is but simple justice to his memory, and alike due to the natural curiosity of the reader, that his career should be as fully and impartially portrayed as the materials will permit.

He was the second son of James Ferguson, afterward Lord Pitfour, of Pitfour, an eminent advocate, and for twelve years one of the Scotch Judges, and was born in Aberdeenshire, Scotland, in 1744. His mother was Anne Murray, daughter of Alexander, Lord Elibank. His father, and his uncle, James Murray, Lord Elibank, were regarded as men of large culture, equal, in erudition and genius, to the authors of the Scottish Augustan age. Having acquired an early education, "young Ferguson," says a British writer, "sought fame by a different direction, *but was of equally vigorous and brilliant powers.*" When only in his fifteenth year, a commission was purchased for him, and he entered the army July twelfth, 1759, as a Cornet, in the second or Royal North British Dragoons, serving in the wars of Flanders and Germany, wherein he distinguished himself by a courage as cool as it was determined. He soon evinced the great purpose of his life—to become conspicuously beneficial by professional skill and effort.

Young Ferguson joined the army in Germany soon after the engagement on the plains of Minden. Some skirmishing took place in the subsequent part of that year. On the thirtieth of June, 1760, the Dragoons, to which he was attached, with other corps, drove the French cavalry from the field, and chased their infantry in disorder through Warbourg, and across the Rymel river, gaining from the Commander-in-Chief the compliment of having performed " prodigies of valor." On the twenty-second of August, the Dragoons defeated a French party near Zierenberg, making a brilliant charge, and deciding the contest. In the following month they captured Zierenberg, with two cannon and three hundred prisoners. During the year 1761, the Dragoons were similarly employed; but suffered much from the bad quality of the water. Ferguson becoming disabled by sickness, was sent home, and remained the most of the time in England and Scotland from 1762 until 1768.

On the first of September, in the latter year, a commission of Captain was purchased for him in the seventieth regiment of foot, then stationed in the Caribbee Islands, in the West Indies, whither he repaired, and performed important service in quelling an insurrection of the Caribs on the Island of St. Vincent. These Caribs were a mixture of the African with the native Indian tribes; they were brave, expert in the use of fire-arms, and their native fastnesses had greatly aided them in their resistance to the Government. The troops suffered much in this service.

The regiment remained in the Caribbee Islands till 1773. About this period, Captain Ferguson was stationed a while in the peaceful garrison of Halifax, in Nova Scotia; and disdaining inglorious ease, he embarked for England, where he assiduously employed his time in acquiring military knowledge and science. When the disputes between the Mother country and her Colonies were verging toward

4

hostilities, the boasted skill of the Americans in the use of
the rifle, was regarded as an object of terror to the British
troops. These rumors operated on the genius of Ferguson,
and he invented a new species of rifle, which could be
loaded with greater celerity, and fired with more precision
than any then in use. He could load his newly constructed
gun at the breech, without using the ramrod, and with such
quickness and repetition as to fire seven times in a minute.

He was regarded as the best rifle shot in the British
army, if not the best marksman living—excepting, possibly, his old associate, George Hanger ;* and in adroitness
and celerity in loading and firing, whether prostrate or

---

* This possible exception should be somewhat qualified. The British writers, including
several who knew whereof they wrote, unite in ascribing this high character to Ferguson's
skill in the use of his improved rifle. Major Hanger, in his *Life and Opinions*, written
after Ferguson had been twenty years in his grave, claims not simply equal, but superior
skill. The redoubtable Major relates, with no little *naïvete*, this ludicrous anecdote, as
occurring in New York City, in 1782, when Sir Guy Carleton had become Commander-in-
Chief of the British forces. Sitting opposite the Major at dinner one day, Sir Guy said:
"Major Hanger, I have been told that you are a most skilful marksman with a rifle-gun—I
have heard of astonishing feats that you have performed in shooting." Thanking him for
the compliment, I told his Excellency, that "I was vain enough to say, with truth, that
many officers in the army had witnessed my adroitness. I then began to inform Sir Guy
how my old deceased friend, Colonel Ferguson, and myself, had practiced together, who, for
skill and knowledge of that weapon, had been so celebrated, and that Ferguson had ever
acknowledged the superiority of my skill to his, after one particular day's practice, when
I had shot three balls into one hole." Sir Guy replied to this : "I know you are very
expert in this art." Now, had I been quiet, and satisfied with the compliment the Commander-in-Chief paid me, and not pushed the matter further, it had been well for me ; but I
replied: "Yes, Sir Guy, I really have reduced the art of shooting with a rifle to such a
nicety, that, at a moderate distance, I can *kill a flea* with a single ball." At this, Sir Guy
began to stare not a little, and seemed to indicate from the smile on his countenance, that he
thought I had rather out-stepped my usual out-doings in the art. Observing this, I respectfully replied: "I see by your Excellency's countenance that you seem doubtful of the
singularity and perfection of my art ; but if I may presume so much, as to dare offer a wager
to my Commander-in-Chief, I will bet your Excellency five guineas that I kill a flea with a
single ball once in eight shots, at eight yards." Sir Guy replied : "My dear Major, I am
not given to lay wagers, but for once I will bet you five guineas, provided you will *let the
flea hop*." A loud laugh ensued at the table ; and, after laughing heartily myself, I placed
my knuckle under the table, and striking it from beneath, said : "Sir Guy, I knock under,
and will never speak of my skill in shooting with a rifle-gun again before you."

Neither Ferguson nor Hanger were aware of a remarkable youth at that time in the
Wheeling region. Lewis Wetzel, who had learned to load but a common rifle as he sped
swiftly through the woods with a pack of Indians at his heels. Killing one of a party, four
others singled out, determined to catch alive the bold young warrior. First, one fell a victim to his unerring rifle, then another, and finally a third, in the race for life ; when the
only survivor stopped short, gave a yell of despair and disappointment, saying : "No
catch dat man—gun always loaded."

erect, he is said to have excelled the best American frontiersman, or even the expert Indian of the forest. He often practiced, and exhibited his dexterity in the use of the rifle, both at Black Heath and Woolwich. Such was his execution in firing, that it almost exceeded the bounds of credibility, having very nearly brought his aim at an objective point almost to a mathematical certainty.

On the first of June, 1776, Captain Ferguson made some rifle experiments at Woolwich, in the presence of Lord Townshend, master of ordnance, Generals Amherst and Hawley, and other officers of high rank and large military experience. Notwithstanding a heavy rain, and a high wind, he fired during the space of four or five minutes, at the rate of four shots per minute, at a target two hundred yards distance. He next fired six shots in a minute. He also fired, while advancing at the rate of four miles per hour, four times in a minute. He then poured a bottle of water into the pan and barrel of the rifle when loaded, so as to wet every grain of powder; and, in less than half a minute, he fired it off, as well as ever, without extracting the ball. Lastly, he hit the bull's eye target, lying on his back on the ground. Incredible as it might seem, considering the variations of the wind, and the wetness of the weather, he missed the target only three times during the whole series of experiments. These military dignitaries were not only satisfied but astonished at the perfection of both his rifle and his practice. On one of these occasions, George the Third honored him with his presence; and, towards the close of the year, a patent was granted for all his improvements.

According to the testimony of eye-witnesses, he would check his horse, let the reins fall upon the animal's neck, draw a pistol from his holster, toss it aloft, catch it as it fell, aim, and shoot the head off a bird on an adjacent fence.*
"It is not certain," says the British *Annual Register* for

---

* General J. W. D. DePeyster's *King's Mountain*, in *Historical Magazine* March 1869, p. 100.

1781, "that these improvements produced all the effect in real service, which had been expected from those astonishing specimens of them that were displayed in England."

Anxious to take an active part in the American war, a hundred select men were chosen for his command, whom he took unwearied pains to instruct in the dextrous use of his newly invented rifle. In the spring of 1777, he was sent to America—to him, a much coveted service. Joining the main army under Sir Henry Clinton, he was placed at the head of a corps of riflemen, picked from the different regiments, and soon after participated, under Sir William Howe, in the battle of Brandywine, on the eleventh of September. "General Knyphausen," says a British writer, "with another division, marched to Chad's Ford, against the Provincials who were placed there. In this service the German General experienced very important assistance from a corps of riflemen commanded by Captain Patrick Ferguson, whose meritorious conduct was acknowledged by the whole British army."

In a private letter from Captain Ferguson, to his kinsman, Dr. Adam Ferguson, he details a very curious incident, which occurred while he lay, with his riflemen, in the skirt of a wood, in front of Knyphausen's division. "We had not lain long," says Captain Ferguson, "when a Rebel officer, remarkable by a hussar dress, passed towards our army, within a hundred yards of my right flank, not perceiving us. He was followed by another, dressed in dark green and blue, mounted on a bay horse, with a remarkably high cocked hat. I ordered three good shots to steal near to and fire at them; but the idea disgusting me, I recalled the order. The hussar, in returning, made a circuit, but the other passed within a hundred yards of us, upon which I advanced from the wood towards him. Upon my calling, he stopped; but after looking at me, he proceeded. I again drew his attention, and made signs to him to stop, levelling my piece at him; but he slowly cantered away. As I was within that distance, at which, in the quickest firing, I could have lodged half a dozen balls in or about him, before he was out of my reach, I had only to determine; but it was not pleasant to fire at the back of an unoffending individual, who was acquitting himself very coolly of his duty—so I let him alone. The day after, I had been telling this story to some wounded officers who lay in the same room with me, when one of the surgeons, who had been dressing the wounded Rebel officers, came in, and told us, that they had been informing him that General Washington was all the morning with the light troops, and only attended by a French officer in hussar dress, he himself dressed and mounted in every point as above described. *I am not sorry that I did not know at the time who it was.*"*

A British writer suggestively remarks, in this connection, that, "unfortunately Ferguson did not personally know Washington, otherwise the Rebels would have had a new General to seek." Had Washington fallen, it is difficult to calculate its probable effect upon the result of the struggle of the American people. How slight, oftentimes, are the incidents which, in the course of events, seem to give direction to the most momentous concerns of the human race. This singular impulse of Ferguson, illustrates, in a forcible manner, the over-ruling hand of Providence in directing the operation of a man's mind when he himself is least of all aware of it.

There is, however, some doubt whether it was really Washington whom Ferguson was too generous to profit by his advantage. James Fenimore Cooper relates, in the New York *Mirror*, of April sixteenth, 1831, on the authority of his late father-in-law, Major John P. DeLancey, some interesting facts, corroborating the main features of the story. DeLancey was the second in command of Ferguson's riflemen, and had seen Washington in Philadelphia

* *Percy Anecdotes*, Harper's edition, ii, 52; British *Annual Register*, 1781, 51; *Political Magazine*, 1781, 60; *Hist. of War in America*, iii, 149; Andrews' *Hist of the War*, iv, 84; James' *Life of Marion*, 76-77; Irving's Washington, iv, 51-52; Day's *Pennsylvania Hist. Colls.*, 213; *National Intelligencer*, May, 1831.

the year before the commencement of the war.   " During
the manœuvres which preceded the battle of Brandywine,"
said Mr. Cooper, "these riflemen were kept skirmishing
in advance of one of the British columns. They had crossed
some open ground, in which Ferguson was wounded in the
arm, and had taken a position in the skirts of a thick wood.
While Captain DeLancey was occupied in arranging a sling
for Ferguson's wounded arm, it was reported that an American officer of rank, attended only by a mounted orderly,
had ridden into the open ground, and was then within point-
blank rifle shot.   Two or three of the best marksmen
stepped forward, and asked leave to bring him down.   Ferguson peremptorily refused ; but he went to the wood, and
showing himself, menaced the American with several rifles,
while he called to him, and made signs to him to come in.
The mounted officer saw his enemies, drew his reins, and
sat looking at them attentively for a few moments.

" A sergeant," continues Mr. Cooper, " now offered to
hit the horse without injuring the rider, but Ferguson still
withheld his consent, affirming that it was Washington reconnoitering, and that he would not be the instrument of
placing the life of so great a man in jeopardy by so unfair
means.   The horseman turned and rode slowly away.   To
his last moment, Ferguson maintained that the officer whose
life he had spared was Washington.   I have often heard
Captain DeLancey relate these circumstances, and though
he never pretended to be sure of the person of the unknown
horseman, it was his opinion, from some particulars of dress
and' stature, that it was the Count Pulaski.   Though in
error as to the person of the individual whom he spared,
the merit of Major Ferguson is not at all diminished " by
its supposed correction.

Captain Ferguson, as we have seen, encountered some
American sharp-shooters in the battle as keen and skillful
as himself in the use of the rifle, and received a dangerous
wound which so shattered his right arm, as to forever after

render it useless.* During the period of his unfitness for service, General Howe distributed his riflemen among other corps ; but on his recovery, he again embodied them, and renewed his former active career. When satisfied that he would never regain the use of his right hand, he practiced, and soon acquired the use of his sword, with the left. A writer in the *Political Magazine* for 1781, states that Ferguson was in the battle of Germantown, on the fourth of October ensuing—was there wounded, and there came near bringing his rifle to bear on Washington ; but it is not probable that he was sufficiently recovered of his severe wound received at Brandywine, to have taken the field three weeks afterwards—besides, the authorities show, that it was at Brandywine where he so narrowly escaped the temptation to try the accuracy of his rifle on the American Commander-in-Chief, or some other prominent officer, making observations, and where he was so grievously wounded.

When the British evacuated Philadelphia, in June, 1778, Captain Ferguson accompanied the retiring forces to New York, and, of course, participated in the battle of Monmouth on the way. It was fought on one of the hottest days of the summer, when many of the British soldiers died from the effects of the heat. For some time after reaching New York, Captain Ferguson and his rifle corps were not called on to engage in any active service.

Little Egg Harbor, on the eastern coast of New Jersey, had long been noted as a place of rendezvous for American privateers, which preyed largely upon British commerce. A vast amount of property had been brought into this port, captured from the enemy. " To destroy this nest of rebel pirates," as a British writer termed it, an expedition was fitted out from New York, the close of September, 1778, composed of three hundred regulars, and a body of one hundred Royalist volunteers, all under the command of Cap-

* Beatson's *Naval and Military Memoirs*, vi, 83 ; Mackenzie's *Strictures on Tarleton*, 23.

tain Ferguson.   Captain Henry Colins, of the Navy, transported the troops in eight or ten armed vessels, and shared
in the enterprise.   From untoward weather, they were long
at sea.   General Washington, hearing of the expedition,
dispatched Count Pulaski and his Legion cavalry, and at
the same time sent an express to Tuckerton, as did also
Governor Livingston, giving information, so that four privateers put to sea and escaped, while others took refuge up
the Little Egg Harbor river.   Ferguson's party reached the
Harbor on the afternoon of the fifth of October, and,
taking his smaller craft, pushed twenty miles up the stream
to Chestnut Neck, where were several vessels, about a dozen
houses, with stores for the reception of the prize goods,
and accommodations for the privateers men.   Here were
some works erected for the protection of the place, and a
few men' occupying them ; but no artillery had yet been
placed there   The prize vessels were hastily scuttled and
dismantled, and the small American party easily driven into
the woods, when Captain Ferguson's force demolished the
batteries, burning ten vessels and the houses in the village.
The British in this affair had none killed, and but a single
soldier wounded.   Had he arrived sooner, Ferguson intended to have pushed forward with celerity twenty miles
farther, to "The Forks," which was accounted only thirty-
five miles from Philadelphia.   But the alarm had been
spread through the country, and the local militia had been
reinforced by Pulaski's cavalry, and five field pieces of
Colonel Proctor's artillery ; so the idea of reaching and
destroying the stores and small craft there, had to be abandoned.

Returning the next day, October the seventh, down the
river, they reached two of their armed sloops, which had got
aground on their upward passage, and were still fast.
They were lightened, and got off the next morning.   During the delay, Captain Ferguson employed his troops,
under cover of the gunboats, in an excursion on the north

shore, to destroy some principal salt works, also some stores, dwellings, and Tucker's Mill; these were sacked and laid in ashes—all, as was asserted by the British, being the property of persons concerned in privateering, or "whose activity in the cause of America, and unrelenting persecution of the Loyalists, marked them out as the objects of vengeance." As those persons were pointed out by the New Jersey Tory volunteers, who accompanied the expedition, we may well imagine that private pique, and neighborhood feuds, entered largely into these proscriptions.

To cover Ferguson's expedition, and distract the attention of Washington, Sir Henry Clinton had detached Lord Cornwallis with five thousand men into New Jersey, and General Knyphausen with three thousand into Westchester county. Learning of Colonel Baylor's dragoons being at old Tappan, Cornwallis selected General Grey to surprise them which he effected much in the same manner as Ferguson subsequently struck Pulaski's infantry, unawares—eleven having been killed outright, twenty-five mangled with repeated thrusts, some receiving ten, twelve, and even sixteen wounds. It was a merciless treatment of men who sued for quarter. Among the wounded were Colonel Baylor and Major Clough —the latter, mortally; and about forty prisoners taken, mostly through the humane interposition of one of Grey's Captains, whose feelings revolted at the orders of his sanguinary commander—the same commander who had, the year before, performed a similarly bloody enterprise against Wayne, at Paoli.

Recalling these predatory parties to New York, Sir Henry Clinton directed Admiral Gambier to write Captain Colins in their joint behalf, that they thought it unsafe for him and Captain Ferguson to remain longer in New Jersey. But Captain Colins' vessels being wind-bound for several days, gave Captain Ferguson time for another enterprise. On the evening of the thirteenth of October, some deserters from Pulaski's Legion gave information of that corps being posted, within striking distance, eleven miles up the river; when Ferguson formed the design of attempting their surprise.

The chief of these deserters was one Juliet, a renegade from the Hessians the preceding winter, who was sent by the Board of War to Pulaski, without a commission indeed, but with orders to permit him to do the duty of a Sub-Lieutenant in the Legion. This man was treated with such disrespect by Lieutenant-Colonel Baron De Bosen, whose high sense of honor led him to despise a person, who, even though a commissioned officer, could be guilty of deserting his colors, that the culprit determined to revenge himself in a manner that could not have been foreseen or imagined. Under pretence of fishing, he one day left the camp with five others, and as they did not return at the proper time, and it could not be supposed that Juliet would have the hardihood to rejoin the enemy, they were thought to have been drowned. But Juliet had the duplicity to debauch three of the soldiers, and the other two were forced to go with them.

Pulaski's corps, as the deserters correctly stated, consisted of three companies of infantry, occupying three houses by themselves, under the Lieutenant-Colonel Baron De Bosen; while Pulaski, with a troop of cavalry, was stationed some distance beyond, with a detachment of artillery, having a brass field piece. Accordingly Ferguson selected two hundred and fifty men, partly marines, leaving in boats at eleven o'clock on the night of the fourteenth; and, after rowing ten miles, they reached a bridge at four o'clock the next morning, within a mile of Pulaski's infantry. The bridge was seized, so as to cover their retreat, and fifty men left for its defence. DeBosen's infantry companies were surrounded and completely surprised, and attacked as they emerged from their houses. "It being a night attack," says Ferguson, in his report, "little quarter could, of course, be given"—so they cut, and slashed, and bayoneted, killing all who came in their way, and taking only five prisoners.

The Americans, roused from their slumbers, fought as well as they could.

The hapless Baron De Bosen, on the first alarm, rushed out, armed with his sword and pistols; and though he was a remarkably stout man, and fought like a lion, he was soon overpowered by numbers and killed. So far, at least, as the double-traitor, Juliet,* was concerned, revenge on De Bosen seems to have been his object; and his voice was distinctly heard exclaiming, amid the din and confusion of the strife: "This is the Colonel—kill him!" De Bosen's body was found pierced with bayonets. Lieutenant De La Borderie, together with some forty of the men, were also among the slain. It was a sad and sanguinary occurrence.

On the first alarm, Pulaski hastened with his cavalry to the support of his unfortunate infantry, when the British, hearing the clattering hoofs, giving note of their approach, fled in disorder, leaving behind them arms, accoutrements, hats, blades, etc. Pulaski captured a few prisoners; but between the place of conflict and the bridge was very swampy, over which the cavalry could scarcely walk. Reaching the bridge, they found the plank thrown off, to prevent pursuit by the cavalry. The riflemen, and some of the infantry, however, passed over on the string-pieces, and fired some volleys on the rear of the retreating foe, which they returned. "We had the advantage," says Pulaski, "and made them run again, although they out-numbered us." As the cavalry could not pass the stream, Pulaski recalled his pioneers; and he adds, in his report, that his party cut off about twenty-five of Ferguson's men in their retreat, who took refuge in the woods, and doubtless subsequently rejoined their friends. Ferguson's loss, as he reported it, was two killed, three wounded, and one missing.

---

* Juliet seems not to have been crowned with honors by the British on his return. A British Diary of the Revolution, published in Vol. iv of the *Historical Magazine*, p. 136, under date Newport, R. I., January 11th, 1779, states: "In the fleet from Long Island arrived several Hessians, among them is one Lieutenant Juliet, of the Landgrave regiment who deserted to the Provincials when the Island was besieged by them, and then went back to New York. *He is under an arrest.*"

He attempted to excuse the butchery of Pulaski's unsuspecting infantry, by alleging that he learned from the deserters, who came to him, that the Count had, in public orders, forbade all granting of quarters—information which proved to be false, and which Ferguson should never have trusted, especially on the word of deserters. It is creditable, however, to his humanity, amid the excitements and horrors of war, that he refrained from wantonly destroying the houses of non-combatants, though they sheltered the personal effects of his enemies. " We had an opportunity," says Ferguson, in his report to Sir Henry Clinton, "of destroying part of the baggage and equipage of Pulaski's Legion, by burning their quarters, but, as the houses belonged to some inoffensive Quakers, who, I am afraid, have sufficiently suffered already in the confusion of a night's scramble, I know, Sir, that you will think with us, that the injury to be thereby done to the enemy, would not have compensated for the sufferings of these innocent people."

As the fleet were going out of Little Egg Harbor, the Zebra, the flag-ship, grounded, and to prevent her from falling into the hands of the Americans, Captain Colins ordered her set on fire ; and as the fire reached her guns, they were discharged, much to the amusement of the Americans, who beheld the conflagration. Besides their military operations, Judge Jones, the Royalist historian of New York, states of Ferguson and his men, that they " plundered the inhabitants, burnt their houses, their churches, and their barns ; ruined their farms ; stole their cattle, hogs, horses, and sheep, and then triumphantly returned to New York "—evidently conveying the idea that this mode of warfare was not honorable to those who ordered, nor to those who were engaged in it.

Irving denounces Ferguson's enterprise as " a marauding expedition, worthy of the times of the buccaneers." Sir Henry Clinton, on the other hand, reported it to the Home Government, as a " success. under the direction of that very active and zealous officer, Ferguson," while Admiral Gambier pronounced it "a spirited service." Ferguson fully accomplished the purpose for which he set out—the destruction of the vessels, stores, and works at Little Egg Harbor; and, in addition, inflicted a severe blow on a portion of Pulaski's Legion.*

During the campaign of 1779, Captain Ferguson was engaged in several predatory incursions along the coast, and on the Hudson—having been stationed awhile at Stony Point before its capture by Wayne; steadily increasing the confidence of his superiors, and extorting the respect of the Americans for his valor and enterprise. On the twenty-fifth of October, in this year, he was promoted to the rank of Major in the second battalion of the seventy-first regiment, or Highland Light Infantry, composed of Frasers, Campbells, McArthurs, McDonalds, McLeods, and many others of the finest Scotch laddies in the British service.

When Sir Henry Clinton fitted out his expedition against Charleston, at the close of 1779, he very naturally selected Major Ferguson to share in the important enterprise. A corps of three hundred men, called the American Volunteers, was assigned for his command—he having the choice of both officers and soldiers; and for this special service, he had given him, the rank of Lieutenant-Colonel. At his request, Major Hanger's corps of two hundred Hessians were to be joined to Ferguson's. Early in February, the seventy-first regiment and Ferguson's corps were sent from Savannah to Augusta; and, early in March, the American Volunteers formed a part of the Georgia troops, who were ordered, under General Patterson, to march towards Charleston, and join the main force under Sir Henry Clinton.

---

* Touching this Little Egg Harbor expedition, see reports of Sir Henry Clinton, Admiral Gambier, Captains Ferguson and Colins, in *Almon* x. 150–56; Pulaski's report, Pennsylvania *Packet*, October 20, 1778; Rivington's *Royal Gazette*, October 24, 1778; *Political Magazine*, 1781. p. 60; Marshall's *Washington*, revised edition, i. 270–71; *Reply to Judge Johnson*, vindicating Count Pulaski, by Paul Bentalou, senior captain in Pulaski's Legion, 1826. 36–37; Irving's *Washington*, iii. 472–75; Bancroft's *History*, x, 152; Lossing's *Field Book*, ii. 529; Barber & Howes' *New Jersey*, 108–9; and Jones' *History of New York During the Revolutionary War*, i, 287.

On the thirteenth of the month, Lieutenant-Colonel Ferguson, with his Volunteers, and Major Cochrane, with the infantry of Tarleton's Legion, were ordered forward to secure the passes at Bee Creek, Coosahatchie, and Tully Finny bridges, about twenty-six miles in advance of the army, which was as promptly effected as the obstacles in the way would permit. It was a toilsome march through swamps and difficult passes, having frequent skirmishes with the opposing militia of the country. These active officers, with their light troops, received intelligence of two parties of mounted Americans at some distance in advance, and at once resolved to surprise them by a night attack—a kind of service for which Colonel Ferguson had an especial fitness, and in which he took unusual delight.

Arriving at nine o'clock in the evening near the spot from which he meant to dislodge the Americans, at Mc-Pherson's plantation, Ferguson discovered that they had decamped, and he consequently took possession of their abandoned position, camping there for the night, and awaiting the arrival of the main British force, who were to pass near it the next morning. Major Cochrane, with his party, piloted by another route, through swamps and by-ways, arrived, before morning, just in front of Ferguson's camp; and, judging by the fires that the Americans were still there, led his men to the attack with fixed bayonets. Ferguson, expecting that the American party might return, had his picket guard out, who, seeing the approach of what they regarded as an enemy, gave the alarm, when the Legion rushed upon them, driving them pell-mell to Ferguson's camp, where the aroused American Volunteers were ready to receive them. "Charge!" was the word on both sides; and, for a little season, the conflict raged. Ferguson, wielding his sword in his left hand, defended himself, as well as he could, against three assailants, who opposed him with fixed bayonets, one of which was unfortunately thrust through his left arm. When on the point of falling, amid the confusion and clashing of arms, Major Cochrane and Colonel Ferguson, almost at the same moment, recognized each other's voices, and exerted themselves to put a stop to the mistaken conflict. Two of Ferguson's men, and one of the Legion, were killed in this unhappy affair, and several wounded on both sides. Lieutenant McPherson, of the Legion, received bayonet wounds in the hand and shoulder.

But for the timely recognition, on the part of the commanders, of the mutual mistake, Colonel Ferguson would most likely have lost his life—"a life," says Major Hanger, "equally valuable to the whole army, and to his friends."

"It was melancholy enough," wrote a participant in the affair, near three weeks afterwards, "to see Colonel Ferguson disabled in both arms; but, thank God, he is perfectly recovered again." Tarleton commends "the intrepidity and presence of mind of the leaders," in this casual engagement, as having saved their respective parties from a more fatal termination. "The whole army felt for the gallant Ferguson," says Hanger; and the peculiar circumstances attending this unlucky conflict, long furnished the camp and bivouac with a melancholy topic of conversation.*

The fleet having crossed the bar, and gained the water command thence to Charleston, enabled Sir Henry Clinton to bestow more attention than he had hitherto done, to cutting off the communications of the Americans between the city and country. A body of militia, together with the remains of three Continental regiments of light dragoons, led by Colonel Washington and others, and all under the command of General Huger, were stationed at Biggin Bridge, near Monk's Corner, about thirty miles from Charleston. To destroy or disperse this party, and thus prevent supplies of food and reinforcements of men to the beleaguered city, was a capital object with Sir Henry Clinton; and its immediate execution was assigned to Colonel

---

* Tarleton's *Campaigns*, 7-8; Mackenzie's *Strictures on Tarleton*, 23; Hanger's *Reply to Mackenzie*, 24-25; *Siege of Charleston*, 158-59.

Tarleton and his Legion, to be seconded by Lieutenant-Colonel Ferguson and his riflemen. Tarleton was dashing, tireless, and unmerciful. "Ferguson," says Irving, "was a fit associate for Tarleton, in hardy, scrambling, partisan enterprise; equally intrepid and determined, but cooler, and more open to impulses of humanity."

As a night march had been judged the most advisable, Tarleton and Ferguson moved, on the evening of April thirteenth, from Goose creek, half way from Charleston, to strike, if possible, an effective blow at Huger's camp. Some distance beyond, a negro was descried attempting to leave the road, and avoid notice. He was seized, and was discovered to be a servant of one of Huger's officers. A letter was taken from his pocket, written by his master the preceding afternoon, which, with the negro's intelligence, purchased for a few dollars, proved a fortunate circumstance for the advancing party. They learned the relative positions of Huger's forces, on both sides of Cooper river, and had in him a guide to direct them there, through unfrequented paths and by-ways.

Destitute of patrols, Huger was, in effect, taken completely by surprise; and the bold and sudden onset, about three o'clock in the morning of the fourteenth, quickly scattered the astonished Americans. They had, indeed, some slight notice of the attack; but they were not properly prepared for it. The cavalry was posted on the side of the river where the first approach was made, and the infantry on the opposite bank. "Although," says Ramsay, "the commanding officer of the American cavalry had taken the precaution of having his horses saddled and bridled, and the alarm was given by his videttes, posted at the distance of a mile in front; yet, being entirely unsupported by infantry, the British advanced so rapidly, notwithstanding the opposition of the advanced guard, that they began their attack on the main body before they could put themselves in a posture of defence." Then Major Cochrane, with Tarleton's Legion, quickly forced the passage of Biggin Bridge, and drove General Huger and the infantry before him. " In this affair," says James, " Major James Conyers, of the Americans, distinguished himself by a skillful retreat, and by calling off the attention of the enemy from his sleeping friends to himself. In this surprise, the British made free use of the bayonet ; the houses in Monk's Corner, then a village, were afterwards deserted, but long bore the marks of deadly thrust and much blood-shed."

Several officers, who attempted to defend themselves, were killed or wounded. The assailing party lost but one officer and two privates wounded, with five horses killed or disabled. General Huger, Colonel Washington, and Major Jameson, with most of their troops, fled to the adjacent swamps and thickets ; while three Captains, one Lieutenant, and ten privates were killed ; one Major, one Captain, two Lieutenants, and fifteen privates were wounded, and sixty-four officers and men, including the wounded, were made prisoners. Some two hundred horses, from thirty to forty wagons, and quite a supply of provisions and military stores, were among the trophies of the victors. If it was not a " shameful surprise," as General Moultrie pronounced it, it was, at least, a very distressing affair for the Americans. Poor General Huger, and his aid, John Izard, remained in the swamp from Friday morning, the time of the surprise, till the succeeding Monday ; it was a long fast, and the exposure produced severe sickness on the part of the General, causing him to retire awhile from the service.*

Among the American wounded was Major Vernier, a French officer, who commanded the remains of the Legion of Count Casimir Pulaski, who had lost his life at Savannah the preceding autumn. " The Major," says Steadman, a British historian and eye-witness, " was mangled in the most shocking manner ; he had several wounds, a severe

---

* Ramsay's *Revolution*, ii, 64; Moultrie's *Memoirs*, ii, 72; Tarleton's *Campaigns*, 15-17; Steadman's *American War*, ii, 182-83; James' *Life of Marion*, 36-37; *Siege of Charleston*, 124, 164; Simm's *South Carolina in the Revolution*, 125, 138; Irving's *Washington*, iv, 51-52.

one behind his ear. This unfortunate officer lived several hours, reprobating the Americans for their conduct on this occasion, and even in his last moments cursing the British for their barbarity, in having refused quarter after he had surrendered. The writer of this, who was ordered on this expedition, afforded every assistance in his power, and had the Major put upon a table, in a public house in the village, and a blanket thrown over him. In his last moments, the Major was frequently insulted by the privates of the Legion." Such merciless treatment of a dying foe, was eminently befitting the savage character of Tarleton and his men.

British historians repel, with indignant language, the charge of permitting the violation or abuse of females to go unpunished; yet Commissary Steadman relates a case highly derogatory of the conduct of some of Tarleton's Legion. In the course of this maraud, several of the dragoons broke into the house of Sir John Colleton, in the neighborhood of Monk's Corner, and maltreated and attempted violence upon three ladies residing there—one, the wife of a Charleston physician, a most delicate and beautiful woman, was most barbarously treated; another lady received one or two sword wounds; while an unmarried lady, a sister of a prominent American Major, was also shamefully misused. They all succeeded in making their escape to Monk's Corner, where they were protected; and a carriage being provided, they were escorted to a house in that region. The guilty dragoons were apprehended, and brought to camp, where, by this time, Colonel Webster had arrived and taken the command. " Colonel Ferguson," says Steadman, " was for putting the dragoons to instant death ; but Colonel Webster did not conceive that his powers extended to that of holding a general court-martial.*

---

* It must not be inferred that Colonel Webster, who was the next year killed at Guilford, was indifferent to such offences; for, we are assured, that to an officer under his command, who had so far forgotten himself as to offer an insult to a lady, he hurled many a bitter imprecation, and had him immediately turned out of the regiment.—*Political Magazine*, 1781, 342.

The prisoners were, however, sent to head-quarters, and, I *believe*, were afterwards tried and whipped." This decisive action on the part of Colonel Ferguson was highly creditable to his head and his heart. "We honor," says Irving, " the rough soldier, Ferguson, for the fiat of 'instant death,' with which he would have requited the most infamous and dastardly outrage that brutalizes warfare." Tarleton, possessing none of the finer feelings of human nature, failed to second Ferguson's efforts to bring the culprits to punishment; for, "afterwards, in England, he had the effrontery to boast, in the presence of a lady of respectability, that he had killed more men, and ravished more women, than any man in America." *

The long protracted siege of Charleston was now drawing to a close. In the latter part of April, Colonel Ferguson marched down with a party, and captured a small redoubt at Haddrell's Point, half a mile above Sullivan's Island; and, on the seventh of May, he obtained permission to attack Fort Moultrie, and while upon the march for that object, he received intelligence of the surrender of the Fort to Captain Hudson, who was relieved of the command by Colonel Ferguson.† And shortly thereafter, General Lincoln gave up the city he had so long and so valiantly defended.

---

* Steadman's *American War,* ii, 183; Irving's *Washington,* iv, 52–53; Garden's *Anecdotes,* Field's Brooklyn edition, 1865, ii, App'x viii; Mrs. Warren's *Hist. Am. Revolution,* ii, 197.

† *Siege of Charleston,* 165-66; Tarleton's *Campaigns,* 50.

CHAPTER IV.

1780—May—July.

*Colonel Ferguson sent to the District of Ninety Six.—Organizing the
Local Militia.—Major Hanger's account of the up-country inhabi-
tants—his own bad reputation.—Ferguson's seductive promises to
the people.—The Tory, David Fanning.—Ferguson's adaptation to
his Mission—Mrs. Jane Thomas' adventure.—Colonel Thomas repels
a Tory assault at Cedar Spring.—Ferguson advances to Fair Forest.
—Character of the Tories—Stories of their plunderings.—Colonels
Clarke and Jones of Georgia—the latter surprises a Tory camp.—
Dunlap and Mills attack McDowell's camp on North Pacolet.—
Captain Hampton's pursuit and defeat of the Tories.*

On the reduction of Charleston, Sir Henry Clinton
was, for the ensuing few weeks, busily employed in issuing
proclamations and forming plans for the complete subjugation of the Carolinas and Georgia.   He had on the eighteenth of May, dispatched Lord Cornwallis with a strong
force on the north-east side of the Santee to Camden ; while
Colonel Ferguson, at the same time, with a hundred and
fifty to two hundred men of the Provincial corps, marched
from Nelson's Ferry via Colonel Thomson's, Beaver creek,
and the Congaree Store, crossing the Saluda above the
mouth of Broad river ; thence on to Little river and Ninety
Six, where they arrived on the twenty-second of June. They
performed their marches in the cool of the morning, and now
and then apprehended prominent Whigs on the route.   His
orders were to have a watch-care over the extended district
of country from the Wateree to the Saluda, well nigh a
hundred miles. Resuming his march he passed on to
Ninety Six, whence, after a fortnight's rest, he advanced
some sixteen miles, and selected a good location on Little

river, where he erected some field works, while most of his Provincials pushed on to the Fair Forest region.* This camp was at the plantation of Colonel James Williams, in what is now Laurens County, near the Newberry line, where the British and Tories long maintained a post, a part of the time under General Cunningham, till the enemy evacuated Ninety Six the following year.†

Sir Henry Clinton had directed Major Hanger to repair with Colonel Ferguson to the interior settlements, and, jointly or separately, to organize, muster, and regulate all volunteer corps, and inspect the quantity of grain and number of cattle, etc., belonging to the inhabitants, and report to Lord Cornwallis, who would be left in command of the Southern Provinces.‡ The powers of this warrant were very extensive to meet the exigencies of the case. It was needful that commissioners should be sent out properly authorized to receive the submission of the people, administer oaths of fealty, and exact pledges of faithful Royal service. It was needful, also, that the young men of the country should be thoroughly drilled and fitted for recruits for Cornwallis' diminished forces ; and it was equally necessary for that commander to know where the necessary supplies of grain and meat could be found. It will thus be seen how comprehensive was this mission and its purposes.

Nor were these the only powers vested in these officers. All Royal authority had, for several years, been superseded by enactments and appointments of the newly created State, and these, of necessity, must be ignored. So Colonel

---

* Tarleton's *Memoirs*, 26, 80, 87, 100; O'Neall's *Hist. of Newberry*, 197.

† Williams' place was about a mile west of Little river, and between that stream and Mud Lick creek, on the old Island Ford road, followed by General Greene when he retreated from Ninety Six, in 1781. Ferguson's camp was near the intersection of a road leading to Laurens C. H., about sixteen miles distant. MS. letters of General A. C. Garlington, July 19th and 28th, 1880, on authority of Colonel James W. Watts, a descendant of Colonel Williams and Major T. K. Vance and others. D. R. Crawford, of Martin's Depot, S. C., states that three miles above the old Williams' place, on the west side of Little river, opposite the old Milton store, must have been an encampment, as old gun barrels and gun locks have been found there.

‡ Hanger's *Life and Opinions*, ii, 401-2.

Ferguson and Major Hanger had superadded to their military powers, authority to perform the marriage service. Whether they had occasions to officiate, we are not informed. However this may have been, the Major evidently formed no high estimate of the beauties of the up-country region. "In the back parts of Carolina," says Major Hanger, "you may search after an angel with as much chance of finding one as a parson; there is no such thing—I mean, when I was there. What they are now, I know not. It is not impossible, but they may have become more religious, moral, and virtuous, since the great affection they have imbibed for the French. In my time, you might travel sixty or seventy miles, and not see a church, or even a schism shop—meeting-house. I have often called at a dog-house in the woods, inhabited by eight or ten persons, merely from curiosity. I have asked the master of the house: 'Pray, my friend, of what religion are you?' 'Of what religion, sir?' 'Yes, my friend, of what religion are you—or, to what sect do you belong?' 'Oh! now I understand you; why, for the matter of that, *religion does not trouble us much in these parts.*'

"This distinguished race of men," continues Hanger, "are more savage than the Indians, and possess *every* one of their vices, but *not one* of their virtues. I have known one of these fellows travel two hundred miles through the woods, never keeping any road or path, guided by the sun by day, and the stars by night, to kill a particular person belonging to the opposite party. He would shoot him before his own door, and ride away to boast of what he had done on his return. I speak only of back-woodsmen, not of the inhabitants in general of South Carolina; for, in all America, there are not better educated or better bred men than the planters. Indeed, Charleston is celebrated for the splendor, luxury, and education of its inhabitants: I speak only of that *heathen race* known by the name of *Crackers.*" *

Such were Major Hanger's representations of the back-

---

* Hanger's *Life and Opinions*, ii, 403-5.

woods people of Carolina in his recorded reminiscences of twenty-one years thereafter. His slurs and insinuations on the virtues and morals of the " angels," probably referring to the females of the country, may well be taken with many grains of allowance, coming, as they do, from the intimate friend and associate of the profligate Prince Regent of England, and Colonel Tarleton, both in turn the keeper of the beautiful, but fallen " Perdita ;" and, moreover, his own reputation in America was that of a sensualist. The probabilities are, that he met with well-deserved rebuffs and rebukes from the ladies of the up-country of Carolina, and did not long remain there to thrust his insults upon a virtuous people. As if anticipating his own rich deservings, he gives, in his " Life," and " Advice to ye Lovely Cyprians," a portrait of himself, dressed in his regimentals, and suspended from a gibbet. Yet, in the end, he " robbed the hangman of his fees," and the gallows of its victim.

In a letter from Lord Cornwallis to Sir Henry Clinton, June thirtieth, 1780, he mentioned having dispersed Lieutenant-Colonel Balfour's detachment from the Forks of the Santee, by the Congarees, to Ninety Six, while he and Lieutenant-Colonel Innes, and Major Graham, are giving orders for the militia of those districts ; and then adds, confirmatory of Major Hanger's representation of the mixed character of Colonel Ferguson's services : " I have ordered Major Ferguson," says his Lordship, " to visit every district in the Province as fast as they get the militia established, to procure lists of each, and to see that my orders are carried into execution. I apprehend that his commission of Major-Commandant of a regiment of militia, can only take place in case a part of the second-class should be called out for service, the home duty being more that of a Justice of Peace than of a soldier." *

Major Hanger did not remain many weeks with Colonel Ferguson in the Little river region ; for, early in August,

* *Life and Cor. of Lord Cornwallis*, i, 486.

he entered Tarleton's Legion as Major, to which he had
recently been appointed, and participated in the battle of
Camden, and in the affair at Charlotte.   In his reckless
manner of expression, the Major remarks, that had he
remained with Ferguson, he might have shared the same
fate as he did at King's Mountain; and, "if, indeed, as
Mahomet is said to have done, I could have taken my flight
to Paradise on a jackass, that would have been a pleasant
ride ; but Fate destined me for other things."

"We come not," declared Ferguson, "to make war on
women and children, but to relieve their distresses."   This
sounded grateful and pleasant to the ears of the people — a
large majority of whom, under the leadership of the Cunninghams, Fletchall, Robinson, and Pearis, were at heart
Loyalists, and honored the King and Parliament.   To
Colonel, Ferguson's standard, while encamped at Little
river, the Tories of the country flocked in large numbers.
Companies and regiments were organized, and many officers commissioned for the Royal service.   David Fanning,
who had long resided in Orange and Chatham Counties, in
the North Province, subsequently so notorious as a Tory
leader for his dare-devil adventures and bloody work generally, was among those who repaired to Ferguson's encampment; and evidently, on his personal recommendation and
influence, secured, in July, from Colonel Ferguson, commissions, from Ensign to Captain, for no less than sixty-two
persons in the five Counties of Anson, Chatham, Cumberland, Orange, and Randolph, in North Carolina, whose
names and residence he records in his published *Narrative*.
Fanning and Captain Richard Pearis had received General
Williamson's submission, and granted protection to him
and his followers; and three days thereafter to Colonel
Pickens.   Colonel Robert Cunningham had taken the command in the Ninety Six region, and formed a camp of
Loyalists ;* and British authority was fully recognized in
all the up-country of South Carolina.

* Fanning's *Narrative*, 12, 13, 19-21.

The younger men were thoroughly drilled by Colonel Ferguson and his subordinates in military tactics, and fitted for active service. No one could have been better qualified for this business than the distinguished partisan whom Sir Henry Clinton had selected for the purpose. He seemed almost a born commander. His large experience in war, and partiality for military discipline, superadded to his personal magnetism over others, eminently fitted him for unlimited influence over his men, and the common people within his region. He was not favored, however, with a commanding personal presence. He was of middle stature, slender make, possessing a serious countenance ; yet it was his peculiar characteristic to gain the affections of the men under his command. He would sit down for hours, and converse with the country people on the state of public affairs, and point out to them, from his view, the ruinous effects of the disloyalty of the ring-leaders of the rebellion — erroneously supposing that it was the leaders only who gave impulse to the popular up-rising throughout the Colonies. He was as indefatigible in training them to his way of thinking, as he was in instructing them in military exercises. This condescension on his part was regarded as wonderful in a King's officer, and very naturally went far to secure the respect and obedience of all who came within the sphere of his almost magic influence.*

Parties were sent out to scour the north-western portion of South Carolina, and apprehend all the Rebel leaders who could be found. Among those who had taken protection, and were yet hurried off as prisoners to Ninety Six, was Colonel John Thomas, Sr., of the Fair Forest settlement, then quite advanced in life. His devoted wife rode nearly sixty miles to visit him, and convey to him such comforts as she had it in her power to bestow. While there, Mrs. Thomas overheard a conversation between some Tory women, of which her quick ear caught these ominous

* *Political Magazine*, March, 1781, 125.

words: "The Loyalists intend, to-morrow night, to surprise the Rebels at Cedar Spring." This intelligence was enough to thrill a mother's heart, for Cedar Spring was but a few miles beyond her Fair Forest home, and with the Whig force were many of her friends and neighbors, and some even of her own children. No time was to be lost—she intuitively resolved to do her best to apprise them of the enemy's intention before the meditated blow could be struck. She started early the next morning, and reached Cedar Spring that evening in time to give them warning of the impending danger, when she quietly repaired to her home, conscious of having done her duty to her country, as well as performed an act of the noblest humanity.*

This was on the twelfth day of July.† Colonel John Thomas, Jr., the son of our heroine, had succeeded his father in command of the Fair Forest regiment, and headed the small band, some sixty in number, now encamped at the Cedar Spring.‡ Joseph McJunkin was one of the party. It seems to have been a camp formed for collecting the regiment, and drilling them, preparatory to joining Sumter. On receiving the timely intelligence of the intended British attack, Colonel Thomas and his men, after a brief consultation, retired a small distance in the rear of their camp fires, and awaited the impending onset. The enemy, one hundred and fifty strong, rushed upon the camp, where they expected to find the luckless Rebels pro-

---

* In crediting Mrs. Jane Thomas with this heroic act, we are aware that Mills, in his *Statistics of South Carolina*, has accorded it to Mrs. Mary Dillard; but the uniform testimony of the Thomas family, including Major McJunkin, who married a daughter of Colonel Thomas, gives the narrative as we have substantially related it. The occasion of her visit to Ninety Six, and residing in the neighborhood of Cedar Spring, go far to sustain this view of the matter. Mrs. Dillard, on the other hand, lived fully thirty miles south-east of Cedar Spring, and south of the Enoree river, in Lauren's District—and on the route Tarleton pursued when on his way to attack Sumter at Blackstock's on Tyger; and Tarleton relates, that "a woman on horseback had viewed the line of march from a wood, and, by a nearer road, had given intelligence" to Sumter. That woman was Mrs. Dillard.

† Compare McCall's *Georgia*, ii, 310; Moore's *Diary*, ii, 351; and Allaire's *Diary*, July 14th and 15th.

‡ Cedar Spring derived its name from a large cedar tree, that formerly ornamented the banks of this fine spring, which is about fifty feet in circumference. It has three principal fountains or sources of supply, which force the water from the bowels of the earth, forming a beautiful basin three feet deep. The water is impregnated with a small portion of lime.

foundly enwrapped in slumber; but, on the contrary, they were wide awake, and astonished the assailants with a volley of rifle balls. Several were slain, and the survivors scampered off badly demoralized. It was a short, quick, and decisive affair. Among the slain was a Tory named John White, well known to Major McJunkin, and who, in the early part of the war, had declined bearing arms against the Indians, on the trumped-up plea of being a non-combatant.* It was fortunate for Thomas' party, that this was a night attack, as the enemy had no opportunity of discovering their decided superiority; and doubtless retired with the belief that the Americans must have numbered several hundred. This embodying of the friends of liberty in the Fair Forest settlement, probably hastened the movement of Ferguson to that quarter.

When Colonel Ferguson left his camp on Little river, he crossed the Enoree at Kelly's Ford, and encamped in the Fork, at the plantation of Colonel James Lyles, who was then in service farther east, with Sumter. John Robison and others of this region were plundered by Ferguson's men. The desperate, the idle, the vindictive, who sought plunder or revenge, as well as the youthful Loyalists, whose zeal or ambition prompted them to take up arms, all found a warm reception at the British camp; and their progress through the country was " marked with blood, and lighted up with conflagration." Irving graphically describes the character of these Tory recruits : " Ferguson," says Irving, " had a loyal hatred of Whigs, and to his standard flocked many rancorous Tories, beside outlaws and desperadoes, so that with all his conciliating intentions, his progress through the country was attended by many exasperating excesses."

To coerce the Whigs to submission, and embody the Tories, and train them for war, Ferguson kept moving about the country, and sending out his detachments in every

---

* Major McJunkin's MS. Statement, among the Saye papers; Mr. Saye's *Memoir* of McJunkin, also Judge O'Neall's, in the *Magnolia* Magazine for Jan., 1843; *Hist. Presbyterian Ch. of So. Carolina*, 534.

direction. In the prosecution of these designs, he marched
into Union District, camping on the south side of Tyger
river, about half a mile below Blackstock's Ford, where
the cripple spy, Joseph Kerr, made such observations as he
could, and returned with the intelligence to Colonel Mc-
Dowell, that about fifteen hundred of the enemy were
penetrating the country ;* and thence Ferguson passed into
the settlement then called "The Quaker Meadow," but
since known as the Meadow Woods. On Sugar creek,
a southern tributary of Fair Forest creek,† resided a
number of determined Whigs named Blasingame, one of
whom was arrested. Thence Ferguson moved up into
the Fair Forest settlement, on the main creek of that
name, camping at different times at McClendon's old field ;
then between where J. McIlwaine and J. H. Kelso since
lived ; thence to where Gist resided a few years since, and
thence to Cunningham's. He camped a while at Fair Forest
Shoal, in Brandon's Settlement ; and subsequently for three
weeks on a hill, on the present plantation of the Hon. John
Winsmith, eleven miles south of Cedar Spring, and two
south of Glenn's Springs. During this period of several
weeks, the Tories scoured all that region of country daily,
plundering the people of their cattle, horses, beds, wearing
apparel, bee-gums, and vegetables of all kinds—even wresting the rings from the fingers of the females. Major Dunlap and Lieutenant Taylor, with forty or fifty soldiers, called
at a Mrs. Thomson's, and taking down the family Bible
from its shelf, read in it, and expressed great surprise that
persons having such a book, teaching them to honor the
King and obey magistrates, should rebel against their King
and country ; but amid these expressions of holy horror,

* Kerr's MS. personal statement, communicated by Colonel J. H. Wheeler; Hunter's
Sketches of Western North Carolina, 120-21.

† " What a *fair forest* is this! " exclaimed the first settlers. The name attached itself
to the place, and then to the bold and lovely mountain stream, which sweeps on till its
waters mingle with those of Broad river.—Rev. James H. Saye's *Memoir of Major Joseph
McJunkin*, and *Sketches of the Revolutionary History of South Carolina*, an interesting
newspaper series published over thirty years ago.

these officers suffered their troops to engage in ransacking and plundering before their very eyes.

From what we have seen, it is not wonderful that the Tories were soon as heartily despised by the British officers as by their own countrymen, the Whigs. But Ferguson was not the man to be diverted from his purpose by any acts of theirs of treachery and inhumanity. The crown had honors and rewards to bestow, and his eye rested upon them. He knew that "the defender of the faith" generally gave much more cash and more honors, for a single year of devoted service in military enterprises, than for a life-time spent in such pursuits as exalt and ennoble human nature.

The horses of Ferguson's men were turned loose in to any fields of grain that might be most convenient. Foraging parties brought in cattle to camp for slaughter, or wantonly shot them down in the woods and left them. As many Whigs as could be found were apprehended, not even excepting those who had previously taken protection. A few had been prompted to take protection, rather than forsake their families, trusting thereby to British honor to secure them from molestation; but they were soon hurried off to Ninety Six, and incarcerated in a loathsome prison, where they well nigh perished for want of sustenance. But most of those, at this time, capable of bearing arms, had retired to North Carolina, or were serving in Sumter's army; so that Ferguson had an excellent opportunity to drill his new recruits, and support his men by pillaging the people. Occasionally small parties of Whigs would venture into the neighborhood—about often enough to afford the enemy good exercise in pursuing them while within striking distance.*

Such an invasion as Ferguson's, with its terrors and aggravations, and the up-rising of the Tories in the western part of North Carolina, under the Moores, and Bryan, soon led to blows, with all the sufferings attendant on war and

---

*Saye's MSS., and *Memoir of McJunkin.*

carnage. The barbarities meted out to the Americans at Buford's defeat, sarcastically denominated by the Whigs as *Tarleton's quarters*, very naturally tended to embitter the animosities of the people. The Moores were signally defeated, in June, at Ramsour's Mill, and Bryan and his followers subsequently driven from the country.

A noted partisan of Georgia, Colonel Elijah Clarke, now comes upon the scene. A native of Virginia, he early settled on the Pacolet, whence he pushed into Wilkes County, Georgia, where the Revolutionary out-break found him. He was one of those sturdy patriots, well fitted for a leader of the people—one who would scorn to take protection, or yield one iota to arbitrary power. When British detachments were sent into various parts of Georgia, it became unsafe for such unflinching Whigs as Clarke longer to remain there. He and his associates resolved to scatter for a few days, visit their families once more, and then retire into South Carolina, where they hoped to find other heroic spirits ready to co-operate with them in making a stand against the common enemy. Some small parties had already left Georgia, and passing along the western frontiers of South Carolina, had sought the camp of Colonel Charles McDowell, who was then embodying a force on the southwestern borders of the North Province.

On the eleventh of July, one hundred and forty well-mounted and well-armed men met at the appointed place of rendezvous; and, after crossing the Savannah at a private ford in the night, they learned that the British and Loyalists were in force on their front. Clarke's men concluded that it would be hazardous to continue their retreat on that route with their present numbers. As they were volunteers, and not subject to coercion, Colonel Clarke was induced to return to Georgia, suffer his men to disperse for a while, and await a more favorable opportunity to renew the enterprise. The majority of the party returned.

Colonel John Jones, of Burke County, however, objected

to a retrograde movement, and proposed to lead those who would go with him, through the woods to the borders of North Carolina, and join the American force in that quarter. Thirty-five men united with him, choosing him for their leader, and John Freeman for second in command, pledging implicit obedience to their orders. Benjamin Lawrence, of South Carolina, a superior woodsman, and well acquainted with the country, now joined the company, and rendered them valuable service as their guide. Passing through a disaffected region, they adroitly palmed themselves off as a Loyalist party, engaged in the King's service ; and, under this guise, they were in several instances, furnished with pilots, and directed on their route.

When they had passed the head-waters of the Saluda, in the north-eastern part of the present county of Greenville, one of these guides informed them, that a party of Rebels had, the preceding night, attacked some Loyalists a short distance in front, and defeated them—doubtless the British repulse at Cedar Spring, as already related, and which occurred some twenty-five 'or thirty miles away. Jones expressed a wish to be conducted to the camp of those unfortunate Loyalist friends, that he might aid them in taking revenge on those who had shed the blood of the King's faithful subjects. About eleven o'clock on that night, July thirteenth, Jones and his little party were conducted to the Loyalist camp, where some forty men were collected to pursue the Americans who had retreated to the North. Choosing twenty-two of his followers, and leaving the baggage and horses in charge of the others, Colonel Jones resolved to surprise the Tory camp. Approaching the enemy with guns, swords, and belt-pistols, they found them in a state of self-security, and generally asleep. Closing quickly around them, they fired upon the camp, killing one and wounding· three, when thirty-two, including the wounded, called for quarter, and surrendered. Destroying the useless guns, and selecting the best horses, the Loyalists were paroled as prisoners of war; when the pilot, who did not discover the real character of the men he was conducting until too late to have even attempted to prevent the consequences, was now required to guide the Americans to Earle's Ford on North Pacolet river, where a junction was formed the next day with Colonel McDowell's forces. As McDowell had that day made a tedious march with his three hundred men, they, too, were in a fatigued condition.

Within striking distance of McDowell's camping ground, some twenty miles in a nearly southern direction, was Prince's Fort, originally a place of neighborhood resort in time of danger from the Indians, in the early settlement of the country, some twenty years before. This fort, now occupied by a British and Tory force, under Colonel Innes, was located upon a commanding height of land, near the head of one of the branches of the North Fork of Tyger, seven miles north of west from the present village of Spartanburg. Innes, unapprised of McDowell's approach, detached Major Dunlap, with seventy dragoons, accompanied by Colonel Ambrose Mills, with a party of Loyalists, in pursuit of Jones, of whose audacious operations he had just received intelligence.

McDowell's camp was on rising ground on the eastern side of the North Pacolet, in the present county of Polk, North Carolina, near the South Carolina line, and about twenty miles south-west of Rutherfordton; and Dunlap reaching the vicinity on the opposite side of the stream during the night, and supposing that Jones' party only was encamped there, commenced crossing the river, which was narrow at that point, when an American sentinel fled to camp and gave the first notice of the enemy's presence.* Dunlap, with his Dragoons and Tories, dashed instantly, with drawn swords, among McDowell's men, while but few of them

---

* McCall, in his *Hist. of Georgia*, asserts that the sentinel fired his gun, but James Thompson, one of Joseph McDowell's party, states as in the text, which seems to be corroborated by the complaint of Col. Hampton, and the general surprise of the camp.

were yet roused out of sleep. The Georgians being nearest to the ford, were the first attacked, losing two killed and six wounded ; among the latter was Colonel Jones, who received eight cuts on his head from the enemy's sabres. Freeman, with the remainder, fell back about a hundred yards, where he joined Major Singleton, who was forming his men behind a fence ; while Colonels McDowell and Hampton soon formed the main body on Singleton's right. Being thus rallied, the Americans were ordered to advance, when Dunlap discovering his mistake as to their numbers, quickly retreated across the river, which was fordable in many places, and retired without much loss ; its extent, however, was unknown, beyond a single wounded man who was left upon the ground.

Besides the loss sustained by the Georgians, six of McDowell's men were killed, and twenty-four wounded. Among the killed were Noah Hampton, a son of Colonel Hampton, with a comrade named Andrew Dunn. Young Hampton, when roused from his slumbers, was asked his name ; he simply replied " Hampton," one of a numerous family and connection of Whigs, too well known, and too active in opposition to British rule, to meet with the least forbearance at the hands of enraged Tories ; and though he begged for his life, they cursed him for a Rebel, and ran him through with a bayonet. Young Dunn also suffered the same cruel treatment. Colonel Hampton felt hard towards Colonel McDowell, his superior officer, as he wished to have placed videttes beyond the ford, which McDowell opposed, believing it entirely unnecessary. Had this been done, due notice would in all probability have been given, and most of the loss and suffering have been averted.*

---

* McCall's *Hist. of Georgia*, ii. 308–12 ; Saye's MSS. ; MS. pension statements of General Thomas Kennedy. of Kentucky, Robert Henderson, and Robert McDowell ; Moore's *Diary of the Revolution*, ii, 351, gives the date of the Pacolet fight as occurring "in the night of July fifteenth," and this on the authority of Govenor Rutledge, who was then at Charlotte. Judging from Allaire's *Diary*, it must have been the night before. The particulars of the killing of young Hampton and Dunn are derived from the MS. communications of Adam, Jonathan, and James J. Hampton, grandsons of Colonel Hampton.

The reason, presumably, why Colonel McDowell was over-confident of security was, that he had, the day before, detached his brother, Major Joseph McDowell, with a party to go on a scout, and ascertain, if possible, where the Tories lay ; but taking a wrong direction, he had consequently made no discovery.* Not returning, Colonel McDowell very naturally concluded that there was no portion of the enemy very near, and that he and his weary men could, with reasonable assurance of safety, take some needed repose. It was that very night, while Major McDowell was blundering on the wrong route, that Dunlap was able to advance undiscovered, and make his sudden attack.

Before sunrise the ensuing morning, fifty-two of the most active men, including Freeman and fourteen of his party, mounted upon the best horses in the camp, were ordered to pursue the retreating foe, under the command of Captain Edward Hampton. After a rapid pursuit of two hours, they overtook the enemy, fifteen miles away ; and making a sudden and unexpected attack, completely routed them, killing eight of them at the first fire. Unable to rally his demoralized men, who had been taken unawares, Dunlap made a precipitate, helter-skelter retreat towards Fort Prince, during which several of his soldiers were killed and wounded. The pursuit was continued within three hundred yards of the British fort, in which three hundred men were securely posted. At two o'clock in the afternoon, Hampton and his men returned to McDowell's camp, with thirty-five good horses, dragoon equipage, and a considerable portion of the enemy's baggage, as the trophies of victory, and without the loss of a single man. It was a bold and successful adventure, worthy of the heroic leader and his intrepid followers.

It is not a little remarkable, that three successive night fights should have occurred within a few miles of each

---

* Statement of Captain James Thompson, of Madison County, Georgia, one of Major McDowell's party, preserved among the Saye MSS.

other, and the two latter as military sequences of the former. First, the Tory attack on Colonel Thomas, at Cedar Spring, on the evening of the thirteenth of July; then Colonel Jones' surprise of the remnant of this Loyalist party, on the night of the fourteenth; and finally, the attack of Dunlap and Mills, in retaliation, on Colonel McDowell's camp, at Earle's Ford of North Pacolet, on the night of the fifteenth. And in all three of these affairs, the Tories got the worst of it.

McCall's *Georgia*, ii, 312–13; and MS. pension statement of Jesse Neville, one of Hampton's party. It may not be inappropriate, in this connection, to add a few words relative to the hero of this courageous exploit. Captain Hampton was a brother of Colonels Wade, Richard, and Henry Hampton, of Sumter's army. He was a very active partisan, and reputed one of the best horsemen of his time. In May, 1775, with his brother, Preston Hampton, he was delegated by the people of the frontiers of South Carolina to visit the Cherokees, and see if, by a suitable "talk," they could not be made to comprehend the causes of the growing differences between the Colonies and the mother country. They met with a rude reception, Cameron and the British emissaries instigating the Indians to oppose their views; and Cameron made them prisoners, giving their horses, a gun, a case of pistols and holsters, to the Indians. By some means, they escaped with their lives.

The following year, 1776, while Edward Hampton was, with his wife, on a visit to her father, Baylis Earle, on North Pacolet, the Cherokees made an incursion into the valleys of Tyger, massacring Preston Hampton, his aged parents, and a young grandchild of theirs. Edward Hampton served on Williamson's expedition against the Cherokees, in the summer and autumn of that year; and though only a Lieutenant, he had the command of his company, and distinguished himself in a battle with the enemy, receiving the special thanks of his General for his bravery and good conduct on the occasion.

After the destruction of the Hampton family, on the Middle Fork of Tyger, where he resided, he seems to have made his home for a season on a plantation he possessed at Earle's Ford, where his father-in-law, Mr. Earle, resided. That he was the Captain Hampton who led the dashing foray against Dunlap on his retreat to Prince's Fort, is partially corroborated by Dr. Howe, in his *History of the Presbyterian Church in South Carolina*, p, 542, though erroneous as to the place of the occurrence; but Jesse Neville's pension statement renders the matter conclusive, supplying the first name of his Captain, which McCall fails to give in his details of that affair.

Captain Hampton was killed the ensuing October, at or near Fair Forest creek, in the bosom of his family, by Bill Cunningham's notorious "Bloody Scout." He was in the prime of life, and in his death his country lost a bold cavalier. He was the idol of his family and friends. His descendants in Georgia, Mississippi, and Texas, are among the worthiest of people. Baylis Earle became one of the early judges of Spartanburg District, and was living in 1826, in his eighty-ninth year—MS. statement of Colonel John Carter, Watauga, May 30th, 1775; MS. letter of Colonel Elijah Clarke to General Sumter, October 29th, 1780; Governor Perry's sketch of the *Hampton Family*, in the *Magnolia* Magazine, June, 1843, with a continuation, which appeared in the South Carolina papers, in 1843, written by Colonel Wade Hampton, Sr., father of the present Senator Hampton, of that State.

CHAPTER V.

1780—July—August.

When Colonel McDowell became convinced that Ferguson's movement to the north-western portion of South Carolina, threatened the invasion of the North Province also, he not only promptly raised what force he could from the sparsely populated settlements, on the heads of Catawba, Broad and Pacolet rivers, to take post in the enemy's front and watch his operations; but dispatched a messenger with this alarming intelligence to Colonels John Sevier and Isaac Shelby, on Watauga and Holston, those over-mountain regions, then a portion of North Carolina, but now of East Tennessee; urging those noted border leaders to bring to his aid all the riflemen they could, and as soon as possible. Sevier, unable to leave his frontier exposed to the inroads of the Cherokees, responded at once to the appeal, by sending a part of his regiment under Major Charles Robertson; and Shelby, being more remote, and having been absent on a surveying tour, was a few days later, but joined McDowell, at the head of two hundred mounted riflemen, about the twenty-fifth of July, at his camp near the Cherokee Ford of Broad river.

Colonel Clarke did not long remain in Georgia. While there, he and his associates were necessarily compelled to secrete themselves in the woods, privately supplied with food by their friends. This mode of life was irksome, and soon became almost insupportable, without the least prospect of accomplishing anything beneficial to the public. The regiment was re-assembled, in augmented numbers, when, by a general desire, Colonel Clarke led them along the eastern slope of the mountains, directing their course towards North Carolina, where they could unite with others, and render their services useful to their country. Without mishap or adventure, they were joined by Colonel Jones, as they neared the region where they expected to find friends in the field. Clarke was soon after joined by the brave Captain James McCall, with about twenty men, from the region of Ninety Six. For want of confidence in Colonel Mc-Dowell's activity, or from some other cause, Clarke pushed on, and joined Sumter on or near the Catawba.

The story of the captivity of Captain Patrick Moore, a noted Loyalist, now claims our attention. He had probably escaped from the slaughter at Ramsour's Mill, on the twentieth of June, when his brother, Colonel John Moore safely retired to Camden. Anxious for the capture of Captain Moore, Major Joseph Dickson and Captain William Johnston were sent out, in the fore part of July, with a party to apprehend this noted Tory leader, and others of his ilk, if they could be found. The veteran Captain Samuel Martin, who had served in the old French and Indian war, was one of the party. On Lawson's Fork, of Pacolet river, near the Old Iron Works, since Bivingsville, and now known as Glendale,* the parties met, and a skirmish ensued, in which Captain Johnston and the Tory leader had a personal rencontre. Moore was at length

---

* Glendale is located on the Southern side of Lawson's Fork, while the Old Iron Works were on the same bank, fully half a mile above, where the old road once crossed the stream. " These Works," says Mills, in 1826 " were burnt by the Tories, and never rebuilt."

overpowered and captured; but in the desperate contest, Johnston received several sword wounds on his head, and on the thumb of his right hand. While bearing his prisoner towards the Whig lines, a short distance away, he was rapidly approached by several British troopers. Quickly attempting to fire his loaded musket at his pursuers, it unfortunately missed, in consequence of the blood flowing from his wounded thumb, and wetting his priming. This misfortune on his part enabled his prisoner to escape; and, perceiving his own dangerous and defenceless condition, he promptly availed himself of a friendly thicket at his side, eluded his pursuers, and shortly after joined his command.*

At this time, or soon after, Moore had command of Fort Anderson, or Thicketty Fort, as it was more generally called, situated a quarter of a mile north of Goucher Creek, and two and a half miles above the mouth of this small water-course, which empties into Thicketty Creek, a western tributary of Broad river, uniting with that stream a few miles above its junction with Pacolet. It was a strong fortress, built a few years before for defence against the Cherokees, and was surrounded by a strong abatis, well fitted for a vigorous defence. It became a great place of resort and protection for Tory parties. They would sally forth from Thicketty Fort, and plunder Whig families in every direction—so that women and children were often left without clothing, shoes, bread, meat, or salt.

In the absence of Captain Nathaniel Jeffries, of that region, one of these plundering parties visited his house, appropriated such articles as they chose, built a fire on the floor, abused Mrs. Jeffries as the meanest of all Rebels, and drove off the horses and cattle. On another occasion, the house of Samuel McJunkin, in Union District, a warm patriot, but too old for active military service, was visited by a party under Patrick Moore. They stayed all

---

* Hunter's *Sketches of Western North Carolina*, 242; MS. Pension Statement of Captain Samuel Martin.

night; and, when about to depart, stripped the family of bed-clothes and wearing apparel. A noted Tory, Bill Haynesworth, seized a bed-quilt, and placed it upon his horse, when McJunkin's sturdy daughter, Jane, snatched it, and a struggle ensued for the possession. The soldiers amused themselves by exclaiming—"Well done, woman!" —"Well done, Bill!" For once Moore's gallantry predominated over his love of plunder; and he swore roundly if Jane could take the quilt from Haynesworth, she should have it. Presently in the fierce contest, Bill's feet came in contact with some dirty slime in the yard, and slipped from under him, and he lay prostrate and panting on the ground. Jane, quick as thought, placed one foot upon his breast, and wresting the quilt from his grasp, retired in triumph, while poor Bill sneaked off defeated and crest-fallen. This brave woman was the sister of Major McJunkin.

Nor was Miss Nancy Jackson, who lived in the Irish Settlement, near Fair Forest creek, less demonstrative in defence of her rights; for she kicked a Tory down the stairs as he was descending, loaded with plunder. In his rage, he threatened to send the Hessian troops there the next day, which obliged the heroic girl to take refuge with an acquaintance several miles distant.*

The intrepid Sumter, hearing of Ferguson's inroads beyond Broad river, directed Colonel Clarke and his Georgians, together with such persons in his camp as resided in that region, and desired to aid in its protection, to repair to that quarter. Captain William Smith, of Spartanburg, and his company, availed themselves of this privilege. Arriving at the Cherokee Ford, they met Colonel McDowell, when Colonel Shelby, together with Colonel Clarke, Colonel Andrew Hampton and Major Charles Robertson, of Sevier's regiment, were detached with six hundred men, to surprise Thicketty Fort, some twenty

---

*MS. Saye papers; Saye's *Memoir of McJunkin;* Mrs. Ellet's *Women of the Revolution,* i ,162.

miles distant. They took up the line of march at sunset, and surrounded the post at day-break the next morning. Colonel Shelby sent in Captain William Cocke, a volunteer—in after years, a United States Senator from Tennessee—to make a peremptory demand for the surrender of the garrison ; to which Moore replied that he would defend the place to the last extremity. Shelby then drew in his lines to within musket shot of the enemy all around, with a full determination to make an assault.

Shelby's gallant " six hundred " made so formidable an appearance, that on a second message, accompanied, we may well suppose, with words of intimidation, Moore, perhaps fearing another Ramsour's Mill onslaught, relented, and proposed to surrender, on condition that the garrison be paroled not to serve again during the war, unless exchanged, which was acceded to—the more readily, as the Americans did not care to be encumbered with prisoners. Thus ninety-three Loyalists, with one British Sergeant-Major, stationed there to discipline them, surrendered themselves without firing a gun ; and among the trophies of victory were two hundred and fifty* stand of arms, all loaded with ball and buck-shot, and so arranged at the port-holes, with their abundant supplies, that they could, had a Ferguson, a Dunlap, or a De Peyster been at their head, have resisted double the number of their assailants.†

Among the spoils taken at King's Mountain, was the fragment of a letter, without date or signature—probably a

* This is Shelby's statement; the MS. Cocke papers say " one hundred and fifty stand of arms were taken."

† The leading facts relative to the capture of Thicketty Fort are taken from Haywood's *History of Tennessee*, 64; Ramsey's *Annals of Tennessee*, 214; Memoir of Shelby, in *National Portrait Gallery*, written by Colonel Charles S. Todd, Shelby's son-in-law, and which appeared, revised, in the *Western Monthly Magazine*, in 1836; Breazeale's *Life as it Is*, 50—all which statements closely follow a MS. account written by Shelby himself; MS. statement, preserved among the Saye papers, of John Jeffries, son of the plundered woman mentioned in the narrative; MS. papers of Hon. William Cocke furnish the name of the fort; MS. pension statements of William Smith, of Lincoln county, Tennessee, Alex. Mc-Fadden, of Rutherford county, North Carolina, and John Clark, of Washington county, Tennessee, corroborating, in a general way, the facts of the capture; and in a personal interview with Silas McBee, of Pontotoc county, Mississippi, in 1842, he confirmed Shelby's statement that ninety-four was the number of Moore's party captured. McBee lived on Thicketty at the time of the capture of Moore and his men.

copy of a dispatch from Ferguson to Lord Cornwallis—in which this account is given of Thicketty Fort, Moore, and his surrender of the place: "It had an upper line of loopholes, and was surrounded by a very strong abatis, with only a small wicket to enter by. It had been put in thorough repair at the request of the garrison, which consisted of neighboring militia that had come to [the fort]; and was defended by eighty men against two or three hundred banditti without cannon, and each man was of opinion that it was impossible [for the Rebels to take it.] The officer next in command, and all the others, gave their opinion for defending it, and agree in their account that Patrick Moore, after proposing a surrender, acquiesced in their opinion, and offered to go and signify as much to the Rebels, but returned with some Rebel officers, whom he put in possession of the gate and place, who were instantly followed by their men, and the fort full of Rebels, to the surprise of the garrison. He plead cowardice, I understand.†"

The capture of Thicketty Fort occurred on Sunday, the thirtieth of July, as the connecting circumstances indicate, and Lieutenant Allaire's *Diary* proves. Shelby and his men, loaded with the spoils of victory, returned at once to McDowell's camp near the Cherokee Ford.

McDowell's force at this time could not have exceeded a thousand men, while Ferguson's must have reached fifteen to eighteen hundred. It was, therefore, the policy of the Americans to maintain their position near Cherokee Ford, guard against surprise, and harass their adversaries, until they should be able, with augmented numbers, to expel them from the country. Shortly after the Thicketty expedition, Colonel McDowell again detached Colonels Shelby, and Clarke, with Colonel William Graham, with a combined force of six hundred mounted men, to watch the movements of Ferguson's troops, and whenever possible, to cut off his foraging parties. They directed their course down Broad

---

† Ramsey's *Tennessee*, 215.

river some twenty-five miles to Brown's creek, in now
Union county, where it was agreed they should assemble,
and which was a better situation than the Cherokee Ford,
to observe the operations of the British and Tories. But
when only a few of the parties fairly began to collect at
that point, a superior force of the enemy forced them to
retire, when they bore off some thirty or forty miles to the
upper portion of the Fair Forest settlement, within the
present limits of Spartanburg. On the way, they seem to
have gotten their force together. By watching their opportunity, they hoped to gain some decided advantage
over their opponents, whom they well knew they would
encounter in large numbers in that quarter. Hearing
of these bold Rebel troopers, Ferguson made several ineffectual attempts to surprise them. But our frontier heroes
were too watchful to be caught napping. Clarke and
Shelby, with their men, were constantly on the alert—having no fixed camp, so that they were difficult to find.

On the evening of August seventh, Clarke and Shelby,
with their troops, stopped for refreshment—and, if not disturbed, for a night's repose—on Fair Forest creek, nearly
two miles west of Cedar Spring, at a point where the old
road crossed that stream, leading thence to Wofford's Iron
Works, and thence onward to the Cherokee Ford. Several
trusty scouts were sent out to make discoveries, who returned before day the next morning, with the intelligence
that the enemy were within half a mile of them. About
the same moment, the report of a gun was heard, in the
direction of the British party, which was afterward ascertained to have been fired by one of Dunlap's men—one who
felt some compunctions of conscience at the idea of surprising and massacring his countrymen, but who, protesting
that it was accidental, was not suspected of treachery.
The Americans, from prudential motives, retreated toward
the old Iron Works, on Lawson's Fork of Pacolet, leaving
Cedar Spring apparently a mile to the right; and taking

position not very far from the old orchard on the Thompson place, which was some three or four miles from the ford over Fair Forest, and something like a mile and a half from the Iron Works, and about a mile from Cedar Spring.   Here

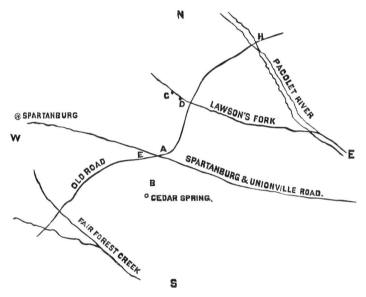

PLAT OF REGION NEAR CEDAR SPRING.

A—Thompson's Place and Peach Orchard. B—Where one part of the battle is said to have been fought. C—Old Iron Works. D—Glendale or Bivingsville. E—Peach Tree Grave. F—Pacolet Hill. G—Cedar Spring.

suitable ground was chosen, and the men formed for battle, when the spies came running in with the information that the enemy's horse were almost in sight.   Before their retirement from their former temporary camp at Fair Forest, Josiah Culbertson, one of the bravest of young men, who had recently joined Shelby, had obtained permission to return home, two or three miles distant on Fair Forest, spend the night, and make such observations as he might, of any enemy in that quarter.   About day-light the next morning, he rode fearlessly into the encampment he had left the evening before, supposing it still to be occupied

by his American friends, not knowing that they had decamped, and Dunlap had just taken possession of it.   But
Culbertson was equal to the emergency, for, seeing everything so different from what it was the previous evening, he
was quick to discover his mistake ; and with extraordinary
coolness and presence of mind, he rode very leisurely out
of the encampment, with his trusty rifle resting on the pom-
mel of his saddle before him.   As he passed along, he observed the dragoons getting their horses in readiness, and
making other preparations indicating an immediate renewal
of their line of march.   No particular notice was taken of
him in the British camp, as it was supposed that he was one
of their own men, who had got ready for the onward movement before his fellows.   But when out of sight, he dashed
off with good speed in the direction he inferred that Clarke
and Shelby had gone, and soon overtook his friends, and
found they had chosen their ground, and were prepared for
the onslaught.

Major Dunlap was an officer of much energy and
promptitude, and soon made his appearance, with a strong
force, part Colonial dragoons and part mounted militia,
and commenced the conflict.   The Whigs were as eager
for the fray as the over-confident Britons.   The action
lasted half an hour, and was severely contested.   Dunlap's mounted volunteer riflemen, it is said, who were in
front, recoiled, giving back at the very first fire of their opponents, and their commander found it difficult to rally
them.   Having at length succeeded, he placed himself at
the head of his dragoons, and led them on to renew the
contest, followed by the mounted riflemen, who were, however, averse to coming into very close quarters.   Dunlap's
dragoons, with their broad-swords, played a prominent part
in the action ; and from the disproportion of Tories killed
over the dragoons, according to the British account, which
is doubtful, it would appear that Clarke and Shelby's riflemen must have been busy in picking them off.   During the

mentioned the circumstance of his ceasing, in the midst of the battle, to witness, with astonishment and admiration, the remarkable and unequal struggle Clarke was maintaining with his foes. In the fierce hand-to-hand contest, he received two sabre wounds, one on the back of his neck, and the other on his head—his stock-buckle saving his life ; and he was even, for a few minutes, a prisoner, in charge of two stout Britons ; but, taking advantage of his strength and activity, he knocked one of them down, when the other quickly fled out of the reach of this famous back-woods Titan. Clarke was every inch a hero, and was indebted to his own good pluck and prowess for his escape from his enemies, with only slight wounds, and the loss of his hat, in the *melée.**

Culbertson, with his characteristic daring, had a personal adventure worthy of notice. Meeting a dragoon, some distance from support, who imperiously demanded his surrender, the intrepid American replied by whipping his rifle to his shoulder and felling the haughty Briton from his horse. When the dead were buried the next day, this dragoon was thrown into a hole near where he lay, and covered with earth. He happened to have at the time some peaches in his pocket, from which a peach tree grew, and for many years after, bore successive crops of fruit. The grave is yet pointed out, but the peach tree has long since disappeared. A worthy person in that region recently died nearly a hundred years of age, who used to reláte that he had, in early life, eaten fruit from that tree.† The graves of some twenty or thirty others, who fell in this engagement, says Governor Perry, were yet to be seen as late as 1842.

---

* McCall mentions that Colonel Clarke and his son were wounded both at Wofford's Iron Works and at Musgrove's, giving the particulars as occurring at the latter; while Shelby notices their having been wounded only at the former, instancing his heroic rencontre there ; and an eye-witness, William Smith, of Tennessee, relates that Clarke received a sword wound in the neck, and lost his hat near Wofford's, returning to McDowell's camp bare-headed.

† MS. letters of N. F. Walker, Esq., of Cedar Spring, June 15th and July 7th, 1880.

It is questionable, however, if so many, on both sides, were killed in the action.*

By some adroit management, a number of British prisoners were captured, and at length Dunlap was beaten back with considerable loss. Mills states that he was pursued a mile, but could not be overtaken. About two miles below the battle-ground, Dunlap's fugitives were met by Ferguson with his whole force, who together advanced to the Iron Works, from which, as they came in sight, a few hours after the action, Clarke and Shelby were compelled to make a hasty retreat, leaving one or two of their wounded behind them—not having time or conveniences to convey them away; but they were treated by Ferguson with humanity, and left there when he retired. As Clarke and Shelby expected, Ferguson now pursued them, with the hope of regaining the prisoners. The American leaders retired slowly, forming frequently on the most advantageous ground to give battle, and so retarding the pursuit, that the prisoners were finally placed beyond recapture.

Three miles north-east of the old Iron Works, they came to Pacolet; just beyond which, skirting its northeast border, rises a steep, rocky hill, fifty to sixty feet high, so steep where the road passed up at that day, that the men, in some cases, had to help their horses up its difficult ascent. Along the crest of this hill or ridge, Shelby and Clarke displayed their little force; and when Ferguson and his men came in view, evincing a disinclination to pursue any farther, the patriots, from their vantage-ground, bantered and ridiculed them to their hearts' content. But Ferguson, having maintained the chase four or five miles,

---

* Major A. J. Wells, of Montevallo, Alabama, a native cf Spartanburg, narrates a singular incident which must relate to this battle. After the war, the widow of a Tory came to the neglected burial place, and had the fallen dead disinterred, from which she readily selected the remains of her husband, for he was six and a half feet high, and piously bore them to her distant home for a more Christian interment.

now abandoned it, with nothing to boast of, save his superior numbers.*

Mr. Saye's account of this affair, as gathered from the traditions of the neighborhood, and published thirty-three years ago, may very properly supplement the narrative just related—with the passing remark, that what he describes as the battle at the peach-orchard, was probably but one of the episodes of that day's heroic exploits, and yet it may have been the principal one: Shelby's force occupied a position near the present site of Bivingsville. Various attempts were made to fall upon the Americans by surprise ; but these schemes were baffled. About four miles from Spartanburg Court House, on the main road to Unionville, is an ancient plantation known as ' Thompson's Old Place.' It is an elevated tract of country, lying between the tributaries of Fair Forest Creek on one side, and those of Lawson's Fork of Pacolet on the other—and about midway between Cedar Spring and the Iron Works.

A road leading from North Carolina to Georgia, by the way of the Cherokee Ford of Broad river, passed through this place, and thence by or near the Cedar Spring. A person passing from the direction of Unionville towards Spartanburg Court House, crosses this ancient highway, after passing which, by looking to the right, the eye rests upon a parcel of land extending down a hollow, which was cleared and planted in fruit trees prior to the Revolutionary war. Beyond this hollow, just where the road enters a body of woodland, there are yet some traces of a human habitation. In this orchard, two patrol parties met from the adverse armies. The party from Dunlap's camp were in the orchard gathering peaches ; the Liberty men fired on them, and drove them from the place. In turn, the victors entered the orchard, but the report of their guns brought out

---

* MS notes of conversations with the late Colonel George Wilson, of Nashville. Tennessee, who derived the facts from his father-in-law, Alexander Greer, one of Major Robertson's men on the expedition. MS. letters of Hon. Simpson Bobo and A. H. Twichell, showing the locality of the Pacolet hill.

a strong detachment from the Cedar Spring, as well as a reinforcement from Shelby. The commander of the patrol, when he saw the enemy approaching, drew up his men under cover of the fence along the ridge, just where the old field and woodland now meet, and where traces of an old residence are now barely visible. Here he awaited their approach.

The onset was furious, but vigorously met. The conflict was maintained against fearful odds till the arrival of reinforcements from Shelby's camp. The scale now turned, and the assailants now fell back. The whole force of Shelby and Clarke were soon in battle array, confronted by the whole British advance, numbering six or seven hundred men. The struggle was renewed with redoubled fury. The Liberty men drove back their foes, when the whole British army came up. A retreat was now a matter of necessity. Such is the local tradition ; but local tradition, especially in this case, is extremely liable to error and confusion, from the fact that but few of the people of that quarter were present in the action—for the actors were mostly from other States, and probably strangers to the neighborhood. Thus far, Mr. Saye's narrative.

Only two British accounts of the action at Cedar Spring have come to our knowledge—one bears date Savannah, Georgia, August twenty-fourth, 1780. It appeared in Rivington's *New York Royal Gazette*, of September fourteenth, copied into the *London Chronicle*, of November sixteenth, ensuing. It has every appearance of being a one-sided and diminuitve statement of the affair : " We learn from Augusta, that a Captain of the Queen's Rangers, with twenty-four dragoons, and about thirty militia, lately charged about three hundred Rebels above Ninety Six. Whilst they were engaged, Colonel Ferguson happily got up with some men to the assistance of our small party, which obliged the enemy to take to their heels. Fifty of the Rebels were killed and wounded ; a Major Smith was among the slain,

Engraved by J.C.Buttre

HON. SAMUEL HAMMOND.

OF GEORGIA
A.D. 1781.

and a Lieutenant-Colonel Clarke was wounded, and died next day. Our loss is said to be one dragoon and seven militia killed."

Allaire supplies the other account : " Got to the ground the Rebels were encamped on, at four o'clock on Tuesday morning, August eighth. They had intelligence of our move, and were likewise alarmed by the firing of a gun in our ranks ; they sneaked from their ground about half an hour before we arrived. Learning that the Rebel wagons were three miles in front of us at Cedar Springs, Captain Dunlap, with fourteen mounted men, and a hundred and thirty militia, were dispatched to take the wagons. He met three Rebels coming to reconnoitre our camp ; he pursued, took two of them, the other escaped, giving the Rebels the alarm. In pursuit of this man, Dunlap and his party rushed into the centre of the Rebel camp, where they lay in ambush, before he was aware of their presence. A skirmish ensued, in which Dunlap got slightly wounded, and had between twenty and thirty killed and wounded— Ensign McFarland and one private taken prisoners. The Rebel loss is uncertain—a Major Smith, Captain Potts, and two privates were left dead on the field. Colonel Clarke, Johnson [Robertson,] and twenty privates were seen wounded. We pursued them five miles, to the Iron Works ; but were not able to overtake them, they being all mounted."

Among the slain was Major Burwell Smith, who had contributed greatly to the settlement of the frontier portion of Georgia, where he had been an active and successful partisan in Indian warfare, and his fall was deeply lamented by Colonel Clarke and his associates. Captain John Potts* and Thomas Scott were also among the slain. Besides Colonel Clarke's slight wounds with a sabre, Major Charles Robertson, a volunteer from the Watauga troops, and Cap-

---

*This is stated on the anthority of Colonel Graham, who participated in the action, corroborated by Lieutenant Allaire's *Diary.* A. H. Twichell, Esq., of Glendale, states as the tradition of an old resident of that region, that an American officer named Potter was shot out of a peach tree at Thompson's place. This doubtless refers to Captain Potts.

tain John Clarke, the youthful son of the Colonel, yet in his teens, and several others, were also wounded in the same manner. This close hand-to-hand sabre fighting, which McCall describes, contradicts his previous description of the action as if it were simply a "distant firing" upon each other. It shows, too, that the back-woods riflemen did not take to their heels on the approach of the dragoons with their glittering broad-swords.

It is not easy to determine the actual strength of the parties engaged in this spirited contest, nor their respective losses. McCall does not specify how many on either side took part in the conflict—only that the Americans were out-numbered; erroneously naming Innes as the British com-mander; and states that the enemy pursued Colonel Clarke to Wofford's Iron Works, where he had chosen a strong position from which the British endeavored to draw him, and that a distant firing continued during the after-noon, until near night; that the Americans lost four killed and five or six wounded, while the enemy lost five killed and eleven wounded. Mills mentions in one place in his work, that Clarke's force was one hundred and sixty-eight, in another, one hundred and ninety-eight, evidently ignorant of the presence of Colonels Shelby and Graham, with their followers; that Ferguson and Dunlap combined, numbered between four and six hundred, of which Dunlap's advance consisted of sixty dragoons and one hundred and fifty mounted volunteer riflemen; that the Americans had four killed and twenty-three wounded, all by the broad-sword; while Dunlap lost twenty-eight of his dragoons, and six or seven of his Tory volunteers killed, and several wounded. Shelby, in Haywood, states Ferguson's full force at about two thousand strong—which Todd augments to twenty-five hundred—of which Dunlap's advance was reputed at six or seven hundred; that the strength of the Americans was six hundred; and acknowledges that ten or twelve of the latter were killed and wounded, but does not state the loss of their assailants. Colonel Graham gives no numbers, but asserts that many of the enemy were killed. These several statements differ very much from the British reports, and from each other.

In Shelby's account as originally published in Haywood's *Tennessee*, and then in Ramsey's, the number of prisoners taken is stated at "twenty, with two British officers," which in Todd's memoir of Shelby, are increased to "fifty, mostly British, including two officers;" and Colonel Graham in his pension statement, places the number at only half a dozen, and Allaire at only two.

As to the particular time in the day in which the contest took place, there is also quite a variety of statements. Mills places it before day, when so dark that it was hard to distinguish friend from foe—his informant doubtless referring, not to Dunlap's fight, but to the prior attack upon Colonel Thomas, at Cedar Spring, which he so signally repelled.

McCall states that it occurred in the afternoon; Shelby is silent on this point; while Governor Perry's traditions convey the idea that it was in the morning or fore part of the day, and in this he is corroborated by Captain William Smith,* as well as by the MS. *Diary* of Lieutenant Allaire.

Colonel Graham only refers to the time of day inferen-

---

* Captain Smith was born in Bucks County, Pennsylvania, September 20th, 1751, and early settled in what is now Spartanburg County, South Carolina. He served in Captain Joseph Wofford's company on the Snow campaign, in 1775; and the next year as Lieutenant on Williamson's expedition against the Cherokees. In 1777, he was made a Captain in the militia and was stationed in Wood's Fort on Tyger. In December, 1778, he was ordered to Georgia, serving under General Lincoln; and shared in the battle of Stono, in June, 1779; in the contests, as we have seen, near Wofford's Iron Works, Hanging Rock, and Musgrove's Mill, in August, 1780; and subsequently at the battle of Blackstocks, in the siege of Fort Granby, at Guilford Court House, Quinby Bridge, the affair at the Juniper, and the capture of some British vessels at Watboo Landing under Colonel Wade Hampton. In the latter part of the war he ranked as Major. After the war, he was chosen County Judge, member of Congress from 1797 to 1799, and State Senator for twenty years. Few men served the public longer or more faithfully in military and civil life than Judge Smith. He died June 22d, 1837, in the eighty-sixth year of his age. His widow survived till October 2d, 1842.

tially, by stating that it was "several hours" after the action before Ferguson, with his combined force, came in sight, when Shelby and his men precipitately retired.

Precisely where the fight took place has also been a subject of dispute—the result, no doubt, of the general vagueness of the descriptions. Mills says it occurred at the Green Springs, meaning Cedar Spring, near Wofford's old Iron Works; Shelby says at Cedar Spring, as does Samuel Espy, of North Carolina, who was also in the action. Had these two men, and Mills' informant, stated the locality with more exactitude, they might, and probably would, have said, that they named the Cedar Spring as a permanent landmark, near which the contest transpired, and so located it—the same as Gates' defeat is frequently referred to as having occurred at Camden, when it really took place some seven miles distant. Colonel Graham, one of the prominent officers in that affair, refers to it as "at Wofford's Iron Works;" Alexander McFadden, a survivor of the contest, speaks of it as "the battle of Wofford's Iron Works;" while McCall, the historian, says the enemy pursued the Americans "to Wofford's Iron Works, where they chose their ground, and awaited the attack."

William Smith, of Tennessee, another survivor of the contest says, "we had a battle near Wofford's Iron Works;" and Captain William Smith, of Spartanburg, who was an intelligent officer in the fight, and resided within a few miles of the battle-ground the most of his long life, states that the contest took place "near the old Iron Works." His son, Hon. John Winsmith, in a historical address he made at Cedar Spring, in 1855, and verbally repeated to the writer in 1871, describes the hill, then covered with timber, nearly half a mile north-east of Cedar Spring, as the locality of the battle. It is possible that the first half-hour's contest, where Clarke had his desperate personal rencontre with unequal odds, may have taken place near this hill, as Dr. Winsmith believes. "On this locality," says N. F. Walker, "within my recollection, a musket-barrel was found, and near where we think the dead were buried."*

But as Cedar Spring seems not to have been on the old route pursued by the contending parties, the weight of evidence, and all the circumstances, go to show that the chief fighting was "near the old Iron Works," as Captain William Smith positively asserts. Mr. Saye's traditions of the neighborhood, collected there prior to 1848, fix the locality of, at least, one portion of the contest, at the old orchard on the Thompson place, between the Cedar Spring and the old Iron Works, about one mile from the former, and nearly two from the latter. The fact that the graves of the Tory dead, including the one from which the peach tree sprung, are near the old Thompson orchard, and between it and Cedar Spring, sufficiently attest the locality where, at least, the principal part of this notable passage at arms occurred.

More space has been devoted to these two somewhat blended affairs—the one at the Cedar Spring, where Colonel Thomas repulsed the enemy, and the other near Thompson's peach-orchard—than, perhaps, their real importance in history would seem to warrant. At the period of their occurrence, they exerted a marked influence on the people of the upper region of Carolina, as demonstrating what brave and determined men could accomplish in defense of their own and their country's rights; and how successfully they could meet an insolent foe, alike in ambush, or on the battle-field. As no contemporary records of these events have come down to us, save the vague and unsatisfactory British ones which we have given entire, and the traditionary accounts have become more or less intermixed and confused, it seemed proper to sift them as thoroughly as possible, and present the simple narrative of the occurrences as the facts seem to indicate.

---

* It may well have been at this hill where the previous Tory attack was made on Colonel Thomas. It was a fit place, then covered with timber, to have formed his successful ambuscade.

The difficulty has hitherto been, on the part of historical writers, in attempts to blend the two affairs, when the
time, details, and different commanding officers, all go very
clearly to prove that they were entirely distinct, and had
no connection whatever with each other.   It is due to the
Rev. Mr. Saye, to state that he was the first person who
discovered the incongruity of applying the details to a single action ; but he was unable to fix their respective dates,
or determine which took the precedence of the other in
point of time.   McCall's *History of Georgia* has furnished
the key to unlock the difficulty with reference to the time
of the attack on Thomas' force at Cedar Spring, and all the
circumstances go to confirm it ; while the hitherto unpub-
lished *Diary* of Lieutenant Allaire determines the date of
the affair near Wofford's Iron Works.*

---

* The authorities consulted in the preparation of this notice of the action near Cedar
Spring and Wofford's Iron Works, are : McCall's *Georgia*, ii, 314; Haywood's *Tennessee*,
64–65; Mills' *Statistics of South Carolina*, 256,738–39 ; Todd's *Memoir of Shelby ;* Governor
Perry's account in the *Magnolia* Magazine, August, 1842 ; New York *Royal Gazette*, September 14th, 1780; *London Chronicle*, November 16th, 1780; Saye's *Memoir of McJunkin*,
and the Saye MSS.; MSS. of Dr. John H. Logan ; Allaire's MS. *Diary;* Winsmith's *Address*, 1855 ; together with the MS. pension statements of Colonel William Graham, Captain William Smith, of Spartanburg, Samuel Espy, Alexander McFadden, and William
Smith, of Tennessee, all participants in the action ; also MS. notes of conversations with
Colonel George Wilson, of Tennessee.   I am indebted to N. F. Walker, Esq., of Cedar
Spring, and A. H. Twichell, Esq., of Glendale, for traditions, and descriptions of the
localities connected with the battle and the retreat.

Ramsay, Moultrie, Lee's *Memoirs*, Johnson's *Greene*, and other early writers, do not
even notice this action ; nor such modern historians as Bancroft, Hildreth, and Stevens.
Lossing, Wheeler, Simms, Ramsey's *Tennessee*, and O'Neall's *Newberry* briefly refer to it ;
while Mrs. Ellet, in her *Women of the Revolution*, and her *Domestic History of the Revolution*, simply copies from Mills, misapplying the story of Mrs. Dillard's adventure.

I have not cited what passes for Colonel Hammond's account of the battle, in a newspaper series, and also in Johnson's *Traditions of the Revolution*, simply because he could
not have written it ; but it was evidently manufactured from Mills' *Statistics*, with some
imaginary interlardings, to give it a new appearance.   Dawson, in his *Battles of the United
States*, has given a chapter on this affair, based on the pretended Hammond narrative.

CHAPTER VI.

1780—August 18.

Returning from their Fair Forest expedition, Clarke
and Shelby's men needed a little repose. McDowell soon
after removed his camp from the Cherokee Ford, taking
post, some ten miles below, on the eastern bank of
Broad River, at Smith's Ford. By his faithful scouts,
Colonel McDowell was kept well informed of Ferguson's
movements and out-posts. Learning that a body of some
two hundred Loyalists were stationed at Musgrove's Mill,
some forty miles distant on the Enoree, to guard the rocky
ford at that place, it was regarded as a vulnerable point—
all the more so, since Ferguson, with his main force, was
stationed considerably in advance, between that place and
the American encampment, thus tending to lull into security
those in their rear.

The term of enlistment of Colonel Shelby's regiment
was about to expire, and that enterprising officer was
desirous of engaging in another active service before retiring to his home on the Holston. Colonels Shelby and

Clarke were appointed to lead a party of mounted men to surprise or attack the Loyalists at Musgrove's. With Clarke was Captain James McCall and Captain Samuel Hammond. Colonel James Williams, whose home was in that region, but who had been driven from it, had, on the sixteenth of August, joined McDowell with a few followers—prominent among whom were Colonel Thomas Brandon, Colonel James Steen, and Major McJunkin ; and these united with Shelby and Clarke, together with several other experienced officers, who volunteered to share in the enterprise, among whom were Major Joseph McDowell, the brother of the Colonel, Captain David Vance, and Captain Valentine Sevier, and with the latter, a number of Watauga and Nolachucky riflemen.

It was largely rumored, that a military chest was either at Musgrove's, or was being conveyed from Ninety Six to Ferguson's camp ; and the Whigs hoped to intercept it on the way. Whatever influence this prospect of obtaining British treasure may have exerted on the volunteers, as we hear no more of the chest, we may conclude that it was a camp yarn, gotten up for the occasion ; or, if a reality, it certainly eluded the grasp of the adventurers.

Secrecy and dispatch were necessary to success. A night march was therefore chosen, when less likely to be observed, and cooler for the horses to travel. Shelby and his two hundred adventurous followers left camp an hour before sun-down, on the seventeenth of August. Williams, Brandon, and their men, were well acquainted with the country, and knew the best route to effect their purpose. They traveled through the woods until dark, when they fell into a road, and proceeded on all night, much of the way in a canter, and without making a single stop — crossing Gilky's and Thicketty creeks, Pacolet, Fair Forest, and Tyger, with other lesser streams, and passing within three or four miles of Ferguson's camp on their left, which was, at this time, at Fair Forest Shoal, in Brandon's settlement, some twenty-six miles from Smith's Ford; and from Fair Forest Shoal, it was still twelve or fourteen miles to Musgrove's. It was a hard night's ride.

Arriving, near the dawn of day, within a mile nearly north of Musgrove's Ford, the Whig party halted at an old Indian field, and sent out a party of five or six scouts to reconnoitre the situation. They crossed the mouth of Cedar Shoal Creek, close to the Spartanburg line, a short distance below Musgrove's Mill, and then passed up a by-road to Head's Ford, a mile above Musgrove's, where they forded the Enoree, and stealthily approached sufficiently near the Tory camp to make observations. Returning the same route, when on the top of the river ridge, west of Cedar Shoal creek, they encountered a small Tory patrol, which had passed over at Musgrove's Ford, during their absence above, and thus gained their rear. A sharp firing ensued, when one of the enemy was killed, two wounded, and two fled precipitately to the Tory camp. Two of the Americans were slightly wounded, who, with their fellows, now promptly returned to Shelby and Clarke's halting place, with the intelligence they had gained, and the particulars of their skirmish.

This firing, and the speedy arrival of the two patrolmen, put the Tory camp in wild commotion. Colonel Innes, Major Fraser, and other officers who had their headquarters at Edward Musgrove's residence, held a hurried council. Innes was for marching over the river at once, and catching the Rebels before they had time to retreat; while others contended for delay, at least till after breakfast, by which time, it was hoped, a party of one hundred mounted men, who had gone on a patrol, eight miles below, near Jones' Ford, would return, and thus add very materially to their strength. But Innes' counsels prevailed, lest they should miss so fine an opportunity "to bag" a scurvy lot of ragamuffins, as they regarded the adventurous Americans. So leaving one hundred men in camp as a reserve, preparations were made for an immediate advance to meet the unexpected invaders.

Meanwhile, Shelby and Clarke had taken position on a timbered ridge, some little distance east of Cedar Shoal creek, and within about half a mile of Musgrove's Ford and Mill. At this juncture, a countryman, who lived near by, came up, giving information that the British had been reinforced the preceding evening, by the arrival of Colonel Alexander Innes, from Ninety Six, with two hundred men of the Provincial regiments, and one hundred Tories, destined to join Colonel Ferguson. A British writer represents, that Innes' detachment consisted of a light infantry company of the New Jersey Volunteers, under Captain Peter Campbell; a company of De Lancey's Provincial Battalion, under Captain James Kerr, together with about one hundred mounted men of his own regiment, the South Carolina Royalists. This could not have included the regular garrison previously stationed there, apparently under the command of Major Fraser. Captain Abraham De Peyster, of the King's American regiment, as well as the noted Loyalist partisan, Captain David Fanning, were also there; while Colonel Daniel Clary was encamped there, at the head of the Tories of that region.

So minute were the circumstances of the information communicated by the countryman, that no doubt was entertained of its truth; and to march on and attack the enemy appeared rash, and to attempt a successful retreat, wearied and broken down as the horses were, seemed almost impossible. Colonel Shelby and his associates instantly concluded, that they had no alternative—fight they must. Securing their horses in their rear, they resolved to improvise a breast-work of logs and brush, and make the best defense possible. Their lines were formed across the road, at least three hundred yards in length, along the ridge, in a semi-circle, and both protected and concealed by a wood. Old logs, fallen trees and brush were hurried into place, so that in thirty minutes they had a very respectable protection, breast-high. Shelby occupied the right—Clarke the left; and Williams in the center, though with no special command, for the whole force formed one extended line. A party of some twenty horsemen were placed on each flank, shielded, as much as possible, from the enemy's observation—Josiah Culbertson having the command of that on Shelby's right; and Colonel Clarke had a reserve of forty men within calling distance.

Captain Shadrach Inman, who had figured prominently in battling the British and Tories in Georgia, was sent forward, with about twenty-five mounted men, with orders to fire upon, and provoke the enemy to cross the ford, and skirmish with them, at his discretion; and retire, drawing the British into the net which Shelby and Clarke had so adroitly prepared for them. This stratagem, which was the suggestion of the Captain himself, worked admirably, for the British infantry seemed elated with their success in driving Inman at the point of the bayonet; but the Whig Captain kept up a show of fighting and retreating. While the enemy were yet two hundred yards distant from the American breast-works, they hastily formed into line of battle; and as they advanced fifty yards nearer, they opened a heavy fire, pretty generally over-shooting their antagonists. When trees were convenient, the frontiermen made use of them, while others were shielded behind their rudely constructed barrier, and, to some extent, availed themselves also of a fence extending along the road. The Americans had been cautioned to reserve their fire "till they could see the whites of the Tories' eyes;" or, as another has it, "till they could distinguish the buttons on their clothes"—nor even then to discharge their rifles, until orders were given, when each man was "to take his object sure." These orders were strictly obeyed.

The British center, on whom Inman made his feigned attacks, seeing him retire in apparent confusion, pressed forward, under beat of drum and bugle charge, in pursuit, but in considerable disorder, shouting: "Huzza for King George!" On approaching within seventy yards of the American lines, they were unexpectedly met with a deadly fire, from which they at first recoiled. But their superiority in numbers enabled them to continue their attack, notwithstanding the advantage which the breast-work gave the Americans. A strong force, composed of the Provincials, led on by Innes and Fraser, forming the enemy's left wing, drove, at the point of the bayonet, the right wing under Shelby from their breast-work. It was a desperate struggle—Shelby's men contending against large odds, and the right flank of his right wing gradually giving away, whilst his left flank maintained its connection with the centre at the breast-work. The left wing, opposed by the Tories, retained its position; and, seeing Shelby in need of succor, Clarke sent his small reserve to his aid, which proved a most timely relief. At this critical moment, as Innes was forcing Shelby's right flank, the British leader was badly disabled, fell from his charger, and was carried back—shot, it was reported, by one of the Watauga volunteers, William Smith, who exultingly exclaimed, "I've killed their commander," when Shelby rallied his men, who raised a regular frontier Indian yell, and rushed furiously upon the enemy, who were gradually forced back before the exasperated riflemen. Culbertson's flanking party acted a conspicuous part on this occasion.

It was unfortunate for the enemy, that, in this desperate contest, one Captain was killed, and five out of seven of the surviving officers of their Provincial corps were wounded. Besides Innes, shot down by Smith, another Watauga rifleman, Robert Beene, wounded Major Fraser, who was seen to reel from his horse. Captain Campbell, together with Lieutenants Camp and William Chew, were also among the wounded.*

---

* Colonel Innes was a Scotchman. He was probably a *protege* of his countryman, Alexander Cameron, the British Indian Agent among the Cherokees; and was, it would appear,

These heavy losses had a very disheartening effect upon the British troops. And the Tories, failing to make any impression on Clarke's line, and having already lost several of their officers, and many of their men, began to show signs of wavering, when Captain Hawsey, a noted leader among them, who was striving to re-animate the Loyalists, and retrieve the fortunes of the day, was shot down. In the midst of the confusion that followed, Clarke and his brave men, following Shelby's example, pushed forth from their barrier, yelling, shooting and slashing on every hand. It was in the *melée*, when the British defeat was too apparent, that the Tory Colonel Clary had the opposite bits of his horse's bridle seized at the same moment by two stalwart Whigs. He had, however, the ingenuity and presence of mind to extricate himself from his perilous situation by exclaiming—" D—n you, don't you know your own officers ! " He was instantly released, and fled at full speed.*

The British and Tories were now in full retreat, closely followed by the intrepid mountaineers. It was in this exciting pursuit that the courageous Captain Inman was killed, while pressing the enemy, and fighting them hand-to-hand. He received seven shots from the Tories, one, a musket ball, piercing his forehead. He fell near the base of a Spanish oak that stood where the modern road leaves the old mill road, and where his grave was still pointed

---

an assistant commissary at the Long Island of Holston, at one time; and in the fall of 1777, returned to the Cherokee nation, taking up his quarters with Cameron. He was commissioned Colonel of the South Carolina Royalists, January 20, 1780; in 1782, he was Inspector General of the Loyalist forces. Colonel Hanger, in his *Reply* to Mackenzie's *Strictures* states that Innes was living retired in 1789, probably on half-pay.

Of Major Fraser, who was wounded in this engagement, we have no further knowledge. Captain Campbell was of Trenton, New Jersey, settled in New Brunswick, after peace was declared, on half-pay, dying in Maugersville in that Colony in 1822, and was buried at Frederickton. Lieutenant Chew retired at the close of the war, on half-pay, to New Brunswick, dying at Frederickton, in 1812, aged sixty-four. Of Lieutenant Camp's career, before or after the affair at Musgrove's Mill, we have no information.

* Colonel Clarey was a prominent citizen of Ninety Six District ; and surviving the war, remained in the country. Notwithstanding his great error in siding with the Tories, he was greatly beloved, and, in after life, performed all the duties of a good citizen, until peacefully gathered to his fathers. He had, a few years since, a grandson, Colonel Clary, living in Edgefield County, and other decendants.

out but a few years since.   Great credit is justly due to
Captain Inman for the successful manner in which he
brought on the action, and the aid he rendered in conducting it to a triumphant issue.

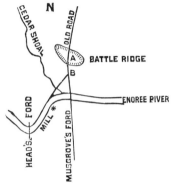

Plat of Region near Musgrove's Mill.
A. Graves. B. Where Captain Inman was
killed, at the junction of the old and new roads.

The yells and screeches
of the retreating British and
Tories as they ran through
the woods, and over the hills
to the river—loudly intermingled with the shouts of
their pursuers, together with
the groans of the dying and
wounded, were terrific and
heart-rending in the ex-
treme.   The smoke, as well
as the din and confusion,
rose high above the exciting
scene.   The Tories ceased to make any show of defense
when half way from the breast-works to the ford.   The
retreat then became a perfect rout; and now, with reckless speed, they hastened to the river, through which they
rushed with the wildest fury, hotly pursued by the victorious
Americans with sword and rifle, killing, wounding or capturing all who came in their way.

Many of the British and Tories were shot down as they
were hastening, pell-mell, across the Enoree at the rocky
ford.   After they were fairly over, one, not yet too weary
to evince his bravado, and attract attention for the moment,
turned up his buttock in derision at the Americans; when
one of the Whig officers, probably Brandon or Steen, said
to Golding Tinsley : *   "Can't you turn that insolent brag-

---

* This old soldier, who did much good service in the up-country of South Carolina
during the Revolution, was born in Culpeper County, Virginia, in or about 1756, as stated in
his pension papers, and settled in South Carolina about 1771.   He early served in the
Rangers. He participated in the battle of Stono, the seige of Savannah, and took an active
part in the actions at Musgrove's Mill, King's Mountain, and Blackstocks. He had two
brothers killed by the Tories in the Fair Forest region during the war. He lived to enjoy
a pension, dying in Spartanburg County, May 11th, 1851, aged about ninety-five years.

gart over?" "I can try," responded Tinsley, who was known to possess a good rifle, when, suiting the action to the word, he took prompt aim, and fired—and sure enough, *turned him over*, when some of his comrades picked the fellow up, and carried him off. Another instance of sharp-shooting is mentioned: One of the enemy, who had re-crossed the ford, betook himself to a convenient tree, which, however, did not fully protect his person, for Thomas Gillespie, one of the Watauga riflemen, brought his rifle to bear on the Tory's partially exposed body, and the next moment he bit the dust.

It is related, that while the firing was yet kept up, on the north side of the Enoree, an intrepid frontierman, Captain Sam Moore, led a small party of ten or twelve men up the river, and crossing the stream at Head's Ford, rushed down upon a portion of the enemy with such impetuosity and audacity as to impress them with the belief that they were but the vanguard of a much larger force, when they incontinently fled, and Moore rejoined his victorious friends over the river.

Some interesting incidents connected with, and following the battle, deserve a place in this connection. So many of the British and Tory reserve as could, mounted to the top of Musgrove's house, that they might witness the contest, not doubting for a moment that King George's men could and would bear down all before them. They saw the heroic Inman deliver his successive fires and retreat, followed closely by Innes' pursuers; and supposed this little band constituted the whole of the Rebel party. To these house-top observers, the bold invaders were beaten back—routed; when they threw up their hats, indulging in shouts that made the old hill in the rear of Musgrove's resound again, with echoes and re-echoes, in commemoration of their imaginary victory. At length, reaching the concealed Whigs, a tremendous fire burst upon their pursuers, which caused a deathly paleness on the countenance of some fifty of the reserve party, who were it was said, paroled British prisoners, doing duty contrary to the laws of war—they, especially, dreading the consequences of a possible capture at the hands of the Americans. Their shoutings ceased— they peered anxiously, with bated breath, towards the contending parties. At length they raised the cry of despair: "We are beaten—our men are retreating;" and long before the Tories had re-crossed the river, these demoralized Britons had seized their knap-sacks, and were scampering off towards Ninety Six at their liveliest speed.

The large patrolling party which had been down the river near Jones' Ford, heard the firing, and came dashing back at full speed; and while descending the steep hill, east of the old Musgrove domicile, their bright uniforms and flashing blades and scabbards reflected the rays of the morning sun just rising in its splendor. They reined up their panting steeds before Musgrove's, the commanding officer eagerly inquiring what was the matter. A hurried account of the battle was given, which had terminated so disastrously some thirty minutes before; when, rising in his stirrups, and uttering deep and loud imprecations, the cavalry commander ordered his men to cross the river. They dashed at full speed over the rocky ford, splashing the water, which, with the resplendent sun-rays, produced miniature rainbows around the horses. They were too late, for the victorious Americans had retired with their prisoners, leaving the British troopers the melancholy duty of conveying their wounded fellows to the hospital at Musgrove's.

For many miles around, every woman and child of the surrounding country, who were able to leave their homes, visited the battle-ground—some for plunder, some from curiosity, and others for a different purpose. It was chiefly a Tory region, the few Whigs having retired from motives of personal safety, joining Sumter and other popular leaders. The most of these visitors were of Loyalist families;

and it was interesting to witness them, as well as the few Whig ladies present, turning over the bodies of the slain, earnestly examining their faces, to see if they could recognize a father, husband, son, or brother. Not a few went away with saddened hearts, and eyes bedewed with tears.

Sixteen Tories were said to have been buried in one grave, near the mouth of Cedar Shoal creek—the particular spot long since defaced and forgotten. Several were interred between the battle-ground and ford, but a stone's throw below where George Gordon resided some thirty years since, on the west side of the old road; while others were buried in the yard of the late Captain Philemon Waters, midway between the ford and battle-field, opposite the dogwood spring, and others yet were buried in a grave-yard, just below Musgrove's house. A burial spot is still pointed out on the battle-ridge, just east of the old road.

It was a complete rout on the part of the British and Tories. They seem to have apprehended, that the Whig forces, in the flush of victory, might push on to Ninety Six, then believed to be in a weak and defenceless condition. The Tory leader, Fanning, states, that after the battle, the British retreated a mile and a quarter, where they encamped for the remainder of the day; and, in the night, marched off towards Ninety Six, under the command of Captain De Peyster. This probably refers to only a part of the enemy; for the larger portion must have remained, if for nothing else, at least to take care of their wounded. Another British writer, Mackenzie, represents, that in the retreat from the battle-ground, they were conducted by Captain Kerr to the southern bank of the Enoree, where they remained till reinforced by Lieutenant-Colonel Cruger from Ninety Six. "Captain Kerr," says the Georgia historian, McCall, "finding that resistance would be in vain, and without hope of success, ordered a retreat, which was effected in close order for four miles, resorting to the bayonet for defence in flank and rear. The pursuit was con-

tinued by the victors, until the enemy took refuge in Musgrove's Mill," which was on the south side of the Enoree, in
the north-east corner of the present county of Laurens,
noted on Mills' *Atlas of South Carolina* as Gordon's Mill.

Colonel Williams' official account represents that the
main fight—the one at the breast-work—lasted only fifteen
minutes, when the enemy were obliged to retreat, and were
pursued two miles ; and that Colonel Innes was reported to
be wounded by two balls—one in the neck and the other
breaking the thigh—and that three Tory Captains were
slain. "The enemy declared they suffered exceedingly in
the action with Colonel Williams ; that Captain Campbell,
an officer in high repute, of the regulars, among others,
was killed,"* and Governor Rutledge confirms the fact that
"one British Captain " was among the slain.

Shelby states, that the action continued an hour before
the enemy were repulsed in front of the breast-work ; while
McCall asserts, that it was "but a few minutes after the
contest began, when so many of the Provincial officers were
either killed or wounded, and "the men tumbled down in
heaps, without the power of resistance," when the survivors
retreated under Captain Kerr.† Probably Colonel Williams'
recollection of the length of the battle before the retreat,
written within a few days thereafter, is approximately correct ; and possibly well nigh an hour may have been consumed by the time the enemy were driven across the ford, and
took refuge in the mill. "This action," says Colonel Hill's
manuscript, "was one of the hardest ever fought in the
country with small arms alone ; the smoke was so thick as

---

* Statement in *Virginia Gazette*, September 27th, 1780, of William Allman, of Colonel
Stubblefield's regiment of Virginia militia, who was captured at Gates' defeat, and subsequently escaped from Camden.

† Captain James Kerr was probably a resident of Long Island or Connecticut, from
whose refugees most of the Queen's Rangers were raised, in which corps he was a Captain.
After the war, he retired on half-pay, first to New Brunswick, and then to King's county,
Nova Scotia, where he was made Colonel of the militia. He died at Amherst, in that
Province, in 1830, at the age of seventy-six, leaving a widow, who survived him ten years,
dying at seventy-four. Three sons and a daughter preceded him to the grave, but twelve
children survived him.

to hide a man at the distance of twenty rods." Shelby described this battle as "the hardest and best fought action he ever was in "—attributing this valor and persistency to "the great number of officers who were with him as volunteers."

It must be confessed, that the Provincials and Tories, before their final rout, fought bravely. Their dragoons, but lately raised, and indifferently disciplined, behaved with much gallantry, fighting on the left with Innes. They all exhibited, more or less, the training they had received under that superior master, Ferguson. The British loss, in this affair, was sixty-three killed, about ninety wounded, and seventy prisoners—a total of not far from two hundred and twenty-three, out of four or five hundred, which is an unusually large proportion for the number engaged in the action. The American loss was only four killed and eight or nine wounded. This disparity in killed and wounded, resulted largely from over-shooting* on the part of the enemy, and the decided advantage which the trees and breast-works afforded the Whigs for their protection. The skill of the frontiermen in the use of their rifles was never better displayed nor more effective; while, in the retreat, the loss fell almost exclusively on the panic-stricken British and Tories.

Anxious to improve the advantage they had so signally gained, Shelby and his heroic compeers at once resolved to pursue the demoralized Tories, and make a dash for Ninety Six, which they learned was in a weak condition; and

---

* Richard Thompson, of Fair Forest, when a boy of some twelve or fourteen years, while on his way with his mother to visit his father, then imprisoned at Ninety Six, passed over the battle-ground at Musgrove's a few days after its occurrence, and observed the bullet marks on the trees—those of the British and Tories generally indicating an aim above the heads of their antagonists, while those of the Whigs were from three to five feet above the ground. He learned from his father and other prisoners at Ninety Six, that the fugitives reported the Whig strength in that action as five thousand; and such was the consternation of the garrison of Ninety Six on receipt of the news of the battle, that had the victorious Whigs showed themselves there, it would have been difficult for Colonel Cruger and his officers to have prevented a general stampede.—Saye's MSS., and *Memoir of McJunkin.*

being only some twenty-five miles distant, they could easily reach there before night. Returning to their horses, and mounting them, while Shelby was consulting Colonel Clarke, Francis Jones, an express from Colonel McDowell, rode up, in great haste, with a letter in his hand from General Caswell, who had, on the sixteenth, shared in General Gates' total defeat near Camden, apprising McDowell of the great disaster, and advising him and all officers commanding detachments to get out of the way, or they would be cut off; McDowell sending word that he would at once move towards Gilbert Town.   General Caswell's handwriting was fortunately familiar to Colonel Shelby, so he knew it was no Tory trick attempted to be played off upon them.   He and his associates instantly saw the difficulty of their situation ; they could not retire to McDowell's camp, for his force was no longer there—Gates' army was killed, captured and scattered—and Sumter's, too, was soon destined to meet the same fate ; in their rear was Cruger, with whatever of Innes' and Fraser's detachments remained, with Ferguson's strong force on their flank.   There was no choice—further conquests were out of the question.   So Ninety Six was left unvisited by the mountaineers—doubtless for them, a fortunate circumstance, as they were without cannon, and Colonel Cruger, who commanded there, was no Patrick Moore, as his brave defence of that garrison against General Greene and his thousands, the following year, sufficiently attested.   It was, therefore, determined in a hasty council on horseback, that they would take a backwoods route, to avoid and escape Ferguson, and join Colonel McDowell on his retreat towards Gilbert Town.

Hurriedly gathering the prisoners together, and distributing one to every three of the Americans, who conveyed them alternately on horseback, requiring each captive to carry his gun, divested of its flint, the whole cavalcade were ready in a few minutes to beat a retreat, as they knew full well that Ferguson would be speedily apprised of their

success, and make a strenuous effort, as he did at Wofford's
Iron Works, to regain the prisoners. Here an amusing
incident occurred. Riding along the ranks, viewing the
prisoners, Colonel Williams recognized among them an old
acquaintance in the person of Saul Hinson, very diminutive
in size, who had the previous year served under his command at the battle of Stono, when the Colonel pleasantly
exclaimed: "Ah! my little Sauly, have we caught you?"
"Yes, Colonel," replied the little man, "and no d—d great
catch either!" Saul's repartee only caused a laugh, and
neither that nor his false position subjected him to any thing
beyond the common restraint of a prisoner.

Some of the few wounded, who were not able to ride,
were necessarily left ; and, it is pleasant to add, they were
humanely cared for by the British, and especially by the
Musgrove family. Among them was one Miller, shot
through the body, whose injuries were believed to be mortal.
A silk handkerchief was drawn through the wound to cleanse
it. His parents, from the lower part of the present county
of Laurens, obtained the services of an old physician, Dr.
Ross, to attend to their wounded son, though it is believed
the British surgeons were not wanting in their professional
attentions. He at length recovered.

The Whig troopers, encumbered with their prisoners,
now hurried rapidly away in a north-westerly direction.
instead of a north-easterly one towards their old encampment. They passed over a rough, broken country, crossing
the forks of Tyger, leaving Ferguson on the right, and
heading their course towards their own friendly mountains.
As they expected, they were rapidly pursued by a strong
detachment of Ferguson's men.* Wearied as the mountaineers and their horses were, with scarcely any refreshment
for either, yet Shelby's indomitable energy permitted them

---

* This detachment could not have been led by Captain De Peyster, as supposed by
Colonel Shelby, for that officer, as the Tory annalist, Fanning, asserts, accompanied him
from Musgrove's to Ninety Six the night after the battle, doubtless to notify Cruger of the
disaster, and obtain reinforcements.

no rest while danger lurked in the way. Once or twice
only they tarried a brief period to feed their faithful
horses; relying, for their own sustenance, on peaches and
green corn—the latter pulled from the stalks, and eaten in
its raw state as they took their turn on horse-back, or trotted
on foot along the trail, and which, in their hungry condition, they pronounced delicious. They were enabled, now
and then, to snatch a refreshing draught from the rocky
streams which they forded.

Late in the evening of the eighteenth, Ferguson's party
reached the spot where the Whigs had, less than thirty minutes before, fed their weary horses; but not knowing how
long they had been gone, and their own detachment being
exhausted, they relinquished further pursuit. Not aware of
this, the Americans kept on their tedious retreat all night,
and the following day, passing the North Tyger, and into
the confines of North Carolina—sixty miles from the battle-
field, and one hundred from Smith's Ford, from which they
had started, without making a stop, save long enough to
defeat the enemy at Musgrove's. It was a remarkable
instance of unflagging endurance, in the heat of a southern summer, and encumbered, as they were, with seventy
prisoners. No wonder, that after forty-eight hours of such
excessive fatigue, nearly all the officers and soldiers became
so exhausted, that their faces and eyes were swollen and
bloated to that degree that they were scarcely able to see.

Reaching the mountain region in safety, they met Colonel McDowell's party, considerably diminished in numbers,
as we may well suppose. Colonel Shelby, with the approbation of Major Robertson, now proposed that an army of
volunteers be raised on both sides of the mountains, in sufficient numbers, to cope with Ferguson. All of the officers,
and some of the privates, were consulted, and all heartily
united in the propriety and feasibility of the undertaking.
It was agreed that the Musgrove prisoners should be sent
to a place of security; that the over-mountain men should

return home to recruit and strengthen their numbers; while Colonel McDowell should send an express to Colonels Cleveland and Herndon, of Wilkes, and Major Winston, of Surry, inviting and urging them to raise volunteers, and join in the enterprise; and that Colonel McDowell should, furthermore, devise the best means to preserve the beef stock of the Whigs of the Upper Catawba valleys and coves, which would undoubtedly be an early object of Ferguson's attention; and McDowell was, moreover, to obtain information of the enemy's movements, and keep the over-mountain men constantly apprised of them.*

As the term of service of their men having expired, Colonel Shelby and Major Robertson, with their Holston and Watauga volunteers, parted company with Colonel Clarke, leaving the prisoners in his charge, and took the trail which led to their homes over the Alleghanies. Colonels McDowell and Hampton, with their Burke and Rutherford followers, now less than two hundred in number, remained in the Gilbert Town region till forced back by the arrival of Ferguson shortly after. Colonel Clarke, after continuing some distance on his route, concluded to take the mountain trails and return to Georgia, transferring the prisoners to Colonel Williams, who, with Captain Hammond, conducted them safely to Hillsboro. There, meeting Governor Rutledge, of South Carolina, who supposing Williams had the chief command of the expedition, as his report was so worded as to convey that idea, conferred on him as a reward for the gallant achievement, the commission of a Brigadier-General in the South Carolina militia service, and, at the same time, promoted Captain Hammond to the rank of a Major. But Shelby, Clarke, Brandon, Steen, McCall, McDowell, and McJunkin, who battled so manfully at Musgrove's, were kept in the back-ground, receiving no merited honors for their services and their suf-

---

* MS. Statements of Major Joseph McDowell, and Captain David Vance, preserved by the late Robert Henry, of Buncombe Co., N. C., and both participants in this expedition.

ferings; yet they, nevertheless, continued faithfully to serve their country without a murmur.

Lord Cornwallis, on the twenty-ninth of August, wrote to Sir Henry Clinton: "Ferguson is to move into Tryon county with some militia, whom he says he is sure he can depend upon for doing their duty, and fighting well; but I am sorry to say, that *h;s own experience*, as well as that of every other officer, is totally against him."* This is a tacit acknowledgment, that Ferguson's detachments were decidedly worsted in the several affairs at Cedar Spring, with Colonel Jones beyond the head-waters of Saluda, at Earle's Ford, near Wofford's Iron Works, and at Musgrove's. So good a judge of military matters as Lord Cornwallis would not have made such a report, had not the disastrous results extorted the reluctant confession.

Some comparison of the principal authorities consulted, which appear more or less contradictory in their character, may not inappropriately be made in concluding this chapter. Dawson, vaguely referring to the Shelby statements, says they "differ so much from the contemporary reports, that I have not noticed them." Colonel Shelby was in every sense a real hero in war, and the details he furnishes are no doubt reliable. But in after life, he appears, perhaps imperceptibly, little by little, to have magnified the numbers, losses and prisoners in some of the contests in which he was engaged—notably so of the Musgrove affair. The venerable historian of Tennessee, Dr. J. G. M. Ramsey, states in a letter before the writer, that he closely followed a manuscript narrative of Governor Shelby in what he records of the battle at Musgrove's—the same that Haywood had used before him; in which the British force is given as four or five hundred, reinforced by six hundred under Colonel Innes from Ninety Six, not, however, stating the strength of the Whigs; that more than two hundred prisoners were taken, with a loss on the part of the victors of only six or seven killed. In his statement to Hardin, Colonel

* Correspondence of Cornwallis, i, 58–59.

Shelby puts both the British and American strength at about seven hundred—the former reinforced by six or seven hundred more ; that over two hundred of the enemy were killed, and two hundred made prisoners, with a Whig loss of Captain Inman and thirty others. Colonel Todd, in his sketch of his father-in-law, Governor Shelby, gives the enemy's force at Musgrove's at five or six hundred, reinforced by six hundred under Innes ; but discards Shelby's exaggerated account of losses and prisoners, adopting McCall's instead.

Colonel Williams' report, on the other hand, gives the American force at two hundred, and the British originally the same, reinforced by three hundred, killing sixty of the enemy, and taking seventy prisoners, while the Americans sustained a loss of only four killed, and seven or eight wounded. Governor Abner Nash, of North Carolina, writing September tenth, 1780, says : "Colonel Williams, of South Carolina, two days after this (Gates') defeat, with two hundred men, engaged four hundred of the British cavalry, in a fair open field fight, and completely defeated and routed them, killing sixty-three on the spot, and taking seventy-odd prisoners, mostly British." Orondates Davis, a prominent public character, writing from Halifax, North Carolina, September twenty-seventh, 1780, states : "Colonel Williams, of South Carolina, three [two] days after Gates' defeat, fell in with a party of the enemy near Ninety Six, and gave them a complete drubbing, killing seventy on the spot, and taking between sixty and seventy prisoners, mostly British, with the loss of four men only." These two statements, written, doubtless, on Williams' information, appear in the *North Carolina University Magazine* for March, 1855. McCall speaks of the British force as three hundred and fifty, and the Americans about equal, stating the British loss at sixty-three killed, and one hundred and sixty wounded and taken, the Americans losing only four killed and nine wounded ; while Mills, who does not report the numbers engaged, gives the British loss at eighty-six killed, and seventy-six taken. Major James Sevier stated the Whig force at two hundred and fifty, as he learned it from his neighbors who participated in the action immediately after their return home; and Major McJunkin placed the British strength at three hundred, and the Americans at half the number.

Shelby's accounts, and those who follow them, give the date of the action as August nineteenth; but the eighteenth has the weight of authority to sustain it—Williams' report, Governor Nash's letter, September tenth, 1780, Ramsay's *Revolution in South Carolina*, 1785, Moultrie, Gordon, McCall, Mills, Lossing, O'Neall, and Dawson.

Note—Authorities for the Musgrove's Mill expedition: Colonel Williams' report which General Gates, September 5, 1780, forwarded to the President of Congress, published in *Pennsylvania Packet*, September 23, *Massachusetts Spy*, October 12, *London Chronicle*, December 21, 1780, Scots' *Magazine*, December, 1780; Almon's *Remembrancer*, xi, 87, and the substance, evidently communicated by Governor Rutledge, in *Virginia Gazette*, September 13, 1780. Ramsay's *Revolution*, ii, 137; Moultrie's *Memoirs*, ii, 220; Mackenzie's *Strictures*, 25–26; Fanning's *Narrative*, 12–13; Gordon's *History*, iii, 449; McCall's *Georgia*, ii, 315–17. Shelby's accounts in Haywood's *Tennessee*, 65–67; Ramsey's *Tennessee*, 217–19; *American Whig Review*, December, 1848; Todd's memoir of Shelby in *National Portrait Gallery*, and in *Western Monthly Magazine* August 1836; Breazeale's *Life as it is*, 51–52; Wheeler's *North Carolina*, ii, 57–58, 1co; Hunter's *Sketches of Western North Carolina*, 337–39. Mills' *Statistics*, 255–56, 764; O'Neall's *History Newberry*, 71, 265, 312–13; Lossing's *Field Book*, ii, 444–45; Dawson's *Battles*, i, 620–22; Howe's *History Presbyterian Church of South Carolina*, 526. MS. papers of Robert Henry. Also Saye's *Memoir of McJunkin*, and Saye MSS; MSS. of Dr. John H. Logan, furnishing many traditions from the Musgrove family; Colonel William Hill's MS. Narrative of the Musgrove affair, derived from "an officer of high standing" who participated in the engagement—the date and details going to show that Colonel Shelby was his authority; they had met on the King's Mountain campaign. Pension statement of Captain Joseph Hughes. MS. notes of conversations with Major James Sevier, son of Colonel John Sevier; also with Major Thomas H. Shelby, son of Colonel Isaac Shelby, and Colonel George Wilson, of Tennessee.

The pretended narrative of Colonel Samuel Hammond, in Johnson's *Traditions*, has not been relied on. It, for instance, refers to the express, who brought intelligence of Gates' defeat, also bringing news of Sumter's disaster at Fishing Creek, when, in fact, it did not occur, until several hours later of the same day, and in a distant county. Colonel Hammond, of course, never wrote anything of the kind.

CHAPTER VII.

1780—Summer and Autumn.

Incidents of the Up-country.—Major Edward Musgrove.—Paddy Carr and Beaks Musgrove.— The Story of Mary Musgrove.—Samuel Clowney's Adventure.—William Kennedy's Forays Against the Tories.—Joseph Hughes' Escape.—William Sharp Bagging a British and Tory Party.— Tories' Attack on Woods, and how dearly he sold his life.—Plundering Sam. Brown.

Several interesting incidents transpired during the summer and early autumn of 1780, in the region of the present counties of Laurens, Spartanburg, and Union, while Colonel Ferguson yet held sway in that quarter. The more striking of them deserve to be preserved in the history of the times, as exhibiting something of the rancor and bitterness engendered by civil warfare.

Edward Musgrove, whose name has been perpetuated by the battle just narrated, fought near his residence, was a native of England, and one of the earliest settlers of the upper country of South Carolina. He had received a good education, and was bred to the law. Possessing fine abilities, large hospitality and benevolence, he was a practical surveyor, giving legal advice, and drawing business papers for all who needed them, for many miles around. He was very popular, and exceedingly useful, in all the region, of which his noted mill on the Enoree was the center.

Major Musgrove, for he bore that title, was a man a little above medium height, of slender form, prematurely gray, and possessed much firmness and decision of character. He had passed the period of active life when the Revolutionary war commenced, and was then living with his third wife—too old to take any part in the bloody strife;

but with trembling lips, he plead each night for a speedy return of peace and good will among men. He lived to see his prayers answered, dying in 1792, in the seventy-sixth year of his age, and was buried in the little grave-yard, just behind the site of his house, near the old mill.

Beaks Musgrove was a son of the Major's by his first wife. Partaking of the spirit of the times, and inspired by such British leaders as the Cunninghams and Colonel Ferguson, he was induced to join the King's standard. Patrick Carr, better known as Paddy Carr, was one of the fearless Captains who served under Colonel Clarke, of Georgia. He had been an Indian trader on the frontiers of that Province, and was, on occasion, quite as reckless and brutal as the worst specimens among the Red Men of the forest. Hunting for Beaks Musgrove, he suddenly darted into Major Musgrove's, at a moment when Beaks had come in to change his clothing, and get some refreshments, and had leaned his sword against the door-post, while his pretty sister, Mary, was engaged in preparing him a meal. Carr had dodged in so quietly and unexpectedly, that Beaks was taken entirely by surprise, and without a moment's notice to enable him to attempt his escape.

" Are you Beaks Musgrove? " inquired Carr.

" I am, sir," was the frank and manly reply.

" You are the man, sir, I have long been seeking," was the stern response of the Whig Captain..

Mary Musgrove, seeing the drawn sword of her brother in Carr's possession, earnestly inquired: "Are you Paddy Carr?"

" I am," he replied.

" I am Mary Musgrove, Mr. Carr, and you must not kill my brother, " at the same time imploringly throwing herself between them.

Carr was evidently touched by the plea of artless beauty, and struck with young Musgrove's manliness and fine soldierly appearance, and said: " Musgrove, you look like a man who would fight."

"Yes," responded Musgrove, "there are circumstances under which I would do my best."

"Had I come upon you alone," said Carr, "in possession of your arms, would you have fought me?"

"Yes—sword in hand," rejoined Musgrove.

Carr seemed pleased with his new acquaintance, who was now so completely in his power, and boldly proposed to him to become a member of his scout at once, and swear never again to bear arms against the Americans. By this time, Carr's men, who had been stationed in the cedar grove some distance from the house, came up, to observe what was transpiring, and, if need be, to render aid to their leader.

Mary Musgrove, seeing her brother disposed to accede to Carr's proposition, with a view, probably, of saving his life, still had her fears awakened for his safety, and boldly challenged the Captain's motives. "Captain Carr," she asked, "I hope you do not intend to persuade my brother to leave me, and then, when the presence of his sister is no longer a restraint, butcher him in cold blood—pledge me, sir, that such is not your purpose."

"I'll swear it," replied Carr, solemnly. Beaks Musgrove joined his party, but at heart he was a Tory still. He, however, continued some time with Carr, constantly gaining upon that bold leader's confidence; but there is no record or tradition tending to show how long the native baseness of his heart permitted him to sustain his new character. There is no evidence that he ever after bore arms against his country—perhaps he feared the terrible retribution Carr would certainly have visited upon him, had he falsified the solemn oath he had taken. About the close of the war, he quit the country, and never returned. He left a son, who became a Baptist preacher, displaying, it is said, much of the eccentricity and acuteness of the celebrated Lorenzo Dow.

By his second marriage, to a Miss Fancher, Major Mus-

grove had two daughters, Mary and Susan, aged respectively some twenty-five and twenty-three years, at the period
of the war troubles of 1780–81 ; and both were akin to the
angels in their unwearied acts of mercy to the wounded and
the suffering in those trying times.   They were young
women of marked attractions, both of mind and body;
Mary, especially, was a young lady of rare beauty of person, possessing a bright intellect, and much energy of character.   She was the renowned heroine of Kennedy's popular story of " Horse-Shoe Robinson ; " and, in all the up-
country of South Carolina, he could not have chosen a more
beautiful character in real life with which to adorn the
charming pages of his historical romance.   In Mary Musgrove's case—

<blockquote>" Beauty unadorned is adorned the most."</blockquote>

Both of these noble sisters fell early victims to the con-
sumption—Mary dying about one year, and Susan about
two years, after the war—both unmarried, and both quietly
repose in the little grave-yard beside their revered parents.

When Mary Musgrove was about passing away, she
selected her sister, and three other young ladies of the
neighborhood, to be her pall-bearers.   Her body being very
light, they bore it to its final resting-place on silk handkerchiefs.   Just as they were lowering the coffin into the grave,
a kind-hearted lady present, the wife of a noted Tory, came
forward to render some little assistance, when a member of
the family, knowing Mary's devoted Whig principles,
gently interposed and prevented it.   Such was the tender
respect shown to the memory of the worthy heroine of the
Enoree.*

A remarkable adventure of Samuel Clowney will next

---

* Among Dr. Logan's MSS., is an interesting statement, to which we are indebted for
these particulars, from the late Captain P. M. Waters, son of Margaret Musgrove, the
oldest daughter, by his last marriage, of Major Musgrove—a girl of twelve summers at the
time of the memorable battle near her father's, in 1780.   She married Ladon Waters, and
survived till 1824; and by her retentive memory these traditions, and several of those
related in the preceding chapter, were preserved.

demand our attention. He was a native of Ireland, and first settled on the Catawba river, in North Carolina, finally locating in South Carolina. He was a most determined Whig, and had joined Colonel Thomas at the Cedar Spring, early in July. Obtaining with several others a brief leave of absence, to visit their friends, and procure a change of clothing, they set off for the settlement on the waters of Fair Forest, known as Ireland or the Irish Settlement, on account of the large number of settlers from the Emerald Isle. On their route, the party left, with a Mrs. Foster, some garments to be washed, and appointed a particular hour, and an out-of-the-way place, where they should meet her, and get them, on their return to camp.

In accordance with this arrangement, when the party reached Kelso's creek, about five miles from Cedar Spring, they diverged from the road through the woods to the appointed place, leaving Clowney, and a negro named Paul, to take charge of their horses until they should return with the washing. Presently five Tories, making their way to a Loyalist encampment in that quarter, came to the creek; when Clowney, conceiving himself equal to the occasion, and giving the negro subdued directions of the part he was to act, yelled out in a commanding tone: "Cock your guns, boys, and fire at the word;" and then advancing to the bank of the stream, as the Tories were passing through it, demanded who they were? They answered: "Friends to the King." To their utter astonishment, not dreaming of a Whig party in the country, they were peremptorily ordered by Clowney to come upon the bank, lay down their arms, and surrender, or "every bugger of them would be instantly cut to pieces." Being somewhat slow in showing signs of yielding, Clowney sternly repeated his demand, threatening them, with his well-poised rifle, of the fatal consequences of disobedience; when the terror-stricken Tories, believing that a large force was upon them, quietly surrendered without uttering a word.

Paul took charge of their guns, when Clowney, giving some directions to his imaginary soldiers to follow in the rear, ordered the prisoners "right about wheel," when he marched them across the creek, directly before him, till he at length reached the rest of his party at Mrs. Foster's washing camp. They were then conducted to Colonel Thomas' quarters. The prisoners were not a little chagrined, when they learned that their captors consisted of only two persons—one of whom was an unarmed negro. After arriving safely at Cedar Spring, his Colonel, when told that Clowney and the negro alone had captured the whole party, seemed at first a little incredulous that they could accomplish such a feat.

" Why, Paddy," said the Colonel, "how did you take all these men?"

"May it plase yer honor," he replied, exultingly, " by me faith, I *surrounded* them!"

Clowney was a real hero. This achievement of his at Kelso's creek is well attested by many who knew him. One of his acquaintances, in his terse way, described him as "a little dry Irishman;" and though he belonged to the Presbyterian Church, like all of his Celtic race of that day, without being intemperate, he could not refrain from getting *dry* once in a while, and dearly loved "a wee bit of the crathure" occasionally. He possessed a remarkable talent for sarcasm and invective; but he was, nevertheless, a most kind-hearted, benevolent man, greatly beloved by all who knew him. His brogue was quite rich, and this, combined with a fund of genial Irish wit, made him a fascinating companion. He died September twenty-seventh, 1824, in his eighty-second year. His son, William K. Clowney, who was a graduate of South Carolina College, and became a prominent lawyer, represented his native district four years in Congress.*

---

* MS. Logan papers; MS. notes of conversations with Dr. Alexander Q. Bradley, of Alabama, and General James K. Means, a son-in-law of Clowney's, in 1871; Howe's *History of Presbyterian Church in South Carolina*, 534-35; Dr. Moore's Life of Lacey 32.

Five miles south of Unionville, in the present county of Union, was Fair Forest Shoal. There Colonel Thomas Brandon resided; but his military position required his presence elsewhere much of the time during the active period of the Revolution. His place, during his absence, was well supplied by a few resolute Whigs, among whom were old 'Squire Kennedy, his son William, Joseph Hughes, William Sharp, Thomas Young, Joseph McJunkin, and Christopher Brandon.

Among these brave and active patriots, William Kennedy stood conspicuous. He was of French Huguenot descent—the race to which Marion belonged. He was tall, handsome, and athletic. His perception was quick, his sagacity equal to any emergency, and his ability sufficient for a great commander. But he persistently refused to accept any office, choosing rather to serve as a common soldier. He was regarded as the best shot with his rifle of any person in all that region. Whether on foot or horseback, at half-speed or a stand-still, he was never known to miss his aim. His rifle had a peculiar crack when fired, which his acquaintances could recognize; and when its well-known report was heard, it was a common remark— "*there is another Tory less.*"

Although he held no commission, yet the men of the neighborhood acknowledged him as their leader when danger was nigh, and their feet were ever in the stirrup at his bidding. His efforts were often called into requisition by the plundering excursions of the Tories sent out under the auspices of Ferguson, Dunlap, and their subordinate officers. He and his comrades often saved their settlement from being over-run by these scouting parties. The crack of Kennedy's rifle was sure to be heard whenever a Tory was found; and it was the well-known signal for his friends to hasten to his assistance. He seemed almost to "snuff the battle from afar;" and the flush of determination would suffuse his manly countenance whenever he had reason to believe the enemy were near.

9

On one occasion, a British and Tory scouting party penetrated the settlement, and began their customary work of plundering the women and children of every thing they possessed, whether to eat or to wear. One of Kennedy's runners went to the hiding-place of Christopher Brandon and two companions—for they were, in the language of the times, out-lyers, and could not with safety stay at home for fear of being massacred by the Tories—and notified them of an enterprise on foot. They mounted their horses, and hastened at half-speed to the place of rendezvous. Pursuing an unfrequented cow-path through a dense forest, they stopped a moment at a small branch crossing their trail, to permit their jaded horses to quench their thirst, and then renew their journey. The crack of a rifle scattered the brains of one of Brandon's companions on his clothes and in his face, the same ball grazing his cheek, the dead body of the victim tumbling into the brook beneath. The two survivors put spurs to their horses, when more than a dozen rifles were fired at them from an unseen enemy behind the trees; but they fortunately escaped uninjured. The Tory party had heard the galloping of the horses of Brandon and his friends, and laid in wait for them.

Reaching the place of meeting, some fifteen or twenty had assembled under their bold leader, Kennedy, and were ready for a hot pursuit. They overtook the Tory band a few minutes before sunset. They were plundering a house in a field a few rods from the public road; and the Whig pursuers had their attention first attracted by the cries of the woman and her children. The Tories had a sentinel outside, who fired as the Whigs came near; and, on the alarm, those within instantly dashed out, mounted their horses, and fled. The Whigs divided, each pursuing his man at full speed. Kennedy directed young Brandon, who was inexperienced, to keep near him, and only fire when told to do so. The leader of the Tory party, whose name was Neal, was the one singled out and pursued by Kennedy. He fled

through an open field, towards the woods, at some distance
away ; but Kennedy kept the road, running nearly parallel
with the fugitive, till he reached an open space in the hedge-
row of bushes that had partially obstructed the view, when
he suddenly called out *whoa!* to his horse, who had been
trained instantly to obey; and, as quick as thought, the
crack of Kennedy's rifle brought Neal tumbling to the
ground. He was stone-dead when Kennedy and Brandon
came up, having been shot through the body in a vital part.
The distance of Kennedy's fire was one hundred and forty
yards. More than half of the Tory party was killed.
" Not one was taken prisoner," as Brandon related the
adventure in his old age, " for it occurred but seldom—our
rifles usually saved us that trouble." Re-taking the Tory
booty, it was all faithfully restored to the distressed woman
and children.*

On the heights at Fair Forest Shoal was an old stockade
fort or block-house. Many tragic incidents occurred there,
and in its neighborhood. A Tory, whose name has been
forgotten, had, with his band, done much mischief in that
region ; and, among other unpardonable sins, had killed
one of William Kennedy's dearest friends. The latter
learned that the culprit was within striking distance, and
called his friends together, who went in search of him.
The two parties met some two or three miles from the
block-house, when a severe contest ensued. The Tories
were routed ; and the leader, who was the prize Kennedy
sought, fled. Kennedy, Hughes, Sharp, McJunkin and
others pursued. The chase was one of life or death. The
Tory approached the bank of Fair Forest at a point, on a
high bluff, where the stream at low water was perhaps
twenty or thirty yards over, and quite deep. The fleeing

---

* MS. notes of Hon. Daniel Wallace, communicated to William Gilmore Simms, the
distinguished novelist and historian of South Carolina, and kindly furnished the writer by
Mr. Simms' daughter, Mrs. Edward Roach, of Charleston. Mr. Wallace was a native of
the up-country of South Carolina, and represented his district in Congress from 1847 to
1853. He died a few years since.

Loyalist, hemmed around by his pursuers on the bluff, just where they aimed to drive him, hesitated not a moment, but spurred his horse, and plunged over the bank, and into the stream below—a fearful leap. His pursuers followed, and at the opposite bank they made him their prisoner.

Their powder being wet by its contact with the water, they resolved to take their captive below to the block-house and hang him. When they arrived there, the officer in command would not permit him to be disposed of in that summary manner, but ordered him to be taken to Colonel Brandon's camp, a considerable distance away, to be tried by a court martial. Kennedy was placed at the head of the guard, but the Tory begged that Kennedy might not be permitted to go, as he apprehended he would take occasion to kill him on the way. Evidently intending to make an effort to escape, he did not wish the presence of so skillful a shot as Kennedy. His request, however, was not heeded. He took an early occasion to dash off at full speed; but Kennedy's unerring rifle soon stopped his flight, and his remains were brought back to the foot of the hill, near the block-house, and there buried. The Tory's grave was still pointed out within a few years past.*

The name of Joseph Hughes has been mentioned as one of the faithful followers of William Kennedy. Both were proverbially brave—Hughes was probably the more reckless of the two—possessed more of a dare-devil character. Early one morning, he left his hiding-place, as one of the honored band of out-lyers, who preferred freedom at any sacrifice rather than tamely yield to the oppression around them, and visited his humble domicile, to see his little family, residing on the west side of Broad river, near the locality of the present village of Pinckneyville. He approached his house cautiously on horse-back, and when within a rod, three Tories suddenly sprang out of the door, and presenting their guns, said exultingly:—

* Wallace Manuscript.

"You d—d Rebel, you are our prisoner!"

"You are d—d liars!" defiantly yelled Hughes, as he instantly spurred his horse to his full speed. As he cleared the gate at a single leap, all three fired, but missed their mark, and he escaped without a scratch. These Tories had watched for him all night, and had just entered the house to get their breakfast as he rode up. They were naturally quite chop-fallen, when, having taken so much pains to secure so plucky an enemy of the King, they found themselves, in the end, so completely foiled in their purpose.*

On another occasion, when a scouting party of British and Tories was passing through what is now Union County, committing robberies, as was their wont, when they little suspected it, their footsteps were dogged by William Sharp, one of Kennedy's fearless heroes, with two associates. At Grindal Shoals, a notable ford of Pacolet, they came upon the enemy. It was in the night, and very dark, which concealed their numbers, and favored their daring enterprise. The first intimation the British and Tories had of danger, was a bold demand on the part of Sharp and his associates for them to surrender instantly, or they would be blown into a region reputed pretty hot. In the surprise of the moment, they begged for quarter, and laid down their arms, to the number of twenty. The victors threw their guns into the river, before their prisoners discovered their mistake, and drove the captives to the nearest Whig encampment in that region.†

In a quiet nook in Spartanburg lived a man named Woods—on one of the Forks of Tyger, we believe. He was not known as particularly demonstrative or combative among his neighbors, but was a true patriot, and unflinching in times of danger. One day, when at home with his wife, he found his house surrounded by a party of determined Tories. Seeing so overwhelming a superiority of

---

* Wallace Manuscript.
† Wallace Manuscript.

numbers against him, Woods, who had closed his house against them, proposed if they would, in good faith, agree to spare his own and wife's lives, they might come in unopposed, and take whatever they wanted, otherwise, as he had two guns, he would sell his life as dearly as possible. They would make no promises, but demanded an unconditional surrender. Woods commenced the unequal battle, availing himself of a crack between his house-logs, which served him as a port-hole, and kept up a brisk firing, his heroic wife loading his guns for him as fast as either was empty, till he had killed three of his assailants. They now became more desperate than ever, and, through the same crack, managed to send a ball which broke Mrs. Woods' arm. In the confusion of the moment, while Woods was assisting his wife, the Tories seeing his fire had slackened, rushed up to the door which they battered down, and captured the intrepid defender. They took him a few rods away, into a copse of wood, where they soon beat him to death with clubs. Mrs. Woods was spared, and recovered.*

In what was originally a part of Tryon, now Lincoln County, North Carolina, were many Loyalists. Among them was Samuel Brown, who had been reared there, and proved himself not only an inveterate Tory, but a bold and unscrupulous plunderer. He had a sister, Charity Brown, who must have been a rough, reckless, bad woman. For quite a period, the two carried on very successful plundering operations—including horses, bed-clothes, wearing apparel, pewter-ware, money, and other valuable articles. Sometimes they had confederates, but oftener they went forth alone on their pillaging forays. About fifteen miles west of Statesville, North Carolina, three miles above the Island Ford, there is a high bluff on the western side of the Catawba river, rising three hundred feet high, at a place known as the Look-Out Shoals. About sixty feet from the

---

* MS. notes of conversations, in 1871, with Major A. J. Wells, of Montevallo, Alabama, a native of Spartanburg County, South Carolina.

base of this bluff, under an over-hanging cliff, was a cave of considerable dimensions, sufficient to accommodate several persons, but the opening to which is now partially closed by a mass of rock sliding down from above. This cave was the depository for the plunder taken by stealth or violence from the poverty-stricken people in the country for many miles around; for their depredations extended from the Shallow Ford of Yadkin to the region embracing the several counties of the north-western portion of South Carolina.

Sam Brown was once married to the daughter of a man residing near the Island Ford, but his wife, disliking the man, or his treatment of her, left him and returned to her father; and in revenge for harboring and protecting her, Brown went one night and killed all his father-in-law's stock. A poor old blind man, named David Beard, living on Fourth creek, near what is now called Beard's bridge, about seven miles east of Statesville, had a few dollars in silver laid up, which Brown unfeelingly filched from him. Beard reproached him for his wrongs and cruelties, and reminded him that he would have a hard account to render at the day of judgment for robbing a person in his poor and helpless condition.

"It's a long trust," retorted Brown; "but sure pay," promptly rejoined Beard.

So notorious had become the robber's achievements, that he was known in all that region as *Plundering Sam Brown*. Among the Tories, he was designated as Captain Sam Brown. As early as the Spring of 1778, he was associated with the Tory leader, David Fanning; and they were hiding in the woods together on Reaburn's creek, in now Laurens County, South Carolina, for the space of six weeks, living entirely upon what they killed in the wilderness, without bread or salt. There were too many watchful Whigs in this region to suit Brown's notions, so he wended his way to Green river, in what is now Polk County, in the south-western part of North Carolina.

The advent of Colonel Ferguson to the up-country of South Carolina proved a perfect God-send to such hardened wretches as Brown. They could now dignify their plundering with the sanction of his Majesty's faithful servants, Colonel Ferguson, Colonel Innes, and Major Dunlap. To such an extent had the people of the Spartanburg region been raided and over-run, during the summer of 1780, by these persistent pillagers, that the men had been compelled to fly to the distant bodies of Whigs under McDowell or Sumter, or become out-lyers in the wilderness. This left a comparatively open field for the marauders, and they were not slow to avail themselves of it. Captain Brown and his followers made frequent incursions in that quarter. He ventured, on one occasion, to the house of Josiah Culbertson, on Fair Forest, accompanied by a single associate named Butler, and inquired of Mrs. Culbertson for her husband. But this young woman, the daughter of the heroic Mrs. Colonel Thomas, gave him some pretty curt and unsatisfactory answers. Brown became very much provoked by this spirited woman, and retorted in much abusive and indecent language ; assuring her, furthermore, that he would, in a few days, return with his company, lay her house in ashes, kill her husband, and plunder and murder the principal Whigs of the neighborhood. After a good deal of *tongue lashing*, and bravado of this character, Brown and Butler rode off, leaving Mrs. Culbertson to brood over her painful apprehensions.

Brown's cup of iniquity was running over, and the day of retribution was at hand. Fortunately, Culbertson returned home that night, accompanied by a friend, Charles Holloway, who was as brave and fearless as himself. The story of Brown's visit, his threats and insolence, very naturally roused Culbertson's feelings—indignation and resentment pervaded his whole nature. Beside this disgraceful treatment of his wife, Brown had apprehended the elder Colonel Thomas, the father of Mrs. Culbertson, soon after the fall of Charleston, and carried him, two of his sons, and his negroes and horses, to the British, at Ninety Six. Culbertson determined to capture the redoubtable plunderer, or rid the country of so great a scourge. Holloway was equally ready for the enterprise.

Early the next morning, reinforced by William Neel, William McIlhaney, and one Steedman,* they followed the tracks of the two marauders some ten or twelve miles, when they discovered Brown's and Butler's horses in a stable on the road-side, belonging to Dr. Andrew Thompson, in the region of Tyger river, where they had stopped for rest and refreshment. Culbertson's party now retraced their steps some distance, hitched their horses out of sight, and crept up within shot of Thompson's, posting themselves behind the stable, and eagerly watched the appearance of the Tory free-booters. At length Brown stepped out of the house into the yard, followed by Butler; and as the Tory Captain was enjoying lazily a rustic yawn, with his hands locked over his head, he received a shot from Culbertson's deadly rifle, at a distance of about two hundred yards. The ball passed directly through his body, just below his shoulders, and making a desperate bound, he fell dead against the door-yard fence. Holloway's fire missed Butler, the ball lodging in the door-jamb, just behind him; but without waiting to learn the fate of his leader, or to secure his horse, he fled to the woods and escaped. Brown was an active, shrewd, heartless man—the terror of women and children wherever his name was known. Butler, it is believed, took the hint, and never re-appeared in Spartanburg.

One tradition has it, that Brown's life of robbery and out-lawry commenced even before the Revolution, which may very well have been so. The amount of money con-

---

* In a MS. letter of Colonel Elijah Clarke to General Sumter, October 29th, 1780, occurs this statement: " I am to inform you, that the Tories killed Captains Hampton and Stidman, at or near Fair Forest "—the latter, perhaps, the associate of Culbertson, in his successful foray against Brown, and for that very reason he probably lost his life, in retaliation, on the part of Brown's friends.

cealed by him was supposed to be large—the fruits of his predatory life; and frequent searches have been made to find the hidden treasure. In his secluded cave, he kept a mistress, but she professed ignorance of his localities of deposit. A small sum only has been discovered by accident. The probabilities are, he never accumulated much money, as the frontier people whom he plundered were poor, and but little specie was in circulation beyond the immediate neighborhood of the British troops.

After the death of her despicable brother, poor Charity Brown fled westward to the mountain region of what is now Buncombe and Haywood, and before her death, it is related, she made some revelations where to find valuables buried in the vicinity of the cave at the Look-Out Shoals; and among articles subsequently discovered, were twelve sets of pewter-ware, which had been concealed in a large hollow tree. This, in the course of time, had been blown down by the wind, and thus revealed this long hidden booty of the robbers of the Catawba. It is currently stated by the superstitious of that region, that when one comes near the cave, and tries to bring his batteau to land at the base of the cliff, he hears a fearful noise—not proceeding from the cave, so far above the water, but from the rock at the bottom.

However this may be, Culbertson and Holloway, after their successful work at Thompson's, deliberately wiped their guns, reloaded them, and were again prepared for any perilous adventure. Not very long after Brown's death, which was a source of rejoicing among the Whigs in all that region, Culbertson received word, that a noted Tory, whom he knew, then in North Carolina, threatened to kill him, in retaliation for Brown's death. They met one day unexpectedly, and instantly recognized each other, when both fired their rifles almost simultaneously; Culbertson's cracked a moment first—the Tory fell dead, while the Whig rifleman escaped unhurt.

Such sanguinary relations of civil warfare make one's

blood almost curdle in the veins. The unmerciful conduct of Tarleton at Buford's defeat, had engendered a feeling of savage fury on the part of the Whigs, and as bitterly reciprocated on the part of the Tories, which, in time, amounted to the almost utter refusal of all quarter. So that in the Carolinas and Georgia, the contest became, to a fearful extent, a war of ruthless bloodshed and extermination.* General Greene, a few months later, wrote thus freely of these hand-to-hand strifes: "The animosity," he said, "between the Whigs and Tories, rendered their situation truly deplorable. There is not a day passes but there are more or less who fall a sacrifice to this savage disposition. The Whigs seem determined to extirpate the Tories, and the Tories the Whigs. Some thousands have fallen in this way in this quarter, and the evil rages with more violence than ever. If a stop can not be put to these massacres, the country will be depopulated in a few months more, as neither Whig nor Tory can live."†

---

* The authorities for the story of *Plundering Sam Brown* are : Fanning's Narrative ; obituary notice of Josiah Culbertson, in the Washington, Indiana, *Weekly Register*, October 17th, 1839, with comments thereon, by Major McJunkin, preserved among the Saye MSS.; Ex-Governor B. F. Perry's sketch of Culbertson. in the *Orion* Magazine, June, 1844; Johnson's *Traditions*, 423 ; and sketch of Sam Brown, by Rev. E. R. Rockwell, of North Carolina, in the *Historical Magazine*, October, 1873.

† Greene's *Life of Greene*, iii, 227.

CHAPTER VIII.

August, 1780—March, 1781.

Cornwallis' Hanging Propensities.—Sumter a thorn in his Lordship's side.—Dispersion of Whig Bands.—Ferguson's Success in Training the Loyal Militia.—Action of the Alarmed Tory Leaders.—Ferguson Moves into Tryon County.—Colonel Graham Repels a Party of Plunderers.—Ruse for Saving Whig Stock.—Mrs. Lytle and her Beaver Hat.—Engagement on Cane Creek, and Major Dunlap wounded.—Apprehension of Jonathan Hampton.—Dunlap's Insolence.—Sketch of Dunlap's Career and Death.

Lord Cornwallis' success at Camden had, like the mastiff fed on meat and blood, made him all the more fierce for further strife and carnage. Two days after Gates' defeat, his Lordship wrote to Lieutenant-Colonel Cruger, at Ninety Six: "I have given orders that all the inhabitants of this Province, who had submitted, and who have taken part in this revolt, should be punished with the greatest rigor; that they should be imprisoned, and their whole property taken from them or destroyed; I have likewise directed that compensation should be made out of their effects to the persons who have been plundered and oppressed by them. I have ordered, in the most positive manner, that every militia man who had borne arms with us, and had afterwards joined the enemy, *should be immediately hanged.* I have now, sir, only to desire that you will take the most vigorous measures to extinguish the rebellion, in the district in which you command, and that you will obey, in the strictest manner, the directions I have given in this letter, relative to the treatment of the country."[*]

These sanguinary orders were, in many cases, most faithfully obeyed—Tarleton, Rawdon, Balfour and Browne, particularly demonstrating their fitness for carrying into effect these tyrannical measures.

Sumter, by his plucky and frequent attacks on several British detachments, had proved himself a thorn in his Lordship's side. He had made a bold push against Lieutenant-Colonel Turnbull at Rocky Mount; then practically defeated Major Carden and the Tory Colonel Bryan, at Hanging Rock; and finally captured Fort Carey, and a large convoy, below Camden. These were audacious things to do, evincing great contempt of his Majesty's Government, and of his Lordship's power and consideration in the Province. Turnbull, after Sumter's attack, had retired to Ferguson's quarters, on Little river; and Ferguson meanwhile, had pushed further north to the Fair Forest region. On his great victory over Gates, Cornwallis directed Turnbull and Ferguson to immediately put their corps in motion, and push on, if possible, to intercept Sumter's retreat towards North Carolina with his prisoners and spoils of victory. Tarleton was also sent in his pursuit, overtaking and surprising him at the mouth of Fishing creek, only two days after Gates' melancholy disaster near Camden.

As we hear nothing more of Turnbull in the Ninety Six region, it is to be presumed that he was, not long after, recalled to the eastern part of South Carolina. The orders of Lord Cornwallis, which must have reached Colonel Ferguson shortly after the affair at Musgrove's Mill, seem to have set that officer's forces in motion. After driving Clarke, Shelby, and Williams out of the Province, it only remained to pay his attention to McDowell's party, at Smith's Ford, on Broad river. On receipt of General Caswell's letter, announcing the disaster of Gates, and advising

---

the subject-matter of this letter; but he wrote a similar one, the same month, fully as blood-thirsty in its tone, to Lieutenant-Colonel Balfour, which is given in Sparks' *Washington*, vii, 555–6.

the independent detachments to retire beyond the reach of the victorious British, McDowell's force mostly disbanded and scattered—some of them, perhaps, like Shelby's men, because their term of service had expired; while others, it may be, like Clarke's Georgians, because they were volunteers at pleasure. What was left of McDowell's command —less than two hundred, apparently—retired to their own mountain region of North Carolina, in the counties of Rutherford and Burke.

That Ferguson, during the period he held command in the up-country, had been both untiring and successful, is well attested by a report of Lord Cornwallis to the Home Government, August twentieth, 1780: "In the district of Ninety Six," says his Lordship, "by far the most populous and powerful of the Province, Lieutenant-Colonel Balfour, by his great attention and diligence, and by the active assistance of Major Ferguson, who was appointed Inspector-General of the militia of this Province by Sir Henry Clinton, had formed seven battalions of militia, consisting of above four thousand men, and entirely composed of persons well-affected to the British Government, which were so regulated, that they could, with ease, furnish fifteen hundred men, at a short notice, for the defense of the frontier, or any other home service. But I must take this opportunity of observing, that this militia can be of little use for distant military operations, as they will not stir without a horse; and, on that account, your Lordship will see the impossibility of keeping a number of them together without destroying the country." Turning their horses into fields of grain, and eating out one settlement, they would soon necessarily have to remove to another.

Only five days before the action at Musgrove's, while Ferguson and his troops were encamped at Fair Forest Shoal, in Brandon's Settlement, an important meeting was held there by the Loyalist officers and their men. The North Carolina battalion under Colonel Ambrose Mills, and the six South Carolina battalions—Cunningham's,Kirkland's,Clary's, King's, Gibbs' and Plummer's were there in camp, while Lieutenant-Colonel John Philips,battalion, and another, were stationed at Edward Mobley's settlement, in the adjoining county of Fairfield, some twenty-five miles distant. All the Colonels seem to have been absent—Clary at Musgrove's; but all the battalions were represented at the meeting. Lieutenant-Colonel Philips, Lieutenant-Colonel W. T. Turner, Majors Daniel Plummer, Zachariah Gibbs, and John Hamilton, and Adjutant Thomas D. Hill, Jr., being present.

These Loyalist chiefs, who had flattered themselves that the Rebellion was, to all intents and purposes, quelled, and that they would soon be made lords and masters over the conquered communities, now began to realize that the Whigs of the country would not "down" at their bidding—that Sumter, Marion, McDowell, Williams, Shelby, Clarke, Thomas, Brandon, McJunkin, and other leaders, were in arms, boldly attacking Tory parties whenever they could meet them on anything like an equal footing. The Loyal militia, when danger began to stare them in the face, showed signs of weakening and lagging. It was, therefore, important, as "the Rebels were again in the field," as they expressed it, that they should provide severe punishments for all of their Loyalist delinquents; that their horses, cattle, grain, and arms should be forfeited; and they should be brought to trial, and punished in person as they deserved. They furthermore gave it as their unanimous expression, that whoever should act a treacherous part by abandoning the Royal cause, deserting his battalion, or disobeying the orders of his commanding officers, is a worse enemy to the King and country than even the Rebels themselves, and that all good Loyalists should assist in the defense of the country, and that whoever neglects to assemble, and do service in the Loyal militia, should be made to serve in the regular army.*

Lord Cornwallis, on the twenty-ninth of August, announced to Sir Henry Clinton: "Ferguson is to move into Tryon county with some militia, whom, he says, he can depend upon for doing their duty and fighting well; but I am sorry to say that his own experience, as well as that of every other officer is totally against him." It is not a little singular, that his Lordship, with his poor opinion of the fighting qualities of the Tories, should have ordered Ferguson so far beyond the reach of succor, in case of danger. As he could not spare any detachment of regulars to give them countenance, he probably hoped that the Whigs were so far cowed and dispersed, that they would not give Ferguson any serious opposition.

As McDowell, Clarke, Shelby, and Williams had retired to the back parts of North Carolina, Ferguson, after awhile, followed into that quarter. His detachments, however, during the heats of summer, performed many of their movements at night, and kept beating about in various directions, sometimes in the North Province and sometimes in the South, in search of prominent Whig leaders, over-awing all opposition, plundering whenever they found anything which they needed or coveted, and administering the 'oath of allegiance to all who would take it, with liberal tenders of pardon to those who had been active and prominent participators in the rebellion. Many submissions were made; but oftener, when Ferguson's and Dunlap's parties would call for the head of a Whig family, he was pretty certain, nine cases out of ten, not to be found at home—where he was, his wife and children could not say, for, in truth, they seldom knew, for the patriots and out-lyers beat about quite as much as those in quest of them.

In consequence of this state of affairs, the old people,

---

* MS. record obtained by Colonel Sevier from a Tory Colonel at King's Mountain, as given in Ramsey's *Tennessee*, 216–17.

together with the women and children, would frequently
gather at the strongest and largest house in their region,
taking with them all their arms, ammunition, and such household goods as they needed, or could not conceal, with sometimes a few men in vigorous life for their protection. Such
a gathering in Colonel William Graham's neighborhood
took place at his residence, near the west bank of Buffalo
creek, in then Lincoln, now Cleveland county, about eight
miles north of King's Mountain, and about seven miles
south-east of the present village of Shelby. It was a large,
hewn-log-house, weather-boarded, and, to some extent, fortified; well fitted for a successful defence against any party
with small arms alone, and who were not prepared to prosecute a regular siege.

Sometime in September, one of these Tory marauding
parties, consisting of about twenty-three in number, suddenly made their appearance before Graham's Fort. The
only persons there capable of bearing arms, for the defence
of the many helpless people, old and young, congregated
there, were Colonel Graham, David Dickey, and the Colonel's step-son, William Twitty, a brave youth of nineteen;
but they were fearless and vigilant. The Tory party
demanded admittance, but were promptly refused by Colonel Graham and his associates. A warm attack was commenced, the Tories firing several volleys, without doing
much damage, yelling out at the top of their voices, after
each discharge, "d—n you, won't you surrender now?"

One fellow, John Burke, more venturesome than the
rest, ran up to the house, and through a crack aimed at
young Twitty, when Susan Twitty, the sister of the young
soldier, seeing his peril, jerked her brother down just as
the gun fired, the ball penetrating the opposite wall. She
then looked out of the aperture, and saw Burke, not
far off, on his knees, re-loading for another fire; and
quickly comprehending the situation, exclaimed: "brother
William, now's your chance—shoot the rascal!" The next

10

instant young Twitty's gun cracked, and the bold Tory was shot through the head. So eager was Miss Twitty to render the good cause any service in her power, that she at once unbarred the door, darted out, and brought in, amid a shower of Tory bullets, Burke's gun and ammunition, as trophies of victory. She fortunately escaped unhurt. It was a heroic act for a young girl of seventeen.* Losing one of their number killed, and three wounded, the Tories at length beat a retreat. Anticipating that the enemy, smarting under their repulse, would return with increased numbers, Colonel Graham and friends retired to a more distant place of safety, when a large Tory party re-appeared, with no one to oppose them, and plundered the house of clothing and other valuables, and carried off six of Colonel Graham's negroes.†

Another instance where a party of the enemy fared no better, occurred during the Tory ascendency in 1780. Adam Reep, a staunch Whig, returning home, after a tour of service under Colonel Graham, to visit his family, on the western bank of the Catawba river, in Lincoln County, had scarcely reached his humble domicile, when a party of ten or twelve Tories, under the leadership of a British officer, made their appearance just at the gray of the evening. Reep, who, like a good minute man, was always on the watch, had barely time to close and bar his doors, when he mounted his ladder with his faithful rifle; and through some port-holes in the loft of his house, he blazed away at his enemies, wounding two of them, when the party fell back

---

* This noble heroine subsequently married John Miller, and died the 14th of April, 1825, at the age of sixty-two years. Her son, Hon. W. J. T. Miller, represented Rutherford County, in the Legislature of North Carolina, in 1836–40, and subsequently Cleveland County, when it was organized, and where he still resides an honored and useful citizen.

Mrs. Miller's brother, William Twitty, who aided so gallantly in the defense of Graham's Fort, was born in South Carolina, July 13th, 1761; he served at King's Mountain, and lived at Twitty's Ford, on Broad river, where he died February 2d, 1816, in his fifty-fifth year. He has many worthy decendants, among them William L. and Dr. T. B. Twitty, grandsons, the latter residing at the old homestead.

† MS. pension statement of Colonel Graham, and MS. correspondence of Hon. W. J. T. Miller, William L. Twitty, and Dr. T. B. Twitty.

to a safer distance, and finally retired with their disabled comrades.*

Colonel Ferguson encamped awhile at Gilbert Town, some three miles north of the present village of Rutherfordton. For many miles around people wended their way to the head-quarters of this noted representative of the British crown; thinking, as Charleston had fallen, Gates been defeated, Sumter surprised and dispersed, and the various detachments lately in force in the Spartanburg region were disbanded or scattered, that the Whig cause was now utterly prostrate and hopeless. Many of those who now took the oath of allegiance to the British Government, subsequently excused their conduct on the plea that the country was over-run, and that this was the only course by which they could save their property, secure themselves and families from molestation, and at the same time preserve the stock of the country for the supply of the needy patriots thereafter.

While in this mountain region, Ferguson found he had a case of small-pox developing itself. It was one of his officers, who was left in a deserted house, taking his favorite charger with him. And there the poor fellow died in this lonely situation; and it is said his neglected horse lingered around till he at length died also. It was a long time before any of the country people would venture to visit the solitary pest-house—

> "And there lay the rider, distorted and pale,
> With the dew on his brow and the rust on his mail."

Finally some one ventured there and carried off the sword, holsters, and pistols, selling them to John Ramsour, who gave them, nearly thirty years after, to Michael Reinhardt.†

Ferguson led a detachment to surprise Colonel McDowell at the head of Cane creek. An engagement took place with McDowell's troops, who had been beating about the

---

* MS. statement of W. M. Reinhardt, Esq., of Lincolnton, North Carolina, who many years ago had the facts from Reep himself.

† MS. statement of W. M. Reinhardt, son of Michael, who yet preserves these relics of a century ago.

mountain country, since retiring from Smith's Ford on
Broad river, and were now retreating towards the Watauga
in East Tennessee. The British force encamped at the noted
White Oak Spring, a mile and a half east of the present
village of Brindletown, in the south-eastern part of Burke
County as now constituted, and on the direct road from
Morganton to Gilbert Town. McDowell learning their
position, and too weak to meet the enemy on anything like
equal terms, concluded to waylay them on renewing their
southward march. He, therefore, selected a fitting spot for
an ambuscade at Bedford's Hill, some three miles south-
west of Brindletown, in the south-eastern corner of
McDowell County, and something like fifteen miles from
Gilbert Town. This hill was a small round elevation about
a quarter of a mile from the base of the South Mountains
then covered with timber and surrounded by a soft swamp ;
located on the eastern side, and just below, the Upper
Crossing of Cane creek, now known as Cowan's Ford—
which ford the hill commanded. If forced to retire, the
Whigs had an easy access to the mountains close by, where
they would be safe against almost any force that the enemy
could send against them.

Here McDowell's party awaited the coming of the British
force, and, as they were passing the ford, an indecisive fight
transpired. The enemy, after receiving the unexpected
fire of McDowell's backwoodsmen, rallied, and beat back
the Americans, killing, among others, one Scott, of Burke
County, while standing beside the late James Murphy, of
that region. By the heroic efforts especially of Major
Joseph McDowell—the Colonel's brother, Captain Thomas
Kennedy, and one McKay, the Whigs were again brought
into action. Major McDowell was particularly active,
swearing roundly that he would never yield, nor should his
Burke boys—appealing to them to stand by and die with
him, if need be. By their united bravery and good bushwhacking management, in which their real wickedness was

concealed, and by their activity and well directed rifle-shots they succeeded in inflicting considerable execution on their antagonists—killing several, and, among others, wounding Major Dunlap. The British now retired to Gilbert Town, conveying their disabled commander with them, who was severely wounded in the leg; while McDowell's party, numbering about one hundred and sixty only, directed their retreat up the Catawba valley, and over the mountains, for the friendly Watauga settlements.

Quite a number of human bones were brought to light, some forty years ago, at the point where this Cane creek fight occurred—the remains of the British and Tories who fell in this spirited contest. This action occurred, according to Lieutenant Allaire's MS. *Diary*, on the twelfth of September; and had its influence, as the sequel will show, in rousing the people over the mountains, as well as in Wilkes and Surry, to embody under their gallant leaders, and strike a decisive blow against the bold invader, Ferguson.*

It has been stated, near the close of the chapter on the Musgrove's Mill expedition, that Shelby and his associates on that service had agreed, that as soon as they could collect the necessary force, they would embody their several detachments, and attack Ferguson. It was correctly anticipated that so soon as that British leader and his forces should exhaust the beef supply in the Spartanburg region, he would be quite certain to advance into Rutherford and Burke Counties, in North Carolina, where, in the latter especially, there were large stocks of fine cattle; and it was

---

* MS. letter of Colonel Isaac T. Avery, October 19th, 1860, to Hon. D. L. Swain; MS. pension statements of General Thomas Kennedy, Colonel William Graham, James Blair, William Walker, and Matthew Kuykendall; General Lenoir's *Account of King's Mountain*, appended to this volume; MS. correspondence of Colonel S. McDowell Tate, of Morganton; T. A. Lewis, of Brindletown; M. O. Dickerson and A D. K. Wallace, of Rutherfordton, North Carolina; the venerable Andrew B. Long, of Rutherford County, whose father, at the time of this action a boy of ten years, resided on Cane creek; and Wm. L. and Dr. T. B. Twitty also of Rutherford County.

Lieutenant Allaire's *Diary* not only supplies the date of this little engagement, but serves to corroborate the tradition of the country, that McDowell's men were drawn up "on an eminence"—Bedford's Hill apparently; that, according to this account, the Whigs were worsted, losing one private killed, Captain White wounded, seventeen prisoners, and twenty pounds of powder while the British had one killed, and two wounded—Captain Dunlap, one of them, receiving two wounds.

enjoined on Colonel Charles McDowell, to devise the best
means possible to preserve these stocks from the grasp of
the British and Tories.

Colonel McDowell called the leading men of the Upper
Catawba valley together, and suggested, simply to meet the
present emergency, that they should repair to Gilbert Town,
take British protection, and thereby save the Whig stock,
so necessary for the support of the country, from being
appropriated by the enemy ; that no man would thereby
become a Tory at heart, but would merely exercise a wise
stroke of public policy—that the end would justify the
means and render the country a good service. Daniel
Smith, afterwards Colonel, Captains Thomas Lytle and
Thomas Hemphill, Robert Patton, and John McDowell, of
Pleasant Garden—better known as Hunting John McDowell
—absolutely refused to engage in any such course, and
stated that they would drive all the stock they could collect
into the deep coves at the base of the Black Mountain ; that
others might, if they would, take protection and save the
remainder that could not be readily collected and concealed.
Captain John Carson, a distinguished Indian fighter, afterwards known as Colonel Carson, Benjamin and William
Davidson, and others, were designated to take protection,
and thus save many valuable herds of cattle from the grasp
of the enemy.* It was a very ungracious act on their part ;
but Carson and his associates deemed it justifiable under
the circumstances—suggested and urged, as it was, by
Colonel McDowell, in behalf of the Whig cause. While
they accomplished the object they had in view, their
motives, in the course of time, were unjustly misjudged
and impugned.†

---

* MS. statements of General Joseph McDowell and Colonel David Vance, made in 1797,
and preserved by the late Hon. Robert Henry—all participants in the King's Mountain
campaign.

† Hon. Samuel P. Carson, a distinguished member of Congress, and son of Colonel Carson, resented an aspersion on his venerable father's character, when charged with having
been a Tory, which resulted in an unfortunate duel, and the death of his antagonist.

As had been anticipated by the patriots, Ferguson, either in full force, or with a strong detachment, penetrated into the very heart of Burke County—as far as Davidson's "Old Fort," in the extreme western part of then Burke, now McDowell county;[*] and a few miles farther north, up the Catawba Valley, as far as the old Edmondson place, since McEntyre's, on Buck creek at the foot of the Blue Ridge. On their way thither, the British force was supplied with beef, corn, and other necessaries, by one Wilson, an Irishman, who afterwards migrated to Tennessee, and for which he received a draft on the British Government from which, probably, he never received any avails.[†]

While in the region of Old Fort, a detachment of the enemy, under the command, it is believed, of Col. Ferguson, concluded to pay a visit to Captain Thomas Lytle, a noted Whig leader, who resided some four miles south-west of that locality on Crooked creek. Mrs. Lytle, a spirited woman, heard of this intended visitation a little in advance of the approach of the party, and concluded she would don her nice new gown and beaver hat, in procuring which for his young wife, Captain Lytle had spent nearly all his Continental money. It was pardonable of Mrs. Lytle to make this display, for there were no meetings or public gatherings, in that frontier mountain region, in those troublous times, where she could appear in her gaudy array of new finery. She naturally felt a secret satisfaction, as her husband was not in the way of danger, that this occasion had presented itself, in which she could gratify the feelings of a woman's pride in making what she regarded as an uncommonly attractive appearance. She took unusual pains in making up her toilet; for though she was no Tory, she yet supposed that Colonel Ferguson was a gentleman, as well as a prominent British officer.

---

[*] MS. Correspondence of Colonel Silas McDowell.

[†] MS. letter of Colonel Isaac T. Avery, November 2d, 1860, on authority of Major Ben Burgin, whose memory went back to the Revolution.

At length, the Colonel, at the head of his squadron, leisurely rode up toward the house. He halted in front of the door, and inquired if he could have the pleasure of a few moments' conversation with Captain Lytle? Mrs. Lytle stepped to the door in full costume—probably the best dressed lady the Colonel had seen since he left Charleston— and dropping him a polite courtesy, in accordance with the fashion of that day, invited him to alight and come in. He thanked her, but his business, he said, required haste; that the King's army had restored his authority in all the Southern Provinces, and that the rebellion was virtually quelled; that he had come up the Valley to see Captains Lytle and Hemphill, and a few others, who had served in the Rebel army against the King, and that he was the bearer of pardons for each of them.

" My husband," Mrs. Lytle replied, " is from home."

" Madame," inquired the Colonel, earnestly, "do you know where he is ? "

" To be candid with you, Colonel," said Mrs. Lytle, " I really do not; I only know that he is out with others of his friends whom you call Rebels."

" Well, madame," replied Ferguson, deprecatingly, " I have discharged my duty; I felt anxious to save Captain Lytle, because I learn that he is both brave and honorable. If he persists in rebellion, and comes to harm, his blood be upon his own head."

" Colonel Ferguson," she responded, thoughtfully but firmly, " I don't know how this war may end; it is not ununlikely that my husband may fall in battle; all I positively know is, that he will never prove a traitor to his country."

" Mrs. Lytle," said the Colonel, patronizingly, "I admire you as the handsomest woman I have seen in North Carolina—I even *half way* admire your zeal in a bad cause; but, take my word for it, the rebellion has had its day, and is now virtually put down. Give my kind regards to Captain Lytle, and 'tell him to come in. He will not be asked to compromise his honor; his verbal pledge not again to take up arms against the King, is all that will be asked of him." He then bowed to Mrs. Lytle, and led off his troop. A straggler in the rear rode back, and taking off his old slouched hat, made her a low bow, and with his left hand lifted her splendid beaver from her head, replacing it with his wretched apology, observing with mock gravity, "Mrs. Lytle, I can not leave so handsome a lady without something by which to remember you." As he rode off, she hallooed after him: "You'll bite the dust for that, you villain!" Thus Mrs. Lytle momentarily enjoyed the occasion of arraying herself in her best; but, as she afterwards confessed, she paid dearly for the gratification of her pride, and long mourned the loss of her beautiful beaver hat.*

Colonel McDowell had completely outwitted Ferguson and his plundering Tory followers; and the hungry horde, who invaded the Upper Catawba Valley with high hopes and expectations, returned to their camps near Gilbert Town *without any beef cattle* as a recompense for all their toils and troubles.

After the affair at Cane creek, and the final retirement beyond the mountains of the last remnant of embodied Whig forces in the western region of the Carolinas, Ferguson thought the matter decided. When William Green rode up with a troop of cavalry, and tendered his and their services for the defense of the King's cause, Ferguson thanked them for their loyalty; but declined their acceptance, as the country was subdued, and everything was quiet.

It was reported to Colonel Ferguson, that Jonathan Hampton, a son of Colonel Andrew Hampton, residing in the vicinity of Gilbert Town, held the King's authority in

---

* MS. correspondence with the late Colonel Silas McDowell, of Macon County, North Carolina, in 1873-74, who had these particulars from Mrs. Lytle herself. Colonel McDowell thought it was Tarleton who visited Captain Lytle's, but it could not have been, as his "Campaigns" and map of the route of his excursions show that he was never above Cowan's Ford on the Catawba, while it is certain that Colonel Ferguson was in Burke County. Captain Lytle died not very far from 1832, at the age of about eighty-three years and his venerable companion gently passed away about the same time.

great contempt; that he had the hardihood to accept a commission of Justice of the Peace from the Rebel Government of North Carolina, and had, only recently, ventured, by virtue of that instrument, to unite Thomas Fleming and a neighboring young lady in the holy bonds of wedlock. It was a high crime and misdemeanor in British and Tory eyes. So a party of four or five hundred men were dispatched, under Majors Plummer and Lee, to visit the Hampton settlement, four or five miles south-west of Gilbert Town, to apprehend young Hampton, and possibly entrap his father at the same time. But the Colonel had left the day before, and re-united with McDowell's forces. Riding up to young Hampton's cabin, they found him sitting at the door, fastening on his leggings, and getting himself in readiness to follow his father to the Whig camp in some secluded locality in the mountain coves of that region.

At this moment, James Miller, and Andrew and David Dickey, three Whig friends, came within hailing distance, and hallooed: "Jonathan, are those men in the yard, friends or foes!"

Hampton, without exercising ordinary prudence, replied: " Boys, whoever you are, they are d—d Red Coats and Tories—clear yourselves!"

As they started to run, the Tories fired two or three volleys at them; but they fortunately escaped unhurt. Perhaps Hampton presumed somewhat upon his partially crippled condition that forbearance would be shown him, for he was reel-footed; yet he managed to perform many a good service for his country, and, as in this case, would lose sight of self, when he could hope to benefit his friends. Mrs. Hampton chided him for his imprudence, saying: "Why, Jonathan, you are the most unguarded man I ever saw."

The Tory party cursed him soundly for a d—d Rebel, and Major Lee knocked him down, and tried to ride over him, but his horse jumped clear over his body without touching him. Lee had just before appropriated Hampton's horse as better than his own, and it may be that the animal recognized his master, and declined to be a party to his injury. While Major Plummer was courteous and considerate, Major Lee was rude and unfeeling in the extreme. Hampton, and his wife's brother, Jacob Hyder, were made prisoners; and those who had Hampton in charge, swore that they would hang him on the spot, and began to uncord his bed for a rope for the purpose, when Mrs. Hampton ran to Major Plummer with the alarm, and he promptly interposed to prevent the threatened execution.

Some of the disappointed Tories, who thirsted for his blood, declared in his presence, that Ferguson would put so notorious a Rebel to death the moment he laid eyes on him. Major Plummer informed Hampton if he could give security for his appearance the next day at Gilbert Town, he might remain over night at home. He tried several Loyalists whom he knew, but they declined; and finally Major Plummer himself offered to be his security. According to appointment, the next day Hampton presented himself to Ferguson, at Gilbert Town, who proceeded to examine his case. When asked his name, he frankly told him, adding, that, though in the power of his enemies, he would never deny the honored name of Hampton. Major Dunlap, then on crutches, entering the room, inquired of Colonel Ferguson the name of the Rebel on trial? "Hampton," replied Ferguson. This seemed to rouse Dunlap's ire, who repeated thoughtfully: "Hampton—Hampton— that's the name of a d—d fine-looking young Rebel I killed a while since, on the head of Pacolet," referring to the affair at Earle's Ford, when Noah Hampton, a brother of the prisoner, was murdered in cold blood. Dunlap added: "Yes; I now begin to recall something of this fellow; and though a cripple, he has done more harm to the Royal cause than ten fighting men; he is one of the d—dest Rebels in all the country, and ought to be strung up at once, without fear or favor."

Jonathan Hampton had, indeed, been an unwearied friend of the Whig cause. He was a good talker; he kept up the spirits of the people, and helped to rally the men when needed for military service. Even in his crippled condition, he would cheerfully lend a helping hand in standing guard; and, when apprehended, was about abandoning his home to join his father and McDowell in their flight to Watauga. But Ferguson was more prudent and humane than Dunlap, and dismissed both Hampton and Hyder on their parole. Hampton observed when Ferguson wrote the paroles, he did so with his left hand; for, it will be remembered, his right arm had been badly shattered at Brandywine, the use of which he had never recovered. Hyder tore up his parole, shortly after leaving Ferguson's presence; but Hampton retained his as long as he lived, but never had occasion to use it, as Ferguson shortly after retired to King's Mountain, and the region of Gilbert Town was never after invaded by a British force.*

Major James Dunlap, who figured so prominently in the military operations in Spartanburg during the summer of 1780, now claims at our hands a further and final notice. Of his origin, we have no account. He must have been a man of enterprise, for he was commissioned a Captain in the Queen's Rangers, a partisan corps, November twenty-seventh, 1776. This corps had been raised during the summer and autumn of that year, from native Loyalists, mostly refugeeś from Connecticut, and from the vicinity of New

---

*MS. correspondence of Adam and James J. Hampton, sons of Jonathan Hampton, in 1873–74; MS. letter of Colonel Isaac T. Avery, October 19th, 1860; and MS. letter of Colonel Silas McDowell, July 13th, 1873.

This sterling patriot, Jonathan Hampton, was born on Dutchman's creek, Lincoln County, near the Catawba river, North Carolina, in 1751; and when nearly grown, he removed with his father, and settled on Mountain creek, four or five miles south-west of Gilbert Town. He was many years clerk of the Rutherford court, and five years represented the County in the State Senate in the early part of the present century. He died at Gilbert Town, October 3d, 1843, at the venerable age of ninety-two years. Of his large family, but one son survives—Jonathan Hampton, Jr., now eighty-five years of age.

York, by Colonel Robert Rogers, who had distinguished himself with a corps of Rangers on the frontiers of New York and Canada, during the French and Indian war of 1755–60. The month before Dunlap had become a Captain in the corps, Rogers had been surprised at Mamoroneck, on Long Island Sound, losing nearly eighty killed and captured, together with sixty stand of arms.*

Such was the daring and good service of the Queen's Rangers at Brandywine, September eleventh, 1777, that the British Commander-in-chief particularly complimented them "for their spirited and gallant behavior in the engagement,"† in which they suffered severely. The ensuing year they shared in the operations around Philadelphia, and in New Jersey. In the affair at Hancock's House, near Salem, New Jersey, on the night of the twentieth of March, 1778, Captain Dunlap bore a prominent part. The order was a most sanguinary one:—" *Go—spare no one— put all to death—give no quarters!* " The house was garrisoned by twenty men, under Captain Carleton Sheppard; and with them were four Loyalist prisoners—Judge Hancock, the owner of the house, and three other Quakers— one of whom was Charles Fogg, "a very aged man." All were asleep, and the work of death by the sword and bayonet was quick and terrible. Some accounts represent that all, others two-thirds, of the occupants, garrison and prisoners, were horribly mangled by Dunlap and his fiendish associates—among them were Judge Hancock and some of his Quaker brethren. Simcoe, of the Rangers, speaks of this undesigned destruction of their friends as "among the real miseries of war," though he had no tears to shed for the score or two of patriots who fell without resistance.‡

Dunlap and the Queen's Rangers shared in the British retreat from Philadelphia to New York, and in the battle of

---

* Lossing's *Field Book of the Revolution*, ii, 615.

† Simcoe's *Journal*, 319.

‡ Johnson's *History of Salem*, New Jersey; Barber and Howe's *Historical Collections of New Jersey*, 426–28; Lossing's *Field Book*, ii, 139; Simcoe's *Journal*, 51–52.

Monmouth, in June, 1778. On the thirty-first of August ensuing, the Rangers participated in a bloody affair near King's Bridge, on the Hudson. A party of Americans and friendly Stockbridge Indians were drawn into an ambuscade, which resulted in the loss of nearly forty—fully twenty of whom were Indians, either killed or desperately wounded, and among the slain were Ninham, their chief, and his son of the same name.* The following year, besides some garrison duty at Oyster Bay, the Rangers served on foraging and scouting parties, during which they encountered some occasional skirmishing. In one of these forays, at Brunswick, New Jersey, they were unexpectedly fired upon by the Americans in ambush ; and among other casualties, their commander, Lieutenant-Colonel Simcoe, was taken prisoner. Sir Henry Clinton, early in 1780, declared that the history of the corps had been a " series of gallant, skilful, and successful enterprises against the enemy, without a reverse, and have killed and taken twice their own numbers." †

Such were the services of the Queen's Rangers, and the experience of Captain Dunlap, prior to his engaging in the expedition against Charleston, in December, 1779. He would seem to have been one of the picked officers of Colonel Ferguson, for his select partisan corps for this new enterprise. Dunlap shared in the siege and capture of Charleston, doubtless in the same operations, as described in a previous chapter, in which Ferguson's corps was engaged, and was sent to the western borders of South Carolina, under Ferguson, immediately after the fall of Charleston. His attack on McDowell's force at Earle's Ford, on North Pacolet, and the affair near Cedar Spring and Wofford's Iron Works, together with the engagement at Cane creek, where he was severely wounded, have already been related.

---

* *Continental Journal*, September 17th, 1778; Simcoe's *Military Journal*, 83–86, and accompanying diagram; *Massacre of the Stockbridge Indians*, by Thomas F. De Voe, in *Magazine of American History*, September, 1880.

† Simcoe's *Journal*, introductory memoir, x.

Major Dunlap has left behind him an unenviable reputation. The bloody work he performed at the Hancock House, and his share in the destruction of Ninham and his Stockbridge warriors, would appear to have been in the line of his taste and character. "He had," says Judge Johnson, in his *Life of Greene*, "rendered himself infamous by his barbarity." "His severities," said Major James Sevier, one of the King's Mountain men, "incensed the people against him." It is certain he was an advocate for hanging Whigs for no other crime than sympathizing with their suffering country; his brutal language to this effect, in the presence of, and concerning Jonathan Hampton, must be fresh in the reader's remembrance. That such a man, characterized by such practices, should, sooner or later, come to an untimely end, is neither strange nor unexpected.

Snuffing the approaching storm, Ferguson suddenly abandoned his camp at Gilbert Town to avoid the approach of the over-mountain men. Dunlap, upon his crutches, and in such a hurried retreat, was in no condition to accompany the retiring forces. William Gilbert, with whom he was stopping while recovering from his wound, was a loyal friend of King George; and while he himself seems to have gone off with Ferguson, Mrs. Gilbert and the family remained to take proper care of the invalid. A soldier of the name of Coates was left to wait upon him, but who, not long after, provoking the mortal ire of a negro of Gilbert's, was killed by him, and his remains consumed in a coal-pit.

This event of ill-omen was speedily followed by an almost tragic occurrence. The avenger of blood was nigh. Two or three men from Spartanburg rode to the door of the Gilbert house, shortly after Ferguson had commenced his retreat for King's Mountain, when the leader, Captain Gillespie, asked Mrs. Gilbert if Major Dunlap was not up stairs? She frankly replied that he was, probably supposing that the party were Loyalists, and had some important communication for him. They soon disabused her of their character and mission, for they declared that he had been instrumental in putting some of their friends to death, and, moreover, had abducted the beautiful Mary McRea, the affianced of Captain Gillespie, as she would not encourage his amorous advances, and kept her in confinement, trusting that she would in time yield to his wishes ; but death came to her relief, she probably dying broken-hearted. They had now come for revenge ; Gillespie, particularly, uttering his imprecations on the head of the cruel destroyer of all his earthly hopes. So saying, they mounted the stairs, when Gillespie abruptly approached Dunlap, as he lay in bed, with the inquiry : " Where is Mary McRea? "   " In heaven," was the reply ; whereupon the injured Captain shot him through the body ; and quickly remounting their horses, Gillespie and his associates bounded away towards their Spartanburg homes. This is the tradition, sifted and collated, as preserved in the Hampton family.*

Colonel Silas McDowell, who visited his old friend, Jonathan Hampton, in 1831, heard him relate the story of Dunlap being shot, but could only recall the main fact, that the perpetrator of the act, some friend of Noah Hampton, whom Dunlap had boasted of slaying, had rushed to the Major's up-stairs room, and shot him through the body as he lay on his couch.   M. O. Dickerson, Esq., of Rutherfordton, has had substantially the same relation from Mr. Hampton. The old Gilbert house was then standing, and Hampton pointed out to both these visitors the stain of Dunlap's blood still discernible upon the floor ; and there are others, still living, who have seen it also. This venerable building, in which the early courts of the County were held, when about to fall from age, was taken down some four or five years since, by its present owner, J. A. Forney, Esq., who

---

* MS. correspondence with the late venerable Adam and James J. Hampton, in 1873–74 ; and the present venerable Jonathan Hampton, in 1880, sons of the patriot, Jonathan Hampton, Sr.

M. O. Dickerson states that it has been handed down as the opinion of some of the old people of that region, that Mrs. Gilbert and her son made way with the unfortunate Major Dunlap ; but this seems to have been a cruel and baseless suspicion.

FERGUSON'S HEAD-QUARTERS.

has preserved the blood-stained floor-plank. While these traditions differ somewhat in their details, all having a common origin from the old patriarch, Jonathan Hampton, Sr., they all agree in the general conclusion, that Dunlap was shot in retaliation for alleged cruelties—either in killing Whigs, or abducting Miss McRea, or both; and all coincide in the belief, that the redoubtable Major was killed outright, and buried about three hundred yards south of the Gilbert house, the grave being still pointed out, marked by a granite rock at the head and foot.*

Major James Holland lived at Gilbert Town for many years, and was a prominent character. In 1783, he represented Rutherford County in the State Senate; in 1786 and 1789, he was in the House of Commons, and served a term in Congress from 1795 to 1797. In this latter year, he was again chosen to a seat in the State Senate, and then served five consecutive terms in Congress, from 1801 until 1811. The late venerable Adam Hampton wrote in 1873: "I will relate to you what I heard Major James Holland say in reference to Major Dunlap's grave. He said that in 1809, while serving as a member of Congress at Washington, he dreamed that a quantity of gold was buried with Dunlap, and, on his return home, he opened the grave, and found sixty-one guineas."

From all these traditions and relations, it would ordinarily be concluded, that Dunlap assuredly died of the wound inflicted by Captain Gillespie. It is quite clear, however, that he did not. We can only suppose that, when shot, he was left unconscious, or feigned death; and when Gillespie's party departed, it was reported, for his safety, that he was killed and buried near by; and it is possible, that the Major may have had his servant, Coates, secrete his money there before the latter was murdered by the negro. Though in a Tory region, it would not have been

---

* MS. letters of Adam, James J., and Jonathan Hampton, Jr., and M. O. Dickerson, W. L. and Dr. T. B. Twitty, and Miss N. M. McDowell.

11

safe to have had it known that Dunlap was still alive; for
Gillespie, or others, would surely have come to make the
work of death more certain next time.   He was too feeble,
with this additional wound, to be removed at once to Ninety
Six—the nearest British fort, after Cornwallis had fled from
Charlotte; and it was fully ninety miles from Gilbert Town
to Ninety Six, in a direct course, and considerably more by
such by-ways as it would have been necessary to pursue, in
order to avoid the intervening Whig settlements.   Hence
the necessity of circulating this report of his death, which
must have been well kept, and which the Hampton family
fully credited, and which Major James Sevier corroborated,
in a general way, to the writer, in 1844, by asserting, that
for his cruelties, Dunlap had been killed by a party of
Whigs at Gilbert Town.   But as Major Sevier made no
mention of having heard anything concerning Dunlap on
the night of the third of October, when he and his fellow-
mountaineers were at Gilbert Town, the wounded Major
must, at that time, have been secreted somewhere in the
neighboring hills or fastnesses for safety.   And even after
the war, as Gilbert was well known, and had figured somewhat in public life, he may have deemed it good policy to
refrain from revealing the fact that he or his family had so
long concealed Dunlap, and perhaps secretly aided him in
effecting his escape to Ninety Six.

As soon as he was able to ride, it would seem, he was
conveyed to Ninety Six; and if any gold had been buried
by Coates in his behalf, near by, for safe keeping, Major
Dunlap must have been unable to find it, for had the Gil-
berts secreted it for him, they would have known the place
of its concealment.   We find him at Ninety Six, in March,
1781, and sufficiently recovered for active service.   He was
sent with a party of seventy-six dragoons on a foraging
expedition.   Receiving intelligence of this plundering maraud, General Pickens detached Colonel Clarke and Major
McCall with a sufficient force to attack him.   On the

twenty-fourth of March, they came up with him encamped at Beattie's Mill, on Little river, some twenty-two miles from Ninety Six. Dispatching a party to take possession of a bridge over which Dunlap would necessarily pass on his return, the main body advanced and took him by surprise. He retired into the mill and some neighboring outhouses, but which were too open for protection against riflemen. "Recollecting," as the historian, McCall, asserts, "his outrageous conduct to the families and friends of those by whom he was attacked, Dunlap resisted for several hours, until thirty-four of his men were killed and wounded—himself among the latter—when a flag was hung out, and they surrendered," else all would have been sooner or later picked off by Clarke's and McCall's unerring riflemen. In General Pickens' report, as published by Congress, the number is stated as thirty-four of the enemy killed, and forty-two taken; so the wounded must have been included among the captives. The prisoners were sent to Watauga settlement, in East Tennessee, for safe keeping.

"The British account of this affair," adds McCall, "stated that Dunlap was murdered by the guard having him in charge, after his surrender; but such was not the fact—for he died of his wounds the ensuing night." It is evident from General Greene's general order of the subsequent sixteenth of April, that Dunlap was taken prisoner, and nothing could have been said in Pickens' first report of the action relative to the Major's death; hence it could hardly have occurred so soon after his surrender as McCall states. But McCall errs in supposing that Dunlap was not killed by his guard, or by some one with their connivance. It was covered up, as much as possible, by those who perpetrated the act; but General Pickens, whose high sense of honor revolted against such turpitude, even against an officer of Dunlap's infamous character, "offered a handsome reward for the murderers," as General Greene subsequently testifies in a letter to the British Colonel Balfour, accompanied with a copy of Pickens' order proclaiming the reward.

Thus wretchedly perished, at the hands of his enemies, Major James Dunlap. While the manner of his taking off is to be regretted, it must be confessed that he had little reason to expect better treatment. He had led a life of military savagery, and his "outrageous conduct" to the families of Clarke's and McCall's men, was perfectly in keeping with his previous actions, and very naturally provoked the retaliation of those whom he had so grievously wronged.*

His rank was Captain in the Queen's Rangers, and apparently Major in the special service to which he was assigned in Ferguson's corps. As the commission of his successor in the Rangers—Bennet Walpole—bore date March twenty-ninth, 1781, that very likely fixes the time of Dunlap's death. His name last appears in the Royal Army List, published in New York in 1781, which was probably issued before his death in March had been learned. Had he been killed in the preceding October at Gilbert Town, his name would doubtless have disappeared, and that of his successor taken its place. It is certain that Dunlap belonged to the Queen's Rangers, and there was no other person of his name and rank either in the Rangers or any other Provincial corps; so it is not possible that there could have been two Major Dunlaps killed—one at Gilbert Town, and the other at or near Beattie's Mill.

---

* *Maryland Journal*, May 1st and 8th, 1781; *Massachusetts Spy*, June 14th, 1781; McCall's *Georgia*, ii, 361; Gordon's *Am. Rev.*, iv, 167; Johnson's *Life of Greene*, ii, 107, 135, 195; Gibbes' *Doc. History*, 1781–82, 169; Greene's *Greene*, iii, 232; MS. pension statements of Absalom Thompson and Joel Darcy.

McCall gives the date of the affair at Beattie's Mill as March 21st; but Pickens' report, as published by Congress, says it occurred on the 24th of that month, and his authority would seem to be most reliable.

Credit is due to Charles R. Hildeburn, Esq., of Philadelphia, for the christian name of Major Dunlap, with the date of his commission in the Rangers, and that of his successor. Mr. Hildeburn has given special attention to the leaders in the Loyalist corps, and learned the facts in question from the rare Royal Army Lists, published in New York from 1777 to 1783.

CHAPTER IX.

July—October, 1780.

Gathering of the King's Mountain Clans.—Williams' failure to get command of Sumter's men—his tricky treatment of Sumter.—Ferguson sends a threat to the over-mountain men.—Shelby's patriotic efforts to turn the scales on Ferguson.—Sevier, McDowell, Hampton, and Campbell unite in the Enterprise—Cleveland invited to join them.—Sevier's success in providing Supplies for the Expedition. —Rendezvous at the Sycamore Shoals.—Preparations for the March. —Parson Doak commends the men to the protection of the Good Father.— Their March over the mountains.— Joined by Cleveland and Winston. — Campbell chosen to the Chief Command. — McDowell's mission for a General Officer.

Colonel Williams, as we have seen, was honored by Governor Rutledge, in September, with a commission of Brigadier-General in the South Carolina militia, in recognition of his having been, as the Governor was led to believe, the chief commander of the Whigs at the battle of Musgrove's Mill. Governor Nash, of North Carolina, had given him permission to recruit, within that State, not to exceed a hundred horsemen. With his commission in his pocket, he at once repaired to Sumter's camp, on the Catawba Reservation, east of the river of that name. He had it publicly read, and then ordered the officers and men to recognize his right to command them, declaring that Sumter had no proper authority to do so.

Here a serious difficulty arose. At this period, Sumter bore the title and performed the office of a General; but he had, in fact, no commission. He had been chosen by his own men, who, forced to leave their homes, had banded together for their mutual safety, and the better, as occasion should offer, to strike an effective blow at an insolent enemy.

Thus gathered together, acting pretty much on their own volition, rather than by any special authority, they chose Sumter their leader, which they believed they had a perfect right to do, as South Carolina, in its then inchoate condition, was unable to grant them any pay, or furnish them supplies of any kind. Governor Rutledge, for safety, had retired to North Carolina.

But they had another reason why they declined to recognize Williams as their commander. They cherished an old grudge against him. While Sumter was organizing his force, in the early summer, on Clem's Branch of Sugar creek, east of the Catawba, Williams and some of his neighbors of the Little river region, had retired to the northward with such of their moveable property as they could convey to a place of safety till more quiet times— probably to Granville County, North Carolina, where the Colonel had formerly lived, and where he had family relations still residing. On his return, he repaired to Sumter's camp, and frankly confessed, as he had brought no men, he could claim no command; but he, nevertheless, wished to serve his country in some position of usefulness. Colonel Hill, who knew him, suggested that General Sumter needed an efficient Commissary; and upon mentioning the matter to the General, he accordingly commissioned Williams to serve in that capacity.

Major Charles Miles, with twenty-five men and four teams and wagons, was assigned to this service under Colonel Williams. So matters went along smoothly enough, and satisfactorily to all concerned, to all outward appearances, till after the battle of Hanging Rock, on the sixth of August. While Sumter was encamped on Cane creek, in Lancaster District, one morning, about the twelfth of that month, it was discovered that Williams had decamped, without dropping a hint to Sumter on the subject, taking with him Colonel Brandon and a small party of followers, mostly of the Fair Forest region, together with a number of public horses, and considerable provisions and camp equipage.

Sumter and his subordinates were not a little vexed at this treatment. As they regarded it, Williams had been not only ungrateful for the position conferred upon him, but had betrayed a public trust. Colonel Lacey, one of Sumter's best officers, a man of much personal prowess, was dispatched, with a small guard, in pursuit of the fugitives, with a view at least of recovering the public property. He overtook them encamped on the west side of the Catawba, but finding Williams' party too strong to attempt coercive measures, Lacey resorted to other means to accomplish his purpose. Inviting Williams to take a walk with him, he suddenly, when out of reach of the camp, presented a pistol at his breast, threatening him with instant death if he should make the least noise, or call for assistance. With his pistol still aimed, Lacey expostulated with him on the baseness of his conduct, when Williams pledged his word and honor that he would take back all the public property, and as many of the men as he could prevail upon to return with him. Not confiding in his word, Lacey exacted an oath to the same purpose, with which Williams readily complied. But once free from restraint, he neither regarded the one nor the other, but retired to Smith's Ford, on Broad river, where he joined Colonel McDowell's forces, and participated, immediately thereafter, in the successful expedition against the enemy at Musgrove's Mill. *

During the summer, Sumter had been operating mostly east of the Catawba. Williams' home was considerably to the southwest of that stream, and he tried to justify himself, no doubt, by arguing that his own particular region had the strongest claim upon his attention, and a man who would not provide for his own family and people was worse than an infidel. However this may be, there can be no good

---

* The details of this affair are taken from Colonel Wm. Hill's MS. narrative.

excuse for his conduct. He should have sought a more manly and honorable way of effecting his object, as Colonel Clarke had done before him.

Sumter, his officers and men, were unanimous in resolving to have nothing to do with Williams. They regarded his conduct in leaving the camp as he did the preceding month, as treacherous, and unbecoming an honorable officer. Williams, meeting with such a reception—and he could hardly have expected any other—was not slow to take his departure. A council of the field officers of Sumter's command was soon after convened, in which it was judged best to make a full representation to Governor Rutledge of the condition of the brigade, and their reasons for refusing to accept Williams as their commander. Five prominent officers were accordingly selected to wait upon the Governor, at Hillsboro, four of whom were Colonels Richard Winn, Henry Hampton, John Thomas, Jr., and Charles S. Myddelton; Colonel Thomas Taylor was probably the other. Meanwhile, it was agreed that Sumter should retire until a decision was reached and the difficulty settled, Colonels Lacey and Hill to command the troops during the interim.*

Williams seems to have received some intimation, while in Sumter's camp, that his conduct would soon be properly represented to Governor Rutledge; and having claimed more with regard to his command at Musgrove's than the facts would warrant, he probably deemed it best not to lay his new grievances before the Governor, but repair at once to the field, and endeavor, by brilliant service, to cause his past derelictions to be overlooked and forgotten.

It is now necessary to give a succinct account of the circumstances which led the over-mountain men so soon again to re-pass the Alleghanies, and appear on their eastern border. Though separated by high mountains and broad forests from their brethren of the Carolinas,

---

* Colonel Hill's MS. narrative.

they heartily sympathized with them, and were even ready to aid them in their struggles against the common enemy. Shelby, the McDowells and their compeers, it will be remembered, while retiring, in August, before Ferguson's pursuers, from the Musgrove's Mill expedition, resolved that as soon as they could have a needed rest, and strengthen their numbers, they would re-cross the mountains, and "beard the lion in his den." The summer heats and exposures had retarded their renewal of the enterprise; their crops had doubtless demanded their attention; and, above all, the neighboring Cherokees were inimical and threatening. And so they tarried, watching on the borders.

But a circumstance transpired that tended to arouse them from their ease and sense of security. When Ferguson took post at Gilbert Town, in the early part of September, remembering how the mountain men had annoyed him and his detachments on the Pacolet, at Thicketty Fort, near Wofford's iron works, and at Musgrove's, he paroled Samuel Philips, a distant relative of Colonel Isaac Shelby, whom he had taken prisoner—perhaps one of the wounded left at Wofford's or Musgrove's, now recovered—with a verbal message to the officers on the Western waters of Watauga, Nolachucky, and Holston, that "if they did not desist from their opposition to the British arms, he would march his army over the mountains, hang their leaders, and lay their country waste with fire and sword." *

This threat accomplished more than Ferguson bargained for. Philips, residing near Shelby's, went directly to him with the message, giving him, in addition, such intelligence as he could impart concerning the strength, locality, and intentions of the enemy. Of the Loyalists composing the major part of Ferguson's command, some had previously

---

* Shelby's King's Mountain Narrative, 1823; Haywood's *Hist. Tennessee*, 67; Shelby's statement, in the *American Whig Review*, Dec., 1846, 580; General Joseph Graham's account, in the *Southern Literary Messenger*, September, 1845.

been on the Western waters, and were familiar with the Watauga settlements, and the mountain passes by which they were reached. One of them had been subjected, the past summer, to the indignity of a coat of tar and feathers, by the light-horsemen of Captain Robert Sevier, on Nolachucky; and, in resentment, proposed to act as pilot to Ferguson.*

In a few days, Shelby went some forty miles to a horse-race, near the present village of Jonesboro, to see Colonel Sevier, the efficient commander of the militia of Washington County, embracing the Watauga and Nolachucky settlements, to inform him of Ferguson's threatening message, and concert measures for their mutual action. The result was that these brave leaders resolved to carry into effect the plan Shelby and associates had formed the previous month, when east of the mountains—to raise all the men they could, and attempt, with proper assistance, to surprise Ferguson by attacking him in his camp; or, at any rate, before he should be prepared to meet them. If this was not practicable, they would unite with any corps of patriots they might meet, and wage war against the enemies of their country; and should they fail, and the country eventually be over-run and subdued by the British, they could take water, float down the Holston, Tennessee, Ohio, and Mississippi, and find a home among the Spaniards in Louisiana. It was known to them, that Colonel Charles McDowell and Colonel Andrew Hampton with about one hundred and sixty men, had retired before Ferguson's forces from Cane creek and Upper Catawba, arriving at Colonel John Carter's on the eighteenth of September, and were now refugees mostly encamped on the Watauga.† Some of McDowell's officers were seen and consulted by Shelby and Sevier before they parted. Colonel Sevier engaged to see others of them, and bring them all into the

---

* Ramsey's *Tennessee*, 223.

† MS. letter Colonel Joseph Martin, Long Island of Holston, Sept. 22, 1780.

measure ; while Shelby, on his part, undertook to procure the aid and co-operation of Colonel William Campbell, of the neighboring County of Washington, in Virginia, with a force from that region, if practicable. A time and place for the general rendezvous were appointed—the twenty-fifth of September, at the Sycamore Flats or Shoals, on the Watauga.

Colonel Shelby had necessarily much to do in getting his own regiment of Sullivan County men in readiness for the expedition. He wrote to Colonel Campbell, who resided forty miles distant, explaining the nature of the proposed service, and urging him to join in it with all the men he could raise for that purpose. The letter was sent by the Colonel's brother, Captain Moses Shelby. It was the plan of Lord Cornwallis to lead his army from Char-lotte to Salisbury, there to form a junction with Ferguson's corps ; and, preliminary to the further invasion of North Carolina and Virginia, to incite the Southern Indians not only to invade the Holston and Watauga settlements, but proceed, if possible, as high up in South-West Virginia as Chiswell's Lead Mines, and destroy the works and stores at that place, where large quantities of lead were pro-duced for the supply of the American armies. And as the destruction of the Mines and their product was a capital object with the British, the Tories high up New river, and in the region of the Lead Mines, had also been encouraged to make an attempt in that direction. Colonel Campbell had been diligently engaged, for several weeks. with a part of his regiment, in suppressing this Tory insurrection, and had just returned from that service when Colonel Shelby's letter arrived.

Campbell replied, that he had determined to raise what men he could, and march down by the Flour Gap, on the southern borders of Virginia, to be in readiness to oppose Lord Cornwallis when he should advance from Charlotte, and approach that State ; that he still thought this the better policy, and declined uniting with Sevier and Shelby on the proposed expedition. Colonel Shelby promptly notified Colonel Sevier of Campbell's determination, and at the same time issued an order for all the militia of Sullivan County to hold themselves in readiness to march at the time appointed. As the Cherokee towns were not to exceed eighty to one hundred miles from the frontiers of Sullivan, and much less from the Watauga settlements; and as it was known that the Cherokees were preparing to make a formidable attack on the border people, in the course of a few weeks, Colonel Shelby felt an unwillingness to draw off, for a distant service, all the disposable force of the counties of Sullivan and Washington at so critical a period, and leave hundreds of helpless families exposed to the tomahawk and scalping-knife.

He, therefore, immediately wrote a second letter to Colonel Campbell by the same messenger, urging his views more fully, and stating that without his aid, he and Sevier could not leave sufficient force to protect their frontiers, and at the same time lead forth a party strong enough to cope with Ferguson. About the same time he wrote also to Colonel Arthur Campbell, the cousin and brother-in-law of Colonel William Campbell, and who was the County Lieutenant or superior military officer of the County, informing him of Ferguson's progress and threats, and telling the touching story of McDowell's party, driven from their homes and families; and appealing to the County Lieutenant, whether it would not be possible to make an effort to escort and protect the exiles on their return to their homes and kindred, and drive Ferguson from the country. Colonel Arthur Campbell had just returned from Richmond, where he had an interview with Governor Jefferson, and learned that vigorous efforts were being made to retrieve the late misfortunes near Camden, and repel the advances of the enemy now flushed with victory.

Both Colonels Arthur and William Campbell, on full

reflection, regarded the proposed expedition with favor, and sent back word that they would co-operate with Colonels Shelby and Sevier to aid their friends to return to their homes beyond the mountains, and punish their Tory oppressors; Colonel Arthur Campbell informing Shelby, through the messenger, Mr. Adair, of the Governor's sentiment, and the efforts that would soon be made by Congress to check the progress of the enemy. "The tale of McDowell's men," says Colonel Arthur Campbell, "was a doleful one, and tended to excite the resentment of the people, who of late had become inured to danger by fighting the Indians, and who had an utter detestation of the tyranny of the British Government."*

At a consultation of the field officers of Washington County, it was agreed to call out one-half of the militia, under Colonel William Campbell, for this over-mountain service. That day, the twenty-second of September, the order was made for the men, who seemed animated with a spirit of patriotism, and speedily prepared for the expedition. An express was, at the same time, sent to Colonel Cleveland, of Wilkes County, North Carolina, to apprise him of the designs and movements of the men on the Western waters, and request him to meet them, with all the troops he could raise, at an appointed place on the east side of the mountains. The express doubtless took the shortest route, crossing New river not far from the Virginia and North Carolina line, and thence to Wilkes County; and probably the thirtieth of September, and the Quaker Meadows, were the time and place of meeting. Colonel Campbell went to the place of rendezvous by way of Colonel Shelby's, while his men, who had assembled at the first creek below Abingdon, marched down a nearer way —by the Watauga road.

The whole country was animated by the same glowing spirit, to do something to put down Ferguson and his Tory gang, who threatened their leaders with the halter, and

* MS. statement of Colonel Arthur Campbell.

their homes with the torch. "Here," exclaimed the young second wife of Colonel Sevier, pointing to a youth of nearly sixteen, "Here, Mr. Sevier, is another of your boys who wants to go with his father and brother Joseph to the war; but we have no horse for him, and, poor fellow, it is too great a distance for him to walk." Horses, indeed, were scarce, the Indians having stolen many of them from the settlers, but young James Sevier, with or without a horse, went on the expedition.

Colonel Sevier endeavored to borrow money on his private responsibility, to fit out his men for this distant service—for there were a few traders in the country who had small supplies of goods. What little money the people had saved, had been expended to the last dollar to the Entry Taker of Sullivan County, John Adair, the State officer, for the sale of the North Carolina lands—the same person, doubtless, whom Colonel Shelby had sent as his express to Colonel Arthur Campbell. Sevier waited upon him, and suggested that the public money in his possession be advanced to meet the military exigencies at this critical juncture. His reply was worthy of the man and the times: "Colonel Sevier," said he, "I have no authority by law to make that disposition of this money; it belongs to the impoverished treasury of North Carolina, and I dare not appropriate a cent of it to any purpose; but, if the country is over-run by the British, our liberty is gone. Let the money go, too. Take it. If the enemy, by its use, is driven from the country, I can trust that country to justify and vindicate my conduct—so take it."* Thus between twelve and thirteen thousand dollars were obtained, ammunition and necessary equipments secured, Colonels Sevier and Shelby pledging themselves to see the loan refunded or legalized by an act of the Legislature, which they effected at the earliest practicable moment.†

---

*This sturdy patriot subsequently settled in Knox County, Tennessee, where he died in April. 1827, at the age of ninety-five years.

†Ramsey's *Tennessee*, 226.

GOV: JOHN SEVIER.

On Monday, the twenty-fifth of September, at the place of rendezvous, at the Sycamore Flats or Shoals, at the foot of the Yellow Mountain, on the Watauga, about three miles below the present village of Elizabethtown, Colonel Campbell's two hundred men assembled, together with Colonel Shelby's and Lieutenant-Colonel Sevier's regiments of two hundred and forty men each. There McDowell's party had been for some time in camp; but Colonel McDowell himself, as soon as the expedition had been resolved on, hurried with the glad news over the mountains, to encourage the people, obtain intelligence of Ferguson's movements, and hasten the march of Colonel Cleveland and the gallant men of Wilkes and Surry. While yet in camp, all hearts were gladdened by the unexpected arrival of Colonel Arthur Campbell, with two hundred more men from his County, fearing the assembled force might not be sufficient for the important service they had undertaken; and uniting these new recruits with the others, this patriotic officer immediately returned home to anxiously watch the frontiers of Holston, now so largely stripped of their natural defenders.*

Mostly armed with the Deckard† rifle, in the use of which they were expert alike against Indians and beasts of the forest, they regarded themselves the equals of Ferguson and his practiced riflemen and musketeers. They were little encumbered with baggage—each with a blanket, a cup by his side, with which to quench his thirst from the mountain streams, and a wallet of provisions, the latter principally of parched corn meal, mixed, as it generally was, with maple sugar, making a very agreeable repast, and withal full of nourishment. An occasional skillet was taken along for a mess, in which to warm up in water their parched meal, and cook such wild or other meat as fortune

---

* MS. statement of the King's Mountain Expedition, by one of Campbell's men—the writer not known—sent me by the late Governor David Campbell, of Abingdon, Virginia.

† A century ago the Deckard or Dickert rifle was largely manufactured at Lancaster, Pennsylvania, by a person of that name. It was, for that period, a gun of remarkable precision for a long shot, spiral grooved, with a barrel some thirty inches long, and with its stock some three and a half or four feet, carrying bullets varying from thirty to seventy to the pound of lead. The owner of a Deckard rifle at that day rejoiced in its possession.

should throw in their way. The horses, of course, had to pick their living, and were hoppled out, of nights, to keep them from straying away. A few beeves were driven along the rear for subsistence, but impeding the rapidity of the march, they were abandoned after the first day's journey.

Early on the twenty-sixth of September, the little army was ready to take up its line of march over mountains and through forests, and the Rev. Samuel Doak, the pioneer clergyman of the Watauga settlements, being present, invoked, before their departure, the Divine protection and guidance, accompanied with a few stirring remarks befitting the occasion, closing with the Bible quotation, "The sword of the Lord and of Gideon;" when the sturdy, Scotch-Irish Presbyterians around him, clothed in their tidy hunting-shirts, and leaning upon their rifles in an attitude of respectful attention, shouted in patriotic acclaim: "The sword of the Lord and of our Gideons!"*

Then mounting their horses, for the most of them were provided with hardy animals, they commenced their long and difficult march. They would appear to have had some trouble in getting their beeves started, and probably tarried for their mid-day lunch, at Matthew Talbot's Mill, now known as Clark's Mill, on Gap creek, only three miles from the Sycamore Shoals. Thence up Gap creek to its head, when they bore somewhat to the left, crossing Little Doe river, reaching the noted "Resting Place," at the Shelving Rock, about a mile beyond the Crab Orchard, where, after a march of some twenty miles that day, they took up their camp for the night. Big Doe river, a bold and limpid mountain stream, flowing hard by, afforded the campers, their horses and beef cattle, abundance of pure and refreshing water.† Here, a man of the name Miller resided, who shod several of the horses of the party.

---

* "This," writes the venerable historian, Dr. J. G. M. Ramsey, "is the tradition of the country, and I fully believe it."—MS. letter, June 21st, 1880.

† It is not altogether certain that the over-mountain men camped here the first night; but such is the tradition, and such the probabilities. If they did not, then they went on beyond the mountain summit, accomplishing some twenty-eight miles, which, with the trouble of driving cattle, would seem quite improbable. It is only by concluding that

The next morning, Wednesday, the twenty-seventh, probably weary of driving the cattle, some of which had stampeded, they killed such as were necessary for a temporary supply of meat, thus considerably delaying the march that day. Relieved of this encumbrance, they pressed forward some four miles, when they reached the base of the Yellow and Roan Mountains. "The next day" —evidently after leaving the Sycamore Shoals,—says Ensign Robert Campbell's diary, "we ascended the mountain;" which they did, following the well-known *Bright's Trace*, through a gap between the Yellow Mountain on the north, and Roan Mountain on the south. The ascent was not very difficult along a common foot-path. As they receded from the lovely and verdant Crab Orchard valley, "they found," says Campbell's diary, "the sides and top of the mountain covered with snow, shoe-mouth deep; and on the summit," adds the same diarist, "there were about a hundred acres of beautiful table-land, in which a spring issued, ran through it, and over into the Watauga." Here the volunteers paraded, under their respective commanders, and were ordered to discharge their rifles; and such was the rarity of the atmosphere, that there was little or no report.* This body of table-land on the summit of the mountain has long been known as "*The Bald Place*," or, "*The Bald of the Yellow.*"

An incident transpired while the troops were at "the Bald" that exerted no small influence on the campaign. Two of Sevier's men, James Crawford and Samuel Chambers, here deserted; and when they were missed, and their object suspected—that of apprising Ferguson of the approach of the mountain men—instead of bearing to the

---

they camped at the celebrated "Resting Place," on the night of the twenty-sixth, that we can reconcile Campbell's diary and the traditions of the oldest and best informed people along the route, as to the other camping places till they reached the Catawba, on the night of the thirtieth, as stated by Campbell, Shelby, and Cleveland, in the official report of the expedition, and by Shelby in his several narratives.

*MS. letter of Dr. J. G. M. Ramsey, July 12, 1880. "This fact," adds the Doctor, "was related to me by several of the old King's Mountain soldiers."

right, as they had designed, the troops took the left hand, or more northerly route, hoping thereby to confuse the enemy should they send spies on the southern trail, and make no discoveries.*

After the parade and refreshments,† the day was well-nigh spent, and the mountaineers passed on a couple of miles descending the eastern slope of the mountains into Elk Hollow —a slight depression between the Yellow and Roan mountains, rather than a gap; and here, at a fine spring flowing into Roaring creek, they took up their camp for the night.‡

Descending Roaring creek, on the twenty-eighth, four miles, they reached its confluence with the North Toe river, and a mile below they passed Bright's place, now Avery's; and thence down the Toe to the noted spring on the Davenport place, since Tate's, and now known as Child's place, a little distance west of the stream, where they probably rested at noonday. Some thirty years ago an old sword was found near this spring, supposed to have been lost by some of the mountaineers.§ As they descended from the mountains, they reached a country covered with verdure, where they enjoyed an atmosphere of almost summer mildness. They followed the ravines along the streams the most of the way, but over a very rough, stony route—exceedingly difficult, and not unfrequently dangerous, for horses to pursue.

The mountain scenery along their route is scarcely exceeded for wildness and romantic grandeur, in any other part of the country—several of the towering peaks, among the loftiest in the United States, exceeding six thousand

---

* Haywood's *Tennessee*, on authority of Colonel Shelby, says this desertion occurred on "the top" of the mountain ; and Robert Campbell, in his King's Mountain Narratives, states that the deserters "left the army on the Yellow mountain;" and Dr. Ramsey practically confirms these statements by asserting that it transpired on the second day.

† Captain Christopher Taylor, of Sevier's regiment, states, in his pension deposition, that in a conference of the officers, held on Yellow Mountain, Colonel Campbell was appointed to the chief command. No other account confirms this statement, and Captain Taylor must have had in mind the subsequent action to that effect.

‡ Campbell's diary; MS. correspondence of the late ex-Governor David Campbell, and of Hon. Wm. B. Carter.

§ MS. letter of W. A. McCall, Aug. 25, 1880.

five hundred feet in height. The bright, rushing waters tumbling over their rocky beds, and the lofty blue mountains in the distance, present a weird, dreamy, bewildering appearance. "Here," says a graphic writer on the mountain region of North Carolina, "if we were to meet an army with music and banners, we would hardly notice it; man, and all his works, and all his devices, are sinking into insignificance. We feel that we are approaching nearer and nearer to the Almighty Architect. We feel in all things about us the presence of the great Creator. A sense of awe and reverence comes over us, and we expect to find in this stupendous temple we are approaching, none but men of pure hearts and benignant minds. But, by degrees, as we clamber up the winding hill, the sensation of awe gives way—new scenes of beauty and grandeur open upon our ravished vision—and a multitude of emotions swell within our hearts. We are dazzled, bewildered, and excited, we know not how, nor why; our souls expand and swim through the immensity before and around us, and our being seems merged in the infinite and glorious works of God. This is the country of the fairies; and here they have their shaded dells, their mock mountains, and their green valleys, thrown into ten thousand shapes of beauty. But higher up are the Titan hills; and when we get among them, we will find the difference between the abodes of the giants and their elfin neighbors."

After a hard day's march for man and beast, they at length reached Cathey's, or Cathoo's, plantation — since Cathey's mill, at the mouth of Grassy creek, a small eastern tributary of North Toe river; and here they rested for the night.† Some twenty miles were accomplished this day. Their parched corn meal, and, peradventure, some

---

* C. H. Wiley's *North Carolina Reader*, 68, 77.

† Campbell's diary. The MS. correspondence of Thomas D. Vance, W. A. McCall, Hon. Wm. B. Carter, W. H. Allis, G. W. Crawford, Dr. J. C. Newland, Hon. J. C. Harper, Colonel Samuel McDowell Tate, Hon. C. A. Cilley, Mrs. Mary A. Chambers, Dr. J. G. M. Ramsey, and Major T. S. Webb, has been of essential importance in helping to determine and describe the route and its localities of the King's Mountain men.

remaining beef rations, formed a refreshing repast, with appetites sharpened by the rough exercise of so tedious a jaunt over hills and dales, and rocks, and mountain streams.

On Friday, the twenty-ninth, the patriot army pursued its winding way up the valley of Grassy creek to its head, some eight or nine miles, when they passed through Gillespie's Gap in the Blue Ridge; emerging from which they joyfully beheld, here and there, in the distance, in the mountain coves and rich valleys of the heads of the Upper Catawba, the advanced settlements of the adventurous pioneers. Here the troops divided—Campbell's men, at least, going six or seven miles south to Henry Gillespie's, and a little below to Colonel William Wofford's Fort, both in Turkey Cove; while the others pursued the old trace in an easterly direction, about the same distance, to the North Cove, on the North Fork of the Catawba, where they camped for the night in the woods, on the bank of that stream, just above the mouth of Hunnycut's creek. On a large beech tree, at this camp, several of the officers cut their names,* among them Colonel Charles McDowell; who had, by arrangement, several days preceded the troops from the camp of the Burke and Rutherford fugitives on the Watauga.

At this point Colonel McDowell rejoined his overmountain friends, imparting to them such vague and uncertain intelligence as he had been able to learn of Ferguson and his movements. Colonel McDowell had repaired to his Quaker Meadow home, and exerted himself, by sending messengers in every direction, to rouse the people; he had despatched James Blair, as an express, to hasten forward Colonel Cleveland with the men of Wilkes and Surry. Blair reached Fort Defiance, a distance of some thirty miles, where he probably met Cleveland and his men

---

* This venerable tree, about 1835, was accidentally charred by burning logs, in clearing land, causing it to die. W. A. McCall, who still resides there, saw the tree and read the names many times.

advancing; but he did not accomplish his mission without imperilling his life, for he was wounded by a stealthy Tory by the way.*

Colonel Campbell's party visited the Turkey Cove settlement, though some miles out of the way, with a view to gaining intelligence. Henry Gillespie, near whose cabin some of the troops camped, a hardy Irishman, who had perhaps been a dozen years in the country, and from whom the neighboring Gap took its name, was acting a neutral part in the war—probably, from his exposed situation, as his only recourse to save himself and family from destruction by the Indians, instigated, as they were, by British emissaries stationed among them. Gillespie was kept at camp during the night; but he really had no secrets to reveal and was set at liberty the following morning.†

Ensign Campbell's diary states: "The fourth night, the twenty-ninth, we rested at a rich Tory's, where we obtained an abundance of every necessary refreshment." This evidently refers to Colonel Wofford, for he was wealthy, and well-to-do for that day; while his near neighbor, Gillespie, was poor, and his little cabin and small surrounding improvements, were sufficient evidence of it. But this is a cruel and unjust imputation upon the memory of so worthy a man as William Wofford. Descended from ancestry from the north of England, he was born near Rock creek, in then Prince George, now Montgomery County, Maryland, about twelve miles above Washington City, on the twenty-fifth of October, 1728. Of his early life, we have no knowledge; but he most likely served among the Maryland troops in the French and Indian war raging on the frontiers of that and the neighboring Colonies in his younger days.

Colonel Wofford was a man of enterprise, early mi-

---

* Blair's MS. pension statement.
† Henry Gillespie died at the Turkey Cove, about 1812, at the age of well-nigh eighty years, leaving two sons, David and William.

grating to the upper country of South Carolina, where, on Pacolet river, he erected noted iron works. He was one of the leading patriots of that region, and served as Lieutenant-Colonel on Williamson's Cherokee campaign of 1776.* Early in 1779, he was in service in pursuit of the fugitive Tory party under Colonel John Moore, when fleeing from North Carolina to Georgia; and, in the spring and summer of that year, he served in Georgia and South Carolina, under General Lincoln,† and doubtless shared in the battle of Stono.

It was probably on the fall of Charleston, when his iron works were destroyed, that he, to avoid the British and Tories who were over-running South Carolina, retired to the Upper Catawba, purchasing a fine tract of nine hundred acres, with improvements, of one Armstrong, an enterprising pioneer in the Turkey Cove. At his new home, he erected a fort for his own and neighbors' protection against the Indians, and built a small grist-mill. It is barely possible that Colonel Wofford may have been prevailed upon by the frontier settlers of Burke county, to unite with Captain John Carson and others, to take protection from Colonel Ferguson when he invaded the Upper Catawba valley, merely as a temporary *ruse* to preserve their stock and other property from those rapacious plunderers. But of this, there is no evidence, save the vague allusion of Ensign Campbell. At all events, Colonel Wofford was no Tory, and never lifted a finger against his country. It is quite evident, that Colonel Campbell gained no important intelligence from either Colonel Wofford or Henry Gillespie, simply because they were not the men to have confided to them the secrets of the Loyalists, and consequently had nothing to impart.‡

---

*Dr. John Whelchel's MS. pension statement.

†Capt. Matthew Patton's MS. pension statement.

‡ Colonel Wofford subsequently gave much attention to the surveying of lands; and, several years after the war, removed to what is now Habersham county, Georgia, where he became an influential citizen, and died near Toccoa Falls, about 1823, at the age of about

The respective divisions—the one at the Turkey Cove, and the other at the North Cove—had marched some fifteen miles this day. Colonel Charles McDowell must have been able to inform the troops, whom he happily met at the North Cove, that Ferguson was yet at and near Gilbert Town; that Cleveland and Winston, at the head of the Wilkes and Surry men, were approaching in strong force; and that the South Carolina parties under Lacey and Hill, and Williams' separate corps, were at no great distance. That Ferguson was still reposing in fancied security within striking distance, and that strong Whig reinforcements were at hand, were matters of good omen; and tended, in no small degree, to encourage and inspirit the patriots in their combined efforts and self-denials to rid their suffering country of a powerful, invading foe.

On Saturday morning, the thirtieth of the month, the troops at the North Cove took up their line of march, passing over Silver and Linville mountains, then along a dividing ridge, and down Paddie's creek to the Catawba. They probably rested at mid-day, delaying a while for the detachment from Turkey Cove, who had several miles farther to march in order to overtake them. When reunited, and refreshed, they pushed on, as the old trail then ran, from the mouth of Paddie's creek, down the northwest bank of the Catawba, crossing the mouth of Linville river,* and thence to the Quaker Meadows, the noted home

---

ninety-five years, being able to read and write without spectacles to the last. General Wm T. Wofford, of Bartow county, Georgia, is his great grandson.

A daughter of Colonel Wofford's was, in after years, married to David Gillespie, the oldest son of Henry Gillespie. David Gillespie was a youth of some fourteen years when the over-mountain men marched to King's Mountain. All through life he was very observant, and possessed a most retentive memory; and from him these facts were derived about a portion of the mountaineers going to Turkey Cove, and the others to the North Cove, and about the detention of his father in camp over night. We are indebted to Wm. A. McCall, of North Cove, for these traditions, which he had from his grandfather, David Gillespie, and to some extent, corroborated by Arthur McFall, an old hunter of the Revolutionary period, who frequently made his home with Gillespie. At the venerable age of about ninety-two, David Gillespie died in Turkey Cove, in 1859.

* This fine mountain stream was named from this circumstance. In the latter part of the summer of 1766, William Linville, his son, and a young man, had gone from the lower Yadkin to this river to hunt, where they were surprised by a party of Indians, the two

of Colonel Charles and Major Joseph McDowell. Here they encamped for the night, after a long and wearisome march, especially on the part of Campbell's corps, who had accomplished well-nigh thirty-one miles this day, and the others about twenty-three.* The McDowells did all within their power to render the mountaineers comfortable around their cheerful camp-fires—Major McDowell particularly bidding them to freely avail themselves of his dry rails in kindling their fires for their evening repast, and for their night's enjoyment.†

Here they had the joyous satisfaction of being joined by the troops from Wilkes and Surry, under the leadership of Cleveland and Winston—reported at the time, for effect, at eight hundred, but really numbering only three hundred and fifty. When the people of the Yadkin region heard of Ferguson's advance into Burke county, and of the engagement so near them, at the head of Cane creek, between McDowell and the British and Tory forces, it exerted a powerful influence in arousing them for active service. Some of them, under Colonel Cleveland, had been on the head of New river, suppressing the Tory insurrection in that quarter; and when they received tidings of the approach of the over-mountain men, they were already embodied, waiting to march at the tap of the drum—if not, indeed, actually *en route* to join their distant brethren. West from Wilkesboro, some eight or ten miles, they crossed the Yadkin at the mouth of Warrior creek; thence bearing to the south-west, some eighteen or twenty miles, they

---

Linvilles killed, the other person, though badly wounded, effecting his escape. The Linvilles were related to the famous Daniel Boone.

* We are indebted to Mr. McCall for the route of march of the King's Mountain men from the North Cove to the Quaker Meadows, derived from his grandfather, David Gillespie. Beside Mr. McCall's tradition, John Spelts and the venerable Major Samuel G. Blalock, declare that they marched by way of Quaker Meadows and Morganton. Captain A. Burgin and J. C. Whitson both of McDowell County, North Carolina, state, on the authority of aged people of the Upper Catawba valley, related to them many years since, that the over-mountain men assuredly took the route by the Quaker Meadows on their outward march.

† MS. notes of conversations with John Spelts, of Marshall county, Miss., in 1844, a venerable survivor of Major McDowell's King's Mountain men.

reached old Fort Defiance ; and thence some eight or ten miles across Warrior mountain, to Crider's Fort,* where the village of Lenoir is now located. Here Philip Evans, one of the Surry men, received a severe injury by a fall from his horse, which rendered it necessary to leave him there for recovery.†

But a worse accident befell Lieutenant Larkin Cleveland, a younger brother of the Colonel. It was some ten miles from Crider's Fort, crossing the Brushy mountain, to Lovelady's Ford of the Catawba. While crossing the river, Lieutenant Cleveland, with the advance, after having passed a narrow defile between a rocky cliff and the stream, was shot by some concealed Tories in the cliff, severely wounding him in the thigh. The Loyalists had learned of Colonel Cleveland's march, and had resolved on his destruction, hoping thereby to cripple the expedition and possibly defeat its object. Colonel Cleveland and his brother very much resembled each other in size and general appearance; and the Tories probably mistook the latter for the Colonel.

The men in the rear, on hearing the volley, rushed forward to surround the daring party in ambush, and, if possible, to effect their capture ; but the birds had flown. Sending the wounded Lieutenant in a canoe up the river, the troops forded the stream without further trouble, and advancing half a dozen miles, passed through Morganton—or what was shortly after so named in honor of General Daniel Morgan, the hero of the Cowpens ; and, about two miles west

---

* Hon. J. C. Harper, of Patterson, Caldwell County, N C., writes: '' Fort Crider was situated on a small eminence within the present limits of Lenoir. It had a hill on the east, and another on the west. Some forty years ago, I heard old Henry Sumter relate, that when the fort was built, a hunter came along, and declared it was not safe, as he could shoot a man in it from either of the hills. On this being disputed, a coat was hung on a stick within the stockade, and the hunter, at the first fire, sent his ball through it from the top of the western hill. It was a remarkable shot for a gun of those days.''

† Evans' MS. pension statement. Mr. Evans recovered in good season to aid in guarding the prisoners on the return of the King's Mountain men; and to share under Major McDowell, in Morgan's glorious victory at the Cowpens, January 17, 1781. He was a native of Rowan County, N. C., born June 17, 1759; and died in Greenville County, S. C., June 19, 1849, at the age of ninety years.

of that point, they again reached and re-crossed the Catawba, meeting with a joyful reception by the McDowells and the mountaineers at the Quaker Meadows. Here Lieutenant Cleveland was confided to the care of the widowed mother of the McDowells, who bestowed every attention upon the unfortunate officer. Though he in time recovered, he was a cripple for life.*

Sunday morning, October the first, dawned brightly upon the mountaineers at their camp, at the Quaker Meadows—a gratifying continuation of the fine weather that had enabled them so comfortably, and with such satisfactory progress, to pass the mountain ranges.· Resuming their march, with a better road, they made a more rapid advance, passing the Pilot mountain, near the present village of Brindletown—a noted beacon for travelers, prominently discernible for many miles away. In the afternoon a rain storm set in, and they early encamped in a gap of the South mountain, near where the heads of Cane and Silver creeks interlock each other, and not very far from the scene of the fight three weeks before, between the British and Tory forces and Colonel McDowell's party. This day's march numbered some eighteen miles.

So wet did the next day, Monday, prove, that the army remained in their camp. The little disorders and irregularities which began to prevail among the troops, unaccustomed to discipline and restraint, occasioned no little uneasiness among the commanding officers. As if by instinct, the field officers of the several corps met that evening for consultation. Colonel McDowell, as the senior officer, presided. It was suggested that inasmuch as the troops were from different States, no one properly had the right to command the whole, and it was important that there should be a military head to their organization; and, to this end,

---

* MS. statement of Elijah Callaway; and MS. letters of Shadrach Franklin and Jeremiah Cleveland—the two latter nephews of the wounded Lieutenant. Callaway was a stout lad of some eleven years at that time, a resident of Wilkes county, and well acquainted with the Clevelands.

that a messenger be sent to General Gates, at his head-quarters, wherever they might be, informing him of their situation, and requesting him to send forward a general officer to take the command. This was agreed to.

Anything looking like delay was not in accordance with the views of Shelby and his associate officers—expedition and dispatch were all-important at this critical juncture. It was now proposed, to meet the emergency, that the corps commanders should convene in council daily, to determine on the measures to be pursued the ensuing day, and appoint one of their number as officer of the day, to put them in execution, until they should otherwise determine. Colonel Shelby, not quite satisfied with this suggestion, observed that they were then within sixteen or eighteen miles of Gilbert Town, where they supposed Ferguson to be, who would certainly attack them if strong enough to do so, or avoid them, if too weak, until he could collect more men, or obtain a reinforcement, with which they would not dare to cope, and hence it behooved them to act with decision and promptitude. They needed, he continued, an efficient head, and vigorous movements ; that all the commanding officers were North Carolinians, save Colonel Campbell, who was from Virginia ; that he knew him to be a man of good sense, and warmly attached to the cause of his country ; that he commanded the largest regiment, and closed by proposing to make Campbell commanding officer, until a general officer should arrive from head-quarters, and that they march immediately against the enemy.

Colonel Campbell thereupon took Colonel Shelby aside and requested him to withdraw his name, and consent to serve himself. Shelby replied that he was the youngest Colonel present—which was true ; that he had served under Colonel McDowell, who was too slow for such an enterprise, who would naturally take offence should he be elevated to the command over him ; that while he (Shelby) ranked Campbell, and as the latter was the only officer from

Virginia, if he pressed his appointment, no one would object. Colonel Campbell felt the force of this reasoning, and consented to serve. The proposition was approved and adopted.

Shelby's object in suggesting Colonel Campbell's appoinment, is best explained by himself. "I made the proposition," says Shelby in his pamphlet, in 1823, "to silence the expectations of Colonel McDowell to command us—he being the commanding officer of the district we were then in, and had commanded the armies of militia assembled in that quarter all the summer before against the same enemy. He was a brave and patriotic man, but we considered him too far advanced in life, and too inactive for the command of such an enterprise as we were engaged in. I was sure he would not serve under a younger officer from his own State, and hoped that his feelings would, in some degree, be saved by the appointment of Colonel Campbell." In his narrative, in the *American Review*, December, 1848, Governor Shelby makes no reference to McDowell's age, but simply states, that he "was too slow an officer" for the enterprise.

Though Colonel Shelby speaks of McDowell's age as objectionable for such a service, it really deserved little, if any, consideration. He was then only some thirty-seven years of age *—Colonel Cleveland was some years older, and Shelby himself, the youngest of the Colonels, was only seven years his junior. It may be curious to note, that "Old Put," then in active service, was twenty-five years older than McDowell, General Evan Shelby, the Colonel's father, who, the year before, commanded an important expedition against the Chicamauga Indian towns, was

---

* There is much diversity in the authorities as to General McDowell's birth-year. It is assumed, in this connection, that he was born in 1743, as stated in Wheeler's *Hist. of North Carolina*, published while Captain Charles McDowell, a son of the General, was still living, and who is believed to have furnished the statement. Other accounts, of a traditional character, place his birth, one in 1740, and another in 1742; while his tomb-stone, giving the date of his death, March 31, 1815, says he was "about seventy years of age." If this latter be true, then he was still younger, born about 1745.

twenty-three years older, General Stark fifteen, Washington eleven, Marion ten, Sumter at least four, and General Greene one. The real objection to Colonel McDowell was not so much his age, as his lack of tact and efficiency for such a command; and, it has been hinted, moreover, that his conduct at the Cane creek affair was not without its influence in producing the general distrust entertained of his fitness to lead the mountain men on this important service. The expression was quite general, that General Morgan or General Davidson should be sent to take the command; the former, especially, who had gained such renown at Saratoga, and had recently joined General Gates, was highly esteemed by the mountaineers.*

Colonel McDowell, who had the good of his country at heart more than any title to command, submitted gracefully to what was done; but observed, that as he could not be permitted to command, he would, if agreeable, convey to head-quarters the request for a general officer. This was warmly approved, as it was justly declared that he was well acquainted with the situation of the country, and could, better than any other, concert with General Gates a plan of future operations, and they would await his return. The manner in which this was presented gratified McDowell, who at once set off on his mission, leaving his men under the command of his brother, Major Joseph McDowell.† Passing through Burke county, McDowell's command, particularly, was considerably increased‡ by relatives, friends

---

* This statement of the action of the officers in council at the South Mountain camp is made up largely frdm Shelby's narratives; that in Haywood and Ramsey's *Histories of Tennessee*, his pamphlet of 1823, and his Hardin account in the *American Review* of December, 1848. The late Colonel Wm. Martin, of Tennessee, also furnished his recollections as derived in conversations with Colonel Cleveland. John Spelts, one of the King's Mountain men, related several facts connected with this council.

† Of the result of McDowell's mission, we have no information, save that he called at the camp of Lacey and Hill, and their South Carolinians, and Williams and his corps, at Flint Hill, a dozen miles or so to the eastward of the head of Cane creek He doubtless visited General Gates, at Hillsboro; but as the news of the King's Mountain victory reached there nearly as early as Colonel McDowell, there was no occasion for any action in the premises.

‡ Shelby's narrative, 1823.

and neighbors; and there John Spelts,§ or Continental
Jack, as he was familiarly called by his associates, first
joined Shelby's regiment, but fought under McDowell.
Colonel Campbell now assumed the chief command; in
which, however, he was to be directed and regulated by the
determination of the Colonels, who were to meet every day
for consultation.

Everything was now arranged quite satisfactorily to the
Whig chiefs; and their men were full of martial ardor,
anxious to meet the foe, confident of their ability, with
their unerring rifles, to overthrow Ferguson and his Loyalist followers, even were their numbers far greater than they
were represented.

§ MS. notes of conversations with Spelts. in 1844. He was a jolly old soldier, then in
his ninety-fourth year, and from him were derived many interesting reminiscences of the
Revolution.

CHAPTER X.

September—October, 1780.

*Further Gathering of the King's Mountain Men.—Williams' North
Carolina Recruits.—Movements of Sumter's Force under Hill and
Lacey.—Troubles with Williams.—March to Flint Hill.—The
Mountaineers at their South Mountain Camp.—Patriotic Appeals
of the Officers to their Men.—Resumé of Ferguson's Operations in
the Upper Catawba Valley.—Alarming Intelligence of the Ap-
proach of the Back Water Men.—Why Ferguson Tarried so long
on the Frontiers.—British Scheme of Suppressing the Rebellion by
the Gallows.—Ferguson Flees from Gilbert Town.—Sends Messen-
gers for aid to Cornwallis and Cruger.—Frenzied Appeal to the
Tories.— Ferguson's Breakfast Stolen by Saucy Whigs.— His
Flight to Tate's Ferry.—Dispatch to Lord Cornwallis.—Takes
Post on King's Mountain, and Description of it.—Motives for
Lingering there.*

It will be remembered, that Governor Nash had granted
to Colonel Williams, a South Carolinian, the privilege of
organizing a corps of mounted men within the North Province. Under this authority, he enlisted about seventy, chiefly
while encamped at Higgin's plantation, in Rowan County.
Colonel Brandon and Major Hammond were quite active
in this service. The call for recruits was dated September
twenty-third; and was headed: "A call to arms!—Beef,
bread, and potatoes." These implied promises of good
fare were more easily made than fulfilled—probably based
on the fact that Governor Nash had given orders to the
commissaries of that State to furnish the party "such supplies as may be necessary." Colonel Hill tells us, that
these North Carolinians who enrolled under Williams, were
men who shirked duty under their own local officers; and
besides the tempting offer of "beef, bread, and potatoes,"
Colonel Williams had furthermore promised what was re-

garded as still better in the estimation of men of easy
virtue—the privilege of plundering the Tories of South
Carolina of "as many negroes and horses as they might
choose to take."

This little force, as Major Hammond states in his pension application, constituted "the largest portion of Williams' command at King's Mountain;" and with them the
Colonel pushed forward some sixty or seventy miles south-
west of Salisbury, where, after crossing the Catawba at the
Tuckasegie Ford, on the second of October, he found
Sumter's command under Colonels Hill and Lacey, in the
forks of the main and south branches of that stream.* This
party, to the number of about two hundred and seventy, had
retired from South Carolina for their own safety, and to be
in readiness to form a junction with others whenever they
could hope thereby to render useful service to their suffering country.   Williams marched into the camp of Sumter's
men; and as Sumter himself, and the most of his principal
officers were still absent—the latter, endeavoring to arrange
with Governor Rutledge with reference to the command,
Williams probably thought it a favorable opportunity to
read again, as he did, his commission of Brigadier, and
with an imperious air, commanded the officers and men to
submit to his authority.   Colonel Hill frankly told him, in
no gingerly language, that there was not an officer nor a
man in the whole body who would, for a moment, yield
obedience to him; that commissioners had been sent to the
Governor with proofs of the baseness of his conduct, as
they regarded it, whose return was soon expected.   Evidently fearing, from what he saw around him, that he
might be subjected to worse treatment than a mere denunci-

---

*Colonel Hill's Manuscript Narrative; Major Hammond's and Andrew Floyd's pen-
sion statements; Colonel Williams' letter to General Gates, October 2, 1780, in the gazettes
of the day, and Almon's *Remembrancer*, xi, 158.

By some unaccountable mistake, or misprint, this letter of Colonel Williams, is dated
"Burke County;" when all the other authorities, Hill. Floyd, Hammond and Whelchel—
the two latter of Williams' party—combine to show, beyond a doubt, that they were at this
time in Lincoln County, west or south-west of Tuckasegie Ford.

ation of words, Williams thought it prudent to beat a safe retreat, which he did, forming his camp some distance apart from the other.

Colonels Hill and Lacey had previously designed to form a junction with General Davidson, of North Carolina, to whom they had sent an express, who gave them, in return, information, probably derived through a messenger from Colonel McDowell on his earliest return from Watauga, that there was, by this time, a considerable body of men from both sides of the mountains, marching with a view of measuring swords and rifles with the redoubtable Ferguson. With this gratifying intelligence, they crossed the Catawba at Beattie's Ford, and that evening received the call already related, from Colonel Williams. That day Colonels Graham·and Hambright had joined the South Carolinians, with a small party of some sixty men from Lincoln County.

On that evening Colonel Hill suggested to Colonel Lacey, that, as they might have to encounter a superior force in a short time, they had better conciliate Colonel Williams, though his followers were but few, if they could do so without recognizing his right to command them. Lacey coincided with this view. It was therefore proposed that the troops should be arranged into three divisions —the South Carolinians proper, Graham and Hambright's party, and Williams' followers, who, by this time, would seem to have been joined by Captain Roebuck's company— perhaps some twenty or thirty in number; and choose a commanding officer for the whole, the orders and movements of the corps to be determined by all the officers. When the matter was submitted to him the next morning, he "spurned" the offer, as Colonel Hill informs us, renewing the intimation, that by virtue of his Brigadier's commission, he would command the whole. He was plainly told, that if he would not accept the honorable offer made him, he should absent himself, and not attempt to march with the South Carolina and Lincoln County men, or the

13

consequences might be more serious than would be agreeable to him. Seeing no prospect of carrying his point,
Williams finally acceded to the proposition, and an officer
was chosen to command the whole. That day the spies
came in with the intelligence, that the mountain men were
advancing through a valley between a large and small
mountain—probably referring to the South Mountain, at
the head of Cane creek.

This party of South Carolinians and their associates
marched through Lincoln County, crossing the upper forks
of Dutchman's creek, proceeding on to Ramsour's Mill,
on the South Fork of Catawba; thence bearing somewhat south-westwardly, crossing Buffalo and First Broad
rivers, to Flint Hill*—now sometimes known as Cherry
Mountain, in the eastern part of Rutherford County—a
great place of modern summer resort, where cherries in
their season abound.† From the flinty rocks along the
mountain sides gush many clear and cool springs, the
heads of neighboring streams. The hill was covered with
timber, as was doubtless the surrounding country, rendering
the locality a most inviting camping ground.‡ Here, on the
third of October, the South Carolinians, the Lincoln men,
and Williams' party, took up their temporary quarters. On
the day of their arrival at Flint Hill, Colonel McDowell
called on them while on his mission to Hillsboro;§ but the
designs of the mountain men to make a push for Ferguson
were not fully resolved on till after the Colonel's departure.
His intelligence, therefore, was not sufficiently decisive to
warrant them in taking up their line of march in any direction; and so they patiently awaited further developments
of the plans and movements of the mountaineers.

Let us return to the mountain men whom we left in camp

---

*MS. pension statements of Dr. John Whelchel, of Williams' party, and Andrew
Floyd, of Graham's men.
†Colonel J. R. Logan's MS. correspondence.
‡MS. letter of W. L. Twitty.
§Shelby's narrative in *American Review*, December, 1848.

in the gap at South Mountain, some sixteen or eighteen miles north of Gilbert Town. It was now supposed that the decisive contest between the Tories of the Western Carolinas and their Whig antagonists would be fought at that place. The officers of the mountaineers were more or less experienced, and felt an abiding confidence of success. Thinking it a good occasion, before taking up the line of march on the morning of October the third, to address a few stirring words to the patriotic army, Colonel Cleveland requested the troops to form a circle, and he "would tell them the news," as he expressed it. Though a rough, uncouth frontiersman, and weighing at this time fully two hundred and fifty pounds, Cleveland possessed the happy faculty of inspiring men with much of his own indomitable spirit. Colonel Sevier was active in getting the men into form, assuring them that they would hear something that would interest them. Cleveland came within the circle, accompanied by Campbell, Shelby, Sevier, McDowell, Winston, and other officers; and taking off his hat, said with much freedom and effect:

"Now, my brave fellows, I have come to tell you the news. The enemy is at hand, and we must up and at them. Now is the time for every man of you to do his country a priceless service—such as shall lead your children to exult in the fact that their fathers were the conquerors of Ferguson. When the pinch comes, I shall be with you. But if any of you shrink from sharing in the battle and the glory, you can now have the opportunity of backing out, and leaving; and you shall have a few minutes for considering the matter."

"Well, my good fellows," inquired Major McDowell, with a winning smile on his countenance, "what kind of a story will you, who back out, have to relate when you get home, leaving your braver comrades to fight the battle, and gain the victory?"

"You have all been informed of the offer," said Shelby;

" you who desire to decline it, will, when the word is given, march three steps to the rear, and stand, prior to which a few more minutes will be granted you for consideration." At length the word was given by the officers to their respective commands, that "those who desired *to back out* would step three paces in the rear." Not a man accepted the unpatriotic privilege. A murmur of applause arose from the men on every hand, who seemed to be proud of each other, that there were no slinks nor cowards among their number. "I am heartily glad," said Shelby, "to see you to a man resolve to meet and fight your country's foes. When we encounter the enemy, don't wait for the word of command. Let each one of you be your own officer, and do the very best you can, taking every care you can of yourselves, and availing yourselves of every advantage that chance may throw in your way. If in the woods, shelter yourselves, and give them Indian play; advance from tree to tree, pressing the enemy and killing and disabling all you can. Your officers will shrink from no danger—they will be constantly with you, and the moment the enemy give way, be on the alert, and strictly obey orders." *

These appeals to the mountain men were adroitly put, and had a good effect. Each soldier felt that he could implicitly rely on his fellows to stand by him to the last. The troops were now dismissed, with directions to be ready to march in three hours—and have provisions prepared for two meals, and placed in their knapsacks. Cleveland and McDowell seem to have obtained some liquor, and added that "when the men were ready for the march, they should have a 'treat.'" † They marched down Cane creek a few miles, making slow progress, and encamped for the night with the usual guards on duty. The next day, October the fourth, they renewed the march, fording and re-fording Cane creek many times, as the trail then ran, and at night

---

* MS. notes of conversations with John Spelts, whose memory of this gathering, and the remarks of Cleveland, McDowell and Shelby, was clear and vivid.

† Spelts' recollections.

reached the neighborhood of its mouth, in the region of Gilbert Town. They learned this day from Jonathan Hampton, that Ferguson had retreated from Gilbert Town ; and also received information that it was his purpose to evade an engagement with them.*

In order to give a proper view of the movements of the opposing parties, it is now necessary to recur to Ferguson and his Tory followers. It will be remembered, that Ferguson's troops made an excursion, during the month of September, into the Upper Catawba Valley, in then Burke, now McDowell County ; and that several of the patriots, Captain John Carson among them, were prevailed on by the Whig leaders to take protection, simply as a *ruse* by which to save as much of the stock of the country as possible. The scheme worked to a charm, not merely in benefiting the Whigs, but by Captain Carson's shrewd management, it produced, in the end, a telling effect on the few Tories of that region. Ferguson began to suspect that Carson and his friends were deceiving him, and saving more cattle than probably belonged to them, and resolved that he would not be thus foiled by such backwoods diplomacy. So he fitted out a party from camp to go in quest of beeves thus attempted to be smuggled out of harm's way, and lay in a good supply of meat. Carson accompanied the foraging expedition. A large herd was found roaming about the extensive cane-brakes, where David Greenlee since resided ; but Carson was close-mouthed about their ownership until the Tory party had slaughtered over a hundred head of fine young cattle, when he quietly observed, that he expected that they were the property of Joseph Brown, Dement, and Johnstone, who had joined Ferguson, and were then in his camp. These men got wind of the transaction, made inquiries, and ascertained that it was indeed their stock that had been so unceremoniously appropriated for his Majesty's troops. They were not a little chop-fallen and disgusted,

---

*General Joseph Graham's narrative; MS. correspondence with Jonathan Hampton, Jr.

and the affair was soon noised abroad, and had quite a dispiriting effect upon the Loyalists of the country. Ferguson declared that the Rebels had out witted him.*

A little incident, worthy of relation, occurred while the British troops were encamped at Davidson's place, since McIntyre's, two miles west of Captain Carson's. A soldier was tempted to kill a chicken and enjoy a savory meal, but he happened to be discovered by Mrs. Davidson, who promptly reported the theft to Ferguson. The British commander had the culprit immediately punished, and gave the good lady a dollar in compensation for the loss.† This act was certainly creditable to Ferguson's sense of justice; but it was, like an oasis in the desert, a circumstance of very unfrequent occurrence.

Returning from this excursion, Ferguson and his Tory marauders camped a while at the White Oak Spring, near Brindletown. Their camp was in close proximity to the lofty peak known in all that region as Pilot Mountain, almost isolated in the midst of a comparatively level country— so named, as tradition has it, from its having been the landmark of the Indians in their wanderings, and the guide by which the Tory foraging parties, in 1780, directed their course when returning from their plundering expeditions. One of these parties captured Robert Campbell, too old for active service, while at breakfast, at his home on Camp Creek, twelve miles north-east of Rutherfordton, and conveyed him to the camp at White Oak Spring.

Reference has heretofore been made to the fight at Cowan's Ford, on Cane creek. One traditon‡ places the

---

* MS. narrative of Vance and McDowell, preserved by Robert Henry.

† MS. letter of Governor D. L. Swain, of Chapel Hill, North Carolina, February 8th, 1854, to General John G. Bynum, on authority of D. M. Smith, of Asheville, North Carolina, a grandson of Mrs Davidson, communicated by Rev. W. S. Bynum, of Winston, North Carolina.

‡ MS. correspondence of Wm. L. Twitty, who derived the tradition from Wm. Monteith, and he from Wm. Watson, a worthy Revolutionary hero who was in the fight, and who died in 1854, at the venerable age of ninety-five years. It may be added, in this connection, that old Wm. Marshall, in his lifetime, placed several large blocks of granite on the spot where this contest is said to have taken place, to identify the locality, and commemorate the occurrence. This would go to prove, that *some* Revolutionary event must have transpired at that point.

locality of this contest some three miles above Cowan's Ford, at the old Marshall place, now Jonathan Walker's, on the west branch of that stream. One Hemphill was killed; Captain Joseph White, John Criswell, and Peter Branks were wounded in this affair.* It was a sort of drawn battle, on a small scale, neither party caring to renew the conflict. Ferguson and his officers seemed to prefer camping on or near some hill or elevation; so while prosecuting their retreat, they took post on the top of a high hill at Samuel Andrews' place, twelve miles north of Gilbert Town. Here the stock, poultry, and every thing they could make use of, were unfeelingly appropriated; while the unfortunate owner, Andrews, and his Whig neighbors, had fled for safety to the neighboring Cane creek mountains.† At length the jaded troops, with their disabled Major, Dunlap, reached their old locality at Gilbert Town —the men encamping on Ferguson's Hill, while Dunlap was conveyed to Gilbert's residence.

On the thirtieth of September,‡ little dreaming of any impending danger, Ferguson was suddenly awakened from his sense of security. The two Whig deserters, Crawford and Chambers, arrived from the camp of the mountaineers on the top of the Yellow Mountain, with the alarming intelligence of the rapid approach of "the Back Water men," as Ferguson termed them. He rightly judged, that if his threats of hanging, fire, and sword had no effect on them, they were coming with a full determination to fight him with desperation. He had furloughed many of his Tory followers to visit their families, under promise of rejoining him on short notice. He had been tarrying longer than he otherwise would, in the hope of intercepting Colonel Clarke, who had laid siege to Augusta, Georgia,

---

* MS. pension statements of Captain James Withrow and Richard Ballew.

† MS. correspondence of A. B. Long and W. L. Twitty.

‡ Colonel Cruger's letter to Ferguson, of 3d October, 1780, refers to the latter's dispatch of September 30th, with the alarming news of "so considerable a force as you understand is coming from the mountains. * * * I don't see how you can possibly [defend] the country and the neighborhood you are now in. The game from the mountains is just what I expected."—Ramsey's *Tennessee,* 242.

from the fourteenth to the sixteenth of September, and would have completely succeeded, had not Colonel Cruger arrived from Ninety Six with a party of relief, when Clarke was compelled to make his way northward, along the eastern base of the mountains.

Cruger promptly apprised Ferguson of Clarke's operations and retirement. In the pursuit, quite a number of the Whigs were taken prisoners by the British and their Tory and Indian allies, and several were scalped. Captain Ashby and twelve other captives were hanged under the eyes of Colonel Browne, the British commandant of Augusta, who was twice disabled during the seige, and was smarting under the effect of his wounds; thirteen who were delivered to the Cherokees were killed by the tomahawk, or by tortures, or thrown into fires. Thirty altogether were put to death by orders of the vindictive and infamous Browne. Lieutenant William Stevenson, one of Ferguson's corps, in writing from Gilbert Town, on the twenty-fifth of September, probably gave vent to the prevalent feelings of Ferguson's men when he said, referring to the pursuit and capture of Clarke's men: "Several of whom they *immediately hanged, and have a great many more yet to hang. We have now got a method that will soon put an end to the rebellion in a short time, by hanging every man that has taken protection, and is found acting against us.*"* Hanging men "*immediately*" after they were made prisoners, plainly implies that no opportunity was given to prove or disprove whether they had ever taken protection or not. But this practice of *immediate hanging* was simply carrying into effect Lord Cornwallis' inhuman orders to Cruger and Balfour.

Ferguson was quite as anxious to waylay the remnant of Clarke's partisans as were Cruger and Browne to have him do so. It is not improbable, that in furloughing so many of his Tory recruits, as he had recently done, to visit

* Almon's *Remembrancer* for 1781, xi, 280–81.

their homes, Colonel Ferguson may have had in view, that their scattered localities might enable them to obtain early notice of the approach of Clarke's fugitives, and promptly apprise him of it. Thus watching and delaying in order to entrap the Georgia patriots, proved his own speedy destruction. When the two deserters from Sevier's regiment brought him intelligence of his threatened danger from the mountaineers, he was not slow to realize his situation. He sent out expresses in all directions, strongly appealing to the Royalists to hasten to his standard with all possible expedition, and to render him every assistance in their power in this critical emergency.

He evidently had a triple object in view by taking this circuitous course. He hoped still, peradventure, to intercept Clarke; he anxiouly desired to strengthen his own force by re-inforcements, and to collect on his route his furloughed South Carolina Loyalists, and prevent their being cut up in detail; and he attempted, moreover, to play off a piece of strategy, which, if successful, would relieve him of the danger of too close a proximity to these swarming mountaineers—by misleading them as to the objective point of his retreat, and thus indulging the hope that they might make a dash, by the nearest route, to intercept him before his expected arrival at Ninety Six. Had Ferguson, with his three or four days' start, taken the most direct easterly course to Charlotte, he could easily have accomplished his purpose, as it was only some sixty miles distant in a straight line, and could not have exceeded eighty by the then zig-zag routes of travel.

Leaving Gilbert Town on the twenty-seventh of September, Ferguson moved to the Green river region in quest of Clarke. Three days later, while in camp at James Step's place, receiving the alarming intelligence of the rapid approach of the Back Water men, in strong force, he promptly notified Lord Cornwallis of his danger, and of the consequent necessity of his hastening towards his Lordship's head-quarters ; and probably hinting that a re-inforcement or escort adequate to the occasion, would prove a most opportune occurrence. This dispatch was confided to Abram Collins and Peter Quinn, who resided on the borders of the two Carolinas, and were well acquainted with the route. His injunctions to them were to make the utmost expedition, and deliver the letter as soon as possible. They took the most direct course, crossing Second Broad river at Webb's Ford ; thence by way of what is now Mooresboro to First Broad river at Stice's Shoal ; and thence on to Collins' Mill on Buffalo, when they bore south-east to King's Mountain. Proceeding on to Alexander Henry's, a good Whig, they disguised their true character and mission, and there obtained refreshments. Immediately renewing their journey, with undue haste, excitèd the suspicions of Mr. Henry's family, that they were engaged in some mischief boding no good to the public welfare. Mr. Henry's sons, inspired by a patriotic feeling, proposed to follow and apprehend them ; and pursued so closely on their trail, that the miscreants got wind of it in the vicinity of the present Bethel Presbyterian Church, and secreted themselves by day, and traveled stealthily by night, crossing the Catawba at Mason's Ferry. Thus was the dispatch delayed, so that it did not reach Cornwallis till the morning of the seventh of October—the day of Ferguson's final overthrow.* These details are interesting as showing the cause of Cornwallis' failure to re-inforce Ferguson in his time of peril and need.

In addition to this dispatch to Lord Cornwallis for succor, Ferguson also wrote on the thirtieth of September to

---

*General Joseph Graham's King's Mountain narrative gives this statement in brief ; many of the particulars were furnished for this work by Colonel J. R. Logan, of Cleveland County, North Carolina. "Collins," adds Colonel Logan, "after the war, entered very valuable lands on Buffalo Creek in this County. He was often in jeopardy on account of his notorious counterfeiting practices, and frequently in jail ; but always had friends enough to help him out. He died in poverty near Stice's Shoal on First Broad river. Peter Quinn led a worthier life, and became the progenitor of very numerous descendants—some of them, in this County, and in the West, highly respectable people."

Colonel Cruger, commanding at Ninety Six, calling for a large militia re-inforcement—how large is not stated, but several regiments ; when Cruger replied that there were only half that number * all told.   And as a *ruse*, Ferguson gave out word, that he was going to Ninety Six, and to give countenance to the deception, started in that direction, making quite a detour southwardly from a direct course to Charlotte.

The fond hope of capturing Clarke and his intrepid folowers was, it would seem, almost an infatuation with Ferguson.   He could not bear the thought of leaving the country without accomplishing this important object, if it were possible to do so.   He had his scouts out in the direction of the mountains, and was vigilant in seeking information from the quarter where Clarke was supposed to be directing his course.   On Sunday, the first of October, while beating about the country, he visited Baylis Earle's, on North Pacolet, a dozen miles south-west of Denard's Ford. Captain William Green and his company made up a part of this force ; and while at Earle's, they killed a steer, destroyed four or five hundred dozen sheaves of oats, and plundered at their pleasure. †   They then marched to Denard's Ford, ‡ making their camp there for the night. While at this Ford, the old crossing of Broad river, half a mile below the present Twitty's Ford, and some eight miles from Gilbert Town, Ferguson issued the following energetic appeal—apparently almost a wail of despair—addressed " to the inhabitants of North Carolina," and, doubtless, similar ones to the Loyalists of South Carolina also:

---

* Ramsey's *Tennessee*, 242.

† MS. letter of Baylis Earle, September 11th, 1814, to Major John Lewis and Jonathan Hampton, communicated by Hon. W. P. Bynum.

‡ MS. letters of Hon. W. J. T. Miller, Dr. J. B. Twitty, W. L. Twitty, A. D. K. Miller, and Colonel J. R. Logan fix the locality of Denard's Ford as *near* the present Twitty's Ford ; and the venerable Samuel Twitty, a colored man, now eighty-six years old, and raised in that neighborhood, says the old ford, half a mile below the present Twitty's Ford and under a large oak tree that long stood there, was often pointed out to him in his boyhood as Ferguson's crossing place.   The MS. McDowell-Vance narrative says Ferguson crossed at Twitty's Ford, which practically confirms these traditions.   The *Virginia Gazette* and the old land records of Rutherford County determine the orthography of the name Denard, instead of Donard, as Wheeler has it in his *History of North Carolina.* Allaire's *Diary* also confirms this mode of spelling the name.

"Denard's Ford, Broad River,   }
          Tryon County, *October* 1, 1780. }

"Gentlemen:—Unless you wish to be eat up by an in-
undation of barbarians, who have begun by murdering an
unarmed son before the aged father, and afterwards lopped
off his arms, and who by their shocking cruelties and irregularities, give the best proof of their cowardice and want of
discipline; I say, if you wish to be pinioned, robbed, and
murdered, and see your wives and daughters, in four days,
abused by the dregs of mankind—in short, if you wish or
deserve to live, and bear the name of men, grasp your
arms in a moment and run to camp.

"The Back Water men have crossed the mountains;
McDowell, Hampton, Shelby, and Cleveland are at their
head, so that you know what you have to depend upon.
If you choose to be degraded forever and ever by a
set of mongrels, say so at once, and let your women turn
their backs upon you, and look out for real men to protect
them.

"PAT. FERGUSON, *Major 71st Regiment.*" *

An amusing incident occurred in this neighborhood. The
British had captured Andrew Miller, and were conveying
him along with them. Lewis Musick, who had just returned
from the unfortunate attack on Augusta, joined Anthony
Twitty, an elder brother of the William Twitty who conducted himself so bravely in the defence of Graham's Fort,
as formerly related; and being well mounted, they concluded to take a scout, and see what discoveries they could
make. Coming to the main road, it seemed to them as
though the whole line of travel for more than a mile was
alive with Red Coats, Ferguson and his dragoons among

---

* *Virginia Gazette*, November 11, 1780; Wheeler's *North Carolina*, ii, 103; Ramsey's
Tennessee, 233. It is exceedingly doubtful if any such barbarities were perpetrated upon
the Tories as Ferguson's proclamation asserts. It must have been a figment of the imagination, invented for effect.

them. The Whig scouts had a good view of them, and as they passed David Miller's place, one of the enemy and a negro remained behind, the latter going to the spring to catch his horse. The soldier — or Red Coat, as Twitty preferred to call him — proved to be Ferguson's cook; and, it seems, was completing the preparation of a savory meal, to take along for the Colonel's breakfast, who had been too busy in getting his troops started to enjoy his morning's repast. Twitty and Musick retired behind a field, where they hitched their horses in some bushes, determined to get ahead of the two loiterers and capture them. Beside the road, there was a fallen tree, the top of which was yet thickly covered with leaves, where they secreted themselves, awaiting the advance of the supposed officer and his servant. The negro, in about fifteen minutes, came dashing along some fifty yards in front. Twitty was to rush out and take the negro, while Musick was to prevent the Red Coat in the rear from shooting him; and the colored fellow was seized so suddenly that he made no defence. Musick demanded the Red Coat to surrender, who seeming unwilling to do so, Twitty leveled his gun at him, with a severe threat if he did not instantly obey. At this moment the negro put spurs to his horse and escaped.

But the white captive was dismounted, and hurried off half a mile or more, and talking loudly by the way, as if to attract the attention of pursuers, he was plainly admonished that another utterance would forfeit his life. After that, he was quiet enough. Once out of danger of being overtaken, the Whig scouts examined their prisoner, and ascertained that he was Ferguson's cook—not so much of a dignitary, after all, as they had supposed, and learned that Ferguson was then on the lookout to intercept Colonel Clarke and his men on their retreat from Augusta. Twitty and his companion paroled the soldier-cook, retaining the captured meal, which they appropriated to their own use, and Ferguson lost his breakfast.

Before releasing their prisoner, however, the Whig scouts found means to pen a hurried note to Ferguson, informing him, that when they ascertained that the person they had taken was his cook, they concluded that the British commander could not well dispense with so important a personage, and he accordingly sent him back, trusting that he would restore him to his butlership. Overtaking the Colonel, the cook delivered the note, cursing his eyes if he had not been taken prisoner by a couple of Rebel buggers, as he termed them, and proceeded to curse and denounce them at a terrible rate. Ferguson quietly restrained his temper, and told him he was wrong to speak of them so harshly, as they had used him well, and permitted him to return after a very brief captivity. Thus Andrew Miller, who was present, subsequently reported the interview.*

From Denard's Ford, Ferguson and his troops, according to Allaire's *Diary*, marched on Monday afternoon, the second, only four miles, where they formed a line of action, and lay on their arms all night. But the enemy they so confidently expected, did not make their appearance. Much precious time was thus spent to no purpose. All this, under ordinary circumstances, would indicate indecision ; but the British commander, it seems, still lingered, hoping to intercept Clarke and his Georgia patriots, and delayed for the return of his men whom he had furloughed to visit their families, and the hoped-for militia from the region of Ninety Six, and, after crossing Broad river at Denard's, purposely bore off to the left, instead of continuing on the direct road south to Green river *en route* for either Cowpens or Ninety Six, hoping thereby to elude the vigilance of the Back Water men.

---

* MS. narrative of Anthony Twitty, written in September, 1832; MS. letters of Drs. T. B. and W. L. Twitty, on authority of Mrs. Jane Toms and others. Twitty was born in Chester County, Pennsylvania, November 29th, 1745, and was much engaged in scouting service during the Revolution. Judge W. P. Bynum, of Charlotte, North Carolina, kindly communicated Twitty's MS. narrative.

It is possible, moreover, that Ferguson might have felt the necessity of feeling his way cautiously out of his difficulties; that while evading the mountaineers on the one hand, he should not run recklessly into other dangers, it might be equally as formidable; for Lord Cornwallis had, on the twenty-third of September, apprised him that Colonel Davie's party of Whig cavalry had marched against him, which Ferguson's apprehensions, and Tory fears, may have magnified into a much larger body than eighty dragoons. Nothing, however, was gained by these tardy operations; and, in these fruitless efforts at strategy, Ferguson, had he realized it, might have exclaimed, with the Roman dignitary, "I have lost a day!" For he could have marched from Denard's Ford to the neighborhood north of Cowpens from sunrise to sunset, instead of consuming two days in its accomplishment.

Allaire's *Diary* informs us, that on the third, Ferguson marched six miles to Camp's Ford of Second Broad river, thence six farther to Armstrong's, on Sandy Run, where the troops refreshed; then, as they reckoned distance, pushed on seven miles to Buffalo creek, a mile beyond which they reached Tate's plantation—making twenty miles this day, the route being north of main Broad river. At Tate's, Ferguson tarried two full days, probably awaiting intelligence as to the movements of the Whigs, which he doubtless received on the evening of the fifth, for the army renewed its march at four o'clock on Friday morning, the sixth. During this day Colonel Ferguson sent the following dispatch to Lord Cornwallis, without date; but the connecting facts fix the time as here indicated:

"My Lord:—A doubt does not remain with regard to the intelligence I sent your Lordship. They are since joined by Clarke and Sumter *—of course are become an

---

* A small squad of Clarke's men did, about this time, join the mountain men; and Sumter's force, under Colonel Lacey, soon after effected a junction. Ferguson, probably from his spies and scouts, learned of these parties and their intentions.

object of some consequence. Happily their leaders are obliged to feed their followers with such hopes, and so to flatter them with accounts of our weakness and fear, that, if necessary, I should hope for success against them myself; but numbers compared, that must be but doubtful.

"I am on my march towards you, by a road leading from Cherokee Ford, north of King's Mountain. Three or four hundred good soldiers, part dragoons, would finish the business. *Something must be done soon.* This is their last push in this quarter, etc.

"PATRICK FERGUSON."*

It is evident from this dispatch, that Ferguson, when penning it, had no other design than to march resolutely forward and join his Lordship at Charlotte. Had he then in contemplation the taking post on King's Mountain, and there awaiting succor, and there deciding the mastery with his tireless pursuers, he would likely have indicated it in his letter. So he simply said: "I am on my march towards you, by a road leading north of King's Mountain;" and, at the same time, tacitly plead for a re-inforcement, apparently aware by this time, that though he had succeeded in his strategic effort to throw the Back Water men off his trail, they were yet doggedly pursuing him.

Lieutenant Allaire says it was sixteen miles from Tate's place to "Little King's Mountain." Ferguson marched up the old Cherokee Ferry road, between the waters of Buffalo and King's creeks, crossing the western branch of this latter stream where Whisnant's mill is now situated; thence on the old Quarry road to main King's creek; and soon after crossing which, he bore off to King's Mountain. Or, as Reverend Robert Lathan describes it, Ferguson "pushed on up the ridge road between King's and Buffalo creeks, until he came to the forks, near Whitaker's Station, on the present Air-Line railroad. There he took the right prong, leading across King's creek, through a pass in the

---

* Almon's *Remembrancer* for 1781, xi, 280; Tarleton's *Campaigns*, quarto edition, 193.

VIEW OF KING'S MOUNTAIN, NORTH CAROLINA.

mountain, and on in the direction of Yorkville. Here, a short distance after crossing the creek, on the right of the road, about two hundred and fifty yards from the pass,"* he came to King's Mountain. Ferguson's dispatch to Cornwallis, already cited, and written during the day before the battle, shows conclusively, that this mountain bore its prefix of "King's" at that time,† and that its subsequent occupancy by the King's troops had nothing to do in giving to it this appellation.

That portion of it where the action was fought, has little or no claim to the distinction of a mountain. The King's Mountain range is about sixteen miles in length, extending generally from the north-east, in North Carolina, in a south-westerly course, sending out lateral spurs in various directions. The principal elevation in this range, a sort of lofty, rocky tower, called *The Pinnacle*, is some six miles distant from the battle ground. That portion of the oblong hill or stony ridge, now historically famous, is in York County, South Carolina, about a mile and a half south of the North Carolina line. It is some six hundred yards long, and about two hundred and fifty from one base across to the other; or from sixty to one hundred and twenty wide on the top, tapering to the South—"so narrow," says Mills' *Statistics*, "that a man standing on it may be shot from either side." Its summit was some sixty feet above the level of the surrounding country.

Ferguson's observing eye was attracted to this commanding eminence; and regarding it as a fit camping place, he concluded to tarry there. This was on the evening of the sixth of October. He apparently awaited the expected return of furloughed parties of Loyalists under Major Gibbs and others; and he fondly hoped, too, to be soon re-inforced by Tarleton, and the militia from the dis-

---

* Pamphlet *Historical Sketch of the Battle of King's Mountain,* Yorkville, South Carolina, 1880.

† "It took its name" says Moultrie's *Memoirs,* "from one King, who lived at the foot of the mount with his family." The name of King's Creek had also the same origin.

14

trict of Ninety Six. Rejoined by his Loyalist forces, and
strengthened by re-inforcements, he no doubt flattered
himself with gaining a crushing victory over the Back
Water men, whom he never failed to belittle, and whom
he heartily despised. He had for months untiringly
drilled the men under his banner; his detachments under
Patrick Moore, Innes and Dunlap, had met with
repeated disasters, which he anxiously desired a suitable opportunity to retrieve before joining his Lordship
at Charlotte. He prided himself in his skill in the use of
fire-arms, and his success in inspiring others with something
of his own feelings of invincibility; and, above all things,
he coveted a fitting occasion to put to the test his long and
patiently drilled Loyalists, as soon as he could do so with
a reasonable hope of success. This hope he saw in
the expected "three or four hundred good soldiers—part
dragoons"—hinting, doubtless, at Tarleton's Legion cavalry, even if the expected militia should fail him; when he
could, in his own estimation, do up the business for the
daring Back Water men, and extricate himself from his
impending danger. Cherishing such hopes, he thought it
unwise to retire too precipitately to Charlotte. Such a
retreat-might betray signs of fear—suggesting, perhaps,
that he shirked the opportunity he had long pretended to
court, and he might thereby lose the chance of a life-time
of distinguishing himself on the glorious field of Mars, and
winning undying honors and fame from his King and
country. These visions of glory were too tempting, and he
yielded to their seductive influences. "The situation of
King's Mountain," said Arthur McFall, one of his Loyalist
followers, "was so pleasing that he concluded to take post
there, stoutly affirming that he would be able to destroy or
capture any force the Whigs could bring against him."* "So
confident," says Shelby, "was Ferguson in the strength of
his position, that he declared that the Almighty could not

---

*MS. letter of Wm. A. McCall, to whom McFall made the statement.

drive him from it." * The McDowell–Vance narrative
states, that Ferguson declared, that "he was on King's
Mountain, that he was king of that mountain, and God
Almighty could not drive him from it." This impious
boast was doubtless made to encourage his confiding followers.

There was a spring on the north-west side of the mountain, one of the sources of Clark's Fork of Bullock's creek,
from which a needful supply of water could be obtained,
though not very convenient; but the country, wild as it
then was, was unable to furnish anything like the necessary
amount of provisions requisite for such a body of men. It
was a stony spot, where lines could not easily be thrown
up; there was, however, an abundance of wood on the hill
with which to form abatis, and defend his camp; but Ferguson took none of these ordinary military precautions, and
only placed his baggage-wagons along the north-eastern
part of the mountain, in the neighborhood of his head-
quarters, so as to form some slight appearance of protection.
And thus he remained nearly a whole day, and as Mills
states, "inactive and exposed," † awaiting the return of his
furloughed men, and the expected succors; but these anx-

---

*Shelby's narrative in *American Review*, December 1848, corroborated by Todd's memoir of Shelby; Colonel Hill's MS. statement; MS. notes of conversations with James
Sevier and John Spelts, both King's Mountain men and General Lenoir's narrative.

Since this chapter was put in type, George H. Moore, LL. D., of the Lenox Library, has
called the author's attention to, and kindly loaned him a copy of a rare, if not hitherto unknown pamphlet, *Biographical Sketch, or Memoir of Lieutenant Colonel Patrick Ferguson*,
by Adam Ferguson, LL. D., Edinburgh, 1817, in which this paragraph, relative to Colonel
Ferguson's retreat occurs: "He dispatched a messenger to Lord Cornwallis, to inform his
Lordship of what had passed,—of the enemies he had to deal with,—of the route he had
taken to avoid them; earnestly expressing his wish, that he might be enabled to cover a
country in which there were so many well affected inhabitants; adding that for this purpose,
he should halt at King's Mountain, hoping that he might be there supported by a detachment from his Lordship, and saved the necessity of any further retreat. This letter having
been intercepted, gave notice to the enemy of the place where Ferguson was to be found;
and though a duplicate sent on the following day was received by Lord Cornwallis, it came
too late to prevent the disaster which followed."

If such a dispatch was sent to Lord Cornwallis, it must have been written after
Ferguson had arrived at King's Mountain, and concluded to take post there. Certain it is,
that Ferguson sent several dispatches to Lord Cornwallis after he commenced his retreat
from Gilbert Town, the burthen of which evidently was to express his great anxiety for a
re-inforcement.

† *Statistics of South Carolina*, 1826, p. 778.

ious hopes were doomed to bitter disappointment.   Instead
of the coveted re-inforcements, as the sequel will show, came
the hated Back Water men, worse, if possible, than were
the Mecklenburg hornets to Cornwallis and his army.

His infatuation for military glory is the only explanation
that can be given for Ferguson's conduct in lingering at
King's Mountain.   When he left Green river, he knew
full well that the mountaineers, in strong force, were pressing hard upon him, and he marched towards Charlotte,
but not expeditiously.   He knew, too, that the Back
Water men had, by their various unions, become "of some
consequence," as he frankly admitted in his dispatch to
Lord Cornwallis.   Concluding, therefore, that "something
must be done," as he expressed it, to check the onward
progress of the mountain men—that this was "their last
push in this quarter," he was not slow in properly esti-
mating the strength and prowess of his enemy; and
keenly realized his pressing need for "three or four
hundred good soldiers," if he hoped to meet and vanquish the coming horde of Back Water "barbarians."
The possible failure of his Lordship to receive his dispatches, seems not to have entered into Ferguson's calculations; and he did not fully realize the dangers besetting
him—the meshes with which the patriots were preparing to
entrap him.   He knew, indeed, that "the Campbells were
coming;" but the haughty Scotsman relied this time too
much on the pluck and luck which had hitherto attended
him.   In his own expressive language, a direful "inunda-
tion" was impending.   Unprepared, as he was, to meet it,
ordinary military prudence would have dictated that he
should make good his retreat to Charlotte without a moment's delay.   Within some thirty-five miles of his Lordship's camp, he could easily have accomplished the distance in a few hours; yet he lingered two days at Tate's,
and one on King's Mountain, deluded with the hope of
gaining undying laurels, when Fate, the fickle goddess, had
only in store for him defeat, disaster, and death.

CHAPTER XI.

October, 1780.

Uncertainty of Ferguson's Route of Retreat.—A small Party of Georgians join the Mountain Men.—Whig forces over-estimated.—Report of a patriot Spy from Ferguson's Camp.—Williams' attempt to Mislead the Mountaineers.—Lacey sets them Right.— The South Carolinians' treatment of Williams.—Selecting the fittest Men at Green river to pursue Ferguson.—Arrival at the Cowpens.— The Tory, Saunders —his ignorance of Ferguson, his Beeves and his Corn.—Story of Kerr, the cripple Spy.— Gilmer, the cunning Scout, duping the Tories.— The Cowpens Council, further selection of Pursuers, and their Number.—Night March to Cherokee Ford.—Straying of Campbell's Men.— Groundless Fears of an Ambuscade.—Crossing of Broad river.—Stormy Time.— Jaded Condition of Men and Horses. — Tory Information.— Gilmer's Adventures.— Plan of Attacking Ferguson.—Colonel Graham Retires.—Chronicle assigned Command of the Lincoln Men.— Young Ponder Taken.—Ferguson's Dress.— Pressing towards the Enemy's Camp.

Leaving Ferguson, for the time being, at his chosen position on King's Mountain, we will return to the mountaineers, whom we left encamped, on the night of the fourth of October, near the mouth of Cane creek, in the neighborhood of Gilbert Town. The *game* they had been seeking had fled. It was generally reported that Ferguson had gone some fifty or sixty miles southwardly, and later assurances from two men, represented that he had directed his course to Ninety Six, well-nigh a hundred miles away.* The defences of that fort had been recently repaired and strengthened,† and it was strongly garrisoned, it was said, with four hundred regulars and some militia. The probability was that it would resist an assault by small arms, and

---

* Moore's *Life of Lacey*, 16.
† Tarleton's *Campaigns*, 169, 183.

the mountaineers had none others; but they were not to be thwarted in their purpose, for they had made many a sacrifice of personal comfort, and had traveled many a weary mile, in order to vanquish, if possible, the great Tory leader of the South. They, however, learned Ferguson's real strength, and were determined to pursue him to Ninety Six, or wherever else he might see fit to go. Here, before renewing their march, the mountain men killed some beeves for a supply of fresh food.

While Colonel Clarke, of Georgia, and his followers, were retreating from that unhappy country, with their families, and were aiming to cross the mountains to the friendly Nolachucky settlements, they were met by Captain Edward Hampton, who informed them that Campbell, Shelby, Sevier, and McDowell were collecting a force with which to attack Ferguson. Major William Candler and Captain Johnston, of Clarke's party, filed off with thirty men and formed a junction with the mountaineers, near Gilbert Town.* Not very long thereafter, at what was called Probit's place, on Broad river, Major Chronicle, with a party of twenty men from the South Fork of Catawba, joined the mountain men.† Every such addition to their numbers was hailed with delight; and the whole force was, for purposes of policy, greatly exaggerated by the leaders, to inspire both their own men and the enemy with the idea of their great strength and invincibility.‡

---

* McCall's *History of Georgia*, ii, 336. McCall mistakes in stating that Colonel Clarke and his Georgia fugitives retired to Kentucky for the safety of their families. That is of itself improbable; but a MS. letter of Clarke to General Sumter, of October 29th, 1780, asserts that it was to the Nolachucky settlement they repaired.

† Vance-McDowell narrative, and MS. letter of R. C. Gillam, of Asheville, North Carolina, to Dr. J. H. Logan, communicating an interview with the venerable Robert Henry, one of Chronicle's men.

‡ MS. statement of General Joseph McDowell and Colonel David Vance, preserved by the late Hon. Robert Henry, of Buncombe county. North Carolina.

Supposing the numbers reported correctly, the whole force assembled for the King's Mountain expedition did not exceed eighteen hundred and forty men, viz: Campbell's force, 400; Shelby's, 240; Sevier's, 240; McDowell's, 160, increased in Burke to probably 180; Cleveland and Winston's, 350; Candler's, 30; Lacey's, 270; Williams', 70; and Hambright's, including Chronicle's, 60. Yet they were represented as numbering three thousand by Major Tate, who was in the action. See General Davidson's letter, October 10th,

Pursuing the same route Ferguson had taken, they passed over Mountain creek and Broad river, at Denard's Ford, when they seem to have lost the trail of the fugitives, whose place of detour to the left they did not happen to discover. They constantly sent out scouts, lest any parties of Tories might be roving through the country, and take them unawares. John Martin and Thomas Lankford, of Captain Joseph Cloud's company, of Cleveland's regiment, while out spying, were waylaid near Broad river, by a party in ambush, who fired at them, severely wounding Martin in the head. Lankford escaped unhurt. The Tories captured their horses and Martin's gun, leaving Martin for dead. At length recovering his senses, the wounded soldier managed to reach the camp of his friends. The shot had fortunately been broken of their force by his hat, and only penetrated through the skin of his temples, and John Death-eridge succeeded in picking them all out of the wound. Unfit for further service at that time, Martin was conveyed home.*

1780. Gordon's *American War* says, they "amounted to near three thousand;" and this was copied into the first edition of Marshall's *Life of Washington.* In Steadman's *American War*, the number is given as "upward of three thousand." Governor Shelby, in his *American Review* narrative, states that "a Whig prisoner taken by Lord Cornwallis represented to him that the patriot force numbered three thousand riflemen;" and other reports to the British at this period made the number still larger. Judge Johnson, in his *Life of Greene*, has magnified it to "near six thousand."

There is, after all, some reason to suppose that the Whig force was over-estimated in the official report of Campbell, Shelby, and Cleveland. Campbell's regiment, according to Ensign Robert Campbell, one of the officers of that corps, amounted to "near four hundred," and Shelby's and Sevier's together to only three hundred. The MS. account heretofore cited, written by one of Campbell's men, whose name is unknown, states that Shelby and Sevier's united force numbered three hundred and fifty, and McDowell's one hundred and fifty; that Williams', the South Carolinians, and the few Georgia troops, amounted to about three hundred and fifty; placing Campbell's at four hundred and fifty, and Cleveland and Winston's at four hundred—making a total of sixteen hundred. Colonel Arthur Campbell's manuscript only gives the number of McDowell's party at one hundred and fifty. In Shelby's narrative, in the *American Review*, it is stated that the Williams party numbered "from two to three hundred refugees" which, united with the others, "made a muster-roll of about sixteen hundred." It was, perhaps, this total number that Major Tate reported to General Davidson, and which the General misunderstood as the selected portion for the battle.

*MS. pension statement of Thomas Shipp. John Martin, one of the heroic soldiers of that part of Surry County, now constituting Stokes, North Carolina, was born in Essex County, Virginia, in 1756; and, in 1768, his parents settled near the Saura Mountain, in Stokes. During the Revolution, Martin was very active, sometimes serving as a private

The mountain men, after crossing Broad river, went on some two and a half miles, to what is now Alexander's Ford of Green river, accomplishing not over twelve or thirteen miles this day, the fifth of October. Many of the horses had become weak, crippled, and exhausted, and not a few of the trampers foot-sore and weary. Their progress was provokingly slow, and Campbell and his fellow leaders began to realize it. They determined to select their best men, best horses, and best rifles ; and, with this chosen corps, pursue Ferguson unremittingly, and overtake him, if possible, before he could reach any post, or receive any re-inforcements. The Whig chiefs were not a little perplexed as to the course of Ferguson's retreat, and the objective point he had in view ; and some of the men began to exhibit signs of getting somewhat discouraged. But all doubts and perplexities were soon happily dissipated, as we shall presently learn.

While Ferguson was encamped at Tate's place, an old gentleman called on him, who disguised the object of his visit. The next morning, October fifth, after traveling all night, some twenty miles or more, Ferguson's visitor, well known to many of the troops as a person of veracity, arrived at the camp of the South Carolinians at Flint Hill, and gave the following information : that he had been several days with Colonel Ferguson, and had, by his plausible address, succeeded in impressing the British commander

---

volunteer, and sometimes as a lieutenant, in fighting the British and Tories. In February, 1776, he served a tour under Colonel Joseph Williams against the Scotch-Tories, at Cross creek, who were defeated just before their arrival ; and in the fall of that year, he went on General Rutherford's expedition against the Cherokees. In a skirmish with the Tories, he wounded and captured one of their leaders, Horton, who died shortly afterwards. In July, 1780, he went in pursuit of the fleeing Tory leader, Colonel Samuel Bryan, and participated in the fight at Colson's, under Colonel William Lee Davidson. But for the grievous wound he received near Broad river, he would have shared in the dangers and glories of King's Mountain. He was stationed, in September, 1781, at Guilford, and shortly after at Wilmington, where he heard the joyful news of Cornwallis' surrender.

After the war, he became a colonel in the militia ; in 1798 and 1799, he served as a member in the House of Commons ; and was long a magistrate, presiding for thirty years in the County Court. He was a man of infinite humor and irony possessing a keen perception of the ludicrous. Several characteristic anecdotes are preserved of him in Wheeler's *History of North Carolina.* He died at his home, near the Saura Mountain, April 5th, 1823, leaving many children to inherit his virtues. The late General John Gray Bynum was his grandson, as is the Hon. William P. Bynum, of Charlotte.

with the belief that his aged visitor was a great friend to
the Royal cause; that Ferguson, the evening before, had
sent an express to Lord Cornwallis, at Charlotte, announcing that he knew full well that the Back Water men were
in hot pursuit; that he should select his ground, and boldly
meet them; that he defied God Almighty himself and all
the Rebels out of h—l to overcome him; that he had
completed the business of his mission, in collecting and
training the friends of the King in that quarter, so that he
could now bring a re-inforcement of upwards of a thousand
men to the Royal army; but as the intervening distance,
thirty to forty miles to Charlotte, was through a d—d rebellious country, and as the Rebels were such cowardly rascals,
that instead of meeting him in an open field, they would
resort to ambuscades, he would, therefore, be glad if his
Lordship would send Tarleton with his horse and infantry
to escort him to head-quarters.*

During the day, Williams and Brandon were missed
from the camp, and Colonel Hill was informed that they
had taken a pathway that led to the mountains.   After sunset they were seen to return.   Colonel Hill, who had been
on the watch for them, now inquired where they had been,
as they had not been seen the greater part of the day.   At
first, they appeared unwilling to give any satisfactory information.   Colonel Hill insisting that they should, like honorable men, impart whatever knowledge they may have gained,
for the good of the whole, Williams at length acknowledged that they had visited the mountain men on their
march south from the neighborhood of Gilbert Town, and
had found them a fine set of fellows, well armed.   When asked
further by Colonel Hill where they were to form a junction
with them, he answered, "At the Old Iron Works, on Lawson's Fork."   Hill remarked, that that would be marching
directly out of the way from Ferguson; that it was undoubt-

---

* Hill's MS. narrative.   Colonel Hill, recording his recollections thirty-four years after
this event, makes the evident mistake that the old man visited Ferguson on King's
Mountain.

edly the purpose of the mountain men to fight Ferguson, who had sent to Cornwallis for Tarleton's horse and infantry to go to his relief, and this re-inforcement might be expected in a day a two; that, if the battle was not fought before Tarleton's arrival, it was very certain it would not be fought at all; that Ferguson, who had been bitter and cruel in his efforts to crush out the Whigs and their cause, was now in South Carolina, within striking distance, and it appeared as if Heaven had, in mercy, sent these mountain men to punish this arch-enemy of the people.

Colonel Hill states, that Williams seemed for some moments to labor under a sense of embarrassment; but finally confessed, that he had made use of deception in order to direct the attention of the mountaineers to Ninety Six. Hill then inquired if they had any cannon with them. Williams said "no," and then added, that such men with their rifles would soon reduce that post. Colonel Hill relates: "I then used the freedom to tell him, that I plainly saw through his design, which was to get the army into his own settlement, secure his remaining property, and plunder the Tories." In the course of the conversation, Williams said, with a considerable degree of warmth, that the North Carolinians might fight Ferguson or let it alone; but it was the business of the South Carolinians to fight for their own country. Colonel Hill took the occasion further to inform him, that, notwithstanding he had taken such unwarrantable means to avoid an action with Ferguson, by his efforts to mislead the mountain men, he would endeavor to thwart his purposes.

Leaving Williams to his own reflections, Colonel Hill at once informed Colonel Lacey what the former had done—that, to use a huntsman's phrase, he had been putting their friends on the wrong scent; that should they not be correctly informed before the ensuing day, Ferguson might escape; and as he, Colonel Hill, was unfit to make a night ride, with his arm still in a sling from the severe wound he received at Hanging Rock, he desired Colonel Lacey to go at once to the camp of the mountaineers, as he was better able to travel, and give them a just representation of Ferguson's locality, and the necessity for the greatest expedition in attacking him while yet within reach, and before Tarleton could come to his aid.

Taking Colonel Hill's horse, who was a good night traveler, with a person for pilot who was acquainted with the country, Lacey started on his mission at about eight o'clock in the evening; and on crossing the spur of a mountain, they unfortunately strayed from the trail, and Lacey began to be suspicious that his guide was playing him false, and was endeavoring to betray him into the hands of the enemy. So strong was this conviction, that he twice cocked his gun to kill the suspected traitor; but the pilot's earnest pleas of innocence prevailed.

At length they regained the path, and, after a devious journey of some eighteen or twenty miles, reached the camp of the mountain men, at Green river, before day. Lacey was at once taken in charge, blind-folded, and conducted to the Colonels' quarters, where he introduced himself as Colonel Lacey. They at first repulsed his advances, taking him to be a Tory spy. He had the address, however, to convince them that he was no impostor. He informed them of Ferguson's position, his strength, and urged them, by all means, to push forward immediately, and that, by combining the Whig forces, they could undoubtedly overwhelm the Tory army, while delay might prove fatal to their success, as Ferguson had appealed to Lord Cornwallis for re-inforcements.* These views met with a hearty response from the sturdy mountaineers.

---

* Hill's MS. narrative, and Dr. M. A. Moore's pamphlet *Life of General Edward Lacey*, pp. 16-17. Dr. Moore states that Lacey's journey from the camp of the South Carolinians to that of the mountaineers was sixty miles; but from Colonel Hill's representation of the time consumed by Lacey and his pilot, it is an evident mistake. The distance from Flint Hill, across a somewhat rough and broken country, to the old ford on Green river, is as stated in the text.

It should be added, in this connection, that Major Chronicle, who probably personally knew Colonel Lacey, must, on this visit of the latter, have been absent on a scout or with a foraging party.

Colonel Lacey learned from the Whig leaders that Williams and Brandon had represented to them that Ferguson had gone to Ninety Six; and that by agreement, the mountain men were to form a junction with the South Carolinians at the Old Iron Works, on Lawson's Fork of Pacolet. This tallied precisely with the opinion Colonel Hill had formed, judging from Williams' confession of deception, in order to lead the mountaineers to the region of Ninety Six, where his own interests were centered. When Campbell and his associates learned of the *ruse* Williams had attempted to palm off upon them, they felt not a little indignant, as they had come so far, and suffered so many privations, for the sole purpose, if possible, of crushing Ferguson. The Cowpens was agreed on as the proper place for the junction of the forces the ensuing evening.

Williams seemed intent on carrying his point of getting control of Sumter's men, and marching them towards Ninety Six. On the morning of Friday, the sixth of October, he went the rounds of the camp of the South Carolinians, ordering the officers and men to prepare to march for the Old Iron Works; but Colonel Hill followed quickly upon his heels, exposing his designs, and directing the men to await Colonel Lacey's return, that they might know to a certainty to what point to march, in order to form the expected union with their friends from the West. Colonel Hill animadverted upon the folly of making a foray into the region of Ninety Six simply for the sake of Tory booty, when Ferguson, with his strong force, would be left in their rear, thoroughly acquainted with all the mountain gaps, and fords of the streams, to entrap and cut them off. Colonel Hill then ordered all who loved their country, and were ready to stand firmly by it in its hour of distress, to form a line on the right; and those who preferred to plunder, rather than courageously to meet the enemy, to form a line on the left. Colonel Hill adds, that he was happy that the greater portion took their places on the right, leaving but the few followers of Williams to occupy the other position.

Upon the return of Colonel Lacey, about ten o'clock, the troops renewed their march, with the expectation of uniting with the mountaineers at the Cowpens that evening. Colonel Williams, with his followers, hung upon the rear, as if he thought it unsafe to march by himself at a distance; and when the pinch came, he abandoned the idea of going with his party alone to the region of Ninety Six. By this time, such was the spirit of animosity cherished by the Sumter men against Williams and his followers, that they shouted back affronting words—even throwing stones at them, the whole day.* About sunset, after a march of some twenty miles, the South Carolinians arrived at the place of their destination.

The over-mountain men now demand our attention. They reached the ford of Green river on the evening of the fifth of October. Strong guards were placed around the camp, relieved every two hours—"mighty little sleep that night," said Continental Jack sixty-four years thereafter. The whole night was spent in making a selection of the fittest men, horses, and equipments for a forced march, and successful attack on the enemy. The number chosen was about seven hundred;† thus leaving of the footmen and those having weak horses, judging from the aggregate given in the official report of the campaign, about six

* These details of the movements and differences of Sumter's corps and Williams and his party, are taken from the interesting MS. narrative of Colonel William Hill. Seeing no reason to discredit the statements of this sturdy patriot, they have been used freely, the better to illustrate the difficulties of the times, and especially those attending the King's Mountain campaign.

† Narrative of Ensign Robert Campbell, who served on the expedition; corroborated by Elijah Callaway's MS. narrative, in 1843. General Wm. Lenoir says " five or six hundred " Campbell's and Callaway's statements in this case seem the most probable. General Lenoir's recollections as to the number of footmen is very erroneous, placing them at about fifteen hundred.

Spelts stated, that some fifty odd footmen followed in the rear, he among the number; and old " Continental Jack" insisted that though at first they were not able to keep up with the horsemen, yet they overtook them, before reaching King's Mountain, and shared in the fight. James Sevier testified to the fact, that a number of footmen actually followed and took part in the action.

hundred and ninety, and somewhat less, according to the statement of the unknown member of Campbell's regiment. These were placed under the command of Major Joseph Herndon, an excellent officer of Cleveland's regiment, while Captain William Neal was left in special charge of Campbell's men. Colonel Campbell, realizing that the footmen might yet be needed in his operations, and knowing that Neal was an officer of much energy of character, had selected him for this service; and gave directions to him, and to Major Herndon also, to do every thing in their power to expedite the march of the troops confided to their charge, by urging them forward as rapidly as possible.

Colonel Lacey's opportune visit to the camp of the mountaineers was fortunate. Some, at least, of the Whig leaders, as tradition has it, began to doubt the policy of continuing the uncertain pursuit, lest by being led too far away, their prolonged absence from their over-mountain homes might invite a raid from the hostile Cherokees upon their feebly protected families. Lacey's information and spirited appeals reassured the timid, and imparted new courage to the hopeful.* Instead of directing their course, as they otherwise would have done, to the Old Iron Works, on Lawson's Fork of Pacolet, some fifteen miles out of their way, they marched direct for the Cowpens, starting about daybreak on the morning of the sixth of October. They took a southerly direction to Sandy Plains, following a ridge road well adapted for travel; † thence bearing southeasterly to the Cowpens, a distance of some twenty-one miles altogether, reaching the place of rendezvous soon after sunset, a short time after the arrival of the South Carolinians and their associates, under Colonels Hill, Lacey, Williams, and Graham.‡ On the way, they passed near where several large bodies of Tories were assembled; one,

---

* MS. letter of the late Dr. Alex. Q. Bradley, Marion, Ala., December 29, 1871.

† MS. letter of Dr. T. B. Twitty, of Twitty's Ford of Broad river.

‡ Hill's MS. narrative. In the narrative of Major Thomas Young, one of Williams' party, in the *Orion* magazine, the idea is conveyed that the mountaineers arrived first and were engaged in killing beeves.

numbering six hundred, at Major Gibbs', about four miles to the right of the Cowpens, who were intending to join Ferguson the next day; but the mountain men were after Ferguson, and would not be diverted from their purpose, and lose precious time, to strike at these lesser parties.[*] The riflemen from the mountains had turned out *to catch Ferguson*, and this was their rallying cry from the day they had left the Sycamore Shoals, on the Watauga.[†]

While the main object was kept steadily in view—not to be tempted away from the direct pursuit of Ferguson, yet it was deemed of sufficient importance to endeavor to make a night attack on this party at Major Gibbs'. The only account we have of this enterprise is preserved in Ensign Campbell's diary: "On passing near the Cowpens, we heard of a large body of Tories about eight miles distant, and, although the main enterprise was not to be delayed a single moment, a party of eighty volunteers, under Ensign Robert Campbell, was dispatched in pursuit of them during the night. They had, however, removed before the mountaineers came to the place, and who, after riding all night, came up with the main body the next day." Ensign Campbell adds, that "a similar expedition was conducted by Captain Colvill, with no better success, but without causing delay,"—and this, too, must have been the same night, though he places it as occurring on the following one.[‡]

For an hour or two on the evening of the sixth, there was a stirring bivouac at the Cowpens. A wealthy English Tory, named Saunders, resided there, who reared large numbers of cattle, and having many pens in which to herd his stock—hence the derivation of Cow-pens. Saunders, was,

---

[*] Shelby, as cited in Haywood's *Tennessee*, 70; and Ramsey's *Tennessee*, 234. Dr. Hunter, in his *Sketches*, 306, gives the number of the Tory party at Major Gibbs' as "four or five hundred," which is perhaps quite as large as it really was.

[†] Hunter's *Sketches*.

[‡] MS. Diary of Ensign Robert Campbell, kindly communicated by Rev. D. C. Kelley, D. D., of Leeville, Tenn. This diary is a different document from the King's Mountain narrative, by the same writer.

at the time, in bed—perhaps not very well, or feigning sickness ; from which he was unceremoniously pulled out, and treated pretty roughly. When commanded to tell at what time Ferguson had passed that place, he declared that the British Colonel and his army had not passed there at all ; that there was plenty of torch pine in his house, which they could light, and search carefully, and if they could find any track or sign of an army, they might hang him, or do whatever else they pleased with him ; but if they made no such discoveries, he trusted they would treat him more leniently. Search was accordingly made, but no evidence of an army passing there could be found.* Several of the old Tory's cattle were quickly shot down and slaughtered for the supply of the hungry soldiers ; and the bright camp fires were everywhere seen lighting up the gloomy surroundings, and strips of beef were quickly roasted upon the coals and embers ; while fifty acres of corn found there were harvested in about ten minutes.† The weary men and horses were refreshed—save a few laggards who were too tardy in cooking their repast.

Joseph Kerr, the cripple spy, was at this time a member of Colonel Williams' command. Either from Flint Hill, or shortly before reaching there, he had been sent to gain intelligence of Ferguson, and found him encamped—apparently at noon-day, on the sixth of October—at Peter Quinn's, six or seven miles from King's Mountain ; and designed marching to that point during the afternoon of that day. It was a region of many Tories, and Kerr found no difficulty in gaining access to Ferguson's camp ; and having been a cripple from his infancy, passed unsuspected of his true character, making anxious inquiries relative to taking protection, and was professedly gratified on learning

---

* MS narrative of Vance and McDowell, preserved by the late Hon. Robert Henry.

† Silas McBee's statement to the author in 1842. Mr. McBee was born November 24, 1765, and was consequently not quite fifteen when he served on this campaign. He died in Pontotoc County, Mississippi, January 6th, 1845, in his eightieth year. He was a member of the first legislature of Alabama, and was a man much respected by all who knew him.

good news concerning the King's cause and prospects. After managing, by his natural shrewdness and good sense, to make all the observations he could, he quietly retired, making his way, probably in a somewhat circuitous course, to rejoin his countrymen. As they were on the wing, he did not overtake them till the evening of that day, at the Cowpens, when he was able to report to the Whig chiefs Ferguson's movements and position, and that his numbers did not exceed fifteen hundred men.* This information was much more recent than had come through the old man who made his report at Flint Hill, on the morning of the fifth; and it tended to corroborate the correctness of the general tenor of the intelligence. And it served to strengthen the faith of the mountain men, that with proper energy on their part, and the blessing of Providence, they would yet overtake and chastise the wily British leader and his Tory allies, after whom they were so anxiously seeking.

It was deemed important to gain the latest intelligence of Ferguson's present position, for he might not now be where he was when seen by Kerr. Among others, Enoch Gilmer, of the South Fork of Catawba, was proposed by Major Chronicle, of Graham's men. It was objected that Gilmer was not acquainted with the country through which Ferguson was believed to have marched. Chronicle replied, that Gilmer could acquire information better than those familiar with the region, for he could readily assume any character that the occasion might require; that he could cry and laugh in the same breath, and all who witnessed him would firmly believe that he was in earnest in both; that he could act the part of a lunatic so appropriately that even those best acquainted with him, if not let into the secret, would not hesitate a moment to believe that he was actually deranged; that he was a

---

* MS. pension statement of Joseph Kerr; Hunter's *Sketches of Western North Carolina,* 121. After the war, Kerr removed to White County, Tennessee, where he received a pension in 1832 for his Revolutionary services, and subsequently died at a good old age.

15

shrewd, cunning fellow, and a stranger to fear.   He was
selected among others, and started off on his mission.

He called at a Tory's house not many miles in advance,
and represented to him that he had been waiting on Ferguson's supposed route from Denard's Ford to Ninety Six,
intending to join his forces ; but not marching in that direction, he was now seeking his camp. The Tory, not suspecting Gilmer's true character, frankly related all he knew
or had learned of Ferguson's movements and intentions ;
that, after he had crossed Broad river at Denard's Ford, he
had received a dispatch from Lord Cornwallis, ordering him
to rejoin the main army ; that his Lordship was calling in his
outposts, making ready to give Gates a second defeat, reduce
North Carolina, stamping out all Rebel opposition as in
Georgia and South Carolina, when he would enter Virginia
with a larger army than had yet marched over American
soil.* Gilmer returned to the Cowpens before the troops
took up their line of march that evening.   All this was about
on a par with the ordinary British boasting of the times ;
but did not furnish the Whig leaders with the intelligence
they more particularly desired relative to Ferguson's present
plans and whereabouts.

Meanwhile a council was held, in which the newly joined
officers, save Colonel Williams, participated ; and Colonel
Campbell was retained in the chief command—" in courtesy," says Colonel Hill, " to him and his regiment, who had
marched the greatest distance."   Men and horses refreshed,
they started about nine o'clock on their night's march in
quest of Ferguson. To what extent the North and South
Carolinians, who joined the mountain men at the Cowpens,
added to their numbers, is not certainly known ; but
as they were less jaded than the others, they probably
reached about their full quota of four hundred, as is
generally understood—Williams had, a few days before,
called them in round numbers, four hundred and fifty,

---

*Vance and McDowell narrative, as preserved by Robert Henry.

including his own corps; while Colonel Hill is silent in his narrative as to their strength. Thus the combined force at the Cowpens was about eleven hundred, and nearly all well armed with rifles. Here a prompt selection was made by the officers from the several parties just arrived from Flint Hill—so that the whole number of mounted men finally chosen to pursue and attack Ferguson, was about nine hundred and ten, besides the squad of uncounted footmen, who were probably not so numerous as Spelts supposed. They may be estimated, *pro rata*, according to the relative strength of their respective corps, about as follows: Chosen at Green river—Campbell's men, two hundred; Shelby's, one hundred and twenty; Sevier's, one hundred and twenty; Cleveland's, one hundred and ten; McDowell's, ninety; and Winston's, sixty;—total, seven hundred. Additional troops selected at the Cowpens: Lacey's, one hundred; Williams', sixty; and Graham and Hambright's, fifty;—total, two hundred and ten; and making altogether nine hundred and ten mounted men.* The squad of uncounted footmen should be added to the number. The little party of Georgians seem to have been united with Williams' men, and served to swell that small corps; Chronicle's South Fork boys helped to make up the Lincoln force under Graham; while the few footmen doubtless generally joined their respective corps, though some, like Spelts, united with the column most convenient to them when the time of trial arrived.

---

* The official report signed by Campbell, Shelby and Cleveland, says nine hundred was the number selected; Shelby's account in Haywood and Ramsey, and in the *American Review* says nine hundred and ten; Colonel Hill's MS. narrative gives nine hundred and thirty-three as the number. Ramsey's *Revolution in South Carolina*, 1785; Gordon's *American War*, 1788; and Moultrie's *Memoirs*, 1802, all give the number as nine hundred and ten. So does General Graham in his King s Mountain narrative. General Davidson, in his letter to General Sumner, October 10. 1780. says sixteen hundred was the number selected—a palpable error, or exaggeration—which was copied by Marshall into the first edition of his *Life of Washington*

"It is not easy," says Rev. Mr. Lathan, "to determine with any degree of certainty, the exact number of Americans engaged in the battle of King's Mountain." It is as accurately known as the numbers are in military operations generally, by following the official and other reliable reports, and discarding palpable errors and exaggerations—such for instance, as that which this writer gives that the South Carolinians under Hill and Lacey "amounted to near two thousand."

It proved a very dark night, and to add to the un-pleasantness and difficulty of the march, a drizzly rain soon set in, which, Shelby says, was, at least part of the time, excessively hard. While the road was pretty good, as Silas McBee represents, who was raised on Thicketty creek in that region, yet, from the darkness brooding over them, the pilots of Campbell's men lost their way, and that corps became much confused, and dispersed through the woods, so when morning appeared the rear portion were not more than five miles from the Cowpens, as Hill's manuscript informs us. Discovering the absence of the Virginians, and divining the cause, men were sent from the front at the dawn of day, in all directions, till the wanderers were found, who had taken a wrong trail, and were now put on the right road.

Once reunited, with the light of day to guide them, they pushed forward uncommonly hard. They had designed crossing Broad river at Tate's, since Deer's Ferry, as the most direct route to King's Mountain ; and, as they neared that locality, they concluded to bear down the river, some two and a half miles, to the Cherokee Ford, lest the enemy, peradventure, or some portion of them, might be in posses-sion of the eastern bank of the stream at Tate's crossing, and oppose their passage.* It was near daylight, when on the river hills, in the neighborhood of the Cherokee Ford, Gilmer was sent forward to reconnoitre at the Ford, and discover, if possible, whether the enemy might not have waylaid the crossing at that point, with a design of attack-ing their pursuers in the river. While awaiting Gilmer's return, orders were given to the men to keep their guns dry, for it was yet raining. After some little time, Gilmer's well-known voice was heard in the hollow near by, singing *Bar-ney Linn*, a favorite jolly song of the times, which was suffi-

---

* Shelby in *American Review;* Hill's MS. narrative; Vance and McDowell's state-ment; General Joseph Graham's sketch in *Southern Literary Messenger,* September, 1845; General Lenoir's narrative in Wheeler's *North Carolina,* ii, 106 ; MS. notes of conversa-tions with Silas McBee.

cient notice that the way was clear. As they reached the river, it was about sunrise. Orders were given, that those having the largest horses should stem the current on the upper side of the stream. Not much attention was paid to the order. Though the river was deep, it was remarked that not a solitary soldier met with a ducking.* They had now marched some eighteen miles since leaving the Cowpens, and were yet some fifteen miles from King's Mountain.

After passing the river, Gilmer was again sent forward to make discoveries, and dashed off at full gallop. The officers rode at a slow gait in front of their men—the latter, as if getting somewhat wearied of the pursuit, would sometimes indulge in an oath, adding that if they were to have a battle, they could wish to engage in it, and have it soon over. Some three miles above the Cherokee Ford, they came to Ferguson's former encampment, where they halted a short time, taking such a snack as their wallets and saddlebags afforded—scanty at best, and many entirely destitute. Coming to a cornfield by the roadside, the mountain men would soon pull it, cutting some of the raw corn from the cob for their own sustenance, and hauling a supply for their horses.

The rain continued to fall so heavily during the forenoon, that Colonels Campbell, Sevier and Cleveland concluded from the weary and jaded condition of both men and beasts, that it was best to halt and refresh. Many of the horses had given out. Riding up to Shelby, and apprising him of their views, he roughly replied with an oath: " I will not stop until night, if I follow Ferguson into Cornwallis' lines." Without replying, the other Colonels returned to their respective commands, and continued the march. The men could only keep their guns dry by wrapping their bags, blankets, and hunting shirts around the locks,

---

* MS. notes of conversations with Silas McBee ; Lenoir's narrative ; and Benjamin Sharp's statement in the *American Pioneer*.

thus leaving their own persons unpleasantly exposed to the almost incessant stormy weather which they had encountered since leaving the Cowpens. Proceeding but a mile after the proposed halt, they came to Solomon Beason's, who was a half-Whig, half-Loyalist, as occasion required, where they learned that Ferguson was only eight miles in advance; and there, too, they had the good fortune to capture a couple of Tories, who, at the peril of their lives, were made to pilot the army to King's Mountain—one, as related by McBee, accompanying Shelby, the other Cleveland. They gave some account of the situation of the enemy, which revived the hopes of all, that they would soon gain the object they were so anxiously seeking. Another gratifying circumstance was, that the rain ceased about noon, and cleared off with a fine cool breeze. When the mountaineers had advanced five miles further, some of Sevier's men called at the house of a Loyalist, seeking information, when the men would only say that Ferguson was not far away. As they departed, a girl followed the riflemen out of the building, and inquired: "How many are there of you?" "Enough," was the reply, "to whip Ferguson, if we can find him." "He is on that mountain," she said, pointing to the eminence three miles distant.*

After traveling several miles, the officers in front descried the horse of Gilmer, the scout, fastened at a gate about three-fourths of a mile ahead. They gave whip to their steeds, and rode at full speed to the place; and on going into the house, found Gilmer sitting at the table eating. "You d—d rascal," exclaimed Colonel Campbell, "we have got you!" "A true King's man, by G—," replied Gilmer. In order to test the scout's ability to sustain his assumed character, Campbell had provided himself with a rope, with a running noose on it after the style of a lasso,

* MS. notes of conversations with Colonel George Wilson, of Nashville, Tennessee, in 1844, derived from Alexander Greer, one of Sevier's men. Greer was a noble specimen of the pioneer soldier; became a Colonel of militia in after years, and died on Duck river, Bedford County, Tennessee, in February, 1810.

and threw it over Gilmer's neck, swearing that they would hang him on the bow of the gate. Chronicle begged that he should not be hung there, for his ghost would haunt the women, who were present and in tears. Campbell acquiesced, saying they would reserve him for the first convenient over-hanging limb that they should come across on the road. Once fairly beyond sight of the house, a few hundred yards, the rope was detached from Gilmer's neck, and he permitted to remount his horse. He then stated the intelligence he had gained: That on reaching the house, and finding it occupied by a Tory family, he declared that he was a true King's man; and wished to ascertain Ferguson's camp, as he desired to join him. Finding the two women at the house warmly attached to the King's cause, he could not repress his joy, so gave each a hearty sympathizing smack; the youngest of whom now freely related, that she had been in Ferguson's camp that very morning, which was only about three miles away, and had carried the British commander some chickens; that he was posted on a ridge between two branches where some deer hunters had a camp the previous autumn. Major Chronicle and Captain Mattocks stated that the camp referred to was theirs, and that they well knew the ground on which Ferguson had taken post—a spur of King's Mountain.

As they now had recent knowledge of Ferguson's position, the officers led by Campbell rode a short distance by themselves, agreeing upon a plan of attack, and freely reported it to the men for their encouragement; assuring them that by surrounding Ferguson's army, and shooting at them on their part up-hill, there would consequently be no danger of our men destroying each other, and every prospect of success would be theirs. It was a question, whether the mountaineers were numerous enough to surround the entire ridge on all sides—for they did not then know its exact length. But the scheme was heartily approved by all. The officers without stopping, began to agree upon the position each corps was to occupy in the attack.

Colonel William Graham, who was at the head of the Lincoln men, and had rendered good service the past summer in connection with Shelby in the Spartanburg region, and had so successfully defended his fort on Buffalo creek, received at this point certain intelligence that his wife was in a precarious condition, some sixteen miles away, near Armstrong's Ford on the South Fork, and his presence was imperatively demanded at the earliest possible moment. When he stated the case to Colonel Campbell, the latter replied that if he could venture to remain, share in the impending battle, and carry the tidings of victory to his companion, it would prove the best possible intelligence to her. Turning to Chronicle, also from the South Fork, Campbell inquired, as if the Major knew something of the urgency of the case—"Ought Colonel Graham to have leave of absence?" "I think so, Colonel," responded Chronicle; "as it is a woman affair, let him go." Leave of absence was accordingly granted; and David Dickey, much against his wishes, was assigned as an escort. Campbell, judging that Major Chronicle was a younger and more active officer than Lieutenant-Colonel Hambright, observed to the Major —"Now you must take Graham's place;" and turning to Hambright, Campbell asked if he had any objections. He generously said, it was his wish that Chronicle should do so, as he best knew the ground. As this was satisfactorily arranged, Chronicle exclaimed, "Come on, my South Fork boys," and took the lead.[*]

When within two or three miles of King's Mountain, Sevier's advance managed to capture two or three more Tories, who were out spying, from whom corroborative information was derived of the position of Ferguson's camp, and of the locality of his picket guard.[†]   Soon after, a

---

[*] This statement concerning Gilmer's adventures the plan of the battle, and Colonel Graham, is taken from the MS Vance-McDowell narrative, and no doubt this portion was furnished by Robert Henry, one of Chronicle's party.

[†] Benjamin Sharp's statement; MS. notes of conversations with Colonel George Wilson, derived from Alexander Greer; Lathan's *Sketch,* 14.

youth, named John Ponder,* some fourteen years of age, was met riding in great haste, while another account says he was captured in an old field—probably taking a circuitous course for Charlotte. Colonel Hambright knowing that this lad had a brother and other relatives in Ferguson's camp, caused his prompt arrest. On searching him, a fresh dispatch from Ferguson to Cornwallis was found, manifesting great anxiety as to his situation, and earnestly renewing his request for immediate assistance. The substance of the dispatch was made known to the men, without, however, mentioning Ferguson's strength, which he seems to have given, lest his numbers should tend to discourage them. Interrogating young Ponder as to the kind of dress Ferguson wore, he replied that while that officer was the best uniformed man on the mountain, they could not see his military suit, as he wore a checked shirt, or duster, over it. Colonel Hambright at once called the attention of his men to this peculiarity of Ferguson's dress : " *Well, poys,*" said he, in his broken Pennsylvania German accent, "*when you see dot man mit a pig shirt on over his clothes, you may know who him is, and mark him mit your rifles.*" †

As they approached within a mile of the enemy, they met George Watkins, a good Whig, who had been a prisoner with Ferguson ; and having been released on parole, was now on his way home. He was able to give the very latest information, with the assurance that the enemy still maintained their position on the mountain. Here a brief halt was made. Hitherto the men had been mostly unembodied—marching singly, or in squads,

---

*General Joseph Graham, in his King's Mountain narrative, gives the name as Fonderin, which Dr. Hunter in his *Sketches* repeats. But Colonel J. R. Logan, who has lived all his life of some seventy years in the King's Mountain region, and whose grandfather, William Logan, was in the battle, states that all the aged persons of that section of country unite in declaring that the youth's name was John Ponder. A Mr. Dover, says Colonel Logan, was likewise met on the march, and imparted some information to the Whig leaders of Ferguson's movements and whereabouts; and the families of the Ponders and Dovers still reside in York County, South Carolina, and Cleveland County, North Carolina, while Ponder's Branch of King's creek is a well-known stream in that quarter.

†General Graham's King's Mountain narrative; MS. correspondence of Abram Hardin; Hunter's *Western North Carolina*, 306-7.

as might best suit their convenience; "but little subordi-
nation," says Colonel Hill, "had been required or expected." The men were now formed into two lines, two
men deep—Colonel Campbell leading the right line, and
Colonel Cleveland the left.* The officers renewedly adopted
the plan of attack already suggested, to surround the enemy;
but Williams, as Colonel Hill states, dared not appear at the
council, in consequence of his recent effort to mislead the
Whig Colonels. The strictest orders were given that no
talking would be allowed on the march, which was faithfully
obeyed, every man seeming as dumb as the poor brute that he
rode.† It was somewhere near this point, that Major Winston
was detached, with a portion of the Wilkes and Surry troops,
to make a detour, apparently south of the Quarry road, to
gain the right of Ferguson.‡

After passing Whistnant's Mill creek, the mountaineers
followed the ridge road past what is now the Antioch Baptist church, thence northerly till they intersected the road
leading from North Carolina to Yorkville, along which
latter they marched to the right, a nearly south-easterly
course, crossing Ponder's Branch, and another upper prong
of King's creek, by way of Colonel Hambright's subsequent
improvements, and through a gap in the mountain to the
battle hill. Or, as General Graham describes the line of
March after passing King's creek, "they moved up a branch
and ravine, between two rocky knobs; beyond which the
top of the mountain and the enemy's camp upon it, were in
full view, about a hundred poles in front."

This route by way of Antioch church and Ponder's
Branch was quite circuitous, north of the old Quarry road.
The traditions of the King's Mountain region are more or
less contradictory; but the statements of the best informed
indicate this as the course pursued;§ and probably this

---

* James Crow's statement.
† Statement of Hon. John F. Darby of St. Louis, derived from his grandfather, one of
Campbell's men.
‡ General Lenoir's narrative.
§ MS. statement of Colonel J. R. Logan.

indirect way was taken in order to cut off the enemy's retreat, should they attempt a flight towards Charlotte when the Whigs should make their formidable appearance. In the rear of trees and bushes, on the east side of King's creek, a little above where the Quarry road passes that stream, the mountaineers arrived at about three o'clock in the afternoon, when the word " halt" was given. Then they were ordered to " dismount and tie horses ; " next to " take off and tie up great-coats, blankets, etc., to your saddles," as it had been rainy the preceding night, and till within the past three hours ; and a few men were designated to take charge of the horses. Then came the final general order: " Fresh prime your guns, and every man go into battle firmly resolving *to fight till he dies!"* * No such word as fail entered into the composition or calculations of Campbell and his men. Never was the war-cry of the ancient Romans more ceaseless and determined, that *Carthage must be destroyed*, than was that of the mountaineers—*to catch and destroy Ferguson!*

---

*Hon. J. F. Darby's narrative : General Graham's statement ; Shelby's memoir in *American Review* ; Latham's *Sketch of King's Mountain*.

CHAPTER XII.

King's Mountain Battle, October 7th, 1780.

Ferguson and his Men Resolve to Fight.— The Bayonet their Main Reliance.—British Strength.—Character of the Provincial Rangers.— Different Classes of Loyalists Described.— Traits of the Mountaineers.— The Holston Men, and Frontier Adventures.—Assignment of the Whig Corps to the Attack.—Campbell's Appeal to his Men. — Winston's mis-Adventures.—Cleveland not the First to Commence the Action.—Surprising the Enemy's Picket.—Shelby's Column Annoyed by the Enemy.—Campbell's Men Rush into the Fight—Attack on the British Main Guard.— The Virginians Advance up the Mountain.—March of Cleveland's Men—Patriotic Speech of their Commander—Drive in a Picket.—Movements of Lacey's Men.— Campbell's Corps Driven before the Bayonet—Rally, and Renew the Contest.—Shelby, too, Retired before the Charging Columns.— The Right and Left Wings take part in the Action.—Culbertson's Heroism.—Captain Moses Shelby Wounded.—Ensign Campbell Dislodging Tories from their Rocky Ramparts.—Terrific Character of the Conflict.—Amusing Incident of one of Lacey's Men.—Heroic Efforts of Campbell and his Corps.—Ensign Campbell's Good Conduct.— Captain Edmondson's Exploit and Death.— Lieutenant Reece Bowen's Disdain of Danger, and his Lamented Fall.—Campbell's Active Efforts and Heroic Appeals.—Death of Major Chronicle.— The South Fork Boys Charged, and Several Wounded.— Robert Henry Transfixed, and yet Survived all his Associates.— William Twitty and Abram Forney.—Cleveland and his Men.— Lieutenant Samuel Johnson and other Wounded Officers.—Intrepidity of Charles Gordon and David Witherspoon.—Singular Adventure of Charles Bowen and Colonel Cleveland.

Ferguson had carefully posted his Provincial corps and drilled Loyalists along the crest of the mountain, extending from nearly one end to the other. They had no thought of retreating from their pursuers. We have, indeed, no evidence that they really knew that the Back Water men were

DIAGRAM OF THE BATTLE OF KING'S MOUNTAIN.

so closely upon them. It is true that one account states, that the British descried in the far distance "a thick cloud of cavalry,"* apparently referring to thick clouds of dust produced by a large body of horsemen; but this could not have been so, for the country was then covered with timber, which would have prevented any such discovery; and it had, moreover, rained many successive hours during the preceding night and the fore part of that day, so that there was no dust from which any clouds could arise. At any rate, the enemy maintained their position, either hopefully or sullenly determined to fight to the last.

Ferguson's Provincials—or Rangers, as Tarleton terms them—were not a permanent corps, but made up for special service, from other Provincial bodies—the King's American Regiment, raised in and around New York, the Queen's Rangers, and the New Jersey Volunteers. These Colonial troops were clad, in the early part of the war, in green; afterwards, as a rule, they wore scarlet coats.† The Provincials were well trained, and Ferguson relied largely upon them in consequence of their practised skill in the use of the bayonet; and, in case of necessity, for such of his Tory troops as were without that implement, he had provided each with a long knife, made by the blacksmiths of the country, the butt end of the handle of which was fitted the proper size to insert snugly in the muzzle of the rifle, with a shoulder or button two inches or more from the end, so that it could be used as an effective substitute for a bayonet.

What was the exact strength of Ferguson's force cannot with certainty be determined. Tarleton says, beside his corps of Rangers — which numbered about one hundred — he had not far from one thousand Loyal Militia,‡ while some British accounts put the number as low as eight hun-

---

*History of the War in America, Dublin, 1785, iii, 149.
† MS. Correspondence of Gen. J. W. DePeyster.
‡ Southern Campaigns, 156.

dred. The American official report, professing to gain the
information from the enemy's provision returns of that day,
gives the number as eleven hundred and twenty-five ; and
this tallies pretty closely with Tarleton's statement. There
is, however, some reason to suppose that about two hundred
Tories left camp that day, perhaps on a scout, but more
likely on a foraging expedition.

It is fitting, in this connection, to speak of the character
of these Loyalists, here arrayed on King's Mountain, and
about to engage in a memorable conflict against their common country—for they were all, or nearly all, save Ferguson himself, natives of the Colonies. Now that Dunlap was
separated from them, Ferguson's corps of Rangers seem to
have been quite as unobjectionable a class of men as the
temptations and unrestrained recklessness of war ordinarily
permit the military to be ; and, though they had fled before
Captain Hampton in their retreat from Earle's Ford of North
Pacolet, and had recoiled before the galling fire of Shelby
and Clarke near Cedar Spring, the summer preceding, yet
they were experienced soldiers, and were by many accounted as brave and reliable as any British troops in America.

But who were the Tories proper? They were made up
of different classes of citizens who sympathized with, or
took up arms for the King, and fought against their fellow-
citizens who were bravely contending for the liberties of
their country. Those of them who remained after the war,
in their old localities, were sadly abused and villified as long
as they lived. They hardly dared to offer an apology for
their conduct. They were numerous in many of the States,
and have left many descendants, not a few of whom are
among the most worthy and respected in the communities
where they reside ; yet none of them boast of their relation-
ship to the Loyalists. It has been the fashion to stigmatize
the Tories without stint and without discrimination, heap-
ing all manner of reproaches upon them and their class
generally. The issue of the war, and the general verdict

of the Whigs, who had suffered not a little in the seven years' conflict, seemed to justify these severe judgments.

No one now supposes that he would have been a Tory, had it been the will of Providence that he should have been an actor in the scenes of the Revolution a century ago. As he reads the history of the stirring events connected with the war, he concludes, that had he been there, he would, as a matter of course, have been on the right side, periling life and fortune at every hazard in the cause of freedom.

It is easy enough for us to imagine, when we read of deeds of humanity, generosity, and noble daring, that we, too, would have acted in a similar manner had we been in the same situation as those persons were who performed them. Few know, till they are tried, what they would do under certain circumstances. One's associations, surroundings, and temptations oftentimes exert an overpowering influence. Let us judge even the Tories with as much charity and leniency as we can. Some of them were cajoled into the British service, and not a few forced into it under various pretenses and intimidations.

Rev. James H. Saye, who has spent his life of over seventy years in Georgia and South Carolina, and had much intercourse with the survivors of the Revolution in his day, made the various classes of Tories a special subject of study and inquiry, including the influences that prompted their unhappy choice, and grouped them into six principal divisions :

I. There were some men in the country conscientiously opposed to war, and every sort of revolution which led to it, or invoked its aid. They believed that they ought to be in subjection to the powers that be ; and hence they maintained their allegiance to the British crown. The Quakers were of this class. They were then far more numerous in the Carolinas than now. They were, religiously, non-combatants ; and the weight of their influence naturally fell on the wrong side.

2. There were many persons who really knew nothing of the questions at issue in the contest. The world has always been cursed with too large a stock of men of this class, whose days are passed in profound ignorance of everything which requires an exertion of intellect, yet often the most self-conceited beings that wear the human form—perfect moles, delighting in nothing so much as dirt and darkness. This class followed their cunning and intriguing leaders in the Revolution, and were easily and naturally led into the camp of the Loyalists.

3. Another class thought the Government of George the Third too good to exchange for an uncertainty. They practically said: "Let well enough alone; a little tax on tea won't hurt us; and as for principles and doctrines, leave them to the lawyers and parsons."

4. Another class thought that, however desirable the right of self-government might be, it was then quite out of the question, unless his most gracious Majesty might be pleased to grant it; and they believed that the fleets and armies of Great Britain were perfectly invincible, while defeat and utter ruin to all engaged in it must follow rebellion against the King.

5. There was another class who claimed no little credit for shrewdness and management; who prided themselves on being genteel and philosophical. If they ever had scruples of conscience, they amounted to very little; if any religious principles, they imposed no self-denial, and forbade no sensual gratification. If they had a spark of patriotism or love for their King, it could only be kindled by fuel from the Government coffers. The needle is no truer to the pole than were these people to the prospect of gain. War is usually a great distributor of money; they wanted a liberal share, and wanted to acquire it easily. On the fall of Charleston, when Sir Henry Clinton issued his proclamation, these money-worshipers discovered in it a bow of promise. Pardon was offered to all rebels with one excep-

tion; and that exception embraced many persons of large estates, and a still greater number possessing comfortable means. Here the shadow of a golden harvest flitted before their longing eyes. The excepted Whigs had property enough to make many rich, if informed against by the zealous advocates of the crown; or, if plundered and appropriated without taking the trouble of making any report of the matter. Feelings of humanity and tenderness were not cultivated or regarded—it was enough that the proscribed Whigs had well-cultivated farms, negroes, horses, cattle, or other desirable property, and that they had, in their estimation, justly forfeited all by rebelling against the King and his Government. This class became the sycophants to Royal authority, and the army of plunderers during the war; and once hardened in pillaging, they soon became reckless of life and virtue.

6. There was yet another class which had a large following among the Tories—a class, too, which either on account of its numbers, industry, or general influence, gave character to a large portion of the whole fraternity. When a Revolutionary soldier was asked, " What sort of men were the Tories?" The almost invariable reply was, "A pack of rogues." An eminent example of this class was found in the person of Plundering Sam Brown, already described, a notorious robber years before the war commenced; yet, like other men who had wealth or the means of acquiring it, he had numerous friends and followers. He had the shrewdness to perceive that the field was well suited to his tastes and habits; and accordingly rallied his retainers, joined Ferguson, and for a time proved an efficient ally. Though he had been an outlaw for many years, yet few brought to the Royal standard a larger share of talent for cunning and inhumanity for the position assigned him. He now enjoyed the liberty of plundering under the sanction of law and authority, and of arresting, for the sake of reward, those who had long been known as the stanch de-

16

fenders of honesty and justice. The notorious Captain David Fanning, Bloody Bill Bates, and Bloody Bill Cunningham were men of the same infamous character — unfeeling, avaricious, revengeful, and bloody.

Here, then, were the conscientious class of Loyalists; an ignorant class; an indifferent class; a cowardly class; a covetous, money-making class; and a disappointed, roguish, revengeful class. It must not be supposed that these characteristics were never combined. Several of them had a natural affinity for each other, and were almost invariably found united in the same person. The non-combatants, the cowards, and the indifferent were not found among those arrayed on King's Mountain; but Ferguson's force, aside from the young men who had enlisted under his standard, and a few worthy but misguided people, was largely made up of the worst characters which war evolves from the dregs of mankind.*

In the confronting ranks was a very different class of men. Those from the Holston, under Campbell, were a peculiar people—somewhat of the character of Cromwell's soldiery. They were, almost to a man, Presbyterians. In their homes, in the Holston Valley, they were settled in pretty compact congregations; quite tenacious of their religious and civil liberties, as handed down from father to son from their Scotch-Irish ancestors. Their preacher, Rev. Charles Cummins, was well fitted for the times; a man of piety and sterling patriotism, who constantly exerted himself to encourage his people to make every needed sacrifice, and put forth every possible exertion in defense of the liberties of their country. They were a remarkable body of men, both physically and mentally. Inured to frontier life, raised mostly in Augusta and Rockbridge Counties, Virginia, a frontier region in the French and Indian war, they early settled on the Holston, and were accustomed from their childhood to border life and hardships; ever ready at the tap

---

* Saye's *Memoir of McJunkin.*

of the drum to turn out on military service; if, in the busiest crop season, their wives, sisters, and daughters could, in their absence, plant, and sow, and harvest. They were better educated than most of the frontier settlers, and had a more thorough understanding of the questions at issue between the Colonies and their mother country. These men went forth to strike their country's foes, as did the patriarchs of old, feeling assured that the God of battles was with them, and that He would surely crown their efforts with success. They had no doubts nor fears. They trusted in God—and kept their powder dry. Such a *thing* as a coward was not known among them. How fitting it was, that to such a band of men should have been assigned, by Campbell's own good judgment, the attack on Ferguson's choicest troops—his Provincial Rangers. It was a happy omen of success—literally the forlorn hope—the right men in the right place.

Lacey's men, mostly from York and Chester Counties, South Carolina, and some of those under Shelby, Sevier, Cleveland, Williams, Winston, and McDowell, were of the same character—Scotch-Irish Presbyterians; but many of them, especially those from the Nolachucky, Watauga, and lower Holston, who had not been very long settled on the frontiers, were more of a mixed race, somewhat rough, but brave, fearless, and full of adventure. They were not a whit less patriotic than the Virginians; and were ever ready to hug a bear, scalp an Indian, or beard the fiercest Tories wherever they could find them. Such, in brief, were the salient characteristics of the mountaineers, and the men of the up-country of the Carolinas, who were about to engage in deadly conflict with Ferguson and his motley followers.

The decisive moment was now at hand, and the mountaineers were eager for the fray. Campbell and his corps commanders had arranged their forces into two divisions, as nearly equal as they could conveniently form them, each party to attack opposite sides of the mountain. Campbell was to lead his Virginians across the southern end of the ridge, and south-east side, which Shelby designates as the column of the right center ; then Sevier's regiment, Mc-Dowell's and Winston's battalions, were to form a column on the right wing, north-east of Campbell, and in the order named, under the command of Lieutenant-Colonel Sevier. Of these, Winston had, it will be remembered, made a detour some distance to the south of Ferguson, in order the more promptly to gain the position assigned him, and per-adventure lend a helping hand in retarding the enemy, should they conclude that a hasty retreat was the better part of valor.

Shelby's regiment was to take position on the left of the mountain, directly opposite to Campbell, and form the left center—Campbell's left and Shelby's right coming together ; and beyond Shelby were respectively Williams' command, including Brandon, Hammond, and Candler ; then the South Carolinians under Lacey, Hathorne, and Steen, with the remainder of the Wilkes and Surry men under Cleveland, together with the Lincoln troops under Chronicle and Ham-bright, all under the direction of Colonel Cleveland. By this disposition was the patriot force arranged in four col-umns—two on either side of the mountain, led respectively by Colonels Campbell and Sevier on the right, and Shelby and Cleveland on the left. It is reasonable to presume that, as Winston had been detached, when a mile away, to gain his assigned position on the right, that Chronicle and Ham-bright were also early ordered to gain the extreme left por-tion of the mountain, so that these two parties should meet each other, and thus encompass the enemy on that end of the ridge.

Before taking up the line of march, Campbell and the leading officers earnestly appealed to their soldiers—to the higher instincts of their natures, by all that was patriotic and noble among men, to fight like heroes, and give not an inch of ground, save only from the sheerest necessity, and then only to retrace and recover their lost ground at the earliest possible moment. Campbell personally visited all the corps; and said to Cleveland's men, as he did to all, " that if any of them, men or officers, were afraid, to quit the ranks and go home; that he wished no man to engage in the action who could not fight; that, as for himself, he was determined to fight the enemy a week, if need be, to gain the victory."* Colonel Campbell also gave the necessary orders to all the principal officers, and repeated them, so as to be heard by a large portion of the line, and then placed himself at the head of his own regiment, as the other officers did at the head of their respective commands.† Many of the men threw aside their hats, tying handkerchiefs around their heads, so as to be less likely to be retarded by limbs and bushes when dashing up the mountain. ‡

At length the several corps started for the scene of conflict, marching two men deep, led on by their gallant officers. Both the right and left wings were somewhat longer in reaching their designated places than had been expected. When Winston's party had marched about a mile, they reached a steep hill, losing sight of the other columns, and evidently of King's Mountain also. Some men riding in view directed them to dismount from their horses, and march up the hill, which was immediately done, with the anticipation of meeting the enemy on its summit; but, before they had advanced two hundred paces, they were again hailed, disabused of their error, and directed to re-mount their horses and push on, as King's Mountain was yet a mile away. They now ran down the declivity with great precipitation to their horses, and, mounting them, rode, like so many fox hunters, at an almost break-neck speed, through rough woods and brambles, leaping branches and

---

*Statement of Joseph Phillips, one of Cleveland's men.

† MS. narrative of Gov. Campbell.

‡ Mrs. Ellet's *Women of the Revolution*, iii, 293.

crossing ridges, without a proper guide who had a personal knowledge of the country. But they soon fell upon the enemy, as good luck would have it, at the very point of their intended destination.

It was an erroneous idea of the South Carolina historian, Ramsay, that Cleveland's men, who had been compelled to make something of a circuit to reach their appointed position in the arrangement for the onslaught, were the first to commence the action, and the first to receive a bayonet charge from the enemy. The official report, to which Cleveland gave the sanction of his signature, states that Shelby and Campbell's regiments began the attack. Such was the nature of the ground, and the thick, intervening foliage of the trees, that the Whigs were not discovered till within a quarter of a mile of Ferguson; when the enemy's drums beat to arms, and the shrill whistle of their commander was distinctly heard, notifying his followers to repair to their places in the ranks, and be ready for hot work, for they well knew that no child's play was in reserve for them.

A select party of Shelby's men undertook to surprise a picket of the enemy, of whose position they had previous knowledge, and accomplished their purpose without firing a gun or giving the least alarm. This exploit seems to have occurred some distance from the mountain, and was hailed by the army as a good omen.* Orders had been given to the right and left wings, that when the center columns were ready for the attack, they were to give the signal by raising a regular frontier war-whoop, after the Indian style, and rush forward, doing the enemy all the injury possible; and the others hearing the battle-shout and the reports of the rifles, were to follow suit. The first firing was heard on the north side of the mountain †—evidently made by the enemy upon Shelby's column, before they were in position to engage in the action. It was galling in

---

* Sharp's narrative in the *American Pioneer*.
† Young's auto-biography in the *Orion* magazine.

its effect, and not a little annoying to the mountaineers, some of whom, in their impatience, complained that it would never do to be shot down without returning the fire. Shelby coolly replied, "press on to your places, and then your fire will not be lost." *

But before Shelby's men could gain their position, Colonel Campbell had thrown off his coat, and while leading his men to the attack, he exclaimed at the top of his voice, —"Here they are, my brave boys; *shout like h—l, and fight like devils!*" The woods immediately resounded with the shouts of the line, in which they were heartily joined, first by Shelby's corps, and then instantly caught up by the others along the two wings.† When Captain De Peyster heard these almost deafening yells—the same in kind he too well remembered hearing from Shelby's men at Musgrove's Mill,—he remarked to Ferguson: "These things are ominous—these are the d—d yelling boys!"‡ And when these terrific shouts saluted Ferguson's ears, he expressed fears for the result.§

About the time the Virginians advanced to the conflict, Major Micajah Lewis, with his brother, Captain Joel Lewis, both of the Wilkes and Surry troops, with Captain Andrew Colvill, of the Virginia regiment, had been designated by Colonel Campbell to make a dash on horseback upon the British main guard, half way up the spur of the mountain; and having swept them out of the way, to fall back, dismount, and join the others in the general advance. Here the first heavy firing took place between the contending parties, the guard commencing it. The mountaineers raised the Indian war-whoop and rushed upon the foe, who soon retreated, leaving some of their men to crimson the earth with their blood.‖

---

* Graham's sketch in the *Southern Literary Messenger*, and Foote's *North Carolina.*

† Statement of John Craig, one of Campbell's men; conversations with Gov. David Campbell, in 1844

‡ Statement, in 1844, of Col George Wilson.

§ Gov. Campbell's statement.

‖ MS. statement of J. L. Gray, and his communication in the *Rutherford Enquirer,* May 24th, 1859.

One of the mountaineers came within rifle shot of a British sentinel before the latter perceived him; on discovering the American, he discharged his musket, and ran with all his speed towards the camp on the hill. This adventurous Whig, who had pressed forward considerably in advance of his fellows, quickly dismounted, leveled his rifle, firing at the retreating Briton, the ball striking him in the back of the head, when he fell and expired.* Among the slain of the Virginians was Lieutenant Robert Edmondson, and John Beatty, the ensign of Colvill's company, while Lieutenant Samuel Newell, also of Colvill's corps, was wounded. Retiring down the hill, Newell passed Colonel Campbell and Major Edmondson hurrying on the regiment into action.

But Newell was too good a soldier to give up at the very commencement of the fight; and returning some distance, he came across a horse, mounting which he rode back to the lines to perform his share in the conflict.†

What terse, patriotic utterances were made by the several Whig leaders to their heroic followers, have been mainly lost to history. Such words had their intended effect at the time: but all were too intent on the exciting scenes before them, to treasure up in their memories these outbursts of patriotism. Cleveland and his men, while passing around to the left of the mountain, were somewhat retarded by a swampy piece of ground then saturated with water; ‡ but, getting clear of this, Cleveland discovered an advance picket of the enemy, when he made the following characteristic speech to his troops—not, under the circumstances, in a very formal manner we may well conclude, but, most likely, by piece-meal, as he rode along the lines:

"My brave fellows, we have beaten the Tories, and we can beat them again. They are all cowards: if they had

---

* This incident is given on authority of a writer in the *Rutherford Enquirer*, May 24th, 1859 signing himself "J. L. G."—J. L. Gray.

† Statements of Lieutenant Newell and Ensign Robert Campbell.

‡ Sharp's narrative.

the spirit of men, they would join with their fellow-citizens in supporting the independence of their country. When you are engaged, you are not to wait for the word of command from me. I will show you, by my example, how to fight; I can undertake no more. Every man must consider himself an officer, and act from his own judgment. Fire as quick as you can, and stand your ground as long as you can. When you can do no better, get behind trees, or retreat; but I beg you not to run quite off. If we are repulsed, let us make a point of returning, and renewing the fight; perhaps we may have better luck in the second attempt than the first. If any of you are afraid, such shall have leave to retire, and they are requested immediately to take themselves off." * But a single man, John Judd, intimated a preference to remain behind—" to hold the horses," as he expressed it; while, to redeem the honor of the family, his brother, Rowland Judd, went forward, and acted the part of a brave soldier in the trying conflict.† The distance that Cleveland's men had to march, with the swampy nature of their route, delayed them some ten minutes in reaching the place assigned them. But they nobly made amends for their delay by their heroic conduct in the action. The picket that they attacked soon gave way, and they were rapidly pursued up the mountain.

Doctor Moore asserts, that it has always been the tradition in the King's Mountain region, that inasmuch as Colonel Lacey rode the express, and gave the patriots at Green river the true situation of Ferguson, Colonel Campbell gave him the honor of commencing the battle—the friends of Campbell, Shelby, Sevier, Winston, and Roebuck have for each also claimed the same honor; that Lacey led on his men from the north-western and most level side of the mountain, engaging the attention of the foe, while Cleve-

---

* Ramsay's *Revolution in South Carolina*, 1785, ii, 182-83. This speech was derived apparently from Colonel Cleveland himself.

† MS. correspondence of Col. H. A. Brown, formerly of Wilkes County, N. C., now of Maury County, Tennessee.

land and the other leaders marched to their respective places of assignment, completely encircling Ferguson's army. * Judging from the official report, this tradition has no substantial foundation; yet Lacey, no doubt, anticipated Cleveland, and perhaps some of the other regimental and battalion commandants, in engaging the attention of the enemy, and taking part in the conflict.

Where Campbell's men ascended the mountain to commence the attack was rough, craggy, and rather abrupt—the most difficult of ascent of any part of the ridge; but these resolute mountaineers permitted no obstacles to prevent them from advancing upon the foe, creeping up the acclivity, little by little, and from tree to tree, till they were nearly at the top—the action commencing at long fire. † The Virginians were the first upon whom Ferguson ordered his Rangers, with doubtless a part of his Loyalists, to make a fixed bayonet charge. Some of the Virginians obstinately stood their ground till a few of them were thrust through the body; but being unable, with rifles only, to withstand such a charge, they broke and fled down the mountain—further, indeed, than was necessary. ‡ In this rapid charge, Lieutenant Allaire, of Ferguson's corps, overtook an officer of the mountaineers, fully six feet high; and the British Lieutenant being mounted, dashed up beside his adversary, and killed him with a single blow of his sword.§ But the British chargers did not venture quite to the bottom of the hill, before they wheeled, and quickly retired to the summit. Campbell's men ran across the narrow intervening valley to the top of the next ridge. Colonel Campbell and Major Edmondson, about half way between their men and the enemy, were loudly vociferating to their Virginians to halt and rally; and Lieutenant Newell, now mounted, joined them in this effort. The men were soon formed, and

---

* *Life of Lacey*, 17-18.
† Statement of James Crow, of Campbell's men.
‡ Statement of Lieutenant Newell.
§ Lieutenant Allaires' narrative in the New York *Royal Gazette*, Feb. 24, 1781.

again led up by their heroic commander to renew the contest. * It was during this attack that Lieutenant Robert
Edmondson, the younger, of Captain David Beattie's company—for there were two Lieutenants of the Virginians of
that name—was wounded in the arm. He then sheltered
himself behind a tree, with one of his soldiers, John Craig,
who bandaged up his limb. By this time Campbell's men
were successfully rallied, and were returning to the charge,
when Edmondson exclaimed, " Let us at it again ! "† Of
such grit was Campbell's Holston soldiers composed ; and
as long as there was any fighting to be done for their
country, and they could stand upon their feet, they never
failed to share largely in it.

Colonel Shelby has briefly stated his knowledge of this
heroic movement of Campbell and his men. " On the first
onset," says Shelby, " the Washington militia attempted
rapidly to ascend the mountain ; but were met by the British
regulars with fixed bayonets, and forced to retreat. They
were soon rallied by their gallant commander, and some of
his active officers, and by a constant and well-directed fire
of our rifles we drove them back in our turn, and reached
the summit of the mountain. "‡ Or, as cited by Haywood,
and understood to be also from a statement by Shelby :
" Campbell, with his division, ascended the hill, killing all
that came in his way, till coming near enough to the main
body of the enemy, who were posted upon the summit, he
poured in upon them a most deadly fire. The enemy, with
fixed bayonets, advanced upon his troops, who gave way
and went down the hill, where they rallied and formed, and
again advanced. *The mountain was covered with flame
and smoke, and seemed to thunder.*"§

While Ferguson's Rangers were thus employed in their
dashing bayonet charge against Campbell's column, Shelby

* Statements of Newell, and David Campbell, afterwards of Campbell's Station, Tenn.
† John Craig's statement.
‡ Shelby's letter to Col. Arthur Campbell. Oct. 12, 1780.
§ Haywood's *Tennessee,* 71.

was pressing the enemy on the opposite side and south-
western end of the mountain; so that the Provincials found
it necessary to turn their attention to this body of the
mountaineers. "Shelby, a man of the hardiest make, stiff
as iron, among the dauntless singled out for dauntlessness,
went right onward and upward like a man who had but one
thing to do, and but one thought—to do it."* But brave
as he and his men were, they, too, had to retreat before the
charging column, yet slowly firing as they retired. When,
at the bottom of the hill, Shelby wanted to bring his men to
order, he would cry out—"Now, boys, quickly re-load your
rifles, and let's advance upon them, and give them
another h—l of a fire!"†

Thus were Campbell's and Shelby's men hotly engaged
some ten minutes before the right and left wings reached
their points of destination, when, at length, they shared in
completely encompassing the enemy, and joined in the
deadly fray. Ferguson soon found that he had not so much
the advantage in position as he had anticipated; for the summit of the mountain was bare of timber, exposing his men to
the assaults of the back-woods riflemen, who, as they
pressed up the ridge, availed themselves of the trees on its
sides, which afforded them protection, and which served to
retard the movements of the British charging parties. As
the enemy were drawn up in close column on the crest of
the mountain, they presented a fair mark for the rifles of the
mountaineers, † and they suffered severely by the exposure.
The famous cavalry Colonel, Harry Lee, well observed of
Ferguson's chosen place for battle—it was "more assailable
by the rifle than defensible with the bayonet."§

Among the keenest of the sharp-shooters under Shelby
was Josiah Culbertson, so favorably noticed elsewhere in
this work. He had been selected with others to get pos-

---

* Bancroft, x, 338.
† MS. statement of Gen. Thomas Love, derived from Captain David Vance.
‡ Shelby's narrative in the *American Review.*
§ Lee's *Memoirs of the War* revised edition, N. Y., 1872, p. 200.

Painted by Jouitt.   Eng. by A.B.Durand.

ISAAC SHELBY.

Isaac Shelby

session of an elevated position, for which a Tory Captain and a party under him stoutly contended; but Culbertson and his riflemen were too alert for their antagonists, and pressing closely upon them, forced them to retire to some large rocks, where Culbertson at length shot their leader in the head, when the survivors fled, and soon after with their fellows were compelled to surrender. *

Captain Moses Shelby, a brother of the Colonel, received two wounds in the action—the last through his thigh near his body, disabling it, so that he could not stand without help. He was assisted down to a branch, some distance from the foot of the mountain, and was left with his rifle for his defence, should he need it. Seeing one of the soldiers coming down too frequently to the branch under plea of thirst, Captain Shelby admonished him if he repeated his visit he would shoot him; that it was no time to shirk duty. †

But a portion of the Tories had concealed themselves behind a chain of rocks in that quarter, from which they kept up a destructive fire on the Americans. As Campbell's and Shelby's men came in contact at the south-western end of the ridge, Shelby directed Ensign Robert Campbell, of the Viginians, to move to the right, with a small party, and endeavor to dislodge the enemy from their rocky ramparts. Ensign Campbell led his men, under fire of the British and Tory lines, within forty steps of them; but discovering that the Whigs had been driven down the hill, he gave orders to his party to post themselves, as securely as possible, opposite to the rocks and near to the enemy, while he himself went to the assistance of Campbell and his fellow officers in bringing the regiment to order, and renewing the contest. These directions were punctually obeyed, and the watching party kept up so galling a fire with their well-plied rifle shots, as to compel

---

* Washington, Indiana, *Weekly Register*, Oct. 17, 1839.
† Captain Moses Shelby's Statement. Conversation with Maj. Thomas H. Shelby, son of Governor Shelby, in 1863.

Ferguson to order a stronger force to cover and strengthen his men behind their rocky defence; but, towards the close of the action, they were forced to retire, with their demoralized associates, to the north-eastern portion of the mountain.*

The battle now raging all around the mountain was almost terrific. "When that conflict began," exclaimed the late eloquent Bailie Peyton, of Tennessee, "the mountain appeared volcanic; there flashed along its summit, and around its base, and up its sides, one long sulphurous blaze." † The shouts of the mountaineers, the peals of hundreds of rifles and muskets, the loud commands and encouraging words of the respective officers, with every now and then the shrill screech of Ferguson's silver whistle high above the din and confusion of the battle, intermingled with the groans of the wounded in every part of the line, combined to convey the idea of another pandemonium.

Colonel Lacey and his gallant South Carolinians, who had seen hard service under Sumter on many a well-fought field, rushed forward to share in the contest. At the very first fire of the enemy, Colonel Lacey's fine horse was shot from under him. With a single exception these South Carolinians, mostly from York and Chester, proved themselves worthy of the high reputation they had gained on other fields. That exception was an amusing one—a man who, at heart, was as true a patriot as could be found in the Carolinas; but who constitutionally could not stand the smell of powder, and invariably ran at the very first fire. When about going into action to fight Ferguson and his Tories, his friends, knowing his weakness, advised him to remain behind. "No," said he, indignantly, "I am determined to stand my ground to-day, *live or die.*" True to his instinct, at the very first fire he took to his heels, as

---

* Ensign Campbell's narrative; his statement, also, as published in 1823.
† Mr. Peyton's speech in Congress, January 16th, 1834.

usual. After the battle was over, when he returned, his friends chided him for his conduct. "From the first fire," said he, by way of apology, "I knew nothing whatever till I was gone about a hundred and fifty yards; and when I came to myself, recollecting my resolves, I tried to stop; *but my confounded legs would carry me off!*" * But fortunately his associates were made up of better material, and rendered their country good service on this occasion.

No regiment had their courage and endurance more severely tested than Campbell's. They were the first in the onset—the first to be charged down the declivity by Ferguson's Rangers—and the first to rally and return to the contest. Everything depended upon successfully rallying the men when first driven down the mountain. Had they have become demoralized as did the troops at Gates' defeat near Camden, and as did some of Greene's militia at Guilford, they would have brought disgrace and disaster upon the Whig cause. When repulsed at the point of the bayonet, the well-known voice of their heroic commander bade them "halt!—return my brave fellows, and you will drive the enemy immediately!"† He was promptly obeyed, for Campbell and his officers had the full confidence and control of their mountaineers. They bravely faced about, and drove the enemy, in turn, up the mountain. In these desperate attacks, many a hand-to-hand fight occurred, and many an act of heroism transpired, the wonder and admiration of all beholders; but there were so many such heroic incidents, where all were heroes, that only the particulars of here and there one have been handed down to us. Ensign Robert Campbell, at the head of a charging party, with singular boldness and address, killed Lieutenant McGinnis, a brave officer of Ferguson's Rangers. ‡

Captain William Edmondson, also of Campbell's regiment, remarked to John McCrosky, one of his men, that

---

* Moore's *Life of Lacey*, 18.
† Statement of David Campbell, of Campbell's Station, who shared in the action.
‡ Ramsey's *Tennessee*, 240.

he was not satisfied with his position, and dashed forward into the hottest part of the battle, and there received the charge of DePeyster's Rangers, discharged his gun, then clubbed it and knocked the rifle out of the grasp of one of the Britons. Seizing him by the neck, he made him his prisoner, and brought him to the foot of the hill. Returning again up the mountain, he bravely fell fighting in front of his company, near his beloved Colonel. His faithful soldier, McCrosky, when the contest was ended, went in search of his Captain, found him, and related the great victory gained, when the dying man nodded his satifaction of the result. The stern Colonel Campbell was seen to brush away a tear, when he saw his good friend and heroic Captain stretched upon the ground under a tree, with one hand clutching his side, as if to restrain his life blood from ebbing away until the battle was over. He heard the shout of victory as his commander and friend grasped his other hand. He was past speaking; but he kissed his Colonel's hand, smiled, loosed his feeble hold on life, and the Christian patriot went to his reward.*

Lieutenant Reece Bowen, who commanded one of the companies of the Virginia regiment, was observed while marching forward to attack the enemy, to make a hazardous and unnecessary exposure of his person. Some friend kindly remonstrated with him—" Why Bowen, do you not take a tree—why rashly present yourself to the deliberate aim of the Provincial and Tory riflemen, concealed behind every rock and bush before you?—death will inevitably follow, if you persist." "Take to a tree," he indignantly replied—" no !—never shall it be said, that I sought safety by hiding my person, or dodging from a Briton or Tory who opposed me in the field." Well had it been for him and his country, had he been more prudent, and, as his

---

* Ramsey's *Tennessee*, 240-41 ; General John S. Preston's *Address* at the King's Mountain Celebration in October, 1855, p. 60. Ramsey states, that Captain Edmondson received a mortal wound in the breast, while Charles Bowen, one of his soldiers, says he was shot in the head. He may have been shot both in the head and body.

superiors had advised, taken shelter whenever it could be found, for he had scarcely concluded his brave utterance, when a rifle ball struck him in the breast. He fell and expired. *

The " red-haired Campbell—the claymore of the Argyle gleaming in his hand, and his blue eye glittering with a lurid flame," wherever he was, dashing here and there along the line, was himself a host. His clarion voice rang out above the clash of resounding arms and the peals of successive riflery, encouraging his heroic mountaineers to victory. And thus the battle raged with increased fury—the mountain men constantly gaining more confidence, and steadily lessening the number of their foes.

Nor were the other columns idle. Major Chronicle and Lieutenant Colonel Hambright led their little band of South Fork boys up the north-east end of the mountain, where the ascent was more abrupt than elsewhere, save where Campbell's men made their attack. As they reached the base of the ridge, with Chronicle some ten paces in advance of his men, he raised his military hat, crying out— "Face to the hill!" He had scarcely uttered his command, when a ball struck him, and he fell; and William Rabb, within some six feet of Chronicle, was killed almost instantly thereafter. The men steadily pressed on, under the leadership of Lieutenant Colonel Hambright, Major Joseph Dickson, and Captains Mattocks, Johnston, White, Espey and Martin—a formidable list of officers for so small a body of men; but they all took their places in the line, and fought with determined heroism. Before they reached the crest of the mountain, the enemy charged bayonet—said to have been led by DePeyster—first firing off their guns, by which Robert Henry supposed that Captain Mattocks and John Boyd were killed, and William Gilmer, a brother of the

---

* Garden's *Anecdotes*, second series, p. 272, presumably communicated for that work by Judge Peter Johnston, of Abingdon, Virginia, a distinguished officer of Lee's Legion during the Revolution, and the ancestor of the present Gen. Joseph E. Johnston, and Hon. John W. Johnston, United States Senator from that State.

17

noted scout, and John Chittim wounded—the latter of Captain Martin's company, was shot in his side, making an orifice, through which, according to tradition, a silk handkerchief could be drawn, and yet he recovered, living to a good old age. *

One gallant young fellow, Robert Henry, then in his sixteenth year, had taken his position behind a log stretched across a hollow ; and was getting ready to give the enemy another shot, when the bayonet chargers came dashing along. One of the enemy was advancing rapidly on young Henry, who was in the act of cocking his gun, when his antagonist's bayonet glanced along Henry's gun-barrel, passing clear through one of his hands, and penetrating into his thigh. Henry, in the *melée*, had shot the Tory, and both fell to the ground—the young Whig hero completely transfixed. Henry was pretty well enveloped in powder-smoke ; but sad and helpless as was his condition, he could not help observing that many of his South Fork friends were not more than a gun's length ahead of the Tory bayonets, and the farthest could not have exceeded twenty feet, when they fired, with deadly effect, upon their pursuers, and retired to the bottom of the hill, quickly re-loading, and in turn chasing their enemies up the mountain.

William Caldwell, one of Henry's companions, seeing his situation, pulled the bayonet out of his thigh ; but finding it yet sticking fast to the young soldier's hand, gave the wounded limb a kick with his boot, which loosened the bloody instrument from its hold. Henry suffered more in the operation of extracting the bayonet, than when the Briton made the effective thrust, driving it through his hand and into his thigh. Again upon his feet, he picked up his gun with his uninjured hand, and found it empty—how, he could not tell ; but supposed, as he received the terrible bayonet thrust, that he must, almost instinctively, have touched the trigger, and discharged his rifle, and that the

---

* MS. letter of Dr. C. L. Hunter.

ball must have cut some main artery of his antagonist, as he bled profusely.*

Another incident of the battle : When William Twitty, who behaved so gallantly in the defence of Graham's Fort the preceding summer, and now serving among the South Fork or Lincoln boys, discovered that his most intimate crony had been shot down by his side, he believed that he knew from the powder-smoke, from behind which tree the fatal ball had sped ; and watching his opportunity to avenge the death of his friend, he had not long to wait, for soon he observed a head poking itself out from its shelter, when he quickly fired, and the Tory fell. After the battle, Twitty repaired to the tree and found one of his neighbors, a well-known Loyalist, with his brains blown out.†

Abram Forney, a brave soldier of Captain William Johnston's company, of the Lincoln men, used in after years to relate this incident of the battle : When the contest had become warm and well-maintained on both sides, a small party of Whigs, not relishing the abundance of lead flying all around them, and occasionally cutting down some gallant comrade at their side, concluded to take temporary shelter behind an old hollow chestnut tree—a mere shell—which stood near, and from its walls to pour forth a destructive fire upon the enemy. The British, however, presently observed the quarter whence this galling fire proceeded, and immediately returned their compliments in

---

* MS. narrative of Robert Henry ; MS. letter of Robert C. Gillam, Sept 29th, 1858, giving statements derived from an interview with Mr. Henry.

Mr. Henry was born in a rail pen, in then Rowan, now Iredall County, North Carolina, January 10th, 1765. Full of patriotism, though young, he shared in the trials and perils of the Revolution, and in due time recovered from the severe wounds he received at King's Mountain. In 1795, he was one of the party who ran the boundary line between North Carolina and Tennessee. He subsequently studied law, and practised his profession many years in Buncombe County. He served in the House of Commons in 1833 and 1834. He was a clear and forcible public speaker ; and his memory deserves to be held in grateful remembrance for preserving the narrative of the King's Mountain campaign and battle, so frequently cited in this work. He died in the new County of Clay, North Carolina, January 6th, 1863, within four days of attaining the patriarchal age of ninety-eight years, and he was undoubtedly the last of the heroes of King's Mountain.

† MS. correspondence of Wm. L. Twitty, grandson of William Twitty.

the shape of a few well-aimed volleys at the old shell, completely perforating it with balls, and finally shivering it in pieces.*

When Cleveland's regiment hastened to their appointed place of attack, under a heavy fire while on the way, their brave commander exclaimed, pointing significantly to the mountain, "Yonder is your enemy, and the enemy of mankind!" They were soon hotly engaged with the Loyalists lining the brow of the eminence before them. From the Colonel down to the humblest private they all heartily detested Tories, and fought them with a resolute determination to subdue them at all hazards. They sought all natural places of protection—trees, logs, rocks, and bushes; when Cleveland would, ever and anon, vociferously urge onward and upward his troops—"a little nearer to them, my brave men!" And the men of Wilkes and Surry would then dart from their places of concealment, and make a dash for more advanced positions. Occasionally one of their number would fall, which only served to nerve on the survivors to punish the Tories yet more effectually.

In one of these bold and dashing forays, Lieutenant Samuel Johnson, of Captain Joel Lewis' company, was more adventurous than prudent, and found himself and men in a most dangerous and exposed position, which resulted in the loss of several of his soldiers, and receiving himself a severe wound in the abdomen. Three bullet holes were made in one skirt of his coat, and four in the other. After Lieutenant Johnson had fallen, and while the contest was yet fiercely raging around him, he repeatedly threw up his hands, shouting—"*Huzza, boys!*" The salvation of his life was attributed to the scanty amount of food he had taken during the three days preceding the battle, so difficult had it been to obtain it. † Of his fellow officers of Cleveland's regiment who were also among the wounded, were Major

---

* Dr. C. L. Hunter, in *Wheeler's North Carolina*, ii, 245.
† Pension statement of Johnson's widow, substantiated by surviving witnesses.

Micajah Lewis, Captain Joel Lewis, Captain Minor Smith, and Lieutenant James M. Lewis ; the three wounded Lewises were brothers, and a noble triumvirate they were. Daniel Siske and Thomas Bicknell were among the killed of the Wilkes regiment, as the manuscript records of that county show.

Many a mortal combat and hand-to-hand rencontre, took place in this part of the line. Charles Gordon, apparently a young officer, made a quick, bold movement into the midst of the enemy, seizing a Tory officer by his cue, and commenced dragging him down the mountain, when the fellow suddenly drew and discharged his pistol, breaking Gordon's left arm ; whereupon the latter, with his sword in hand, killed the officer outright. The whole affair was but the work of a moment, and was regarded at the time as an intrepid act—a prodigy of valor. * David Witherspoon, also of Cleveland's regiment, in getting into close quarters, discovered one of the enemy prostrate on the ground, loading and firing in rapid succession. Witherspoon drew his rifle on him and fired, when the Red Coat, wounded, pitched the butt of his gun, in submission, towards his antagonist, throwing up his hands imploring mercy ; and when Witherspoon reached him, he found his mouth full of balls, chewing them so as to make them jagged, and render the wounds they might inflict more fatal. †

Early in the engagement, Colonel Cleveland's noble steed, "Roebuck," received two wounds, and he had to dismount ; yet, unwieldly as he was, he managed under the excitement surrounding him, to keep fully up with his men,

---

* MS. statements of Rev. Z. H. Gordon, and Mrs Sarah C. Law, nephew and niece of the hero of this adventure. Charles Gordon was a native of the Fredericksburg region, in Virginia, early settling in what subsequently became Wilkes County, North Carolina, where he filled public positions, and became a Major in the militia. He married a daughter of General Lenoir, dying near what is now Patterson, Caldwell County, in that State, March 24, 1799, at the age of about thirty-seven years. Charles G. McDowell, of Shufordsville, N. C., and the lady of Hon James C. Harper of Patterson, are his grand-children, and Mrs. C. A. Cilley. of Lenoir, N. C., is his great grand-daughter.

† MS. letter of Col. J. H. Witherspoon, a son of David Witherspoon, Nov. 25, 1880, giving the incident as related to him by his father.

and, with rifle in hand, gallantly fulfilling all the duties of
the occasion ; until he was at length remounted, one of his
men bringing him another horse. *   An incident occurred,
near the close of the contest, of an exciting character, and
which very nearly cost the heroic Colonel his life.   Charles
Bowen, of Captain William Edmondson's company, of
Campbell's regiment, heard vaguely that his brother, Lieutenant Reece Bowen, had been killed, and was much distressed and exasperated in consequence.   On the spur of
the moment, and without due consideration of the danger
he incurred, he commenced a wild and hurried search for
his brother, hoping he might yet find him in a wounded
condition only.   He soon came across his own fallen Captain Edmondson, shot in the head, and dying ; and hurrying from one point to another, he at length found himself
within fifteen or twenty paces of the enemy, and near to
Colonel Cleveland, when he slipped behind a tree.

At this time, the enemy began to waver, and show
signs of surrendering.   Bowen promptly shot down the first
man among them who hoisted a flag ; and immediately, as
the custom was, turned his back to the tree, to re-load,
when Cleveland advanced on foot, suspecting from the
wildness of his actions that he was a Tory, and demanded
the countersign, which Bowen, in his half-bewildered state
of mind, had, for the time being, forgotten.   Cleveland,
now confirmed in his conjectures, instantly levelled his rifle
at Bowen's breast, and attempted to shoot ; but fortunately
it missed fire.   Bowen enraged, and perhaps hardly aware
of his own act, jumped at and seized Cleveland by the
collar, snatched his tomahawk from his belt, and would in
another moment have buried it in the Colonel's brains, had
not his arm been arrested by a soldier, named Buchanan, who
knew both parties.   Bowen, now coming to himself, recollected the countersign, and gave it—" Buford ;" when
Cleveland dropped his gun, and clasped Bowen in his arms

* Sharp's narrative.

for joy, that each had so narrowly and unwittingly been restrained from sacrificing the other.*   Well has a noble
South Carolina orator, a grandson of the illustrious Campbell, described him—"Cleveland, so brave and yet so
gentle!" †

---

* Bowen's MS. pension statement, 1832, then of Blount County, Tennessee.
† Gen. John S. Preston's King's Mountain Address,1855, p. 60.

CHAPTER XIII.

The Battle.—October 7th, 1780.

All the different corps fought well at King's Mountain. The Burke and Rutherford battalion, under McDowell and Hampton, performed their full share in the engagement. Among Hampton's men was William Robertson, who during the fight was shot completely through the body, the ball entering at one side, and passing out at the other. He fell quite helpless to the ground. His wound was apparently mortal, and chancing to recognize one of his neighbors lying down near him, he anxiously inquired if he, too, was wounded. The reply was, that his gun was choked, or something of the kind, and would not fire. Robertson then gave him his rifle. "Give me your shot-bag, also, old fellow," he added, for his own supply was exhausted. With his own hand the fallen patriot delivered him his ammunition. But God was better to the wounded hero than his fears; for in due time he recovered, and raised a family, living near Brittain, in Rutherford County, on the farm now occupied by William L. Twitty. *

Thomas Robertson, a brother of the wounded man, was posted behind a tree, when a Tory neighbor, named Lafferty, discovering him, called him by name; and Robertson peering around the tree to see, if he could, who had spoken to him, when a ball sped quickly past him, cutting the bark of the tree near his head. Robertson instantly fired back, before his antagonist could regain his position, mortally wounding the tricky Tory, who was near enough to exclaim, and be heard, "Robertson, you have ruined me!" "The d—l help you," responded the Whig, and then re-loading his rifle, renewed the fight for freedom. A Tory named Branson was wounded and fell; and seeing his

---

* Gen. Lenoir, in Wheeler's *North Carolina*, ii, 107; MS. correspondence of Wm. L. Twitty, who derived the incident from A. B. Long.

Whig brother-in-law, Captain James Withrow, of Hampton's men, begged his relation to assist him. "Look to your friends for help," was the response, evincive of the bitterness that existed between the Whigs and Loyalists in those times. *

All of Captain William Lenoir's company of Cleveland's regiment, save half a dozen, remained behind with the other footmen at Green river, while the Captain himself went forward in a private capacity, falling into line wherever he found it most convenient—fighting "on his own hook." He fell in immediately behind Winston's men, in front of the right hand column, where he could see what was going on under McDowell and Hampton. He says he advanced the nearest way toward the enemy, under a heavy fire, until he got within thirty paces. He noticed the particular instance of bravery just related of William Robertson. "About that time," he adds, "I received a slight wound in my side, and another in my left arm; and, after that, a bullet went through my hair above where it was tied, and my clothes were cut in several places."† Participating in this close and hotly-contested action, it is sufficiently evident, was no child's play to those engaged in it.

Sevier's column at length gained the summit of the hill, driving the enemy's left flank upon his center. ‡ But they were not subjected to any bayonet charges—save a portion of the left, who hastened to the support of Campbell's regiment, when hard pressed, and became intermingled with them. Captain Robert Sevier was mortally wounded towards the close of the action, and becoming faint and thirsty, was assisted, by his brother, Joseph Sevier, some distance to a hollow, where there was a spring of water.

The last time Campbell and Shelby's men were driven down the declivity, the mountaineers learned in some way—

---

*MS. correspondence of W. L. Twitty, who adds, that the gun that Thomas Robertson used in the battle, is in the possession of one of his decendants.
† General Lenoir's narrative, in Wheeler's *North Carolina*, ii, 107.
‡ Official report of the Colonels to General Gates.

perhaps by deceptive shouting on the part of the enemy—that Tarleton with his horse had come, which seemed for the moment to have a dispiriting effect; when the officers, including Colonel Sevier, rode along the line, calling upon the men to halt, assuring them that Tarleton was not there; and if he were, they could also make him, like Ferguson's Rangers, turn their backs, and flee up the mountain. This time the riflemen pressed upon the enemy with the utmost firmness and determination. *

In the beginning of the action, Colonel Campbell's famous *Bald Face*, a black horse, proving skittish, he exchanged him with his namesake, a Mr. Campbell, of his own corps, for a bay animal; and *Bald Face* was sent to the rear, and placed in charge of the Colonel's servant, John Broddy, who was a tall, well-proportioned mulatto, and in the distance very much resembled his master. † Broddy's curiosity prompted him to ride up within two hundred yards of the raging battle, saying " he had come to see what his master and the rest were doing." ‡ Broddy, with his coat off, and sitting upon *Bald Face*, unwittingly deceived Colonels Shelby and Sevier, Captain Moses Shelby, and perhaps others, into the belief that it was Colonel Campbell himself, intently watching at a respectful distance, the progress of the engagement. But Campbell was all this time in the thickest of the fight, riding his bay

---

* Conversations with Colonel G. W. Sevier, son of Colonel Sevier.

† Colonel Cleveland was something of a wag. While in camp, *en route* for King's Mountain, the obese and jolly Colonel walked up to Campbell's markee, and seeing him at the entrance and very much resembling his servant, pretended to mistake him for the latter, and accosted him with—" Halloo, Jack, did you take good care of my noble Roebuck when you fed your master's horse ?—Ah! I ask your pardon, Colonel Campbell ; you and your servant look so much alike, led to the mistake!" The joke was received, as it was given, in the best of good humor, and was much enjoyed among the officers. This anecdote was related to the author in 1843, by Benjamin Starritt, of Fayette County, Tenn., who was one of Lee's Legion in the Revolution, Lee's and Campbell's corps fought together at the battle of Guilford ; and Starritt personally knew Cleveland, and had two brothers-in-law under Sevier at King's Mountain.

‡ No doubt others of the sons of Africa, beside Broddy, aided in menial occupations on the campaign. It is worthy of record, that " there is a tradition in the King's Mountain region," says Colonel J. R. Logan, " that something more than a dozen negroes were under arms in the battle, in behalf of liberty, and demeaned themselves bravely."

horse till he became exhausted, when he abandoned him, and was the remainder of the battle at the head of his men, on foot, with his coat off and his shirt collar open.*

It was during that critical period of the battle, when the final rally of the Virginians had been made, and after Colonel Campbell's horse had given out, that the intrepid chief ascended the mountain on foot, several paces in advance of his men; and, having reached the point of the ridge, he climbed over a steep rock, and took a view of the position of the enemy within a very short distance of their lines, and discovered that they were retreating from behind the rocky rampart they had hitherto occupied with so much security to themselves, and injury to the mountaineers, when he rejoined his men unharmed. †

Colonel Williams, who felt offended that his merit—and his superior rank, also—had not been recognized by the other Colonels, at first refused to take part in the battle; ‡ but he could not, after all, when the pinch came, resist so glorious an opportunity to do his country service, and redeem, it may be, the errors of the past. Williams wheeled chivalrously into line on the left of Shelby, exclaiming to his followers, "Come on, my boys—the old wagoner never yet backed out." § Though his numbers were few, Williams

---

*Statements of Lieutenant Newell and James Snodgrass, of Campbell's regiment, and Thomas Maxwell of Shelby's men, together with the published account of General John Campbell, in the *Richmond Enquirer*, June 24, 1823, with the appended letter of "J. C.," dated Washington County, Virginia, June 13, 1823; corroborated by statements of Ex-Governor David Campbell, of Abingdon, Va., to the author. General Campbell asserts in his article, that Andrew Evins also declared that Colonel Campbell rode his bay horse in the action until he gave out.

William Moore, Israel Hayter, James Keyes, Benjamin White, William Anderson, of Campbell's regiment; Jacob Norris, James Pierce, and Gideon Harrison of Sevier's; and Joseph Phillips, of Cleveland's, also testify to the fact that it was Colonel Campbell's bay, not his bald faced horse that he rode in the action. Much confusion grew out of the mistake that it was *Bald Face* that Campbell rode on the field, and on which he was supposed to have retired to a place of safety long before the conclusion of the battle. Several of Campbell's own men, and those who were nearest to him, and had the best means of knowing, unite in declaring that this is a grievous error. See, also, *Southern Literary Messenger* September, 1845; and Foote's *Sketches of North Carolina*. 271.

† Ensign Robert Campbell's narrative; *Holston Intelligencer*, October, 1810.

‡ MS. letter of Dr. M. A. Moore to Dr. J. H. Logan.

§ Dr. C L. Hunter, in Wheeler's *North Carolina*, ii, 246.

had several good and experienced partisan officers—
Brandon, Hammond, Hayes, Roebuck and Dillard among
them ; and their intrepid example had an inspiring effect
upon the men under their command.

Among the "bravest of the brave" who fought under
Williams and Brandon, was William Giles, some of whose
heroic adventures in the Union region in South Carolina,
have already been related. The battle-field of King's
Mountain was a fitting scene for such a fearless spirit.
During the contest, into which he entered with his accustomed zeal, he received a ball through the back of his neck,
and fell as if dead. William Sharp, his fellow-hero, his neighbor, his friend and relation, stopped a moment, brushed away
a tear from his eye, saying—"Poor fellow, he is dead ; but
if I am spared a little longer, I will avenge his fall." After
firing his rifle several times, Sharp, to his astonishment, saw
Giles raise himself up, rest upon his elbow, and commence
loading his gun. He had got *creased*, as it is said of horses
when shot through the upper part of the neck, and falling
helpless to the ground, after a while recover. Giles was soon
upon his feet again, fought through the battle, and lived to
a good old age. His son of the same name, in after years
represented both York and Union Counties in the South
Carolina Legislature.*

Thomas Young, also under Williams and Brandon, relates a touching incident. An uncle of his, one McCrary,
was then a prisoner with the British on Edisto Island ; and
his wife, for fear her husband would be hung, compelled
her youthful son, Matthew McCrary, to turn out and join
Ferguson. "Just after we had reached the top of the hill,"
says Young, "Matthew discovered me, and ran from the
British line, and threw his arms around me for joy. I told
him to get a gun and fight ; he said he could not ; when I
bade him let me go, that I might fight." Whether young
McCrary found a gun, and shared in the engagement, we

---

* MS. notes of Hon. Daniel Wallace.

are not informed; but certain it is, the lad had thrown away his British rifle, and the enemy had one less follower among their number. *

"I well remember," continues Young, "how I behaved. Ben Hollingsworth and I took right up the side of the mountain, and fought our way, from tree to tree, up to the summit. I recollect I stood behind one tree, and fired until the bark was nearly all knocked off, and my eyes pretty well filled with it. One fellow shaved me pretty close, for his bullet took a piece out of my gun-stock. Before I was aware of it, I found myself apparently between my own regiment and the enemy, as I judged from seeing the paper which the Whigs wore in their hats, and the pine twigs the Tories wore in theirs, these being the badges of distinction.

"On the top of the mountain," Mr. Young adds, "in the thickest of the fight, I saw Colonel Williams fall, and a braver or a better man never died upon the field of battle. I had seen him but once before, that day—it was in the beginning of the action, as he charged by me at full speed around the mountain. Toward the summit a ball struck his horse under the jaw, when he commenced stamping as if he were in a nest of yellow jackets. Colonel Williams threw the reins over the animal's neck—sprang to the ground, and dashed onward. The moment I heard the cry that Colonel Williams was shot, I ran to his assistance, for I loved him as a father, he had ever been so kind to me, almost always carrying a cake in his pocket for me and his little son, Joseph. They carried him into a tent, and sprinkled some water in his face. As he revived, his first words were, 'For God's sake, boys, don't give up the hill!' I remember it as well as if it had occurred yesterday. I left him in the arms of his son Daniel, and returned to the field to avenge his fall." †

---

* Saye's *Memoir of McJunkin.*

† Narrative of Major Thomas Young, drawn up by Col. R. J. Gage, of Union County, S. C., and published in the *Orion* magazine, Oct. 1843.

In one of the charges on the enemy, Major Hammond, of Williams' corps, full of his usual dash and intrepidity, broke through the British lines with a small squad of brave followers, when the enemy attempted to intercept their return. Seeing his own and soldiers' perilous situation, Hammond instantly faced about, ordering his men to join him in cutting their way back, which, by dint of the most heroic efforts, they successfully effected. *

A singular incident occurred, which Major Hammond used to relate in connection with the contest. One of the men in his command had fought in many a battle, and had always proved himself true as steel. On the night preceding the action—in some snatch of sleep, perhaps, while on the march—he had a presentiment, that if he took part in the impending battle he would be killed. Before reaching King's Mountain, he concluded that he would, for once in his life, be justifiable, under the circumstances, in skulking from danger, and thereby, as he believed, preserve his life for future usefulness to his country. So he stole off, and hid himself. He was missed, when an orderly went in search of him, and finally discovered him in an out-of-the-way place, all covered up, head and body, with his blanket. Though taken to the front, he soon found means to absent himself again ; but his lurking place was again found, and he once more hurried to the front, just before the final attack. He evidently now made up his mind to do his duty, and let consequences take care of themselves ; and during the action he had posted himself behind a stump or tree, and evidently peering his head out to get a shot, received a fatal bullet in his forehead, killing him instantly. Subsequently learning the cause of his singular conduct in endeavoring to evade taking part in the contest, Major Hammond regretted that he had not known it at the time, so that he could have respected the soldier's conscientious convic-

* Obituary notice of Col. Samuel Hammond, September, 1842, written by his son-in-law, James H. R. Washington, corroborated by Mrs. Washington to the author, as related to her by her father.

tions ; but, at the moment, suspecting that he was under the cowardly influence of fear, the Major could not, and would not, tolerate anything of the kind in his command. *

And thus the battle waged with alternate advances and repulses, the columns of Campbell and Shelby having been two or three times driven down the mountain at the point of the bayonet—the last one almost a rout; but the brave mountaineers had learned from experience when to stop in their retreat, face about, and push back their assailants. In this last desperate repulse, some of the Whig riflemen were transfixed, while others fell head-long over the cliffs.†
When one column would drive the enemy back to their starting place, the next regiment would raise the battle-cry —" Come on, men, the enemy are retreating ;" and when the Provincials and Loyalists would make a dash upon this party of mountain men, and would, in turn, be chased back by them, then the other Whig riflemen, who had just before been driven down the hill, would now advance, returning the shout—" Come on, men, the enemy are retreating !" ‡
Thus, as one of Campbell's men expressed it—" When the enemy turned, we turned." § " Three times," says Mills' *Statistics*, " did the Britons charge with bayonet down the hill ; as often did the Americans retreat ; and the moment the Britons turned their backs, the Americans shot from behind every tree, and every rock, and laid them prostrate." It was the happy fruition of Shelby's perpetual battle cry— "Never shoot until you see an enemy, and never see an enemy, without bringing him down." ‖

By this time the two wings of the mountaineers were pressing the enemy on both sides of the mountain, so that Ferguson's men had ample employment all around the emi-

---

* Dr. A. L. Hammond's sketch of King's Mountain battle, in *Charleston Courier*, June 21, 1859.
† Hamilton's *Republic of the United States*, ii, 161.
‡ General Graham's narrative.
§ James Crow's statement.
‖ Niles' *National Register*, iv, 403.

nence, without being able to repair to each other's relief, however much they needed it. At length the Provincial Rangers and their fellow chargers, led by the intrepid De-Peyster, began to grow weary and discouraged—steadily decreasing in numbers, and making no permanent inroads upon their tireless opposers, who, when beaten down the mountain, did not choose to stay there simply to oblige their enemies. From the south-western portion of the ridge, the Rangers and Tories began to give way, and were doggedly driven by Campbell and Shelby, aided by some of Sevier's men, and perhaps others, intermingled with them.

Near the close of the action, Lieutenant-Colonel Hambright, while encouraging his men, received a shot through his thigh, making an ugly wound—the ball passing between the thigh bone and his saddle, cutting some arteries, and filling his boot with blood. Discovering that the Colonel was wounded, Samuel Moore, of York County, South Carolina, proposed to assist him from his horse, which he declined, assigning as a reason, that it would distract the attention of his men, and, as he did not feel sick nor faint, he preferred to remain with them as long as he could sustain himself in the saddle. Then pressing forward, he exclaimed in his broken German: " Huzza, my prave poys, fight on a few minutes more, and te battle will be over !" Hearing this encouraging shout, Ferguson, it is said, responded : "Huzza, brave boys, the day is our own !" * It was among the last of the British leader's utterances to animate his men in a hopeless struggle.

Dr. Ramsay, in his *History of Tennessee*, asserts that the Tories had begun to show flags in token of surrender, even before Ferguson was disabled, seeing which, he rode up, in two instances, and cut them down with his sword. It was

---

* MS correspondence of the venerable Abraham Hardin, who knew Colonel Hambright, and of Gill. Hambright, his descendant. Colonel Hambright, during the action, had his hat perforated with three bullet holes, and this memorial of the battle was long retained in the family. Though his wound was a serious one, he soon recovered ; but as some of the sinews of his thigh were cut, he ever after had a halt in his walk.

18

suggested to him by some of his officers, that it was useless
to prolong the contest, and throw their lives away. The
slaughter was great, the wounded were numerous, and
further resistance would be unavailing. But Ferguson's
proud heart could not think of surrendering; he despised
his enemies, and swore " he never would yield to such a
d—d banditti." Captain DePeyster, his second in command, having the courage of his convictions, and " convinced from the first of the utter futility of resistance at the
point selected, advised a surrender, as soon as he became
satisfied that Ferguson would not fall back upon the (supposed) rapidly advancing relief. He appears to have urged
the only course which could have saved the little army,
viz : a precipitate, but orderly, retreat upon less exposed
points, for the purpose of assisting the General-in-
Chief in his attempt to re-inforce the detachment—so important to future and ultimate success—by drawing back,
nearer to some point, which alone, re-inforcements could
reach, and where, alone, they could be made available.
This advice was founded on what the event proved : that
the British were about to be slaughtered to no purpose, like
' ducks in a coop,' without inflicting any commensurate loss.
The event proved the justice of this counsel." *

At length, satisfied that all was lost, and firmly resolving
not to fall into the hands of the despised "Back-Water men,"
Ferguson, with a few chosen friends, made a desperate attempt to break through the Whig lines, on the south-eastern side of the mountain, and escape. The intrepid British
leader made a bold dash for life and freedom, with his sword
in his left hand, cutting and slashing till he had broken it.
Colonel Shelby mentions the sword incident, and Benjamin
Sharp corroborates it ; while several others unite in testifying to the fact that he spurred his horse, and rushed out,
attempting to escape. †   Before the action commenced, it

---

* Gen. DePeyster, in *Historical Magazine*, March, 1869, 195.

† Shelby's narrative in *American Review* ; Shelby, as cited in Haywood's *Tennessee*,
71 ; Sharp's statement in *American Pioneer*, February, 1843; MS. account of King's

was well known that Ferguson wielded his sword in his left hand, and that he wore a light or checked duster or hunting-shirt for an outer garment, and the admonition had gone from soldier to soldier—" Look out for Ferguson with his sword in his left hand, wearing a light hunting-shirt !" *

One of Sevier's men, named Gilleland, who had received several wounds, and was well-nigh exhausted, seeing the advance of Ferguson and his party, attempted to arrest the career of the great leader, but his gun snapped ; when he called out to Robert Young, of the same regiment— " There's Ferguson—shoot him !" † " I'll try and see what Sweet-Lips can do," muttered Young, as he drew a sharp sight, discharging his rifle, when Ferguson fell from his horse, and his associates were either killed or driven back. Several rifle bullets had taken effect on Ferguson, apparently about the same time, and a number claimed the honor of having shot the fallen chief—among them, one Kusick, another of Sevier's sharp-shooters. ‡ Certain it is, that Ferguson received six or eight wounds, one of them through the head. He was unconscious when he fell, and did not long survive. It was in the region of Sevier's column that he received his fatal shots ; and not very far, it would seem, from where Colonel Shelby had posted Ensign Robert Campbell to watch the motions of the enemy so strongly ensconced behind the range of rocks.

Ensign Campbell gives us some further insight into Ferguson's attempt at flight. It was, as he represents, when

Mountain by an unknown member of Campbell's corps; Hon. Wm. C. Preston's *Defence of Colonel Campbell*, 1822; MS. correspondence of Ex-Governor David Campbell, and Dr. A. Q. Bradley ; conversations with Colonel Thomas H. Shelby. Mills, in his *Statistics of South Carolina*, asserts that "Ferguson attempted to force his way ;" and Wheeler's *North Carolina* declares that " he made a desperate move to break through the American lines." The *Political Magazine*, for February, 1781, states while " advancing to reconnoitre the enemy, who were retiring, he fell by a random shot."

* Statements of James and George W. Sevier ; Silas McBee, Colonel George Wilson. Colonel Thomas H. Shelby, and others. Mrs. Ellet, in her *Women of the Revolution*, iii, 293, speaks of the check-shirt disguise.

† Gilleland recovered from his wounds, and lived many years.

‡ Conversations with James and George W. Sevier, and Colonel George Wilson ; and MS. correspondence of Dr. J. G. M. Ramsey.

Colonels Campbell and Shelby were pressing the enemy from the south-western extremity of the mountain, and Ferguson's men were falling fast on every hand. He had sent DePeyster with the Provincial Rangers to strengthen the front; and in reaching the point assigned him, he had to pass through a blaze of riflery, losing many of his men in the effort. Ferguson's small cavalry corps, under Lieutenant Taylor—consisting of twenty men, made up from his Rangers—were ordered to mount, and press forward to aid DePeyster in his heroic purpose; but as fast as they mounted, they were mostly picked off by the Whig marksmen. Driven to desperation, Ferguson endeavored to make his escape, accompanied by two Loyalist Colonels, all mounted, who charged on that part of the line which they thought was most vulnerable—" in the quarter where Sevier's men were," as related by James Sevier, one of their number, and Benjamin Starritt, derived from his two brothers-in-law, who served in Sevier's regiment; and, as Ensign Campbell stated, " on that part of the line defended by his party." As soon as Ferguson reached the Whig front, he fell; and the other two officers, attempting to retreat, soon shared the same fate. One of these Tory officers killed was, doubtless, Colonel Vezey Husband, and the other—not a Colonel, as Ensign Campbell supposed— but Major Daniel Plummer.

Some accounts represent that Colonel Williams sought a personal encounter with Ferguson, determined to kill him, or die in the attempt. This is more romantic than probable. It could hardly have been so, since Ferguson was shot some distance from where Williams must have received his wounds, and on the opposite side of the hill; and the accounts pretty well agree, that Williams was wounded at the very close of the conflict, when the enemy had begun to exhibit their white flags, * while Ferguson was shot from

---

* Mills, in his *Statistics of South Carolina*, states, that Colonel Williams " had the good fortune to encounter personally in battle Colonel Ferguson, who attempted to force

his horse some little time before. The suggestion made by Colonel Hill, in his manuscript narrative, that Colonel Williams was shot by some of Lacey's men, who were inimical to him, and had sworn to take his life, is hardly credible; and, for the honor of humanity, we are constrained to discard so improbable and unpatriotic a supposition.

The last desperate grapple between Campbell's men— assisted by Shelby's—and the enemy, just before the close of the engagement, lasted twenty minutes*—and within

his way at this point. They both fell on the spot, being shot, it was supposed, by a ball from the British side—it was the last gun fired.''

Dr. Ramsay, the Tennessee historian, asserts that Colonel Williams "fell a victim to the true Palmetto spirit, and intemperate eagerness for battle. Toward the close of the engagement, he espied Ferguson riding near the line, and dashed toward him with the gallant determination of a personal encounter. 'I will kill Ferguson, or die in the attempt!' exclaimed Williams; and spurring his horse in the direction of the enemy, received a bullet as he crossed their line. He survived till he heard that his antagonist was killed, and his camp surrendered; and amidst the shouts of victory by his triumphant countrymen, said : 'I die contented ;' and with a smile on his countenance, expired."

The late Dr. A. L. Hammond, son of Major Hammond, in an article on King's Mountain battle, in the *Charleston Courier*, June 21, 1859, stated that "Williams' horse, wounded and snorting with foam and blood at every bound, dashed forward. Ferguson turned to receive him; their swords crossed—nothing more, for at that instant a deadly volley came from both sides, and the two combatants fell mortally wounded."

Ensign Robert Campbell states, that "Colonel Williams was shot through the body, near the close of the action, in making an attempt to charge on Ferguson; he lived long enough to hear of the surrender of the British army, when he said : 'I die contented, since we have gained the victory.' "

Dr. John H. Logan, the historian of the *Up-Country of South Carolina*, has preserved among the MS. traditions he gathered many years ago, this account of Colonel Williams death : Williams and Ferguson fell nearly at the same time, on the eastern side of the mountain. Williams, from a more favorable position than those occupied by Campbell and Hambright, saw the magic influence of Ferguson's whistle. Dashing to the front, his horse throwing bloody foam from his mouth that had been struck by a ball, he was heard to exclaim—"I'll silence that whistle or die in the attempt!" Quickly Ferguson was no more; and soon after, a ball from the enemy laid Williams mortally wounded on the hillside.

Still more romantic is Simms' statement in his *History of South Carolina :* "Tradition reports that Williams and Ferguson perished by each other's hands ; that, after Ferguson had fallen by the pistol of Williams, and lay wounded on the ground the latter approached and offered him mercy ; and that his answer was a fatal bullet from the pistol of the dying man !"

Much more probable is the statement of Dr. John Whelchel, of Williams' command, doubtless an eye-witness, and a man of much intelligence. In his pension declaration, he states that Colonel Williams received his fatal shot "immediately after the enemy had hoisted a flag to surrender." Lieutenant Joseph Hughes, of Brandon's men, makes a similar statement. The narrative of Thomas Young already cited, also tends to divest these romances of any claim to historic probability.

*"A British surgeon," says Lieutenant Newell, referring, doubtless, to Dr. Johnson, "stated that he held his watch, and that the storm lasted twenty minutes."

thirty or forty yards of each other; and was the most hotly contested part of the action. Campbell was on foot at the head of his regiment—so much advanced in front as to be in danger from the fire of his own men; and his courageous words were—"Boys, remember your liberty! Come on! come on! my brave fellows; another gun—another gun will do it! D—m them, we must have them out of this!" *   It was one incessant peal of fire-arms. The enemy made a firm stand; but after a while they were forced to retire some distance along the crest of the mountain, towards their camp at the north-eastern extremity, when they halted again for a few moments. The brave men of Campbell and Shelby were sensibly aided by the heroic bravery of the left wing under Cleveland, Lacey and Williams, who pressed, with shouts of victory, upon the Tories in that quarter, which tended to re-animate the Virginians and the Sullivan troops, who, with re-doubled fury, fought like tigers. They drove Ferguson's surviving Rangers and the Tories before them to where their wagons were, behind which they made a rally; but they were soon driven from this covert, down into a sunken or hollow place, by which time the Rangers were mostly killed or disabled, and the Loyalists quite demoralized. †

Campbell's column was two or three times driven down, or partly down the mountain; Shelby says he was three times repulsed—and Doctor Ferguson, in his *Memoir* of his kinsman, Colonel Ferguson, declares that the Provin-cials, with their bayonets "repulsed the enemy in three several attacks." One part of Cleveland's line was charged once in the flank, and another portion was twice driven before the bayonet; while Chronicle and Hambright's Lincoln men were once, at least, forced down the hill. Mc-Dowell's corps received a bayonet charge, as Thomas Ken-

---

Newell's and Sharp's statements.

† Statements of Lieutenant Newell, James Crow, and Henry Dickenson, of Campbell's regiment.

BATTLE OF KING'S MOUNTAIN—FERGUSON'S DEATH CHARGE.

nedy, one of the Captains, testifies. Sevier's column, save those intermingled with Campbell's men, was not charged during the action; nor was Williams' battalion;* nor is it known that Lacey's or Winston's columns suffered from these bayonet charges.

When the Provincials and Loyalists charged the Americans down the mountain, they seem to have reserved their fire till the termination of their pursuit; and having discharged their rifles, they retreated with great precision, reloading as they retraced their steps †—as they had learned very skillfully to do by the example and instructions of Ferguson; but while they were thus deliberately retiring, the sharp-sighted riflemen below them, taking deadly aim, would pick them off at every moment. Long experience proves, that marksmen in a valley have the advantage of those on a hill, in firing at each other, which is probably owing to the terrestrial refraction. ‡ The forest-hunters, though apprised of this fact, often shoot too high when their object is below them. Be this as it may, the English shot whistled over the heads of the Americans, rattling among the trees and cutting off twigs, while the bullets of the mountaineers produced dreadful effect—the British losses having been nearly three times that of their antagonists. Lieutenant Allaire states that the North Carolina Loyalists, seeing that they were surrounded, and numbers being without ammunition, were the first to give way, which naturally threw the rest of the Tories into confusion. § This may have been so, and yet the official report of Campbell and his associates be also true, that the greater part of the enemy's guns at the surrender were still charged.

As Robert Henry, of Hambright's and Chronicle's party,

---

*So James Sevier and Silas McBee, of those regiments, respectfully stated to the author.

† Communicated verbally, in July, 1842, by Samuel Handley, of Pontotoc County, Miss., as derived from his father, Captain Samuel Handley, Sr., who served in Sevier's regiment at King's Mountain.

‡ Mills' *Statistics*. 779.

§ Allaire's MS. Diary; and his newspaper narrative, also.

who had been transfixed by a Tory bayonet, was making his way at the very close of the engagement to Clarke's Branch to quench his thirst, he unexpectedly met Colonel Graham on his large black steed, accompanied by David Dickey, who, wielding his sword around his head, exclaimed —"D—m the Tories!" * He had heard the firing while on his way to his sick wife, and could not resist the impulse to return, and share in the battle. † Just before the final surrender of the enemy, when there was much intermingling of the mountaineers, Colonel Shelby had the hair on the left side of his head scorched off, which was noticed by Colonel Sevier, who met him at this moment—so narrowly did the heroic Shelby escape losing his life by Tory bullets.‡ With their men forced into a huddle near their tents and wagons, the surviving British officers could not form half a dozen of them together; and the demoralized Tories were being shot down like sheep at the slaughter.

The fall of Ferguson is represented by Lieutenant Allaire as having occurred " early in the action;" and Captain Ryerson, another of his corps officers, only states that DePeyster, after the loss of Ferguson, maintained his ground as long as it was possible to defend it. Tarleton states, that when Ferguson was shot, after nearly an hour's fighting, " his whole corps was thrown into total confusion ; no effort was made after this event, to resist the enemy's barbarity, or revenge the fall of their leader." In the *Memoir of General Samuel Graham*, a Captain under Lord Cornwallis—a work prepared from the General's manuscripts—it is stated, that after the fall of Ferguson, and many of his men, " the remainder, after a short resistance, were overpowered, and compelled to surrender." A

---

* Robert Henry's MS. narrative, appended to the statements of Vance and McDowell.

† That night, Colonel Graham's only child, Sarah, was born, who, when she grew to womanhood, became the wife of Abram Irvine, who was several years Sheriff of Rutherford County. The venerable Dr. O. B. Irvine, of Greenville, S. C., is one of several children of this marriage.

‡ Shelby s letter, August 12, and Colonel John Sevier's, August 27, 1812.

writer in the London *Political Magazine*, for February, 1781, asserts that when Ferguson fell, Captain DePeyster, the next in command, "immediately hoisted the white flag —that is, his white handkerchief; an officer close by him, enraged at such timidity, made a stroke at him with his sabre, and almost cut off his hand; nevertheless the surrender went on."

Allaire and Ryerson, his fellow officers, not only acquit DePeyster of the charge of timidity, but declare that his conduct was, in all "respects, proper;" and Captain Ryerson adds, that he "behaved like a brave good officer." Of course, the hand-cutting incident had no foundation. Ramsay, the South Carolina historian, states that "no chance of escape being left, and all prospect of successful resistance being at an end, the second in command sued for quarter." Gordon, in his *History*, and Mackenzie, in his *Strictures*, adopt this view of the matter: And Ensign Robert Campbell, of the Virginia regiment observes, that as soon as Ferguson fell, "Captain DePeyster raised a flag, and called for quarters; it was soon taken out of his hand by one of the officers on horseback, and raised so high that it could be seen by our line."

But there were other white flags or emblems displayed by the enemy, either with or without the sanction of De-Peyster. A man was mounted on horseback with a white handkerchief as a token of submission; but he was quickly shot down by the half-crazed Bowen, as already related; when another was mounted on the same horse, and set out for the display of the emblem of surrender, who soon shared the same fate, but a third met with better success— Major Evan Shelby received it, and, with others, proclaimed the surrender. By this time white handkerchiefs were also displayed in various quarters on guns and ramrods. "Our men," says Shelby, "who had been scattered in the battle, were continually coming up, and continued to fire, without comprehending, in the heat of the moment, what had happened." Many of the young men, it was said for their apology, knew not the meaning of a white flag under such circumstances; while others had become embittered, and were crying out—"Give them Buford's play!"*— no quarters, as Tarleton had, the preceding May, so savagely treated Colonel Buford and his party. "When the British," says Mills' *Statistics of South Carolina*, "found themselves pressed on all sides, they hung out white handkerchiefs upon guns and halberds. Few of the Americans understood the signal, and the few that did, chose not to know what it meant; so that, even after submission, the slaughter continued, until the Americans were weary of killing." This is a sad confession, but impartial truth demands that the record be faithful, though, in this case, there is reason to believe that the latter part of Mills' statement is somewhat exaggerated.

Among those still engaged in this work of death was young Joseph Sevier, who had heard that his father, Colonel Sevier, had been killed in the action—a false report, originating, probably, from the fact of the Colonel's brother, Captain Robert Sevier, having been fatally wounded; and the young soldier kept up firing upon the huddled Tories, until admonished to cease, when he excitedly cried out, with the tears chasing each other down his cheeks—"The d—d rascals have killed my father, and I'll keep loading and shooting till I·kill every son of a b—h of them." Colonel Sevier now riding up, his son discovered the mistake under which he had labored, and desisted. †

But the Whig leaders were active in their efforts to put a stop to the further firing of the patriots. The subdued Tories were everywhere crying "quarters!"—"quarters!" "D—m you," exclaimed Shelby, "if you want quarters, throw down your arms!" ‡ Benjamin Sharp, of Camp-

---

* Shelby's narrative, 1823 ; General Graham's statement ; certificate of John Long, of Shelby's men.

† Statement of Colonel George W. Sevier.

‡ Certificate of John Sharp, of Shelby's regiment, 1823.

bell's regiment, who witnessed this scene, thus describes it:
" At the close of the action, when the British were loudly
calling for quarters, but uncertain whether they would be
granted, I saw the intrepid Shelby rush his horse within
fifteen paces of their lines, and command them to lay down
their arms, and they should have quarters. Some would
call this an imprudent act; but it showed the daring bravery
of the man." *

Andrew Evins, a member of Captain William Edmondson's company, of the Virginia regiment, was, with others,
still firing on the demoralized Tories, when Colonel Campbell came running up, and knocked up the soldier's gun,
exclaiming—" Evins, for God's sake, don't shoot! It is
murder to kill them now, for they have raised the flag!"†
Campbell, as he rushed along, repeated the order—" Cease
firing!—for God's sake, cease firing!"‡ Thus was Colonel
Campbell mercifully engaged in saving the discomfited
Loyalists from further effusion of blood—no officer could
have acted more tender or humane; and he passed on
around the prisoners, on foot, still seeking to promote their
safety and protection.

Captain DePeyster, who had succeeded Ferguson in
the command, sitting on his grey horse, expostulated with
Colonel Campbell, referring to the firing on his flag—" Colonel Campbell, it was d—d unfair," and then repeated it;
but Campbell, probably thinking it no time to bandy words
with the British leader, simply ordered him to dismount;
and called out, " officers, rank by yourselves; prisoners,
take off your hats, and sit down." § The enemy at this
time had been driven into a group of sixty yards in length,
and less than forty in width. ‖ The mountaineers were
ordered to close up in surrounding the prisoners, first

---

* *American Pioneer*, February, 1843, 69.
† Evins' statement, 1823.
‡ Letter of General George Rutledge, May 27th, 1813.
§ James Crow's statement, May 6, 1813.
‖ General Graham's narrative.

in one continuous circle, then double guards, and finally four deep. * Colonel Campbell then proposed to his troops three *huzzas for Liberty*, which were given in hearty acclaim, making the welkin ring, and the hills resound, with their shouts of victory.†

An occurrence now transpired, that, for a few moments, changed the whole scene in that quarter; and threatened, for a brief period, the most tragic consequences. It is known, as a British account relates it, that " a small party of the Loyal militia returning from foraging, unacquainted with the surrender, happening to fire on the Rebels, the prisoners were immediately threatened with death, if the firing should be repeated."‡ Whether it was the volley from this party, who probably scampered off; or whether from some of the Tories in the general huddle, exasperated perhaps that proper respect was not instantly paid to their flag, now fired upon, and mortally wounded Colonel Williams, who was riding towards the British encampment; and, wheeling back, said to William Moore, one of Campbell's regiment—" I'm a gone man !" §

Colonel Campbell was close at hand when this unhappy event transpired; and doubtless reasoned, that if the fatal firing proceeded from an outside party, it was the precursor of Tarleton's expected relief; if from the surrendered Tories, at least some considerable portion of them were inclined to spring a trap on the Whigs, shoot down their leaders, and make a bold attempt to escape, when the patriots were measurably off their guard, and least prepared for it; and acting on the spur of the moment, he resolved on stern military tactics to quell the intended mutiny, by instantly

---

* Captain Christopher Taylor's statement : conversations with John Spelts.
† Statements of John Craig; MS. narrative of Robert Henry.
‡ *South Carolina Gazette,* December 20, 1780; and *Scot's Magazine,* January, 1781. The editor of the *Gazette* evidently derived his statement from Lieutenant Allaire, of Ferguson's Rangers, judging from a comparison of the details there given, with a more elaborate narrative in Rivington's *Royal Gazette,* New York, February 24, 1781, which General J. Watts DePeyster attributes, from internal evidence, to that officer, and which Lieutenant Allaire's MS. *Diary* fully corroborates.
§ Statement of William Moore.

ordering the men near him—the men of Williams and Brandon's command—to fire upon the enemy. The order was quickly obeyed by the soldiers who had been so treacherously deprived of their intrepid leader ; " and," said Lieutenant Joseph Hughes, one of Brandon's party, " we killed near a hundred of them." But the probabilities are, that those who fired, and those who suffered from it, were not very numerous. It was, however, a sad affair ; and in the confusion of the moment, its origin and its immediate effects were probably little understood by either party ; and doubtless Colonel Campbell himself deeply regretted the order he had given to fire upon an unresisting foe. *

---

* These particulars may be somewhat erroneous and exaggerated ; but there must be a basis of truth in them. It is due to the high reputation that Colonel Hughes sustained in his day, to accord candor and good intentions to his statements generally. In his pension application, in 1833, he briefly states : " Was at King's Mountain, where General Williams was mortally wounded, after the British had raised their flag to surrender, by a fire from some Tories. Colonel Campbell then ordered a fire on the Tories, and we killed near a hundred of them after the surrender of the British, and could hardly be restrained from killing the whole of them."

That Colonel Hughes' statements are worthy of respect, a brief reference to some of the more salient points of his Revolutionary services, and the good character he bore during the war, and for more than half a century thereafter, are only necessary to be cited. He was born in what is now Chester County, South Carolina, in 1761, his parents having retired there temporarily from the present region of Union County, on account of Indian troubles. He served, in 1776, on Williamson's Cherokee expedition, and subsequently in Georgia. Governor Rutledge, early in 1780. commissioned him a Lieutenant, and he fought under Sumter at Rocky Mount and Hanging Rock ; and then shared in the heroic action at Musgrove's Mill. His dare-devil character, and adventurous services, in the up-country region of South Carolina, during the summer and autumn of 1780, have already been related. In one of these Tory encounters, Hughes had a lock of hair cut from his head, Captain Samuel Otterson a slight wound on his chin, while a third person received a cut across his cheek—all from the same shot.

Then we find him taking part, in the memorable engagements at King's Mountain, Hammond's Store. and Cowpens. Though yet a Lieutenant, he commanded his company in this latter action. He was not only a man of great personal strength, but of remarkable fleetness on foot. As his men, with others, broke at the Cowpens, and fled before Tarleton's cavalry ; and though receiving a sabre cut across his right hand, yet with his drawn sword, he would out-run his men, and passing them. face about, and command them to stand, striking right and left to enforce obedience to orders ; often repeating with a loud voice : " You d—d cowards. halt and fight—there is more danger in running than in fighting, and if you don't stop and fight, you will all be killed !" But most of them were for awhile too demoralized to realize the situation, or obey the commands of their officers. As they would scamper off, Hughes would renewedly pursue, and once more gaining their front, would repeat his tactics to bring them to their duty. At length the company was induced to make a stand. on the brow of a slope, some distance from the battle-line, behind a clump of young pines that partially concealed and protected them from Tarleton's cavalry. Others now joined them for self-protection. Their guns were quickly loaded,

The firing upon the British and Tories was at length suppressed. Colonel Shelby, fearing that the enemy might yet, perhaps, feel constrained, in self-defence, to resume their arms, and which they could with such facility snatch up as they lay before them, exclaimed : " Good God ! what can we do in this confusion ? " " We can order the prisoners from their arms " said Captain Sawyers. " Yes," responded Shelby, "that can be done"; and the prisoners were accordingly forthwith marched to another place, with a strong guard placed around them. *

The surviving British leaders were prompt to surrender their swords to the first American officer that came near them. Ferguson's sword was picked up on the ground ; and, according to one account, it passed into Colonel Cleveland's possession ; but with more probability, according to others, it fell into the hands of Colonel Sevier. Captain DePeyster delivered his sword, as some assert, to Colonel Campbell; while others declare it was to Major Evan Shelby. Captain Ryerson, who was wounded, tendered his sword to Lieutenant Andrew Kincannon, of

---

and they were themselves again. Morgan galloped up and spoke words of encouragement to them. The next moment the British cavalry were at them; but the Whigs reserved their fire till the enemy were so near, that it was terribly effective, emptying many a British saddle, when the survivors recoiled. Now Colonel Washington gave them a charge—the battle was restored, when Howard and his Marylanders with the bayonet swept the field. Such is the account related by Christopher Brandon to Daniel Wallace. Tarleton acknowledges, that " an unexpected fire from the Americans, who came about as they were retreating, stopped the British, and threw them into confusion," when a panic ensued, and then a general flight. It was a high and worthy compliment from his old commander, Colonel Brandon, who declared, that, at the Cowpens, " *Hughes saved the fate of the day.*"

As a deserved recognition of these meritorious services, he was promoted to a Captaincy early in 1781, when he was scarcely twenty years of age ; and led his company with characteristic valor, at the battle of Eutaw Springs. The Tories had killed his father during the war, and many a dear friend, and his animosity against the whole race was alike bitter and unrelenting. In 1825, he removed to Alabama, first to Green County, and then to Pickens, where he died, in September, 1834, in his seventy-fourth year. For more than twenty of the closing years of his life, he was an elder in the Presbyterian church ; and the rough, and almost tiger-like partisan, became as humble and submissive as a lamb. He rose to the rank of Colonel in the militia. He was tall and commanding in his appearance, jovial and affable in conversation ; yet his early military training rendered him, to the last, stern and rigid in discipline. In all that makes up the man, he was a noble specimen of the Revolutionary hero.

* Ramsey's *Tennessee*, 239 ; MS. correspondence of Dr. Ramsey.

Campbell's regiment, who was, at that moment, endeavoring to check the firing on the surrendered Tories; but not regarding himself as the proper officer to receive this tender of submission, the Lieutenant, without due reflection, courteously invited the British Captain to be seated; who looking around, and seeing no seat, promptly squatted himself upon the ground, Kincannon entering into conversation with him. Adjutant Franklin, of Cleveland's regiment, now coming up, received Ryerson's sword, the latter remarking: " You deserve it, sir !" * Colonel Campbell was stalking around among the enemy in his shirt sleeves, and his collar open, and when some of the Americans pointed him out as their commander, the British, at first, from his unmilitary plight, seemed to doubt it, but a number of officers now surrendered their swords to him, until he had several in his hands, and under his arm.†

It is proper to advert briefly to Ferguson's conduct in the battle. It was that of a hero. He did all that mortal man could have done, under the circumstances, to avert the impending catastrophe. He was almost ubiquitous—his voice, his presence, and his whistle everywhere animated his men, either to renew their bayonet charges, or maintain a firm stand against the steadily encroaching mountaineers. But he trusted too much to the bayonet against an enemy as nimble as the antelope. ‡ " He had," says Doctor Ferguson, " two horses killed under him, while he remained untouched himself; but he afterwards received a number of wounds, of which, it is said, any one was mortal, and dropping from his horse, expired, while his foot yet hung in the stirrup." §
This, if we may credit Lee's *Memoirs of the War in the*

---

* Judge J. F. Graves' sketch of his grandfather, Jesse Franklin, in the second series of Caruthers' *Incidents in the Old North State*, pp. 203-4; MS. statement of Elijah Callaway; MS. correspondence of Dr. A. N. Kincannon, of Missouri, and John L. Worth, of Mt. Airy, N. C.

† Lieutenant William Russell, James Snodgrass, James Keys, David Campbell, Henry Dickenson, and David Beattie, of Campbell's regiment, and William King, and George Rutledge, of Shelby's men.

‡ Johnson's *Greene*, i, 306.

§ *Memoir of Colonel Ferguson*, 33.

South, and Burk's *History of Virginia*, happened after fifty minutes' fighting; or some ten or fifteen minutes before the final close of the action; and about three minutes before the flag was displayed for surrender, according to Thomas Maxwell, one of Shelby's men.

As long as Ferguson lived, his unyielding spirit scorned to surrender. He persevered until he received his mortal wounds. His fall very naturally disheartened his followers. For some time before that fatal event, there was really nothing to encourage them, save the faintest hope which they vainly cherished of momentary relief from Tarleton. Animated by the brave example of their heroic leader, and still confiding in his fruitful military resources, they had maintained the unequal contest under all disadvantages. Losing his inspiration, they lost all—with him perished the last hope of success. *

Colonel Ferguson not only made a sad mistake in delaying a single moment at King's mountain with a view to a passage at arms with his pursuers; but he committed, if possible, a still more grievous error in the supposed strength of his position. " His encampment," says the South Carolina historian, Ramsay, " on the top of the mountain was not well chosen, as it gave the Americans an opportunity of covering themselves in their approaches. Had he pursued his march on charging and driving the first party of the militia which gave way, he might have got off with the most of his men; but his unconquerable spirit disdained either to flee or to surrender." The historian, Gordon, takes the same view: "Major Ferguson was overseen in making his stand on the mountain, which, being much covered with woods, gave the militia, who were all riflemen, the opportunity of approaching near, with greater safety to themselves than if they had been upon plain, open ground. The Major, however, might have made good his retreat, if not with the whole, at least with a great part of his men, had he pursued

---

* Stedman's *American War*, ii, 223.

his march immediately upon his charging and driving the first detachment; for though the militia acted with spirit for undisciplined troops, it was with difficulty that they could he prevailed upon to renew their attack, after being charged with the bayonet. They kept aloof, and continued popping; then gathered round, and crept nearer, till, at length, they leveled the Major with one of their shots."

General Simon Bernard, one of the most distinguished engineers, and aids-de-camp of the great Napoleon, and subsequently in the United States engineer service, on examining the battle-ground of King's Mountain, said: " The Americans, by their victory in that engagement, erected a monument to perpetuate the brave men who had fallen there; and the shape of the hill itself would be an eternal monument of the military genius and skill of Colonel Ferguson, in selecting a position so well adapted for defence; and that no other plan of assault but that pursued by the mountain-men, could have succeeded against him." *

One of our best historical critics, General DePeyster, observes: " Ferguson set an inordinate value on the position which he had selected, which, however strong against a regular attack, was not defensible against the attacks which were about to be directed upon it. How grievously he erred as to the intrinsic availability of King's Mountain as a military position, was evinced by his remark that ' all the Rebels from h—l could not drive him from it.' It is true, he was not driven from it; but its bald, rocky summit merely served, like the sacrificial stone of the Aztecs, for the immolation of the victims." †

The historian, Lossing, who visited the battle-field thirty odd years ago, justly observes: " It was a strange place for an encampment or a battle, and to one acquainted with the region, it is difficult to understand why Ferguson and his band were there at all." ‡

---

* Ramsey's *History of Tennessee*, 239.
† *Historical Magazine*, March, 1869, 194.
‡ *Pictorial Field Book of the Revolution*, ii, 423.
19

It is useless to speculate on what might have changed the fate of the day; yet a few suggestions may not be out of place in this connection. Trivial circumstances, on critical occasions, not unfrequently produce the most momentous consequences. Had Tarleton, for instance, suddenly made his appearance before or during the battle—had the detachment at Gibbs' plantation, near the Cowpens, or Moore's foraging party, vigorously attacked the mountaineers in the rear, during the progress of the engagement, and especially during the confusion consequent upon the repulses of Campbell's and Shelby's columns; or had Ferguson chosen suitable ground on the plains, and in the woods, where his men could have availed themselves of shelter for their protection, and fought on an equality with their antagonists, the result might have been very different, and Ferguson have been the hero of the hour—and, it may be, the fate of American Independence sealed. But in God's good Providence, such a fatal blow was not in store for the suffering patriots.

Most of the accounts represent that the British Colonel was killed out-right. He is said to have received six or eight bullet holes in his body—one penetrating his thigh, another re-shattering his right arm just above the elbow; and yet he continued to raise his sword in his left hand,* till a rifle ball piercing his head, put an end to further fighting or consciousness.† In falling from his horse, or while

---

* MS. statement of Elijah Callaway, in 1842.

† Ramsay, Gordon, Smith, in his *American War*, Moultrie, Judge James, Mills and Foote are among the American writers, who unite in declaring that Ferguson "received a mortal wound." Stedman, Mackenzie, and Lamb, British writers, all of whom were connected with the British service at the time, make the same assertion. The *Columbian Magazine*, 1792, p. 323, states also that he received a mortal wound. Dr. John Whelchel, of Williams' men, asserts in his pension statement, that Ferguson "fell mortally wounded;" and William White, of Lacey's regiment, in his pension application, says "he was mortally wounded, and died a short time afterwards."

The place where Ferguson fell is indicated on the diagram of the battle-field, near the brow of the south-eastern portion of the mountain, opposite to McDowell's column, but probably where Sevier's men had advanced at the close of the conflict. when the enemy had been forced to that quarter. That locality was pointed out, fully fifty years ago, by William Logan, a survivor of the battle, to his grandson, the present Col. J. R. Logan, and in which, Arthur Patterson, a cotemporary of the Revolution, and familiar with King's Mountain all his life, coincided.

being conveyed to the rear, a silver whistle dropped from his vest pocket, which was picked up by one of his soldiers, Elias Powell, who preserved it many years ; * and Powell, and three others, as John Spelts relates, were seen, at the close of the surrender, bearing off, in a blanket, their fallen chief to a spring near the mountain's brow, on the southern side of the elevation ; and there gently bolstered him up with rocks and blankets. One of the Tories, who had just grounded his gun, taking in the situation, and true to his plundering instincts, ran up, and was in the act of thrusting his hand into the dying man's pockets, when the unfeeling intruder was repelled by one of the attendants, who, rudely pushing him away, exclaimed with a sarcastic oath—" Are you going to rob the dead? " † A little after, Colonel Shelby rode up, and thinking perhaps that Ferguson might yet be sensible of what was said to him—though he evidently was not—exclaimed : " Colonel, the fatal blow is struck—we've Burgoyned you? " ‡ The life of this restless British leader soon ebbed away. Some of the more thoughtless of the Whig soldiery, it is said, committed an act which we would fain be excused from the pain of recording. " The mountaineers, it is reported, used every insult and indignity, after the action, towards the dead body of Major Ferguson." §

So curious were the Whigs to see the fallen British chief, that many repaired to the spot to view his body as it lay in its gore and glory. Lieutenant Samuel Johnson, of Cleveland's regiment, who had been severely disabled in the action, desired to be carried there, that he, too, might

---

* Powell was one of the young men induced to enlist under Ferguson's banner, and became much attached to his commander. He was taken prisoner to Hillsboro, where he was paroled. and returned to his widowed mother, who lived at what is known as Powellton, two miles east of Lenoir, Caldwell County, on the western frontier of North Carolina. There he lived until his death, May 5th, 1832. The silver whistle then went to one of his decendants, who removed West, and having since died, the relic has been lost sight of. John Spelts related, that Ferguson had a yet larger silver whistle, a foot in length, which fell into the hands of Colonel Shelby.

† Statement of Spelts.

‡ Related by Spelts and Thomas H. Shelby, a son of the Colonel.

§ Tarleton's *Campaigns*, 165.

look upon the dying or lifeless leader of the enemy whom he
had so valiantly fought; when Colonel Cleveland, and two
of the soldiers, bore the wounded Lieutenant to the place
of pilgrimage;* and even the transfixed Robert Henry, amid
his pains and sufferings, could not repress his curiosity to
take a look at Ferguson. It was probably where he was
conveyed, and breathed his last, that he was buried—on
the south-eastern declivity of the mountain, where his mortal
remains, wrapped, not in a military cloak, or hero's coffin,
but in a raw beef's hide,† found a peaceful sepulture.

The tradition in that region has been rife for more than
fifty years, that Ferguson had two mistresses with him, perhaps nominally cooks—both fine looking young women.
One of them, known as Virginia Sal, a red haired lady, it is
related, was the first to fall in the battle, and was buried in
the same grave with Ferguson, as some assert; or, as others
have it, beside the British and Tory slain; while the other,
Virginia Paul, survived the action; and after it was over,
was seen to ride around the camp as unconcerned as though
nothing of unusual moment had happened. She was conveyed with the prisoners at least as far as Burke Court
House, now Morganton, North Carolina, and subsequently
sent to Lord Cornwallis' army.‡

That almost envenomed hate which the mountaineers
cherished towards Ferguson and his Tory followers, nerved
them to marvellous endurance while engaged in the battle.
They had eaten little or nothing since they left the Cowpens
some eighteen hours before—much of the time in the rain,
protecting their rifles and ammunition by divesting themselves of their blankets or portions of their clothing; and they
had been, since leaving Green river, for over forty hours,
without rest or repose. "I had no shoes," said Thomas
Young, "and of course fought in the battle barefoot, and,

* Statement of Lewis Johnson, a son of the Lieutenant.
† MS. letter of Dr. W. J. T. Miller, July 30, 1880.
‡ MSS. of Dr. John H. Logan; MS. letters of James J. Hampton, Dr. C. L. Hunter,
Colonel J. R. Logan, and Dr. W. J. T. Miller.

when it was over, my feet were much lacerated and bleeding." * Others, too, must have suffered from the flinty rocks
over which they hurriedly passed and re-passed during the
engagement. As an instance of the all-absorbing effect of
the excitements surrounding them, when the next morning
the mountaineers were directed to discharge their guns, " I
fired my large old musket," said Young, " charged in time
of the battle with two musket balls, as I had done every time
during the engagement; and the recoil, in this case, was
dreadful, but I had not noticed it in the action." †

Taking it for granted that the Loyalist force under
Ferguson at King's Mountain was eight hundred, it may
be interesting to state what little is known of the respective
numbers from the two Carolinas. In Lieutenant Allaire's
newspaper narrative, he refers to the North Carolina regiment, commanded by Colonel Ambrose Mills, as numbering " about three hundred men." A Loyalist writer in the
London *Political Magazine*, for April, 1783, who apparently once resided in the western part of North Carolina,
asserts that the Loyalists of the Salisbury district—which
embraced all the western portion of the North Province—
who were with Ferguson, numbered four hundred and
eighty. Deducting the absent foraging party under Colonel
Moore, who was a North Carolinian, and whose detachment
may be presumed to have been made up of men from that
Province, we shall have about the number mentioned by
Allaire remaining. This would suggest that about three
hundred and twenty was the strength of the South Carolina
Loyalists.

As the North Carolina Tories were the first to give way,
according to Allaire, and precipitate the defeat that followed,
it only goes to prove that they were the hardest pressed by
Campbell and Shelby, which is quite probable ; or, that the
South Carolinians had been longest drilled for the service,

---

* Rev. James H. Saye's MS. conversations with Thomas Young, of Union County,
South Carolina, March 27, 1843.

† Saye's MSS.

and were consequently best prepared to maintain their ground. It is not a little singular, that so few of the prominent Loyalist leaders, of the Ninety Six district, were present with Ferguson—only Colonel Vesey Husband, of whom we have no knowledge, and who, we suppose, was in some way associated with the South Carolina Tories, together with Majors Lee and Plummer. Where were the other Loyalist leaders of that region—Colonels Cunningham, Kirkland, and Clary, Lieutenant-Colonels Philips and Turner, and Majors Gibbs, Hill, and Hamilton? Some were doubtless with the party whom the Whigs had passed at Major Gibbs' plantation, near the Cowpens, or possibly with Colonel Moore's detachment; others were scattered here and there on furlough; but they were not at King's Mountain, when sorely needed, with all the strength they could have brought to the indefatigable Ferguson. That freebooter, Fanning, with his Tory foragers, who were beating about the country, fell in with Ferguson five days before his defeat;* but preferring their independent bushwhacking service, they escaped the King's Mountain disaster.

Paine, in his *American Crisis*, berated the Loyalists as wanting in manhood and bravery, declaring: " I should not be afraid to go with an hundred Whigs against a thousand Tories. Every Tory is a coward, for a servile, slavish, self-interested fear is the foundation of Toryism; and a man under such influence, though he may be cruel, can never be brave." Yet, it must be confessed, that the Loyalists evinced no little pluck and bravery at King's Mountain. But they had been specially fitted for the service, and under the eye of a superior drill-master, as few Americans had been in either army; and it had been justly said, that, on this occasion, they fought with halters around their necks; and they, too, were expert riflemen.

The British Southern leaders were not only surprised

---

* Fanning's Narrative, 13.

and amazed beyond measure, but were filled with alarm at
the unexpected appearance of so formidable a force—
largely exaggerated as it was—from border settlements
of which they had not so much as heard of their existence.
Lord Rawdon, in his letter of October twenty-fourth, 1780,
referring to Ferguson's miscarriage, and the men who
confronted and defeated him, says: "A numerous army
now appeared on the frontier, drawn from Nolachucky,
and other settlements beyond the mountains, whose very
names had been unknown to us;" and Mackenzie, one
of Tarleton's officers, probably mistaking Nolachucky, in
what is now East Tennessee, for Kentucky, states in his
Strictures: "The wild and fierce inhabitants of Kentucky,
and other settlements westward of the Alleghany mountains, under Colonels Campbell and Boone," then naming
the other leaders, "assembled suddenly and silently;" and
adding, that these mountaineers "advanced with the intention to seize upon a quantity of Indian presents, which they
understood were but slightly guarded at Augusta, and which
were, about that time, to have been distributed among a
body of Creek and Cherokee Indians assembled at that
place."

This erroneous statement of Mackenzie's has been
adopted by Stedman in his *History of the American War*,
and by Dr. Ferguson, in his *Memoir of Colonel Ferguson.*
So critical a student of American history as Gen. J. W.
DePeyster, has fallen into the error, that the "dark and
bloody ground" of Kentucky contributed her quota of
fighting men for King's Mountain battle.* But none of the
King's Mountain men came from that region, though many
of them subsequently became permanent settlers there; and
so far from Colonel Boone having participated in the campaign, he was hundreds of miles away, in his beloved
Kentucky. The day before King's Mountain battle, while
he and his brother, Edward Boone, were out buffalo hunting,

---

* *Historical Magazine*, March, 1869. p. 190.

the latter was shot dead by a party of Indians, concealed in a cane-brake, some fifteen or twenty miles from Boonesboro, and the former made good his escape to that settlement; and, the day of the contest on King's Mountain, he was with a party in pursuit of the Indians who had killed his brother. Nor is it in any sense true, that the plunder of Indian goods at Augusta was their object—all the facts go to disprove any such intention. This, however, seems to have been one of the motives held out by Colonel Clarke to his men in his attack on Augusta, as stated by Lee in his *Memoirs*.

There is no great discrepancy among the different authorities as to the length of time occupied by the engagement—if we discard, as we must, Mills' inordinate mistake, that "the battle began between eight and nine o'clock in the morning, and lasted till night." A writer in the *Virginia Argus*, of December eleventh, 1805, evidently a survivor of Campbell's men, says, "in forty-two minutes we made them beg for quarters," referring, doubtless, to the time of Ferguson's fall, and the running up of the white flag. General Davidson, in his letter to General Sumner, states, three days after the action, on the authority of Major Tate, of Lacey's corps, who was in the engagement, that it lasted "forty-seven minutes." Lee, in his *History of the Southern Campaigns*, who was subsequently associated in service with Campbell, declares that after "the battle had raged for fifty minutes," Ferguson was shot, when the fire of the enemy slackened, and their surrender followed. Burk, in his *History of Virginia*, makes the same statement. This fixes the time, as nearly as we can ascertain it, when Ferguson fell. There would seem to have been but little resistance on the part of the enemy after the loss of their commander; it could have been prolonged a few minutes only at most. Both Tarleton and Stedman, British authorities, state that the action lasted " near an hour."

In Colonel Shelby's letter to his father, written October twelfth, 1780, he says: " the battle continued warm for an hour;" and he wrote the same day to Colonel Arthur Campbell, that " the firing was kept up with fury, on both sides, for near an hour." But Campbell, Shelby, and Cleveland, in their official account, assert that " a flag was hoisted by Captain DePeyster, their commanding officer— Major Ferguson having been killed a little while before; " that " the engagement lasted an hour and five minutes." The British Captain Ryerson who shared in the contest, states in his account in Rivingston's New York *Royal Gazette*, of March twenty-first, 1781, that " the action lasted an hour and five minutes, very hot indeed; " and Lieutenant Allaire, another British contestant, says, in his newspaper narrative, that " the action was severe for upwards of an hour; " and, in his MS. *Diary*, he is more explicit, stating that it lasted " an hour and five minutes." The probabilities are that Doctor Johnson, who timed by his watch the last desperate attack of Campbell's and Shelby's corps, also noted the duration of the battle, from its commencement to the final suppression of the firing on the Tories; and that Campbell and his associates derived from him their knowledge of the length of the engagement, and which may be regarded as correct.

The exact strength and losses of the British at King's Mountain can only be approximately determined. Ferguson's Rangers may be set down at one hundred—though they may have somewhat exceeded that figure. The general estimate is, in round numbers, one thousand militia or Loyalists, which would make a total of eleven hundred; or, perhaps eleven hundred and twenty-five, as the American official report has it, founded on the provision returns of that day. In General Lenoir's account it is stated, that " not a single man of them escaped that was in camp at the commencement of the battle." This is probably true, and goes to show that the party of foragers who returned at the close of the battle and fired on the Americans, mortally wounding Colonel Williams, had left previously without coming under this category. It is pretty evident that a detachment left camp that morning—doubtless on a foraging expedition; and this returning party were probably a portion of the number. Gordon, in his *American War*, usually good authority, says four hundred and forty escaped; and Haywood's *Tennessee* gives the same statement, evidently copied from Gordon; while Mills' *Statistics of South Carolina* gives the number as three hundred. Judge Johnson, in his *Life of General Greene*, says two hundred escaped; and this accords with the statement of Alexander Greer, one of Sevier's men, who adds that they were under Colonel Moore,* perhaps the Tory commander at Ram-

---

* Whether Colonel John or Patrick Moore is the one referred to, is not certain—probably the former, as Colonel Ferguson seemed not to have formed a good opinion of the conduct of Patrick Moore in failing to defend Thicketty Fort the preceding July. Moses Moore, the father of Colonel John Moore, was a native of Carlisle, England, whence he migrated to Virginia in 1745, marrying a Miss Winston, near Jamestown, in that Province; and in 1753, settling in what is now Gaston County, North Carolina, eight miles west of Lincolnton. Here John Moore was born; and being a frontier country, when old enough he was sent to Granville County, in that Province, for his education. When the Revolution broke out, he became a zealous Loyalist; and led a party of Tories from Tryon County, in February, 1779, to Georgia, and uniting with Colonel Boyd on the way, they were defeated by Colonel Pickens at Kettle Creek. Boyd was mortally wounded, and Moore escaped to the British army in that quarter; and is said to have participated in the defence of Savannah. In December following, he was in the service near Moseley's Ferry, on the Ogeechee.

He subsequently returned to North Carolina, a Lieutenant-Colonel in Hamilton's corps of Loyalists, and prematurely embodied a Tory force, near Camp Branch, about half a mile west of his father's residence; thence marched about six miles north to Tory Branch, and thence to Ramsour's Mill, on the South Fork, where he was disastrously defeated, June 20th, 1780, escaping with thirty others to Camden. His regiment, the Royal North Carolinians, participated in Gates' defeat, losing three killed and fourteen wounded—among the latter, Colonel Hamilton. It is doubtful if Moore participated in the action, as he was about that time under suspension, threatened with a court martial for disobedience of orders in raising the Loyalists at Ramsour's before the time appointed by Lord Cornwallis; but it was at length deemed impolitic to bring him to trial. Escaping from King's Mountain, we next find him with Captain Waters, and a body of Tories, defeated by Colonel Washington at Hammond's Store, South Carolina, December 28th, 1780. Though a family tradition coming down from a sister to her grandson, John H. Roberts, of Gaston County, represents that Moore went to Carlisle, England, and was lost track of; yet the better opinion is founded on a statement by a North Carolina Loyalist, published in the *Political Magazine*, London, April, 1783, that he was taken prisoner by Colonel Wade Hampton, near the Wateree, and hanged. He left no family.

A few words about Colonel Patrick Moore may not be inappropriate in this connection. He was of Irish descent, and a native of Virginia. He early settled on Thicketty creek in the north-western part of South Carolina, where he commanded Fort Anderson or Thicketty Fort, which he surrendered, without firing a gun, to Colonel Shelby and associates. He was subsequently captured by a party of Americans, according to the tradition in his family, near Ninety Six, and was supposed to have been killed by his captors, as his remains were afterwards found, and recognized by his great height—six feet and seven inches. His death probably occurred in 1781. He left a widow, who survived many years, a son and three daughters; and his descendants in South Carolina and Georgia are very worthy people.

sour's Mill. Joseph Kerr, one of Williams' men, after enumerating the killed and prisoners of the enemy, adds—" the balance escaped." General Alexander Smythe, who lived on the Holston, said in a speech in Congress, in 1829, " only twenty-one escaped "—referring, perhaps, to that party of foragers who mortally wounded Colonel Williams. Andrews, in his *History of the War*, says "very few escaped;" and Tarleton mentions about picking up some of the fugitives.

We may conclude that Moore's foraging detachment numbered about two hundred; which would have left about nine hundred altogether under Ferguson with whom to fight the battle. The British Lieutenant Allaire says, the Loyalists consisted of eight hundred, and Ferguson's corps of one hundred,* which tallies pretty well with Tarleton's account in his *Southern Campaigns*, of about one thousand Loyal militia, supposing that two hundred of them were on detached service at the time of the battle; and it agrees also with Lord Rawdon's statement, made towards the close of October, that Ferguson had " about eight hundred militia " in the engagement—to this, of course, should be added his one hundred Provincial Rangers. Allaire, and other British writers, assuming as true that the exaggerated account of the entire Whig strength, including those in the rear, was well-nigh three thousand, assign as a reason of their overwhelming defeat, the great superiority of their antagonists—three to one, as they assert, against them. In point of fact, the numbers of the opposing forces were about equal; and it was their persistency, their pluck, and excelling in the use of the rifle, that gave the mountaineers the victory.

Both in Allaire's New York *Gazette* and MS. *Diary*

---

* Allaire's account in the New York *Royal Gazette*, February 24, 1781; and in his MS. *Diary*, kindly communicated by his grandson, J. DeLancey Robinson, of New Brunswick. Stedman gives Ferguson's as nine hundred and sixty; Mrs. Warren, in her *History of the Revolution*, eight hundred and fifty. The British historian, Andrews, in his *History of the War*, still further diminishes the number—killed and wounded upwards of three hundred, and four hundred prisoners.

accounts, he states that the British lost on the field and in prisoners, as follows: Of the Provincial corps, Colonel Ferguson, Lieutenant McGinnis and eighteen privates, total, twenty killed; Captain Ryerson and thirty-two Sergeants and privates, total, thirty-three wounded—making the killed and wounded together, fifty-three; two Captains, four Lieutenants, three Ensigns, one Surgeon, and fifty-four Sergeants and privates, including the wounded, making a total of sixty-four prisoners—showing, according to this account, only thirty-one of Ferguson's corps who escaped being killed or wounded. This, however, is a manifest error, for the fifty-three killed and wounded, and thirty-one uninjured men would add up only eighty-four, whereas, Lieutenant Allaire concedes that there were, at the commencement of the battle, one hundred of Ferguson's corps. In this estimate of prisoners, he did not probably include the survivors of Lieutenant Taylor's twenty dragoons, and ten wagoners, taken from the Rangers—more than enough to make up the full complement assigned to the Provincials by that officer. He also states, that the Loyalists lost "in officers and privates, one hundred killed, ninety wounded, and about six hundred prisoners." Reckoning the prisoners at six hundred and ten, and the killed and wounded as Allaire reports them, would make up the full amount of the supposable Tory force—eight hundred.

It is stated in the official report of Campbell and his associates, that of Ferguson's corps nineteen were killed, and thirty-five wounded—exceeding Allaire's account by one only; but making of the officers and privates sixty-eight prisoners, which would seem to have included only a part of the wounded; that the Tories had two hundred and six killed, one hundred and twenty-eight wounded, and forty-eight officers and six hundred privates made prisoners —thus accounting for a total of Provincials and Loyalists of eleven hundred and three.

Only five days after the battle, Colonel Shelby, in a

letter to his father, stated the loss of Ferguson's corps at thirty killed, twenty-eight wounded, and fifty-seven prisoners; that the Tories had one hundred and twenty-seven killed, one hundred and twenty-five wounded, and six hundred and forty-nine prisoners; or both classed together, one hundred and fifty-seven killed, one hundred and fifty-three wounded, and seven hundred and six prisoners—total, one thousand and sixteen. Here is a difference of the killed of the Tories alone, of seventy-nine, between Shelby's statement to his father, and the official account, which he is supposed to have drawn up, and signed a few days later, in conjunction with Campbell and Cleveland. This discrepancy is unaccountable, except on the supposition that the official statement was designed, as Colonel Shelby alleges in his narrative of 1823, to "give tone to public report," and confessing, withal, that it was "inaccurate and indefinite." The probabilities are that the figures of the patriots, as to the extent of the losses of the enemy, were considerably over-estimated for public effect; and that the prisoners were somewhat "upward of six hundred," as stated in General Greene's manuscripts,[*] and which Allaire practically confirms by stating that they were "about six hundred."

"Exaggeration of successful operations," wrote Colonel Lee to General Greene, "was characteristic of the times;"[†] and this was, perhaps, excusable in this instance, since a total defeat of the enemy, like that of Ferguson's at King's Mountain, was a circumstance of rare occurrence, and the Whigs probably thought it was well to make the most of it to revive the drooping spirits of the people. Love of country predominated over any mere questions of casuistry; and thus Shelby and his associates were not over-nice about the matter of the enemy's numbers, so that they were only represented sufficiently large to make a decided impression

---

[*] Greene's *Life of General Greene*, iii, 78.

[†] Greene's *Greene*, iii, 222.

on the minds of all classes, encouraging the friends of freedom, and equally depressing their enemies.

Of the killed and wounded of the Americans, it is less
difficult to get at the facts ; or at least they are not involved
in such contradictory statements as those relating to the
British losses.   Colonel Shelby, in his letter to his father,
October twelfth, 1780, mentions six officers and twenty three
privates killed, and fifty-four wounded ; but adds, that he
believes, with more accurate returns, the killed will prove
to be thirty-five, and the wounded between fifty and sixty.
Colonel Campbell, in his letter of October twentieth, places
the number at about thirty killed, and sixty wounded.
In the official report, made out apparently somewhat later,
and hence more reliable, the killed are stated at twenty-
eight, and the wounded at sixty-two.

In the command of Williams, Brandon, Steen and Hammond, we have no record of any loss save that of their
gallant leader, and the person, whose name is unknown,
who had a presentiment of his death ; and William Giles,
as already related, slightly wounded.   Among the South
Carolinians under Lacey and Hawthorn, no killed are
reported, save, perhaps, David Duff and William Watson,
who probably belonged to this corps, and but one wounded,
Robert Miller, of Chester County, who was badly disabled
in his thigh.   In both of these commands there were probably other losses.   Of the Rutherford men under Colonel
Hampton, John Smart * and Preston Goforth were killed,
and Major James Porter and William Robertson wounded :
but of McDowell's Burke County men, we have no knowledge of any deaths or disabilities.

The Lincoln County men, considering their small number, suffered considerably in the engagement—Major
Chronicle, Captain Mattocks, William Rabb, John Boyd,
and Arthur Patterson, killed, and Moses Henry mortally

---

* Smart was killed by a Tory named Hughes. In after years, John Smart Jr. hearing
of Hughes in West Tennessee, started on a mission to seek the Tory's life, but never
returned.—W. L. Twitty.

wounded; Lieutenant-Colonel Hambright, Captain Espey, Robert Henry, William Gilmer, John Chittim, * and William Bradley, wounded. There must have been other losses; for of Captain Samuel Martin's company of about twenty men, he relates in his pension statement, that four were killed, and two mortally wounded.

Of Sevier's regiment, William Steele, John Brown, and Michael Mahoney, are known to have lost their lives in the contest; while Captain Sevier was mortally, and one Gilleland and Patrick Murphy severely wounded. Near the close of the action, Captain Sevier, while stooping to pick up his ramrod, received a buck-shot wound near his kidney; after the action, the British Surgeon, Doctor Johnson, endeavored to extract the shot, but failed in the effort; dressed his wound, saying if he would remain quiet awhile, the shot could be extracted, and he would probably recover; but if he attempted to return home at once, his kidneys would inflame, and about the ninth day he would expire. Fearing to be left behind, lest the Tories might wreak their vengeance on him, he started on horse-back for his Nolachucky home, accompanied by his nephew, James Sevier. On the ninth day, when at Bright's Place on the Yellow Mountain, preparing their frugal meal, he was suddenly taken worse, and died within an hour, and his remains, wrapped in his blanket, were interred beneath a lofty mountain oak.

After the battle, among the stores captured from the enemy was a keg of rum, some of which was conveyed to the wounded Pat Murphy, with which to bathe his wound. He had been shot across the windpipe in front, cutting it considerably. Pat held the cup while a companion gave the wound a faithful bathing; this done, he swallowed the remainder, remarking with much *sang froid*, "a little *in* was as good as *out*." †

* Chittim was placed on the invalid roll of pensioners in 1815, drawing seventy-two dollars a year, till his death, December 24, 1818.

† Statement of the late Major John Sevier, a son of Colonel Sevier.

Colonel Shelby's regiment no doubt suffered from losses in the action; but the particulars are wanting, save that Captain Shelby, William Cox, and John Fagon were wounded. As Shelby's men encountered hard fighting, and were repeatedly charged down the mountain, they must necessarily have lost some of their number, and had more wounded than the three whose names are mentioned.

Of the Wilkes and Surry men, under Cleveland and Winston, we have only the names of two men killed— Thomas Bicknell, and Daniel Siske, of Wilkes County; Major Lewis, Captains Lewis, Smith, and Lenoir, Lieutenants Johnson and J. M. Smith, Charles Gordon, and John Childers wounded—the latter badly. Where so many officers were disabled, there must have been several others of this gallant regiment killed and wounded.

Colonel Campbell's Virginians, who fought so nobly and persistently throughout the action, met with severer losses than any other regiment engaged in this hard day's contest. Of the killed were Captain William Edmondson, Lieutenants Reece Bowen, William Blackburn, and Robert Edmondson, Sr., Ensigns Andrew Edmondson, John Beattie, James Corry, Nathaniel Dryden, Nathaniel Gist, James Philips, and Humberson Lyon, and private Henry Henigar. Lieutenant Thomas McCulloch, and Ensign James Laird, who were mortally wounded, died a few days thereafter. Captain James Dysart, Lieutenants Samuel Newell, Robert Edmondson, Jr., and eighteen privates wounded,* of whom were Fredrick Fisher, John Skeggs Benoni Banning, Charles Kilgore, William Bullen, Leonard Hyce, Israel Hayter, and William Moore, who recovered. The names of the other ten disabled Virginians have not been preserved.

So badly wounded was William Moore, that his leg had to be amputated on the field. He was necessarily left at

---

* Samuel Newell's letter to General Francis Preston, states that Campbell's regiment had thirty-five killed and wounded. As fourteen were killed including two officers who shortly after died of their wounds, it would leave twenty-one wounded, three of whom were officers.

some good Samaritan's; but when his associates returned to their distant Holston homes, and told the story of their victory, and its cost in life and suffering, his devoted wife, on learning her husband's terrible misfortune, though in the month of November, mounted her horse and rode all the long and dreary journey to the neighborhood of King's Mountain—such was the intrepidity of the frontier women, as well as the men, of those trying times; and having nursed him until sufficiently recovered, she conveyed him home, and he lived to a good old age,* dying in 1826, after having received from the Government an invalid pension for thirty-seven years.

It is remarkable, that thirteen officers to only a single private of Campbell's men, were killed or mortally wounded during the battle—nearly one-half of the fatalities of the whole Whig force engaged in the contest. This disparity of losses between the leaders and privates is a striking proof how fearlessly the officers exposed themselves in rallying the regiment when broken, and leading on their men by their valor and heroic examples to victory. One-third of the wounded were of Campbell's regiment. Another remarkable fact is, that of eight Edmondsons of the Virginia troops, engaged that day, three were killed, and one was wounded—all prominent and efficient officers of that corps; the survivors having been William Edmondson, the major of the regiment, and privates John, Samuel, and William Edmondson.

Thus the names of those who fell and those who were disabled, of the several Whig regiments, so far as we have been able to collect them, number twenty-six killed, and a nameless one of Hammond's men, who fell, who had a premonition of his fate; and thirty-six wounded. There must have been several others killed, beside those whose names are given in the several lists, and some twenty-six

* MS. Statements of the late Governor David Campbell, and Wm. G. G. Lowry, Clerk of the Court of Washington County, Virginia—the latter a great grandson of this patriotic couple.

20

additional ones wounded. It does not appear that there was a single Surgeon among the Americans, and Doctor Johnson only, of three Surgeons of Ferguson's men, survived, who seems to have generously attended the wounded of the Whigs, as well as those of his own corps. But the frontier people were much accustomed, from necessity, with splints, bandages, and slippery elm poultices, to treating gun-shot wounds and other disabilities.

Not very long after the close of the action, Captain John Weir, of that part of Lincoln now comprising Gaston County, arrived with his company, having heard of the advance of the mountaineers; and may have heard, in the distance, the reports of the eighteen hundred rifles and muskets of the Whigs and Tories that reverberated from King's Mountain over the surrounding country.* Captain Robert Shannon, a brave Irishman, also of Lincoln County, hastened with his company likewise to the field of battle. And not a few of the scattered settlers of that region, men and women, repaired to the battle-ground to learn the news, and render whatever aid they could under the circumstances. Among them was Mrs. Ellen McDowell, and her daughter Jane, having heard the firing from their house, went to the scene of strife, where they remained several days nursing and attending to the wounded soldiers.

After the battle quite a number were appointed to count up the losses; but their reports were so contradictory that little reliance could be placed in them—apparently repeating the process of counting them, in some instances, so that

---

* Captain Weir was born in Ireland, in 1743, where he early married a Miss McKelvey. Their eldest son was born in Ireland, soon after which they emigrated to America, settling on Buffalo Creek, at what is now known as Weir's Bridge, in Gaston County, North Carolina. Weir was early commissioned a Captain, and was much engaged in scouting service during the Revolution. His activity in the Whig cause excited the ire of the Tories. Just before the battle of the Cowpens, he was caught and severely whipped by a Tory party, and left in the woods securely tied to a tree; but was fortunately soon after found, and released by his friends. On another occasion, his wife was whipped by the Tories for refusing to divulge to them the place of her husband's concealment. She died, August 11, 1819, and he on the 4th of September following, in his seventy-sixth year. Both were long members of the Presbyterian church, and left many worthy descendants.

the aggregate results greatly exceeded the facts in the case. Among the natural rocky defenses, where many of the Tories had posted themselves, upwards of twenty of their dead bodies were found, completely jammed in between the rocks, who had been shot directly through the head * — so fatally accurate was the aim of the mountain-riflemen when their antagonists ventured to peep out from their chosen fastnesses.

Some considerable time was necessarily employed in getting the prisoners properly secured, and in giving such attention to the wounded Whigs as the circumstances would permit; Colonel Williams being taken into one of the British markees, as were doubtless many others. Doctor Johnson, of Ferguson's corps, seems to have been the good Samaritan of the occasion, rendering such professional services as he could, alike to the Whigs and his brother Provincials; while the wounded of the poor Loyalists appear to have been left pretty much to their fate.

The truth is, that rarely, if ever, did a body of eighteen hundred fighting men come into conflict, with so litttle provisions to supply their wants. The Americans, in their desperate pursuit of the enemy, trusting to luck, had literally nothing; while Ferguson had been scarcely any more provident in securing needful supplies. The country in the immediate vicinity of King's Mountain was but sparsely settled at that period. " It was dark again we got the prisoners under guard," says the unknown chronicler of Campbell's regiment, who left us his narrative of the campaign and battle.

Many a souvenir was appropriated by the victors. Captain Joseph McDowell, of Pleasant Garden, secured some of Ferguson's table service—six of his china dinner plates, and a small coffee cup and saucer; several of which interesting war trophies are yet retained among his descendants.† Colonel Shelby obtained the fallen Chieftain's

---

* Statements of Silas McBee and John Spelts to the author.

† MS. letters of Mrs. R. M. Pearson, and Miss N. M. McDowell, grand-daughters, and Miss Anna M. Woodfin, a great grand-daughter, of Captain McDowell.

famous silver whistle, while the smaller one fell to the lot of
Elias Powell; and Colonel Sevier secured his silken sash,
and Lieutenant-Colonel's commission, and DePeyster's
sword.   Colonel Campbell secured at least a portion of his
correspondence.   Ferguson's white charger, who had
careered down the mountain when his master was shot from
his back, was, by general consent, assigned to the gallant
Colonel Cleveland, who was too unwieldy to travel on foot,
and who had lost his horse in the action.   Samuel Talbot,
turning over Ferguson's dead body, picked up his pistol,
which had dropped from his pocket.   His large silver watch,
as round as a turnip, fell into the hands of one of Lacey's
men; and Doctor Moore, in his *Life of Lacey*, says he
frequently saw it; that it traded for about forty-five or fifty
dollars as a curiosity.

" Awful, indeed," says Thomas Young, " was the scene
of the wounded, the dying and the dead, on the field, after
the carnage of that dreadful day."*   " We had," observed
Benjamin Sharp, " to encamp on the ground with the dead
and wounded, and pass the night amid groans and lamentations."†   " My father, David Witherspoon," remarks his
son, " used to describe the scenes of the battle-ground the
night after the contest as heart-rending in the extreme—
the groans of the dying, and the constant cry of "water!
water!"‡   "The groans of the wounded and dying on the
mountain," said John Spelts, " were truly affecting—
begging piteously for a little water; but in the hurry, confusion, and exhaustion of the Whigs, these cries, when
emanating from the Tories, were little heeded."§

> "The red rose grew pale at the blood that was shed,
> And the white rose blushed at the shedding."

Such was the night on King's Mountain immediately

---

* Young's *Memoir* in the *Orion* magazine.
† Sharp's narrative in the *American Pioneer.*
‡ MS. letter of Colonel J. H. Witherspoon, of Lauderdale County, Alabama, No-
vember, 1880.
§ Conversations with Spelts, in December, 1843.

succeeding the battle. While these surrounding sufferings touched many a heart, others had become more or less hardened, believing, so far as the Tories were concerned, that their wretched condition, brought upon themselves, was a just retribution from high heaven for their unnatural opposition to the efforts of their countrymen to throw off the chains of political bondage forged by the British Government. The Whigs, weary as they were, had to take turns in guarding the prisoners, with little or no refreshment; and caring, as best they could, for their own over three-score wounded, with no little fear, withal, lest Tarleton should suddenly dash upon them. It was a night of care, anxiety and suffering, vividly remembered, and feelingly rehearsed, as long as any of the actors were permitted to survive.

CHAPTER XIV.

October, 1780.

Battle Incidents.—Long Sam Abney Coerced into Ferguson's Army.—
Death of Arthur Patterson.—Drury Mathis' Rough Experience.—
A Tory Woman Finding her Slain Son.—Fatality of the Riflemen.—
Preston Goforth and three Brothers Killed.—A Brother Kills a
Brother.—The Whig and Tory Logans.—William Logan Noticed.—
Preparing to Retire—Burning Captured Wagons—Horse-Litters
for the Wounded.—Gray's Kindness to a Wounded Tory.—A
Termagant Prisoner Released.—Messengers Sent to the Foot-Men.—
Arms Captured—Tories made to Carry Them.—Trophies of Vic-
tory.—A Whig Woman Refusing to Share in the Plunder.—Rumor
of Tarleton's Approach.—Burial of the Whig and Tory Dead.—
Treatment of Ferguson Considered.—Re-Interment of Remains.—
March of the Army.—Death of Colonel Willams.—Camp at Broad
River.—Willams' Burial—Discovery of his Long-Forgotten Grave.
—Six Tory Brothers Escape.—Notice of Colonel Walker.—Bran-
don's Barbarity.—Campbell Protecting the Prisoners.—Gray's Retort
to a Tory Vixen.—Gray's Services.—Suffering for Food.—Feeding
Prisoners on Corn and Pumpkins.—Billeting the Wounded.—March
to Bickerstaff's Old Fields.

In a contest like that on King's Mountain, lasting over
an hour, with eighteen hundred men engaged in mortal
combat, and with repeated charges and repulses, many a
battle-incident occurred of an interesting or exciting character. A number of them have already been related while
detailing the services of the several corps engaged in the
action ; but others, of a more general nature, or where Loyalists were referred to, may very appropriately be grouped
in this connection.

Samuel Abney—better known as Long Sam Abney, to
distinguish him from others of the name—a resident of
Edgefield County, South Carolina, was a Whig both in

principle and practice. Upon the fall of Charleston, and the occupation of Ninety-Six and Augusta by a strong British force, the great body of the people were forced to submit—to take protection, which they understood to mean neutrality ; but which the British leaders construed very differently. They were treated as conquered Rebels, and, in many instances, were compelled to take up arms in defence of a Government which they loathed, and to fight against their country's freedom to which their hearts were devoted. Such was Abney's situation. He was forced into Ferguson's Loyalist corps, and was marched to King's Mountain.

At the commencement of the battle, he stationed himself behind a rock, where he would be secure from the balls of either side, determined not to fight against his countrymen. He could not, and would not, take part in shooting his own friends, was his secret thought and resolution. But amid the shower of bullets flying in every direction, he was not so safe as he had flattered himself ; for while leaning on his rifle, and probably indulging in the curiosity of taking a view of the combatants, he unintentionally exposed his person more than he had designed, when a ball penetrated the fleshy part of his arm. This made him " a little mad," as he expressed it ; still he had, as yet, no thought of taking part in the contest. Presently, however, he was struck with another ball ; which made him " mighty mad," and he then turned in and fought with the bravest and boldest of Ferguson's troops. Before the action was over, he was riddled with bullets, as he related the story of the fight— seven balls taking effect on his person. He was left in a helpless, unconscious condition, among the slain and wounded on the battle-field ; but fortunately the frost of the ensuing night revived him. He crawled to a neighboring branch, and slacked his burning thirst. He was subsequently found by one of the people of that region, who compassionately conveyed him to his home, and bound up his wounds; and, after many days, he recovered, and returned to his friends. He lived to a good old age, and used merrily to relate how he was shot, and how he was provoked to shoot back again, at King's Mountain. *

In the neighborhood of King's Mountain, on King's creek, resided old Arthur Patterson, an Irishman, who was devoted to the Whig cause, as well as his several sons who were settled around him. On the morning preceding the battle, a party of Ferguson's foragers ranging along that stream, came across three of the young Pattersons, Arthur, Jr., Thomas and William, together with James Lindsay; arrested and marched them to camp, where they were placed under guard, awaiting trial. The same day, learning of the apprehension of his sons, the aged father of the Pattersons started for the camp, to see if he could do anything towards effecting their release. Meanwhile the Whigs suddenly made their appearance, encircled the mountain, and commenced their attack. During the progress of the action, while the Americans were pressing the enemy, the guards were ordered to take their places in the line of defence, and aid, if possible, in checking the advance of the mountaineers. Left to themselves, amid the confusion of the battle, the prisoners resolved to make a push for freedom. Lindsay, together with William and Arthur Patterson, Jr., ran through an opening in the British lines, and escaped unharmed—Arthur with a portion of the rope, with which he had been fastened, still dangling from his neck. Thomas Patterson, possessing perhaps more of a belligerent nature, watched his opportunity, between fires, and made a bold dash for the Whig lines, reaching Shelby's corps, where he picked up the rifle of a wounded soldier, and fought bravely until victory was proclaimed. His aged father was less fortunate. His old Irish blood, as he came in view of the noble army of patriots, was stirred within

---

* *Random Recollections of the Revolution*, by Hon. J. B. O'Neall, in the *Southern Literary Journal*, August, 1838, pp. 106-7.

him ; and hoping that he might aid in liberating both his sons and his country, he warmly joined in the fray, and was killed. *

Drury Mathis, who resided at Saluda Old town, on the Saluda, in South Carolina, some two and a half miles above the mouth of Little river, had united his fortunes with Ferguson. In the third charge which was made against Campbell's men, Mathis was badly wounded, and fell to the ground. The spot where he had fallen was half way down the mountain, where the balls from the Virginians fell around him almost as thick as hail. He used to relate, that as the mountaineers passed over him, he would play possum ; but he could plainly observe their faces and eyes ; and to him those bold, brave riflemen appeared like so many devils from the infernal regions, so full of excitement were they as they darted like enraged lions up the mountain. He said they were the most powerful looking men he ever beheld ; not over-burdened with fat, but tall, raw-boned, and sinewy, with long matted hair—such men, as a body, as were never before seen in the Carolinas. With his feet down the declivity, he said he could not but observe that his Loyalist friends were very generally over-shooting the Americans ; and that if ever a poor fellow hugged mother earth closely, he did on that trying occasion. After the battle —the next day, probably—he was kindly taken to a house in that region, and nursed till his wound had healed, when he returned to Ninety-Six, an humbled, if not a wiser man. He lived to enjoy a green old age ; but used stoutly to swear that he never desired to see King's Mountain again. †

Thomas Mullineaux, a youth, lived with his mother, some two miles from the mountain. He used to relate, in his old age, that when the firing began, his mother and the family were sitting down to a late dinner. Presently a neighboring woman came running in, wringing her hands,

---

* MS. letters of Colonel J. R. Logan, Dr. W. J. T. Miller, Abraham Hardin; Hunter's *Sketches*, 311 ; Moore's *Lacey*, 18 ; *The Carolinian*, Hickory, North Carolina, Oct. 1st, 1880.
† MS. papers of Dr. John H. Logan.

and uttering her deep lamentations over the dangers surrounding her son, who had enlisted under the banners of
Ferguson.   After the firing had, at length, ceased, and
all was still again, as if nothing had occurred to disturb the
peace that had brooded over the mountain from time
immemorial, the poor woman hastened, with a heavy heart,
accompanied by young Mullineaux, to the scene of action.
Turning up the faces of the dead and wounded Tories,
scattered along the sides, and upon the crest of the mountain, she at length discovered the gory body of her son
pierced by a rifle ball.   It was a heart-rending scene.*

The fatality of the sharp-shooters at King's Mountain
almost surpasses belief.   Riflemen took off riflemen with
such exactness, that they killed each other when taking
sight, so instantaneously that their eyes remained, after
they were dead, *one shut and the other open*—in the usual
manner of marksmen when leveling at their object.†   Wilkinson, in his *Memoirs*, refers to " the Southern States, rent
by civil feuds, bleeding by the hands of brothers ; " and cites
an incident in point at King's Mountain, related to him by
Colonel Shelby, " *that two brothers, expert riflemen, were
seen to present at each other, to fire and fall at the same
instant*—their names were given to me, but they have
escaped my memory." ‡

It is not improbable that these two brothers who confronted and killed each other, as related by Colonel Shelby,
were of the Goforth family, of Rutherford County, North
Carolina.   At least, four brothers—Preston Goforth on the
Whig side, and John Goforth and two others in the Tory
ranks—all participated in the battle, and all were killed.
It was a remarkable fatality. §

Another instance of brother killing a brother, during the
engagement, is thus related :   A Whig soldier noticed a

---

* Dr. J. H. Logan's manuscripts.
† Lamb's *Journal.* 308.
‡ Wilkinson's *Memoirs*, i, 115.
§ MS. Correspondence of W. L. Twitty.

good deal of execution in a particular part of his line from a
certain direction on the other side. On close observation,
he discovered that the fatal firing on the part of Ferguson's
men, proceeded from behind a hollow chestnut tree, and
through a hole in it. He concluded to make an effort to
silence that battery, and aimed his rifle shots repeatedly at
the aperture. At length the firing from that quarter ceased.
After the battle, his curiosity prompted him to examine the
place, and discovered that he had killed one of his own
brothers, and wounded another, who had joined the Loyalist
forces, and concealed themselves in the rear of this tree.
So much did the patriot brother take the circumstance to
heart, that he became almost deranged in consequence.*

There were four brothers, all of Lincoln County, North
Carolina, who shared in the battle—William and Joseph
Logan, on the Whig side, and John and Thomas Logan
among Ferguson's forces. William Logan belonged to
Mattock's company, and was close by his Captain when he
fell—the fatal ball having passed a hollow dead chestnut
tree. Joseph Logan, the other Whig brother, was a Baptist
preacher; and, during the engagement, he, with a Presbyterian minister, wrestled with the Lord in prayer, as in
olden times, to stay up the hands of their friends. Thomas
Logan, one of the Tory brothers, had his thigh badly
broken, and was left on the field of battle; while his
brother, John Logan, was taken among the prisoners, and
afterwards died a pauper.† These political divisions in
families, which were not unfrequent, were exceedingly
unpleasant, engendering much bitterness and animosity.

---

* Rev. E. R. Rockwell, of Cool Spring, North Carolina, in *Historical Magazine*,
September, 1867, p. 181.

† MS. Correspondence of Colonel J. R Logan. His grandfather, William Logan, who
shared in the glories of King's Mountain, was a native of Virginia, born in 1749, descending from Scotch-Irish ancestry. Before the war, he married Jane Black, and settled in
Lincoln County, North Carolina. He did good service at King's Mountain, and rendered
himself useful during the continuance of the contest, for which in his advanced years he
drew a pension. After the war he settled on main Buffalo creek, on the border of York
County, South Carolina, where he died in 1832, at the age of eighty-three years, having
dropped dead in the field while feeding his cattle. He left five sons and two daughters, and
was long a worthy member of the Baptist church.

In the morning, after the battle, a man was discovered on the top of the mountain—one of the Tories, it is believed —with a bullet hole through his head, a rifle ball having entered his forehead, and passed out at the back part of his cranium ; and strange to say, he was still alive, and sitting in an upright posture on the ground. Some of his brains had oozed out on either side of his head; and though unconscious, he was yet breathing. It was proposed by those who saw him, that they would gently lay him down ; and, on doing so, he instantly expired.*

On Sabbath morning, October the eighth, the sun shone brightly, the first time in several days, and the patriots were early astir—prompted thereto by two very pressing motives. One was, that they might get on their return route as quickly as possible, to secure a much needed sup- ply of provisions ; the other to hasten beyond the reach of the dreaded Colonel Tarleton, an encounter with whom was very undesirable, encumbered as they were with so many prisoners, and the necessary care and conveyance of their own wounded. Seventeen baggage wagons were, according to Colonel Shelby's letter to his father, among the trophies of victory ; and these, says Ramsey's *Tennes- see*, were drawn by the men across their camp-fires and consumed. To have attempted to carry them along, would have retarded their march over a rough country ; and the wounded could be best borne on the journey on horse-litters, by fastening two long poles on either side of two horses at tandem, leaving a space of six or eight feet between them, stretching tent-cloth or blankets between the poles, on which to place a disabled officer or soldier.

In rambling that morning among the Tory wounded, who lay scattered about—all who could had crept to the branch to quench their raging thirst—James Gray, of the Rutherford troops, discovered an old acquaintance wounded

---

*J. L. Gray's MS. narrative, derived from James Gray, one of the King's Mountain men.

in the ankle, and unable to walk. Gray was fully aware, that the unfortunate man was not one of those disreputable Tories who had joined the King's standard, like Plundering Sam Brown, simply for the sake of being protected in rapine and plunder. He had joined Ferguson from conscientious motives, believing it his duty to fight for the Royal Government. Gray feeling kindly towards his old friend, took out his pocket-handkerchief, bound up his broken limb, and did whatever else he could to ameliorate his unhappy condition. Nor was this kindness thrown away. Recovering from his wound, the Loyalist became a useful citizen to his country; and, as long as he lived, he manifested the strongest friendship for Gray, who had shown him compassion in the day of his distress. *

Among the prisoners, Colonel Shelby discovered some officers who had fought under his banner, a few weeks previously, at Musgrove's Mill. They declared that they had been forced to join Ferguson, or fare worse; and when their cases had been inquired into, and their representations found to be correct, their misfortunes were commisserated, and they were henceforth regarded as friends. † Here a woman was liberated from captivity, who had been taken prisoner in Burke County during Colonel Ferguson's invasion of that region in the month preceding. She was a regular termagant—especially excited by the presence of Tories, and in this instance, her ire had probably been provoked by the reckless plunder of her property, and she had apparently been apprehended because she gave them a piece of her tongue, in a manner quite too loose and reckless to suit the fastidious notions of his Majesty's representatives in the backwoods of America. ‡ Once again free in body, as her unruly member always had been, she renewedly indulged her propensity, we may well judge, of saying ugly things of Ferguson and his men to her heart's content.

* J. L. Gray's MS. statement, and *Rutherford Enquirer*, May 24, 1859.
† Shelby, in *American Review*, December, 1848.
‡ MS. statement of W. L. Twitty, derived from Colonel W. H. Miller.

Early that morning, Colonel Campbell ordered two of his men, William Snodgrass and Edward Smith, to return on the route on which the army had advanced, so as to meet the party of footmen, and prevent their further approach in the direction of King's Mountain. Declining a guard, because, as the messengers said, the patriots already had the whole population of that region, either as soldiers or prisoners, they went on, without any mishap or adventure, to Broad river—apparently at the Cherokee Ford—where they met their countrymen. They imparted to them the joyful tidings of victory, and turned their course, in obedience to orders, up the stream. *

According to the official report of Colonel Campbell and associates, fifteen hundred stand of arms were captured ; but in Colonel Shelby's letter to his father, written five days after the battle, twelve hundred is the number stated—and a portion of these were supernumerary, designed for new recruits. " The prisoners," says Shelby, " were made to carry their own arms, as they could not have been carried in any other way." The flints were taken from the locks ; and, to the more strong and healthy Tories, two guns each were assigned for conveyance. When ready to start on the day's journey, the prisoners were marched, in single file, by the spot where the rifles and muskets were stacked, and each was directed to shoulder and carry the arms allotted to him. Colonel Shelby, with his sword drawn, stood by, among others, to see that the order was strictly obeyed. One old fellow came toddling by, and evinced a determination not to encumber himself with a gun. Shelby sternly ordered him to shoulder one without delay. The old man demurred, declaring he was not able to carry it. Shelby told him, with a curse, that he was able to bring one there, and he should carry one away ; and, at the same time gave him a smart slap across his shoulders with the flat side of his sword-blade. The old fellow, discovering

---

* MS. letter of Wm. Snodgrass to Ex-Governor David Campbell, August 15th, 1842.

that he could not trifle with such a man as Shelby, jumped at the gun-pile, shouldered one, and marched away in double-quick time. *

There were not a few other articles, military and personal, that fell into the hands of the victors. These seem to have been retained by those who possessed themselves of them—as the troops, be it remembered, had not engaged in the service by any order of Congress, or of their respective States. It was entirely a volunteer movement—no baggage-wagons, no commissaries, no pay, and no supplies. General Lenoir adds, that by the victory of King's Mountain, " many militia officers procured swords who could not possibly get any before ; neither was it possible to procure a good supply of ammunition."

If the soldiers, who had marched so far and suffered so much, in order to meet and conquer Ferguson and his army, were not unwilling to appropriate to their own use the trophies of victory, there is at least one recorded instance in which a sturdy Whig woman of the country refused to profit by the spoils of war. Two brothers, Moses and James Henry, of the Lincoln troops, residing in what is now Gaston County, fought bravely in the battle ; Moses Henry sealing his devotion to his country with his life's blood—dying, not long thereafter, in the hospital at Charlotte, of the wound he received in the action. His brother, James Henry, while passing through the woods near the scene of the conflict, a few days after the engagement, found a very fine horse, handsomely equipped with an elegant saddle, the reins of the bridle being broken. The horse and equipments had belonged, as he supposed, to some officer of the enemy. He took the animal home with him, greatly elated with his good luck ; but his patriotic mother meeting him at the gate, immediately inquired whose horse it was? He replied, that he judged that it had be-

*Shelby's narrative in the *American Review*; Ramsey's *Tennessee*, 242; General Lenoir's statement; T. L. Gray's MSS.; *Rutherford Enquirer*, May 24th, 1859.

longed to some British officer. "James," said the mother, sternly, "turn it loose, and drive it off the place, for I will not have the hands of my household soiled with British plunder." Colonel Moses Henry Hand, a worthy citizen of Gaston County, is a grandson of Moses Henry who was mortally wounded at King's Mountain. *

At length the patriot army was ready to commence its long and tedious return march, encumbered with their wounded, and over six hundred prisoners. A report was prevalent that morning, that Tarleton's cavalry was pressing on, and would attempt to rescue the prisoners, † and inflict punishment upon the audacious mountaineers; but while it was only camp rumor, brought in by people from the surrounding country, whose curiosity had prompted them to visit the battle-field, yet the Whig leaders deemed it wise to waste no time unnecessarily. Much of the morning had been consumed in preparing litters for the wounded.

When the army marched, some ten o'clock in the forenoon, Colonel Campbell remained behind with a party of men to bury their unfortunate countrymen.‡ The British Lieutenant Allaire states, that before the troops moved, orders were given to his men by Colonel Campbell, that should they be attacked on the march, to fire on and destroy the prisoners. We have no means of determining whether such orders were given on the supposition of Tarleton's possible pursuit, and attempt to rescue the captives; or it may be, if there was any foundation for the statement, it was made in a modified form.

A place of sepulture was selected, upon a small elevation, some eighty or a hundred yards south-east of Ferguson's head-quarters; large pits were dug, and a number of the slain placed together, with blankets thrown over them, and thus hurriedly buried.§ Tarleton asserts, on some

* Hunter's *Sketches*, pp. 296-97.
† MS. letter of Wm. Snodgrass to Governor Campbell; Mills' *Statistics,* 779; conversations with Silas McBee and John Spelts, survivors of the battle.
‡ Statement of Joseph Phillips, one of Cleveland's men.
§ MS. letters of Wm. Snodgrass and John Craig, of Campbell's regiment.

reports he had heard, that the mountaineers used every insult and indignity towards the dead body of Ferguson ; *and Hanger, an officer at that time in Tarleton's corps, declares that such was the inveteracy of the Americans against the British leader, that while they buried all the other bodies, they stripped Ferguson's of its clothes, and left it naked on the field of battle, to be devoured by the turkey-buzzards of the country. †

Colonel Ferguson's biographer repeats the statement that his body was stripped, and his surviving comrades were denied the privilege of bestowing upon his remains the honors of a soldier's burial ; but that the neighboring people subsequently accorded to him a decent interment. ‡ Mills, in his *Statistics of South Carolina*, remarks, that the victors, dreading the arrival of Tarleton, " hastened from the scene of action ; nor durst they attend to the burial of the dead, or to take care of the wounded, many of whom were seen upon the ground, two days after the battle, imploring a little water to cool their burning tongues ; but they were left to perish there, and this long hill was whitened with their bones."

That Ferguson's elegant clothing, under his duster or hunting-shirt, may have been taken, and that even some indignities may have been shown by an excited soldiery, towards the British leader's lifeless body, is quite possible ; if so, it is strange that two officers of his corps, much devoted to him, Lieutenant Allaire and Captain Ryerson, should make no mention of any such circumstance in their narratives of King's Mountain battle. At all events, when Colonel Campbell detailed a party of his troops to remain behind to bury the American dead, he directed a number of the British prisoners to dig pits for the interment of their fallen companions, and at the same

---

* Tarleton's *Campaigns*. quarto edition, 165.

† Hanger's *Life and Opinions*, ii, 406.

‡ Dr. Ferguson's *Memoir*, 35.
21

time, detained Doctor Johnson to attend to the wounded of the enemy before his final departure.* That the grave-pits were shallow, and the work of sepulture hastily performed, is very likely, for the reception of both the American and British remains; but all was undoubtedly done that well could be, under the circumstances, with such limited facilties as they possessed, and in their half-starved condition, and, withal, threatened, as they supposed, with a visit from Tarleton's Legion. The British dead were interred in two pits—one a very large one, probably where the Tories were laid, side by side; the other, a smaller one, where doubtless the men of Ferguson's corps were buried.†

The wolves of the surrounding country were soon attracted to the spot by the smell of flesh and blood; and for several weeks they revelled upon the carcasses of the slain—some of which had been overlooked and left unburied, while others were scratched out of their shallow graves by these prowlers of the wilderness. Vultures and wolves divided the human plunder; and so bold and audacious did the latter grow, gorging on flesh, that they, in some instances, showed a disposition to attack the living, when visiting the scene of the battle. And long after the war, it is said, that King's Mountain was the favorite resort of the wolf-hunter.‡

---

* MS. letter of Wm. Snodgrass to Governor Campbell, August 15th, 1842; Benjamin Sharp's statement in the *American Pioneer*. These acts of kindness on the part of Colonel Campbell, effectually disprove the supposition of Carrington, in his *Battles of the Revolution*, that the Tory wounded were deliberately slaughtered by the victorious patriots.

† MS. correspondence of Abraham Hardin.

† Doctor Logan's MSS., and his *History of Upper South Carolina*, 68; MS. correspondence of Colonel J. R. Logan; Mills' *Statistics*, 779.

It may be added, in this connection, that in 1815, through the instrumentality of Doctor William McLean, of Lincoln County, North Carolina, a day was set apart, and the scattered human bones on the mountain, dragged away from their former resting places by the voracious wolves, were collected together, and re-interred; and the old monument or head-stone of dark slate rock erected at the expense of Doctor McLean, who delivered a suitable address on the occasion. The monument bears this inscription: On the east side—"Sacred to the memory of Major William Chronicle, Captain John Mattocks, William Robb, and John Boyd, who were killed at this place on the 7th of October, 1780, fighting in defence of America." On the west side: "Colonel Ferguson, an officer of his Britannic Majesty, was defeated and killed at this place, on the 7th of October, 1780."— Mills' *Statistics*, 779; Hunter's *Sketches*, pp. 289, 311; MS. correspondence of Abraham Hardin.

When the army took up its line of march, strongly guarding their prisoners, the tenderest possible care was bestowed on the suffering wounded, conveyed on the horse-litters—and of none more so than on the heroic Colonel Williams. In the early part of the afternoon, when about three miles south-west of the battle ground, on the route towards Deer's Ferry on Broad river, the little guard having him in charge, discovering that life was fast ebbing away, stopped by the road-side at Jacob Randall's place, since long the homestead of Abraham Hardin, where he quietly breathed his last. His death was a matter of sincere grief to the whole army. His friends resolved, at first, to carry his remains to his old home, near Little river, in Laurens County; but soon after changed this determination. Marching some twelve miles from the battle ground, they encamped that night near the eastern bank of Broad river, and a little north of Buffalo creek, on the road leading to North Carolina, and within two or three miles of Boren's or Bowen's river and known also as Camp's creek. Here at the deserted plantation of a Tory named Waldron as Allaire has it—or Fondren, as Silas McBee remembered the name*—they found good camping ground, with plenty of dry rails and poles for their evening fires, and happily a sweet potato patch sufficiently large to supply the whole army.

" This," says Benjamin Sharp, " was most fortunate, for not one in fifty of us had tasted food for the last two days and nights—since we left the Cowpens." During the evening Colonel Campbell and party rejoined the patriots; and the footmen arrived whom they had left at the ford of Green river, and who had made commendable progress in following so closely upon the mounted advance; and who

---

*Col. J. R. Logan fully corroborates McBee's statement—that instead of Waldron, as Allaire has it, the name of the owner of the plantation where Williams was buried, was Matthew Fondren, connected with the Quinns of that region—so states Mrs. Margaret Roberts, *nee* Quinn, now nearly ninety years of age, and reared in that locality. Fondren was subsequently thrown from a chair or gig, and killed.

had, moreover, the good fortune to secure a temporary supply of food—live beef cattle, probably; so that the hungry mountaineers, almost famished, now enjoyed a happy repast.*

The next morning, for want of suitable conveyance, the friends of Colonel Williams concluded to bury his remains were they were. They were accordingly interred with the honors of war, between the camp of the patriots and the river, a little above the mouth of Buffalo creek—on what was long known as the Fondren, then the old Carruth place, now belonging to Captain J. B. Mintz.† Having performed this touching service, and fired a parting volley over the newly made grave of one of the noted heroes of the war of independence, the army, late in the day, renewed its line of march apparently up Broad river; and after passing what Allaire calls Bullock's creek, but what is evidently Boren's river they took up quarters for the night on its northern bank, having accomplished only two and a half miles. Beside the burial of Colonel Williams, the precarious condition of the wounded, probably, retarded the progress of this day's march, and time was needed for recuperation.

Tuesday, the tenth, was a busy day. The course pursued would seem to have been still up main Broad river, crossing First Broad and Sandy run, in a north-westerly direction, towards Gilbert Town, and camping in the woods that night, probably not very far from Second Broad river, after having accomplished a march of twenty miles. An incident occurred on this part of the route,

---

* Snodgrass MS. letter to Governor Campbell; Sharp's narrative; General Lenoir's statement; Allaire's MS. *Diary;* and conversations with Silas McBee.

† MS. correspondence of Colonel J. R. Logan and Abraham Hardin. Colonel Logan adds, that he learned from Captain Mintz that a tradition had been handed down that Colonel Williams was buried in that neighborhood, and no little pains had been taken to identify the grave by various people, and even by some of Colonel Williams' descendants, but without success. At length Captain Mintz employed some men to shrub off a field long overgrown, and requested them to watch for the long-forgotten grave; and sure enough, they found a grave with a head and foot stone composed of a different kind of rock from those abounding there, and well overgrown with grape vines. Though there was no inscription on the head-stone, there is no doubt it is the grave of " Old King's Mountain Jim."

worthy of notice. Among the prisoners were six brothers named Gage, who had joined Ferguson in consequence of the Tory influences surrounding them. During the second day's march, one of the Gages was taken ill, when the officer of the day, who probably could not provide any means for his conveyance, and possibly surmising that he was feigning sickness, in order to seek an opportunity to escape, or delay the Whigs so that Tarleton might overtake them, urged the sick prisoner to keep pace with the others. His brothers, to save him from possible calamity, took turns in carrying him on their backs; and they adopted the plan of availing themselves of their peculiar situation to lag as much behind as possible, with a view of taking advantage of the first considerable stream they should have occasion to pass, in the night, to fall down in the water, and suffer the rear guard to ride over them. Their scheme succeeded, and they thus escaped in the darkness unobserved.* The Whigs kept up their march of evenings, so long as they thought it necessary to place themselves beyond the reach of British pursuit.

During Wednesday, the eleventh, the army marched twelve miles, and encamped at Colonel John Walker's, according to Allaire's *Diary*. Colonel Walker, one of the prominent Whig leaders of the country, resided some five miles north-east of Gilbert Town, on the east side of Cane creek, half a mile above its mouth, and a mile below the present Brittain church.† There seems to have been

---

* Conversations with Benjamin Starritt, in 1843.

† Colonel Walker was born on Bohemia Creek, New Castle County, Delaware, in 1728. When grown, he settled on the South Branch of Potomac, Hampshire County, Virginia, where he married Elizabeth Watson. He served as a volunteer under Colonel Washington, and shared in Braddock's disastrous defeat in 1755. He shortly after removed to North Carolina, settling first on Leeper's Creek, in now Lincoln County, and served on Colonel Grant's campaign against the Cherokees in 1761. He subsequently located on Crowder's Creek; and, in 1768, at the mouth of Cane Creek, where he purchased a fine tract of four hundred acres for a doubloon. He was a man of marked character and prominence, holding several commissions under the Colonial Government—Colonel Commandant of Tryon County, and Judge of the Court for many years. On the breaking out of the Revolution, sharing in the sympathies of the people, he resigned his Loyal offices, and was among the foremost in signing the Articles of Association, pledging resistance to British encroachments,

individual cases of savage severity, even to murder, exercised towards the prisoners. Colonel Brandon, a rough, impulsive Irishman, discovering that one of the Tories, who had been carrying a couple of the captured guns, had dodged into a hollow sycamore by the road-side, dragged him from his hiding place, and completely hacked him to pieces with his sword.* Hints and innuendoes have been occasionally thrown out against Colonel Campbell himself as guilty of heartless cruelty to the Tory prisoners;† but the following extract from his *General Order*, at the camp below Gilbert Town, October eleventh, 1780, probably in the early part of the day, should be a complete vindication of his memory and good name from such a charge: " I must," he said, " request the officers of all ranks in the army to endeavor to restrain the disorderly manner of slaughtering and disturbing the prisoners. If it cannot be prevented by moderate measures, such effectual punishment shall be executed upon delinquents as will put a stop to it." ‡

It would appear that the army, on its march this day, passed through Gilbert Town; and resting there awhile, the prisoners were placed in a pen, in which Ferguson, when stationed there, had confined captured Whigs. When the British held full sway in that quarter, a Tory woman there was asked what the leaders were going to do with their Rebel prisoners in the bull-pen? " We are going," she tartly replied, " to hang all the d—d old Rebels, and take their wives, scrape their tongues, and let them go." This

---

in August, 1775; and. the same month, served as a member of the Convention at Hillsboro. His sons took an active part in the war, one of whom, Felix Walker, represented Rutherford County seven years in the House of Commons, and six in Congress. Colonel Walker, in 1787, removed to the mouth of Green river, in Rutherford County, where he died January 25th, 1796, in his sixty-eighth year. He was one of the pioneer fathers of Western Carolina. For most of the facts in this note, we acknowledge our indebtedness to the *Memoirs of Hon. Felix Walker*, edited by his grandson, Samuel R Walker.

* Conversations with the late Dr. A. Q. Bradley, who had this incident from one of Brandon's men.

† Statements of Henry Blevins, John Lang and Jacob Isely. appended to Shelby's King's Mountain pamphlet, 1823; and W. A. Henderson's published Lecture on Governor John Sevier. at Knoxville, Tennessee, in January, 1873.

‡ Copied from the original, furnished by General John S. Preston; Bancroft, x, 340.

same Loyalist lady, now when the changes of fortune had so suddenly reversed matters, again visited the prison-pen, where her husband, who had joined Ferguson's forces, was among those in confinement; and, with eyes filled with tears, touchingly· inquired of James Gray, one of the guard, "What are you Whigs going to do with these poor fellows?" Retorting in her own slang language, to annoy and humble her, he replied: "We are going to hang all the d—d old Tories, and take their wives, scrape their tongues, and let them go." This severe response completely confounded the termagant, against whose friends and cause the battle had gone, and she silently retired.*

Remaining in camp at Walker's during Thursday, the twelfth, the baggage of the British leaders was divided among the Whig officers, save a small portion granted to Captain DePeyster and his associates for a change. Colonel Shelby, referring to the tardy movements of the troops, observes: "Owing to the number of wounded, and the destitution of the army of all conveyances, they traveled slowly, and in one week had only marched about forty miles." † Another trying circumstance was, that in consequence of the contending armies having either occupied, or repeatedly traversed, this sparsely settled region, during the preceding two or three months, the people were completely

---

* MS. statement of J. L. Gray, derived from his grandfather, Jámes Gray; *Rutherford Enquirer,*. May 24th, 1859.

James Gray, who generously bound up. with his handkerchief, the broken ankle of a Tory acquaintance at King's Mountain, and treated the Tory woman with a touch of his biting sarcasm, was a worthy Revolutionary soldier. He was born in Augusta County, Virginia, in 1755, and settled in Tryon. since Rutherford County, North Carolina, prior to the Revolution. He served throughout the war, a part of the time in Captain Miller's company. He took part in Rutherford's campaign against the Cherokees in 1776; in the fight at Earle's on North Pacolet; in chasing Dunlap to Prince's Fort; and was in Captain Edward Hampton's company at the capture of Fort Anderson, on Thicketty creek. It was, as he used to relate, a matter of great satisfaction to him. that he aided in capturing at King's Mountain some of his Tory acquaintances who had formerly pursued him when unable to defend himself. He served in Captain Inman's company at the siege of Ninety Six, in 1781; and not long after was appointed a Captain, and guarded the stations at Earle's, Russell's, Waddleton's and White Oak. Captain Gray lived to enjoy a pension, and died in Rutherford County, October 21st, 1836, at the good old age of eighty-one years.

† *American Review,* December, 1848.

stripped of provisions, and both the patriots and their prisoners suffered greatly for want of the necessaries of life.
"The party," says the British Lieutenant Allaire, "was
kept marching two days without any kind of provisions."

Thomas Young, in his narrative, refers to the army
arriving on Cane creek with the prisoners, "where," he adds,
"we all came near starving to death. The country was
very thinly settled, and provisions could not be had for love
or money. I thought green pumpkins, sliced and fried,
about the sweetest eating I ever had in my life." * The poor
prisoners fared worse, for their food was uncooked. When
camped for the night, they were fed, while surrounded by a
cordon-guard, like so many farmer's swine—corn upon the
ear, and raw pumpkins, being thrown to them, which the
hungry fellows would seize with avidity. † To expedite the
march of the army, Colonel Campbell issued an order on
the thirteenth, while yet encamped at Walker's place,
directing that all the wounded who were not able to march
with the army, should be billeted in the best manner possible, the several companies to which they belonged providing the necessary assistance for their removal to places
selected for them. ‡ This was probably intended to lighten
the army of a part of its encumbrance ; but we judge, it was
found impracticable in that settlement, in consequence of
the scarcity of provisions. That day, according to Allaire's
Diary, the troops moved, with their prisoners, five or six
miles, north-east of Walker's to Bickerstaff's, or Biggerstaff's Old Fields, since known as the Red Chimneys, where
a stack of chimneys long stood after the house had decayed
and been demolished. This locality is on Robertson's
creek, some nine miles north-east of the present village of
Rutherfordton.

---

* *Orion* Magazine, October, 1843.

† Conversations with John Spelts, an eye-witness to these scenes ; and also with Benjamin Starritt.

‡ Colonel Campbell's MS. order, preserved by General Preston.

CHAPTER XV.

October—November, 1780.

Colonel Campbell Denounces Plundering.—Complaints against Tory Leaders.—Their Outrages on the Whigs.—A Court called to Consider the Matter.—Retaliation for British Executions Demanded.—A Law Found to Meet the Case.—Charges against Mills, Gilkey, and McFall.—Colonel Davenport Noticed.—Number of Tories Tried and Condemned.—Case of James Crawford.—One of the Prisoners Released.—Cleveland Favoring Severe Measures.—Motives of the Patriots Vindicated.—Shelby's Explanation.—Tories Executed—their Names and Residence.—Paddy Carr's Remarks, and Notice of Him.—Baldwin's Singular Escape.—Further Executions Stopped.—Tories Subsequently Hung.—Rumor of Tarleton's Approach.—Whigs Hasten to the Catawba.—A Hard Day's March—Sufferings of Patriots and Prisoners.—Major McDowell's Kindness.—Mrs. McDowell's Treatment of British Officers.—Some of the Whig Troops Retire.—Disposition of the Wounded. —Prisoners Escape—One Re-taken and Hung.—March to the Moravian Settlements.—Bob Powell's Challenge.—Official Account of the Battle Prepared.—Campbell and Shelby Visit General Gates. —Cleveland left in Command.—His Trial of Tories.—Escape of Green and Langum.—Cleveland Assaults Doctor Johnson.—Colonel Armstrong Succeeds to the Command.—Escape of British Officers.

While encamped at Bickerstaff's, on Saturday, the fourteenth, Colonel Campbell issued a *General Order*, deploring the "many deserters from the army," and the felonies committed by them on the poverty-stricken people of the country. "It is with anxiety," he adds, "that I hear the complaints of the inhabitants on account of the plundering parties who issue out of the camp, and indiscriminately rob both Whig and Tory, leaving our friends, I believe, in a worse situation than the enemy would have done;" and appeals to the officers "to exert themselves in suppressing

this abominable practice, degrading to the name of soldiers."
He further orders that none of the troops be discharged,
till the prisoners can be transferred to a proper guard. *
But some of the prisoners were soon to be disposed of in a
manner evidently not anticipated when the order just issued
was made known to the army.

During this day, an important occurrence transpired at
Bickerstaff's. The officers of the two Carolinas united in
presenting a complaint to Colonel Campbell, that there
were, among the prisoners, a number who were robbers,
house-burners, parole-breakers, and assassins. The British
victory near Camden had made, says General Preston,
" Cornwallis complete master of South Carolina. This
power he was using with cruelty, unparalleled in modern
civilized conquest; binding down the conquered people
like malefactors, regarding each Rebel as a condemned
criminal, and checking every murmur, answering every
suspicion with the sword and the fire-brand. If a suspected
Whig fled from his house to escape the insult, the scourge
or the rope, the myrmidons of Ferguson and Tarleton
burned it down, and ravished his wife and daughters; if a
son refused to betray his parent, he was hung like a dog;
if a wife refused to tell the hiding-place of her husband, her
belly was ripped open by the butcher-knife of the Tory;
and to add double horror and infamy to the deep damna-
tion of such deeds, Americans were forced to be the instru-
ments for perpetrating them. That which Tarleton (beast,
murderer, hypocrite, ravisher as he was,) was ashamed to
do, he had done by Americans—neighbors, kinsmen of his
victims. I draw no fancy picture—the truth is wilder far
than the fabulist's imagination can feign." †

Bancroft touchingly depicts the sad condition of the
people, where unchecked Toryism had borne sway : " The
sorrows of children and women," he says, " robbed and

---

* MS. Order preserved by General Preston.
† King's Mountain *Address, October*, 1855, 49.

wronged, shelterless, stripped of all clothes but those they wore, nestling about fires they kindled on the ground, and mourning for their fathers and husbands," were witnessed on every hand; and these helpless sufferers appealed to all hearts for sympathy and protection. Colonel Campbell, on the strength of the complaints made to him, was induced to order the convening of a court, to examine fully into the matter. The Carolina officers urged, that, if these men should escape, exasperated, as they now were, in consequence of their humiliating defeat, they would commit other enormities worse than their former ones.* The British leaders had, in a high-handed and summary manner, hung not a few of the captured patriots at Camden, and more recently at Ninety Six, and Augusta; and now that the Whigs had the means of retaliation at their command, they began to consider whether it was not their duty to exercise it; thinking, probably, that it would have a healthful influence upon the Loyalists—that the disease of Toryism, in its worst aspects, was disastrous in its effects, and heroic treatment had become necessary.

Colonel Shelby, with others, seems to have taken this view of the subject. When the mountaineers "reached Gilbert Town," says Shelby, "a week after the battle, they were informed by a paroled officer, that he had seen eleven patriots hung at Ninety Six a few days before, for being Rebels. Similar cruel and unjustifiable acts had been committed before. In the opinion of the patriots, it required retaliatory measures to put a stop to these atrocities. A copy of the law of North Carolina was obtained, which authorized two magistrates to summon a jury, and forthwith to try, and, if found guilty, to execute persons who had violated its precepts."† This law providing capital punishment, must have had reference to those guilty of murder, arson, house-breaking, riots, and other criminal offences.

---

* Ensign Robert Campbell's King's Mountain narrative.

† Shelby, in *American Review*, December, 1848.

" Colonel Campbell," says Ensign Campbell, " complied, and ordered a court-martial to sit immediately, composed of the field officers and Captains, who were ordered to inquire into the complaints which had been made. The court was conducted orderly, and witnesses were called and examined in each case—the consequence was, that thirty-two were condemned." *

Under the law as cited by Colonel Shelby, while the tribunal was, no doubt, practically, a court-martial, it was nominally, at least, a civil court, with two presiding justices. There was no difficulty on this point, for most of the North Carolina officers were magistrates at home—Colonel Cleveland, and four or five others, of the Wilkes regiment alone filling that position. The jury was composed of twelve officers—Lieutenant Allaire, in his *Diary*, denouncing it as " an infamous mock jury." " Under this law," says Shelby, " thirty-six men were tried, and found guilty of breaking open houses, killing the men, turning the women and children out of doors, and burning the houses. The trial was concluded late at night ; and the execution of the law was as summary as the trial."

How much of the evidence, hurriedly adduced, was one-sided and prejudiced, it is not possible at this late day to determine. Colonel Ambrose Mills, the principal person of those condemned, was a man of fair reputation, and must have been regarded chiefly in the light of being a proper and prominent character upon whom to exercise retaliatory measures ; and yet it was necessary to make some specific charge against him—the only one coming down to us, is that related by Silas McBee, one of the King's Mountain men under Colonel Williams, that Mills had, on some former occasion, instigated the Cherokees to desolate the frontier of South Carolina, which was very likely without foundation. It was proven against Captain Walter Gilkey, that he had called at the house of a Whig ;

* *Annals of the Army of Tennessee*, 1878.

and inquiring if he was at home, was informed by his son, a youth, that he was absent, when the Tory Captain immediately drew his pistol, discharged it, wounding the lad in the arm, and taking his gun from him. Recovering from his wound, this youth was now with the mountaineers, and testified against his would-be murderer. Gilkey's aged father was present, and offered in vain his horse, saddle and bridle, and a hundred dollars in money, as a ransom for his son.*

Another case somewhat similar to Gilkey's, was that of John McFall, a noted Tory leader of Burke County. Heading a party of mounted Loyalists, McFall dashed up to the house of Martin Davenport, on John's river, hoping to capture or kill him, as he was a prominent Whig, and had, more than once, marched against the Tories, under Colonel Cleveland and Major McDowell. But they failed to find him, as he was absent in the service. The Tory band vented their spleen and abuse on Mrs. Davenport, and directed her to prepare breakfast for them; and McFall ordered the lad, William Davenport, then in his tenth year, to go to the corn crib, procure some corn, and feed the horses in the trough prepared for such use at the hitching post. After getting their meal, and coming out to start off, McFall discovered that the horses had not been fed, and asked the little fellow roughly why he had not done as he had bidden him? The spirited little Rebel replied: "If you want your horses fed, feed them yourself." Flying into a passion, McFall cut a switch and whipped him smartly.

At the trial at Bickerstaff's, when McFall's case was reached, Major McDowell, as the proper representative of Burke County, whence the culprit hailed, was called on to give his testimony; when, not probably regarding McFall's conduct as deserving of death, he was disposed

---

* Conversations with Silas McBee; narrative of Ensign Robert Campbell; MS. correspondence of W. L. Twitty, as related by the venerable John Gilkey, of Rutherford County, N. C., in no way related to his Tory namesake.

to be lenient towards him.   Colonel Cleveland, who, it would appear, was one of the presiding justices, had his attention attracted from his paper, upon which he was making some notes, by hearing McFall's name mentioned, now spoke up—" That man, McFall, went to the house of Martin Davenport, one of my best soldiers, when he was away from home, fighting for his country, insulted his wife, and whipped his child ; and no such man ought to be allowed to live." *   His fate was sealed by this revelation ; but his brother, Arthur McFall, the old hunter of the mountains, was saved through the kind intervention of Major and Captain McDowell, believing, as he had been wounded in the arm at King's Mountain, it would admonish him not to be found in the future in bad company. †

Benjamin Sharp represents that the number of Tories condemned to the gallows was upwards of forty, Thomas Maxwell and Governor David Campbell say thirty-nine, Shelby thirty-six, General Lenoir and Ensign Campbell thirty-two, while Ramsey's *Tennessee*, Lieutenant Allaire, Benjamin Starritt and others, give the number as thirty. Starritt asserts that those upon whom sentence of death had been pronounced, were divided into three classes of ten each

---

* MS. pension statement of Richard Ballew, of Knox County, Ky , formerly of Burke County. N C. ; MS. letters of Hon. J. C. Harper, and Captain W. W. Lenoir, who had the particulars from William Davenport himself. Colonel Davenport was born in Culpeper County, Virginia, October 12, 1770. His mother dying about the close of the Revolution of small-pox, his father removed to the mountain region, on Toe river, in now Mitchell County ; a hunter's paradise, where he could indulge himself in his favorite occupation of hunting, and where his son William killed the last elk ever seen in North Carolina. Colonel William Davenport became a man of prominence, representing Burke County in the House of Commons in 1800, and in the Senate in 1802. He possessed an extraordinary memory, was a most excellent man ; and was the chief founder of Davenport Female College at Lenoir. He married the widow of Major Charles Gordon, one of the King's Mountain heroes ; and lived for many years in the Happy Valley of the Yadkin, three and a half miles above Fort Defiance, where he died August 19, 1859, in the eighty-ninth year of his age.

† MS. correspondence of W. A. McCall, Esq., of McDowell County, N. C., who knew Arthur McFall very well. He used to speak kindly of the McDowells befriending him, and said that Colonel Cleveland had little mercy on Americans who were caught fighting with the British. Arthur McFall spent most of his life as a hunter in the mountains, making his home, when in the settlements, with old acquaintances. He was a man after Daniel Boone's own heart ; and died about the year 1835, on Grassy Creek, at the venerable age of between ninety and a hundred years.

—Colonel Mills heading the first class, and James Crawford the second class. It will be remembered that Crawford, who lived at the head of French Broad river, belonged to Sevier's regiment; and while at " The Bald " of the Yellow Mountain on their outward march, had enticed Samuel Chambers, an inexperienced youth, to desert with him, and they gave Ferguson information of the plans and approach of the mountaineers. It is said, that when Ferguson had taken post on King's Mountain, and a week had elapsed since the renegades brought the report, that he had caused Crawford to be tried and condemned for bringing false intelligence; and the evening of the seventh of October had been set for his execution. However this may have been, Colonel Sevier interceded in Crawford's behalf, as he could not bear to see his old neighbor and friend suffer an ignominious death, and had him pardoned. He subsequently removed to Georgia. Young Chambers' guilt was excused on account of his youthfulness. * Judged by the laws of war, Crawford was a deserter; and in view of the injury he tried to inflict on the Whig cause, he as richly deserved the halter as André, and doubtless much more than any of his Tory associates.

As Abram Forney, one of the Lincoln troops, was surveying the prisoners, through the guard surrounding them, he discovered one of his neighbors, who only a short time before King's Mountain battle, had been acting with the Whigs; but had been over-persuaded, by some of his Tory acquaintances, to join the King's troops. Upon seeing him, Forney exclaimed—" Is that you, Simon?" "Yes," he replied, quickly, " it is, Abram, and I beg you to get me out of this bull-pen; if you do, I will promise never to be caught in such a scrape again." When it was, accordingly, made to appear on the day of trial, that he had been unfortunately wrought upon by some Tory neighbors, such a mitigation of his disloyalty was presented as to induce the court

---

* MS. notes of conversations with James and George W. Sevier, and Benjamin Starritt.

to overlook his offence, and set him at liberty.   Soon afterwards, true to his promise, he joined his former Whig
comrades, marched to the battle of Guilford, and made a
good soldier to the end of the war. *

So far as the evidence goes, Colonel Cleveland was
probably more active and determined than any other officer
in bringing about these severe measures; though Colonel
Brandon, it was well known, was an inveterate hater of
Tories; and Colonel Shelby seems to have aided in finding a State law that would meet these cases.   It is said
that Cleveland had previously threatened to hang certain
Tories whenever he could catch them;† and Governor
Rutledge, shortly after this affair, ascribed to him the chief
merit of the execution of several " noted horse thieves and
Tories" taken at King's Mountain. ‡

The Southern country was then in a very critical condition, and there seemed to be a grave necessity for checking,
by stern and exemplary punishment, the Tory lawlessness
that largely over-spread the land, and impressing that
class with a proper sense of the power and determination
of the Whigs to protect their patriot friends, and punish
their guilty enemies.   Referring to the action at Bickerstaff's, Ensign Campbell well observes: " The officers on
that occasion acted from an honorable motive to do the
greatest good in their power for the public service, and to
check those enormities so frequently committed in the States
of North and South Carolina at that time, their distress
being almost unequalled in the annals of the American
Revolution."   The historian, Bancroft, errs in supposing
that these executions were the work of lawless " private
soldiers." §   The complaints against the Tory leaders were
made by the officers of the western army from the two
Carolinas, and the court and jury were composed exclu-

---

* Hunter's *Sketches*, pp. 266–67.
† Gordon's *American Revolution*, iv., 466; Mrs. Warren's *Revolution*, ii, 252.
‡ *Russell's Magazine*, 1857, i, 543.
§ *History of the United States*, x, 339.

sively of officers—and all was done under the form and sanction of law.

While the jurist-historian, Johnson, could have wished that the conquerors of Ferguson had been magnanimous, and spared these miserable wretches from the gallows, yet as an act of justice and public policy he vindicates their conduct. Many severe animadversions, he observes, have been showered on the brave men who fought at King's Mountain for this instance of supposed severity. War, in its mildest form, is so full of horrors, that the mind recoils from vindicating any act that can, in the remotest degree, increase its miseries. To these no act contributes more than that of retaliation. Hence no act should be ventured upon with more solemn deliberation, and none so proper to be confined to a commander-in-chief, or the civil power. But the brave men who fought in the affair at King's Mountain, are not to be left loaded with unmerited censure.

The calmest and most dispassionate reflection upon their conduct, on this occasion, will lead to the conviction, that if they committed any offence, it was against their own country—not against the enemy. That instead of being instigated by a thirst of blood, they acted solely with a view to put an end to its effusion; and boldly, for this purpose, took upon themselves all the dangers that a system of retaliation could superinduce. The officers of the American army, who, twelve months afterwards, hazarded their lives by calling upon their General to avenge the death of Hayne, justly challenge the gratitude and admiration of their country; but the men of King's Mountain (for it is avowed as a popular act, and not that of their chief alone), merit the additional reputation of having assumed on themselves the entire responsibility, without wishing to involve the regular army in their dangers. And this was done in the plenitude of British triumph, and when not a man of them could count on safety for an hour, in anything but his own bravery and vigilance.

22

But what was the prospect before them? They were all proscribed men; the measures of Lord Cornwallis had put them out of the protection of civilized warfare; and the spirit in which his proclamations and instructions were executed by his officers, had put them out of the protection of common humanity. The massacres at Camden had occurred not six weeks before, and those of Browne, at Augusta, scarcely half that time. Could they look on and see this system of cruelty prosecuted, and not try the only melancholy measure that could check it? The effect proved that there was as much of reflection as of passion in the act; for the little despots who then held the country, dared prosecute the measure no farther. Another and an incontestible proof that blind revenge did not preside over the counsels that consigned these men to death, is drawn from the deliberation with which they were selected, and the mildness manifested to the residue of the prisoners.

It has been before observed, that, in the ranks of Colonel Ferguson, there were many individuals notorious as habitual plunderers and murderers. What was to be done with these? There were no courts of justice to punish their offences;* and, to detain them as prisoners of war, was to make them objects of exchange. Should such pests to society be again enlarged, and suffered to renew their outrages? Capture in arms does not exempt the deserter from the gallows; why should it the cold-blooded murderer? There was no alternative left; and the officers, with all the attention to form that circumstances would permit, and more—a great deal, it is believed—than either Browne or

---

* Such was the distraction of the times, that South Carolina, during the period of 1780-81, was without a civil government, Governor Rutledge having been compelled to retire from the State, and the Lieutenant Governor and some of the Council were prisoners of war. Nor during a portion of the war did North Carolina fare much better. At one time, one of her high judicial officers, Samuel Spencer, could only execute the laws against Tories with threats and attempted intimidation : the Governor, at one period, was captured and carried away. When Cornwallis invaded the State, the prominent officials fled, carrying the public records to Washington County, Virginia, on the lower frontiers of Holston, as a place of asylum and security, as is shown by a MS. letter of Colonel Arthur Campbell to Hon. David Campbell, September 15, 1810.

Cornwallis had exhibited, could only form a council, and consign them to the fate that would have awaited them in the regular administration of justice. *

It is but just and proper, in this connection, to give the views of Colonel Shelby, one of the conspicuous actors in this whole affair; and he seems to justify it wholly as a measure of retaliation: It is impossible, he observes, for those who have not lived in its midst, to conceive of the exasperation which prevails in a civil war. The execution, therefore, of the nine Tories at [near] Gilbert Town, will, by many persons, be considered an act of retaliation unnecessarily cruel. It was believed by those who were on the ground to be both necessary and proper, for the purpose of putting a stop to the execution of the patriots in the Carolinas by the Tories and British. The event proved the justice of the expectation of the patriots. The execution of the Tories did stop the execution of the Whigs. And it may be remarked of this cruel and lamentable mode of retaliation, that, whatever excuse and pretenses the Tories may have had for their atrocities, the British officers, who often ordered the execution of Whigs, had none. Their training to arms, and military education, should have prevented them from violating the rules of civilized warfare in so essential a point. †

Early in the evening, the trials having been brought to a conclusion, a suitable oak was selected, upon a projecting limb of which the executions were to take place. It was by the road side, near the camp, and is yet standing, known in all that region as the *Gallows Oak*. Torch-lights were procured, the condemned brought out, around whom the troops formed four deep. It was a singular and interesting night scene, the dark old woods illuminated with the wild glare of hundreds of pine-knot torches; and quite a number of the Loyalist leaders of the Carolinas about to be launched

---

* Johnson's *Life of Greene*, i. pp. 309-11.

† *Conversations with Governor Shelby*, in *American Review*, December, 1848.

into eternity. The names of the condemned Tories were—Colonel Ambrose Mills, Captain James Chitwood, Captain Wilson, Captain Walter Gilkey, Captain Grimes, Lieutenant Lafferty, John McFall, John Bibby, and Augustine Hobbs. They were swung off three at a time, and left suspended at the place of execution. According to Lieutenant Allaire's account, they died like soldiers—like martyrs, in their own and friends' estimation. "These brave but unfortunate Loyalists," says Allaire, "with their latest breath expressed their unutterable detestation of the Rebels, and of their base and infamous proceedings; and, as they were being turned off, extolled their King and the British Government. Mills, Wilson and Chitwood died like Romans." *

Among the small party of Georgians who served in the campaign, was the noted Captain Paddy Carr, heretofore introduced to the reader. Devoid, as he was, of the finer feelings of humanity, he was deeply interested in, and greatly enjoyed these sickening executions. If there was

---

* Allaire's MS. *Diary;* and his statements as given in the *Scot's Magazine* and Rivington's *Royal Gazette.*

It may be well to give the authorities for the names of the Loyalist leaders who suffered on this occasion. Lord Cornwallis, in his correspondence, names Colonel Mills, as do several historians; Allaire gives the names of Captains Wilson and Chitwood; Gilkey is referred to by Ensign Campbell, and specifically named by Silas McBee, and the venerable John Gilkey; Captain Grimes is mentioned in Ramsey's *Tennessee*, and Putnam's *Middle Tennessee;* McFall's name has been preserved by Richard Ballew, John Spelts, and Arthur McFall—eye-witnesses, and his prior acts at Davenport's are related by Hon. J. C. Harper and Captain W. W. Lenoir, who derived them from William Davenport; the names of Lafferty and Bibby have been communicated by W. L. Twitty, as the traditions of aged people of Rutherford County, N. C., where they, as well as Chitwood lived, whose name is likewise preserved in the memories of the aged inhabitants of that region; and the name of Hobbs is alone remembered by Silas McBee.

Colonel Mills resided on Green river, in Rutherford County; Captain Wilson, in the Ninety Six region, South Carolina; Chitwood, Lafferty, Bibby, and probably Gilkey, in Rutherford; McFall, in Burke County; Hobbs most likely in South Carolina; and Grimes in East Tennessee, where he was a leader of a party of Tory horse-thieves and highwaymen, and where some of his band were taken and hung. He fled to escape summary punishment, but justice overtook him in the end. His bandit career in Tennessee is noticed in Ramsey's *History* of that State, pp. 179, 243; and Putnam's *Middle Tennessee*, 58.

General DePeyster, in his able *Address on King's Mountain*, before the New York Historical Society, January, 4, 1881, has inadvertently fallen into the error of including Captain Oates as among those executed with Colonel Mills, citing Mrs. Warren's *History* as authority. Lord Cornwallis, in his letter to General Smallwood, November, 10, 1780, states that Captain Oates was taken by the Americans near the Pedee, in South Carolina, and "lately put to death."

anything he hated more than another, it was a Tory; and, it may be, much of his extreme bitterness grew out of the fact, that he knew full well how intensely he, in turn, was hated by the Loyalists. Pointing at the unfortunates, while dangling in mid-air, Carr exclaimed: " Would to God every tree in the wilderness bore such fruit as that !" *

After nine of the Loyalist leaders had been executed, and three others were about to follow suit, an unexpected incident occurred. Isaac Baldwin, one of these condemned trio, had been a leader of a Tory gang in Burke County, who had sacked many a house, stripping the unfortunate occupants of food, beds and clothing ; and not unfrequently, after tying them to trees, and whipping them severely, would leave them in their helpless and gory condition to their fate. While all eyes were directed to Baldwin and his companions, pinioned, and awaiting the call of the executioners, a brother of Baldwin's, a mere lad, approached,

---

* J. L. Gray's MS. statement; Rutherford *Enquirer*, May 24, 1859.

The Revolutionary war produced few characters so singular and so notorious as Patrick Carr. He was by birth an Irishman, and settled in Georgia before the commencement of the war. It is only in the latter part of the contest we are able to trace him. He shared as a Captain under Colonel Clarke in the heroic attack on Augusta, in September, 1780; then retired to the Carolinas, and joined the mountaineers under Major Candler, and fought at King's Mountain. The following month we find him under Sumter at Blackstocks; in May, 1781, engaged in forays against British and Tory parties in Georgia, waylaying and defeating them, extending little or no mercy to any of them. In November, 1781, when Major Jackson surprised the British post at Ogeechee, and its commander, Johnson, was in the act of surrendering his sword to Jackson, Carr treacherously killed Captain Goldsmith. Johnson and his associates, judging that no quarters would be given them, instantly sprang into their place of defence, and compelled the Americans to retire with considerable loss. A notorious Tory by the name of Gunn had concerted a plan to kill Colonel Twiggs, and subsequently fell into the Colonel's hands, when Carr insisted that Gunn should be hung; but Twiggs, more humane, protected the prisoner from harm. In 1782, Carr was made a Major, and, in the spring and early summer, marched with a force over the Altamaha, where he had two skirmishes with whites and Indians. On one occasion, Carr was praised for his bravery, when he replied that had not God given him too merciful a heart he would have made a very good soldier. It is related that he killed eighteen Tories on his way back from King's Mountain and Blackstocks to Georgia ; and one hundred altogether during the war, with his own hands! Certain it is, the Tories stood in great awe of him. He was murdered, in August, 1802, in Jefferson County, Georgia, where he long resided ; and, it is said, the act was committed by descendants of the Tories. In December following, the Jefferson County troop of Light Horse assembled at his place of interment, Lieutenant Robinson delivering a brief eulogy, when the military fired a volley over his grave. Though "a honey of a patriot, " Paddy **Carr** left a name

" ———————————————— to other times,
        Mixed with few virtues, and a thousand crimes."

apparently in sincere affection, to take his parting leave. He threw his arms around his brother, and set up a most piteous screaming and lamentation as if he would go into convulsions, or his heart would break of sorrow. While all were witnessing this touching scene, the youth managed to cut the cords confining his brother, who suddenly darted away, breaking through the line of soldiers, and easily escaping under cover of the darkness, into the surrounding forest. Although he had to make his way through more than a thousand of the best marksmen in the world, yet such was the universal admiration or feeling on the occasion, that not one would lift a hand to stop him. *

Whether the escape of Baldwin produced a softening effect on the minds of the Whig leaders—any feelings of forbearance towards the condemned survivors; or whether, so far as retaliation, or the hoped-for intimidating influence on the Tories of the country, was concerned, it was thought enough lives had been sacrificed, we are not informed. Some of these men must have been tried within the scope of the civil law, for crimes committed against society; while others must have been tried and condemned for violations of the usages of war; † and yet, after all, the *moral effect* would seem to have been the principal motive for these cases of capital punishment.

Referring probably to the two companions of Baldwin after he had effected his escape, we have this statement on the authority of Colonel Shelby: " Three more were tied, ready to be swung off. Shelby interfered, and proposed to

---

* Conversations with John Spelts and Benjamin Starritt; *Memoir of Major Thomas Young;* Johnson's *Life of General Greene,* i. 310.

Baldwin made his way into his old region, in Burke County, where his father resided, on Lower Creek of Catawba ; where some two weeks afterwards, he was espied in the woods by some scouts who gave chase, and finally overtook him, one of the pursuers killing him by a single blow over the head with his rifle. Some forty-five years after this tragedy, a younger brother of Ike Baldwin—probably the one who had so successfully planned his escape at Bickerstaff's—made three ineffectual attempts to kill the man who had brained the Tory free-booter.

† Speech of General Alexander Smyth, in Congress, January 21, 1819, *Niles' Register,* xv., Supplement, 151.

stop it. The other officers agreed; and the three men who supposed they had seen their last hour, were untied."* The inference is, that the officers here referred to, who, with Shelby, exercised the pardoning power, or " put a stop " to further executions, were the presiding officers of the court, in their character of justices, of whom Colonel Campbell could hardly have been one, though a magistrate at home, for the civil court was acting under the laws of North Carolina; and yet Ensign Campbell, in his narrative, speaks of the trials having been conducted before a court-martial, and adds, that, after the nine were executed, " the others were pardoned by the commanding officer; " while another eye-witness, Benjamin Sharp, states that " a court was detailed," and after the nine were hung, " the rest were reprieved by the commanding officer." Nor is the language of the late Governor Campbell less explicit: " A court-martial was ordered and organized to try many of the Tory officers, charged by the officers of North and South Carolina with many offences—such as murdering unoffend-ing citizens not in arms, and without motive, save the brutal one of destroying human life. Thirty-nine were found guilty, nine of whom were executed, and thirty were par-doned by the commanding officer." † Whether the surviv-ors were pardoned by the court in its civil capacity, or by the commanding officer at the instance of a court-martial, the executions ceased. ‡

---

* *American Review*, December, 1848.

† MS. statement by Governor Campbell.

‡ This, however, was not the last of the Tory executions. A few days after King's Mountain battle, while some young men of the surrounding country—Thomas Patterson, who escaped while a prisoner, and fought so bravely in the action, is believed to have been one of the party—were near the battle-ground, looking for horses in the range, they dis-covered one of Ferguson's foragers, who was absent at the time of the engagement. They concluded to capture him; but on showing such an intention, they were surprised at his pluck, in firing on them single-handed—the bullet whizzing close by them without harm. The Tory then betook himself to his heels, but was soon overhauled, and, without much ceremony, was suspended to the limb of a tree by means of one of the halters designed for the horses His carcass was left hanging till it decayed, and dropped to the ground; while the rope dangled from the limb for several years. So relates the venerable E. A. Patterson, a grand-son of young Arthur Patterson, who, while a prisoner on King's Mountain, escaped

One of the reprieved Tories, touched with a sense of the obligation he was under for sparing his life, and perhaps resolved thereafter to devote his energies to the Whig cause, went to Colonel Shelby at two o'clock that night, and made this revelation: "You have saved my life," said he, "and I will tell you a secret. Tarleton will be here in the morning—a woman has brought the news." * No doubt intelligence came that Tarleton had been dispatched by Lord Cornwallis with a strong force for the relief of Ferguson, if relief could be of any service; but as to the particular time of his arrival, that was the merest guess-work, and, with the Tories, the wish was father to the thought. But the Whig leaders, on receiving this information, deeming it prudent to run no risk, but to retire with their prisoners to a place of safety, instantly aroused the camp, picking up everything, sending the wounded into secret places in the mountains, and making every preparation for an early start in the morning. † They marched, according to Allaire's *Diary*, at the early hour of five o'clock, on Sunday, the fifteenth of October.

The poor Loyalist leaders had been left swinging from the sturdy oak upon which they had been executed. No sooner had the Whigs moved off, than Mrs. Martha Bickerstaff, or Biggerstaff, the wife of Captain Aaron Bickerstaff who had served under Ferguson, and been mortally wounded at King's Mountain, with the assistance of an old man who worked on the farm, cut down the nine dead bodies. Eight of them were buried in a shallow trench, some two feet deep; while the remains of Captain Chitwood

---

during the battle; corroborated by the venerable Abraham Hardin. Colonel J. R. Logan communicated Mr. Patterson's tradition of the affair.

Not long after the action at King's Mountain, a couple of Tories were caught and hung on an oak tree, near Sandy Plains Baptist Church, in the edge of Cleveland County, some four miles south-east of Flint Hill. Neither their names, nor the crimes with which they were charged, have been preserved. The tree on which they were executed is still standing, and like that at the Bickerstaff Red Chimneys, is known as the Gallows Oak; it has been dead several years. This tradition has been communicated by the aged father of Daniel D. Martin, of Rutherford County, and Colonel J. R. Logan.

* Shelby's account in *American Review.*

† Shelby's account.

were conveyed by some of his friends, on a plank, half a mile away to Benjamin Bickerstaff's, where they were interred on a hill still used as a grave-yard. About 1855, a party of road-makers concluded to exhume the remains of Colonel Mills and his companions, as the place of their burial was well known. The graves of only four of the number were opened, the bones soon crumbling on exposure. Several articles were found in a very good state of preservation—a butcher knife, a small brass chain about five inches in length, evidently used in attaching a powder-horn to a shot-bag, a thumb lancet, a large musket flint, a goose-quill, with a wooden stopper, in which were three or four brass pins. These articles, save the knife, and a portion of the pins, are preserved by M. O. Dickerson, Esq., of Rutherfordton. *

Shortly after marching from Bickerstaff's, rain began to fall in torrents, and it never ceased the whole day. "Instead of halting," says Benjamin Sharp, "we rather mended our pace in order to cross the Catawba river before it should rise to intercept us." It was regarded as essential to get out of Tarleton's reach, and hence the straining of every nerve, and the exercise of every self-denial, to accomplish so important an object. The sanguinary character of that impetuous British cavalry officer, and the celerity of his movements, as shown at Buford's defeat, at Monk's Corner, and at Sumter's surprise at Fishing Creek, admonished the Whig leaders of the enemy they might have to deal with; and impelled, on this occasion, by the hope of rescuing several hundred British and Tory prisoners was very naturally regarded by the patriots as a powerful incentive for Tarleton to push them to the utmost extremity, and play cut and slash as usual—and hence the supposed necessity of equal exertions on their part to avert so great a calamity. It is not a little singular that, at this very moment, Cornwallis and Tarleton were retreating from Charlotte to

---

* MS. correspondence of W. L. Twitty and Mr. Dickerson.

Winnsboro, South Carolina, with all their might and main—
"with much fatigue," says Lord Rawdon, "occasioned by
violent rains;" fearing that the "three thousand" reported
victorious mountaineers were in hot pursuit. "It was
amusing," said one of the King's Mountain men, "when
we learned the facts, how Lord Cornwallis was running in
fright in one direction, and we mountaineers as eagerly
fleeing in the other." *

In Allaire's newspaper narrative, we have this account
—whether colored or distorted, we have no means of
determining: "On the morning of the fifteenth, Colonel
Campbell had intelligence that Colonel Tarleton was
approaching him, when he gave orders to his men, that
should Tarleton come up with them, they were immediately
to fire on Captain DePeyster and his officers, who were in
the front, and then a second volley on the men. During
this day's march, the men were obliged to give thirty-five
Continental dollars for a single ear of Indian corn, and forty
for a drink of water, they not being allowed to drink when
fording a river; in short, the whole of the Rebels' conduct
from the surrender of the party into their hands, is incredible
to relate. Several of the militia that were worn out with
fatigue, not being able to keep up, were cut down and
trodden to death in the mire."

It was about ten o'clock at night, according to Allaire's
Diary, and as late as two o'clock, according to Shelby, when
the wearied troops and prisoners reached the Catawba, at
the Island Ford, where the river was breast deep as they
forded it. They bivouacked on the western bank of the
river at the Quaker Meadows—the home of Major Mc-
Dowell. "A distance of thirty-two miles," says Allaire,
"was accomplished this day over a very disagreeable road,
all the men worn out with fatigue and fasting, the prisoners
having had no bread nor meat for two days"—and, apparently, not even raw corn or pumpkins. Nor had the Whigs

---

* MS. Notes of conversations with Silas McBee, in 1842.

Jos. Mc.Dowell

fared any better, judging from the statement in the *American Review*, dictated by Colonel Shelby: "As an evidence of the hardships undergone by these brave and hardy patriots, Colonel Shelby says that he ate nothing from Saturday morning until after they encamped Sunday night—[or rather Monday morning]—at two o'clock." Benjamin Sharp throws additional light on the privations of the patriots: "During the whole of this expedition," he states, "except a few days at our outset, I neither tasted bread nor salt, and this was the case with nearly every man; when we could get meat, which was but seldom, we had to roast and eat it without either; sometimes we got a few potatoes, but our standing and principal rations were ears of corn, scorched in the fire or eaten raw. Such was the price paid by the men of the Revolution for our independence."

Here, at McDowell's, some provisions were obtained—not much of a variety, but such as satisfied half-starved men; nor did they seek rest until they had dried themselves by their camp fires, and enjoyed their simple repast. "Major McDowell," says Sharp, "rode along the lines, and informed us that the plantation belonged to him, and kindly invited us to take rails from his fences, and make fires to warm and dry us. I suppose that every one felt grateful for this generous offer; for it was rather cold, it being the last of October, and every one, from the Commander-in-chief to the meanest private, was as wet as if he had just been dragged through the Catawba river."

It is evident from Allaire's *Diary*, that when it was possible, courtesies were extended to the British officers—even when the Whig patriots themselves were camping out on the ground. "We officers," he says, "were allowed to go to Colonel McDowell's, where we lodged comfortably." A little incident transpired on this occasion which the good Lieutenant did not care, perhaps, to record in his *Diary*. Some of these very same officers had visited the residence of the McDowell's, under very different circumstances, the preceding month, when Ferguson had invaded the Upper Catawba Valley, and when the two brothers, Colonel Charles and Major Joseph McDowell, had retired with their little band across the mountains. Their widowed mother was the presiding hostess of the old homestead at the Quaker Meadows; she was a woman of uncommon energy and fearlessness of character—a native of the Emerald Isle. She possessed a nice perception of right and wrong; and, withal, was not wanting in her share of quick temper peculiar to her people.

Some of these visitors, having ransacked the house for spoils, very coolly appropriated, among other things, the best articles of clothing of her two noted Rebel sons; and took the occasion to tantalize the aged mother with what would be the fate of her boys when they should catch them. Charles should be killed out-right, but as for Joe, they would first compel him, by way of humiliation, to plead on his knees for his life, and then would slay him without mercy. But these threats did not in the least intimidate Mrs. McDowell; but she *talked back* at them in her quaint, effective Irish style, intimating that in the whirligigs of life, they might, sooner or later, have a little begging to do for themselves. The changed circumstances had been brought about in one short month, quite as much, perhaps, to the surprise of the good old lady, as to the proud officers of Ferguson's Rangers. Now they appeared again, wet, weary, and hungry; but Mrs. McDowell readily recognized them, and it required not a little kind persuasion on the part of Major McDowell to induce his mother to give those "thieving vagabond Tories," as she termed them, shelter, food, and nourishment. But the appeals of her filial son, of whom she was justly proud, coupled with the silent plea of human beings in their needy, destitute condition, prevailed; and in her Christian charity, she returned good for evil.*

---

* Related by the lady of Ex-Governor Lewis E. Parsons, of Alabama, who derived it from her mother, a daughter of Major Joseph McDowell, of Quaker Meadows.

It was fortunate for the mountaineers that they had succeeded in crossing the Catawba so opportunely, for the next
morning they found it had risen so much as to be past
fording. This obstacle would naturally prevent, for some
time, all pursuit, if indeed any had been made. It was
now arranged that Colonel Lacey's men * should be permitted to return to South Carolina, while most of Shelby's
and Sevier's regiments, with the footmen of the Virginians,
should take their home trail across the mountains. The
mounted men of Campbell's regiment, with the Wilkes and
Surry troops under Cleveland and Winston, and perhaps
McDowell's party, together with a few of Sevier's and
Shelby's young men who preferred to remain in the service,
and who had incorporated themselves into McDowell's
corps, now constituted the escort for the prisoners. Shelby
states, that after the several corps had retired at the Catawba,
there remained not more Whigs than they had prisoners to
guard—about five or six hundred.

The wounded Americans, who had been hid away in the
mountains when the troops marched so hurriedly from
Bickerstaff's, were soon brought forward ; and many of them
were left in Burke County, eight or ten miles above Burke
Court House, where Doctor Dobson, of that neighborhood,
had eighteen of them under his care at one time ; four of
whom were Wilkes and Surry County officers billeted at
a Mr. Mackey's. †

After a needful rest, and the return of fair weather, the
patriots proceeded at two o'clock on Monday afternoon,
October sixteenth, directing their course, by easy marches,
to the head of the Yadkin, and down the valley of that
stream. Fording Upper creek, or the North branch of
the Catawba, and John's river, they encamped that night at
a Tory plantation, not very far beyond the latter stream.

While on the hurried and toilsome march from Bicker-

---

* Pension statements of William White of Lacey's regiment, and William Alexander
of Campbell's men.

† Lieutenant Newell's statement, 1823.

staff's to the Catawba, and especially during several hours of the evening, amid rain and mud, it proved a favorable opportunity for many of the prisoners to give their guards the slip, and effect their escape. Allaire says the number reached a hundred. To put a stop to these numerous desertions, the Whig leaders promulgated severe admonitions of the consequences of any further attempts in that direction; but they did not effectually restrain the daring and adventurous. Having marched fifteen miles during Tuesday, passing through Happy Valley and over Warrior Mountain, the troops, with their prisoners, camped that evening at Captain Hatt's plantation, not very far from Fort Defiance; and, during the night, three of the prisoners attempted to evade their guards, two of them succeeding, while the other was shot through the body, retaken, and executed at five o'clock on the following morning. *

During Wednesday, the eighteenth, the troops forded Elk and Warrior creeks, camping that night on the western bank of Moravian creek, a short distance west of Wilkes Court House, having accomplished eighteen miles; and passing the next day through the Old Mulberry Fields, or Wilkes Court House, they took up their camp at Hagoods' plantation, on Brier creek, having marched sixteen miles this day. While in camp, on Brier creek, Colonel Campbell appears to have discharged some of his Virginians, for he wrote a letter on the twentieth, to his brother-in-law, Colonel Arthur Campbell, giving him a brief account of the battle, but was uncertain as yet what disposition would be made of the prisoners. Taking a late start on Friday, six miles only were accomplished, camping that night at Sales' plantation. Proceeding by slow marches, they passed Salem, arriving at Bethabara, or Old Town, on the twenty-fourth—both Moravian villages— whose people, according to Allaire, were stanch friends of the King, and were very kind to all the prisoners.

---

* Allaire's MS. *Diary.* Capt. Hatt may possibly be designed for Capt. Holt or Hall.

The very first night the British officers had been assigned quarters at Bethabara, Lieutenant Allaire and Doctor Johnson, who were rooming together, were driven from their bed by a violent Whig Captain named Campbell, who, with drawn sword, threatened them with death if they did not instantly obey him. Colonel Campbell was notified of this rudeness, who had the unseasonable intruder turned out of the room; * and this is but another instance of his sense of justice towards helpless prisoners.

Among the Tory captives, was a notorious desperado named Bob Powell. He was a man of unusual size, strong, supple, and powerful. He boasted of his superior ability and agility to out-hop, out-jump, out-wrestle, or out-fight any Whig in the army. He seemed to possess a happier faculty of getting into scrapes, than in getting out. Chained with two accomplices for some bad conduct, he sent word one morning that he wanted to see Colonels Campbell, Shelby and Cleveland, on a matter of importance. When waited on by those officers, he seemed to think that the proposition he was about to submit was a matter of no small consideration—no less than a challenge to wrestle or fight with the best man they could produce from their army, conditioned that, should he prove victor, his freedom should be his reward; should he fail, he would regard his life as forfeited, and they might hang him. Though a couple of guineas were offered to any man who would successfully meet him—probably more with a view of an exhibition of the "manly art," as then regarded by the frontier people, yet no one saw fit to engage in the offered contest. Under the circumstances, all knew full well that Powell would fight with the desperation of a lion at bay; and none cared to run the risk of encountering a man of his herculean proportions, with the stake of freedom to stimulate his efforts.†

It was apparently while at Bethabara, that Colonels

---

* Allaire's MS *Diary*, and his newspaper narrative.
† MS. notes of conversation with John Spelts, an eye-witness.

Campbell, Shelby, and Cleveland made out their official report of King's Mountain battle. Had it been prepared before Colonels Lacey and Sevier had retired at the Quaker Meadows, the names of those two officers would doubtless have been attached to it also.* Colonel Shelby accompanied the troops to Bethabara. He had been deputed to visit General Gates at Hillsboro, to tender the services of a corps of mountaineers, mostly refugees, under Major McDowell, to serve under General Morgan. Colonel Campbell also had occasion to repair to head-quarters to make arrangements for the disposition of the prisoners.

On the twenty-sixth of October, Colonel Campbell issued a *General Order*, appointing Colonel Cleveland to the command of the troops and prisoners until his expected return, especially providing that full rations be issued to the prisoners ; adding, " it is to be hoped, no insult or violence unmerited will be offered them ; no unnecessary injury be done to the inhabitants, nor any liquor be sold or issued to the troops without an order from the commanding officer." † Here we have additional evidence, if any were needed, of Campbell's humanity and good sense.

Colonels Campbell and Shelby had scarcely departed, when new troubles arose in the treatment of the prisoners. Allaire tells us, that one of the Whig soldiers was passing the guard, where the captives were confined, when he rudely accosted them : " Ah ! d—n you, you'll all be hanged !" One of the prisoners retorted—" Never mind that, it will be your turn next ! " For this trifling offence, the poor fellow

---

* Doctor Ramsey, in his *History of Tennessee*, states that the three Colonels visited Hillsboro, and there made out their report. Colonel Cleveland did not go there on that occasion, having been left in command at Bethabara. His name was signed to the report by himself, and not by another, as a comparison of his genuine autograph with the *fac-simile* signature to the report conclusively shows. Perhaps as a compliment, Colonel Cleveland was permitted to head the list, in signing the report, as shown in *fac simile* in Lossing's *Field Book of the Revolution ;* but when General Gates sent a copy, November 1, 1780, to Governor Jefferson, to forward to Congress, he very properly placed Campbell's name first, Shelby's next, and Cleveland's last—and so they appear as published in the gazettes at the time by order of Congress.

† MS. order, preserved by General Preston.

was tried before Colonel Cleveland, and condemned to be hung. Quite a number of people gathered at Bethabara to witness the execution of the unfortunate man ; "but," adds Allaire, "Colonel Cleveland's goodness extended so far as to reprieve him."

About this time, Captain William Green and Lieutenant William Langum, among the Tory prisoners, were tried before Colonel Cleveland. The charge against Green seems to have been, that he had violated the oath he had taken as an officer to support the governments of the State of North Carolina and of the United States, by accepting a British commission, and fighting at King's Mountain. Some of the British officers were present, and remonstrated at the course taken, when Cleveland cut them short, saying : "Gentlemen, you are British officers, and shall be treated accordingly—therefore give your paroles and march off immediately ; the other person is a subject of the State." * Green and Langum were condemned to be executed the next morning. "May be so," coolly remarked Green.

That night, as he and his comrade, Langum, were lying before the camp-fire, under a blanket, Green rolled over so that his hands, fastened with buck-skin straps, came in contact with Langum's face, who seeming to comprehend his companion's intention, worked away with his teeth till he succeeded in unfastening the knot. Green was now able to reach his pocket, containing a knife, with which he severed the remaining cords, and those of Langum. He then whispered to Langum to be ready to jump up and run when he should set the example. Green was above the ordinary size, strong and athletic. The guard who had special watch of them, was in a sitting posture, with his head resting upon his knees, and had fallen asleep. Making a sudden leap, Green knocked the sentinel over, and tried to snatch his gun from him ; but the latter caught the skirt of the fleeing man's coat, and Green had to make a

---

* Gordon's *American Revolution*, iii, pp. 466-67.

23

second effort before he could release himself from the soldier's grasp, and gladly got off with the loss of a part of his
garment.   In another moment both Green and Langum
were dashing down a declivity, and though several shots
were fired at them, they escaped unhurt, and were soon
beyond the reach of their pursuers.   Aided by the friendly
wilderness, and sympathizing Loyalists, they in time reached
their old region of Buffalo creek, in now Cleveland County,
Green at least renouncing his brief, sad experience in the
Tory service, joined the Whigs, and battled manfully thereafter for his country.   Both Green and Langum long survived the war, and were very worthy people. *

   Allaire records an incident, involving, if correctly reported,
rash treatment on the part of Colonel Cleveland towards
Doctor Johnson, whose benevolent acts, it would be supposed, would have commanded the respectful attention of all :
" November the first," writes Lieutenant Allaire, " Doctor
Johnson was insulted and knocked down by Colonel Cleveland, for attempting to dress the wounds of a man whom
the Rebels had cut on the march.   The Rebel officers
would often go in amongst the prisoners, draw their swords,
cut and wound whom their wicked and savage minds
prompted." †   There must have been something unex-
plained in Doctor Johnson's conduct—the motive is wanting
for an act so unofficer-like as that imputed to Colonel Cleveland.   While it is conceded that he was a rough frontier
man, and particularly inimical to thieving and murderous
Tories, yet he was kind-hearted, and his sympathies
as responsive to misfortune as those of the tenderest
woman.   The same day, Colonel Cleveland was relieved
of his command by Colonel Martin Armstrong, his superior

---

*MS. Deposition of Colonel Wm. Porter, 1814, kindly communicated by Hon. W. P.
Bynum ; MS. letters of Jonathan Hampton and Colonel J R. Logan, the latter giving the
recollections of the venerable James Blanton, now eighty-two years of age, who was well
acquainted with both Green and Langum ; statements of Benjamin Biggerstaff and J. W.
Green, furnished by W. L. Twitty. Some of the traditions represent Langum's name as
Lankford.

† Allaire's MS. *Diary*, and his newspaper narrative.

in rank, as well as the local commandant of Surry County, where the troops and prisoners then were.

The British officers had been expecting to be paroled. Colonel Cleveland's remark to them, at Green's trial, would seem to indicate the early anticipation of such an event. "After we were in the Moravian town about a fortnight," says Allaire, "we were told we could not get paroles to return within the British lines; neither were we to have any till we were moved over the mountains in the back parts of Virginia, where we were to live on hoe-cake and milk." Large liberties had been accorded the officers, to enable them to while away the tedium of captivity: so that they sometimes visited the neighboring Moravian settlements, or dined at their friends, in the country.

When Lieutenants Taylor, Stevenson, and Allaire learned that there was no immediate prospect of their receiving paroles, they concluded that they would "rather trust the hand of fate," as Allaire states it in his narrative, and make a desperate effort to reach their friends—taking French leave of their American captors. Accordingly, on Sunday evening, about six o'clock, the fifth of November, they quietly decamped, taking Captain William Gist, of the South Carolina Loyalists, with them; traveling fifteen miles that night to the Yadkin, the fording of which they found very disagreeable, and pushed on twenty miles farther before daylight. Though pursued, the Whigs were misled by false intelligence from Tory sources, and soon gave up the chase.

Traveling by night, and resting by day; sometimes sleeping in fodder-houses, oftener in the woods; with snatches of food at times—hoe-cake and dried beef on one occasion—supplied by sympathizing friends by the way; encountering cold rain storms, and fording streams; guided some of the weary journey by Loyalist pilots, and sometimes following such directions as they could get; passing over the Brushy Mountain, crossing the Upper Catawba, thence over the country to Camp's Ford of second Broad river, the Island Ford of Main Broad, and the old Iron Works of Pacolet; barely escaping Sumter's corps at Blackstock's on Tyger, they at length reached Ninety Six, the eighteenth day after taking their leave of Bethabara, traveling, as they accounted distance, three hundred miles. These resolute adventurers suffered unspeakable fatigues and privations, but successfully accomplished the object of all their toils and self-denials. After resting a day at Ninety Six, they pursued their journey to Charleston.

CHAPTER XVI.

October—December, 1780.

Disposition of King's Mountain Prisoners.—Proposition to Enlist them. —Needed for Exchange.—Congress Refers the Matter to the States where the Prisoners Belong.—How they Dwindled Away.—Colonel Armstrong Blamed.—Remnant Confined at Salisbury.—DePeyster and Ryerson Paroled.—A Plucky Band of Whigs Scare a large Tory Party.—Tarleton Frustrates Cornwallis' Design of Relieving Ferguson.—Intercepting Ferguson's Messengers.—Tarleton at Length in Motion.—His Instructions.—Effect of King's Mountain Victory.—Ewin and Barry Alarm the Neutrals, and they Alarm Cornwallis.—Crowing of David Knox.—Cornwallis flees to South Carolina, with the Imaginary Mountaineers in Pursuit.—A Tricky Guide Misleading the Retiring Troops.—A Panic.—Illness of Cornwallis.—Sickness and Fatality among the Troops.—Privations and Sufferings of the Retrograders.—Aid Rendered by the Tories.— Ninety Six Safe.—Cornwallis Threatens Retaliation for Execution of King's Mountain Prisoners.—Gates and Randall on the Situation.—The Question Met by General Greene.—Cornwallis Drops the Matter.—Case of Adam Cusack.—The Widows and Orphans of Ninety Six District.—Good Words for King's Mountain Victory.— Gates Thanks the Victors.—Washington Takes Courage.—Resolves of Congress.—Greene and Lee Commend the Mountaineers.—Lossing, Bancroft, and Irving on the Result.—The British Leaders Recognize the Disastrous Effects of Ferguson's Miscarriage.—Gates and Jefferson's Encomiums.—King's Mountain Paves the Way for Yorktown and Independence.

General Gates, on the twelfth of October, at Hillsboro, received the joyous intelligence of the victory of King's Mountain; and wrote the next day to Colonel William Preston, near Fort Chiswell, or the Lead Mines, in the Virginia Valley, appointing him to prepare barracks or other works for the reception of the prisoners, and to take the superintendency of them, believing that locality a safe quarter, and where the necessary supplies could be obtained for their support. Colonel Preston assured General Gates that the Lead Mines would be an unsafe place for the prisoners, as there were more Tories in that County, Montgomery, than any other known to him in Virginia; he urged, besides, the further objection of its proximity to Surry and other disaffected regions in North Carolina, and the inimical Cherokees to the south-west. He, therefore, suggested the County of Botetourt, higher up the Valley, as more suitable, and William Madison as a proper and younger person to undertake the service.*

It would seem that General Gates balanced between two modes of disposing of the prisoners—one, to place them where they would be secure from rescue, " to be ready for exchange for our valuable citizens in the enemy's hands ;" the other, a suggestion of Colonel Campbell, to send them to the North, and incorporate them with the army under General Washington. Colonel Campbell was the bearer of General Gates' dispatches on the subject to Governor Jefferson, at Richmond, who finally referred the whole matter to Congress.† That body, on the twentieth of November, recommended to Governor Jefferson to cause the King's Mountain prisoners to be secured in such manner and places as he might judge proper : " That a list of the names of the Tory prisoners be taken, distinguishing the States, County or District to which they severally belong, and transmitted to the Executives of their several States, who are requested to take such order respecting them as the public security, and the laws of the respective States may require." ‡

But various circumstances combined to render all such arrangements of no avail. Starting from King's Mountain with not to exceed six hundred prisoners, they rapidly

---

* MS. letter of Gates to Preston, October 13, and of Preston to Gates, October 27, 1780; Jefferson's *Works*, i, 273.

† MS. letter of Linnæus Smith to General Francis Preston, July 19, 1823.

‡ Journals of Congress, 1780, vi, 374.

dwindled away; the paroles of some of them commenced the second day after the battle; * one hundred, Allaire tells us, escaped during the march the stormy day, and part of the night, before reaching the Quaker Meadows; half a dozen at another time; Allaire and three associates escaping as already related, and still later sixteen soldiers succeeded in getting away from the guard at Bethabara, † while doubtless many others evaded the vigilance of their guards of which we have no record. According to the Moravian accounts, there were never more than three hundred prisoners at Bethabara, fifty of whom were of Ferguson's Provincial corps, and five hundred Whigs to guard them, who remained at that place nineteen days, till all the provisions were consumed. ‡ Prior to the seventh of November, one hundred and eighty-eight, who were inhabitants of the western country of North Carolina, were taken out of Colonel Armstrong's charge by the civil authorities, and bound over, § inferentially for their appearance at court, or for their good behavior; some were dismissed, some paroled, but most of them enlisted—some in the three months' militia service, others in the North Carolina Continentals, and others still in the ten months' men under Sumter. So evident was it to General Gates, that neither the military nor civil officers of North Carolina had any authority over these prisoners, many of whom had been almost constantly in arms against their country since the surrender of Charleston, that he remonstrated with the State Board of War at Salisbury; and Colonel Armstrong was made to answer for the injury thus done to the American cause. The remaining prisoners were then marched under a strong guard to Hillsboro. ‖

---

* MS. parole of Dennis McDuff by Captain George Ledbetter, October 9th, 1780, preserved by Hon. W. P. Bynum.

† Colonel Armstrong to Gen. Gates, November 11th, 1780, among the Gates Papers in the New York Historical Society.

‡ Reichel's *Moravians in North Carolina*, pp. 92-93.

§ Colonel Armstrong to Gen. Gates, November 7th and 11th, 1780.

‖ Burk's *History of Virginia*, iv, 410.

Including the Provincials, only about one hundred and thirty captives remained; and General Greene, when he took the command of the Southern department, early in December, lamented the loss of so many of the King's Mountain prisoners, who, had they been retained, would have been the means of restoring to the service many a noble soldier languishing in British prisons; nor was he without suspicions of something more than folly on the part of those who had taken such liberties to dispose of them. * The jail and a log house near it, at Salisbury, were ordered by General Greene to be picketed in, for the reception of the remaining prisoners, who were directed to erect huts within the pickets, † for their use as cooking and sleeping apartments. " The North Carolina government," wrote Colonel Henry Lee to General Wayne, January seventh, 1781, " has in a great degree baffled the fruits of that victory. The Tories captured were enlisted into the militia or draft service, and have all rejoined the British; I heard General Greene say, yesterday, that his last return made out sixty in jail, and his intelligence from the enemy declares that two hundred of them were actually in arms against us." ‡ In February ensuing, Captains DePeyster and Ryerson were paroled to Charleston, and found on their arrival that they were already exchanged. §

A singular incident occurred, in connection with the King's Mountain campaign, that shows what, with pluck and bravery, a few fearless men may accomplish. Ferguson, it will be remembered, had foraging, and perhaps recruiting, parties out—under Colonel John Moore, Major Zachariah Gibbs, and, very likely, others. One of these parties, estimated at above two hundred and fifty, though probably not so numerous, encamped a night or two pre-

---

* Greene to Washington, December 7th, 1780.

† Greene's *Life of Greene*, iii, pp. 78-79.

‡ *Life of Gen. Henry Lee*, by R. E. Lee, perfixed to *Lee's Memoirs*, revised edition, 1872, p. 33.

§ Captain Ryerson's statement in the *Royal Gazette*, Charleston, October 27th, 1781.

ceding the battle, at a school-house, near Hollingsworth's mill, on Brown's creek, in now Union County, South Carolina, some twenty-five miles south of King's Mountain. Their camp was on a high hill, thickly covered with timber.

A small party of eight or ten Whigs, who were lurking about the thickets along Brown's creek, with a view of gaining intelligence concerning both friends and foes, chanced to capture a solitary Tory, from whom they learned of the design of this large party of foragers to bivouac that night at the school-house near Hollingsworth's. Ready for adventure, the plucky Whigs, though so few in number compared with their adversaries, thought they might gain by strategy what they could not accomplish by main strength; and concluded to make an effort to give the Tory camp, at least, a first-rate scare. They accordingly arranged their plan of proceedings, which was natural and simple. Some time after dark they approached the enemy's camp—spread themselves in open order, around the hill, at some distance from each other, with the understanding that they would advance till hailed by the sentinels, then lie down till the guards fired, when they would arise and rush towards the camp, firing and shouting as best they could.

They moved forward with great caution. The Tory camp-fires threw a glaring light towards the canopy of heaven, and lit up the forest far and near. All was joy and gladness in the camp. The jovial song, and merry laugh, indicated to the approaching Whigs that good cheer abounded in the camp among the friends of King George. In a moment all this was suddenly changed—the sentinels hailed—then they fired, when an unseen foe rushed on through the woods, yelling and screaming at the top of their voices—and bang! bang! belched forth their rifles in quick succession. The poor Tories were taken completely by surprise—a panic ensued; and crying "mercy! mercy!" they dashed through the bushes down the hill at their very best speed. A frightened Tory was proverbially famous in such a race.

The victorious Whigs came into the camp one after another, and peered into the darkness, but could only hear the retreating foragers darting through the woods ; the noise growing fainter at each successive moment ; while the skedaddlers, poor souls, were congratulating themselves on their fortunate escape from a formidable party of Rebels, led on, it might be, by the untiring Sumter, or such a Tory-hater as Tom Brandon, of Fair Forest. The Whigs had now gained full possession of the camp, with none to dispute their victory.   Forage wagons were standing hither and thither, horses hitched to them and to the surrounding trees, guns stacked, cooking utensils lying about the fires, with hats, caps, and articles of clothing scattered in wild confusion.

Till the grey twilight streaked the eastern sky on the following morning, the little patriot band kept close guard, expecting the momentary return of the campers ; but nothing of the kind transpired. The sun rose brightly, and mounted high above the hills, and still no report from the fugitives.   What should be done with the horses, arms, baggage and baggage-wagons, was now discussed by the fearless captors. They transported them from the camp, around the hill to a secluded spot, and maintained a strict watch over their new quarters, and the property they had so adroitly captured.   It must have been the day succeeding Ferguson's defeat, that one of the men on guard discovered a party of a dozen or fifteen horsemen rapidly approaching.   It was thought to be the van of an army— perhaps Ferguson's—coming to recover the spoils ; but the brave Whigs who had made the successful capture, and had guarded the plunder with so much vigilance, resolved to test the matter.

They boldly advanced in a body, hailed the vanguard, while their horses were drinking at the creek.   But the horsemen responded only by a confused flight ; and upon them the patriots discharged their rifles, which disabled one of their horses, so that his rider surrendered in dismay. From him the Whigs learned that his party was just 'from King's Mountain—probably the band who had returned from a foray, and fired upon the mountaineers at the close of the action, mortally wounding Colonel Williams—and were now making the best of their way to their respective homes, or to Ninety Six, having in view no other object than their personal safety. Learning of Ferguson's total defeat, the Whig heroes now ventured to leave their secluded camp, and gather a party to convey away the spoils of war to a place of safety, where they and their friends could divide and enjoy them. *

Lord Cornwallis' fine schemes of North Carolina and Virginia conquest, were destined to a speedy disappointment. Awaiting at Charlotte, for the reception of supplies, and the return of the healthful season, to prosecute his military enterprise, he had reluctantly yielded to the persuasions of Colonel Ferguson to make an excursion into the western borders of North Carolina, to encourage the friends of the Government in that quarter. Though Ferguson gave Cornwallis the assurance that his trained militia could be trusted, yet his Lordship had serious doubts on that head, declaring that Ferguson's "own experience, as well as that of every other officer, was totally against him;" but, in consequence of Ferguson's entreaties, backed with the earnest advice of Colonel Tarleton, the expedition was undertaken, Ferguson promising to return should he hear of any superior force approaching him.

Cornwallis, failing for some time to receive any definite information from Ferguson, evidently commenced to feel anxious concerning his situation. In the *Virginia Gazette*, of October eleventh, 1780, we find among the latest items of intelligence from the southward, one to the effect that " on the thirtieth of September, about eight hundred of the enemy, with two field pieces, were on their march, three miles in

---

* Saye's *Memoir of McJunkin.*

advance from Charlotte, on the road leading to Beattie's Ford, on Catawba river, supposed to be intended to support Major Ferguson, who was, with a party, in the neighborhood of Burke Court House."

If a relief force was sent at all, it was not pushed far enough forward to accomplish the purpose. Tarleton's illness of a fever—yellow fever, as Major Hanger terms it—may have caused procrastination. "Tarleton is bétter," wrote Lord Cornwallis to Ferguson on the twenty-third of September. As he recovered, he was pressed to engage in this service, but found excuses for not undertaking it. "My not sending relief to Ferguson," observed Lord Cornwallis, "although he was positively ordered to retire, was entirely owing to Tarleton himself; he pleaded weakness from the remains of a fever, and refused to make the attempt, although I used the most earnest entreaties." *

Tarleton informs us, that the County of Mecklenburg, in which Charlotte was situated, and the adjoining County of Rowan, were more hostile to England than any other portion of America; that so vigilant were the Whig troops and people of that region, that " very few, out of a great number of messengers, could reach Charlotte, in the beginning of October, to give intelligence of Ferguson's situation." At length Cornwallis received confused reports of Ferguson's miscarriage. He dispatched Tarleton on the tenth of that month, with his Light Infantry, the British Legion, and a three-pounder, to go to the assistance of Ferguson, as no certain intelligence had arrived of his defeat; though it was rumored, with much confidence, by the Americans in the neighborhood of Charlotte. Tarleton's instructions were to re-inforce Ferguson wherever he could find him, and to draw his corps to the Catawba, if, after the junction, advantage could not be obtained over the mountaineers; or, upon the certainty of his defeat, at all events to oppose the entrance of the victorious Americans into South Carolina—

---

* Cornwallis' *Correspondence*, i, 59.

fearing they might seriously threaten Ninety Six and Augusta.*

The effect of King's Mountain battle on the Tories of the country, and on Lord Cornwallis and his officers at Charlotte, may be best inferred from actual facts explanatory of the matter. Robert Henry, who had been so painfully transfixed in a British charge on Chronicle's men, was conveyed to his home on the South Fork, a few miles of the way on Saturday evening after the battle, and the remainder on Sunday, Hugh Ewin and Andrew Barry, two of his brave companions, acting as his escort. On Monday morning these two friends came to see him, and learned the happy effects of a poultice of wet, warm ashes, applied to his wounds by his good mother. While there, several neutrals, as they termed themselves, but really Tories in disguise, called to learn the news of the battle, when the following dialogue took place between them and Ewin and Barry:

" Is it certain," inquired one of the Tories, "that Colonel Ferguson is really killed, and his army defeated and taken prisoners?"

" Yes, it is certain," replied the Whigs, "for we saw Ferguson after he was dead, and his army prisoners of war."

" How many men had Ferguson?"

" Nearly, but not quite, twelve hundred," was the reply.

" Where," asked the Tories, "did the Whigs get men enough to defeat him?"

"They had," responded the patriots, "the South Carolina and Georgia refugees, Colonel Graham's Lincoln County men, some from Virginia, some from the head of the Yadkin, some from the head of the Catawba, some from over the mountains, and some pretty much from everywhere."

" Tell us," eagerly inquired the neutrals, "how it happened, and all about it."

---

* Tarleton's *Campaigns*, pp. 160, 161, 165.

"Well," said Ewin and Barry, "we met near Gilbert Town, and found that the foot troops could not overtake Ferguson, and we took between six and seven hundred horsemen, leaving as many or more footmen to follow; and we overtook Ferguson at King's Mountain, where we surrounded and defeated him."

"Ah!" said one of the Tories, "that will not do—between six and seven hundred surrounding nearly twelve hundred. It would have taken more than two thousand to surround and take Colonel Ferguson."

"But," responded the Whigs, "we were all of us blue hens' chickens—real fighters, and no mistake."

"There must have been," said the Tories, "of your foot and horse over four thousand in all. We see what you are about—that your aim is to catch Lord Cornwallis napping."

Thus ended the dialogue, not more than two hours after sunrise on Monday, the ninth of October; and the neutrals or Tories quickly took their departure. It was reported that they immediately swam a horse across the swollen Catawba, by the side of a canoe, and hastened to give Lord Cornwallis the earliest news of Ferguson's defeat.

As soon as the intelligence reached Charlotte, it produced a great excitement among all classes.

"Have you heard the news," inquired one officer, of the guard?

"No, what news?"

"Why," said the first, "Colonel Ferguson is killed, and his whole army defeated and taken prisoners."

"How can that be," said the doubter—"where did the men come from to accomplish such a feat?"

"Some of them," replied the man of news, "were South Carolina and Georgia refugees, some from Virginia, some from the heads of the Yadkin and Catawba, some from over the mountains, and some from everywhere. They met at or near Gilbert Town, about two thousand desperadoes on horseback, calling themselve blue hens' chickens; and started in pursuit of Ferguson, leaving as many footmen to follow. They overtook Ferguson at a place called King's Mountain, where they surrounded his army, killed that gallant officer, defeated his men, and took the survivors prisoners."

"Can this be true?" despondingly inquired the first officer.

"As true as the gospel," replied the other; "and we may look out for breakers."

"God bless us!" ejaculated the dejected officer of the guard.

David Knox, a kinsman of President Polk, who was a prisoner, but enjoyed the privilege of the town, a man full of fun and frolic, hearing this colloquy, jumped upon a pile of fire-wood beside the street, slapped his hands and thighs, and crowed like a rooster, exclaiming, *Day is at hand!* *

It was accounts like these, largely colored and exaggerated by the fear-stricken Tories, that reached Cornwallis' ears, and so alarmed him that he sent out Tarleton to aid Ferguson, if yet in a condition to be relieved, and finally induced his Lordship to depart in hot haste from Charlotte, with all his army. Tarleton proceeded a south-westerly course, fifteen or twenty miles, to Smith's Ford, below the Forks of the Catawba, where he received certain intelligence of the melancholy fate of Ferguson, and crossed the river "to give protection" as he says, "to the fugitives,"— a small number of whom, he adds, his light troops picked up, all of which must have been the result of his vivid imagination.

At length, while Tarleton was absent, Cornwallis received definite information of Ferguson's downfall; and Tarleton gives a sombre picture of the unhappy influence it exerted upon both the British and Tories. "Added,"

---

* MS. narrative of Robert Henry, who heard the dialogue between the neutrals and Ewin and Barry, and had the particulars of the interview of the British officers, from David Knox himself.

he says, " to the depression and fear it communicated to the Loyalists upon the borders, and to the southward, the effect of such an important event was sensibly felt by Lord Cornwallis at Charlotte Town. The weakness of his army, the extent and poverty of North Carolina, the want of knowledge of his enemy's designs, and the total ruin of his militia, presented a gloomy prospect at the commencement of the campaign. A farther progress by the route which he had undertaken, could not possibly remove, but would undoubtedly increase his difficulties; he, therefore, formed a sudden determination to quit Charlotte Town, and pass the Catawba river. The army was ordered to move, and expresses were dispatched to recall Lieutenant-Colonel Tarleton." *

About sunset, on the evening of the fourteenth of October, the British army took up its line of march towards the Old Nation Ford on the Catawba. They had for a guide William McCafferty, an Irishman, who had for several years been a merchant at Charlotte; remaining there when the enemy came, endeavoring to save his property; but whatever were his professions to the British, he played his new friends a sharp trick—a shabby one, no doubt, in their estimation. About two miles below Charlotte, he led them on a wrong road towards Park's, since Barnett's mill; he at length suggested that they must be out of the way, and he would ride a little to the left to get righted; but as soon as out of their sight, he left them to their fate. They were two miles to the right of the road they intended to have taken—the night was dark, and, being near Cedar creek, they were intercepted by high hills and deep ravines. Endeavoring to file to the left, to regain the right road, they became separated into different parties, and kept up a hallooing to learn which way their comrades had gone. By midnight they were three or four miles apart, and appeared to be panic-struck, lest the Americans

---
* Tarleton's *Campaigns*, 166.

—the dreaded mountaineers—should come upon them in their pitiful situation. They did not get together until noon the next day, about seven miles from Charlotte. Owing to the difficult passes they took, and the darkness of the night, together with the scare that befell them, the rear guard left behind them near twenty wagons, says Tarleton —forty, says General Graham—and considerable booty, including a printing press and other stores, together with the baggage of Tarleton's Legion.*

Reaching the Old Nation Ford, the river was too high to cross with safety. In consequence of a dangerous fever, which suddenly attacked Lord Cornwallis, as the result of heavy rains and severe exposures, and the want of forage and provisions, the army remained two days in an anxious and miserable situation in the Catawba Indian settlement, until his physicians declared that his Lordship's condition would endure the motion of a wagon. Meanwhile, the treacherous pilot, McCafferty, had hastened to the Whig Colonel Davie's encampment, reaching there early in the morning, and communicating the tidings of the enemy's retreat. Davie, with his small squadron of cavalry, hung upon their rear and flanks, but could gain no advantage over them. Crossing the Catawba near Twelve Mile creek, the army at length reached Winnsboro, a distance of some seventy miles, on the twenty-ninth of the month, after a two weeks' march; encountering sickness, difficulties, and privations of the most serious character.

Major Hanger relates, that he and five other officers had the yellow fever, as he terms it, and were placed in wagons when the army evacuated Charlotte; that, in passing swollen streams, the straw on which they lay in the vehicles frequently became wet, which aggravated their sickness, and all, save himself only, died of fatigue and exposure during the first week of the march, and were buried in the woods, while the jaded troops were moving forward as rapidly as possible. So low was Major Hanger reduced, that his bones protruded through his skin, and his life was only saved by the use of opium and port wine.*

But for their Tory associates, the sufferings of the army, great as they were, would have been still more aggravated. For several days in succession it rained without intermission; the soldiers had no tents, and the roads were over their shoes in water and mud. At night the army encamped in the woods, in a most unhealthy climate, and for many days, Stedman adds, they were entirely without rum. The water they drank was frequently as thick as in puddles by the road side. Sometimes they had beef and no bread; at other times bread, or corn, and no beef. For five days the troops were supported upon Indian corn alone, which was gathered as it stood in the field, five ears of which were the allowance for two soldiers for twenty-four hours. The Tory militia taught the regulars how best to adapt it for use. Taking their tin canteens, they would cut them up, and punch holes through the strips with their bayonets, and then use them as a rasp, or grater, on which to grate their corn, and prepare it for cooking. The idea was communicated to the Adjutant-General, and afterwards adopted throughout the army. †

By their acquaintance with the country, being mounted on horseback, and inured to the climate, the Tory militia would go forth daily in quest of provisions, being frequently obliged to pass through rivers, creeks, woods and swamps, to secure beef cattle for the support of the army. "Without their assistance," says Stedman, "it would have been impossible to have supplied the troops in the field." Some of these men, when a creek was reached, difficult, from its steep banks, and its clayey, slippery soil, to cross,

* *Life of Hanger*, ii, pp. 408-11.
† Stedman's *American War*, ii, 224

would take the place of the horses, being harnessed in their stead, and drag the wagons through the stream. Stedman, one of Cornwallis' officers, gives us some inklings of the treatment of these Tory benefactors of their army, by the British officers: "We are sorry to say," observes this candid historian, "that in return for these exertions, the militia were maltreated by abusive language, and even beaten by some officers in the Quarter-Master General's department. In consequence of this ill usage, several of them left the army the next morning forever, choosing to run the risk of meeting the resentment of their enemies, rather than submit to the derision and abuse of those to whom they looked up as friends.*

Cornwallis, with his army, was now at Winnsboro, nearly midway between Camden and Ninety Six, and within supporting distance of either. According to Lord Rawdon, the second in command, it is evident that the British leaders were happy, after all their toils and sufferings, to find that "Ninety Six was safe" †—that the muchdreaded mountaineers had fortunately turned their faces northwardly, instead of towards the fortress where Cruger commanded, and which they might easily have reached long before it could possibly have been relieved by the storm, mud, and sick-bound army *en route* from Charlotte to Winnsboro.

Through the Tories, doubtless, Lord Cornwallis learned in time of the executions by the mountaineers of the Loyalists at Bickerstaff's, near Gilbert Town, and wrote to the American commanders threatening retaliation. General Gates, in transmitting these complaints to Congress, expressed the opinion that "no person ought to be executed, but after legal conviction, and by order of the supreme civil or military authority, in the department where the offence is committed; but I must confess my astonishment at Lord

---

* Stedman, ii, 225.
† Cornwallis' *Correspondence,* i, 496.

Cornwallis' finding fault with a cruelty he and his officers are constantly practising—this is crying rogue first."

Commenting on this passage, Henry S. Randall pertinently observes: "Supreme civil or military authority" was not much better than a name, in the locality and exigency; and was quite as well represented, in our judgment, as it could elsewhere have been, in the intelligent and responsible gentlemen—for emphatically they were such—who, by their own danger and exertions, had done what no formally constituted "authority" was able to do; and, if the victors of King's Mountain hung fewer men than the documents found on British officers clearly proved had been executed of Americans by their orders, they enforced less, we believe, than the full measure of rightful and proper retaliation. And there is not a doubt that the practical effect of the measure was good, not only on the British Lieutenant-General, but on the parricides who were so keen to scent out, among their countrymen, the breakers of enforced and withdrawn paroles. The hunt became less intently amusing, when it was understood that the hunter placed the noose that had strangled his victim, around his own neck, in the event of his capture. *

The threatened retaliation by Cornwallis, addressed in the first instance to General Smallwood, and then to General Gates, was left as a legacy for General Greene, on his succeeding Gates in the command of the Southern department; and he met it in a calm and dignified manner. " I am," he wrote to his Lordship, " too much a stranger to the transactions at Gilbert Town to reply fully to that subject. They must have been committed before my arrival in the department, and by persons under the character of volunteers, who were independent of the army. However, if there was anything done in that affair contrary to the principles of humanity and the law of nations, and for which they had not the conduct of your army as a precedent, I shall be ever ready to testify my disapprobation of it. The

---

* *Life of Jefferson*, i, 282.

first example was furnished on your part, as appears by the list of unhappy sufferers enclosed; and it might have been expected, that the friends of the unfortunate should follow it. Punishing capitally for a breach of military parole, is a severity that the principles of modern war will not authorize, unless the inhabitants are to be treated as a conquered people, and subject to all the rigor of military government. The feelings of mankind will forever decide, when the rights of humanity are invaded. I leave them to judge of the tendency of your Lordship's order to Lieutenant-Colonel Balfour after the action near Camden, of Lord Rawden's proclamation, and of Tarleton's laying waste the country, and distressing the inhabitants, who were taught to expect protection and security, if they observed but a neutrality. Sending the inhabitants of Charleston to St. Augustine, contrary to the articles of capitulation, is a violation which I have also to represent, and which I hope your Lordship will think yourself bound to redress."

The enclosed list referred to was this: "William Stroud and Mr. Dowell, executed near Rocky Mount, without a trial, by order of Lieutent-Colonel Turnbull; Richard Tucker, Samuel Andrews, and John Miles, hanged at Camden by order of Lord Cornwallis; Mr. Johnson, hanged since the action of Blackstocks, by Lieutenant-Colonel Tarleton; about thirty persons hanged at Augusta by Colonel Browne; Adam Cusick hanged at Pedee by one Colonel Mills." *

---

* Gordon's *American War*, iv, pp. 28-29.

The Colonel Mills here referred to, must not be confounded with Colonel Ambrose Mills, of King's Mountain memory, one of the unfortunates executed at Bickerstaff's. William Henry Mills, mentioned by General Greene, belonged in·the Cheraw region, and served in the South Carolina Provincial Congress, early in the contest; but subsequently joined the British, and was made a Colonel. Surviving the war, he retired to Jamaica, and then to England, where he died in 1807.

But from Judge James' *Life of Marion*, and Gregg's *History of the Cheraws*, it is very questionable if Colonel Mills was responsible for the execution of Cusack. Those well-informed writers clearly charge that act upon Colonel Wemyss. Cusack was accused, according to one account, of no other crime than refusing to transport some British officers over a ferry, and shooting at them across the river; while another statement has it, that he shot at the black servant of a Tory officer, John Brockington, whom he knew, across Black creek. Taken prisoner by the enemy, he was tried, and condemned on the evidence of the negro.

Here happily ended the threatened retaliation on the part of Lord Cornwallis for the execution of the Loyalist leaders taken at King's Mountain. It was well that his Lordship refrained from exercising a power that could only have fanned the flames of desolation throughout the southern borders. The inhumanities practiced on both sides in that distracted quarter were already but too deplorable in their character, and needed not fresh provocations to intensify their brutality, or add to the frequency of their occurrence. It was generally said, and believed, that in the district of Ninety Six alone, fourteen hundred unhappy widows and orphans were left to bemoan the fate of their unfortunate fathers, husbands and brothers, killed and murdered during the course of the war.[*]

Good words for the victory and victors of King's Mountain have not been wanting. General Gates returned thanks, through Colonel Campbell and his associates, "to the brave officers and soldiers under your command, for your and their glorious behavior in the action; the records of the war will transmit your names and theirs to posterity, with the highest honors and applause;" and he desired to express the sense he entertained of "the great service they had done their country." General Washington proclaimed the result in *General Orders* to the army, as "an important object gained," and "a proof of the spirit and resources of the country;" while Congress expressed in its resolves, "a high sense of the spirited and military conduct of Colonel Campbell, and the officers and privates of the militia under his command, displayed in the action of October seventh, in which a complete victory was obtained." This marked success over Ferguson, and the heroic conduct of the riflemen at Guilford, convinced General Greene, that "the militia of the back country are formidable." "Campbell's glorious success at King's Mountain," was the terse encomium of Lieutenant-Colonel Lee, of the Legion

---

[*] Moultrie's *Memoirs*, ii, 242.

Cavalry. "It was a sharp action," said Chief Justice Marshall, gained by "the victorious mountaineers."

"No battle," says Lossing, "during the war, was more obstinately contested than this; it completely crushed the spirits of the Loyalists, and weakened, beyond recovery, the royal power in the Carolinas." * "The victory at King's Mountain," observes Bancroft, "which in the spirit of the American soldiers was like the rising at Concord, in its effects like the success at Bennington, changed the aspects of the war. The Loyalists of North Carolina no longer dared rise. It fired the patriots of the two Carolinas with fresh zeal. It encouraged the fragments of the defeated and scattered American army to seek each other, and organize themselves anew. It quickened the North Carolina Legislature to earnest efforts. It encouraged Virginia to devote her resources to the country south of her border. The appearance on the frontiers of a numerous enemy from settlements beyond the mountains, whose very names had been unknown to the British, took Cornwallis by surprise, and their success was fatal to his intended expedition. He had hoped to step with ease from one Carolina to the other, and from those to the conquest of Virginia; and he had now no choice but to retreat." †

When all the circumstances, continues the same distinguished historian, are considered, the hardihood of the conception, the brilliancy of the execution, and the important train of consequences resulting from it, there was nothing in the North more so, except the surrender at Saratoga. It is not to be imagined, that the assemblage of the troops was an accidental and tumultuous congregation of men, merely seeking wild adventures. On the contrary, although each step in the progress of the enterprise seemed to be characterized by a daring impulse, yet the purpose had been coolly conceived, and its execution

---

* *Field Book of the Revolution*, ii, pp. 428-29.
† *History of the United States*, x, 340,

deliberately planned in a temper of not less wisdom than hardihood. *

Irving declares, that "the battle of King's Mountain, inconsiderable as it was in the numbers engaged, turned the tide of Southern warfare. The destruction of Ferguson and his corps gave a complete check to the expedition of Cornwallis. He began to fear for the safety of South Carolina, liable to such sudden irruptions from the mountains; lest, while he was facing to the north, these hordes of stark-riding warriors might throw themselves behind him, and produce a popular combustion in the Province he had left. He resolved, therefore, to return with all speed to that Province, and provide for its security." *

Lord Cornwallis fully recognized the extent of the great disaster. His sudden retreat into South Carolina showed it. Ferguson, he said, "had taken infinite pains with some of the militia of Ninety Six," and had confidence that they would fight well, which his Lordship doubted; and yet Cornwallis suffered him to go on a distant service, without any regulars, artillery, or cavalry for his support, and the result was, as his Lordship acknowledges, that Ferguson was "totally defeated at King's Mountain." The discouraging effect of that crushing disaster on the Tories, may well be judged from Cornwallis' dispatch to Sir Henry Clinton: "The militia of Ninety six," he observes, "on which alone we could place the smallest dependence, was so totally disheartened by the defeat of Ferguson, that of that whole district we could with difficulty assemble one hundred; and even those, I am convinced, would not have made the smallest resistance if they had been attacked." "The defeat of Major Ferguson," wrote Lord Rawdon, "had so dispirited this part of the country, and indeed the Loyal subjects were so wearied by the long continuance of the campaign, that Lieutenant-

---

* MS. statement of Hon. George Bancroft, preserved by General Preston.
† Irving's *Washington*, iv, pp. 193-94.

Colonel Cruger, commanding at Ninety Six, sent information to Lord Cornwallis, that the whole district had determined to submit as soon as the Rebels should enter it;" and, a little later, Lord Cornwallis wrote: "The constant incursions of refugees, North Carolinians, Back Mountain men, and the perpetual risings in different parts of this Province, the invariable successes of all those parties against our militia, keep the whole country in continual alarm, and render the assistance of regular troops everywhere necessary." *

Sir Henry Clinton, the British Commander-in-chief in America, blamed Lord Cornwallis for detaching Ferguson without any support of regular troops, when his Lordship had previously stated, that Ferguson's hopes of success on his Tory militia " were contrary to the experience of the army, as well as of Major Ferguson himself;" and " that his Lordship," wrote Sir Henry, " should, *after this opinion*, not only suffer Colonel Ferguson to be detached without support, but put such a river as the Catawba between him and Ferguson, was a matter of wonder to Sir H. Clinton and all who knew it." †

"Great and glorious!" was the exclamation of General Gates, when the tidings of the grand triumph of the King's Mountain men reached him. " That memorable victory," declared the patriot Jefferson, "was the joyful annunciation of that turn of the tide of success, which terminated the Revolutionary war with the seal of independence." And richly did the heroes, who marched under Campbell's banners, deserve all the praise so generously bestowed upon them. King's Mountain paved the way for the successive advantages gained by the American arms at First Dam Ford, Blackstocks, Cowpens, Guilford, and Eutaw; and ultimately for the crowning victory of York Town, with the glorious fruition of " INDEPENDENCE FOREVER."

---

* Cornwallis' *Correspondence*. i. pp. 63, 80-81, 497-98.

† Clinton's *Observations on Stedman*.

CHAPTER XVII.

Gen. William Campbell.

His Scotch-Irish Ancestry.—His Father an Early Holston Explorer.— William Campbell's Birth and Education.—Settles on Holston.—A Captain on Dunmore's Campaign.—Raised a Company for the first Virginia Regiment in 1775.—Returns for the Defence of the Fron- tiers.—His Military Appointments.—Rencounter with and Hanging of the Bandit Hopkins.—Suppressing Tories up New River.— King's Mountain Expedition—his Bravery Vindicated.—Public Thanks for his Services—Marches to Long Island of Holston.— At Whitzell's Mills and Guilford.—Resigns from Ill-treatment.— Made Brigadier-General.—Serves under LaFayette.—Death and Character.—Notices of his King's Mountain Officers.

The Campbell family, from which the hero of King's Mountain descended, were originally from Inverary, Argyll- shire, connected with the famous Campbell clans of the Highlands of Scotland ; and emigrated to Ireland near the close of the reign of Queen Elizabeth—about the year 1600.   The northern portion of Ireland received, at that period, large accessions of Scotch Protestants, who proved valuable and useful citizens.   Here the Campbells continued to live for several generations, until at length John Camp- bell, with a family of ten or twelve children, removed to America in 1726, and settled first in Donegal, Lancaster County, Pennsylvania, where we find one of his sons, Pat- rick Campbell, born in 1690, serving as a constable in 1729. About 1730, John Campbell, with three of his sons, Patrick among them, removed from Pennsylvania to what was then a part of Orange, now Augusta County, in the rich valley of Virginia.*   Another authority assigns 1738 as the time of this migration.†

---

* MS. statements of Gov. David Campbell ; Foote's *Sketches of Virginia*, second series, pp. 114, 117; Rupp's *History of Lancaster County*, Pa., 185; Mombert's *Lancaster*, 120.
† R. A. Brock, Esq., in *Richmond Standard*, July 10th, 1880.

Among the children of Patrick Campbell, who thus early settled in Western Virginia, was Charles, who seems to have been born in Ireland before the removal of the family to the New World. He became a prominent and efficient pioneer of the Augusta Valley. He early married a Miss Buchanan, whose father, John Buchanan, Sr., had figured in the wars of Scotland; and from this union sprang William Campbell, who subsequently led the Scotch-Irish patriots of the Holston Valley against Ferguson at King's Mountain. He was born in Augusta County in 1745; and, though reared on that remote frontier, and amid the excitements and dangers of the French and Indian war of 1755–63, yet he was enabled, as an only son, to secure the best education under the best teachers of that period—David Robinson, a fine scholar, having been, it is believed, among his instructors, as he was of many others of the youth of Augusta of that day. Young Campbell acquired a correct knowledge of the English language, ancient and modern history, and several branches of the mathematics.*

His father, Charles Campbell, was not only an enterprising farmer of Augusta, but early engaged in western exploration, and in the acquisition of the rich wild lands of the country. In April, 1748, he made an exploring tour down the Holston, in company with Doctor Thomas Walker, Colonel James Patton, James Wood, and John Buchanan, together with a number of hunters and woodmen. It was on this occasion that Campbell located a fine tract on the North Fork of Holston, where valuable salt springs were afterward discovered, for which he obtained a patent from the Governor of Virginia in 1753. It proved a great benefit alike to his descendants and the country. In an old manuscript written apparently in 1750, it is stated that "John Buchanan and Charles Campbell do not go out this fall"—indicating a contemplated removal, probably

---

* Col. Arthur Campbell's MS. Sketch of Gen. William Campbell; Gov. Campbell's MS. correspondence.

to the Holston frontiers. As early as 1742, Charles Campbell was enrolled as a militia-man in the company of John
Buchanan; and, in 1752, he was chosen a Captain, and
doubtless rendered service in the defence of the Augusta
Valley during the long period of Indian irruptions and
disturbances of Braddock's war. In the latter part of his
life he became intemperate, and cut short his career, dying
early in 1767.*

At his father's death, William Campbell, then a young
man of about twenty-two, resolved to remove with his
mother and four young sisters,† to the frontiers of Holston.
They migrated there, locating on a fine tract called Aspenvale, twenty-one miles east of the Wolf Hills, now the
pleasant town of Abingdon, and one mile west of the
Seven Mile Ford. In 1773, he was appointed among the
earliest Justices of Fincastle County, and, in 1774, a Captain
of the militia. Although an only son, and inheriting a
considerable property, he never yielded to the fashionable
follies of young men of fortune. Devoted to the opening
and culture of a plantation in the wilderness, nothing
occurred to interfere with the routine of farm life till the
breaking out of the Indian war in 1774, when he raised a
company of young men, and joining Colonel Christian's regiment, pursued rapidly to overtake Colonel Andrew Lewis,
who had preceded them to Point Pleasant, at the mouth
of the Kenhawa, where a decisive battle was fought, beating
back the Shawanoes and allied tribes. Colonel Christian's
re-inforcement, though they made a forced march, did not
reach the battle-ground till midnight succeeding the engagement. The next morning the army crossed the Ohio, hastening to join Lord Dunmore, with another division, at the Pick-

---

*MS. records of Augusta County, Va.; Winterbotham's *America*, iii, 230; Morse's
Geography, ed 1797: do . ed. 1805 i, 688; Scott's *Geographical Dictionary*, 1805; Guthrie's
Geography. 1815. ii. 472; MS. Diary of Dr. Thomas Walker. which alone shows the correct
date of Charles Campbell's exploration of the Holston Valley.

†The eldest, Elizabeth, married John Taylor; Jane, Thomas Tate; Margaret. Col.
Arthur Campbell; and Ann, Richard Poston—all men of great respectability, leaving
numerous descendants.

away plains on the Scioto, where his Lordship concluded a treaty of peace with the defeated and humbled Indian tribes. Thus was Captain Campbell, with all his zeal to engage in active service, and after having traveled hundreds of miles through the wilderness from south-western Virginia to the heart of the Ohio country, compelled to sheathe his sword, and return again to his peaceful home on the Holston.

The aggressions of the British ministry on the rights of American freemen had already made a deep impression on the minds of the frontier people. While at Fort Gower, at the mouth of the Hockhocking, returning from the Scioto expedition, the troops declared, on the fifth of November, 1774—Captain Campbell, no doubt, among the number—that, " as the love of Liberty, and attachment to the real interests and just rights of America outweigh every other consideration, we resolve that we will exert every power within us for the defence of American Liberty, and for the support of her just rights and privileges." And on the twentieth of January ensuing, Colonels Preston and Christian, Arthur and William Campbell, together with William Edmondson, Reverend Charles Cummings, and other leaders of Fincastle County, comprising the Holston settlements, sent a calm and patriotic address to the Continental Congress, announcing, that "if no pacific measures shall be proposed or adopted by Great Britain, and our enemies attempt to dragoon us out of those inestimable privileges which we are entitled to as subjects, and reduce us to slavery, we declare that we are deliberately and resolutely determined never to surrender them to any power upon earth but at the expense of our lives. These are our real, though unpolished, sentiments of liberty and loyalty, and in them we are resolved to live and die." * These were noble declarations of William Campbell and associates, proclaimed three months before the first clang of arms at Lexington, four anterior to

* *American Archives,* Fourth Series, i, 963, 1168.

the patriotic resolves of the people of Mecklenburg, five before the deadly strife on Bunker Hill, and nearly a year and six months before the immortal Declaration of Independence by Congress.   These sentiments of the men of Holston formed the key-note of their patriotic efforts throughout the Revolution—and they never flagged a moment, while life lasted, till their liberties were secured.

At length war burst upon the country.   Captain Campbell, who had pledged himself at Fort Gower, in 1774, to exert every power within him in the defence of American liberty, and subsequently renewed the solemn declaration "to live and die" in support of the great principles for which Bruce and Wallace, and Hampden and Sydney had, in the past, contended, now entered warmly into the contest, raising the first company in south-western Virginia in support of the common cause, marching to Williamsburg with his hunting-shirt riflemen, in September, 1775, and taking their place in the First Virginia regiment under the command of the famous Patrick Henry.   His commission as Captain bore date December fifteenth of that year. Owing to the regiment's confinement to the inactivities of camp life, and the slights and indignities meted out to him, Henry at length resigned the command, when his men, who were devoted to him, went into mourning.   Lieutenant-Colonel Christian succeeded to the command, and the regiment was placed on Continental establishment, under General Andrew Lewis ; and shared in dislodging Dunmore from Gwyn's Island, July ninth, 1776—the British not fancying a too close contact with the frontier riflemen, exclaimed, as they came in sight, "the shirt-men are coming!" when they, panic-stricken, precipitately evacuated the Island.

Shortly after, intelligence came that the Cherokees, instigated by British agents and emissaries, had attacked the frontiers, when Colonel Christian resigned, and returned to the Holston country to lead an expedition against the hostile Indians. When Captain Campbell heard of these border troubles, he felt not a little uneasy on account of the unprotected situation of his mother and sisters; and wrote to Major Arthur Campbell, expressing the hope that all the women and children in the Holston country might be gathered into forts, thus enabling the men to engage in repelling the enemy, adding: "I have the most cogent reasons for endeavoring to resign, and can, I think, do so with honor; and if I possibly can, I shall be with you soon."* He felt it was his duty to repair to the frontiers, and lend all his aid in their defence. But he was not able to leave the service till near the close of the year, and thus failed to share in Christian's expedition against the Cherokees. But the delay, perhaps, aided him in securing a noble companion for life, in the person of Miss Elizabeth Henry, a sister of his old commander, Patrick Henry—the unrivalled orator and statesman of the Revolution. During this service of over a year in eastern Virginia, Captain Campbell acquired a practical knowledge of military tactics, and the discipline of an army, which proved of great value to him in his subsequent campaigns to King's Mountain and Guilford.

On his return home he found the Cherokees, having been subdued, were quiet for awhile. The large County of Fincastle, embracing much of south-western Virginia and all of Kentucky, was sub-divided; and on the organization of Washington County, in January, 1777, he was continued a member of the Justices' Court, and made Lieutenant-Colonel of the militia, Arthur Campbell having been made County Lieutenant or Colonel Commandant, and Evan Shelby, Colonel. At this term of the court, William Campbell, William Edmondson, and two others were appointed commissioners *to hire wagons to bring up the County salt* allotted by the Government and Council, and receive and distribute the same, making it necessary to wagon the salt

---

* MS. letter, August 1st, 1776.

fully four hundred miles, over rough roads, from Williamsburg.   This was several years before the rich salt wells were
discovered on Colonel Campbell's lands on North Holston.
In the fall of this year, Colonel Campbell, having been
appointed a commissioner for running the boundary line
between Virginia and the Cherokees, probably in fulfill-
ment of stipulations of the treaty at Long Island of Holston,
in July preceding, performed this service, the line extending from the mouth of Big creek to the high knob on
Cumberland Mountain, a few miles west of Cumberland
Gap.*   During the year 1778, he seems to have been
engaged in no special public service.

In the summer of 1779, there was a partial uprising of
Tories in Montgomery County, where Colonel Walter
Crockett, by his energy, succeeded in quelling the insurrection before it had gained much headway.   The same Tory
spirit had extended itself into Washington County—and
even into the Watauga and Nolachucky settlements ; but the
leaders were not open in their movements—rather like
bandits, struck their blows in the dark, under disguises and
conceaiments.   Colonel Campbell was very out-spoken
against them.   His gates were placarded, threatening his
life ; and an attempt was made to take him, of a dark night,
and in a deep forest, by two of these desperadoes, but they
mistook their man—otherwise Colonel Campbell would have
probably lost his life at their hands.

Not long after, when he was returning from the Ebbing
Spring meeting house, where he had been hearing a good
Presbyterian sermon, mounted on horseback, accompanied
by his wife, his cousin John Campbell and family, Captain
James Dysart and wife, James Fullen, a man named Farris,
an African negro named Thomas, and others, he discovered
a man approaching, on horseback, who turned off into the
woods—a suspicious circumstance.   Colonel Campbell did
not personally know him, but John Campbell, who did, told

---

* MS. pension statement of Charles Bickley.

the Colonel that it was Francis Hopkins, the Tory bandit. For a year or more Hopkins had given the County authorities much trouble; they had imposed heavy fines upon him for his rascalities, and had placed him under heavy bonds. He had been found guilty of passing counterfeit money—was ordered imprisoned at Cocke's Fort on Renfroe creek, till the county jail should be completed; and when the new structure was ready for occupancy, it was a ricketty affair, and Hopkins one dark night was released from his confinement by the aid of sympathizing Tories, who pried the jail door from its hinges, and carried it half a mile away. Thus the bandit and counterfeiter evaded further imprisonment, and snapped his fingers at justice. He fled to the nearest British garrison—probably in Georgia—where he obtained a commission, with letters to the Cherokee Indians and the white emissaries among them, urging them to fall upon the frontier settlers with fagot, knife, and tomahawk. He was, in every sense, an infamous Tory, and a dangerous character.

Upon learning the name of the stranger, Colonel Campbell instantly put spurs to his horse, and gave chase to the bandit; and in the course of one or two miles, reaching the deep ford of the Middle Fork of Holston,* about a mile above where Captain Thompson then lived, Hopkins, who was mounted on a fine horse, rode down a steep bluff, some fifteen or twenty feet, plunging into the river. Campbell, by this time, was close in pursuit, and not to be balked, followed the bandit into the water. The fearful leap threw Hopkins from his horse; and, before he could recover, Campbell was at him. They had a long and desperate rencounter in river, the bandit losing his dirk. Hopkins was the strongest man, and came near drowning Campbell, when Fullen and some of the others, who had followed, came to his relief; and, with their assistance, the bandit was, after something of an enforced ducking, subdued and taken to the bank.

---

*This locality is now on James Byar's farm, in Washington County.

25

Hopkins' reckless character was well known—a leader of a mountain clan of desperadoes, who had long infested the country, committing robberies on defenceless people along the thinly populated frontiers. No time was lost—there was no jail in the county that could hold him, and it was dangerous to the community to suffer such a lawless character to roam at large, threatening the lives of such men as William Campbell. On taking the culprit to the bank of the stream, they searched him, finding his commission, with commissions for others, and the letters to the Cherokees, which he had not yet delivered. The horse he rode was stolen but a few hours before; and he had a new halter tied on behind his saddle, evidently intended for another horse, preparatory, perhaps, for a journey, with some accomplice, to the Cherokee country. But the halter, like Haman's gallows, was put to quite a different use from what was designed; for with it, Hopkins, who was insolent to Campbell, was speedily hung to the limb of a convenient sycamore that leaned over the river. When Colonel Campbell rejoined his wife, she eagerly inquired, " What did you do with him, Mr. Campbell?" " Oh, we hung him, Betty—that's all." The whole country rejoiced at this riddance of one of the greatest pests to society. Others of the bandit party were hunted down, and several of them killed—one on Clinch, and another at the lower end of Washington County, or on the borders of the neighboring County of Sullivan, in now Tennessee.

At the ensuing October session of the Virginia Legislature, an act was passed, at the instance of General Thomas Nelson, Jr., one of the signers of the Declaration of Independence, and afterwards Governor of the State, to fully meet the case—though it would seem to have hardly been necessary. The act states, that while the measures for the suppression of " open insurrection and conspiracy " may not have been " strictly warranted by law, it was justifiable from the immediate urgency and imminence of the danger "—hence " that William Campbell, Walter Crockett, and other liege subjects of the Commonwealth, aided by detachments of the militia and volunteers from the County of Washington and other parts of the frontiers, did by timely and effectual exertion, suppress and defeat such conspiracy," and they were declared fully exonerated and indemnified for the act.*

In April, 1780, Colonel Campbell was promoted to the full rank of Colonel, in place of Evan Shelby, Sr., whose residence, it was now determined, was in North Carolina. He served a term in the House of Delegates from early in May, until the twentieth of June, when he obtained leave of absence for the remainder of the session, to engage in an expedition against the Chickamauga towns, Governor Jefferson and his council authorizing him to embody two hundred and fifty militia from Washington and Montgomery counties, and unite with a conjunctive force from the Carolinas.†

But soon after his return home, he found a dangerous enemy in the midst of the white settlements. Two hundred Tories of the New river region, within what is now Grayson County, Virginia, and Ashe County, North Carolina, had risen in arms, with some British officers aiding them, with a view of seizing the Lead Mines, near the present Wytheville ; when Colonel Campbell, by order of Colonel Preston, took the field in August at the head of one hundred and forty or fifty men, and scoured that wild, mountainous country ; and at a place known as the Big Glades, or Round Meadows, approaching a large party of Tories, the latter under cover of a thick fog, fled, dispersing in every direction, and hiding themselves in the mountains, losing only one of their num-

---

*Statement of Colonel Samuel Newell. December 9. 1833, in *The Land We Love*, May, 1867 ; MS. Correspondence of Governor D. Campbell and John B. Dysart; conversations with Colonel Patrick H. Fontaine, a grandson of Patrick Henry, and General Thomas Love ; Henning's *Statutes of Virginia*, x, 195. In *Atkinson's Casket*, for September, 1833, is an interesting story founded on the hanging of Hopkins, having, however, but little resemblance to the real facts in the case.

†*Journal of House of Delegates*, 1780; Gibbes' *Doc. History*, 1776-82, p. 135.

ber in their flight.   Colonel Cleveland on a similar service, had captured Zachariah Goss, one of Plundering Sam Brown's gang of murderers, horse-thieves, and robbers, who was tried and immediately hung at Peach Bottom, on New River, in the presence of Cleveland's and Campbell's parties; while two other villains were very well whipped.   Colonel Campbell then marched to the old Moravian town of Bethabara, in North Carolina, where he made head-quarters for some time, sending out detachments in quest of Tory bands—one penetrating into Guilford County, surprised and dispersed two companies of Tories at night, and captured Captain Nathan Read, one of their leaders, and seventeen others—Captain Eli Branson, another of their leaders, narrowly escaping.   Read was tried, Colonels Cleveland and Martin Armstrong, and Major Lewis sitting upon the court-martial, was found guilty of crimes and misdemeanors, and condemned to be hung— with the alternative presented him of joining the patriots, and serving faithfully to the end of the war, which he declined, meeting his death heroically.   Another party of Tories was dispersed above the Shallow Ford of Yadkin.*

Returning from this expedition, Colonel Campbell led four hundred brave riflemen from Washington County across the Alleghanies to meet Ferguson's Rangers and the united Tories of the Carolinas.   Their utter discomfiture has been fully related; and too much praise cannot well be accorded to "the hero of King's Mountain" for his gallant bearing during the campaign generally, and especially for his heroic conduct in the battle.   It is a matter of regret, that such patriots as Shelby and Sevier should have been deceived into the belief that the chivalric Campbell shirked from the dangers of the conflict, mistaking, as they did, the Colonel's servant in the distance for the Colonel him-

---

* Colonel William Campbell's MSS.; statement of John Spelts, who was out in this service; MS. Pension statements of Colonel Robert Love and James Keys, of Campbell's men; Gibbes' *Doc. History*, 1776–82, p. 137.

self; when well-nigh forty survivors of the battle, including some of Campbell's worthiest officers, and men of Shelby's, Sevier's, and Cleveland's regiments as well, testifying, of their own knowledge, to his personal share in the action, and specifying his presence in every part of the hotly-contested engagement, from the beginning to the final surrender of the enemy at discretion. It is evident that such heroes as Shelby and Sevier had quite enough to do within the range of their own regiments, without being able to observe very much what was transpiring beyond them. And what Shelby honestly supposed was a vague confession by Campbell of unaccountable conduct on his part in the latter part of the action, simply referred to his too precipitate order to fire on the unresisting Tories when Colonel Williams had been shot down after the close of the contest. But in such a victory, without unjustly detracting from Campbell's great merits and rich deservings, there is both honor and fame enough for all his worthy compatriots also. * It may be proper to note, that the sword that Colonel Campbell wielded at King's Mountain, and subsequently at Guilford—his trusty *Andrea di Ferrara*—more than a century old, was used by his Caledonian ancestors in the wars of the Pretenders, and is yet preserved by his Preston descendants. †

Colonel Campbell would have been more or less than mortal, had he not felt a sense of satisfaction for the high praises showered upon him and his associates for the decisive triumph achieved at King's Mountain—emanating from Gates, Washington, the Legislature of Virginia, and the Continental Congress. The latter august body voted, that it entertained " a high sense of the spirited and mili-

---

* Both Colonel William Martin and Elijah Callaway, who were intimately acquainted with Colonel Cleveland, state that he frequently spoke of Campbell's good deportment in the battle; Major Lewis, of Cleveland's regiment, declared that, had it not been for Campbell and his Virginians, Ferguson would have remained master of King's Mountain; and General Lenoir, also of Cleveland's men, testified to Campbell's gallant conduct in the action.

† Colonel Arthur Campbell's Memoir; Campbell's *History of Virginia*, 1860, p. 700.

tary conduct of Colonel Campbell" and his associates;
while the Virginia House of Delegates voted its "thanks
to Colonel Campbell," his officers and soldiers, for their
patriotic conduct in repairing to the aid of a distressed sister State, and after "a severe and bloody conflict," had
achieved a decisive victory; and that "a good horse, with
elegant furniture, and a sword, be purchased at the public
expense, and presented to Colonel William Campbell as a
further testimony of the high sense the General Assembly entertain of his late important services to his country."
To these high compliments of the Legislature, Colonel
Campbell returned the following modest acknowledgment:

"Gentlemen—I am infinitely happy in receiving this
public testimony of the approbation of my country for my
late services in South Carolina. It is a reward far above
my expectations, and I esteem it the noblest a soldier can
receive from a virtuous people. Through you, gentlemen,
I wish to communicate the high sense I have of it to the
House of Delegates. I owe, under Providence, much to
the brave officers and soldiers who served with me; and I
shall take the earliest opportunity of transmitting the
resolve of your House to them, who, I am persuaded, will
experience all the honest heart-felt satisfaction I myself
feel on this occasion." *

Now hurrying to his frontier home on the Holston, he
found that the restless Cherokees had again been at their
bloody work, and Colonel Arthur Campbell had in December, 1780, aided by Colonel Sevier and Major Martin, led
forth a strong force for their chastisement. Colonel William Campbell at once raised additional troops, and marched
as far as the Long Island of Holston, † to succor his kinsman if need be; but it was not necessary, for the Chero-

* *Journals of Congress*, 1780, 367; *Journal of the Virginia House of Delegates*, 1780,
Fall session, pp. 13, 18. The Virginia Legislature subsequently called a County after him,
to perpetuate his name and memory.

† MS. correspondence of Colonel William Martin, one of William Campbell's men, and
of Governor D. Campbell; Haywood's *Tennessee*, 98.

kees were pursued in detached parties by their invaders, many of their warriors were killed, and their settlements desolated.

On the thirtieth of January, 1781, General Greene wrote to "the famous Colonel William Campbell," reminding him of the glory he had already acquired, and urging him "to bring, without loss of time, a thousand good volunteers from over the mountains." Notwithstanding the Cherokees were still troublesome, and threatening the frontiers, the noted Logan, with a northern band, was committing depredations on Clinch, while others were doing mischief in Powell's Valley, yet Colonel Campbell raised over a hundred of his gallant riflemen, and moved forward on February twenty-fifth,* others joining him on the way, until he brought General Greene, about the second of March, a re-inforcement of over four hundred mountaineers. † Lord Cornwallis had imbibed a personal resentment towards Colonel Campbell, as the commander at King's Mountain, threatening that should he fall into his hands, he would have him instantly put to death for his rigor against the Tories—evidently designing to hold him personally responsible for the execution of the Tory leaders at Bickerstaff's. This, instead of intimidating, had the contrary effect; and Campbell, in turn, resolved, if the fortunes of war should place Cornwallis in his power, he should meet the fate of Ferguson. ‡

Could anything have served to give additional spirit to Colonel Campbell, and nerve him to almost superhuman exertions, it was just such a dastardly threat as that uttered by Lord Cornwallis. Campbell and his men were soon called into action. Taking advantage of a thick fog, Lord Cornwallis sent forward a strong force to beat up the quarters of Greene's advance parties—or, as Greene supposed,

---

* *Calendar of Virginia State Papers,* 548, 555.
† *Calendar of Virginia State Papers,* 542; Johnson's *Greene,* i, 438.
‡ Colonel Arthur Campbell's memoir of General William Campbell.

either to intercept his stores, or cut off the Light Infantry, including the riflemen, from the main body. These advance columns met at Whitzell's Mills, on Reedy creek, some seven miles from Greene's camp, where Colonel Otho H. Williams, with Campbell's and Preston's riflemen, and Washington's and Lee's corps, formed on the southern bank of the stream, in front of the ford, and some two hundred yards below the mill. The main object was to protect the mill as long as possible, and enable Greene's provision wagons to load with flour and meal, and get off with the needed supply, which they barely effected. As the British, with their short Yager riflemen in front, approached, they fired in the distance; and when within eighty yards, descending towards the creek, the American riflemen opened on them with deadly effect, one of the officers of the enemy, when shot, bounding up several feet, fell dead; a second discharge on the advancing foe, when only some forty-five yards off, was also very destructive. The enemy had opened their field pieces, but, like the fire of their small arms, was too high, and only took effect among the limbs of the trees. As the atmosphere was heavy, the powder smoke obstructed the enemy's view; while the Americans, below them, had a better opportunity. The fighting was chiefly done by the riflemen, and Lee's Legion, while covered by the regulars; and "Colonel Campbell," says·John Craig, one of his riflemen, "acted with his usual courage."

Having accomplished the object they had in view—the security of the flour and meal,—the Americans retired over the ford, which was some three feet deep, with a rapid current, over a slippery, rocky bottom, with a steep brushy bank on the northern shore to ascend. While effecting this passage, the gallant Major Joseph Cloyd, of Preston's riflemen, observed his old commander on foot, who had been unhorsed in the conflict, and dismounting, aided Colonel Preston, who was now advanced in years and quite fleshy, into the saddle, when both escaped.* "The enemy,"

_____
* MS. notes of conversations with Thomas Hickman, of Davidson County, Ten-

said General Greene, "were handsomely opposed, and suffered considerably."

After no little manoeuvring, the battle of Guilford took place on the fifteenth of March. It was brought on by a sharp action, in the morning, by the advance, consisting of Lee's Legion, and a portion of Campbell's riflemen—in which Lee was supposed to have inflicted a loss of fifty on the part of Tarleton; while the Light Infantry of the Guards were so hard pressed by the riflemen, losing a hundred of their number, that a portion of Tarleton's cavalry went to their relief. In the main battle that soon followed, Lee's Legion and Campbell's riflemen formed the corps of observation on the left flank—the riflemen occupying a woodland position. During the obstinate contest, Campbell's corps fought with the heroic bravery characteristic of their noble leader, and of their own unrivalled reputation. When the enemy charged the Maryland Line, Campbell with his riflemen made a spirited attack on the regiment of Boze, on the British right wing, and drove it back; and when the riflemen, in turn, were charged with the bayonet, having none to repel them, they were obliged for the moment to retire, still loading and firing, however, on their pursuers, and thus, whether charging or retiring, kept up a destructive fire on these veteran German subsidiaries. So severely did Campbell's riflemen handle his right wing, that Lord Cornwallis was obliged to order Tarleton to extricate it, and bring it off. By this time Lee had retired with his cavalry, without apprising Campbell of his movement; and the result was, that the riflemen were swept from the field.*

nessee, and Major Herndon Haralson, of Brownsville, Tennessee, in 1844, and Benjamin Starritt, all participants in the action; Tarleton's *Campaigns*, 135; Stedman, ii, 336; Lee's *Memoirs*, revised ed., 265–67; Greene, in *Letter to Washington*, iii, 260; Johnson's *Greene*, i, 462–63; Greene's *Greene*, iii, 188.

*MS. Notes of conversations with Benjamin Starritt, of Lee's Legion; Tarleton's *Campaigns*, 270–71, 275–76; Stedman, with MS marginal notes by Captain J. R. Whitford, ii, 337, 343; Lee's *Memoirs*, new ed., 276–83; Johnson *Greene*, ii, 6; Lossing's *Field Book*, ii, 402, 403; Bancroft, x, 476–79; Dawson's *Battles*, ii, 665–67. MS. Letter of Hon. W. C. Preston, to the author, July 10th, 1840.

Lee commended Colonel Campbell for the bravery displayed in the action by his battalion; and Greene assured him, that his "faithful services" claimed his General's warmest thanks, and his "entire approbation of his conduct"—adding: "Sensible of your merit, I feel a pleasure in doing justice to it." Displeased with the treatment shown to himself and riflemen—who were the first in the engagement, and the last in the field—Campbell retired in disgust from the service. At his home on the Holston, he announced himself, on the thirty-first of March, as a candidate for the House of Delegates, saying: "The resignation of my military commission, which I could not longer hold with honor, after the treatment I have received, puts it out of my power to serve my country as an officer."[*] Campbell and his, men felt deeply aggrieved—feeling that Lee had abandoned them without notice, and left them to maintain the unequal contest unprotected by cavalry, when Tarleton directed his dragoons against them.

" You have no doubt observed," wrote General William R. Davie, " that Campbell's regiment of riflemen acted with Lee on the left flank of the army. After the main body of the army had been pushed off the field, these troops remained engaged with the Yagers of the regiment of Boze, near the Court House, some of them covered by houses, others by a skirt of thick wood. In this situation, they were charged by the British cavalry, and some of them were cut down. Lee's cavalry were drawn up on the edge of the open ground, above the Court House, about two hundred yards off, and, as Colonel Campbell asserted, moved as this charge was made on his riflemen. On the day after the action, Campbell was extremely indignant at this movement, and spoke freely of Lee's conduct. Lee was, however, sent off the same day, to watch the enemy's movements, and Campbell's regiment were soon discharged."[†]

---

[*] MS. Letter of Colonel Campbell to Colonel Daniel Smith, on Clinch.
[†] Johnson's *Greene*, ii, 16-17, 20.

" Lee's abandonment of Campbell's riflemen," said the late William C. Preston, " at twilight, and without giving notice of his withdrawal, was long regarded by the survivors with the most bitter feelings, which were subsequently revived by the manner in which he sunk their services and sufferings in his published account of the battle." * This, at least, is expressive of the sentiments of Campbell and his men ; and, at this late day, it is difficult to determine whether Lee was excusable, or culpable, for the course he pursued. But well-merited compliments and soothing words, on the part of General Greene, did not change Colonel Campbell's determination to withdraw from the service. He accordingly left camp on the morning of the twentieth ; and returning home resigned his commission in the militia.

Colonel Campbell, as the oldest serving Justice in the County Court, became entitled to a term of the office of Sheriff, but declined the position. He was chosen to represent Washington County in the House of Delegates. The General Assembly convened at Richmond early in May of this year ; but owing to the approach of the enemy, they adjourned to meet at Charlottesville on the twenty-fourth of that month ; and, on June the fourth, they were compelled hurriedly to adjourn to Staunton to escape capture by Tarleton. During the session, disturbed as it was, much important public business was transacted. Colonel Campbell was placed on several of the leading committees, associated with Patrick Henry and other prominent patriots—on privileges and elections, the establishment of martial law, and amendatory of the militia act. General Morgan was again called into service by the Legislature ; and a few days later, on the fourteenth of June, the House of Delegates chose Colonel Campbell a Brigadier General of the militia, to serve under Marquis De La Fayette, then commanding in Virginia, which was concurred in by the

---

* MS. letter to the author, July 10th, 1840.

Senate the following day. On the sixteenth, General Campbell obtained leave of absence for the remainder of the session, and at once repaired to La Fayette's camp for service. He became a favorite of that gallant nobleman, who assigned him to the command of a brigade of light infantry and riflemen. *

While General Campbell was temporarily absent, and his corps was encamped at some point in Cumberland County, a Parson McCrea, of the old established church, who had drawn his salary in tobacco for many a year, visited the camp, and plied his best arguments to discourage the men, representing that the great strength of Cornwallis' army would enable them to slaughter the feeble American force like so many beeves. General Campbell returning, and hearing of this insolent visit, sent a detail of men to apprehend the inter-meddling Parson; and severely reprimanded him for his unpatriotic conduct, saying his age alone excused him from corporal punishment; " but we will show you," added the General, "how we intend to serve Cornwallis." He then ordered the Tory clergyman to prostrate himself flat on his belly across the road, when every soldier stepped over him on their march. We are afraid the good man left in too ill a humor to properly pray for his enemies.

From the published histories, and the gazettes of that day, it would not appear that General Campbell had any share in the battle of Jamestown Ford, fought on the sixth of July, mainly by Wayne's brigade; yet a survivor of La Fayette's army stated that Campbell participated in the attack, and fell back fighting as he retired.† His riflemen, perhaps, formed the reserve of Wayne's attacking party; for some of his riflemen were wounded, and Colonel John Boyer, of his rifle corps, from Rockbridge County, was

---

* *Journals of the Virginia Legislature,* 1781; Colonel Arthur Campbell's memoir.

† MS. notes of conversations with Reverend James Haynes, near Paris, Tenn., in 1844, then eighty-four years of age.

made a prisoner by the enemy. Though Cornwallis affected the most haughty contempt for "the boy" La-Fayette, he must have had some respect for Wayne, the hero of Stony Point, for Campbell, who had taken a little detached army from him at King's Mountain, and for Morgan, who had handled his detachment under Tarleton so roughly at the Cowpens.

While Cornwallis was encamped at Williamsburg, and La Fayette six miles distant on the road leading to Richmond, General Campbell, in command of the light troops, usually kept a picket guard of a dozen or fifteen of his mounted men at the Three Burnt Chimneys, about midway between the hostile camps. For several successive mornings the enemy would send out a superior body of horsemen, and drive in the American picket. Campbell determined to profit by this experience. A short distance in the rear of the Burnt Chimneys was a fine grove by the road-side, surrounding a church. In this grove Campbell posted a large detachment of mounted riflemen, himself at their head; and placed the customary picket at the Burnt Chimneys, with directions to retire on the approach of the expected British cavalry early in the morning. The enemy, as usual, hotly pursued the fleeing Americans under whip and spur, until they reached the grove, when an unexpected volley of rifle balls unhorsed a goodly number of the astonished Britons—killing some twenty or more of their cavalry men, and thirty or forty of their horses. The survivors fled back in dismay, and the picket at the Burnt Chimneys was no more annoyed. *

But General Campbell's services were destined to a sudden termination. Taken with a complaint in his breast, he was conveyed to the residence of Colonel John Syme, his wife's half brother, at Rocky Mills, in Hanover County, where, after a few days' illness, he expired, August the

---

* MS. notes of conversations, in January, 1844, with James Givens, one of Campbell's men, then in his eightieth year.

twenty-second, 1781, in his thirty-sixth year. When La Fayette received intelligence of the death of his friend, he issued a *General Order* announcing the sad event, characterizing General Campbell as " an officer whose services must have endeared him to every citizen, and in particular to every American soldier. The glory which General Campbell has acquired in the affairs of King's Mountain and Guilford Court House, will do his memory everlasting honor, and insure him a high rank among the defenders of liberty in the American cause;" General La Fayette regretting that the funeral was so great a distance from the army, as to deprive him and his officers the privilege of paying to General Campbell the honors due to his rank, and " particularly to his merit," and deputing four field officers to repair to Rocky Mills and, in behalf of the army, pay him their last tribute of respect.

Here his remains reposed until 1823, when his relatives had them removed to his old Aspenvale homestead on the Holston, in now Smyth County, beside his mother, little son, and other relatives, and where a neat monument was erected to his memory. His widow, a son, and a daughter survived him—the widow subsequently uniting in marriage with General William Russell; the son died young; the daughter, Sarah, became the wife of General Francis Preston, and mother of Hon. William C. Preston, General John S. Preston, and Colonel Thomas L. Preston. General Campbell's widow died in November, 1825, aged about eighty; and his daughter, Mrs. Preston, died at Abingdon, Virginia, July twenty-third, 1846, at the age of nearly seventy years.

There was something akin to rivalry between Colonel Arthur Campbell and his brother-in-law, William Campbell, whose sister Margaret he had married. She was a woman of excellent mind, and of uncommon beauty and sprightliness; and withal she possessed no little ambition, which she endeavored to turn to good account in her

husband's behalf. This young wife encouraged him in all
his plans by which he might acquire distinction as a public
man. Her whole mind seemed completely absorbed in
this one great object of her life, to which every other must
bend; no privation, however great, annoyed her in the
smallest degree, if she believed it would contribute to the ac-
quirement of either military or civil reputation for her husband. Her extreme solicitude and promptings to push him
up the ladder of fame, caused him sometimes to make false
steps, and involved him in unnecessary altercations with
his brother-in-law and others. Except these ambitious efforts, and they were always promoted in a manner to gratify her husband, she was among the most exemplary of
women, never having a thought in opposition to his upon
any subject, and believing him to be the greatest man in
the country, not excepting her brother, of whose abilities
she entertained a very exalted opinion.*

Colonel Arthur Campbell was some three years the
senior of William Campbell; this fact, and his having been
in youth a prisoner with the Indians, had given him the
precedence in martial affairs. His military talents, however, were not of the first order, while William Campbell
thought that the experience he had gained on the Point
Pleasant campaign, and during his year's service in the
Williamsburg region, in 1775-76, fairly entitled him to lead
his brother-in-law, who would not acquiesce in this view,
and jealousies were the consequence, and sometimes open
ruptures. There appears to have been a sort of *quasi* understanding between them, that they should take turns in
commanding the Washington force on military expeditions
against the enemy. While Colonel William Campbell led
the troops against the Tories up New river, the men composing the command were only in part from Washington
County; and, hence he was permitted to go on the King's
Mountain campaign, heartily seconded in his efforts by

*MS. letter of Gov. David Campbell to the author, Dec. 12, 1840.

Colonel Arthur Campbell. The latter led the expedition
in December following against the Cherokees; and when,
shortly after, William Campbell received the urgent in-
vitation from General Greene to join him with a band of
riflemen, Colonel Arthur Campbell interposed objections,
nominally on the ground of danger from the Indians, but
probably prompted in fact somewhat by his jealousy of his
brother-in-law's growing fame as a leader in expeditions
against the enemy.

General Campbell had a very imposing personal appearance—the *beau ideal* of a military chieftain with those
who served under him, He was about six feet, two inches
high, possessing a large, muscular, well-proportioned frame
—rather raw-boned; with an iron constitution, capable of almost incredible endurance—and he was as straight as an Indian. His complexion was ruddy, with light colored or red-
dish hair, and bright blue eyes. His countenance presented
a serious—nay, stern appearance; and when not excited expressive of great benevolence; but when his ire was stirred,
he exhibited the fury of an Achilles. On such occasions he
would commit violent and indiscreet acts; he was, however,
easily calmed, particularly when approached by those in
whom he reposed confidence—to such he would yield his
opinions without the slightest opposition. In conversation
he was reserved and thoughtful; in his written communications, expressive and elegant. He was bland in his manners, and courteous to all with whom he had intercourse,
whether high or low, rich or poor. At preaching in the
country, it was his constant custom to look around after sermon was ended, and assist all the women of the neighborhood, especially the more aged, who were not attended,
on their horses.

Of Scottish descent, he inherited the principles and
predilections of his persecuted Presbyterian ancestors
of that northern land. His religious zeal—certainly in
theory—and his devotion to liberty, were alike deep, fer-

vent, and exclusive. In his domestic and social relations, he was the most amiable of men. He would send his servants to aid a poor neighbor, while he would himself plow through the heat of the day in his fields, giving his spare moments to his Bible and his God, endeavoring scrupulously to live up to the golden rule in all his dealings with his fellow men. But he set his face like a flint against the enemies of his country and of freedom, proving himself almost as inflexible as a Claverhouse or a Cumberland toward those who betrayed or deserted the holy cause for which he contended, and for which he died.

But it was as a military genius that he shone preëminent. He had the ability to form able plans—confidence in himself, and indefatigable perseverance to execute them ; and the rare capacity to inspire all under his command with his own confidence and indomitable courage. Had he acted on as conspicuous a stage as Warren or Montgomery, his name and fame would have been as illustrious as theirs. With inferior numbers of undisciplined volunteers, embodied with great celerity, led forth, with scanty supplies, nearly two hundred miles over rugged mountains, he totally defeated Ferguson, one of the most experienced and enterprising of the British partisan leaders—gaining, as he expressed it, " victory to a wish." At Guilford he fully sustained his high reputation, and had the North Carolina militia behaved with the firmness and courage equal to his riflemen, the army of Cornwallis would not have been crippled only, but would, in all probability, have met with irretrievable disaster.

General Campbell never balanced between military duty and prudential maxims. Himself a hater of vice and treason in every form, he was by some deemed too severe in punishing the deviations of others—yet his acts, in his own estimation, were the result of the purest patriotic impulses. Wherever the story of King's Mountain and Guilford is read, and the services of their heroes fully appreciated, it will be found that William Campbell has "purpled o'er his name with deathless glory."

———

Of such of General Campbell's officers as served with him at King's Mountain, and concerning whom facts have been obtained, brief notices will be made. Major William Edmondson—or Edmiston, as frequently written in early days—the second in command of the Virginia regiment in the battle, was descended from Irish ancestry, and born in Cecil County, Maryland, in 1734. While he was yet young, his father removed to what is now Rockbridge County, Virginia, where he grew to years of manhood, receiving a limited education. He early engaged in the old French and Indian war.

Learning of Colonel Byrd's expedition down the Holston, destined against the Cherokees, in 1760, William Edmondson, and his brother Samuel, concluded to enlist, so as to give them an opportunity to examine the lands of the Holston country with a view to future settlement. While on this service, William Edmondson was guilty of the high crime of addressing an officer without taking off his hat, as was required of all soldiers, for which he was severely rebuked, and threatened with punishment. Reaching his comrades in great wrath, Edmondson loaded his rifle, and swore he would shoot the officer who had so grossly insulted him; and it was with great difficulty, that his brother dissuaded him from it. One of the Virginia officers, who knew Edmondson, wrote to Governor Fauquier, that there was a high-spirited soldier in his corps, who, unless commissioned, was likely to get into trouble. †
On the first of August, in that year, the Governor sent

———

* These salient points in the character of General Campbell are drawn from Colonel Arthur Campbell's memoir; Governor D. Campbell's MS. correspondence; and the recollections of Colonel Walter Lewis, who had served under him, in *Atkinson's Casket*, September, 1833, 387.

† MS. letter of Hon. Benjamin Estill, August 21st, 1845.

him an Ensign's commission to serve on that expedition. But when Byrd got pretty well down the Valley, he took to camp, but made no further progress during that nor the following year. In 1763, Governor Fauquier sent Edmondson a commission of Lieutenant in the militia.

Having married a Miss Montgomery, he removed, after the war, to the New river frontiers, in now Grayson County; and subsequently to what now constitutes Washington County, settling on a tract of land received for his military services. In 1774 he was commissioned a Lieutenant in the militia of Fincastle County, served on the frontiers of Clinch and Sandy, and probably in Christian's regiment on the expedition to Point Pleasant and the Scioto: and, in 1776, he was made a Captain, and served on the campaign against the Cherokees in the fall of that year. In 1777, he was appointed a Justice, and failed only a few votes of an election to the House of Delegates. He was, this year, selected by the Legislature one of the commissioners for taking depositions against the claim of Henderson and Company to the Kentucky country. During 1777, he was in service when the treaty was held at Long Island of Holston, and was much engaged, in 1778, in guarding the frontiers. Early in 1779, he commanded a company on Colonel Evan Shelby's Chickamauga expedition; and early in 1780, he was promoted to Major of the Washington regiment, serving on the expedition against the Tories on New river, and then on the King's Mountain campaign. At the close of the year he joined Colonel William Campbell's force, marching to the Long Island of Holston. He was advanced to Lieutenant-Colonel in 1781, and in 1783 to a full Colonel. During 1781 and 1782, he was much in service in protecting the frontiers.

By two marriages—the second to a Miss Kennedy—he had fifteen children, one son, born soon after the death of his revered commander, he named *General William Campbell Edmondson.* He lived to a good old age, dying July thirtieth, 1822, in his eighty-ninth year. He was six feet, two inches high, possessed a vigorous mind; he was bold, manly, open-hearted, and generous. His attachments were strong, and his hatreds bitter. He served at one time as Sheriff of the County, and for many years presided, with great dignity, over the County Court. Judge Estill, who knew him well, declared, that "few more gallant, useful, and honorable men than Colonel Edmondson ever lived in any country."

James Dysart was born in Donegal County, Ireland; his parents dying in his infancy, he was raised by his grandfather, who gave him a plain education. At the age of seventeen he sailed for the New World to seek his fortune, landing, in 1761, at Philadelphia, from which he gradually worked his way to the south-west, until he reached the Holston Valley. In 1770, he joined James Knox and others, in exploring Tennessee and Kentucky, who are known in history as the Long Hunters. In 1775, he married Nancy Beattie, sister of Captain David Beattie, and settled on the Little Holston. During the whole Revolutionary war he was active in frontier service, heading his company; and at King's Mountain he was badly wounded in the left hand, which crippled him for life. In 1781 he was made a Major, and subsequently a Colonel; and once represented Washington County in the Virginia Legislature. In his old age, broken up by surety debts, he removed to Rockcastle County, Kentucky, with his wife, three sons, and three daughters; where he died, May twenty-sixth, 1818, at the age of seventy-four years. He was fond of reading, and had quite a library of books. When it was once suggested to him that he must be lonesome at his frontier home—"I am never lonesome," he replied, "when I have a good book in my hand." He always spoke highly of Colonel William Campbell as a brave man and able commander. In 1806, he was placed on the invalid pension list, drawing a hundred and twenty dollars a year.

Another of Campbell's officers was Captain David Beattie, son of John Beattie, born on Carr's creek, in now Rockbridge County, Virginia, about 1752; and removed with his parents to what is now Washington County, in 1772, settling at the present locality of the Glade Spring Depot. He married Miss Mary Beattie, and raised four sons and a daughter. The Beattie connection forted against the Indians where the Glade Spring church is now situated. Captain Beattie was much engaged in frontier service, and led his company at King's Mountain—his brothers John and William were also along. John Beattie, an Ensign, was killed in the battle, leaving no family. Captain Beattie died in the spring of 1814. He was a man of much energy of character. His brother, William Beattie, survived till April fourth, 1860, at the venerable age of one hundred years—the last of Campbell's King's Mountain men.

Captain Andrew Colvill, an early settler in the Holston Valley, took an active part in the defence of the country. He was, as early as 1776, commanding at Fort Black, and the two following years he was ranging the frontiers, or stationed at Moore's and Cowan's Forts, and distinguished himself at King's Mountain. He died in the autumn of 1797.

Few of the Holston pioneers were more serviceable than Robert Craig. He commanded a company on Christian's Cherokee campaign in the fall of 1776; was much engaged in the defence of the frontiers, and at King's Mountain, where he fought bravely, losing his Lieutenant, William Blackburn, and his Ensign, Nathaniel Dryden. He survived the war.

Of Captain William Edmondson's career, who distinguished himself and lost his life at King's Mountain, we have no further particulars; nor of Captain William Neal, who commanded the footmen in the rear, save that he rose from the rank of ensign in 1777, and survived the war.

Reece Bowen was born in Maryland about 1742. He first emigrated to what is now Rockbridge County, Virginia, and, in 1769, to the waters of Clinch, in what is now Tazewell County. He shared in the battle of Point Pleasant; went to the relief of the Kentucky stations in 1778; and on the King's Mountain campaign, he was Lieutenant of his brother, William Bowen's company. His brother being ill of fever, Reece Bowen succeeded to the command of the company. His heroic death has been already related; he is said to have been shot by a Tory boy, behind a baggage wagon, near the close of the engagement, when Campbell's men were driving the enemy toward the north-eastern end of the mountain. He was remarkable for his herculean strength and great activity. He left a family—his son, Colonel Henry Bowen, lived in Tazewell County to a good old age.

Thomas McColloch had long been prominent among the border men of Holston. Though only a Lieutenant, he commanded a company at King's Mountain, and was mortally wounded in the battle. He died while the army was at Walker's, on their return march, the twelfth of October, and was buried in Little Britain grave-yard. On the rude stone at his grave is this inscription: "Here lies the body of Lieutenant Thomas McColloch, belonging to Colonel Campbell's Virginia regiment, who lost his life in, and for the honorable, just, and righteous cause of liberty, in defeating Colonel Ferguson's infamous company of banditti, at King's Mountain, October seventh, 1780."

William Russell, Jr., who, though only a Lieutenant, commanded Captain Neal's company at King's Mountain, was born in Culpeper County, Virginia, in 1758. He was chiefly raised on the south-western frontier of that State; and, in 1774, he served on an expedition, in Powell's Valley, under Daniel Boone, and was repeatedly in service thereafter; acting as Adjutant to Colonel Campbell at King's Mountain, Whitzell's Mill, and Guilford. He afterwards removed to Kentucky, serving from 1791 to 1794, under Scott, Wilkinson, and Wayne, on their several expeditions against the Indians; and again, in north-western campaigns during the war of 1812–15, having been appointed to the command of a regiment in the regular army in 1808. He rendered much service in civil life, representing Fayette County, in the Virginia Legislature in 1789, and in the Kentucky Legislature thirteen sessions. He was an unsuccessful candidate for Governor in 1824; and died July third, 1825, about sixty-seven years of age.

The two Robert Edmondsons—of whom the elder was killed, and the younger wounded, at King's Mountain—were of Irish descent, and near kinsmen. Both were in the battle of the Long Island Flats of Holston, July twentieth, 1776, when some of the men retreated—young Robert among them. The elder Robert Edmondson interposed, and brought some of them into line, his young kinsman of the number. The elder Edmondson chided the younger for having used profane language during the engagement, for which he was bound to report him to his father. The young man retorted—" You, too, did the very same thing when the men were on the flight." This accusation shocked the good man, who was a strong Presbyterian, and said this charge would be an additional matter to report to the young man's father; whereupon a by-stander mildly said, " It's too true—I heard you." The old soldier, who had unconsciously used rough language under high excitement, now held his peace. He was a good soldier, and killed two or three Indians at the Island Flat battle; he served on Christian's Cherokee expedition in the fall of 1776; was engaged in frontier defense as a Lieutenant in 1777-8, and on Evan Shelby's Chickamauga expedition in 1779.

At King's Mountain, the younger Edmondson was Lieutenant of Beattie's company. He subsequently settled at the Irish station, near Haysboro, seven or eight

miles above Nashville, on the Cumberland. In the fall of
1787, in a scrape with the Indians, at Neely's Bend, he
was badly wounded in the arm ; and it was eight years
after, when an ounce ball was extracted from the arm,
before he recovered. He died in 1816, at the age of sixty-
three. Captain Andrew J. Edmondson, who served under
General Jackson in the Creek war, and at New Orleans,
was his son.

Samuel Newell was born in Frederick County, Virginia, November fourth, 1754, and his parents early settled
on the Holston. He engaged in the service against Tories
in April, 1776, and in the summer following shared in the
battle of Long Island Flats of Holston ; and the same year
was appointed a Sergeant in Captain Colvill's company, and
a Lieutenant in 1777—serving several years on the frontiers. In 1780, he took part in the expedition against the
Tories on New river, and then at King's Mountain, in Colvill's company, where he was badly wounded, from which
he never fully recovered. In December of the same year,
he went on Colonel Arthur Campbell's Cherokee expedition ; and in 1781, was appointed a Captain. He was
much engaged in the protection of the Kentucky road and
Powell's Valley, and had several skirmishes with the Indians—twice, in 1782, overtaking war parties, in one of
which he and his men surrounded an Indian camp, and
his gun alone went off, the others failed, from becoming wet ;
but his single fire killed one Indian and mortally wounded
another. He early removed to French Broad river, in
Tennessee, where he figured among the promoters of the
Franklin Government, was a representative, in 1785, of
Sevier County in the Legislature, and also a member of
the Convention that formed the Franklin Constitution at
the close of that year ; was subsequently a Justice and a
Colonel of militia. In 1797, he removed to what is now
Pulaski County, Kentucky, where he was long presiding
Justice of the County Court ; and about 1838 he removed to

Montgomery County, Indiana, where he died September twenty-first, 1841, at the age of nearly eighty-seven years. He was six feet, one inch in height, of fine presence, and superior abilities. He left numerous descendants. In 1812 he was placed on the invalid pension list, drawing, at first, ninety-six, and subsequently increased to one hundred and eight dollars a year, and still later to two hundred and thirty-one dollars and ninety-three cents.

Andrew Kincannon, a native of the Valley of Virginia, was born October twenty-seventh, 1744. He early settled in the Holston country. He was a blacksmith and gunsmith by trade, and claimed to have made the first horse-shoe in Kentucky, probably in 1775. In February, 1777, he was acting as armorer to the troops stationed at Long Island of Holston; and that year he was appointed an Ensign, and then a Lieutenant in Washington County, and stationed at the Stone Mill on Deer Creek. At King's Mountain, he succeeded to the command of his company, when Captain Dysart was wounded, and was chosen Captain in 1782. A few years after the war, he settled on Tom's Creek, in Surry County, North Carolina, where he had a fine farm and iron works. He married Catherine McDonald; they raised nine children, and left many descendants. He was tall and muscular, of great integrity, and high character. He died in November, 1829, at the age of eighty-five years.

Robert Campbell, a younger brother of Colonel Arthur Campbell, was born in Augusta County, Virginia, May 25, 1755, and emigrated to the Holston in 1771; serving in Christian's regiment on the Shawanoe Campaign in 1774; and was in the battle of Long Island Flats of Holston, in July, 1776, where in advance of his fellows, he was mistaken for an Indian, and came near losing his life, and when within twenty paces of a warrior, who had discharged his gun ineffectually at Campbell, the latter aimed at him in turn, when the savage hero folded his arms, and met his fate with a dignity and firmness worthy of the brightest days of chivalry. Seeing the Indians extending their lines to surround the whites, Campbell gave the alarm in season to counteract it. On Christian's Cherokee campaign, in the fall of 1776, he was a volunteer; and on the march to Highwassee, the troops forded French Broad river to their waists and armpits, then bivouacked on the southern bank during the greater part of a very cold night, without fire, apprehending an attack from the Indians, and renewing their march at the dawn of day, with shivering limbs, literally encased in ice. At King's Mountain, though only an Ensign, he served conspicuously. In December following he was Adjutant to his brother, Colonel Arthur Campbell, on his Cherokee expedition, and at his own request, headed a party of sixty men to destroy Chilhowee. Having accomplished this service, while returning, they had to pass a narrow defile, three hundred yards in extent, lined by two or three hundred warriors; and, without pausing, he directed his men to follow him in single file, and charged through at their best speed, without losing a man, though a heavy volley was fired at them. He served a long period as a Colonel of a regiment, and as a magistrate nearly forty years, in Washington County; then removed, in 1825, to Knox County, Tennessee, where he died December twenty-seventh, 1831, in the seventy-seventh year of his age.*

---

* Some writers have confounded Lieutenant-Colonel Richard Campbell with General William Campbell. In a sketch of the latter, in the first edition of *Appleton's Cyclopedia*, it is stated that he was mortally wounded at the battle of Eutaw Springs, September eighth, 1781; and when told of the success of the American arms, died uttering the same words as Wolfe had done before him, "I die contended." This was true of Richard Campbell, also a native of the Virginia Valley. who was commissioned a Captain in February, 1776, and subsequently a Major, serving in Colonel John Gibson's regiment at Pittsburg. He served on McIntosh's expedition against the Ohio Indians in 1778; and leading a relief party to Fort Laurens, in June, 1779. he commanded that frontier garrison till its evacuation shortly after. Joining General Greene with a regiment of Virginia regulars, he served with distinction at Guilford, Hobkirk's Hill and Ninety Six, sealing with his life's blood his devotion to his country at Eutaw.

CHAPTER XVIII.

Cols. Shelby and Sevier, and their Officers.

Notice of Evan Shelby.—Isaac Shelby's Life and Services.—Officers under him at King's Mountain—Evan Shelby, Jr.—Gilbert Christian—Moses Shelby— James Elliott— John Sawyers—George Maxwell, and George Rutledge.— John Sevier's Life and Services.— His King's Mountain Officers— Jonathan Tipton— Valentine and Robert Sevier—Christopher Taylor— Jacob Brown—Samuel Weir.

Evan Shelby, who was born in Wales in 1720, emigrated, with his father's family, to Maryland, about 1735, settling near North Mountain, in now Washington County, where he became a noted woodsman, hunter, and Indian trader. He figured prominently on the Maryland and Pennsylvania frontiers in the old French and Indian war—first as a Lieutenant, and then as a Captain. On Forbes' campaign, he gave chase to an Indian spy, in view of many of the troops, overtaking and tomahawking him. He subsequently distinguished himself at Point Pleasant, on Christian's campaign, and on the expedition he led against the Chickamaugas. Rising to the rank of Colonel, and then General, he died December fourth, 1794, at the age of seventy-four years.

His son, Isaac Shelby, was born near the North Mountain, Maryland, on the eleventh of December, 1750, where amid the excitements of the Indian wars, he obtained only the elements of a plain English education. In 1771, he was for some time engaged in feeding and herding cattle in the extensive natural ranges west of the Alleghanies; and in the same year, the Shelby connection removed to the Holston country. In 1774, when the Indians became troublesome, Isaac Shelby received the commission of a Lieutenant in the militia at the hands of Colonel William Preston, the County Lieutenant of Fincastle, and took his seat; when his father, who was present, thinking his son had not shown proper respect in the matter, said to him : " Get up, you dog you, and make your obeisance to the Colonel "— whereupon the youthful officer arose, somewhat abashed, and made the *amende honorable.* He served with distinction, as second in command of his father's company, in the memorable battle of Point Pleasant, October tenth, 1774, where the frontier riflemen fought the Shawanoes and allied tribes from sunrise till sundown, gaining a decisive victory. Point Pleasant was then made a garrison, where he remained in service till July, 1775, when Governor Dunmore ordered the disbandment of those troops, lest they might sympathize with, and become obedient to the Whig authorities.

He was now, for nearly twelve months, engaged in exploring the wilds of Kentucky, and in surveying lands for Henderson and Company, who had made a large purchase from the Cherokees. During his absence in 1776, he was commissioned a Captain; and, in 1777, Governor Henry appointed him a Commissary of supplies for the several frontier garrisons, and for the ensuing treaty with the Cherokees at the Long Island of Holston in that year. It was only by his most indefatigable exertions that the large amount of provisions required, could be obtained. The following year he continued his Commissary services, providing for the Continental army, and for General McIntosh's expedition against the Ohio Indians. In the spring of 1779, he pledged his *individual credit* for supplies for his father's troops on the Chickamauga expedition. He was, this spring, elected a member of the Virginia Legislature from Washington County; and, in the fall, he was commissioned a Major by Governor Jefferson for the escort of guards to the Commissioners for extending the boundary line between Virginia and North Carolina. His residence was now found to be within the limits of the latter State, and he was, in November of this year, appointed by Governor Caswell a Colonel and magistrate of the new County of Sullivan, entering upon their duties at the organization of the County in February following.

In the the summer of 1780, Colonel Shelby was in Kentucky, perfecting his claims to lands he had five years before selected and marked out for himself, when the intelligence of the surrender of Charleston reached that country. He returned home in July, determined to enter the service, and remain in it until independence should be secured. He found a message from Colonel Charles McDowell, of Burke County, begging him to furnish all the aid he could towards checking the enemy, who were over-running the three Southern States, and had reached the western borders of North Carolina. In a few days, he crossed the Alleghanies with two hundred mounted riflemen. Their valor and patriotism were shown conspicuously at Thicketty Fort, Cedar Springs and Musgrove's Mill; re-assuring the struggling patriots that the British leaders could not ride, roughshod, over the American people. Shelby's noble efforts in prosecuting the King's Mountain expedition, his magnanimity in securing the appointment of Colonel Campbell to the chief command, and his heroic conduct in the battle, all combine to render his services, at that critical period, of the greatest importance to his country.

The Legislature of North Carolina passed a vote of thanks to Colonels Shelby and Sevier for their good services, directing that an elegant sword should be presented to each of them. General Greene wrote urgently requesting Col. Shelby to join him with a body of mountaineers, which letter miscarried; but a second message was more fortunate, and Shelby and Sevier led five hundred mounted riflemen over the mountains joining General Greene, about the first of November. Shelby was detached with Colonel Maham in an attempt on the British post of Fairlawn, at Colleton's plantation, a few miles from Monk's Corner. When a flag

was sent in, demanding its surrender, the British officer in
command returned for answer, that he would defend it
to the last extremity.   Shelby then went himself, assuring
the commandant that should he be so fool-hardy as to suffer
a storm, every soul would be put to death, as he had under
his command several hundred mountaineers who would
rush in, tomahawk in hand, upon the garrison.   The officer
then inquired if he had any cannon.   " Yes, indeed," said
Shelby, " guns that will blow you to atoms in a moment."
" Then," replied the officer, " I suppose I must surrender,"
which he did—one hundred and five prisoners, with three
hundred stand of arms.   Shelby shortly after obtained leave
of absence, to attend the North Carolina Legislature, of
which he was a member.   Soon after the mountaineers
returned home—not deserters as Judge Johnson describes
them, for the call upon them was for a special service—to
aid in intercepting Cornwallis ; who, having been effectually
intercepted at Yorktown, they felt that they had fulfilled all
that could reasonably be required of them, and retired
to their homes, in a deep snow, early in January ensuing.*

The Legislature of North Carolina soon adjourned, and
Colonel Shelby returning to the Holston, was engaged during spring in preparing for an expedition against the Chickamauga band of Cherokees, and the hostile Creeks at the
sources of the Mobile, in which enterprise he was to have
been joined by two hundred men from Washington County,
Virginia ; but on account of the poverty of that State, the
authorities discouraged the scheme, and reaching Big Creek,
thirty miles below Long Island of Holston, the expedition
was relinquished.   He was, in 1782, again chosen a member
of the North Carolina Assembly, and was appointed one of
the Commissioners to adjust preëmption claims on Cumberland river, and lay off the lands allotted to the officers and

---

* Haywood's *History of Tennessee*, 102-106; Todd's *Life of Shelby*; MS. statement of
Gov. Shelby, apparently addressed to Judge Johnson, controverting his statements about
the pretended desertion of the mountaineers; MS. notes of conversations with James
Sevier, who was in the service, and with Col. George Wilson.

soldiers of the North Carolina line, which service he performed in the winter of 1782-83. In April following, he was married at Boonesborough, Kentucky, to Susanna, daughter of Captain Nathaniel Hart, one of the pioneers of the country, and now settled on his preëmption near Stanford, where he continued to reside for forty-three years.

In January, 1783, Colonel Shelby having been appointed by Governor Harrison and the Council of Virginia, one of the Commissioners to hold treaties with the Western Indians, a conference was held at Long Island of Holston with the Cherokees in July, but nothing of moment was accomplished. The proposed treaty with the Shawnees miscarried; and only Colonels Donelson and Martin met the Chickasaws at French Lick, on Cumberland, in November, and interchanged friendly talks with them. For several years Indian disturbances continued, the Cherokees waylaying the Kentucky road, and inflicting much injury on the travelers to that country. The Kentucky people resolved to march in strong force against Chickamauga, and could only be restrained, in the summer of 1791, in view of an approaching treaty at Knoxville. Colonel Shelby attended—the Indians were surly, when he frankly told them, that there were a thousand riflemen in Kentucky, with their horses all shod, ready to march against them. "Too many—too many," said the Cherokees, and they patched up a temporary peace.

He was a member of the early Conventions held at Danville to secure a separation from Virginia, and of the Convention, in April, 1792, that formed the first Constitution of Kentucky. In May following, he was chosen the first Governor of the new State; and during his four years' term he proved a model Chief Magistrate, lending every aid in his power in supplying troops for quelling the Indian war in the North-west. He was three times chosen an elector, supporting Thomas Jefferson for President; and when the second war with Great Britain burst upon the country, he consented again to serve as Governor, exerting every influence in sustaining the Government, and bringing the conflict to an honorable issue.   The revival of the war spirit reminded North Carolina of its ancient pledge of a sword to Governor Shelby for his King's Mountain services, and it was presented to him in 1813; and he led the Kentucky troops, the same year, on the Canada campaign, which closed with the victory of the Thames.   For this patriotic service, Congress, in 1817, voted him a gold medal.   In 1818, he was appointed, by President Monroe, Secretary of War; but, at his advanced age, preferring the quiet of private life, he declined its acceptance.   In 1818, he was associated with General Jackson in holding a treaty with the Chickasaws, which resulted in the cession of their lands west of the Tennessee to the General Government—his last public service.   He was stricken with paralysis in 1820, disabling his right arm and limb; but his mind continued unimpaired until July eighteenth, 1826, when he died of apoplexy, sitting in his chair—with only his venerable companion present, as he had often expressed his wish that it should be.   The noble patriot of three wars thus quietly passed away, in the seventy-sixth year of his age.

————

Evan Shelby, Jr., who acted as Major in his brother's regiment at King's Mountain, was born in Maryland about 1754.   He was a Lieutenant on Christian's campaign of 1776.   Beside his participation in the King's Mountain expedition, he served as a volunteer at the Cowpens; and, near the close of 1781, with his brother Isaac in South Carolina.   Left on one occasion, with three or four men, to guard quite a squad of horses on an island, a British party of some ninety men came and took the horses; Shelby and his associates escaping.   But they dogged the enemy until they camped in a lane, when, leaving one of their number behind some distance with a horn which he was directed, at the proper time, to blow furiously, Shelby and the others made a bold push on the camp, hallooing "surround! surround them!" This, with the horn, indicating a charge, some of the enemy began to fall back, when the horses, becoming frightened, ran at full speed over the Red-Coats, materially aiding in the stampede. The Whigs killed several of the skedaddlers. Marrying his cousin, Catharine, daughter of Major John Shelby he settled a station about 1790, pretty well up the West Fork of Red river, some fifty miles north-west of Nashville. On the eighteenth of January, 1793, when out hunting, at the mouth of Casey's creek of Little river, in the eastern part of the present county of Trigg, Kentucky, he, with two companions, was killed by hostile Indians—his brother, Moses escaping unhurt.

Gilbert Christian, son of Robert Christian, was born in Augusta County, Va., about 1734, and participated in the border wars of 1755-63. Settling in the Holston country, he commanded a company on Christian's Cherokee campaign, the Chickamauga expedition, and at King's Mountain. He served as a Major on Arthur Campbell's expedition, figured prominently in the Franklin Republic, and acted as a Colonel during the Cherokee war of 1788 till his death, at Knoxville, in November 1793, when returning from the Hightower campaign.

Moses Shelby, born about 1756, was severely wounded at the head of his company at King's Mountain. He served at the siege of Savannah in 1779, at Cowpens, and the capture of Augusta, in 1781—on one of which occasions he received six sabre wounds. After the Indian wars, he settled near New Madrid, Missouri, where he died September seventeenth, 1828, about seventy-two years of age.

James Elliott was an early settler on Holston. From an Ensign in 1777, he rose by good service to the rank of Captain, commanding his company at King's Mountain; and while serving on Colonel Arthur Campbell's Cherokee expedition, he was killed at Tellico, December twenty-eighth, 1780, by a concealed Indian—Colonel Campbell denominating him "a gallant young officer."

27

John Sawyers was born in Virginia in 1745, shortly after his parents arrived from England, who early settled in Augusta County, Virginia. In 1761 young Sawyers was engaged on Colonel Byrd's abortive expedition, and in other frontier service against the Indians. In 1768, he with others explored the Holston Valley, early removed to that frontier, and served at Point Pleasant, on Christian's Cherokee campaign, and on the Chickamauga expedition in 1779, and led a company at King's Mountain. Settling in what is now Knox County, Tennessee, he was made a Major, then a Colonel, and twice chosen a member of the Legislature. He died November twentieth, 1831, aged eighty-six years.

George Maxwell born in Virginia, 1751, early migrated to the Holston. A Lieutenant in 1777, he was much engaged in frontier service, commanding a company at King's Mountain. On the organization of Sullivan County, Tennessee, in 1780, he was made one of the Justices; in 1784, a Major; the next year a Colonel, and member of the Assembly of the short-lived Republic of Franklin; in 1787, a member of the North Carolina Legislature; in 1799, a member of the Tennessee Senate from Hawkins county, where he died November twenty-third, 1822, in his seventy-second year. Of his associates, Captain John Pemberton, and Captain Webb, we have no knowledge.

Col. John Sevier and his Officers.

Near the close of the seventeenth century, the grandfather of the subject of this sketch fled from his native Paris, on account of religious persecution, and settled in London. The family name of Xavier was now Anglicized to Sevier. Here he married a Miss Smith, and had two sons, Valentine and William, who, when scarcely grown, ran away, and took passage for America. This was not far from 1740. Among their fellow-passengers were several young men of a wild and sporting character, from whom Valentine Sevier acquired habits of gambling and dissipation. Landing at

Baltimore, he subsequently married a Miss Joanna Goade, and settled in then Augusta, now Rockingham County, in the Valley of Virginia, six miles south-west of where the little village of New Market was subsequently located. Here he opened a farm, and carried on trade with the Indians. and here John Sevier was born, September twenty-third, 1745. After the Indian war of 1755 broke out, the family removed for safety to Fredericksburg, where they remained nearly two years, and where young Sevier attended school.

Returning to his old home in the Valley, Valentine Sevier found his domicil had been burned by the Indians. The cabins were re-built, and trade re-commenced. John Sevier was sent to Staunton to school; and while there, he one day accidentally fell into a mill-race, and was saved from drowning by the heroic efforts of two young ladies— one of whom subsequently became the wife of George Matthews, one of the heroes of Point Pleasant, and subsequently a Colonel in the Revolution, and Governor of Georgia. He now engaged with his father in trade; and, in 1761, before he had turned of seventeen, he married Miss Sarah Hawkins, cleared up a farm, and engaged in excursions against the Indians—on one occasion, he and his party narrowly escaping a fatal ambuscade by a timely discovery of the trap their enemies had set for them. He laid out the village of New Market, and there for some time he kept a store and inn, and carried on a farm; and then engaged in merchandizing in the neighboring village of Middletown.

About 1771, he visited the Holston country, carrying some goods with him for trade, and repeated the visit in 1772. At the Watauga Old Fields, on Doe river, near its junction with the Watauga, he witnessed a horse-race, where a large, savage fellow, named Shoate, took from a traveling stranger his horse, pretending that he had won him in a bet. Such an act disgusted Sevier with the country, naturally beautiful; but the elder Evan Shelby remarked: "Never mind these rascals: they'll soon take poplar"—meaning canoes, and put off. This Shoate became a noted horse-thief, and was pursued and killed about 1779-80. Late in 1773, John Sevier removed his family to the Holston country, and first located in the Keywood settlement, on the north shore of Holston, half a dozen miles from the Shelbys. Before his removal from Virginia, he had been commissioned a Captain by Governor Dunmore.

He was at Watauga Fort when attacked, July twenty-first, 1776. At day-break, when there were a large number of people gathered there, and the women were out-side milking the cows, a large body of Cherokees fired on the milkers; but they all fortunately escaped to the fort, the gates of which were thrown open for their reception. Among the young girls thus engaged was Catharine Sherrill, who, when she reached the gate, found it shut; but equal to the emergency, she threw her bonnet over the pickets, and then clambered over herself, and, as she jumped within, was caught in the arms of John Sevier—her future husband. A warm attack on the fort ensued, during which Captain Sevier thought he killed one of the Indians. A man stole out of the stockade at night, went to the Holston, when a large party marched to the relief of the beleaguered garrison. It was because the people refused to join and co-operate with the enemies of their country, that the savages were instigated to murder them, destroy their crops and improvements, and drive off their cattle and horses.

John Sevier was among the foremost in the defence of the Watauga and Nolachucky settlements. He had been elected Clerk of the first self-constituted court in 1775; and, in 1776, he was chosen one of the representatives of the united settlements to the North Carolina Convention at Halifax, and took his seat, securing the establishment of the district of Washington. Hastening back home, he reached there in season to serve on Christian's expedition against the Cherokees at the head of a fine company of riflemen; and also, at Colonel Christian's request, he acted as a spy during the campaign. He continued his services, till the conclusion of the treaty at Long Island of Holston in July, 1777. In the fall of that year, he was appointed Lieutenant-Colonel for Washington County. During the period 1777-79, the Indians, Tories and horse-thieves required Colonel Sevier's constant vigilance. In the summer of 1780, he was left in defence of the settlements, while Major Charles Robertson led the Watauga troops on the campaign in South Carolina. During their absence, August fourteenth, having some time previously lost his wife, he was married to Miss Catharine Sherrill.

His gallant services at King's Mountain cannot be too highly extolled. December sixteenth following, he defeated the Cherokees at Boyd's creek, killing thirteen, and taking all their baggage, and then joined Colonel Arthur Campbell on an expedition against the hostile Indian towns. On the third of February, 1781, he was made a full Colonel; and in March, he led a successful foray against the Middle Cherokee Settlements, killing about thirty of their warriors, capturing nine prisoners, burning six towns, and bringing off about two hundred horses.

"What time from right to left there rang the Indian war-whoop wild,
Where Sevier's tall Watauga boys through the dim dells defiled."

Having, in February, been appointed by General Greene one of the Commissioners to hold a treaty with the Indians, a conference took place with the Cherokees at the Long Island of Holston in July, Colonel Sevier and Major Martin attending, but without any permanent results. In the autumn of this year, Colonel Sevier served under Generals Greene and Marion in South Carolina; and, in 1782, he carried on a campaign against the Cherokees.

In November, 1784, he was appointed Brigadier-General, which he declined because of his leadership in the effort to establish the republic of Franklin. During the period of 1784 to 1788, he was made its Governor and defender. He was apprehended by the North Carolina authorities, on a charge of rebellion against the State, and conveyed to Morganton, where he was rescued by a party of his friends ; and returning home, "Chucky Jack" led a campaign against the Indians. As the East Tennesseans were divided in sentiment, the Franklin Republic, after a turbulent career of some four years, ceased to exist. In 1789, General Sevier was chosen a member of the Legislature of North Carolina, when an act of oblivion was passed, and he was re-instated as Brigadier-General. In 1790-91, he was elected to represent the East Tennessee district of North Carolina in Congress. When Tennessee was organized into a Territory, he was appointed by President Washington a Brigadier-General in the militia ; and he continued to protect the frontier settlements, carrying on the Hightower campaign against the Cherokees in 1793. In 1798, he was made a General in the Provisional army.

On the organization of a State Government in 1796, General Sevier was chosen the first Governor, and by successive re-elections was continued in that office till 1801. In 1802, he served as a Commissioner in running the boundary line between Tennessee and Virginia. He again served as Governor from 1803 till 1809, and then a term in the State Senate. He was chosen to a seat in Congress in 1811, serving, during the war, on the important committee on military affairs, till 1815 ; when President Madison appointed him one of the Commissioners, to ascertain the boundary of the Creek territory, and died while on that service, in camp, on the east side of the Tallapoosa, near Fort Decatur, Alabama, September twenty-fourth, 1851, closing a busy, useful life at the age of seventy years. As a proof of the love and veneration of his neighbors and friends, while absent in the Creek country, they had again elected him to Congress without opposition. In the language of the distinguished Hugh L. White, who had served under him in the old Indian wars: "General Sevier was considered in his day, among the most gallant, patriotic, and useful men in the country where he lived." *

Jonathan Tipton was born in Frederick County, Virginia, in 1750. Early settling in what became Washington County, East Tennessee, he was, in February, 1777, made Major, and was engaged in guarding the frontiers; and in 1780, had a fight with the Indians at the mouth of Flat creek, on Nolachucky. He was second in command of Sevier's regiment at King's Mountain; and then served on Arthur Campbell's campaign, leading a detachment against Telassee and Chilhowee. In the fall of 1781, he went on service with Colonels Shelby and Sevier under General Greene, in South Carolina. Major Tipton died in Overton County, Tennessee, January eighteenth, 1833, in his eighty-third year.

Valentine Sevier was born in what is now Rockingham County, Virginia, about 1747, and settled at an early period in East Tennessee. He was a Sergeant, and one of the spies, at the battle of Point Pleasant, where, says Isaac Shelby, "he was distinguished for vigilance, activity, and bravery." He subsequently served in the Indian wars in East Tennessee, and commanded a company at Thicketty Fort, Cedar Springs, Musgrove's Mill, and King's Mountain. He was the first Sheriff of Washington County, a Justice of the court, and rose in the militia to the rank of a Colonel. He removed to the mouth of Red river on Cumberland, now Clarksville, where he was attacked by Indians, November eleventh, 1794, killing and wounding several of his family. After long suffering from chronic rheumatism, he died at Clarksville, February twenty-third, 1800, in his fifty-third year; his widow surviving till 1844 in her one hundred and first year, His younger brother, Robert Sevier, who also commanded a company at King's Mountain, and was mortally wounded in the conflict, was previously much engaged in ridding the Watauga and Nolachucky region of Tories and horse thieves.

Christopher Taylor was born in Bedford County, Vir-

* MS. letter to the author, April 6th, 1839.

ginia, in 1746, and early removed, with a young family, to East Tennessee. He served on Christian's campaign; he was chosen a Captain, in 1778, and ranged the frontiers, serving in 1780, at King's Mountain, and subsequently against the Indians. He was a member of the Jonesborough convention in 1784, and died in Washington County, Tennessee, September tenth, 1833, at the age of eighty-seven.

Jacob Brown was born in South Carolina, December eleventh, 1736; settled on Nolachucky, in 1772, purchasing lands of the Cherokees. He served in the Indian wars, at the head of his company in Sevier's regiment at King's Mountain, and then on Arthur Campbell's expedition. He was made a Major, defeated a party of Indians in the fall of 1781, and died, June twenty-eighth, 1785, from an accidental wound received while out hunting.

Samuel Weir was another of Sevier's Captains at King's Mountain. He was an active participant in the Franklin Republic movement; led a party, in 1793, against Telassee, killing sixteen Indians, and taking four prisoners. In 1793 and 1794, he was a member of the Territorial Legislature, and, in 1796, a member of the Convention that formed the Constitution of Tennessee. He served many years as clerk of Sevier County court; and lived to a good old age. He was fully six feet in height, dark complexioned, and possessed much energy of character.

Other Captains of Sevier's regiment at King's Mountain were Samuel Williams, a member of the Jonesborough Convention of 1784, and a representative of Carter County, in the Legislature in 1799; James Stinson, Jesse Beene, and Thomas Price, who were much engaged against the Cherokees. George Russell, Joel Callahan, Isaac Lane, Andrew Caruthers, and William Robinson, were probably all Lieutenants. Caruthers, a native of Ireland, died in Lincoln County, Tenn., in 1818; and Robinson, a native of Scotland, was among the defeated Regulators at Alamance, in May, 1771, and lived to advanced years, dying also in Lincoln County.

CHAPTER XIX.

Col. Ben. Cleveland, Maj. Joseph Winston and their Officers.

Cleveland's Ancestry.—His Early Life and Hunting Adventures.—Trip to Kentucky.—Elk Hunt and Narrow Escapes.—Revolutionary War.—Suppressing Scotch Tories.—Rutherford's Cherokee Campaign.—Marches to Watauga.—Appointed Colonel.—Serves in Georgia.—New River Scout.— King's Mountain.—Hangs Coyle and Brown.—Captured by Tories and his Rescue.—Riddle and Wells Hung.—Other Tory Brigands Taken—Nichols, Tate, and Harrison.—Thumbing the Notch.—Reforming Tories.—Removes to Tugalo.—Hangs Dinkins.—Appointed Judge.—Anecdote.—Great Size, Death, and Character.

Major Joseph Winston Noticed.—Ben. Herndon.—Micajah and Joel Lewis.—Robert and John Cleveland.— Jesse Franklin.—William Lenoir— John Barton—William Meredith, and Minor Smith.— John Brown and Samuel Johnson.—David and John Witherspoon.— Jo. Herndon, Richard Allen, and Elisha Reynolds.

A beauty of the time of Charles the First—so runs the story—named Elizabeth Cleveland, a daughter of an officer of the palace of Hampton Court, attracted the attention of her sovereign, and an amour was the result. When Oliver Cromwell became the rising star of the empire, the same charms won his sympathies, and a son was born unto them. The mother retired from the public gaze, and subsequently married a Mr. Bridge. When this wild colt of a son grew up, he took his mother's name and was the reputed author of a book—" *The Life and Adventures of Mr. Cromwell, Natural son of Oliver Cromwell,*" published after his death, by consent of his son, first in 1731, a second edition, with a French translation in 1741, and yet another edition in 1760.

The perusal of this work, more than thirty years ago, left on the mind of the writer the strong conviction that it was a romance, and a recent re-examination of it confirms that opinion. Noble, in his learned production on the *Cromwell Family*, published nearly a century since, declares that these pretended *Adventures* are "too marvelous to be true;" and a writer in *Notes and Queries*, in 1856, states that from "the extraordinary adventures related in it," he "considers it a fictitious narrative." Whether or not this work is a romance, or records a series of facts more wonderful than fiction, it is nevertheless true, that Colonel Benjamin Cleveland had a copy of it, to which he used to point with no little pride, claiming his descent through this "Mr. Cleveland," from the illustrious Oliver Cromwell. Others of the Cleveland connection made the same claim.

While Noble, Guizot, and other writers on Cromwell, agree that the renowned Protector, with all his religious seeming, "probably had natural children," yet it is exceedingly doubtful if our King's Mountain hero descended from any such questionable origin. History informs us, that the Clevelands were an ancient family, deriving their name from a tract of country in the North Riding of Yorkshire, England, still called Cleveland. Tradition designates Alexander Cleveland, Sr. and Jr.; and that John Cleveland, with his father, the younger Alexander Cleveland, early migrated to Virginia, and married a Miss Martha Coffee. He settled on the since famous Bull Run, in Prince William County, where he engaged in the employment of a house-joiner. His son, Benjamin Cleveland, the subject of this sketch, was born there May twenty-sixth, 1738; and while yet very young, his father removed some sixty miles to the south-west, locating in a border settlement on Blue Run, some six or eight miles above its junction with the Rapidan, in Orange County, near the line of Albemarle. Not only young Cleveland's parents, but his grandfather Cleveland and wife also settled on Blue Run; the latter couple dying there, about 1770, within three days of each other, when about a hundred years old *; and here his parents lived and died at a good old age.

When about twelve years old, and his parents were both absent, some drunken rowdies called at the house, and began to throw the stools into the fire. Little Ben, satisfied what his father would do were he at home, snatched the old man's rifle from its hooks, and simply said, "gentlemen, do you see this?" They saw it, and the youth's determined attitude, which led them to think discretion the better part of valor, when one of the party said to his fellows: "We'd better be off; we don't know what this excited child might do." So the brave lad put the lawless drunkards to flight, and saved his father's property.

Nor was it inebriates alone that young Cleveland early learned to vanquish. Like Nimrod of old, he became "a mighty hunter;" and, like Daniel Boone, he had an unconquerable aversion to the tame drudgery of farm life, as he regarded it. He spent much of his time from early youth in the wilderness, securing pelts and furs, which found a ready market. The heads of the Dan, Staunton and Pig rivers, in the region that subsequently became Pittsylvania County, was a favorite resort for hunters, and here young Cleveland reaped his forest harvests. Fire hunting, at that day, was a very common mode of entrapping the deer in warm weather, when they repaired to particular localities at night in shallow streams, where they could find succulent food, and be less exposed to tormenting insects. The torchlights of the hunters would so dazzle the fated deer's

---

* This fact is given on the authority of Maj. John Redd, of Henry County, Va., to the writer in 1849. who was born in Orange County, Va., in 1755, and personally knew these old people. If then, Alexander Cleveland, the younger, who died about 1770, was a hundred years old, he must have been born about 1670—only seventeen years after Cromwell became Protector. This would seem to spoil the story of descent from Oliver Cromwell through the pretended "Mr. Cromwell"; and that he must have descended from Alexander Cleveland, Sr., whose birth evidently was considerably anterior to the time of the Protectorate.

attention, that he would stand in amazement watching the strange light, while the wary hunter had only to blaze away at its glaring eyes, and bring down the stupid animal.

There was an old Dutchman in that region who had a good stand for fire-hunting, and young Cleveland concluded he would scare him out of it. Pealing some bark from a tree, he placed it in the water so as to represent a counterfeit deer. The next night, he hid himself near by where he could watch operations. In due time, the Dutch hunter made his appearance—fired on the supposed deer, without apparently bringing him down; then repeated his shot, and still the deer remained unmoved. The Dutchman now becoming alarmed, exclaimed, " Its de duy-vil ;" and quickly abandoned that hunting ground—Cleveland chuckling not a little over the success of his stratagem.

At length young Cleveland married, in Orange County, Miss Mary Graves—of an excellent family, whose father was in quite comfortable circumstances. Tradition tells us that Cleveland took an active part in the French and Indian war ; but the particulars are lost to history. He, no doubt, in that border conflict became initiated into military life, which proved a preparatory school for his Revolutionary services. But his marriage did not reform his idle and reckless habits. He still loved gaming, horse-racing, and the wild frolicking common on the frontiers. In company with Joseph Martin—afterwards General Martin—he put in a field of wheat on Pig river, about the year 1767, where he settled some four years before ; but they were too indolent to fence it properly. When harvest time came, there was something of a crop. As was the custom of the times, they invited their friends to join them in cutting the grain ; for which hilarious occasion some liquor and a fiddler were provided, and a good time was necessary before entering upon the work, which ended in a debauch, and the grain was never harvested.

To break away from such habits and associations,

Cleveland, about 1769, removed, with his father-in-law and family, to North Carolina, and settled, near the foot of the Blue Ridge, on the waters of Roaring Creek, a northern affluent of the Yadkin, in what was then Rowan, afterwards Surry, and a few years later Wilkes County. Here Cleveland, with the aid of Mr. Graves' servants, opened a farm, raised stock, and devoted much of his time to hunting. At some subsequent period, he located on the noted tract, on the northern bank of the Yadkin, fifteen miles below Wilkesboro, known as *the Round About*—taking its name from the horse-shoe shape of the land, nearly surrounded by the river.

From Daniel Boone, who was among the earliest of the pioneers of the Yadkin Valley, Cleveland learned of the Kentucky country—that land of cane and pea-vine, abounding with deer and buffalo. Its wild charms, its rich lands, and its teeming game, rendered it the hunter's paradise. Such attractions as these Cleveland could not resist. In the summer of about 1772, in company with Jesse Walton, Jesse Bond, Edward Rice, and William Hightower, he set out on a trip of hunting and exploration, in quest of the beautiful land of Kentucky. When they had safely passed Cumberland Gap, and entered upon the borders of the famous hunting grounds, with cheerful hopes and glowing prospects, they were unexpectedly met and plundered by a party of Cherokees, of all their guns, horses, peltry, and every thing they possessed, even to their hats and shoes. A poor old shot gun was given in turn, with a couple of charges of powder and shot, when they were threateningly ordered to leave the Indian hunting-grounds. They had no alternative. On their way home, they husbanded their ammunition as long as possible; with one of the charges they killed a small deer—the other was spent ineffectually. They had the good fortune to catch a broken-winged wild goose, and eventually had to kill their faithful little hunting dog, greatly to their regret; and Cleveland, in after years, used to say that this dog was tame, under the circumstances, the sweetest animal food he ever ate. With this scanty supply, and a few berries, they managed to hold out till they reached the settlements, but in a nearly famished condition.

Several months afterwards, Cleveland made up a party of chosen men—among whom was William Hightower, who wended their way to the Cherokee towns, determined to recover the horses that had been taken from them. From some circumstance not now known, Hightower gave name to the Hightower or Etowah river. Cleveland applied to a noted Cherokee chief, known among the whites as Big Bear, who replied that the Indians who had his horses would be likely to kill him as soon as they should learn the object of his mission ; but, he added by way of compliment, "if you were to be killed, I should claim that honor, as one big warrior ought only to be slain by another." Big Bear sent an escort with Cleveland to the several towns to aid him in reclaiming his property. He succeeded without much difficulty, except in the last case. The Indian having the horse, showed fight, raised his tomahawk, and Cleveland cocked his rifle, when his friendly escort interposed, and saved their red brother from a fatal shot, by throwing him to the ground ; but not before he had hurled his battle-axe at his antagonist, which happily did no other harm than cutting away a part of the bosom of Cleveland's hunting shirt. Then Cleveland, at the instance of his Indian guides, mounted his newly recovered horse, which was at hand, and was riding away, when a ball from the rifle of the enraged Cherokee, wounded the animal, but not seriously. Returning to Big Bear's village, that chief increased the guard ; and Cleveland and party retired with their horses in triumph. On their way back to North Carolina, they went by the Tugalo country, which greatly attracted Cleveland's attention.

Reuben Stringer was a noted woodsman of the Upper Yadkin Valley, and was often Cleveland's associate in his hunting adventures. They took an elk hunt together, in the month of August, when these animals were in their prime The elk were large, and very wild, and gradually retired before the advancing settlements. A few years anterior to the Revolutionary war, they were yet to be found at the foot of the mountain ranges on the heads of New river. Pursuing a wounded elk, Cleveland in attempting to intercept him at a rocky point of the river, where he expected the animal would cross the stream, found himself surrounded by a large number of rattle-snakes, coiled, hissing, and fearfully sounding their alarm rattles on every hand. From this dangerous dilemma, his only deliverance seemed to be an instantaneous plunge into the river, which he made without a moment's hesitation, and thus probably escaped a horrid death.

While Stringer was busy one day in preparing a fire for cooking some of their wild meat for a repast, Cleveland spread his blanket on the ground, beneath a cluster of large white oaks, to rest himself, and soon fell asleep. In a few moments he suddenly awakened, in a startled condition— why, he could not tell—and, casting his eyes into the tree-tops above, he discovered a large limb, directly overhead, nearly broken off, hanging only by a slight splinter to its parent stem. He said to his companion, pointing to the object of his alarm: " Look, Reuben, and see what an ugly thing we have camped under !" " It has, indeed, an ugly appearance ; " replied Stringer, "but since it has apparently hung a great while in that condition, it may very likely do so a good while longer." " Ah ", said Cleveland, " as long as it has hung there, there is a time for it to come down, and I will not be in the way of danger," and gathered up his blanket, to spread it in a safer place. As he was passing the fire, he heard a crack above—the splinter had broken, and the limb came tumbling down, plunging its three prongs directly into the ground where Cleveland had but a moment before lain. They pulled over the fallen limb, and found its prongs had penetrated into the earth to the depth of fourteen inches. Stringer congratulated his comrade on his fortunate awaking and removal, "for," he added, "in one minute more, you would have been inevitably killed." "Ah, Reuben," said Cleveland, who was very much of a fatalist, "I always told you that no man would die till his appointed time; and when it comes, there can be no possible escape."

But Cleveland's hunting days were about to end. It was no longer a war with the wild beasts of the forest, but with his fellow men. The story of Colonial taxation by the King and Parliament reached the Yadkin Valley, and Cleveland was among the first to resent the threatened tyranny; and soon came the tidings of Lexington and Bunker Hill. North Carolina was organized into companies, regiments, and brigades; and, on the first of September, 1775, Cleveland was appointed an Ensign in the second regiment, under the command of Colonel Robert Howe. But he seems not to have accepted it, preferring to serve in the militia in his immediate locality, where he judged his presence and efforts would be more useful.

During 1775, when Cleveland's neighbors and friends of the Upper Yadkin Valley had occasion to go to Cross Creek to dispose of their surplus productions, and purchase their supplies of iron, sugar, salt, and other necessaries, they were compelled, before they were permitted to buy or sell, to take the oath of allegiance to the King. When Cleveland heard of these tyrannical acts, and attempts to forestall the politics of the people, he swore roundly that he would like nothing better than to dislodge those Scotch scoundrels at Cross Creek. Nor was an opportunity long wanting. In February, 1776, the Highland Tories of that locality raised the British standard, when Captain Cleveland marched down from the mountains with a party of volunteer riflemen; and, tradition has it, that he reached the front in season to share in the fight, and in the suppression of the revolt. He scoured the country in the region of Wake Forest, capturing several outlaws, some of whom he hung to the trees in the woods; one of whom was Captain Jackson, who was executed within half a mile of Ransom Sutherland's homestead, whose houses and merchandize, Jackson had caused to be laid in ashes a few days after the battle of Moore's Creek Bridge. "I don't recollect," said Colonel Sutherland, in the *North Carolina University Magazine*, for September, 1854, "after Cleveland had done with them, to have heard much more of those wretches during the war." In this service, or at least a part of it, Cleveland was under Colonel James Moore, who had served with credit on the frontiers in the old French and Indian war, and whose determined bravery gave him the *sobriquet* of "Mad Jimmie" among the soldiery; and for years thereafter, Moore was the theme of Cleveland's admiration.

When the Cherokees were inveigled by the British into hostilities, Captain Cleveland, in the summer of 1776, served a tour of duty in scouting on the Western frontier of the State; and, shortly after, getting intelligence that a Tory Colonel Roberts had embodied a number of Loyalists on the northwest side of the Blue Ridge, on the borders of North Carolina and Virginia, he went in quest of them; but hearing of this pursuit, they disbanded and dispersed. In the autumn of that year, when General Rutherford led a strong force against the Cherokees, Cleveland and his company went on the campaign, in the Surry regiment, under Colonel Joseph Williams * and Major Joseph Winston. William Lenoir, who was Cleveland's Lieutenant, was accustomed, in after years, to recount the hardships and privations the troops

---

* Colonel Williams was born in Hanover County, Virginia, March twenty-seventh, 1748; migrated in 1766 to Granville County, North Carolina, where he married Rebecca, daughter of Thomas Lanier, and shortly after settled near the Shallow Ford of Yadkin, in what afterwards became Surry County. When that County was organized, he was made Colonel, and led his regiment on Rutherford's Cherokee campaign in 1776. He shared in defeating the Tory leaders, Colonel Gideon and Captain Hezikiah Wright, at the head of three hundred and ten Loyalists, at the Shallow Ford, October, fifteenth, 1780. Colonel Williams died August eleventh, 1827.

28

had to suffer on that service—often destitute of provisions, without tents, with but few blankets, dressed in clothing made of rude materials, derived from hemp, tow, and the wild nettle. Though often harrassed on their march by parties in ambush, there was no general engagement—Captain Cleveland sharing in the skirmishes and bush-whackings of the campaign. The villages and settlements of the hostile Cherokees were laid waste, their crops and provisions destroyed, and they were compelled to sue for peace.

Such was the high estimate placed on Captain Cleveland's fitness for frontier service, that early in the spring of 1777, he was selected to lead his company to the Watauga settlements, to serve a tour for their protection against the yet troublesome Cherokees. After passing the rugged intervening mountain country, and reaching the Watauga Valley, Cleveland and his men made their head-quarters at Carter's Fort, while the Virginia troops were stationed at the Long Island of Holston. Though scouting was kept up, every pains were taken to bring the Indians to terms. Cleveland's company concentrated, with the other forces, at the Long Island, where the celebrated treaty, in July of that year, was held, and at which Major Winston was one of the Commissioners. When peace was made, the Wilkes troops returned to their distant home.

In the autumn of 1777, Captain Cleveland attended the Legislature—not as a member, but to use his influence for the division of Surry, and the formation of a new County, for the better convenience of the Upper Yadkin settlements. Wilkes County, thus formed, was named in honor of John Wilkes, noted for his steady opposition in Parliament to the American war. In March, 1778, when the new County was organized, Cleveland was placed at the head of the commission of Justices, and was made Colonel of the militia. Henceforth we find Colonel Cleveland in regular attendance as one of the Justices of the County Court, and generally the principal bondsman for the Sheriff and other County officers. He was also often called on to fill other positions—Commissioner for seizing confiscated estates, Superintendent of elections, and County Ranger or Stray Master. In 1778, he was chosen to represent Wilkes County in the House of Commons, and was regarded as one of the popular leaders of the mountain region of the State.

On one occasion, soon after the regiment was organized, it was ordered on service to the frontiers to quell some Tory disturbance. After no little indiscriminate plundering of both Whigs and Tories, they returned home before the expiration of their term of service, with their ill-gotten gains, before Colonel Cleveland was able to join them. He was highly displeased with their conduct, swearing roundly that he would shoot the ring-leaders; but he finally agreed to forgive them on two conditions—the restoration of their dishonorable plunderings, and to the end of the war, turning out on a minute's warning. All who had shared in the disgraceful pillage, returned the spoils of every kind, and were ever after prompt to engage in any service at the shortest notice.

When the British invaded Georgia, in 1778, General Rutherford led a force from the back part of North Carolina, of which at least a portion of Colonel Cleveland's regiment formed a part. They repaired to Georgia, and shared in the winter campaign of 1778-79, which culminated in the disastrous defeat of General Ashe, at Brier Creek, before Lincoln and Rutherford could come to his aid. Returning from this service, Colonel Cleveland was chosen to represent his County in the State Senate. In the summer of 1780, he was constantly employed in suppressing the Tories—first in marching against those assembled at Ramsour's mill, reaching there shortly after their defeat; then in chasing Colonel Bryan's band from the State; and finally in scouring the region of New river in checking the Tory rising in that quarter, capturing and hanging some of their notorious leaders and outlaws.

Then followed his King's Mountain campaign—the great service of his life—the wounding, while on the way, of his brother, Lieutenant Larkin Cleveland, by a Tory party under Captain John Murray, near Lovelady's Shoals; and then hurrying forward to grapple with the indomitable Ferguson. The poet Hayne notices Cleveland in this battle as though he were a very round head of Cromwell's fervor and time:

"Now, by God's grace," cried Cleveland my noble Colonel he,
Resting to pick a Tory off, quite cooly on his knee,—
"Now, by God's grace, we have them! the snare is subtly set;
The game is bagged: we hold them safe as pheasants in a net."

His heroic bearing in the contest, and his exciting rencounter with the half-crazed Bowen, each so fortunately escaping fatal results, have been already related. Besides having assigned to him, by general consent, one of Ferguson's war horses, which lived to an uncommon great age, he carried home with him a snare-drum, to which he pointed with pride as a King's Mountain trophy, as long as he lived.

There can be no question but Colonel Cleveland was conspicuous in bringing about the execution of the Tory leaders at Bickerstaff's. His whole career during the war goes to show that he was severe in his treatment of the Tories— perhaps not unjustly so, considering the times and circumstances of an exposed frontier, when the execution of civil law was so infrequent and uncertain. His brief command over the Tory prisoners at Bethabara has been elsewhere noticed. Sometime in November ensuing, James Coyle or Cowles, and John Brown—or Jones, as Wheeler has it— two notorious Tory plunderers, passing through Lincoln County, robbed the house of Major George Wilfong of everything they could carry away, and then made off with a couple of his horses. Major Wilfong with a party followed the culprits, overtaking them near Wilkesboro, recovered the horses, but the ruffians made good their escape. They had appropriated Wilfong's clothes-line for halters, which the Major left behind, with which to hang the rascals should they ever be taken. Shortly after, as they were returning towards Ninety Six, they were apprehended by some of Cleveland's scouts, and brought to Wilkesboro, where Colonel Cleveland ordered them hung with Wilfong's ropes. All admitted that though the execution was summary, it was nevertheless just.

Early in 1781, when General Greene was manœuvering on the upper border of North Carolina, Colonel Cleveland raised about a hundred riflemen, went to his assistance, serving awhile in the advance parties of light infantry, but returned home from their tour of duty a little before the conflict at Guilford.

To Colonel Cleveland, whose career was replete with perilous adventures, an occurrence now transpired, which at one time threatened the most tragic termination; and which, for its hair-breadth escapes, may be regarded as the most notable event of his life. Some thirty-five miles from his home at the Round-About on the Yadkin, and some twenty north-west of Wilkesboro, and in the south-eastern portion of the present County of Ashe, was a well-known locality, mostly on the northern bank of the South Fork of New river, called *the Old Fields*—which at some previous period, was probably the quiet home of a wandering band of Cherokees. These Old Fields belonged to Colonel Cleveland, and served, in peaceful times, as a grazing region for his stock.

Having occasion to visit his New River plantation, Colonel Cleveland rode there, accompanied only by a negro servant, arriving at Jesse Duncan's, his tenant, at the lower end of the Old Fields, on Saturday, the fourteenth of April, 1781. Unfortunately for the Colonel, Captain William Riddle, a noted Tory leader, son of the Loyalist Colonel James Riddle, of Surry County, was approaching from the Virginia border with Captain Ross, a Whig captive, whom he had taken, together with his servant, and now *en route* for Ninety Six, where a British reward appears to have been paid for prisoners. Riddle, with his party of six or eight men, reaching Benjamin Cutbirth's, some four miles above the Old Fields, a fine old Whig, and an old associate of Daniel Boone, who had only partially recovered from a severe spell of fever. The Tory Captain, probably from Cutbirth's reticence regarding solicited information, shamefully abused him, and placed him under guard.

Descending the river to the upper end of the Old Fields, where Joseph and Timothy Perkins resided—about a mile above Duncan's—both of whom were absent in Tory service, Riddle learned from their women, that Cleveland was but a short distance away, at Duncan's, with only his servant, Duncan, and one or two of the Callaway family there. Every Tory in the country knew full well of Cleveland's inveterate hatred of their race ; how prominently he had figured at King's Mountain, and had given his influence for the Tory executions at Bickerstaff's, and caused the summary hanging of Coyle and Brown at Wilkesboro. Riddle well judged that such a prisoner would be a prize to take along to Ninety Six, or it would prove no small honor to any Loyalist to rid the Rebel cause of so untiring and distinguished a leader in the Southern country.

The prospect of making Cleveland his prisoner was too tempting for Riddle to neglect. His force was too small to run any great risk, and so he concluded to resort to stratagem. He resolved, therefore, to steal Cleveland's horses in the quiet of the night, judging that the Colonel would follow their trail the next morning, supposing they had strayed off, when he would ambuscade him at some suitable place, and thus take " Old Round-About " as he was called, unawares, and at a disadvantage. The horses were accordingly taken that night ; and a laurel thicket selected, just above the Perkins' house, as a fitting place to waylay their expected pursuers. During Saturday, Richard Callaway and his brother-in-law, John Shirley, went down from the neighboring residence of Thomas Callaway to Duncan's, to see Colonel Cleveland, and appear to have remained there over night.

Discovering that the horses were missing on Sunday morning, immediate pursuit was made. Having a pair of pistols, Colonel Cleveland retained one of them, handing the other to Duncan, while Callaway and Shirley were unarmed. Reaching the Perkins' place, one of the Perkins women knowing of the ambuscade, secretly desired to save the Colonel from his impending fate, so she detained him, as long as she could, by conversation, evidently fearing personal consequences should she divulge the scheme of his enemies to entrap him. His three associates kept on, with Cleveland some little distance behind, Mrs. Perkins still following, and retarding him by her inquiries; and as those in advance crossed the fence which adjoined the thicket, the Tories fired from their places of concealment, one aiming at Cleveland, who though some little distance in the rear, was yet within range of their guns. But they generally shot wild—only one shot, that of Zachariah Wells, who aimed at Callaway, proving effectual, breaking his thigh, when he fell helpless by the fence, and was left for dead.* Duncan and Shirley escaped. Cleveland from his great weight—fully three hundred pounds—knew he could not run any great distance, and would only be too prominent a mark for Tory bullets, dodged into the house with several Tories at his heels. Now, flourishing his pistol rapidly from one to another, they pledged to spare his life and accord him good treatment, if he would quietly surrender, which he did.

Wells by this time having re-loaded his rifle, made his appearance on the scene, swearing that he would kill Cleveland; and aiming his gun, the Colonel instantly seized Abi-

---

*Richard Callaway had been grieviously wounded on the head, arms, shoulder, and hand by Tarleton's cavalry, at Sumter's surprise, Aug. eighteenth, 1780, and left for dead; yet recovered, though, he had a crippled hand for life. In due time his broken limb, so badly disabled by Wells' unerring shot, healed up, and he lived many years. He aided in running the boundary line from the White Top Mountains to the Mississippi, and died in Tennessee in 1822.

gail Walters who was present, and by dint of his great strength, and under a high state of excitement, dextrously handled her as a puppet, keeping her between him and his would-be assassin. Wells seemed vexed at this turn in the affair, and hurled his imprecations on the poor woman, threatening if she did not get out of the way, that he would blow her through as well, not appearing to realize that she had as little power as a mouse in the clutches of a ferocious cat. Cleveland getting his eyes on Captain Riddle, whom he knew, or judged by his appearance, to be the leader, appealed to him if such treatment was not contrary to the stipulations of his surrender. Riddle promptly replied that it was, and ordered Wells to desist from his murderous intent, saying that they would take Cleveland to Ninety Six, and make money out of his capture. The terrified woman who had been made an unwilling battery, was now released from Cleveland's grasp as from a vise ; and the whole party with their prisoner and his servant were speedily mounted, and hurried up New river. This stream, so near its source, was quite shallow, and the Tories traveled mostly in its bed to avoid being tracked, in case of pursuit.

Soon after the Tory party had called at Cutbirth's, on their way down the river, young Daniel Cutbirth and a youth named Walters, who were absent at the time, returned ; and encouraged by Mrs. Cutbirth, though only fourteen or fifteen years of age, they resolved that they would take their guns, select a good spot, and ambuscade Riddle on his return, and perhaps rescue whatever prisoners he might have. But on the return of the Tory party the next day, they made so much noise, and gave so many military commands, that led the youthful ambuscaders to conclude that they had received a re-inforcement, and that it would be rashness for two single-handed youths to undertake to cope with numbers so unequal. So Riddle and his party reached Cutbirth's undisturbed, and ordered dinner for himself, men, and prisoners. One of the Cutbirth girls, not engaging willingly in this service, received abuse, and even kicks, from the Tory leader. Their hunger appeased, they proceeded up New river, mostly along its bed, till they reached Elk Creek, up which they made their way in the same manner. Colonel Cleveland, meanwhile, managed unperceived, to break off overhanging twigs, dropping them into the stream to float down as a guide to his friends, who he knew would make an early pursuit. From the head of the south fork of Elk, they ascended up the mountains to what has since been known as Riddle's Knob, in what is now Watauga County, and some fourteen miles from the place of Cleveland's captivity, where they camped for the night.

Early on that Sabbath morning, Joseph Callaway and his brother-in-law, Berry Toney, wishing to see Colonel Cleveland on business matters, called at Duncan's, and learned about the missing horses, and the pursuit; and at that moment they heard the report of the firing at the upper end of the plantation, and hastened in that direction, soon meeting Duncan and Shirley in rapid flight, who could only tell that Richard Callaway had fallen, and Colonel Cleveland was either killed or taken. It was promptly agreed, that Duncan, Shirley, and Toney should notify the people of the scattered settlements to meet that afternoon at the Old Fields, while Joseph Callaway should go to his father's, close by, mount his horse and hasten to Captain Robert Cleveland's, on Lewis' Fork of the Yadkin, a dozen miles distant.* His brother, William Callaway, started forthwith up the river, and soon came across Samuel McQueen and Benjamin Greer, who readily joined him; and all being good woodsmen, followed the Tory trail at best they could, till night overtook them when some distance above the mouth of Elk Creek, and about ten miles from the Old Fields. William Callaway suggested, that he

---

* Joseph Callaway was a member from Ashe County, in the House of Commons, in 1804 and 1806.

and McQueen would remain there, while Greer should return to pilot up whatever men may have gathered to engage in pursuit of the Tories.

By night-fall, Captain Robert Cleveland and others, to the number of twenty or thirty, good and tried men, who had served under Colonel Cleveland, had gathered at the Old Fields, determined to rescue their old commander at every hazard, even though they should follow the Tory party to the gates of Ninety Six. Greer made his appearance in good time, and at once they were on the trail of the enemy.* They reached William Callaway and McQueen awhile before day; and as soon as light began to appear, John Baker joined Callaway and McQueen, to lead the advance as spies. A little after sun-rise, having proceeded four miles, they discovered indications of the enemy's camp on the mountain. But little arrangement was made for the attack; nine men only were in readiness—the others were apparently some distance behind; and only four or five of these were designated to fire on the enemy, the rest reserving their shots for a second volley, or any emergencies that might happen—of these was William Callaway.

Some of the Tories had already breakfasted, while others were busily employed in preparing their morning meal. Colonel Cleveland was sitting on a large fallen tree, engaged, under compulsion, in writing passes for the several members of Captain Riddle's party, certifying that each was a good Whig—to be used, when in a tight place, to help them out of difficulty, by assuming that they were patriots of the truest type, Cleveland's commendation passing unquestioned along the borders of Virginia and the Carolinas. But "Old Round About" had a strong

---

* Greer was one of Cleveland's heroes. One of his fellow soldiers stole his tobacco from him, when he threatened he would whip him for it as soon as he should put his eyes on him. Cleveland expostulated with Greer, telling him his men ought to fight the enemy, and not each other. "I'll give him a *hint* of it, any way," said Greer, and when he met the tobacco pilferer, he knocked him down. *Greer's hint* was long a by-word in all that region.—Col. W. W. Lenoir.

suspicion that their urgency for these passports betokened that the moment they were completed, his days would be numbered; and thus naturally but a poor penman, he purposely retarded his task as much as possible, hoping to gain time for the expected relief, apologizing for his blunders, and renewing his unwilling efforts. Several of the Tory party were now gathering up their horses for an early start, and Cleveland was receiving severe threatenings if he did not hurry up his last passport.

Just at this moment, while Captain Riddle and Zachariah Wells were especially guarding Cleveland and Captain Ross—the former with Cleveland's pistol presented at his breast, and the latter with his gun aimed for instantaneous use, if need be—the relief party were silently creeping up; and the next moment several guns were fired, and the Whigs rushed up, uttering their loudest yells. Colonel Cleveland, comprehending the situation, tumbled off the prostrate tree, on the side opposite to his friends, lest their balls might accidently hit him, and exclaiming, in his joy, at the top of his thundering voice, "*Huzza for brother Bob!—that's right, give 'em h—l!*" Wells alone was shot, as he was scampering away, by William Callaway in hot pursuit, and supposed to be mortally wounded, he was left to his fate; the rest fled with the aid of their fresh horses, or such as they could secure at the moment—Riddle and his wife among the number. Cleveland's servant, a pack-horse for Tory plunder, was overjoyed at his sudden liberation. Cleveland and Ross were thus fortunately rescued; and having gained their purpose, the happy Whigs returned to their several homes. William Callaway was especially elated that he had had the good fortune to shoot Wells, who had so badly wounded his brother, Richard Callaway, at the ambuscade at the Old Fields.

Shortly after this occurrence, Captain Riddle ventured to make a night raid into the Yadkin Valley, where on King's Creek, several miles above Wilkesboro, they surrounded the house where two of Cleveland's noted soldiers, David and John Witherspoon, resided with their parents, and spirited them many miles away in the mountain region on Watauga river, in what is now Watauga County, were both were sentenced to be shot—blindfolded, and men detailed to do the fatal work. It was then proposed, if they would take the oath of allegiance to the King, repair to their home, and speedily return with a certain noble animal belonging to David Witherspoon, known as " the O'Neal mare," and join the Tory band, their lives would be spared. They gladly accepted the proposition—with such mental reservations as they thought fit to make. As soon as they reached home, David Witherspoon mounted his fleet-footed mare, and hastened to Colonel Ben. Herndon's, several miles down the river, who quickly raised a party, and piloted by the Witherspoons, they soon reached the Tory camp, taking it by surprise, capturing three, and killing and dispersing others. So the young Witherspoons fulfilled their promise of returning speedily to the Tory camp, bringing the O'Neal mare with them ; but under somewhat different circumstances from what the unsophisticated Tories expected.

The three prisoners taken were Captain Riddle, and two of his noted associates, named Reeves and Goss. On their arrival at Wilkesboro, a court martial condemned them to be hung ; but as if to curry favor with the soldiers, or get them in a condition so he might escape, Riddle treated them freely to whisky. Learning which, Colonel Cleveland frankly informed him, that it would be useless to waste his whisky in such efforts—that he would be hung directly after breakfast. The three notorious freebooters were accordingly executed, on the hill adjoining the village, on a stately oak, which is yet standing, and pointed out to strangers at Wilkesboro. Mrs. Riddle, who seems to have accompanied her husband on his wild and reckless marauds, was present, and witnessed his execution.

Colonel Cleveland was active at this period in sending out strong scouting parties to scour the mountain regions, and if possible, utterly break up the Tory bands still infesting the frontiers. His Wilkes riflemen had, by this time, acquired a reputation of which they were justly proud. They were generally known as *Cleveland's Heroes,* sometimes as *Cleveland's Bull Dogs;* while the Tories denominated them *Cleveland's Devils.* Cleveland himself rated each of his well-tried followers as the equal of five ordinary soldiers. It was not long before one of these detachments had the good fortune to take Zachariah Wells, who had not yet recovered from the dangerous wound he had received at Riddles' Knob. He was conveyed to Hughes' Bottom, about a mile below Colonel Cleveland's Round-About residence, near the mouth of a small stream known as Hughes' Creek. Here young James Gwyn, a youth of thirteen, with a colored boy with him, was at work in the cornfield, when Colonel Cleveland, who had joined those having the prisoner in charge, of whom Lieutenant Elisha Reynolds, Cleveland's two sons and his brother, formed a part, took the plow lines from the horse, with which to hang Wells to a tree on the river bank.

Young Gwyn, who knew little of the stern realities of war, was shocked at the thought of so summary an execution. Intimately acquainted with Colonel Cleveland, he begged the Colonel not to hang the poor fellow, who looked so pitiful, and was suffering from his former wound, greatly exciting his sympathies. "Jimmie, my son," said Cleveland tenderly, "he is a bad man; we must hang all such dangerous Tories, and get them out of their misery;" while Captain Bob. Cleveland, who was present, was cursing the wincing Tory at a vigorous rate. With tears coursing down his cheeks, the Colonel adjusted the rope, regretting the necessity for hanging the trembling culprit—remembering vividly the rough treatment he had so recently received at the hands of Wells at the Perkins' place, at the Old Fields; and firmly convinced that the lives of the patriots of the Yadkin Valley would be safer, and their slumbers all the more peaceful, when their suffering country was rid of all such vile desperadoes. Such was Cleveland's philosophy, and such his patriotism. Wells soon dangled from a convenient tree, and his remains were buried in the sand and loam on the bank of the Yadkin.

Others of the Tory brigands also fell into the hands of Cleveland's vigilant troopers. One of them was Bill Nichols, a noted and desperate leader, whose wife is said to have been a sister of Captain Willaim Riddle. On one occasion, Nichols had a difficulty with a Whig neighbor named Letcher, snatched his gun from him, and with it shot him down in his tracks. Nichols was speedily executed. At another time, one Tate and eight others were taken by Cleveland and his men, and had them near old Richmond, on the Yadkin, in Surry. When Cleveland was about to execute the leader, Colonel William Sheppard protested against such summary justice. "Why," said Cleveland, "Tate confesses that he has frequently laid in wait to kill you." "Is that so?" inquired Sheppard, turning to the Tory captain. Tate frankly acknowledged that it was true—that he was an influential Whig, and the Loyalists were anxious to have him out of the way. Sheppard now acquiesced in the opinion that Tate was a dangerous man, and that they had best make an example of him. So his fate was fixed, while his associates only suffered imprisonment as other captives of war.

On another occasion Colonel Cleveland visited Colonel Sheppard* at Richmond, where he had two notorious Tory horse-thieves in prison. Cleveland insisted on swinging them to the nearest tree, less they should effect their escape,

---

* Colonel Sheppard was an early settler of Surry County; he commanded a troop of cavalry on Rutherford's Cherokee campaign; and participated largely in opposing the Tories of his region. He represented his County in the State Senate six years, 1777-82; and removing to Orange County, he served again in the Senate in 1793, 1801 and 1803, and was many years a magistrate, He died February eighth, 1822, in his seventy-sixth year.

and yet further endanger the community—at least one of them, whose crimes rendered him particularly obnoxious to the people. One end of a rope was fastened to his neck, when he was mounted on a log, and the other end made fast to the limb of a tree overhead, and the log then rolled from under the culprit. Cleveland now repaired to the jail, and significantly pointed the surviving Tory to his late associate now dangling from the tree. "You have your choice," observed Cleveland sternly, " either to take your place beside him, or cut your own ears off, and leave the country forever." The Tory knew he could not trifle with "Old Round-About," so he called for a knife. A case-knife was accordingly handed him, which he whetted a moment on a brick, then gritting his teeth, he slashed off his own ears, and left with the blood streaming down his cheeks, and was never heard of afterwards. Truly civil wars are both savage and sanguinary in their character.

John Doss was the faithful overseer of Cleveland's plantation while the Colonel was much of the time absent from home during the period of Tory troubles in 1780–81. Bill Harrison, a noted Tory leader of that region, with the aid of his followers, not only stole Cleveland's stock, and destroyed his property, but apprehended his vigilant overseer, took him to a side-hill, placed him on a log, fastening one end of a grape vine around his neck, and the other over a prong of a stooping dogwood; when one of the party went up the hill, so as to gain sufficient propelling power, then rushed down headlong, butting Doss off the log into eternity. It was not long before Harrison was caught, and brought to Cleveland's home. Accompanied by his servant Bill, and one or two others, Cleveland led Harrison to the same dogwood on which he had hung poor Doss.

" I hope you will not hang me, Colonel," faintly observed the trembling wretch." "Why not?" " Because," said the abject Tory, " you know I am a useful man in the neighborhood—am a good mechanic—have worked for you in peaceful days, and can not well be spared; besides I have invented perpetual motion, and if I am now suddenly cut off, the world will lose the benefit of my discovery. I, too, have heard you curse Fanning and other Loyalist leaders for putting prisoners to death—*where are your principles— where your conscience?*" "Where is my conscience," retorted Cleveland; "where are my horses and cattle you have stolen—my barn and fences you have wantonly burned —and where is poor Jack Doss? 'Fore God I will do this deed, and justify myself before high heaven and my country! Run up the hill, Bill, and butt him off the log—I'll show him perpetual motion!" *

It is related, that, on one occasion, when, Colonel Cleveland was absent from home, a Tory horse-thief was brought in for adjudication, and turned over to the care of the Colonel's sons to await their father's return. This not occurring so soon as expected, and fearing if they should undertake to keep their prisoner over night he might give them the slip, or make them trouble, they appealed to their mother, who was engaged in her domestic vocations, and smoking her pipe, what they had best do under the circumstances. Learning the nature of the offense, and that the evidence against the culprit was overwhelming, she asked them what their father would do in such a case? "Hang him," was the prompt reply. "Well, then," said the old lady, "you must hang him," and he was accordingly hung at the gate.†

Punishments were graded according to the offence, and seem to have been administered on the principles of martial law. When an ordinary pilferer was taken to Colonel Cleveland by William Lenoir, he was ordered to have his two thumbs placed in a notch of a tree, and thus made fast, while he received fifteen lashes. This was called *thumbing*

---

*Related in a debate in the North Carolina Legislature, in 1840, by Hon. Hamilton C. Jones, of Rowan.

†Johnson's *Traditions of the Revolution*, 401, corroborated by others.

the notch. Captain John Beverly, in this case, carried the order into execution ; but anxious to meet out full justice to the prisoner, with a little added interest, he did not stop at the number adjudged, but continued to whip the wincing culprit, when Colonel Herndon drew his sword, and struck Beverly, who drew his in return, and a tilt was the result, which, but for the interference of mutual friends might have terminated fatally. A little over five miles above Wilkesboro, on the Burke road, and half a mile west of the village of Moravian Falls, yet stood within a few years " Shad Laws' Oak," on which the notches thumbed by Shadrach Laws, under sentence of Cleveland, were distinctly visible.

The reader must not suppose that Colonel Cleveland always deemed it the best policy to resort to the severest measures with the Tory thieves brought before him for adjudication. Once, it is related, that he had a pretty hard case in hand. "Waste no time," said Cleveland ; " swing him off quick !" " You needn't be in any such d—d hurry about it," cooly retorted the condemned man. Cleveland, who was toddling along behind, pleased with the nonchalance of the fellow, exclaimed, " boys, let him go !" The Tory, touched with such unexpected generosity, turned to Cleveland and said, with no little feeling : "Well, old fellow, you've conquered me ; I'll ever after fight on your side," and proved himself one of the most intrepid of Cleveland's followers.

" Old Round-About " was a keen judge of human nature, and would often set himself at work to reform a class of Tories who had been led astray by unhappy influences. Missing one of this class awhile, and at length meeting him, he saluted him in this kind, familiar style : " Well, Bob, I reckon you are returning from a Tory trip—are you not?" " Yes, Colonel, I am," " Well," continued the Colonel, " I expect when you become rested, you will take another jaunt with them, eh?" " No, Colonel, if I ever go with them again, I'll give you leave to make a button of my

29

head for a halter." "Well, Bob, that shall be the bargain."
So he gives Bob a stiff drink of grog, in accordance with the
fashion of the times, and a hearty dinner, and starts him off
home rejoicing on his way, and swearing that, after all,
"Old Round-About" had a warmer heart, and a kindlier
way with him, than any Tory leader of his acquaintance, and
ever after Bob proved himself as true a Whig almost as the
Colonel himself.

Nor were Colonel Cleveland's efforts restricted to making good Whigs out of refractory Tories. He aimed as well
to make good and industrous citizens. Eleven miles above
Wilkesboro, on the south bank of the Yadkin, resided one
Bishop, one of a class who tried to shirk the responsibilities
of the war, and was wanting alike in patriotism and energy
of character. At heart he was believed to be a Tory. Passing Bishop's on one of his excursions, Cleveland observed
that his corn, from neglect, presented a sorry appearance.
He called Bishop out, and asked him if he had been sick?
He said that he had not. "Have you, then, been fighting
for your country?" "No," said the neutral, "I have not
been fighting on either side." "In times like these," remarked Cleveland, "men who are not fighting, and are able
to work, must not be allowed to have their crops as foul as
yours." The indolent man had "*to thumb the notch*,"
with the admonition that if his corn thereafter was not well
worked, double the punishment would be his portion next
time. It is hardly necessary to add, that Bishop's corn
was henceforth in as fine condition as any man's in the
country.*

Cleveland was literally "all things to all people." By his
severities, he awed and intimidated not a few—restraining
them from lapsing into Tory abominations; by his kindness,
forbearance, and even tenderness, winning over many to the
glorious cause he loved so well.

But the war was now rapidly drawing to a close. In

*MS. correspondence of Col. W. W. Lenoir.

the autumn of 1781, Colonel Cleveland performed his last military service, a three months tour of duty, on the waters of the Little Pedee, in the south-eastern part of the State, under General Rutherford. At this time, the British Colonel Craig was confined to Wilmington, while Fanning and other Tory leaders were yet scouring the country, and needed such a force as the mountaineers to successfully cope with them. Cleveland's men routed several of these scattered Loyalist detachments before returning home.

At the close of the war, Colonel Cleveland, having lost his fine Round-About plantation by a better title, now turned his attention to the fine region of the Tugalo, on the western borders of South Carolina—a country that had greatly attracted him, when, many years before, he returned from the Cherokee Nation with the horses he had reclaimed from their plundering warriors. Though the Indian title was not yet extinguished, he resolved to be among the early squatters of the country. In 1784, he visited the Tugalo Valley, made his selection of a new home in the forks of Tugalo river and Chauga creek, in the present County of Oconee, whither he removed in the following year, accompained by not a few of his kinsmen and old companions in arms.

In November, 1785, the treaty of Hopewell was concluded, by which the Cherokees agreed to bury the hatchet, and relinquish all claim to territory east of the Tugalo. Such obligations usually rest lightly upon Indians, and oftentimes, it must be confessed, they were trespassed upon by their more powerful and covetous white neighbors. While a sort of *quasi* war was yet brewing, the Cherokees stole some of Cleveland's stock, when he buckled on his hunting knife, and went in person to their towns, demanding their restoration within a given time, or the last one of them should pay the forfeit with his life. They were greatly surprised at his enormous size, and judged that it would take a hundred good warriors to cope with him single-handed. The stock were promptly restored.

During these border troubles, one Henry Dinkins, a Tory of the Revolution, who had taken refuge among the Cherokees, inducing a couple of negroes to steal horses and flee with him, made plundering raids on the Tugalo, accompained by these colored men, all well armed and well mounted. Cleveland got wind of their approach, snatched up his rifle, and one night way-laying their trail, captured all three of them. Some assistance coming to his aid, Cleveland concluded that the best disposition to make of Dinkins was to hang him on the spot, which was accordingly done. So notorious was Dinkins' reputation for evil, that the whole country rejoiced at his riddance, without stopping to inquire whether the particular mode of his exit was quite in accordance with the nicities of the law.

Colonel Cleveland served many years as a Judge of the Court of old Pendleton County, with General Pickens and Colonel Robert Anderson at his associates ; Colonel Cleveland "frequently taking a snooze on the bench," says Governor Perry, "while the lawyers were making long, prosy speeches ;" if he snored too loudly, his judicial associates would give him a nudge, and wake him up. He nevertheless administered justice promptly and fairly. In 1793, he lost his election to the Legislature by seven votes only. "We were always afraid," said Mrs. Jane Miller, a daughter of General Pickens, "when Colonel Cleveland came to stay over night with us, lest the bedstead should prove unequal to his ponderous weight." For several years before his death, he became so unwieldly in size, that he could no longer mount his favorite saddle horse, and leave his home—gradually attaining to the enormous weight of four hundred and fifty pounds, and was long unable to rest in bed.

He would spend much of his time sitting on his piazza, dressed in a sort of loose gown, enjoying in the coldest of weather, the fresh air, while others would suffer from the exposure. He was full of good cheer, indulging in jibes and jokes with the passers-by. On one occasion, while occupying his big chair on his porch, he saluted a stranger jocularly: "Halloo, my friend, what's the news this morning from the lower regions?" "Oh, nothing of any moment," the man sportively retorted, "only that Old Horny and his wife had quite a set-to last night—she clamoring for a supply of soap-grease, when he at length pacified her with the assurance, that Colonel Cleveland would soon be there, when her royal highness should enjoy *the fat of the land* to her heart's content." This rough repartee so pleased the jolly Colonel, that he insisted on the stranger stopping with him, and partaking of his hospitalities.

For several summers preceding his death, he suffered from dropsy in his lower limbs, and during the last year of his life his excessive fat considerably decreased, and he, at length, died sitting at breakfast, in October, 1806, in the sixty-ninth year of his age. His wife had preceded him to the grave some half a dozen years. He left two sons and a daughter, whose descendants are numerous and respectable—one of them becoming the wife of General Thomas J. Rusk, one of the leaders in acquiring Texan independence, and subsequently serving ten years in the United States Senate; another, the lady of Governor Charles J. McDonald, of Georgia. In the prime of life, Colonel Cleveland was a little short of six feet, finely proportioned, possessing a pleasing and intelligent countenance.

With scarcely any education, and little improvement in after life, yet Colonel Cleveland, with a naturally vigorous intellect, exerted a commanding influence among a frontier people; and though despotic in his nature, and severe on the Tories, his patriotic activity did much in preserving the western portion of the Carolinas from British and Tory ascendency. North Carolina deservedly commemorated his services by naming a County after him. This noble hero of King's Mountain now sleeps, in the family burial-ground, on his old plantation, beautifully situated in the forks of the Tugalo and Chauga. No monument—no inscription—no memorial-stone point out his silent resting place. The spot is now marked by several large pines that have grown up since his interment—one of them, it is understood, shoots its tall spire from his grave. His old dwelling and out-houses have long since disappeared, but the muse of history will not willingly let die the name and memory of Benjamin Cleveland—to all Tories the terror of terrors, and to all others, the jolly " Old Round-About " of the Yadkin.

———

A branch of the Winston family, originally of Yorkshire, England, settled in Wales, and thence migrated to Virginia. , " The family of Winston," says Alexander H. Everett, " was among the most distinguished in the Colony." One of the Virginia descendants was Samuel Winston, of Louisa County—reputed a brother of the mother of Patrick Henry—who had seven sons all actively engaged in the Revolution. Among them was Joseph Winston, born in Louisa County, June seventeenth, 1746. Receiving a fair education for that day, he joined, at the age of seventeen, a company of rangers, under Captain Philips, who marched from Louisa to the frontiers on Jackson's river, where uniting with Captain George Moffett, making sixty men altogether, they pursued a party of Indians between Forts Young and Dinwiddie, and were drawn into an ambuscade, September thirtieth, 1763. They were fired on from both sides of the trail, and maintained the fight a considerable time ; but, at length, overpowered by numbers, they were forced to give way, scattering as best they could. Several were killed, and, in the *melée*, young Winston had his horse shot from under him, and himself received two wounds, one in the body, and the other through his thigh, rendering him well nigh helpless. He managed to conceal himself till the Indians retired in pursuit of the fugitives, when a comrade

fortunately came to his aid, carried him upon his back for three days, living upon wild roseberries, and at length reached a friendly frontier cabin. Though he in time recovered, the ball in his body was never extracted, and was the source of occasional suffering through life.

In 1769, Joseph Winston and others petitioned the Virginia authorities for a grant of ten thousand acres of land on the lower side of Little Guyandotte; and probably failing to secure it, Mr. Winston migrated about this period to North Carolina, locating on Town Fork of Dan river, in what was long Surry, subsequently Stokes County, North Carolina. In 1775, he was a member of the Hillsboro Convention; and, in February, 1776, he went on the expedition against the Scotch Tories at Cross creek. He was appointed, in this year, Ranger of Surry County, and Major in the militia, serving on Rutherford's expedition against the Cherokees. In 1777, he was a member of the House of Commons, and a Commissioner to treat with the Cherokee Indians. In 1780, he served in Colonel Davidson's expedition in pursuit of Bryans' Tories; was with Cleveland against the Loyalists on New river; in a skirmish at Alamance; and commanded a portion of the right wing at King's Mountain, for which he subsequently was voted an elegant sword by the Legislature of North Carolina.

In February, 1781, he led a party against a band of Tories; had a running fight with them, killing some, capturing others, and dispersing the remainder. He shortly after joined General Greene with a hundred riflemen, and shared in the battle of Guilford. In 1792–3, and again from 1803–7, he represented his district in Congress. He was a Presidential elector in 1800, voting for Jefferson, and in 1812, voting for Madison. Three times he was chosen a member of the State Senate from Surry; and when Stokes County was organized, he was appointed Lieutenant-Colonel, and five times elected to the Senate—the last time in 1812, when the Legislature provided for the presentation of the sword voted him in 1781, and which he thus pertinently acknowledged:

"Mr. Speaker:—I am at a loss for words to express my sense of the honor which the General Assembly has conferred upon me by this grateful present. I trust that the sword, which is directed to be presented to me, will never be tarnished by cowardice, but be wielded in defence of my country's rights and independence."

Colonel Winston died April twenty-first, 1815, in his sixty-ninth year—curiously enough, the same age as his superior, Colonel Cleveland. He was a man of stately form, old school manners, and commanding presence. His home was within view of the lofty mountains of Stokes and Surry, whose "cloud-capt summits seemed within a squirrel's jump of heaven." He left many worthy descendants—three sons born at a single birth.*

Benjamin Herndon was born near Fredericksburg, Virginia, in 1749, and early settled in what is now Wilkes County, North Carolina. He was appointed one of the first Justices of Wilkes County, serving for many years; was Entry Taker of the County; first a Captain, and then Lieutenant Colonel of Cleveland's regiment—in which double capacity he served at King's Mountain, commanding a company of sixty men. He was twice a member of the House of Commons, and twice of the North Carolina Senate. Not long after this last service, in 1786, he removed to Newberry District, in South Carolina, where he died December thirtieth, 1819, in his seventy-first year.

Micajah Lewis, who descended from Welsh ancestors,

---

*Soon after the birth of these triplets, a married sister, who had a babe about a month old, called to visit the mother, and proposed to adopt one of the trio, and thus each would practically have a pair of twins to rear. Mrs. Winston regarded the proposition favorably; and as she sat up in bed, carefully examining all three to determine which to retain, and which one to bestow upon her sister—she at length exclaimed: "I cannot decide for my life—you cannot have any of them, sister; as God has given them to me, he will give me strength to nurse them." And so he did—all of them lived, and were well educated. One of them became a Major-General, another a Judge, and the third a State Senator and Lieutenant Governor of Mississippi; while a brother of theirs, who remained in North Carolina, fought in the war of 1812, became a Major-General, and served in the State Legislature.

was born in Albemarle County, Virginia, in 1755; and early removed to what subsequently became Surry County, North Carolina. He was appointed a Lieutenant in 1776, and was a Captain in service in 1778. He joined General Lincoln in 1779, and shared in the battle of Stono; and, in June 1780, he went in pursuit of Bryan's Tories, and was a Major and Quarter-Master in Cleveland's regiment on the King's Mountain campaign, receiving a wound in the battle. He served as a volunteer at Pyle's defeat, February twenty-fifth, 1781; and, two days afterwards, while out reconnoitering, he was mortally wounded, dying the next day, and was buried at Dickey's plantation, on the Alamance. He had rendered service in the North Carolina line, and was, as General Joseph Graham states, " a real soldier," of " past service and experience."

Joel Lewis was born in Albemarle County, Virginia, August twenty-eighth, 1760; early settled in Surry County; commanded a company at King's Mountain, said to have embraced among its members twenty-two of his own family connections. A colored free man, named Bowman, of his company, claimed to have killed Ferguson; and Captain Lewis secured some of the British commander's arms—one a jewel-hilted poniard, which he retained many years. He married Miriam Eastham, and had eighteen children. In 1784, he was chosen to represent Surry in the House of Commons; and, in 1789, he removed to Nashville, Tennessee, where he was an early hotel-keeper. In 1796, he was a member of the Convention that formed the first Constitution of Tennessee, and was the same year, and again in 1799, elected a State Senator. He held other public positions; and died, near Nashville, November twenty-second, 1816. He left many worthy descendants. His younger brother, James Martin Lewis, born in 1762, who was a Lieutenant at King's Mountain, married Mary, daughter of Colonel Benjamin Herndon, and died at Columbia, Tennessee, in 1830. It is not a little singular, that the three brothers, Micajah, Joel, and James M. Lewis, were all officers, and were all wounded at King's Mountain.

Robert Cleveland, a brother of Colonel Cleveland, was a Captain at King's Mountain, but his company seems to have been mostly among the footmen in the rear. He was born in Virginia, in 1744, and died in Wilkes County, North Carolina, April twenty-sixth, 1812, in his sixty-eighth year. He was one of the North Carolina Electors on the Jefferson ticket for President. His younger brother, Lieutenant Larkin Cleveland, who was so badly wounded at the Catawba while on the march to King's Mountain, settled in Lincoln County, Tennessee, where he died in 1817, in his sixty-seventh year.

John Cleveland, a son of the Colonel, was born in Virginia, about 1760; entered the service very young as a private, afterwards was made a Lieutenant, and was under Colonel Isaacs at Sumter's surprise, August eighteenth, 1780. He led his company at King's Mountain; and on the Raft Swamp expedition under General Rutherford, in the fall of 1781. He was a wild, reckless man—long known by the *sobriquet* of "Devil John." He died in the Tugalo region about 1810. His son, Benjamin Cleveland, was long a prominent citizen of Habersham County, Georgia, a member of the Legislature, an officer in the Creek war, and rose to the rank of a General in the militia.

Jesse Franklin, a Captain and Adjutant in the regiment of his uncle, Colonel Cleveland, was born in Orange County, Virginia, March twenty-fourth, 1760. He settled in Surry County, North Carolina, about 1777, and shared largely with his uncle in the Tory warfare of the times. On one occasion, a Tory party under Jo. Lasefield captured him, and had him ready to swing off, when he said. "You have me completely in your power; but if you hang me, it will prove the dearest day's work you ever performed; for uncle Ben. Cleveland will pursue you like a blood-hound, and he will never cease the chase while a solitary one of you survives." Though they hung him, the bridle with which they did it broke, and he fortunately dropped into the saddle of his horse, bounded away and escaped. Besides his service at King's Mountain, he participated in Guilford battle, and attained to the rank of Major before the close of the war. He was ten years a member of the House of Commons, and two of the State Senate; two years in the lower house of Congress, and twelve in the Senate, retiring in 1813. In 1816, he was appointed by President Madison a Commissioner to hold a treaty with the Chickasaws; and, in 1820, he was elected Governor of North Carolina, serving one term, when his health failing, he declined further public service, and died September twenty-ninth, 1823, in his sixty-fourth year. "He was distinguished." says Wheeler. "for his sincere patriotism, sound sense, and unassuming deportment."

William Lenoir, of French descent, was born in Brunswick County, Virgina, May twentieth, 1751, early removing with his parents to near Tarboro, North Carolina, where he grew to years of manhood. In March, 1775, he settled in what subsequently became Wilkes County; served as a Lieutenant on Rutherford's Cherokee campaign, a Captain at King's Mountain, and at Pyle's defeat; rising, after the war, to the rank of Major General in the militia, and serving many years as Magistrate, Clerk of the Court, County Register, County Surveyor, and Trustee of the State University; three years a member of the House of Commons, and seven of the State Senate. He died at Fort Defiance, May sixth, 1839, nearly eight-eight years of age. He was a man of probity, patriotism and sterling worth; and a County in North Carolina worthily perpetuates his name.

John Barton was an early Wilkes settler, commanding a company in Cleveland's regiment at King's Mountain. He was many years a Magistrate of that County; and, about 1785, he removed to the Tugalo region, on the western borders of South Carolina, where he died in 1827, aged about seventy years. His remains are interred on the eastern slope of Chauga creek, about two miles above Colonel Cleveland's burial place, on his old farm, now owned by Thomas Jenkins.

William Meredith, of Welsh descent, a native of Louisa County, Virginia, early migrated to the Yadkin country, where he became a neighbor of Colonel Cleveland. He was appointed an Ensign in 1776, and took an active part in the war, commanding a company under Cleveland at King's Mountain. He is remembered at a period after the war as a school teacher; and, afterwards removed to the Tugalo country, where he left worthy descendants.

Miner Smith fought heroically at the head of his company at King's Mountain, where he was wounded; and he served, in the autumn of 1781, under General Rutherford, on the Raft Swamp expedition. He disappeared from the Wilkes and Surry region soon after the war—probably migrating to the Tugalo region. Of William Jackson, another of Cleveland's King's Mountain Captains, we have no knowledge.

John Brown was born in Derry County, Ireland, in 1738; migrated to Lancaster County, Pennsylvania, about 1763, where he taught school awhile, and married Jane McDowell. He subsequently removed to Salisbury, North Carolina, and, about 1770, to the Wilkes region on Yadkin. He was among the first board of Magistrates, when Wilkes became a County in 1778; served under Cleveland at King's Mountain, it is believed as a Captain; and three times represented the County in the House of Commons. He died in Wilkes County, in 1812, leaving many worthy descendants. Colonel H. A. Brown, of Maury County, Tennessee, is his grandson.

Samuel Johnson was born near Richmond, Virginia, in 1757, and early settled in the Upper Yadkin Valley. He served as a private on Rutherford's Cherokee campaign in 1776; about 1779 he commanded a mounted Company against Tories in the Fayetteville region, In 1780 he served on Cleveland's New river expedition, and led his company on the King's Mountain campaign; but as the companies were reduced in the re-organization, leaving the footmen behind, he acted in the battle as Lieutenant in Joel Lewis' company. His unique, but effective command in the battle, was: "Aim at the waistbands of their breeches, boys!" He was badly wounded in the action. In 1781, he aided in capturing and breaking up Captain Riddle's band of Tories. He was placed on the invalid pension roll in 1809, and died in Wilkes County, September, fifteenth, 1834, in his seventy-seventh year.

David Witherspoon was a subordinate officer—perhaps a Lieutenant—in Cleveland's regiment at King's Mountain, and his younger brother, John, was a private. They were of Scotch origin, natives of New Jersey, David born in 1758, and John in 1760—collateral relatives of John Witherspoon, President of Princeton College, and a signer of the Declaration of Independence. Early settling in the Yadkin country, they served on Rutherford's Cherokee campaign of 1776, and both followed the fortunes of Cleveland in his warfare against Indians, British and Tories. Their captivity by the Tory Captain Riddle, in the Spring of 1781, led to the breaking up of that dangerous gang of freebooters, as already related. After the war, these brothers represented Wilkes County two years each in the House of Commons. David Witherspoon was long an honored Magistrate, and died while on a visit to South Carolina, in May, 1828; and his brother, who many years before had removed first to Williamson, then Wayne County, Tennessee, died there about 1839.

Major Joseph Herndon, who commanded the footmen, in the rear, on the King's Mountain expedition, was born near Fredericksburg, Virginia, about 1751. He commanded a company on frontier service in 1776; was the first County Surveyor and County Trustee of Wilkes, as well as a member of the County Court. In 1782, 1788, and 1793, he was a member of the House of Commons, and in 1788 a member of the North Carolina Convention. He was a noted gunsmith in his day. He died in Wilkes County in the summer or autumn of 1798.

Richard Allen was born in Baltimore County, Maryland, November twenty-sixth, 1741; settled in what was subsequently Wilkes County in 1770; became a Sergeant in 1775; served on the Cross Creek expedition in February, 1776; early in 1780 he commanded a company for the relief of Charleston; then went in pursuit of Bryan's Tories; and led his company on the King's Mountain campaign, but was prevailed on to remain with the footmen in the rear. He served a tour of duty early in 1781 under General Greene. He was the first Sheriff of Wilkes County, and a member of the House of Commons in 1793. He attained to the rank of Colonel in the militia, and died in Wilkes County, October tenth, 1832, in his ninety-first year.

Elisha Reynolds was born in what became Wilkes County, in April, 1755. He served on Rutherford's campaign in 1776 against the Tories gathered at Ramsour's, in June, 1780; and shortly after against the Tories on New river. He was with the footmen, in the rear, on the King's Mountain campaign; and shortly after Colonel Cleveland's capture by the Tories, early in 1781, he went with Captain Johnson and others, and broke up the Tory gang who captured him. He was a Lieutenant in the latter part of the war, and rendered his country good service. He died December thirteenth, 1836, in his eighty-second year.

CHAPTER XX.

Lacey and Other Whigs.—British and Tory Leaders.

Lacey, Hawthorne, Tate, and Moffett.—Williams, Hammond, Hayes, Dillard, Thompson, and Candler.—Brandon, Steen, and Roebuck,— Maj. McDowell, Capt. McDowell, Kennedy, Vance, and Wood.— Hampton, Singleton, Porter, Withrow, Miller, and Watson.— Hambright, Graham, Chronicle, Dickson, Johnston, White, Espey, Martin, and Mattocks.—British and Tory Leaders.

Sumter's Men Under Lacey and Hawthorn.

Edward Lacey was born in Shippensburg township, Pennsylvania, in September, 1742; and when only thirteen, fascinated with the appearance of soldiery, he ran away, joined the Pennsylvania troops, serving in the pack-horse department, and was in Braddock's defeat. After two year's absence, his father found and took him home. When sixteen, he again ran away, emigrating to Chester District, South Carolina, with William Adair, to whom he bound himself to learn the trade of brick-laying, and from whom he received a good English education. In 1766, he married Jane Harper, and settled on the head waters of Sandy river, six miles west of Chester Court House.

He became a Captain on the breaking out of the Revolution, and served on Williamson's Cherokee Campaign; and when news reached them of the Declaration of Independence, he read that patriotic paper to the army. He lead the detachment that defeated the British Captain Huck, and served with Sumter at Rocky Mount, Hanging Rock, Carey's Fort, and Fishing Creek. At King's Mountain, he led the Chester troops, losing his horse in the action, which was replaced with one of Ferguson's chargers. He again served under Sumter at Fish Dam Ford and Blackstocks ; on Sumter's rounds early in 1781, at Orangeburg, Biggin Church, Quinby Bridge, and Eutaw, and never received a wound, as a gipsey woman assured him, when a youth, that he would not, though destined to pass through many a battle, but would finally get drowned. After the war, he was chosen a Brigadier-General of the militia, a Judge of the County Court, and served many years in the Legislature. In 1797, he migrated first to West Tennessee, and two years later to Livingston County, Kentucky, where he was made County Judge ; and was thrown from his horse while in a fit of catalepsy, in crossing the swollen waters of Deer Creek, and drowned, March twentieth, 1813, at the age of seventy-one years. His widow pined away, surviving her husband only two months. Of their eleven children, ten grew to years of maturity. "General Lacey," says Mills' *Statistics of South Carolina*, "was a cool, intrepid officer, and rendered important services to the State."

James Hawthorn was born in Armagh County, Ireland about 1750, whose father and family early migrated to the frontiers of South Carolina, where the mother, two daughters and her young son, then about twelve years of age, were captured by the Indians—the mother and girls were killed. James Hawthorn was at length surrendered by the Indians, learned the blacksmith's trade in York County, South Carolina, where he married Mary, a daughter of Colonel Thomas Neel. He took an active part in the Revolution, serving in Neel's regiment on the Snow campaign in 1775, on Williamson's Indian expedition in 1776, and as a Captain on the Florida campaign of 1778–79. He served under Sumter at Rocky Mount, Hanging Rock, Carey's Fort, and Fishing Creek.

As Colonel Hill was unable, from a former wound, to lead his regiment at King's Mountain, it devolved on his Lieutenant-Colonel Hawthorn to do so. He was subsequently with Sumter at Fish Dam Ford and Blackstock's, and was wounded on Sumter's rounds in February, 1781; and received a second wound during the course of the war. In after years he migrated to Livingston County, Kentucky, where he lost a fine property, being on the bond of a defaulting Sheriff, and where he died in the latter part of 1809, about fifty-nine years of age. He left several children.

Samuel Tate, who was the Brigade-Major of Sumter's brigade, of which Lacey's and Hawthorn's men formed a part, was of Irish descent on his father's side, and of English on his mother's. He was born and raised on the Santee, near Vance's Ferry, in Orangeburg District, South Carolina, and served under Sumter during the Revolution. He shared in the glory of King's Mountain; and died at the old homestead, near Vance's Ferry, about 1798.

John Moffett was born, about 1742, probably in the Valley of Virginia. He early settled in Chester County, South Carolina, and served as a Captain on the Snow campaign, and against the Cherokees in 1776. He was under Sumter in his operations in the summer of 1780, particularly distinguishing himself at Fishing Creek. His company formed a part of Lacey's regiment at King's Mountain; he afterwards served with Sumter, and also at the Cowpens, attaining the rank of Colonel before the close of the war. He died in DeKalb County, Georgia, in 1829 aged about eighty-seven years.

Williams, Hammond, Hayes, Dillard, and Candler.

James Williams, son of Daniel and Ursula Williams—the father a native of Wales—was born near the old Fork Church, Hanover County, Virginia, in November, 1740. His education was very limited, and his parents dying, he early migrated to Granville County, North Carolina, where

30

his brother, Colonel John Williams was a distinguished jurist, as was also his cousin, Colonel Richard Henderson. Colonel Joseph Williams, of Surry County, in that Province, was also his cousin. Marrying a Miss Clarke, about 1762, he ten years later removed to Little River, in now Laurens County, South Carolina, where he engaged in the combined avocations of farmer, miller and merchant.

Taking a decided part against the mother country, he was chosen one of the representatives, in January, 1775, of the Broad river and Saluda district, to the South Carolina Congress; and soon after one of the local Committee of Safety, and served as a Captain on the Snow campaign in suppressing the Tories. In 1776 he was made Lieutenant-Colonel of Militia, and served on Williamson's expedition against the Cherokees. In 1778, he was defeated for State Senator by the strong Tory influence in his section; and that year led his regiment on the abortive Florida campaign. In 1779, he shared in the affairs at Brier Creek, Stono Ferry, and Savannah, receiving in the latter a spent ball on his forehead. The same year he served on an expedition against the Cherokees, and was engaged a while in guarding prisoners at Ninety Six. He served under Sumter, in 1780, as Commissary, on his expeditions against Rocky Mount and Hanging Rock; then at Musgrove's Mill, and closing his useful life at King's Mountain, where he received a mortal wound, dying the next day, in his fortieth year, leaving eight children, five sons and three daughters.

Fighting and dying, as he did, for his country, Colonel Williams well deserves to be judged in charity. He was every inch a patriot—and a man of strong religious feelings. He was rough, rash and fearless, As a soldier, he was much after the style of Cromwell, and Thomas J. Jackson in more recent times; and it may be added, that his ambition for glory, mingled doubtless with a true love of country, led him, perhaps unconsciously, to the use of means, not over scrupulous, in the accomplishment of his ends. While he differed and chafered with Sumter, Hill and their associates, yet when the tug of war came, he plunged fearlessly into the thickest of the fight, and freely poured out his blood, and yielded up his life, for his country. Let his unquestioned patriotism, like a mantle of charity, cover all his seeming short-comings. The historian, Bancroft, speaks of him as "a man of exalted character, of a career brief but glorious. An ungenerous enemy revenged themselves for his virtues by nearly extirpating his family; they could not take away his right to be remembered by his country with honor and affection to the latest time."

Samuel Hammond was born in Richmond County, Virginia, September twenty-first, 1757; was at the battle of Point Pleasant, in 1774, and at the Great Bridge, in December, 1775. After serving under General Hand at Pittsburg, in 1777–78, he went south, opposing the British in Georgia, at Stono Ferry, and Savannah, in 1779; in 1780, at Cedar Spring, Musgrove's Mill, King's Mountain and Blackstocks; in 1781, at Augusta, Ninety Six, and Eutaw, where he was wounded, retiring from the service at the end of the war with the rank of Colonel of Cavalry. He filled many public positions; in Georgia, a member of the Legislature, commanding against the Indians, and serving a term in Congress; in Missouri, Receiver of Public Moneys, President of the Territorial Council, and member of the Convention that formed the first Constitution; and in South Carolina, a member of the Legislature, Surveyor General, and Secretary of State. He died near Hamburg, in that State, September eleventh, 1842, nearly eighty-five years of age. His services in the Revolutionary war were highly important to the country.

Joseph Hayes, of Laurens County, South Carolina, served first as a Captain, and then as Lieutenant-Colonel, in all, or nearly all, the services performed by Colonel Williams—in Georgia, Brier Creek, Stono, a campaign against the Cherokees, and at Savannah; and in 1780, at Hanging

Rock, Musgrove's Mill, and King's Mountain, when he succeeded to the command of the regiment on the death of Colonel Williams, and served at Blackstock's, Hammond's Store, and Cowpens. On the nineteenth of November, 1781, while Colonel Hayes, Captain Daniel and Joseph Williams—sons of Colonel Williams, respectively eighteen and fourteen years of age—with several others, were besieged at Hayes, Station by Bloody Bill Cunningham, the buildings were fired, and the unhappy inmates forced to surrender, on condition of being treated as prisoners of war. When, in violation of the pledges made them, Colonel Hayes and Captain Williams were about to be hung to the pole of a fodder stack, little Joseph Williams cried out in his heart's agony, "Oh! brother Daniel, what shall I tell mother!" "You shall tell her nothing, you d—d Rebel suckling!" retorted Cunningham, as he hewed him down. Hanging Hayes and the elder Williams, the pole broke, when the bloody monster cut and slashed with his sword, hacking them to pieces. Eleven others perished in the same manner at the hands of Cunningham and his men.

James Dillard was born in Culpeper County, Virginia, about 1755, removing to what is now Laurens County, South Carolina, about 1772. He served as a private in 1775, and, in 1776, in the defence of Charleston. In 1778, he went on the Florida expedition as Sergeant-Major, and served on the frontiers in 1779. He was chosen a Captain in Williams' regiment in August, 1780, serving at King's Mountain, Hammond's Store and Cowpens, and, in 1782, on Picken's expedition against the Cherokees. His heroic wife, Mrs. Mary Dillard, gave Sumter notice of Tarleton's approach toward Blackstock's. He became a Major in the militia, and died December fourth, 1836.

John Thompson, of York County, who had served as a Captain at Rocky Mount, Hanging Rock and Fishing Creek, commanded a company under Williams at King's Mountain, and subsequently fought at Cowpens. Gabriel Brown was another of Williams' Captains.

Major William Candler, who with Captains Carr and Johnston, commanded the small party of Georgians at King's Mountain, and probably under Colonel Williams, was born of English parents, at Belfast, Ireland, in 1738, and was brought to Virginia when a mere child. He married in 1761, Elizabeth Anthony; and the next year migrated to Georgia. In 1771, he was a Deputy Surveyor. During the war, he served under Colonel Clarke—was in the attack on Augusta, at King's Mountain, and Blackstocks, and rose to the rank of Colonel. He was a member of the Legislature in 1784 and 1785; was appointed a Judge; and died at his seat, in Columbia County, in September, 1789, at the age of fifty-one years, leaving several children, his oldest son Henry, having served with him in the war.

Brandon, Steen, and Roebuck.

Thomas Brandon, of Irish descent, was born in Pennsylvania in 1741—his parents, with a colony of Irish Presbyterians, emigrated from that Province to what is now Union County, South Carolina, at the period of 1754-55, and had for several years to fort against the turbulent Cherokees. Serving in the early part of the Revolution, he rose, in 1780, to the command of a regiment, acting much under Sumter. Retiring from that service, with Colonel Williams, he shared in the affair at Musgrove's Mill, then at King's Mountain, Blackstock's, and Cowpens—in the latter killing three of Tarleton's dragoons with his sword. After the war, he was a Justice of the Court, County Ordinary, General of the militia, and frequently a member of one or the other branch of the Legislature. He was a good soldier, but, like Cleveland, a bitter enemy of Tories, who received little mercy at his hands. He died at his residence on Fair Forest, February fifth, 1802, in the sixty-first year of his age.

James Steen, also of Irish descent, was probably a

native of Pennsylvania, and early settled in what is now Union County, South Carolina. In August, 1775, he " was fully convinced, and ready to sign the Continental association," and doubtless led a company on the Snow campaign, as he did the following year against the Cherokees, and, in 1777, commaned at Prince's Fort. In 1779, he served in Georgia, then at Stono, and Savannah ; and performed a tour of duty from November in that year till February, 1780, near Charleston. At this period, he ranked as Lieutenant-Colonel, distinguishing himself at Rocky Mount, Hanging Rock, Musgrove's Mill, King's Mountain, and probably with his superior, Colonel Brandon, at the Cow pens. In the summer of 1781, while endeavoring to arrest a Tory, in Rowan County, North Carolina, he was stabbed by an associate, surviving only a week.

Benjamin Roebuck was born in Orange County, Virginia, about 1755. His father, Benjamin Roebuck, Sr., settled in Spartanburg County, South Carolina, in 1777 ; and the next year the younger Roebuck served as a Lieutenant in Georgia, and was at Stono and Savannah. In 1780, he joined Sumter, and was at Hanging Rock, and subsequently at Musgrove's Mill, commanding a company at King's Mountain, and distinguishing himself at Cowpens, where he had a horse shot under him. About this time, he was promoted to the rank of Lieutenant-Colonel ; and in a fight at Mud Lick with the Tories, March second, 1781, he was badly wounded, the ball penetrating under the shoulder blade, could not be extracted. He was then made prisoner, and conveyed to Ninety Six, where he was incarcerated during the siege. He was subsequently taken to Charleston, and placed on board a prison ship. In August following, he was exchanged, and returned home. He died, unmarried, in 1788, from the effects of his wound. Hon. Simpson Bobo, of Spartanburg, South Carolina, is his nephew.

McDowell and his Officers.

Joseph McDowell, Sr., of Scotch-Irish descent, was born in Ireland in 1715—reared a weaver, married Margaret O'Neil, and early migrated to Pennsylvania. He soon after settled in Winchester, Virginia, where his sons, Charles and Joseph, were born—the latter in 1756. A brother of the elder Joseph McDowell, known in after years as "Hunting John McDowell," early removed to the Catawba Valley, settling that beautiful tract, Pleasant Garden, sometime prior to 1758; and at some period not very long thereafter, his brother Joseph McDowell, Sr., followed to that wild frontier region, locating at the Quaker Meadows, where his family was reared.

In February, 1776, Joseph McDowell, Jr., young as he was, went in his brother's regiment—some accounts state as Major—on the expedition against the Scotch Tories. In July, the Cherokees burst upon the Catawba settlements, killing thirty-seven persons on the tenth and eleventh of that month, and beleaguering a fort, in which were Colonel and Major McDowell, with nine other men, and a hundred and twenty women and children; the Indians were driven off. Major McDowell served, in the ensuing fall, in his brother's regiment, on Rutherford's campaign against the Cherokees; in 1779, on the Stono expedition; early in 1780, after the Tories, sharing in the victory at Ramsour's Mill—"the same Joseph McDowell," says the old pensioner, Joseph Dobson, "who was afterwards General," He was next in service at Earle's Ford on Pacolet, at Musgrove's Mill, King's Mountain and Cowpens. He served a tour, in the spring of 1781, against Cornwallis. In August, 1781, and again in March, 1782, Major McDowell led expeditions, chastising the Cherokees; and in the fall of 1782, he commanded the Burke regiment on a campaign against the same troublesome tribe, under the leadership of his brother, General McDowell.

Colonel McDowell, and his cousin of the same name, were both much engaged in the public service—the former distinguished from the latter, while in the State Legislature, by the appendage of "Jr." to his name. In Burke County they were familiarly known as "Quaker Meadow Joe," or "Congress Joe," and the other as "Pleasant Garden Joe." Colonel McDowell, of the Quaker Meadows, and afterwards of John's river, served in the House of Commons in 1787, 1788, 1791, and 1792; and in 1788, he was a member of the State Convention for the consideration of the Federal Constitution. He served two terms in Congress, 1793-95, and 1797-99, taking an active part in the debates of that body against the Alien and Sedition laws, and other Federal measures of that day. In 1797, he was a Commissioner for running the boundary line between North Carolina and Tennessee.

His death occurred at his home, of apoplexy, August eleventh, 1801, in the forty-fifth year of his age; and he was buried at the Quaker Meadows, where some rude stones, and a large tree at the head of his grave, mark the place of his repose. He married Margaret, daughter of Colonel George Moffett, of Virginia, leaving two sons and six daughters. "He was," says Moore, the North Carolina historian, "the recognized leader of the Republican party in the western Counties, and was as eminent for his sagacious leadership in civil matters as he had been dauntless and successful in the late war. He was no inconsiderable an antagonist in debate, and throughout his life he was the idol of the western people of North Carolina."*

*That it was Joseph McDowell, of the Quaker Meadows, who commanded the Burke troops at King's Mountain, has been called in question—not by any of his associate heroes of the Revolution, nor by the historians of the country, but chiefly by the descendants of his namesake-cousin and brother-in-law, of Pleasant Garden. Both having borne the same name, resided in the same County, and both having unquestionably served in that battle—the younger, of Pleasant Garden, as a Captain under his elder cousin—have led to the confusion and mistake. The descendants of the Captain, who fought in the battle, and brought home as trophies some of Ferguson's table set, still preserved in the family, have drawn therefrom the erroneous conclusion, that he was the Major who commanded the Burke troops on that service.

Of Major McDowell's officers, only brief reference can be made. Joseph McDowell, his cousin, son of " Hunting John McDowell," was born at Pleasant Garden, February twenty-fifth, 1758. He served on Rutherford's campaign, killing an Indian; on scouts against the Indians in Burke County, and commanded a company at King's Mountain. He was a member of the North Carolina Convention of 1788, making several able speeches. He married Mary Moffett, dying in April, 1795, leaving several children. He was a physician by profession, and is regarded as having possessed the brightest intellect of any of the connection.

Thomas Kennedy was born in 1756, and settled when

Colonel Shelby, in his narrative cited by the Tennessee historians, Haywood and Ramsey, and in his pamphlet of 1823, states that Major McDowell, who was at King's Mountain, was the brother of Colonel Charles McDowell; and no less than three survivors of McDowell's command, Captain David Vance, John Spelts, and James Thompson, make the same assertion, fully corroborated by Robert Henry and Benjamin Sharp, two other King's Mountain men. The coincidence of Spelts and Sharp about Major McDowell freely permitting the soldiers to burn his rails at camp at the Quaker Meadows, confirms this view of the matter; as does the anecdote of the treatment of the British captive officers, at the Quaker Meadows, by Mrs. McDowell, the mother of the Major. Henry Rutherford, son of General Rutherford, and General Thomas Love, of Buncombe, both well acquainted with General Joseph McDowell, declared that he was the brother of General Charles McDowell, and the Burke leader at King's Mountain. A letter of the late Hon. N. W. Woodfin, whose lady was of the McDowell connection, makes the same statement, confirmed by Misses Mary and Myra A. Dickson, grand-daughters of General Charles McDowell; and also by Hon. J. C. Harper, derived from Col. Wm. Davenport, who well knew all the McDowells. The late Hon. Joseph J. McDowell, of Ohio, and Harvey H. McDowell, Sr., late of Missouri, sons of General Joseph McDowell, never had a doubt on the subject. The venerable Mrs. Samuel P. Carson, who from her McDowell and Carson connection, has had good opportunities for learning the family traditions, declares that it was Joseph McDowell, of the Quaker Meadows, who led the Burke troops at King's Mountain. The historians, Haywood, Ramsey, Lossing, Wheeler, Hunter, Moore, and Mrs. Ellet, all take the same view.

It has always been undoubted, that the Major McDowell of King's Mountain, was the same who led the North Carolina troops at the Cowpens. Shelby states, in effect, that he arranged for Major McDowell, who had served with him at King's Mountain, to join Morgan's light troops; and General James Jackson, in a letter extant, written in January, 1795, endorsed by General Pickens, both of whom distinguished themselves under Morgan at the Cowpens, and both of whom were associated with McDowell in Congress, refers to Colonel McDowell, " now in Congress," as the commander of the North Carolina militia in that battle.

If, therefore, the statements of those who shared in the campaign, and at Cowpens, and all our historians who refer to the subject, are to be credited, Joseph McDowell, of the Quaker Meadows, was unquestionably the Major who led the Burke troops at King's Mountain. It was doubtless in recognition of his Revolutionary leadership, that he was, in after years, made a General of the militia.

young in Burke County, North Carolina. He was early made a Captain, and was wounded at Ramsour's Mills; then served at Earle's Ford on Pacolet, Cane Creek, King's Mountain, and with Rutherford in the fall of 1781, when he was made prisoner by the Tories. Removing to Kentucky, he had a personal conflict with an Indian on a hill-side, rolling down together, when Kennedy killed him. He served in the Virginia and Kentucky Legislatures, and the Kentucky Convention of 1792; became a General; and died in Garrard County, June nineteenth, 1836.

David Vance, of Scotch-Irish descent, was born in Frederick County, Virginia, about 1748, early removed to Burke County, North Carolina, where he taught school, and became Surveyor, serving at Ramsour's, Musgrove's Mill, and King's Mountain. He was a member of the House of Commons in 1786 and 1791; then removed to Buncombe County, and in 1797, was one of the Commissioners for running the boundary line between North Carolina and Tennessee, and became a Colonel in the militia. He died about 1820. Hons. Z. B. and R. B. Vance, of North Carolina, are his grandsons.

Samuel Wood commanded a company at King's Mountain, as did probably Joseph White, both of whom removed to Lincoln County, Kentucky. Edmund Fear and John Sigman were also Burke County Captains in McDowell's corps.

Hampton and his Officers.

Andrew Hampton, a native of England, migrated first to Virginia, and settled prior to 1751, on Dutchman's Creek on the Catawba, removing before the Revolution to what is now Rutherford County, North Carolina. In 1770, he was made Captain, in 1776, Lieutenant-Colonel, and Colonel, in 1779. While yet a Captain, early in 1776, he served against the Scotch Tories; and early in 1779, pursued Colonel John Moore's Tory party when they fled south.

Early in 1780, he went to the relief of Charleston; subsequently served at Earle's Ford, Thicketty Fort, Cane Creek, and commanded the Rutherford troops at King's Mountain and Blackstock's. He was Sheriff of Rutherford in 1782, and died in October, 1805, leaving many worthy descendants.

Richard Singleton was born in Brunswick County, Virginia, about 1750, settling in what is now Rutherford County, North Carolina, before the Revolution. He led a company against the Scotch Tories; acted as Major in 1780, at Earle's Ford, Cane Creek, and King's Mountain; and on a campaign against the Cherokees, in March, 1782. He served in both branches of the Legislature, in the Convention of 1788, and as Sheriff of Rutherford County. Near the close of the last century, he removed to Lincoln County, Kentucky, where he died at a good old age.

James Porter, of Irish parentage, was born in Pennsylvania, in 1744; settled early in Rutherford, serving as a Major at King's Mountain, where he was wounded; and subsequently removed to Greenville County, South Carolina, where he survived many years, dying childless. His brother, William Porter, was also at King's Mountain, served nineteen years in the Legislature, and was killed by lightning in 1817, at the age of seventy-one years. Robert Porter, a cousin, and man of prominence, was probably an officer at King's Mountain also.

James Withrow, a Captain under Hampton, was born in Virginia, in 1746; settled early in Rutherford; served against the Scotch Tories, at Stono, King's Mountain, Blackstock's, and against the Cherokees. He served eight years in the House of Commons, and died about 1836, at the age of about ninety years, James Miller, of Irish descent, a native of Pennsylvania, and George Ledbetter, also commanded companies under Hampton at King's Mountain. Miller did much service during the war, was made a Colonel in 1781, repressing the Tories, and commanded the Rutherford troops on the expedition against the Cherokees in the fall of 1782. From 1782 to 1787, he was four times State Senator; and died while on a trip to Charleston, about 1812, at Cross Anchor, South Carolina. Ledbetter was a member of the State Convention of 1788, and shortened his days by too free use of spirituous liquors.*

Hambright, Chronicle and their Officers.

Frederick Hambright was born in Germany, in 1727, and, when a youth, was taken to Pennsylvania about 1738.† About 1755, he removed to Virginia, where he married Sarah Hardin; and, about 1760, he migrated to North Carolina, settling near the South Fork, forting awhile against the Indians. In August, 1775, he was a member of the Provincial Congress, He served as a Captain on the frontiers in June, 1776; and, in the fall, on Rutherford's Cherokee campaign. He was made Lieutenant-Colonel in 1779; and, late in that year, he went to the relief of Charleston, serving in Lillington's brigade, and retiring before the surrender of the place. In 1780, he served under Colonel McDowell in the Broad river region; and succeeding Colonel Graham,‡ fought at King's Mountain, where he was badly wounded; and where his son John also did service, rising to the rank of Captain before the close of the war. Twice married, Colonel Hambright

*Major Patrick Watson commanded the Rutherford footmen in the rear, and thus failed to participate in King's Mountain battle. A native of Pennsylvania, he settled in Rutherford in 1764, and died December sixteenth, 1809, in his fifty-eighth year.

†In October, 1738, Adam and Conrad Hambright arrived at Philadelphia from Germany with their families, and probably settled in Lancaster, where the Hambrights have long been prominent citizens.

‡William Graham, born in Augusta County, Virginia, in 1742, settled in North Carolina before the Revolution; served in the Provincial Congress of 1775, and was appointed Colonel of Tryon County, serving on the Snow campaign; then against the Scotch Tories, and on Rutherford's Cherokee expedition. He was chosen a member of the Halifax Convention of 1776. In 1779-80, he went to the relief of Charleston; then served at Thicketty Fort, Cedar Spring, and in defence of his dwelling against Tories. His retirement from the army to visit his sick wife, a little before King's Mountain battle. and his hasty return at its close, have been already related. He died near Shelby, North Carolina, March twenty-sixth, 1835, in his ninety-third year, a pensioner for his Revolutionary services.

was the father of eighteen children ; and died, in March, 1817, in the ninetieth year of his age.

William Chronicle was born on the South Fork of Catawba, now Gaston County, North Carolina, about 1755. In December, 1775, he marched at the head of a company on the Snow campaign, and in 1779, to Georgia ; and afterwards to the relief of Charleston. He was with General Rutherford's rear at Ramsour's, then joining Sumter at Clem's Branch awhile, he was engaged in chasing Tories out of the country. He was probably with Graham at Thicketty Fort and Cedar Spring ; and yielded up his young life, while serving as Major, at King's Mountain. He had attracted the attention of Colonel Campbell before the battle. "He was," says General Graham, "a young man of great promise "—the idol of his friends and soldiers.

Joseph Dickson, of Scotch-Irish stock, was born about 1745 ; married Margaret McEwen, a Scotch lady, and migrated to North Carolina before the Revolution, settling first in Rowan County, and finally in what is now Lincoln. He was a Captain in service as early as April, 1779—and probably much earlier. In June, 1780, he joined General Rutherford, and was engaged in ridding the country of Tories. He was in service under Colonel McDowell, in South Carolina, during that summer ; and served as Major of the Lincoln men at King's Mountain. Early in 1781, he opposed Cornwallis' invasion of North Carolina, and was advanced to the rank of Colonel. He was in this year chosen Clerk of Lincoln Court ; State Senator from 1788 to 1795 ; a General in the militia, and a member of Congress from 1799 to 1801. He removed in 1803, to what is now Caldwell County, and in 1806, to Rutherford County, Tennessee, where he died April fourteenth, 1825, aged about eighty years, and was buried with military and masonic honors.

James Johnston, a native of Scotland, was born about 1742. His father, Henry Johnston, early settled in what is now Lincoln County, North Carolina, where the son became a Captain at the out-break of the Revolution, serving on the Snow campaign; was then chosen a member of the Provincial Congress, of April, 1776; then served on the frontiers, and on Rutherford's Cherokee expedition. Early in 1780, he had the personal conflict with the Tory, Patrick Moore, related elsewhere; and commanded a company at King's Mountain. He served in the State Senate in 1780–82; and died July twenty-third, 1805, leaving seven children. Colonel William Johnston, of Charlotte, is his grandson.

Isaac White, of Scotch-Irish parentage, was born in Chester County, Pennsylvania, in 1760; and migrated, with his elder brother Thomas, to Lincoln County, North Carolina, about 1779. Though young, James White was chosen a Captain, and his brother the Lieutenant of the company; and served at King's Mountain and Cowpens. In 1816, they removed to Bond County, Illinois, James dying in 1821, aged sixty-one years, and Thomas in 1824, at the age of seventy.

Samuel Espey was born in Cumberland County, Pennsylvania, May eighth, 1758; and, in 1770, his father removed to what is now Lincoln County, North Corolina. He served as a soldier in 1776, on the frontiers, and on Rutherford's campaign. In 1779, he was again in service. Early in 1780, he was made a Captain in Graham's regiment, serving at Cedar Spring and King's Mountain, where he had an arm broken in the action. He again served awhile in the spring of 1781; and died in what is now Cleveland County, December twenty-ninth, 1838.

Samuel Martin was born in Ireland in 1732, where he married Margaret McCurdy, and migrated to Pennsylvania. While there, he served in the old French and Indian war. Removing to North Carolina, he served on the Snow campaign in 1775; on the frontiers in 1776; and went to the relief of Charleston in 1779–80. In June, 1780, he was made Captain, serving under Rutherford; and was at the

D. Peyster Capt.
N. Y. Regt.

capture of Rugeley's Tories, and at King's Mountain. In 1781, he opposed Cornwallis at Cowan's Ford, and afterwards served awhile under General Pickens ; and then commanded a company under Colonel William Polk at Eutaw Springs. Surviving his companion, he died in Gaston County, November twenty-sixth, 1836, at the great age of one hundred and four years.

We have no details of the prior life and services of Captain John Mattocks, of the South Fork, who was killed at King's Mountain. His brother Charles participated with him in the battle, and interceded for his Tory brother Edward, who was severely wounded there, and cured of his Toryism. After the war, the family removed to Georgia.

British and Tory Leaders at King's Mountain.

Colonel Ferguson has already been fully sketched in this work. He was a Lieutenant-Colonel in the regular army, and Inspector General of the Loyal Militia of South Carolina, in consequence of which he was sometimes denominated General. The epithet of *"Bull-Dog Ferguson"* was well applied to him, as suggestive of his determination and persistence.

Abraham DePeyster, the second in command at King's Mountain, descended from an ancient and influential family, was born in New York in 1753. He entered the Royal service as Captain in the New York Volunteers—served in the siege of Charleston, Musgrove's Mills, and in Ferguson's operations during the summer and autumn of 1780, distinguishing himself at King's Mountain, where his life was saved by a doubloon in his vest pocket, which stopped a rifle ball, though the coin was bent by its force. He retired on half-pay to New Brunswick, where he was Treasurer and Colonel in the militia, dying about 1798. He was a brave, vigilant, and enterprising officer.

Samuel Ryerson, another of Ferguson's Captains, was

a native of New Jersey, of Dutch descent, early entered the service as a Captain in the New Jersey Volunteers, was wounded at King's Mountain, retired after the war to New Brunswick, where he lived to a good old age.

John Taylor was born near Amboy, New Jersey, May fifteenth, 1742; became a Lieutenant in the New Jersey Volunteers—was assigned to Ferguson's corps, serving under him during the campaign of 1780, and at King's Mountain. He had his leg broken in some action in South Carolina; retired to Weymouth, Nova Scotia, where he died November thirteenth, 1822, leaving descendants.

Anthony Allaire, of Huguenot descent, was born at New Rochelle, Westchester County, New York, February twenty-second, 1755; was commissioned a Lieutenant in the Loyal American Volunteers, serving as Adjutant in Ferguson's corps, in the siege of Charleston, at Monks' Corner, and in the up-country of North and South Carolina, sharing in the action of King's Mountain. The *Diary* he left of the South Carolina campaign is a valuable contribution to history. He retired from the service in 1783, to New Brunswick; and, in 1793, re-entered the service as Lieutenant in the New Brunswick regiment, securing a Captaincy in 1801, shortly before the disbandment of that corps, when he retired on half-pay. He died on his farm, near Fredericton, June ninth, 1838, leaving a daughter who intermarried with Lieutenant John Robinson of the army.

Wm. Stevenson, a native of Monmouth County, New Jersey, was first commissioned a Lieutenant in some Loyal company in December, 1776, and transferred to the New Jersey Volunteers; serving in 1780, in Ferguson's corps, at Charleston and King's Mountain. He retired to Nova Scotia, and died at his old army associate's, Captain Taylor's, at Weymouth, about 1818, quite advanced in years, and without a family.

Duncan Fletcher was a New Yorker, a Lieutenant in the Loyal American Volunteers—assigned to Ferguson's corps during the campaign of 1780, serving at King's Mountain. He subsequently became a Captain; and in 1784, was at Wilmot, Nova Scotia.

John McGinnis, who was killed at King's Mountain, was an Ensign in the New Jersey Volunteers; and, in Ferguson's corps, seems to have acted as Lieutenant for that special service.

Dr. Uzal Johnson, son of Eliphalet Johnson, was born in Newark, New Jersey, April seventeenth, 1757, where he practiced his profession of medicine as early as 1776; in which year he joined the New Jersey Volunteers as Surgeon. He served with great benefit to Ferguson's corps—and to the wounded Americans as well at King's Mountain. After the war, he returned to Newark, and practiced his profession till his death, May twenty-second, 1827, at the age of seventy years.

Of the Loyalist leaders but little can be gleaned from history or tradition. Colonel Ambrose Mills, among the unfortunates who were executed at Bickerstaff's, was born in England, about 1722 and was taken while yet young to Maryland. He married Miss Mourning Stone, settling on James River, and finally removing to the frontiers of South Carolina, where his wife was killed by Indians, during the Indian war of 1755–61, leaving an only son, William. He afterwards married Miss Anne Brown, of the Chester region, sister of the wife of the noted Loyalist leader, Colonel Thomas Fletchall; and, about 1765, settled on Green River, in North Carolina; and by this second marriage had three sons and three daughters. In 1776, he served against the Cherokee Indians. In 1778, Colonel Mills and the notorious David Fanning raised a corps of five hundred men with the design of joining the Royal standard at St. Augustine, when one of the party betrayed their plans. Mills and sixteen others were apprehended, and conveyed to Salisbury jail; Fanning undertaking to rescue him on the way, but his force proved too weak to effect the purpose. Mills was, in course of time, liberated; joined Ferguson with the Loyal militia of his region, fought at Earle's Ford and King's Mountain; and, as viewed a century after the occurrence, he was too severely dealt with at Bickerstaff's. His descendants are among the ablest and best citizens in the South and South-West.

His son, William Mills, was born on James River, Virginia, November tenth, 1746. He was very popular, and served in 1776 against the Indians. He acted as Major under his father at King's Mountain, where he was badly wounded, and left for dead; and was subsequently saved from being executed by the interference of leading Whigs who knew his worth and goodness. In after years, he settled in the mountain region of the south-western portion of North Carolina on Clear Creek, in now Cleveland County. Mills' River and Mills' Gap, in that section, were named after him. He married early in life Eleanor Morris, by whom he had two sons and five daughters. He was a handsome, noble, generous man. He died, in consequence of a fall from his horse on his birthday, November tenth, 1834, at the age of eighty-eight years. He had lived a happy married life of sixty-nine years—his venerable companion surviving him.

Vezey Husbands, who was killed at King's Mountain, and is said to have served as a Colonel there, lived near Lower Creek of Catawba, in Burke County; and was, perhaps a relative of Herman Husbands, of Regulation war notoriety, who was a native of Pennsylvania, of Quaker descent.

William Green, who commanded a company at King's Mountain, and whose escape from captivity has already been related, was born on Buffalo Creek, in now Cleveland County, near the State line, May sixteenth, 1753. He served up to 1780 as a Captain in the Whig cause; was captured by the Tories and held prisoner until released by their defeat at Ramsour's. His only British service was at King's Mountain, which he deeply regretted ; and, to atone for the error, he enlisted in Captain Levi Johnston's company, of ten month's men under Sumter, in 1781–82, and shared in the battle of Eutaw Springs. After the war, he served in the House of Commons in 1798, and fourteen times in the State Senate from 1800 to 1824. He died in Rutherford County, November sixth, 1832, leaving many worthy descendants.

Major Daniel Plummer, who was probably killed at King's Mountain, lived between Fair Forest and Tyger, in now Spartanburg County, South Carolina ; and was represented as " honest and open "—kind and considerate to all. His estate was confiscated. Of Major Lee, who was in, and survived the battle, we have no further information. William Gist, a Tory Captain in the action, lived on Tyger river, South Carolina ; was committed to jail at Charleston, in 1776, for Toryism. His estate was confiscated ; but he did not probably long survive the war, as the General Assembly subsequently granted his wife and children five hundred acres of any of his confiscated lands not already sold. Captain Aaron Biggerstaff, of English descent, of Rutherford County, was one of the Loyalist leaders at Ramsour's ; escaping that disaster, he was mortally wounded at King's Mountain, taken for treatment to what is now Union Court House, where he died. From Allaire's *Diary*, we learn of Captain Townsend, who resided a mile from the Island Ford of Broad river. He received three balls in the battle. and was paroled to his home.

APPENDIX.

Diary of Lieut. Anthony Allaire,

OF FERGUSON'S CORPS.

MEMORANDUM OF OCCURRENCES DURING THE CAMPAIGN OF 1780.

Sunday, March 5th. The following corps marched from Savannah, viz.: Light Infantry, commanded by Maj. Graham; American Volunteers, Lieut. Col. Ferguson; New York Volunteers, Lieut. Col. Turnbull; North Carolinians, Lieut. Col. Hamilton; South Carolinians, Col. Innes; Dismounted Legion, Maj. Cochrane; one company of Georgia Dragoons, Capt. Campbell; and the First Battalion of the Seventy-first regiment, Maj. McArthur—in number about fifteen hundred.

We marched from Savannah at six o'clock in the morning; arrived at Cherokee Hill, nine miles from Savannah, at twelve o'clock, and encamped to refresh ourselves. At three o'clock in the afternoon got in motion, and marched to Abercorn, eight miles from Cherokee Hill; here we encamped and lay all night. Disagreeable, rainy weather.

Monday, 6th. At eight o'clock we got in motion, and marched to Ebenezer, a village situated on Savannah river, eight miles above Abercorn. It contains about twenty houses and a church. The inhabitants are high Dutch. It is garrisoned by our troops; there are four redoubts, but no cannon in any of them.

Tuesday, 7th. Remained at Ebenezer. Pleasant morning, showery evening and very warm. Spent part of the evening with two Indian Captains, John and James; smoked tobacco and drank grog with those two devils incarnate.

Wednesday, 8th. Still remained at Ebenezer. Orders to draw two days' provisions, and be ready to march at reveille beating. Several men taken suddenly ill with pain and swelling of the extremities, occasioned by a weed that poisons where it touches the naked skin, when the dew is on it.

484

Thursday, 9th. The army got in motion ; passed a causeway three-quarters of a mile in length, overflowed with water from two to three feet deep. We marched to a plantation ten miles from Ebenezer, called the Two Sisters, situated on Savannah river. It was formerly a public ferry ; but at present nobody lives at it. The houses are destroyed.

Friday, 10th. The American Volunteers and British Legion marched three miles up the Augusta road to Tuckasse-King. Here we encamped, and took breakfast at ten o'clock in the morning. A Rebel Lieut. Johnson with twenty men surrounded a poor man's house here this morning. They heard we were in motion, but not being certain of it, they came to find out the truth. They did no damage to the family ; neither did they tarry long, being informed that we were in possession of the Two Sisters, they thought it proper for the brothers to take themselves off. This is the first Rebel party we have heard of. At three o'clock in the afternoon received orders to take the ground we left in the morning, where I and part of the detachment lay all night. One division crossed the river—the others to follow as expeditiously as possible.

Saturday, 11th. Crossed the Savannah river ; such a fresh that the boats were brought through woods a mile and a half ; the water was from four to ten feet deep, where in a dry time we might have marched on dry ground. The horses were swum over the river—the current sets down very rapid.

South Carolina, Sunday, 12th. Lay encamped a quarter of a mile from the river in the field where Gen. Moultrie was encamped last summer when our troops were retreating from Charleston. A foraging party of the Dragoons fell in with some Rebel Light Horse ; and Mr. Campbell of the Georgia Dragoons received a slight wound.

Monday, 13th. The American Volunteers and British Legion were ordered forward twenty-six miles, to secure the passes of Bee creek, Coosawhatchie and Tullyfinny Bridge, which we effected. This day passed Turkey Hill, a pleasant country seat belonging to one Mr. Middleton. We took up our ground at dusk, at Coosawhatchie Bridge, where the Rebels opposed our troops last May and got defeated. A cool, pleasant day for marching.

Tuesday, 14th. Found several horses, a quantity of furniture, Continental stores and ammunition, hid in a swamp by one John Stafford, a sort of Rebel commissary who lives at Coosawhatchie, and is, by the by, a cursed fool, which alone prevents his being a d——d rogue. About five o'clock in the afternoon we crossed Tullyfinny Bridge, and proceeded about six miles to Mr. McPherson's. Fifty of the militia on horseback had just left this plantation and gone to John McPherson's. A small party of ours pursued them, but could not come up with them, Maj. Cochrane with the Legion were in pursuit of another party of Rebels on another road ; but being mis-piloted, he arrived just before break of day in front of our picket. He immediately conjectured we were the party he had been in pursuit of all night. He halted and made a position with an intent to attack as soon as it began to be clearly light; but the alertness of our sentinels obliged them to come on sooner than they intended. He immediately, on their firing, rushed on the picket; they gave the alarm, but were driven to the house, where our men ready for the attack, expecting it was Rebels, a smart skirmish ensued. The sad mistake was soon discovered, but not before two brave soldiers of the American Volunteers, and one of the Legion were killed, and several on both sides badly wounded. Col. Ferguson got wounded in the arm by a bayonet, Lieut. McPherson, of the Legion, in the arm and hand.

Wednesday, 15th. Still remained at McPherson's plantation; foraging parties get everything necessary for the army.

Thursday, 16th. Remained at McPherson's plantation, living on the fat of the land, the soldiers every side of us roasting turkeys, fowls, pigs, etc., every night in great plenty; this Mr. McPherson being a great Rebel, and a man of vast property, at present in Charlestown. About thirty Rebels showed themselves this morning, a mile and a half in front of us. A party went out in pursuit of them; but returned without effecting anything—the jockeys being on horseback easily made off.

Friday. Still at McPherson's. Three militia men were brought in prisoners by a scouting party of the American Volunteers, and a number of horses. Received orders to march to-morrow morning.

Saturday, 18th. Marched from McPherson's plantation to Saltketcher, a Rebel party consisting of eighty mititia, commanded by a Maj. Ladson, placed themselves on the north side of the river to oppose our crossing. They were amused by a company of the Legion returning their fire across the river at the place where the bridge formerly was, whilst the Light Infantry and remainder of the Legion crossed the river below, and came in the rear of them before they were aware of it. Here the bayonet was introduced so effectually that a Capt. Mills, and sixteen privates of the Rebels, could not exist any longer, and of course gave up the cause. Four were badly wounded, and one taken prisoner that luckily escaped the bayonet. Maj. Graham, of the Light Infantry, and Maj. Wright, of the Georgia Loyalists, slightly wounded. The former continued to command his battalion, and the latter continued his march. Two privates of the Light Infantry were also slightly wounded. We remained all night at Ogilvies' plantation, on the side of the river called Indian land. This day's march was very tedious—a disagreeable, rainy, cold day, and through a swamp where the water was from two to three feet deep.

Sunday, 19th. Passed Saltketcher river—where the bridge formerly stood, but has been destroyed since the rebellion—in boats, and swam the horses. The causeway on both sides of the river is overflowed with water from two to three feet deep, at the ferry house, about a quarter of a mile from the river. Dr. Johnson dressed the wounds of Maj. Wright and the four Rebels that were bayoneted yesterday. Marched one mile and a half to a tavern kept by Mr. Gibson, who is at present prisoner in Charleston, for not taking up arms when his country so loudly calls for assistance.

Monday, 20th. The army got in motion, marching about two miles. Received orders to halt, the rear guard being fired on ; it proved to be the York Volunteers, getting the boats on the carriages at the river, were fired on by a skulking party of rascals on the other side of the stream. Three poor lads of the York Volunteers were killed. What damage was done to the Rebels we are not certain. Detained by this and repairing of bridges on the road, we only marched seven miles this day. Took up our ground at a place called Godfrey's savannah.

Tuesday, 21st. The army got in motion. Marched to Fish Pond river. Here we were detained to repair the bridge till evening. Before we crossed we moved on about three miles, through a swamp, over an exceeding bad causeway. This day Col. Tarleton, with his dragoons, joined us from Beaufort, where he had been to get horses—his being all lost on the passage from New York. We took up our ground about ten o'clock at night, and remained till ten o'clock next morning.

Wednesday, 22d. The army got in motion at ten in the morning, and marched as far as Horse Shoe, where we again were detained to repair the bridge. After crossing, continued our march to Jacksonsburgh, a village containing about sixty houses, situated on Pon Pon, or Edisto river. The most of the houses are very good ; the people tolerable well to live ; some large store houses for rice, from which they convey it by water to Charleston market. In short, it is a pleasant little place, and well situated for trade, but the inhabitants are all Rebels—not a man remaining in the town, except two, one of whom was so sick he could not get out of bed, and the other a doctor, who had the name of a friend to Government. The women were treated very tenderly, and with the utmost civility, notwithstanding their husbands were out in arms against us.

Thursday, 23d. All the army, except the Seventy-first regiment, and greatest part of the baggage, crossed the river in boats and flats, the bridge being destroyed. Col. Tarleton came up with a party of Rebel militia dragoons, soon after crossing the river at Gov. Bee's plantation. He killed ten, and took four prisoners. Gov. Bee was formerly Lieut. Gov. under His Majesty, is now one of the members of Congress, and Lieut. Gov. of South Carolina.

Friday, 24th. The remainder of the baggage and Seventy-first regiment passed Pon Pon river. The army got in motion about one o'clock in the afternoon, and marched about seven miles, where we halted all night. A flag of truce, consisting of a Capt. Saunders, Capt. Wilkinson, one private and a servant, came in at the rear of the army. Just as we halted they were severely reprimanded by Gen. Paterson for their unmilitary conduct. He told them that they were ignorant of the profession they followed ; and in consequence of their behavior he must detain them all night, and, as to their request, it would not be granted, which was likewise very unmilitary, it being to speak with the prisoners and give them some necessaries. The gentry of the flag were led blind-fold to their lodging. This day Col. Ferguson got the rear guard in order to do his King and country justice, by protecting friends, and widows, and destroying Rebel property ; also to collect live stock for the use of the army, all of which we effect as we go, by destroying furniture, breaking windows, etc., taking all their horned cattle, horses, mules, sheep, fowls, etc., and their negroes to drive them. We had a disagreeable night—very heavy shower, with a great deal of heavy thunder and lightning.

Saturday, 25th. The army got in motion at reveille beating, and marched to Stono, where was formerly a bridge, called Wallace's Bridge. We took up our ground about three o'clock in the afternoon, where we remained all night. Light Infantry and part of the Dragoons went over the river.

Sunday, 26th. Consumed the whole day in passing the baggage and live stock over the river, the bridge that formerly stood here being destroyed, and the one just made very bad. We took up our ground as soon as we got over, on a neck of land that runs down between Stono and Rantowle's, only one mile between the two rivers. This day the Commander-in-chief came to us from James Island, which is six miles distant.

Monday, 27th. Two companies of Light Infantry, American Volunteers, and one company of Dragoons, crossed at Rantowle's in scows; the rest of the army crossed yesterday. Col. Hamilton, of the North Carolinians, and Dr. Smith, of the Hospital, proceeding about a mile in front of the army, to Gov. Rutledge's house, were immediately surrounded by three hundred Continental Light Horse, and they consequently made prisoners. The British Dragoons fell in with them soon after, and had a skirmish; the Rebels soon gave way, and showed them the road, as is customary for them to do. Qr. Master Sergeant McIntosh, of the Georgia Dragoons, badly wounded in the face by a broadsword. Several Dragoons of the Legion were wounded. How many of the Rebels got hurt we can't learn; but they did not keep up the combat long enough for many to receive damage. This morning, Capt. Saunders, that came in with the flag on the 24th, was sent out; his attendant, Capt. Wilkinson, not being mentioned in the body of the flag, is detained as a prisoner of war. We took up our ground on Gov. Rutledge's plantation, about one mile from his house, where we remained all night.

Tuesday, 28th. The army got in motion about nine o'clock in the morning, and marched to Ashley Ferry, where we met the British and Hessians, Grenadiers, Light Infantry and Yagers, under command of Sir H. Clinton. We continued our march down the river about six miles to Lining's plantation; it is situated on Ashley river, nearly opposite Charlestown, and commands an extensive view towards the sea.

Wednesday, 29th. Sir Henry Clinton, with the British and Hessians, Grenadiers, Light Infantry and Yagers, passed over Ashley river to Charleston Neck, early in the morning. Spent the day in viewing Charleston and found it not a little like New York; for Ashley and Cooper rivers form a bay exactly like East and North river at New York.

Thursday, 30th. Incessant firing of small arms on the neck; cannon at short intervals. This firing was at the Commander-in-chief and his family reconnoitring. He forbid the British returning the fire. Lord Cathness, standing by the side of Gen. Clinton, was shot through the body by a musket ball; one Yager killed.

Friday, 31st. Engineers' tools, etc., carried over from Lining's Landing, and broke ground without molestation, under direction of Maj. Moncrieff. Rode two miles to see two redoubts, one of which has six, and the other two thirty-two pounders in them, at the mouth of Wapoo-Cut, a river that runs from Stono to Ashley river, and separates from the main land what is called James Island. Those two redoubts are exactly opposite Charleston.

Saturday, April 1st. Some cannon and mortars moved over Ashley river from Lining's Landing.

Sunday, 2d. Rode down to view our fleet that lay at Stono.

Monday, 3d. Marched to Ashley Ferry to cover the Dragoons of the Legion whilst crossing the river. Marched from this up the river to Henry Middleton's plantation; passed several famous country seats, one called Drayton's Hall, belonging to William Henry Drayton, deceased, who was a member of Congress, and died at Philadelphia. Constant firing at our works from the Rebels all day.

Tuesday, 4th. Constant cannonade from the Rebels, both from their batteries and shipping; one of their ships, endeavoring to move up Cooper river, was fired on from our works, and drove back.

Wednesday, 5th. Constant cannonade from the Rebels at our works on the Neck, in the evening. Our batteries at the mouth of Wapoo-Cut opened, and kept up a warm fire for a few minutes, then the firing ceased on both sides.

Thursday, 6th. Cannonade from the Rebels all day by intervals. In the evening our batteries opened on the Neck, and at Wapoo-Cut fired all night by intervals.

Friday, 7th. Cannonade at intervals as usual,

Saturday, 8th. But little firing from the Rebels. Rainy, disagreeable morning. The Rebels were reinforced with thirteen hundred men last night, commanded by a Gen. Scott. They fired a *feu de joie*, and rang all the bells in town on the occasion. About four o'clock this afternoon the fleet hove in sight, coming up under full sail with a fresh breeze at south west, and passed Fort Moultrie—the Rebel fort that they boasted of on Sullivan's Island, which no fleet could ever pass. They were but a few minutes passing. What damage is sustained we have not yet learned. The Richmond lost her fore top-mast; a cutter lay opposite the fort all the time the fleet was passing, with a flag hoisted to point out the channel. A heavy cannonade from the Rebels' batteries, which the shipping returned as they passed with a spirit becoming Britons.

Sunday, 9th. Admiral Arbuthnot came on shore, and went over to Head-quarters on the Neck. By him we were informed that there were only seven men killed, and fifteen wounded, in passing Sullivan's Island. The shipping damage was so trifling that 'twas not worth mentioning.

Monday, 10th. Nothing extraordinary. Cannonade from our batteries during the night to cover the working parties.

Tuesday, 11th. Col. Ferguson came from Head-quarters. Informs us that the town was summoned to surrender to his Britannic Majesty. Answer was returned, that they thought it necessary as well as their duty to defend it to the last extremity, which they meant to do.

Wednesday, 12th. Received orders to march. The North Carolinians were ordered to join Col. Ferguson. We left Lining's plantation about seven o'clock in the evening, and marched to Bacon's Bridge, twenty-two miles, where we arrived at five o'clock on Thursday morning; very much fatigued. We halted to refresh till seven. Cool weather.

Thursday, 13th. Got in motion at seven o'clock in the morning. Marched through a small village called Dorchester. It contains about forty houses and a church. Continued our march to Middleton's plantation at Goose creek, about fifteen miles from Bacon's Bridge, and ten from Dorchester. Here we met the Legion about one o'clock in the afternoon, and halted till ten at night. Then, in company with them, got in motion and marched eighteen miles to Monk's Corner, being informed that Col. Washington's, Pulaski's, Bland's, and Horry's Light Horse lay here. We arrived just as day began to appear on Friday morning, and found the above enemy here, in number about four hundred, including some militia that arrived the day before, commanded by Gen. Huger. Luckily for them, they were under marching orders, which made them more alert, when the alarm was given, than usual, which alone prevented their being all taken completely by surprise. They made off with great expedition. We pursued, overtook and killed

Pulaski's Major Vernier, wounded a French Lieut. Beaulait,* and one other officer; about sixty privates were taken, fifteen or twenty of whom were wounded. We had but one man wounded, and he very slightly. We took thirty wagons, with four horses in each. A number of very fine horses that belonged to their troops were likewise taken, and converted to British Light horses. Col. Washington and all their officers made but a narrow escape; their baggage, letters, and some of their commissions were taken.

Friday, 14th. Remained at Monk's Corner, collecting the stores, etc. About seven o'clock at night, accidentally a store house caught fire, in which were two casks of powder; was very much alarmed by the explosion, and all got under arms. This confusion was scarcely over when three ladies came to our camp in great distress : Lady Colleton, Miss Betsy Giles, and Miss Jean Russell. They had been most shockingly abused by a plundering villain. Lady Colleton badly cut in the hand by a broadsword, and bruised very much. After my friend, Dr. Johnson, dressed her hand, he, with an officer and twelve men, went to the plantation, about one mile from camp, to protect Mrs. Fayssoux, whom this infamous villain had likewise abused in the same manner. There he found a most accomplished, amiable lady in the greatest distress imaginable. After he took a little blood from her she was more composed, and next morning come to camp to testify against the cursed villain that abused them in this horrid manner. He was secured and sent to Head-quarters for trial.

Saturday, 15th. The army got in motion about twelve o'clock. My friend, Dr Johnson, and myself had the happiness of escorting the ladies to their plantation. Before we got there we were met by a servant informing us that there were more plunderers in the house. This news so shocked Lady Colleton and Mrs. Fayssoux, who were some distance before us, and the young ladies in à carriage, that I am not able to describe their melancholy situation, which was truly deplorable. After their fright was a little over we passed on to their house ; but the ladies fearing to stay alone, Lady Colleton and Mrs. Fayssoux got into the carriage, Miss Giles behind me, and Miss Russell on a horse, which I led for fear he should make off with my fair one ; they passed on with us four miles to a plantation called Mulberry Broughton, and here we bid adieu to our fair companions with great regret, they thinking themselves out of danger of any insults. We this day countermarched to the twenty-three mile house, and halted all night.

Sunday, 16th. Got in motion about three o'clock in the morning,

---

* Beaulait has been very unfortunate since in America. He received seven wounds by a broadsword, in a charge of Campbell's Light Horse, when Charlestown was besieged by Gen. Provost, and two at Monk's Corner, which amounts to nine, four or five of them in the face.—A. A.

and marched to Strawberry Ferry, a branch of Cooper river. Took up the day in passing the army and baggage over the stream. After crossing, marched four miles to Bono Ferry, another branch of Cooper river, where we came up with the baggage of the Thirty-third and Sixty-fourth Regiments, and of the Legion. Here we lay all night, as it took up the night to get this baggage over the river. A Captain's guard from our detachment was sent over to take charge of a store house full of household furniture, brought out of town and deposited at a Maj. Butler's for safety—the store was full of very rich furniture of all kinds.

Monday, 17th. Crossed Bono Ferry and passed on to Miller's Bridge, over a branch of Wando river, where we took up our ground about nine o'clock in the evening. This day passed St. Thomas' church, where we met the Thirty-third regiment.

Tuesday, 18th. Began to fortify at the Bridge, and make a block house in order to keep post here with a few men.

Wednesday, 19th. Maj. Ferguson, with fifty of the American Volunteers, and part of the North Carolinians, moved on to join the Thirty-third and Sixty-fourth regiments, and the British Legion, which had gone forward to attack a Rebel post at Lempriere's Point. The British were coming back; they had marched up to the fort, but found it so strong that it was imprudent to storm it with so few men.

Thursday, 20th. Remained at Miller's Bridge, finishing the block house. Col. Tarleton surprised and took nine sloops with goods, stores, etc., and twenty pieces of cannon.

Friday, 21st. Capt. Ryerson, with forty American Volunteers, a subaltern, and twenty of the Thirty-third, and a subaltern, and twenty of the Sixty-fourth regiments, remained at Miller's Bridge to defend and keep the pass. The remainder of the Thirty-third and Sixty-fourth regiments, American Volunteers, and British Legion, counter-marched twelve miles and took up our ground at St. Thomas' church.

Saturday, 22d. Took possession of the parish house; took up and was under the disagreeable neccessity of detaining a lady of the town, on suspicion of her being a spy.

January 23d. Moved from the house into the woods for the convenience of shade—very warm weather.

Monday, 24th. Lord Cornwallis joined us and took command. About ten o'clock in the evening there was the most tremendous cannonade I ever heard, and an incessant fire of musketry. The Rebels sallied out and took eight of the Light Infantry prisoners, upon which the whole line got under arms; some in their hurry getting out without putting on their coats, were taken by the others for Rebels, and fired on, which unluckily occasioned warm work for a few minutes. Sixty odd of ours got killed and wounded by our own men. The Rebels were repulsed, and they finding their muskets rather an incumbrance threw thirty odd of them away.

Tuesday, 25th. About eight o'clock in the morning got in motion ; were joined by the Twenty-third regiment and Volunteers of Ireland. We proceeded on, passed over Miller's Bridge and Waputa Bridge, took possession of Waputa meeting house, about seven o'clock in the evening, where we halted till two in the morning.

Wednesday, 26th. At two o'clock in the morning got in motion, and marched seventeen miles to Mount Pleasant, opposite Charleston, where we took possession of the ground, on which the Rebels had one eighteen pounder. Here is a ferry from this to a town called Hibban's Ferry ; there are very good barracks here if finished, that were begun before the rebellion. Sullivan's Island is about a half a mile distant from the Point. There is a bridge from the Point to the Island with four arches. The barracks were used for a hospital, in which we took some invalids and a doctor. About six miles from the Point stands Christ Church. This night I might properly sing, "Content with our hard fate, my boys," on the cold ground where I lay—wrapt up in my great coat, with my saddle for a pillow. A blustering cold night.

Thursday, 27th. Got in motion about one o'clock in the morning, and countermarched to Waputa meeting house. Cold north-east wind.

Friday, 28th. Fortified the small house by the side of the meeting house, at ten o'clock at night. Intelligence being received that the Rebels had left the fort at Lempriere's Point, and gone to Charleston, we got in motion and marched down to discover the fact. We arrived about four in the morning, and found the fort occupied by the Navy, a Lieutenant of the Navy, commanding officer. The Rebels were gone to Charleston.

Saturday, 29th. Countermarched to our old grounds at the meeting house. Pleasant weather.

Sunday, 30th. Got in motion at three o'clock in the morning, in company with the York Volunteers, and marched to Lempriere's Point to take post there. We got to our ground about seven o'clock in the evening, where we found four eighteen, two four pounders, and five swivels, that the Rebels left in their fort. A very disagreeable post it is, being nothing but a bank of sand, where, in a windy day, you must keep your eyes shut or have them filled with sand. Here used to be a ferry called Lempriere's Ferry.

Monday, May 1st. Bathed in Wando river.

Tuesday, 2d. Began to fortify Lempriere's Point. Maj. Ferguson, with a detachment of American Volunteers, marched down to Mount Pleasant, stormed and took possession of a little redoubt, located partly on the main, and partly on the bridge that leads to Fort Moultrie. This cuts off the communication from Sullivan's Island, and keeps them on their proper allowance. The Rebels ran off from the redoubt, though it was very strongly situated, after they fired about a dozen shot.

Wednesday, 3d. Still fortifying Lempriere's Point. In the evening began a cannonade on the neck, which continued very heavy all night—an incessant firing of musketry, the cannon chiefly from the Rebels, small arms from us. This night took their hospital ship that lay opposite the town.

Thursday, 4th. Continued fortifying the Point. Rode from Lempriere's Point to Mount Pleasant; dined with Capt. Ord, of the Navy. After dinner rode to Hurdle's [Haddrell's?] Point to view the redoubt which Col. Ferguson stormed the second of May, with only sixty men, and never was more surprised in my life, for twenty men like the American Volunteers would have defied all Washington's Army.

Friday, 5th. Very windy—in danger of losing one's eyes by the blowing of sand. Cold blustering night.

Saturday, 6th. Very disagreeable, windy day. Still at Lempriere's. News just received from Lord Cornwallis, that Lieut. Nash and eleven dragoons that were patrolling, were taken by Washington and Horry's Light Horse near Santee river. Col. Tarleton was immediately ordered to pursue them. He overtook them at the river ; charged and killed a number, and took a Major and thirty privates. The patrolling party that had been taken were in a boat, rowing across the river. Upon their seeing Col. Tarleton, they immediately seized the guard, threw them overboard, rowed themselves back and joined their regiment again. Col. Washington and Horry took to the river and swam across it.

Sunday, 7th. Orders to get ready to march with two days' provision, at a minute's notice. Maj. Ferguson had obtained permission to attack Fort Moultrie. He rode forward with four dragoons to reconnoitre. We were to remain at our post till we got orders for marching. The first news we heard was the fort was in possession of the British ; the Rebels had surrendered themselves prisoners of war. Capitulation was as follows : Capt. Hudson of the Navy summoned the fort on Friday, and received for answer: " Tol, lol, de rol, lol: Fort Moultrie will be defended to the last extremity." On Saturday he sent another flag, and demanded a surrender, acquainting Col. Scott that the Lieutenant with the flag would wait a quarter of an hour for an answer. If the fort was not given up, he would immediately storm it, and put all the garrison to the sword. At this Col. Scott changed the tune of his song, begging that there might be a cessation of arms, that the fort would be given up on the following conditions : that the officers both Continental and militia, should march out with the honors of war, and be allowed to wear their side arms; the officers and soldiers of the militia have paroles to go to their respective homes, and remain peaceably till exchanged ; and the continental soldiers to be treated tenderly. Granted by Capt. Hudson. About eight o'clock Sunday morning, Colonel Scott with his men, about one hundred and twenty, marched out of the fort, piled their arms, Capt. Hudson marched in, took possession of Fort Moultrie, the key to Charleston harbor; which puts it in our power to keep out any forcing enemy that would wish to give the Rebels any assistance. Taken in the fort, fifty barrels of powder, forty-four pieces of cannon, one brass ten inch mortar, three thousand cannon cartridges, five hundred ten inch shells, forty thousand musket cartridges, three month's salt provision, a lot of rice, forty head black cattle, sixty sheep, twenty goats, forty fat hogs, six wagons, two stand of colors, an amazing quantity of lunt;* and, in short, so many other articles which are

* Match-cord for firing cannon.

necessary in a fort that it would take me a week to set them down.

Monday, 8th. Six o'clock in the morning, Sir Henry Clinton sent in a flag, and demanded the surrender of Charleston. General Lincoln requested cessation of hostilities till eight o'clock—from eight to twelve; and the truce continued until four o'clock Tuesday evening when Sir Henry Clinton receiving a very insolent request, sent in word that he plainly saw that Gen. Lincoln did not mean to give up the town; that the firing should commence at eight o'clock in the evening, at which time began a most tremendous cannonade, throwing of carcases and shells into the town, and an incessant fire of musketry all night.

Wednesday, 10th. Firing still continued all day, and very brisk all night.

Thursday, 11th. The town set on fire by a carcase, which burnt several houses. The Rebels sent out a flag soon after; our firing continued without taking notice of their flag. They showed the second flag, which we accepted. It was begging the terms that had been offered the last truce. Sir Henry Clinton answered them the firing should cease until he could send and consult Admiral Arbuthnot. The terms were granted.

Friday, 12th. The gates were opened, Gen. Leslie at the head of the British Grenadiers, Seventh, Sixty-third and Sixty-fourth regiments, and Hessian Grenadiers marched in, and took possession of Charleston, and soon leveled the thirteen stripes with the dust, and displayed the British standard on their ramparts. Still at Lempriere's.

Saturday, 13th. Remained at Lempriere's.

Sunday, 14th. Went to Charleston to view their strong works. Saw the poor Rebel dogs very much chagrined at not being allowed to wear their side arms.

Monday, 15th. Magazine blew up—set the town on fire—burnt several houses. Capt. Collins and Lieut. Gordon, of the artillery, Lieut. M'Leod of the Forty-second regiment, and about thirty privates, perished by the explosion. In what way the accident happened is not certain; 'tis supposed by throwing the captured arms into the magazine, one went off, and set fire to the powder.

Tuesday, 16th. The American Volunteers relieved the Navy, and took command of Fort Moultrie.

Wednesday, 17th. Spent the day in writing letters for New York. Nothing new.

Thursday, 18th, to Sunday, 21st. Lay at Fort Moultrie. Nothing extra.

Monday, 22d. Received orders for marching—went to Charleston.

Tuesday, 23d. About three o'clock in the afternoon returned in a six-oared boat, and had the pleasing view of sixty or seventy large ships coming into the harbor.

Wednesday, 24th. Lay at Fort Moultrie.

Thursday, 25th. The detachment was relieved by British and Hessian Grenadiers. The American Volunteers marched up to Mount Pleasant, and crossed over to Charleston. Marched through the town, and took up their ground just in front of the lines. The horses and baggage with myself crossed from Lempriere's Point to the Ship Yard, which is about two miles from the town.

Friday, 26th. The following corps got in motion about three o'clock in the morning, under the command of Col. Balfour, of the Twenty-third regiment, viz—Light Infantry, commanded by Maj. Graham, three companies of the Seventh by Capt. Peacock, American Volunteers by Maj. Ferguson, and the Prince of Wales American Volunteers by Lieut.-Col. Patterson—in number about six hundred. Marched out to the Ten Mile House, and halted. Made bough houses to cover the men from the heat of the sun. Heavy thunder shower.

Saturday, 27th. Marched at five o'clock in the morning; passed through a piece of low ground covered with magnolias in full bloom, which emitted a most delicious odor. We took up our ground at a plantation about two miles from the Twenty-Three Mile House.

Sunday, 28th. Got in motion at two o'clock in the morning. Marched to Monk's Corner and halted. Dr. Johnson and myself went and dined with Lady Colleton, Miss Russell and Miss Giles, the ladies we protected in their distress when we were here the fourteenth of April.

Monday, 29th. Lay encamped in a wood at Monk's Corner. Spent an agreeable afternoon at Lady Colleton's, with Miss Russell and Miss Giles.

Tuesday, 30th. Got in motion at five o'clock in the morning, and marched to Gen. Moultrie's plantation, at a place called Prussia, where we halted.

Wednesday, 31st. Got in motion at half past four in the morning; marched to Greenland swamp, and halted.

Thursday, June 1st. Got in motion at five o'clock in the morning, and marched to Nelson's Ferry, Santee river. By express were informed that Col. Tarleton, Monday, the 29th, fell in with a body of Rebels.

[Buford's corps] forty miles above Camden. He summoned them to surrender—received an insolent answer, charged them, killed one Lieutenant-Colonel, three Captains, eight Subalterns, one Adjutant, one Quarter-Master, and ninety-nine Sergeants and rank and file. Wounded three Captains, five Subalterns, and one hundred and forty-two rank and file. Made prisoners two Captains, one Subaltern, fifty rank and file. Total killed, wounded and taken prisoners, one Lieutenant-Colonel, eight Captains, fourteen Subalterns, one Adjutant, one Quarter-Master, and two hundred and ninety-one Sergeants, rank and file; three stand of colors taken, two brass six-pounders, two howitzers, two wagons with ammunition, one artillery forge wagon, fifty-five barrels powder, twenty-six wagons loaded with clothing, camp equipage, musket-cartridges, cartridge-boxes, flints, etc., etc. Killed of the Legion, Lieut. McDonald and Ensign Campbell, serving with the cavalry, two privates of the cavalry, and one of the Light Infantry. Total, two Subalterns, and three rank and file. Wounded, Lieut. Patterson, seven dragoons, making eight rank and file of the cavalry, and three of the infantry. Total wounded, one Subaltern, and eleven rank and file.

Friday, 2d. Lay encamped in a pleasant field near Nelson's Ferry. Ordered to be in readiness to march at two o'clock in the morning.

Saturday, 3d. Got in motion two o'clock in the morning. Marched to Campbell's plantation, where we halted in the woods for the convenience of shade. This place is seventy-seven miles from Charleston.

Sunday, 4th. Lay in the woods at Campbell's plantation. Some prize wine shared to the different corps; very convenient time to drink his Majesty's health.

Monday, 5th. Got in motion at two o'clock in the morning, and marched to Cave Hall, St. Matthew's parish. Just below our camp was a remarkably large cave, about an hundred feet deep. There is a room formed by a rock sixty feet long, and forty wide, with famous grand arches formed by nature. Through the middle runs a beautiful stream of water, which heads in a fountain at the farther end of the cave. This day twenty militia men came in, and brought the new-fangled Governor of Georgia prisoner. He was sent to Charleston. He had taken protection from Lord Cornwallis as a private man.

Tuesday, 6th. Got in motion at three o'clock in the morning, and marched thirteeen miles to Col. Thomson's, and halted on the march. Started two bucks; they ran in amongst the men. One of them got caught. The militia were in from all quarters.

Wednesday, 7th. Lay encamped at Col. Thomson's plantation; a field in our rear covered with sensitive plant and passion flower.

Thursday, 8th. Still at Thomson's plantation. A thunder shower every afternoon.

Friday, 9th. Encamped still at Thomson's plantation; wrote a letter to Miss ——.

32

Saturday, 10th. Got in motion and left Thomson's at twelve o'clock at night, and marched eighteen miles to Beaver creek, where we halted. Maj. Graham, and two flank companies of the Prince of Wales American Volunteers, remained at Thomson's. This day a company of militia came in with their arms. A Henry Meholm, an old man eighty-one years of age, this day met us; he had left home with an intention to go to Charleston, and had walked upwards of an hundred miles when he met us. His errand was to get some kind of assistance. He had been plundered by the Rebels, and stripped of everything. What is remarkable, this old gentleman left at home a child between two and three years old.

Sunday, 11th. Got in motion at five o'clock in the morning, and marched five miles and halted.

Monday, 12th. Got in motion at two o'clock in the morning, and marched fourteen miles to Congaree Stores. This day passed a plantation where were about four hundred acres of Indian corn growing— the property of one man.

Tuesday, 13th. Lay at Congaree Stores. Many good friends to Government have suffered much by the Rebels.

Wednesday, 14th. Lay at Congaree Stores. Capt. Peacock and the three companies of Royal Fusileers under his command, remain here; Col. Patterson and his battalion to go to Camden.

Thursday, 15th. Got in motion at twelve o'clock at night, and marched twelve miles to Saluda Ferry; crossed the river and halted.

Friday, 16th. Got in motion at half after four o'clock in the morning, and marched seven miles to the blacksmith's, and halted.

Saturday, 17th. Lay still in the field at the blacksmith's, or High Hill creek.

Sunday, 18th. Got in motion at two o'clock in the morning, and marched fourteen miles to a Capt. Wright's, of Col. Innes' regiment.

Monday, 19th. Got in motion at four o'clock in the morning, and marched to Cook's place, fourteen miles. This Cook is a Rebel Justice and Captain—a great persecutor of friends to Government. He is ordered down to John's Island, a place pointed out for the reception of such infamous villains.

Tuesday, 20th. Got in motion and marched to Davenport's, fourteen miles. He was formerly Captain of militia under Government. He has the name of a Tory from his neighbors; but many of his actions were doubtful.

Wednesday, 21st. Lay encamped at Davenport's, Little river.

Thursday, 22d. Got in motion at twelve, and marched ten miles to the fording place, Saluda river; crossed the men and baggage in a scow, and forded the horses; continued our march six miles to Ninety Six, where we halted. It is a village or country town—contains about twelve dwelling houses, a court-house and a jail, in which are confined about forty Rebels, brought in prisoners by the friends to Government, who have just now got the opportunity, and gladly embrace it, many of them having been obliged before this to hide in swamps to keep from prison themselves. Ninety Six is situated on an eminence, the land cleared for a mile around it, in a flourishing part of the country, supplied with very good water, enjoys a free, open air, and is esteemed a healthy place. Here were condemned seventy-five friends to Government at one court; five were executed—the others got reprieved.

Friday, 23d. Lay in the field at Ninety Six. Some friends came in, four were wounded. The militia had embodied at Tuckasegie, on the South Fork of Catawba river—were attacked by a party of Rebels, under command of Gen. Rutherford. The miltia were scant of ammunition, which obliged them to retreat. They were obliged to swim the river at a mill dam. The Rebels fired on them and killed thirty.* Col. Ferguson, with forty American Volunteers, pushed with all speed in pursuit of the Rebels. It is seventy miles distance from Ninety Six. The militia are flocking to him from all parts of the country.

Saturday, 24th. Took quarters in town, opposite the jail, where I have the constant view of the Rebels peeping through the grates, which affords some satisfaction to see them suffer for their folly. Some of them are magistrates; one the executioner of the five that were hanged here some time in April, 1779.

Sunday, 25th, to Tuesday, 27th. Spent in cleaning, parade, and in the town.

Thursday, 29th, and Friday, 30th. Still at Ninety Six. Nothing extra.

Saturday, July 1st. Took a ride into the country for exercise.

Sunday, 2d, to Saturday, 8th. Still at Ninety Six.

Sunday, 9th. The American Volunteers moved from Ninety Six at seven o'clock in the evening, under the command of Captain DePeyster, and marched seven miles to Island Ford, of Saluda river, on our way to meet a party of Rebels that were making approaches towards our lines. Dr. Johnson and I being late before we left our old quarters, without any guide, got out of the road; found our mistake at a mill, three miles from the road we ought to have taken. It turned out to be no great loss, as we have supplied ourselves with a grist of corn for our horses. We came up to the detachment at one o'clock in the morning. Our baggage had not arrived, which put us to the necessity of going to a house to lodge. We found two women, and spent the night, though not to our satisfaction. It afforded some merry scenes with those two modest country women.

---

*Col. Moore's defeat at Ramsour's Mill, June 20th.

Monday, 10th. Got in motion at five o'clock in the morning; crossed Saluda in a flat; marched nine miles to a Rebel Col. Williams' plantation, where we halted. Mrs. Williams and the children were at home, and were treated with the utmost civility. Col. Williams is with the Rebels, and is a very violent, persecuting scoundrel.

Tuesday, 11th. Got in motion at five o'clock in the morning, and marched eight miles to Indian creek, and halted during the heat of the day at one Ryan's, who is a good friend, and suffered much for his loyalty. Got in motion at six o'clock in the evening, and marched eleven miles to Duncan's creek, where we halted at a Widow Brown's.

Wednesday, 12th. Got in motion at five o'clock in the evening, and forded Duncan's creek and Enoree river. Continued marching to Capt. Frost's, at Padget creek, eight miles from the Widow Brown's. This evening met an express with the disagreeable news of a party of ours consisting of seventeen of the Legion, eighteen York Volunteers, and twenty-five militia being defeated at Col. Bratton's, at Fishing creek.*

Thursday, 13th. Lieut. Hunt of the Legion Cavalry came to our quarters at Capt. Frost's. He was one of the party defeated the twelfth inst. He gave an imperfect account of the affair. Capt. Huck commanded the party consisting of one subaltern and seventeen dragoons of the Legion, three subalterns and eighteen New York Volunteers, twenty-five militia men. They were sent in pursuit of a Rebel party, and arrived at twelve o'clock, Tuesday night, the 11th instant, at Col. Bratton's, at Fishing creek, and were very much fatigued. They thought to rest themselves. Unfortunately a Rebel party commanded by a Col. Lacey came upon them at four o'clock in the morning of the 12th, who were in amongst them, and had possession of every pass before they where apprised of it—except a road leading towards North Carolina, where Captain Huck, with four dragoons, attempted to make off. Huck got shot through the neck, of which he died. Mr. Hunt, with one dragoon, took a foot path leading to a swamp. The militia he could give no account of. We left Capt. Frost's about six o'clock in the evening; forded Tyger river, continued our march twelve miles to Sugar creek. Here we found two hundred militia encamped at Wofford's old field, Fair Forest, under command of Majors Plummer and Gibbs. The Rebels, we hear, are collecting in force at the Catawba Nation and Broad river.

Friday, 14th. Lay encamped at Fair Forest. Every hour news from different parts of the country of Rebel parties doing mischief. Light Infantry of Gen. Browne's corps joined us at twelve o'clock at night.

Saturday, 15th. Went in company with Capt. F. De Peyster, Dr. Johnson, and Lieut. Fletcher, to dine with Col. Fletchall. After dinner went to see his mill, which was a curiosity, having never seen such an one

---

* Capt. Hook or Huck defeated that morning.

before. The water falls fourteen feet perpendicularly down into a tub, fixed with buckets; from this tub runs up a shaft through the stone, and turns, as the cog turns, a double-geared mill. Returning to camp were informed that Capt. Dunlap had been obliged to retreat from Prince's Fort. Capt. Dunlap made an attack upon the Rebels; drove them from their ground, took one prisoner, who informed him that the Rebels were four hundred strong. Upon this information Dunlap thought proper to retreat, as his number was only fourteen American Volunteers and sixty militia. We lost two killed, a sergeant and private wounded, and one prisoner. The loss of the Rebels is uncertain—reports are, twenty or thirty killed. Upon this news arriving, Capt. De Peyster ordered the American Volunteers and militia to get in motion to support Dunlap. Capt. Frederick De Peyster, with one hundred militia men, marched twelve miles to McElwain's creek, where they met Dunlap.

Sunday, 16th. Dunlap with the men under his command marched down to Stephen White's plantation, where the American Volunteers and militia lay.

Monday, 17th. Lay at White's. The militia brought in four prisoners, one lad of fifteen years old, badly wounded in the arms.

Tuesday, 18th. Still at Mitchell's creek. This day Col. Ferguson came to us from Nintey Six; brought news that the Light Infantry were on their march to join us.

Wednesday, 19th. Still at White's plantation, on Mitchell's creek.

Thursday, 20th. Got in motion at five o'clock in the evening, and marched six miles to Fair Forest Ford, where we halted and lay all night.

Friday, 21st. Col. Balfour, with the Light Infantry from Ninety Six, joined us—we still remained at the Ford.

Saturday, 22d. The Light Infantry, American Volunteers, and three hundred militia, got in motion at seven o'clock in the evening; made a forced march of twenty-five miles to Lawson's Fork to surprise a party of Rebels, who, we were informed, lay there. We arrived at James Wood's plantation at six o'clock in the morning; greatly disappointed at finding no Rebels here. We were informed they were at Green river—twenty-five miles farther.

Sunday, 23d. Got in motion at one o'clock in the morning, and countermarched to our old ground, Fair Forest Ford.

Monday, 24th. Very much fatigued; slept all day.

Tuesday, 25th. Col. Balfour with the Light Infantry got in motion at two o'clock in the morning, and marched towards Ninety Six.

Wednesday, 26th. Lay at our old ground, Fair Forest.

Thursday, 27th. Got in motion at nine o'clock in the morning; forded Fair Forest river; marched about three miles and took up our ground in the wood.

Friday, 28th. Got in motion at seven o'clock in the morning, and marched eight miles to Col. Henderson's plantation, Pacolet river. Henderson is prisoner at Charlestown; he has a pretty plantation, with near two hundred acres of Indian corn growing.

Saturday, 29th. Got in motion at eight o'clock in the morning, and marched five miles to Thicketty river and halted; one of the soldiers killed a Continental rattle-snake, with thirteen rattles on.

Sunday, 30th. Got in motion at three o'clock in the morning; countermarched twelve miles to Armstrong's creek, Fair Forest. This day came into camp express from Anderson's fort, a Capt. Cook, aged sixty years, who has buried four wives, and now has his fifth on her last legs.

Monday, 31st. Got in motion at six o'clock in the morning, and marched ten miles to Mitchell's creek, Fair Forest; a very wet, disagreeable day; got thoroughly soaked.

Tuesday, August 1st. Lay at Mitchell's creek. Had intelligence that the Rebels had attacked Col. Turnbull at Rocky Mount, on Sunday the 30th; but could not learn the particulars.

Wednesday, 2d. Got in motion at four o'clock in the morning; marched four miles to Tyger river; forded that stream and continued our march to Capt. Bobo's, and halted. Had intelligence that Col. Turnbull beat off the Rebels; Capt. Hulett got wounded in the head. The Rebels were commanded by Gen. Sumter. He sent in a flag, demanding the post—Rocky Mount. Col. Turnbull sent word that he might come and take it. Sumter endeavored to do so, but was obliged soon to retreat with considerable loss. Col. Turnbull took two prisoners, who had previously been in his camp, drew ammunition, and then joined the Rebels, and were heard to say when firing, "take back your ammunition again." They were both hanged as a reward for their treachery.

Thursday, 3d. Lay at Bobo's; nothing extra.

Friday, 4th. Still at Bobo's. At six o'clock in the evening moved three-quarters of a mile for advantage of ground.

Saturday, 5th. Lay in the woods near Bobo's. Had intelligence that Fort Anderson, in which we had a Sergeant of the American Volunteers, and eighty militia men, was summoned on Sunday the 30th July, and given up in a dastardly manner, without exchanging a single shot.*

Sunday, 6th. Got in motion at seven o'clock in the evening. Left the heights near Bobo's, upon hearing that the Rebels were collecting in force at Ford's Mills. We made a forced march of sixteen miles in order to surprise them; marched all night; got to our ground at Jemmie's creek at six o'clock in the morning of the 7th, where we heard the Rebels had moved seven miles to Phillip's Ford.

---

* Col. Patrick Moore, commanding, taken by Col. Shelby and others.

Monday, 7th. Got in motion at seven in the evening, and made another forced march for them; and fording Jemmie's creek and the South and North branches of Tyger river. Got to the ground the Rebels were encamped on, at four o'clock on Tuesday morning, August eighth. They had intelligence of our move, and were likewise alarmed by the firing of a gun in our ranks; they sneaked from their ground about half an hour before we arrived.

Tuesday, 8th. Learning that the Rebel wagons were three miles in front of us at Cedar Springs, Captain Dunlap, with fourteen mounted men, and a hundred and thirty militia, were dispatched to take the wagons. He met three Rebels coming to reconnoitre our camp; he pursued, took two of them—the other escaped, giving the Rebels the alarm. In pursuit of this man, Dunlap and his party rushed into the centre of the Rebel camp, where they lay in ambush, before he was aware of their presence. A skirmish ensued, in which Dunlap got slightly wounded, and had between twenty and thirty killed and wounded— Ensign McFarland and one private taken prisoners. The Rebel loss is uncertain. A Maj. Smith, Capt. Potts, and two privates, were left dead on the field. Col. Clarke, Johnson [Robertson,] and twenty privates were seen wounded. We pursued them five miles to the Iron Works, but were not able to overtake them, they being all mounted. We countermarched five miles to Cedar Springs, and halted to refresh during the heat of the day. At six in the evening, marched and took a height near the ground the Rebels left.

Wednesday, 9th. Lay on the heights; nothing extra.

Thursday, 10th. Sent the wounded to Musgrove's Mills, Enoree river, to be attended by Dr. Ross. We marched about seven miles to Culbertson's plantation, on Fair Forest. Express arrived from Col. Turnbull at Rocky Mount, with orders to join him. By the express heard that Sumter had attacked Hanging Rock the 6th instant. The North Carolinians were first attacked; they gave way. Brown's corps came up, but were obliged to give way. The Legion Cavalry came in the Rebels' rear, and soon gained the day. Brown's corps suffered much—three officers killed, and three wounded—an hundred men taken prisoners.

Friday 11th. Got in motion at six o'clock in the morning. Marched ten miles to Maj. Gibbs' plantation; lay all night.

Saturday, 12th. Got in motion at seven o'clock in the morning, and marched seven miles to a Rebel Capt. Stripling's plantation. He has taken protection, and as yet has not broken his promise. A Maj. Rutherford* came with a flag; in consequence of his coming in our rear, without giving signal by drum or trumpet, was detained all night, and threatened with imprisonment.

---

* Maj. Rutherford, a son of Gen. Rutherford, distinguished himself at Ramsour's Mill, and was subsequently killed at Eutaw Springs.

Sunday, 13th. Got in motion at five o'clock in the morning, and marched nine miles to Tinker creek. At seven in the evening got in motion and marched five miles to Smith's Mills, on Swift's creek. Here we lay all night.

Monday, 14th. Got in motion at four o'clock in the morning; Marched to the Quaker fording place; forded Tyger river, continued our march to a Rebel Col. James Lisle's plantation. Lisle is in the Rebel service—his family at home.

Tuesday, 15th. Got in motion at seven o'clock in the morning. Marched two miles to Lisle's Ford; forded Broad river—proceeded seven miles to a Mr. Coleman's in Mobley's settlement; halted during the heat of the day. Got in motion at seven o'clock in the evening; marched two miles to the camp of the New York Volunteers, where we got intelligence that Gen. Gates lay within three miles of Camden, with an army of seven thousand men. Col. Turnbull had orders the twelfth to retreat from Rocky Mount, and act as he saw proper—to get to Camden if he could. Sumter appeared with cannon at Rocky Mount, about twelve hours after Col. Turnbull left it, in order to make a second trial for the post. He found not so harsh a reception as his first attempt.

Wednesday, 16th. Got in motion at seven o'clock in the morning, and marched two miles to Mobley's meeting house for convenience of ground.

Thursday, 17th. Got in motion at nine o'clock in the morning, and marched six miles to a Rebel Col. Winn's plantation. Winn is at James Island, a prisoner.

Friday, 18th. Lay at Winn's plantation, waiting news from Camden, having spies out upon every quarter.

Saturday, 19th. Lay at Winn's plantation. An express arrived from Camden with the agreeable news of Lord Cornwallis' attacking and totally defeating Gates' army on the morning of the 16th; twelve hundred were killed and wounded, left on the field; and one thousand prisoners, eight brass field pieces taken, being all the Rebels had in the field, several stand of colors, all their ammunition wagons, a hundred and fifty wagons of baggage, provisions, and stores of different kinds. All this with the trifling loss on our side of not more than ten officers killed and wounded, and two or three hundred non-commissioned officers and privates. We received orders to pursue Sumter, he having the only remains of what the Rebels can call a corps in these parts at present. At six o'clock in the evening our wagons were ordered forward that we might pursue Sumter with vigor. At seven we got in motion. That very moment an express arrived from Col. Innes', who was on his way from Ninety Six to join us, informing us that he had been attacked by a body of Rebels at Musgrove's Mills on Enoree river; that himself, and Major Fraser of his regiment, were wounded, as were Capt. Peter Campbell, Lieuts. Chew and Camp, of Col. Allen's regiment. He wished for support as many of the militia had left him. This, to our great mortification, altered the course of our march. At eleven at night, we got in motion; marched all night; forded Broad river at sun-rising.

Sunday, 20th. Proceeded four miles, and took up our ground at Peter's creek, where we lay all day, fatigued with our night's march, being eighteen miles. While we lay at Col. Winn's, a Mr. Smith was executed for joining the Rebels after he had taken protection, and been allowed to embody himself with our militia.

Monday, 21st. Got in motion at one o'clock in the morning, and marched six miles to a Rebel Capt. Lipham's on Padget creek. Took up our ground at five o'clock in the morning. This morning was so cold that we were glad to hover round large fires as soon as we halted. About one o'clock a Mr. Duncan came to our camp with the agreeable news that Col. Tarleton, with three companies of the Light Infantry, and the Legion Cavalry, fell in with Sumter about twelve o'clock on Saturday, the nineteenth.* He found them all asleep after the fatigue of two nights' rapid retreat. Their horses were all at pasture. The first alarm was the Light Infantry firing upon them. Col. Tarleton, with his usual success, gained a complete victory over Gen. Sumter; took two brass field pieces, made two hundred and fifty prisoners, eight hundred horses, thirty wagons, and retook a hundred of Brown's men that were captured at Hanging Rock. Captain Duncan made his escape from the Rebels during the engagement, he being a prisoner. Got in motion at eleven o'clock in the evening; marched ten miles to Tyger river; forded it at break of day.

Tuesday morning, 22d. Continued our march four miles to Harrison's plantation, on Fair Forest, where we halted.

Wednesday, 23d. Got in motion at six o'clock in the morning, and marched six miles to John Blasingame's plantation, on Sugar creek, where we took up our ground. Col. Ferguson set out for Camden.

Thursday, 24th. Still lay at Blasingame's, on Sugar creek.

Friday, 25th. Still at Blasingame's.

Saturday, 26th. Got in motion at six o'clock in the morning; marched six miles to John Wofford's plantation, on McClure's creek.

Sunday, 27th. Lay at McClure's creek; nothing extra.

Monday, 28th. Got in motion at five o'clock, and marched six miles to Culbertson's plantation, near Fair Forest river.

Tuesday, 29th, to Thursday, 31st. Lay at Culbertson's; nothing extra.

Friday, September 1st. Still remained at Culbertson's. Maj. Ferguson joined us again from Camden with the disagreeable news that we

---

* It was really the preceding day, Friday, 18th.

were to be separated from the army, and act on the frontiers with the militia.

Saturday, 2d. Got in motion at eleven o'clock in the morning; forded Fair Forest river, and marched ten miles to the Iron Works, on Lawson's Fork of Pacolet river. Here was a Rebel militia-man that got wounded in the right arm at the skirmish at Cedar Springs, the eighth of August. The bone was very much shattered. It was taken off by one Frost, a blacksmith, with a shoemaker's knife and carpenter's saw. He stopped the blood with the fungus of the oak, without taking up a blood vessel.

Sunday, 3d. My friend Johnson and I bathed in the stream at the Iron Works.

Monday, 4th. Got in motion at six o'clock in the morning, and marched ten miles to Case's creek, where we halted all night.

Tuesday, 5th. Got in motion at five o'clock in the evening, and marched a mile and a half to Pacolet river, and halted. The fresh was so high we could not ford the river. I took lodging, with my friend Johnson, who was very unwell, at one Coleman's, who is a very warm Tory. His wife and all her children have been stripped of all their clothes, bedding, and other furniture. She was mother of five children in two years.

Wednesday, 6th. Got in motion at eight o'clock in the morning; marched six miles to Buck's creek; dined at one Nelson's. Here was a hearty old man, named William Case, a hundred and nine years old. He is a native of New England. Talks very strong; gives some faint description of New England. His memory began to fail seven years past; he lost his eyesight about eighteen months past; is otherwise very hale; walks amazingly spry, and danced a jig.

Thursday, 7th. Got in motion at seven o'clock in the morning; crossed Buck creek, and the division line of South and North Carolina; marched six miles farther, and halted. Maj. Ferguson, with about fifty of the American Volunteers, and three hundred militia, got in motion at six o'clock in the evening, and marched to Gilbert Town in order to surprise a party of Rebels that we heard were there. Capt. DePeyster and I remained on the ground we took in the morning, with the remainder of the American Volunteers and militia.

Friday, 8th. Got in motion at eight in the morning, and marched six miles to Broad river, and took a height where we halted, and waited orders from Maj. Ferguson.

Saturday, 9th. Remained on the ground; received intelligence from Maj. Ferguson to keep our post. He was returning to keep a good lookout, as the Georgians were coming towards us.

Sunday, 10th. Col. Ferguson joined us about eleven o'clock at night.

Monday, 11th. Got in motion at four o'clock in the evening; forded

Broad river and continued on our march ten miles to one Adair's plantation, and halted.

Tuesday, 12th. Maj. Ferguson, with forty American Volunteers and one hundred militia, got in motion at two o'clock in the morning, and marched fourteen miles through the mountains to the head of Cane creek, in Burke County, in order to surprise a party of Rebels we heard lay there. Unfortunately for us, they had by some means got intelligence of our coming, in consequence of which, Mr. McDowell, with three hundred infamous villains like himself, thought it highly necessary to remove their quarters. However, we were lucky enough to take a different route from what they expected, and met them on their way, and to appearance one would have thought they meant sincerely to fight us, as they drew up on an eminence for action. On our approach they fired and gave way. We totally routed them, killed one private, wounded a Capt. White, took seventeen prisoners, twelve horses, all their ammunition, which was only twenty pounds of powder, after which we marched to their encampment, and found it abandoned by those Congress heroes. Our loss was two wounded and one killed. Among the wounded was Capt. Dunlap, who received two slight wounds. After the skirmish we returned to one Allen's to refresh ourselves. We got in motion about four o'clock in the afternoon, and countermarched about six miles to a Rebel Mr. Jones', where we halted all night.

Wednesday, 13th. Got in motion about eight o'clock in the morning and continued countermarching to a Rebel Col. Walker's plantation where we met Capt. Ryerson and Lieut. Fletcher with the remainder of the American Volunteers and militia. Here we took up our ground, very much fatigued with our enterprise.

Thursday, 14th. Lay still at Col. Walker's. The poor, deluded people of this Province begin to be sensible of their error, and come in very fast. Maj. Ferguson, with thirty American Volunteers, and three hundred militia, got in motion at six o'clock, and marched to the head of Cane creek, and halted at one Wilson's.

Friday, 15th. Capt. DePeyster and I, who remained at Col. Walker's with the remainder of the American Volunteers and militia, got in motion at six o'clock in the morning, and marched twelve miles to one Bowman's, near the head of Cane creek, and halted. This creek is so amazingly crooked that we were obliged to cross it nineteen times in marching four miles. Mrs. Bowman is an exceedingly obliging woman. She had a child about four years old, who had smoked tobacco almost three years. At four o'clock in the afternoon got in motion, and marched a mile and a half to Wilson's, where we joined Maj. Ferguson. At ten o'clock in the evening we got in motion, with the American Volunteers and five hundred militia, leaving Capt. Ryerson and Lieut. Fletcher, with two hundred militia, to guard the baggage, and marched fifteen miles to one John Forsyth's, on the banks of the Catawba, to surprise Col. McDowell. We arrived there about six o'clock in the morning of the 16th. Col. McDowell had left this place the 14th. We countermarched to one Devore's, and halted to refresh ourselves. At three o'clock got in motion; marched to Pleasant Garden Ford, Catawba river; forded it, and continued our march to one George Cathy's plantation, about a mile and a half from Devore's. Pleasant Garden is a very handsome place. I was surprised to see so beautiful a tract of land in the mountains. This settlement is composed of the most violent Rebels I ever saw, particularly the young ladies.

Sunday, 17th. Got in motion and marched two miles to Buck's creek, forded it, and continued our march two miles farther to a Rebel Maj. Davidson's plantation, and halted.

Monday, 18th. Got in motion, countermarched to Buck creek, forded it, and proceeded on five miles to Richey's Ford, on Catawba river, forded it, and marched to a Rebel Alexander Thompson's plantation, six miles farther, and halted.

Tuesday, 19th. Got in motion at five o'clock in the morning, and marched about eleven miles to a Rebel Mr. Hemphill's plantation, and halted. At seven o'clock in the evening, I went about a mile and joined Capt. Ryerson and the militia under his command.

Wednesday, 20th. Got in motion at six o'clock in the morning, and marched a mile and a half to one White's plantation, where we joined Maj. Ferguson again. This day three officers belonging to Cruger and Allen's regiments, joined us from Ninety Six, with fifty militia men.

Thursday, 21st. Got in motion at five o'clock in the morning and marched fourteen miles to a Rebel Samuel Andrew's plantation, and halted. On the march I saw eight wild turkeys.

Friday, 22d. Got in motion at five o'clock in the morning; marched five miles to Col. Walker's plantation, and halted.

Saturday, 23d. Got in motion at nine o'clock in the morning; marched three miles to Gilbert Town; took up our ground on a height about half a mile from the town. This town contains one dwelling house, one barn, a blacksmith's shop, and some out-houses.

Sunday, 24th. Five hundred subjects came in, also a number of ladies. Received intelligence from Col. Cruger, that he had marched from Ninety Six to Augusta, to the assistance of Col. Browne, who was besieged by six hundred Rebels, under the command of Col. Clarke. Fortunately for Col. Browne, the Cherokee Indians, for whom he is agent, were coming to Augusta for their yearly presents. They met the Rebels just as they were going into the town, which obliged them to fight. The Rebels being too numerous, and the Indians unacquainted with field fighting, were obliged to make the best of their way to a fort on one flank of the town, where Col. Browne had retired to. He made a very gallant defence for five days, two of which he was without bread or water. On Col. Cruger's approach, the Rebels moved off with their plunder, of which they had a tolerable share. Col. Cruger arrived time enough to retake the cannon which they had taken from Browne, and about thirty prisoners.

Monday, 25th, and Tuesday, 26th. Lay at Gilbert Town ; nothing extra.

Wednesday, 27th. Got in motion at five o'clock in the morning, and marched three miles to Rucker's Mill, and halted.

Thursday, 28th. Got in motion at five o'clock in the morning ; marched seven miles to Mountain creek, forded it, although very difficult, continued on about a mile farther to Twitty's Ford of Broad river, and took up our ground on its banks. At six o'clock in the evening got in motion, forded the river ; marched two miles to McDaniel's Ford of Green river ; forded it, and marched two miles farther ; halted on the road ; lay on our arms till four o'clock the next morning.

Friday, 29th. We then, at that early hour, moved on three miles to one James Step's plantation, and halted. This man has been very unfortunate in his family ; his wife, who is a very decent woman, was caught by the Indians about a twelvemonth past. They scalped and tomahawked her several times in the head, treated the infant she had in her arms in a most inhuman and savage manner. They mashed its head in such a manner that its recovery is truly astonishing ; but what this poor, unhappy woman seems most to regret is the loss of her oldest son, whom the savages took, and she now remains in a state of uncertainty, not having heard from him since.

Saturday, 30th. Lay at James Step's with an expectation of intercepting Col. Clarke on his return to the mountains ; but he was prudent enough to take another route.

Sunday, October 1st. Got in motion at five o'clock in the morning, and marched twelve miles to Denard's Ford of Broad river, and took up our old ground where we lay the 8th September.

Monday, 2d. Got in motion at four o'clock in the afternoon ; forded Broad river ; marched four miles ; formed in line of action and lay on our arms. This night I had nothing but the canopy of heaven to cover me.

Tuesday, 3d. Got in motion at four o'clock in the morning ; marched six miles to Camp's Ford of Second Broad river, forded it and continued on six miles to one Armstrong's plantation, on the banks of Sandy Run. Halted to refresh ; at four o'clock got in motion ; forded Sandy Run ; marched seven miles to Buffalo creek ; forded it ; marched a mile farther and halted near one Tate's plantation. John West came in camp, who is a hundred and one years of age ; is amazingly strong in every sense.

Friday, 6th. Got in motion at four o'clock in the morning, and marched sixteen miles to Little King's Mountain, where we took up our ground.

Saturday, 7th. About two o'clock in the afternoon twenty-five hundred Rebels, under the command of Brig.-Gen. Williams, and ten Colonels, attacked us. Maj. Ferguson had eight hundred men. The action continued an hour and five minutes ; but their numbers enabled them to surround us. The North Carolina regiment seeing this, and numbers being out of ammunition, gave way, which naturally threw the rest of the militia into confusion. Our poor little detachment, which consisted of only seventy men when we marched to the field of action, were all killed and wounded but twenty ; and those brave fellows were soon crowded as close as possible by the militia. Capt. DePeyster, on whom the command devolved, saw it impossible to form six men together ; thought it necessary to surrender to save the lives of the brave men who were left. We lost in this action, Maj. Ferguson, of the Seventy-first regiment, a man much attached to his King and country, well informed in the art of war ; he was brave and humane, and an agreeable companion ; in short, he was universally esteemed in the army, and I have every reason to regret his unhappy fate. We had eighteen men killed on the spot ; Capt. Ryerson and thirty-two privates wounded of Maj. Ferguson's detachment ; Lieut. McGinnis, of Allen's regiment of Skinner's Brigade, killed. Taken prisoners, Two Captains, four Lieutenants, three Ensigns, and one Surgeon, and fifty-four sergeants rank and file, including the mounted men under the command of Lieut. Taylor. Of the militia, one hundred were killed, including officers ; wounded, ninety ; taken prisoners, about six hundred. Our baggage all taken, of course. Rebels lost Brig.-Gen. Williams, one hundred and thirty-five, including officers, killed ; wounded, equal to ours.

Sunday, 8th. They thought it necessary to move us sixteen miles, to one Waldron's plantation, where they halted.

Monday, 9th. Moved two miles and a half to Bullock creek ; * forded it, and halted on the banks.

Tuesday, 10th. Moved twenty miles and halted in the woods.

Wednesday. 11th. Moved at eight o'clock in the morning ; marched twelve miles to Col. Walker's, and halted.

Thursday, 12th. Those villains divided our baggage, although they had promised on their word we should have it all.

Friday, 13th. Moved six miles to Bickerstaff's plantation. In the evening their liberality extended so far as to send five old shirts to nine of us, as a change of linen—other things in like proportion.

Saturday, 14th. Twelve field officers were chosen to try the militia

---

* Apparently Boren's creek—Bullock's creek was some fifteen or eighteen miles distant.

prisoners—particularly those who had the most influence in the country. They condemed thirty—in the evening they began to execute Lieut.-Col. Mills, Capt. Wilson, Capt. Chitwood, and six others, who unfortunately fell a sacrifice to their infamous mock jury. Mills, Wilson, and Chitwood died like Romans—the others were reprieved.

Sunday, 15th. Moved at five o'clock in the morning. Marched all day through the rain—a very disagreeable road. We got to Catawba, and forded it at Island Ford, about ten o'clock at night. Our march was thirty-two miles. All the men were worn out with fatigue and fasting—the prisoners having no bread or meat for two days before. We officers were allowed to go to Col. McDowell's, where we lodged comfortably. About one hundred prisoners made their escape on this march.

Monday, 16th. Moved at two o'clock in the afternoon. Marched five miles; forded the north branch of Catawba and John's river; halted at a Tory plantation.

Tuesday, 17th. Moved at eight o'clock in the morning. Marched fifteen miles; halted at Capt. Hatt's plantation. Three prisoners attempted to make their escape this night; two succeeded—the other was shot through the body.

Wednesday, 18th. About five o'clock in the morning the Rebels executed the man who unfortunately got wounded in attempting to make his escape. We moved at eight o'clock in the morning, and marched eighteen miles to Moravian creek, and halted.

Thursday, 19th. Moved at eight o'clock in the morning; forded Moravian creek, passed by Wilkes Court House, and marched sixteen miles to one Hagwoods' plantation, and halted.

Friday, 20th. Moved at eleven o'clock in the morning; marched six miles to Mr. Sale's plantation, and halted.

Saturday, 21st. Several Tory women brought us butter, milk, honey, and many other necessaries of life. Moved at ten o'clock in the morning, and marched fourteen miles to Mr. Headpeth's plantation, a great Tory, who is at present with Lord Cornwallis. We lodged at Mr. Edward Clinton's, who is likewise with Lord Cornwallis.

Sunday, 22d. Moved at ten o'clock in the morning. Obtained liberty to go forward with Col. Shelby to Salem, a town inhabited by Moravians. Rode ten miles, and forded Yadkin river at Shallow Ford. Proceeded on fourteen miles farther to Salem. Went to meeting in the evening; highly entertained with the decency of those people, and with their music. Salem contains about twenty houses, and a place of worship. The people of this town are all mechanics; those of the other two Moravian settlements are all farmers, and all stanch friends to Government.

Monday, 23d. Lay at Salem in the evening. Two Continental

officers slept at the tavern, on their way to join their army, One Mr. Simons, a Lieutenant of Col. Washington's dragoons, was exceeding polite, pitied our misfortune in falling into the hands of their militia.

Tuesday, 24th. Moved at ten o'clock in the morning ; marched six miles to the old town called Bethabara. Here we joined the camp again. This town is about as large as the other ; but not so regularly laid out. The inhabitants very kind to all the prisoners. This night Dr. Johnson and I were disturbed by a Capt. Campbell, who came into our room, and ordered us up in a most peremptory manner. He wanted our bed. I was obliged to go to Col. Campbell, and wake him to get the ruffian turned out of the room ; otherwise he would have murdered us, having his sword drawn, and strutting about with it in a truly cowardly manner.

Wednesday, 25th. The men of our detachment, on Capt. DePeyster passing his word for their good behavior, were permitted to go into houses in the town without a guard.

Thursday, 26th, to Saturday, 28th. Nothing extra.

Sunday, 29th. Col. Cleveland waited on Capt. DePeyster and the rest of the officers, and asked us if we, with our men, would come and hear a sermon at ten o'clock. He marched the militia prisoners from their encampment to the town, and halted them ; and sent an officer to our quarters to acquaint us they were waiting for us. We then ordered our men to fall in ; marched to the front of the prisoners ; the whole then proceeded on to a height about half a mile from the town. Here we heard a Presbyterian sermon, truly adapted to their principles and the times ; or, rather, stuffed as full of Republicanism as their camp is of horse thieves.

Monday, 30th. A number of the inhabitants assembled at Bethabara to see a poor Tory prisoner executed for a crime of the following nature, viz : A Rebel soldier was passing the guard where the prisoners were confined, and like a brute addressed himself to those poor unhappy people in this style : "Ah, d—n you, you'll all be hanged." This man, with the spirit of a British subject, answered, "Never mind that, it will be your turn next." But Col. Cleveland's goodness extended so far as to reprieve him.

Tuesday, 30th. Rode to Salem in company with Capt. DePeyster, Dr. Johnson and Mr. Supple. This night very cold ; froze ice a quarter of an inch thick—the first this fall.

Wednesday, November 1st. My friend, Dr. Johnson, insulted and beaten by Col. Cleveland for attempting to dress a man whom they had cut on the march. Col. Armstrong relieved Cleveland in the afternoon, and took the command.

Thursday, 2d. Took a walk with Capt. DePeyster, Dr. Johnson and Mr. Taylor to Bathania, three miles from Bethabara. This town contains about thirty houses ; it is regularly laid out.

Friday, 3d. Heard by a countryman, who was moving his family over the mountains to Nolachucky, that General Leslie had landed at James river, in Virginia.

Saturday, 4th. Dined at a country house.

Sunday, 5th. Set off from Bethabara in company with Lieut. Taylor, Lieut. Stevenson, and William Gist, a militia-man, about six o'clock in the evening. We marched fifteen miles to Yadkin river; forded it, found it very disagreeable. We continued on twenty miles farther to Mr. Miller's plantation, an exceeding good subject. Here we arrived just at daybreak the next morning.

Monday, 6th. Took up our ground in the bushes, about half a mile from the house. At ten o'clock, we sent Mr. Gist to the house for some victuals. He found Mr. Miller at home, who very readily gave us all the assistance that lay in his power. About two o'clock, he brought us some victuals, which we were very happy to see, being very hungry after our fatiguing march the night before. In conversation, which very naturally run upon the safest way, guides, etc., Mr. Miller told us he knew a militia Capt. Turner, and one or two more subjects, then lying in the bushes, who would be very happy to join Lord Cornwallis; and they were also excellent guides. On this we consulted, and thought it prudent to stay all night. Mr. Miller then fetched us a blanket, and immediately set out to find those people.

Tuesday, 7th. Mr. Miller returned informing us that one of those men would be with us at six o'clock in the evening. We waited till seven, but the man not coming, we thought it prudent to go without him. We set out about half after seven; marched six miles to one Carpenter's. When we arrived there, Mr. Carpenter advised us to remain there the remainder of the night, and he would go to Mr. Miller, and send him again for the men. We then consulted, and thought it best to stay a day or two—then to proceed on, without a guide.

Wednesday, 8th. Lay very snug in the bushes. About four o'clock in the afternoon, Mr. Carpenter returned and told us Mr. Miller was gone in search of a guide, and was to return with an answer as soon as possible. Suffered exceedingly with the cold this day.

Thursday, 9th. Heard of the Rebels following us, but they getting false intelligence, returned again, which was much in our favor. In the course of the day, we thought it would be prudent to get the best directions we could, and proceed on, without a guide, rather than remain too long in one place, lest some of those people might be treacherous. We got direction from Mr. Carpenter for sixty miles, and at six o'clock in the evening, set out; marched thirty miles, and halted in the woods at daybreak.

Friday, 10th. Suffered very much with the cold. At six o'clock in the evening set out again. This night saw the moon in an eclipse, and heard several wolves bark. Passed a Rebel party consisting of twelve or fourteen, who lay about twenty yards from the road by a fire; but very fortunately for us, they were all asleep. We marched thirty miles and arrived at Colbert Blair's, just at daybreak.

Saturday, 11th. It began to rain just after we got to Mr. Blair's. Lucky we were indeed. This good man secreted us in his fodder-house, and gave us the best his house afforded.

Sunday, 12th. Remained at Mr. Blair's; a rainy, disagreeable day.

Monday, 13th. Set out from this good man's fodder-house. He conducted us about three miles to a Mr. F. Rider's, who guided us seven miles farther, over the Brushy Mountains, to Catawba river. Mr. John Murray, who lived on the bank of the river, put us over in a canoe, and conducted us three miles to Mr. Ballou's. This old man was about sixty years of age; but his love for his King and his subjects induced him to get up, although very late at night, and guided us seven miles to a Mr. Hilterbrine's. On the way the old man informed us he had two sons who lay out in the woods, who were anxious to go to our army, and were also good guides. He also told us of one Williams, that was a good guide, and who would be glad to go with us. We told the old man we should be very happy to have them, as the road began to grow more dangerous, and we quite unacquainted with the way. This poor old man expressed a great deal of anxiety for our safety, and at last told us he would go the next day and endeavor to find them, and send them to us. We arrived at Hilterbrine's about six o'clock in the morning of the 14th. He received us with great caution, lest we should be treacherous; but when he found we were British officers he was very kind.

Wednesday, 15th. Just as we were drinking a dish of coffee, on a rock, after dusk, those three young men came to us on horseback, which made us very happy. We set out immediately, and marched twenty miles over the Brushy Mountains, where there was nothing but Indian paths. Crossed several small rivers. We arrived at one Sheppard's plantation, just at daybreak of the 16th. This poor family were so completely stripped of everything they had, by the Rebels, that they could give us nothing but a hoe cake, and some dried beef, which was but a very indifferent repast for hungry stomachs. At six o'clock in the evening set out; marched sixteen miles to Camp's Ford of Second Broad river; forded it, and continued on three and a half miles farther to Island Ford of Main Broad river; forded it, and marched one mile to Capt. Townsend's plantation. This man received three balls in the action on King's Mountain, and was at home on parole. He was very happy to see us, and gave us the best his house afforded.

Friday, 17th. Set out at six o'clock in the evening; marched twelve miles to a Mr. Morris'. Here we were told that a party of Rebels were directly in our front; that we had better remain there that night, in which time we could send Mr. Williams, who was with us, and well acquainted with that neighborhood, to get a militia Capt. Robins, who lay out in the woods, and was going to our army in a day or two. This man was so good a guide that it induced us to stay.

Saturday, 18th. Lay in the woods ; fared pretty well.

Sunday, 19th. Mr. Williams returned, but without effecting what he went after. We had a council of safety ; found it necessary to proceed on. We got Mr. Murray to guide us to the main road that leads to the Iron Works, which is twelve miles distant. We set out about three o'clock in the afternoon ; took by-paths. and got in the main road just at dusk. We crossed Pacolet river, Lawson's Fork, and Tyger river ; passed a Rebel guard ; marched thirty-seven miles, and arrived at James Duncan's plantation, half an hour before daybreak of the 20th. About ten o'clock Mrs. Duncan rode out to see if she could get any intelligence of our army, and of the Rebel army, that we might shun the latter. Mrs. Duncan returned in less than an hour, with the disagreeable news that the Rebel army was marching within two miles of us, and were going to encamp at Blackstock's, about four miles from us. This news truly discouraged me. About five o'clock in the evening Mr. Duncan came to us with agreeable news—that Col. Tarleton was in pursuit of the Rebels. At six o'clock a Mr. Jackson came to us, and informed us he had seen Col. Tarleton ; he had also heard he had had an action with Sumter, who commanded the Rebels, but did not know the particulars. He advised us to go to his house and stay all night, as we would be perfectly safe there, and the next morning go to Mr. Smith's, where we could hear the particulars of the action, as there were some of the Legion wounded there. We agreed to what the man said ; staid all night at his house, where we were treated very kindly.

Tuesday, 21st. Mr. Duncan conducted us to Mr. Smith's, where we found six of the Legion wounded.

Wednesday, 22d. Set out from Archey Smith's on horseback, which the subjects in that neighborhood supplied us with. They brought us on thirteen miles to one Adair's. Here we dismounted, and those good people returned. We continued thirteen miles to Williams' Fort, which was commanded by Col. Kirkland, who received us very kindly.

Thursday, 23d. Set out from Col. Kirkland's, who was kind enough to lend us horses as far as Saluda. Left the horses here ; crossed in a scow ; walked a mile to Col. Mayson's ; dined ; got horses and rode to Ninety Six. Arrived at Capt. John Barbarie's * quarters, about eight o'clock in the evening.

Friday, 24th. Remained at Ninety Six ; nothing extra.

Saturday, 25th. Set out for Charleston, Where I arrived the 29th of November ; nothing worth notice on the journey.

---

* Capt. Barbarie belonged to the New Jersey Volunteers ; was captured at Staten Island in 1777 ; doubtless shared in the siege of Charleston. as he did in the siege of Ninety Six, during which he was wounded ; and was again wounded at Eutaw Springs. He received half pay. and settled at St. Johns, New Brunswick. where he became a Colonel of the militia, and a magistrate. He died at Sussex Vale in 1818 at the age of sixty-seven. His son, Andrew Barbarie, was a member of the Assembly of that Province.

KING'S MOUNTAIN BATTLE.

BRITISH ACCOUNTS.

[From *Scot's Magazine*, January, 1781.]

CHARLESTON, *Dec, 27, 1780.*

A gentleman lately come to town has favored us with an account of the base treatment the unfortunate officers and men met with who surrendered prisoners of war, last October, to the Rebel Col. Campbell, in the action of King's Mountain. A small party of the [British] militia returning from foraging, unacquainted with the surrender, happening to fire on the Rebels, the prisoners were immediately threatened with death if the firing should be repeated.

The morning after the action, the prisoners were marched sixteen miles; previous to their march, orders were given by Campbell, should they be attacked, to fire on and destroy every prisoner. The party kept marching for two days without any kind of provisions. On the third day's march all the baggage of the officers was seized, and shared among the Rebel officers.

A few days after, a mock court-martial sat for the trial of the militia prisoners; when, after a short hearing, thirty gentlemen, some of the most respectable characters in that country, had sentence of death passed on them; and at six o'clock the same day they began to execute. Col. Mills and Capt. Chitwood, of North Carolina, Capt. Wilson, of Ninety Six, and six privates, were first executed. The British officers were compelled to attend at the execution of their brave but unfortunate men; who, with manly firmness, avowed their loyalty in their last moments, and with their latest breath expressed their unutterable detestation for the Rebels, and their base and infamous proceedings. The remaining twenty-one were reprieved for a time.

KING'S MOUNTAIN BATTLE.

[From Rivington's *Royal Gazette*, New York, February 24th, 1781.]

Extract from a letter from an officer,* dated Charleston, January 30th, 1781.

This gentleman went from New York with a detachment drawn from the Provincial Brigade, which was commanded by the brave Major Patrick Ferguson. This letter gives the most circumstantial account yet

---

* This letter was evidently enough written by Lieut. Allaire, as a comparison with his *Diary* proves ; and the same test shows that the preceding article from *Scot's Magazine*, was dictated by him.

received of the action at King's Mountain, in South Carolina, Oct. seventh.

I think the last letter I wrote you was from Fort Moultrie, which I left a few days after. We marched to a place called Ninety Six, which is about two hundred miles from Charleston ; we lay there about a fort-night in good quarters, after which we proceeded to the frontiers of South Carolina, and frequently passed the line into North Carolina, and can say with propriety, that there is not a regiment or detachment of his Majesty's service, that ever went through the fatigues, or suffered so much, as our detachment.

That you may have some faint idea of our suffering, I shall mention a few particulars. In the first place we were separated from all the army, acting with the militia ; we never lay two nights in one place, frequently making forced marches of twenty and thirty miles in one night ; skirmishing very often ; the greatest part of our time without rum or wheat flour—rum is a very essential article, for in marching ten miles we would often be obliged to ford two or three rivers, which wet the men up to their waists.

In this disagreeable situation, we remained till the seventh of October, when we were attacked by two thousand five hundred Rebels, under the command of Gen. Williams. Col. Ferguson had under his command eight hundred militia, and our detachment, which at that time was reduced to an hundred men. The action commenced about two o'clock in the afternoon, and was very severe for upwards of an hour, during which the Rebels were charged and drove back several times, with considerable slaughter. When our detachment charged, for the first time, it fell to my lot to put a Rebel Captain to death, which I did most effectually, with one blow of my sword ; the fellow was at least six feet high, but I had rather the advantage, as I was mounted on an elegant horse, and he on foot. But their numbers enabled them to surround us and the North Carolina regiment, which consisted of about three hundred men. Seeing this, and numbers being out of ammunition, which naturally threw the rest of the militia into confusion, our gallant little detachment, which consisted of only seventy men, exclusive of twenty who acted as dragoons, and ten who drove wagons, etc., when we marched to the field of action, were all killed and wounded but twenty, and those brave fellows were soon crowded into an heap by the militia. Capt. DePeyster, on whom the command devolved, seeing it impossible to form six men together, thought it necessary to surrender, to save the lives of the brave men who were left.

We lost in this action, Maj. Ferguson, of the Seventy-first regiment, a man strongly attached to his King and country, well informed in the art of war, brave, humane, and an agreeable companion—in short, he was universally esteemed in the army, and I have every reason to regret his unhappy fate. We lost eighteen men killed on the spot—Capt. Ryerson and thirty-two Sergeants and privates wounded, of Maj. Ferguson's detachment. Lieutenant M'Ginnis of Allen's regiment, Skinner's brigade, killed; taken prisoners, two Captains, four Lieutenants, three Ensigns, one Surgeon, and fifty-four Sergeants and privates, including the wounded, wagoners, etc. The militia killed, one hundred, including officers; wounded, ninety; taken prisoners about six hundred; our baggage all taken, of course.

The Rebels lost Brig.-Gen. Williams, and one hundred and thirty-five, including officers, killed; wounded nearly equal to ours. The morning after the action we were marched sixteen miles, previous to which orders were given by the Rebel Col. Campbell (whom the command devolved on) *that should they be attacked on their march, they were to fire on, and destroy their prisoners.* The party was kept marching two days without any kind of provisions. The officers' baggage, on the third day's march, was all divided among the Rebel officers.

Shortly after we were marched to Bickerstaff's settlement, where we arrived on the thirteenth. On the fourteenth, a court martial, composed of twelve field officers, was held for the trial of the militia prisoners; when, after a short hearing, they condemned thirty of the most principal and respectable characters, whom they considered to be most inimical to them, to be executed; and, at six o'clock in the evening of the same day, executed Col. Mills, Capt. Chitwood, Capt. Wilson, and six privates; obliging every one of their officers to attend at the death of those brave, but unfortunate Loyalists, who all, with their last breath and blood, held the Rebels and their cause as infamous and base, and as they were turning off, extolled their King and the British Government.

On the morning of the fifteenth, Col. Campbell had intelligence that Col. Tarleton was approaching him, when he gave orders to his men, that should Col. Tarleton come up with them, they were immediately to fire on Capt. DePeyster and his officers, who were in the front, and then a second volley on the men. During this day's march the men were obliged to give thirty-five Continental dollars for a single ear of Indian corn, and forty for a drink of water, they not being allowed to drink when fording a river; in short, the whole of the Rebels' conduct from the surrender of the party into their hands is incredible to relate. Several of the militia that were worn out with fatigue, and not being able to keep up, were cut down, and trodden to death in the mire.

After the party arrived at Moravian Town, in North Carolina, we officers were ordered in different houses. Dr. Johnson (who lived with me) and myself were turned out of our bed at an unseasonable hour of the night, and threatened with immediate death if we did not make room for some of Campbell's officers; Dr. Johnson was, after this, knocked down, and treated in the basest manner, for endeavoring to dress a man whom they had cut on the march. The Rebel officers would often go in amongst the prisoners, draw their swords, cut down and wound those whom their wicked and savage minds prompted.

This is a specimen of Rebel lenity—you may report it without the least equivocation, for upon the word and honor of a gentleman, this description is not equal to their barbarity. This kind of treatment made our time pass away very disagreeably. After we were in Moravian Town about a fortnight, we were told we could not get paroles to return within the British lines ; neither were we to have any till we were moved over the mountains in the back parts of Virginia, where we were to live on hoe cake and milk ; in consequence of this, Capt. Taylor, Lieut. Stevenson and myself, chose rather to trust the hand of fate, and agreeable to our inclinations, set out from Moravian Town the fifth of November, and arrived at the British lines the twentieth. From this town to Ninety Six, which was the first post we arrived at, is three hundred miles ; and from Ninety Six to Charleston, two hundred, so that my route was five hundred miles. The fatigues of this jaunt I shall omit till I see you, although I suffered exceedingly ; but thank God am now in Charleston in good quarters."

KING'S MOUNTAIN.

[From Rivington's New York *Royal Gazette*, March 21st, 1781. Copied into a London paper, of April, 30th, and into the Charleston *Royal Gazette* of October 27th following.]

Extract of a letter from an officer taken prisoner at King's Mountain, dated Charleston, S. C., March 4th, 1781 :

Capt. DePeyster and I* were permitted to come within the lines upon paroles, and were made exceedingly happy on our arrival in town, being informed we were exchanged. After our misfortune in losing Maj. Ferguson, the command devolved on Capt. DePeyster ; he behaved like a brave, good officer, and disputed the ground as long as it was possible to defend it against four times our number. The action lasted an hour and five minutes, very hot indeed. I must confess I was pleased, though a prisoner, to see their loss superior to ours. It is an agreeable satisfaction to think, that although they got the better of us, d——n 'em, we made them pay for it. I can assure you, sir, we deserved success, although it was not in our power to command it.

---

* As Lieuts. Allaire, Taylor, and Stevenson had previously escaped from Bethabara, and arrived in Charleston, the only officers left with Capt. DePeyster were Capt. Ryerson and Lieut Fletcher. It was one of these—most likely Capt. Ryerson—who wrote this letter.

COL. WILLIAMS TO GEN. GATES.

BURKE COUNTY, *Oct. 2d, 1780.*

Sir: I am at present about seventy miles from Salisbury, in the fork of the Catawba, with about four hundred and fifty horsemen, in pursuit of Col. Ferguson. On my crossing the Catawba river, I dispatched to different quarters for intelligence, and this evening I was favored with this news, which you may depend on: That Col. Clarke, of the State of Georgia, with one hundred riflemen, forced his way from South Carolina to Georgia. On his route thither, being joined by seven hundred men, he proceeded to the town of Augusta, and has taken it with a large quantity of goods ; but not finding it prudent to continue there, he has retreated to the upper parts of South Carolina, in Ninety Six district, and made a stand with eight hundred brave men.

This moment another of my expresses is arrived from Cols. McDowell and Shelby ; they were on their march, near Burke Court House, with fifteen hundred brave mountain men, and Col. Cleveland was within ten miles of them with eight hundred men, and was to form a junction with them this' day. I expect to join them to-morrow, in pursuit of Col. Ferguson, and under the direction of heaven, I hope to be able to render your honor a good account of him in a few days.

I am, &c.,

MAJ.-GEN. GATES.   JAMES WILLIAMS.

GEN. W. L. DAVIDSON TO GEN. SUMNER.

CAMP, ROCKY RIVER, *Oct. 10th, 1780..*

Sir: I have the pleasure of sending you very agreeable intelligence from the West. Ferguson, the great partisan, has miscarried. This we are assured of by Mr. Tate, Brigade Major in Gen. Sumter's late command. The particulars from that gentleman's mouth stand thus : That Cols. Campbell, Cleveland, Shelby, Sevier, Williams, Brandon, Lacey, etc., formed a conjunct body near Gilbert Town, consisting of three thousand. From this body were selected sixteen hundred good horse, who immediately went in pursuit of Col. Ferguson, who was making his way to Charlotte. Our people overtook him well posted on King's Mountain, and on the evening of the seventh inst., at four o'clock, began the attack, which continued forty-seven minutes. Col. Ferguson fell in the action, besides one hundred and fifty of his men ; eight hundred and ten were made prisoners, including the British, one hundred and fifty of prisoners are wounded. Fifteen hundred stand of arms fell into our hands. Col. Ferguson had about fourteen hundred men. Our people surrounded them, and the enemy surrendered.

"We lost about twenty men, among whom is Maj. Chronicle, of Lincoln County; Col. Williams is mortally wounded. The number of our wounded cannot be ascertained. This blow will certainly effect the British very considerably. The Brigade Major who gives this, was in the action. The above is true. I give you joy upon the occasion."

In forwarding the above to Gen. Gates, Gen. Sumner wrote from Yadkin Ford, eight o'clock in the evening, October 10th: "With great satisfaction I inform you of the defeat of Maj. Ferguson, four o'clock on Saturday afternoon. The particulars I inclose you as I received them a few minutes ago."

GEN. GATES TO GOV. JEFFERSON.

HILLSBORO, *Oct. 12th, 1780.*

Sir: This instant I received the great and glorious news contained in the enclosed letter from Brig.-Gen. Davidson to Gen. Sumner, who directly dispatched it to me by express. We are now more than even with the enemy. The moment the supplies for the troops arrive from Taylor's Ferry, I shall proceed with the whole to the Yadkin. Gen. Smallwood and Col. Morgan are on their way to that post; the latter, with the Light Infantry, was yesterday advanced eighteen miles beyond Guilford Court House; the former, with the cavalry, lay last night thirteen miles on this side that place. I desire your Excellency will dispatch copies of all the letters I now send to the President of Congress.

GEN. GATES' LETTER OF THANKS FOR KING'S MOUNTAIN VICTORY.

HILLSBORO, *Oct. 12th, 1780.*

To the officers commanding in the late defeat of Maj. Ferguson:

Sirs: I received, this morning early, the very agreeable account of your victory over Maj. Ferguson. It gave me, and every friend to liberty, and the United States, infinite satisfaction.

I thank you, gentlemen, and the brave officers and soldiers under your command, for your and their glorious behavior in that action. The records of the war will transmit your names and theirs to posterity, with the highest honor and applause. I desire you will acquaint them with the sense I entertain of the great service they have done their country. I have, this morning, by a special messenger, transmitted intelligence of it to Congress.

I am now only anxious about the disposal of the prisoners, as they must be ready to use in exchange for our valuable citizens in the enemy's hands. Send them under proper guards to Fincastle Court House, Virginia. I will desire the Colonel of that County to have a strong palisade, eighteen feet high out of the ground, instantly set up, within which log huts may be built to cover them. The guard must be without, and the loop-holes eight feet from the ground. Provisions, etc., shall be ordered to be provided for them.

OFFICIAL REPORT.

[From the *Virginia Gazette*, Nov. 18th, and *Massachusetts Spy*, Nov. 30th, 1780.]

A state of the proceedings of the Western Army, from the 25th of September, 1780, to the reduction of Major Ferguson, and the army under his command.

On receiving intelligence that Major Ferguson had advanced as high up as Gilbert Town, in Rutherford County, and threatened to cross the mountains to the western waters, Col. William Campbell, with four hundred men from Washington County, Virginia, Col. Isaac Shelby, with two hundred and forty from Sullivan County of North Carolina, and Lieut.-Col. John Sevier, with two hundred and forty men, of Washington County, assembled at Watauga, on the 25th of September, where they were joined by Col. Charles McDowell, with one hundred and sixty men from the Counties of Burke and Rutherford, who had fled before the enemy to the western waters.

We began our march on the 26th, and on the 30th we were joined by Col. Cleveland, on the Catawba river, with three hundred and fifty men, from the Counties of Wilkes and Surry. No one officer having properly a right to command in chief, on the 1st of October, we dispatched an express to Maj. Gen. Gates, informing him of our situation, and requesting him to send a general officer to take the command of the whole. In the meantime Col. Campbell was chosen to act as commandant till such general officer should arrive. We marched to the Cowpens, on Broad river, in South Carolina, where we were joined by Col. James Williams, with four hundred men, on the evening of the 6th of October, who informed us, that the enemy lay encamped somewhere near the Cherokee Ford, of Broad river, about thirty miles distant from us.

By a council of the principal officers, it was then thought advisable to pursue the enemy that night with nine hundred of the best horsemen, and leave the weak horses and footmen to follow as fast as possible. We began our march with nine hundred of the best men, about eight o'clock the same evening; and, marching all night, came up with the enemy about three o'clock P. M. of the 7th, who lay encamped on the top of King's Mountain, twelve miles north of the Cherokee Ford, in the confidence that they could not be forced from so advantageous a post. Previous to the attack, on the march, the following disposition was made: Col. Shelby's regiment formed a column in the center, on the left; Col. Campbell's regiment, another on the right; with part of Col. Cleveland's regiment, headed in front by Major Winston, and Col. Sevier's regiment, formed a large column on the right wing. The other part of Cleveland's regiment, headed by Col. Cleveland himself, and Col. Williams' regiment, composed the left wing. In this order we advanced, and got within a quarter of a mile of the enemy before we were discovered.

Col. Shelby's and Col. Campbell's regiments began the attack, and kept up a fire on the enemy, while the right and left wings were advancing to surround them, which was done in about five minutes, and the fire became general all around. The engagement lasted an hour and five minutes, the greater part of which time, a heavy and incessant fire was kept up on both sides. Our men in some parts, where the regulars fought, were obliged to give way a small distance, two or three times; but rallied and returned with additional ardor to the attack. The troops upon the right having gained the summit of the eminence, obliged the enemy to retreat along the top of the ridge to where Col. Cleveland commanded, and were there stopped by his brave men. A flag was immediately hoisted by Capt. DePeyster, the commanding officer (Maj. Ferguson having been killed a little before), for a surrender. Our fire immediately ceased, and the enemy laid down their arms, the greatest part of them charged, and surrendered themselves to us prisoners at discretion.

It appears from their own provision returns for that day, found in their camp, that their whole force consisted of eleven hundred and twenty-five men; out of which they sustained the following loss: Of the regulars, one Major, one Captain, two Sergeants, and fifteen privates killed; thirty-five privates wounded, left on the ground, not able to march; two Captains, four Lieutenants, three Ensigns, one Surgeon, five Sergeants, three Corporals, one Drummer, and forty-nine privates taken prisoners. Loss of the Tories—two Colonels, three Captains, and two hundred and one privates killed; one Major, and one hundred and twenty-seven privates wounded, and left on the ground, not able to march; one Colonel, twelve Captains, eleven Lieutenants, two Ensigns, one Quarter-Master, one Adjutant, two Commissaries, eighteen Sergeants, and six hundred privates taken prisoners. Total loss of the enemy, eleven hundred and five men at King's Mountain.

Given under our hands at camp,

WILLIAM CAMPBELL,
ISAAC SHELBY,
BENJ. CLEVELAND.

The losses on our side were—one Colonel, one Major, one Captain, two Lieutenants, Four Ensigns, nineteen privates killed—total, twenty-eight killed ; one Major, three Captains, three Lieutenants, and fifty-five privates wounded—total, sixty-two wounded.

Published by order of Congress,

CHARLES THOMSON, SECRETARY.

———

COL. ISAAC SHELBY TO HIS FATHER, GEN. EVAN SHELBY.

[From the *Virginia Gazette*, November 4th, 1780.]

———

I have herewith the pleasure to acquaint you, that on Saturday, the 7th inst., in the afternoon, we came up with Ferguson and his crew, who lay encamped on the top of King's Mountain. The day was wet, and that Providence who always rules and governs all things for the best, so ordered it that we were close around them before we were discovered, and formed in such position, so as to fire on them nearly about the same time, though they heard us in time to form, and stood ready. The battle continued warm for an hour ; the enemy finding themselves so embarrassed on all sides, surrendered themselves prisoners to us at discretion.

They had taken post at that place with the confidence that no force could rout them ; the mountain was high, and exceedingly steep, so that their situation gave them greatly the advantage ; indeed, it was almost equal to storming a battery. In most places we could not see them till we were within twenty yards of them. They repelled us three times with charged bayonets ; but being determined to conquer or die, we came up a fourth time, and fairly got possession of the top of the eminence. Our loss I have not exactly collected, as the camp has been in such disorder ; but believe the killed to be about thirty-five men, and between fifty and sixty wounded.

A list of the killed, wounded, and prisoners of the British : Killed, Maj. Ferguson, one Captain, two Surgeons, and twenty-six privates. Wounded, one Lieutenant, and twenty-seven privates. Prisoners, one Captain, five Lieutenants, one Surgeon, and fifty privates.

Tories killed : Two Colonels, two Captains, and one hundred and twenty-five privates. Wounded, one hundred and twenty-five. Prisoners, one Colonel, one Major, twelve Captains, eleven Lieutenants, two Ensigns, two Adjutants, one Commissary, one Quarter-Master, eighteen Sergeants, and six hundred privates. Total, one thousand and sixteen ;

and seventeen baggage wagons, and twelve hundred stand of arms taken.

Our loss of killed and wounded : Col. Williams, of South Carolina, Capt. Edmondson, and five Lieutenants, of Virginia, and twenty-three privates of the different States. Wounded fifty-four of the different States.

COL. ISAAC SHELBY TO COL. ARTHUR CAMPBELL.

[From the *Virginia Argus*, October 26th, 1810.]

NORTH CAROLINA, *Oct. 12th, 1780.*

I have herewith the honor to acquaint you, that on Saturday, the 7th inst., in the afternoon, after a forced march of forty-five miles on that day and the night before, a detachment from our little army of mountain men, of about nine hundred, under command of Col. William Campbell, came up with Col. Ferguson, who lay encamped on King's Mountain.

The forenoon of the day was wet, but we were fortunate enough to come on him undiscovered, and took his pickets. We were soon formed in such order as to attack the enemy on all quarters. The Washington and Sullivan regiments began the attack on the front and left flank—the North Carolina regiments, under Cols. Williams, Sevier, and Cleveland, attacked the rear, and the other flank. The firing in about fifteen minutes, became general, and was kept up with fury on both sides for near an hour.

On the first onset, the Washington militia attempted rapidly to ascend the mountain ; but were met by the British regulars with fixed bayonets, and forced to retreat. They were soon rallied by their gallant commander and some of his active officers, and, by a constant and well-directed fire of our rifles, we drove them back, in our turn, and reached the summit of the mountain, where the enemy, being closely surrounded, surrendered prisoners at discretion. Their commander, Col. Ferguson, attempted, a little before the close of the action, to make his escape on horseback, but was intercepted by a few riflemen of the Sullivan regiment, and fell dead when forcing his way.

The post taken by the enemy, gave them confidence that any force the Americans could bring against them, could not defeat them. Truly the situation of the ground gave them greatly the advantage, as the mountain was high, and exceedingly steep in front, and interspersed along the top with craggy cliffs of rocks ; in short, it was almost equal to storming regular works.

The enclosed* list contains an account of the loss of the enemy. Ours is small as to numbers, being about thirty killed, and something over fifty wounded. Among the former are some brave men of our best officers, whose services their countrymen ought long to remember with gratitude.

COL. WM. CAMPBELL TO COL. ARTHUR CAMPBELL.

WILKES COUNTY, CAMP ON BRIER CREEK, *Oct. 20th, 1780.*

Dear Sir: Ferguson and his party are no more in circumstances to injure the citizens of America. We came up with him in Craven County, South Carolina, posted on a height, called King's Mountain, about twelve miles north of the Cherokee Ford of Broad river, about two o'clock in the evening of the 7th inst., we having marched the whole night before.

Col. Shelby's regiment and mine began the attack, and sustained the whole fire of the enemy for about ten minutes, while the other troops were forming around the height upon which the enemy were posted. The firing then became general, and as heavy as you can conceive for the number of men. The advantageous situation of the enemy, being the top of a steep ridge, obliged us to expose ourselves exceedingly ; and the dislodging of them was almost equal to driving men from strong breast-works ; though in the end we gained the point of the ridge, where my regiment fought, and drove them along the summit of it nearly to the other end, where Col. Cleveland and his countrymen were. They were driven into a huddle, and the greatest confusion ; the flag for a surrender was immediately hoisted, and as soon as our troops could be notified of it, the firing ceased, and the survivors surrendered themselves prisoners at discretion.

We fought an hour and five minutes, in which time two hundred and twenty-five of the enemy were killed, and one hundred and thirty wounded ; the rest, making about seven hundred regulars and Tories, were taken prisoners. Ferguson was killed near the close of the action. The victory was complete to a wish ; and I think it was won by about seven hundred men, who fought bravely. I have lost several of my brave friends, whose death I much lament. Maj. Edmondson will give you their names, though I must myself mention Capt. Edmondson, his two brothers, and Lieut. Bowen. My regiment has suffered more than any other in the action. Our loss in the field was, altogether, about thirty killed, and sixty wounded. I must proceed on with the prisoners until I can in some way dispose of them. Probably I may go on to Richmond, in Virginia.

* Not given, but doubtless the same as in the letter to Gen. Evan Shelby.

WASHINGTON'S GENERAL ORDER.

HEAD-QUARTERS, TOTOWAY, *Oct, 27th, 1780,*

The General has the pleasure to congratulate the army on an important advantage lately obtained in North Carolina, over a corps of fourteen hundred men, British troops and new levies, commanded by Col. Ferguson.

The militia of the neighboring Country, under Cols. Williams, Shelby, and others, having assembled to the number of about three thousand men, a detachment of sixteen hundred was sent on horseback to fall in with Ferguson's party, on its march to Charlotte. They came up with the enemy at a place called King's Mountain, advantageously posted, and gave him a total defeat, in which Col. Ferguson, and a hundred and fifty of his men were killed, eight hundred made prisoners, and fifteen hundred stand of arms taken. On our part, the loss was inconsiderable. We have only to regret that the brave Col. Williams is mortally wounded.

These advantages will, in all probability, have a very happy influence on opertions in that quarter, and are a proof of the spirit and resources of the country.*

KING'S MOUNTAIN—A FRAGMENT.
By Col. Arthur Campbell.

Soon after the defeat of the American army under Gen. Gates, the British commander in South Carolina made arrangements to invade North Carolina and Virginia. With this view, he organized a corps of the upland Tories, mostly riflemen, and attached to them two companies of his regular troops, giving the command of the whole to Maj. Patrick Ferguson, of the Seventy-first regiment, an intelligent officer, and well calculated for a separate command. The corps on the first outset, amounted to two thousand men. Orders were also sent to the British Indian agents, to excite the Indians to invade the American settlements west of the mountains ; and, if practicable, to proceed as far as Chiswell's Lead Mines, and destroy the works and stores at that place.

The main body, commanded by Cornwallis in person, was to move along the central road, by way of Salisbury, and form a junction with Ferguson before he entered into Virginia. Ferguson's detachment began the operation by marching towards the mountains ; and, on his way, met with a small regiment of North Carolina militia commanded by Charles and Joseph McDowell. They were attacked, and soon dispersed ; but the Colonel and Major, with a part of the men chose,

---

* Whiting's *Revolutionary Orders*, pp. 123-24.

rather than submit, to pass over the Apalachian mountains, and take refuge among their Whig brethern on the western waters. They arrived in the settlement on Watauga river, without their families, to the number of about one hundred and fifty men. Their tale was a doleful one, and tended to excite the resentment of the western militia, who of late had become inured to danger by fighting the Indians, and who had an utter detestation of the tyranny of the British Government.

At this period, early in September, the County Lieutenant of Washington was in Richmond. There he had an interview with the Governor of Virginia, who detailed the circumstances of Gen. Gates' defeat, the measures about to be taken to retrieve the late misfortune, and to expel the enemy from our country ; and that vigorous resistance everywhere would soon put an end to the war. On the return of the County Lieutenant, Col. Isaac Shelby, of North Carolina, sent to him a trusty messenger to inform him of the progress of Ferguson, and the retreat of McDowell's corps; and also to inquire whether it would be prudent to make an effort to enable the exiles to recross the mountains, and return to their own homes. Mr. Adair, the messenger, was told the Governor's sentiments on the subject of Gates' defeat, and the efforts that would soon be made, by order of Congress, to check the progress of the enemy ; and he was also assured, that if the western counties of North Carolina would raise a force to join Col. McDowell's men, that the officers of Washington County would co-operate to aid their friends to return home.

A consultation was soon had with the field officers, and a resolution agreed on, to order half the militia of Washington County into actual service, under the command of Col. William Campbell. All ranks seemed animated with the same spirit, and the quota was raised and equipped in a few days. An express was sent to Col. Cleveland, of Wilkes County, North Carolina, to let him know what was going on, and to march all the men he could raise, to rendezvous at an appointed place on the east side of the mountains. Cols. Shelby and Sevier acted their part, with like promptitude, in the western counties of North Carolina, and the whole met at Col. McDowell's encampment on Watauga.

On the twenty-eighth [twenty-sixth] of September our little army took up its line of march, and the third day in the evening reached the other side, without any opposition from the enemy. Two days afterwards, Col. Cleveland joined his corps to the main body ; and the day afterwards Col. Williams, with three companies of volunteers from South Carolina. A council of officers was held, and it was agreed that Col. William Campbell, of Virginia, should take command of the whole, and pursue the enemy. Col. Ferguson, after dispersing such parties of the North Carolina militia as were embodied, followed Col. McDowell's men as far as the foot of the great mountains, and after taking some prisoners, and collecting a drove of beeves, he made a hasty retreat to

King's Mountain, in order to be nearer the main army, and on account of the strong encampment that might be formed on the top of it. Our newly elected commander reviewed his men, and selected all that were fit for service of the mounted infantry, and ordered the footmen to follow as they might be able to hold out.

Those who have been familiar with the principal officers who fought on King's Mountain, and those who fought at Cowpens, will readily pronounce that the latter was a mere skirmish compared with the arduous affair on King's Mountain. There our heroes had to act as a forlorn hope—storm the enemy's camp, defended by superior numbers, and disciplined troops. The Virginia regiment alone had more killed than the whole of Gen. Morgan's corps. This proves where the hard fighting was, more than the pompous tale of a partial historian. It was Ferguson's defeat that was the first link in a grand chain of causes, which finally drew down ruin on the British interests in the Southern States, and finally terminated the war of the Revolution.

It has been remarked why so small a number of the Americans were killed at King's Mountain, compared with the loss of the enemy. Our officers accounted for it in this way: The Tories occupied much the least space of ground, and of course were more thickly planted than the extended circle of the Americans around them, so that the fire of our men seldom failed doing execution; besides, when the Virginia regiment reached the summit of the hill, the enemy was crowded, making their retreat to the other end, without returning a shot; and when they were driven into a huddle by meeting the fire of Col. Williams' division, they received a heavy fire before our troops could be notified of the surrender.

———

AN ACCOUNT OF THE MARCH AND BATTLE OF KING'S MOUNTAIN,

By an unknown member of Campbell's regiment.

———

On hearing of a large body of British and Tories assembled in North Carolina, under the command of Col. Ferguson, and threatening to visit Holston river, on the 22d of September, 1780, two hundred and fifty of the militia of Washington County, Virginia, were ordered out under the command of Col. William Campbell; and rendezvoused on Watauga, where they were joined by three hundred and fifty men from the western part of North Carolina under the command of Col. Sevier and Col. Isaac Shelby, together with a party of one hundred and fifty men, under the command of Col. Charles McDowell, who had been driven over the mountains by Col. Ferguson. While we were yet at the place of rendez-
34

vous, Col. Arthur Campbell, believing that there was not a sufficient force to successfully engage with the enemy, ordered out, and came on with two hundred more of the Washington militia, and joined us at Watauga.   Col. Arthur Campbell returned home to take care of the frontiers, which were left bare of men, and were in danger of being attacked by the Indians, who were near neighbors.

A council was held to select a commander, and it was unanimously given to Col. William Campbell.   We began our march from Watauga on the 27th * of September, with nine hundred and fifty men.   With a very bad road, we were four days in passing the mountains, when we arrived at the settlements of North Carolina ; and the next day we were joined by Col. Cleveland, from Wilkes County, and Maj. Winston, from Surry, with four hundred men.   From there we proceeded on, living mostly on parched corn.   We left four hundred footmen behind, not being able to keep up with the horse, and the fifth [sixth] of October, joined Col. Williams, and some Georgia troops, being about three hundred and fifty.   From Col. Williams' camp, we set out about dark, and traveled all that night, expecting to attack the enemy about break of day ; but Col. Ferguson sometime before hearing of our coming, retreated, and took an advantageous position at a place called King's Mountain, where the enemy thought they were very safely posted, and sent to Cornwallis for a re-inforcement.   But Col. Campbell proceeded so precipitately on his march, that we came on them with surprise, on the 7th of October, the sun being about an hour and a half high.

Col. Campbell ordered Col. Williams and Col. Cleveland to the left, and Col. Shelby for a reserve, and attacked on the right himself, making the first onset ; but the action soon became general—Col. Williams and Col. Cleveland acting with great bravery on the left.   Col. Ferguson ordered a charge to be made on the Virginia regiment, which forced some of them to retreat a short distance ; but they were rallied again, but the enemy fell so fast that they were obliged to retire to the top of the mountain.   Col. Shelby with the reserve came up, and in about half an hour the enemy was surrounded.

Too much cannot be said in praise of our brave commander, who exerted himself, animating the men to victory.   We advanced on the enemy, and broke their lines ; but they were rallied three times by Col. Ferguson, but to no effect ; our men pressing so close on them on every side, at length that active British officer, losing all hopes of victory, thought with some others to break through our lines and get off ; but fell in the attempt, Col. Ferguson having two balls through his body, and one through his head.   The enemy then soon surrendered.   The action lasted an hour and five minutes.   The enemy had about two hundred

---

* The official report, and Ensign Campbell's Diary, state that it was the 26th.

and thirty dead on the ground, and a number wounded. We lost some brave officers, and about thirty-five lay dead on the ground. The enemy mostly over-shot us, as we marched up the mountain. It was dark again we got the prisoners under guard. Cornwallis had sent Tarleton with four hundred dragoons to re-inforce Col. Ferguson, but hearing of his retreat, returned.

COL. CAMPBELL'S GENERAL ORDERS.

CAMP BELOW GILBERT TOWN, *Oct. 11, 1780.*

Return of the strength of the different regiments, with the rank and number of the dead and wounded, in the late action, to be immediately made out. Two hundred privates, with the proper and necessary number of officers, to mount guard every morning, who, with the field officers of the day, are to march with the front of the army, and when we camp are to take the charge of the prisoners immediately, to detach the necessary pickets and patrols. I must request the officers of all ranks in the army to endeavor to restrain the disorderly manner of slaughtering and disturbing the prisoners. If it cannot be prevented by moderate measures, such effectual punishment shall be executed upon delinquents as will put a stop to it.

CAMP AT COL. WALKER'S, *Oct. 13, 1780.*

Parole Newburn.

The Deputy Quarter-Masters, under the direction of the Quarter-Master General, to dispose of the wounded of their respective regiments, who are not able to march with the army, in the best manner they can, in the vicinity of this place. The Quarter-Masters to call upon the companies to which the wounded belong, for any necessary assistance for their removal. The Adjutants to wait upon the Brigade-Major at six o'clock every day for the orders. The army to march without fail by ten o'clock.

CAMP AT ————, *Oct. 14, 1780.*

The many desertions from the army, and consequent felonies committed by those who desert, oblige me once more to insist that proper regimental returns be made every morning, noting down the names of those who desert, that such may hereafter be punished with the justice which their crimes deserve; and officers commanding regiments are requested not to discharge any of their troops until we can dispose of the prisoners to a proper guard. The Quarter-Master General to see the ammunition taken from the enemy properly issued to the troops who have not yet drawn any of it. The Commissary-General to send small parties before us upon our route to collect provisions; and he is hereby empowered to call upon the commanding officers of the different regiments for such parties. It is with anxiety I hear the complaints of the inhabitants on account of the plundering parties who issue out from the camp, and indiscriminately rob both Whig and Tory, leaving our friends, I believe, in a worse situation than the enemy would have done. I hope the officers will exert themselves in suppressing this abominable practice, degrading to the name of soldier, by keeping their soldiers close in camp, and preventing their straggling off upon our marches.

CAMP AT BETHABARA, *Oct. 26, 1780.*

Parole Henry.

Col. Cleveland to take the command of the guards now here, and of those who may come to camp until I return, and in the meantime to issue such orders as may be necessary. Should I by letter direct the prisoners and troops to move from here, they are to do it, and go to such place as I shall so direct. The officers and soldiers all to lodge in camp, and to be and remain there from eight o'clock at night, until next morning after guard mounting, under pain of arrest or confinement. The officers ordered on guard, to attend strictly to their duty until they are relieved. The Commissary to issue full rations to the prisoners. The regular officers to continue at the place until I return, unless I shall direct them to be removed with the other prisoners. It is hoped no insult or violence unmerited will be offered to them. My wish is that no unnecessary injury be done to the inhabitants of this place or the adjacent country. No liquor to be sold or issued to the troops without an order from the commanding officer for the time being. This order respects all retailers of spirituous liquors in or near camp, of which they are to be made acquainted.

VOTE OF THANKS OF THE VIRGINIA LEGISLATURE TO COLONEL CAMPBELL.

IN THE VIRGINIA HOUSE OF DELEGATES, *Nov. 10th, 1780.*

RESOLVED, *nemine contradicente,* that the thanks of this House be given to Col. Wm. Campbell, of the County of Washington, and to the officers and soldiers of the militia under his command, who spontaneously equipt themselves, and went forth to the aid of a sister State, suffering distress under the invasion and ravages of the common enemy, and who combined with some detachments of militia from the neighboring States judiciously concerted, and bravely executed, an attack upon a party of the enemy commanded by Maj. Ferguson, consisting of about eleven hundred and forty-five men, British and Tories, strongly posted on King's Mountain; when after a severe and bloody conflict of upwards of an hour, the survivors of the enemy were compelled to surrender themselves prisoners of war. And that Col. Campbell be requested to communicate the contents of this resolution to the gallant officers and soldiers who composed his party.

ORDERED, that Mr. Joseph Jones of King George, Mr. Richard Henry Lee, and Mr. Fleming, be a committee to communicate the foregoing vote of thanks to Col. Campbell.

Test:

JOHN BECKLEY, C. H. D.

IN THE VIRGINIA SENATE, *Nov. 15th, 1780.*

RESOLVED, *nemine contradicente*, that the thanks of this House are justly due to Col. Wm. Campbell, of Washington County, and the brave officers and soldiers under his command, who, with an ardor truly patriotic, in the month of September last, without waiting for the call of Government, voluntarily marched out to oppose the common enemy, at that time making depredations on the frontiers of North Carolina, and on the 7th day of October, by a well-timed, judicious, and spirited attack, with a force inferior to that of Maj. Ferguson, then advantageously posted on King's Mountain, with upwards of eleven hundred men, and by perseverance and gallantry rarely to be met with even among veteran troops, totally defeated the whole party; whereby a formidable and dangerous scheme of the enemy was effectually frustrated.

Test:

WILL. DREW, C. S.

COL. HENRY LEE TO COL. CAMPBELL.

March 17th, 1781.

I am very happy in informing you that the bravery of your battalion, displayed in the action of the 15th, is particularly noticed by the General. It is much to be lamented that a failure took place in the line which lost the day, separated us from the main body, and exposed our retreat. I hope your men are safe, and that the scattered will again collect. Be pleased to favor me with a return of your loss, and prepare your men for a second battle.

I am, most respectfully, your obedient servant,

HENRY LEE, Jun.

COL. CAMPBELL.

GEN. GREENE TO COL. CAMPBELL.

———

HEAD-QUARTERS, *March 19th, 1781.*

Sir:—Your faithful services, and the exertions which you made to second the efforts of the Southern army, on the 15th inst, claim my warmest thanks. It would be ungenerous not to acknowledge my entire approbation of your conduct, and the spirited and manly behavior of the officers and soldiers under you. Sensible of your merit, I feel a pleasure in doing justice to it. Most of the riflemen having gone home, and not having it in my power to make up another command, you have my permission to return home to your friends, and should the emergency of the Southern operations require your further exertions, I will advertise you.

I am, sir, with great esteem, your most humble servant,

NATH'L. GREENE.

COL. CAMPBELL.

———

LA FAYETTE'S ORDERS.

———

August, 25th, 1781.

The General has no doubt but that the army will unite with him in regretting Gen. Campbell's death, an officer whose services must have endeared him to every citizen, and in particular to every American soldier. The glory which Gen. Campbell has acquired at the affairs of King's Mountain and Guilford Court House, will do his memory everlasting honor, and ensure him an high rank among the defenders of liberty in the American cause.

The General wishes it had been possible for himself and the officers of the army, to have paid him those honors to which his rank, but particularly his merit, so highly entitle him ; but his great distance from the army, and our present situation, render it impossible.

The Lieutenant of the County will assemble a corps of militia, and pay military honors to the deceased General. Gen. Stevens is requested to name a deputation of four field officers, who will immediately repair to Rocky Mills, and in the name of the army pay Gen. Campbell their last respects.

LA FAYETTE,

WM. BARBER, D. A. G.

[Extract from a letter from James Monroe, Governor of Virginia, to Robert R. Livingston, Minister Plenipotentiary from the U. S. to France, dated Richmond, Dec. 15th, 1801 :]

Sir: You will forgive my troubling you with an object which I do in confidence that you will execute it with pleasure. The late Gen. William Campbell of this State, a very gallant officer of the militia, rendered important services to his country in a severe encounter with a detachment of the British under the command of Col. Ferguson, on a mountain called King's Mountain, in North Carolina, in the year 1780. In that action, in which Gen. Campbell displayed great gallantry, Col. Ferguson was killed, his party defeated, and by means of it, the *first check given to the British in the South, after a series of unfortunate events.* In consideration of his services on the occasion, and as a testimony of the public acknowledgement of his merit, the General Assembly voted him a horse completely caparisoned, and a sword which the Executive was desired to present him with. It remains to provide the sword, which I have to request you will be so kind as to undertake for the Commonwealth.

DIARY OF MEMORANDUMS.

[From a small book kept by Ensign Robert Campbell.]

At the battle of King's Mountain the Americans had thirty killed, and about sixty wounded ; the British two hundred and twenty-five killed, and something less than that number wounded.

Col. David Campbell, of Campbell's Station, was in Dysart's company at the battle of King's Mountain. Col. Robert Campbell was the Ensign in the same company.

In the expedition to King's Mountain, Col. Campbell, Col. Shelby. and Col. Sevier rendezvoused at the Sycamore Flats, on Watauga, at the foot of Yellow Mountain, on the 25th of September, 1780. Next day, the 26th, they ascended this mountain, mostly on horseback, and encamped at night in the gap of the mountain on the opposite side. The ascent over this part of the mountain was not very difficult. There was a road ; but not one on which wagons could pass. No provisions were taken but such as each man could carry in his wallet or saddle-bags. The sides and top of the mountain were covered with snow, shoe-mouth deep. On the top of the mountain there was about one hundred acres of beautiful table land, in which a spring issued, ran through it, and over into the Watauga. Here the troops paraded. On reaching the plane beyond the mountain, they found themselves in a country covered with verdure, and breathed an atmosphere of summer mildness. The second night—the night of the 27th, they rested at Cathey's plantation. The third day, the 28th, they fell in with Gen. McDowell, and that night held a consultation of the officers. The General was without troops, yet his rank and former services could not easily be overlooked. It was stated in the council, that they needed an experienced officer to command them. Morgan was the man they wanted, and to obviate all difficulties Gen. McDowell offered to be the bearer of their wishes to Gen. Gates. The fourth night, the 29th, they rested at a rich Tory's, where they obtained abundance of every necessary refreshment. On the fifth day, the 30th, they reached the Catawba, and were there joined by Cleveland. Here they dispatched Gen. McDowell to Gen. Gates.

On passing near the Cowpens, they heard of a large body of Tories about eight miles distant ; and although the main enterprise was not to be delayed a single moment, a party of eighty volunteers, under Ensign Robert Campbell, was dispatched in pursuit of them during the night. They had, however, removed before the party came to the place, who, after riding all night, came up with the main body next day. On the next night a similar expedition was conducted by Captain Colvill, with no better success, but without causing any delay.

The battle was fought on Saturday, the 7th day of October, 1780. On the next Saturday, a court martial was held for the trial of the Tories. This is represented in history to have taken place immediately ; but it was the eighth day after the battle.

COL. ROBERT CAMPBELL'S CERTIFICATE.

I was an Ensign in Captain Dysart's company, in the battle of King's Mountain. Frequently saw Col. Campbell riding along our lines animating the men. About the middle of the action, Col. Shelby came riding where I was, and ordered me to follow him to a particular position to the right, to attack some of the enemy that were annoying us. We marched after him some distance, when the enemy fired at us. He then ordered me to form on a spur of the mountain in front, and retired. I there kept up a fire on the enemy until they retired to their main body, at which time I saw their flag raised. At this moment Col. Sevier came riding up, and we marched up with him to the line of surrender. I then discovered I was on the opposite side of the enemy from the Virginia regiment to which I belonged. I went round immediately in search of my brother. Col. Campbell shook me by the hand, and ordered me to mount one of the enemy's horses, and bring in all the men I could to guard the prisoners, which I did. Col. Campbell at this time was in his shirt sleeves.

[From the *Annals of the Army of Tennessee*, Oct., 1878.
MSS. of the Tennessee Historical Society.]

BATTLE OF KING'S MOUNTAIN.

By Ensign Robert Campbell.

The following account of the Battle of King's Mountain was found amongst the papers of James Campbell, deceased. It was written by Robert Campbell, an Ensign in Capt. Dysart's company, who, upon Capt. Dysart being wounded early in the action, commanded the company afterward. The scene is not within the limits of our State, but as we were then a portion of the Territory of North Carolina, and as many of our families had relatives engaged in it, I have thought proper to transcribe it, to be filed with the other historical documents of our Society.   JOHN R. EAKIN.

Nashville, Tenn., 1848.

In the fall of the year 1780, when the American cause wore a very gloomy aspect in the Southern States, Cols. Arthur and William Campbell, hearing of the advance of Colonel Ferguson along the mountains in the State of North Carolina, and that the Whigs were retreating before him, unable to make any effectual resistance, formed a plan to intercept him, and communicated it to the commanding officers of Sullivan and Washington Counties, in the State of North Carolina. They readily agreed to co-operate in any expedition against Col. Ferguson. Col. Arthur Campbell immediately ordered the militia of Washington Co., Virginia, amounting to near four hundred, to make ready to march under command of Col. Wm. Campbell, who was known to be an enterprising and active officer. Cols. Shelby and Sevier raised a party of three hundred, joined him on his march, and moved with forced marches toward Col. Ferguson. At the same time Cols. Williams, Cleveland, Lacey, and Brandon, of the States of North and South Carolina, each conducted a small party toward the same point, amounting to near three hundred. Col. Ferguson had notice of their approach by a deserter that left the army on the Yellow Mountain, and immediately commenced his march for Charlotte, dispatching at the same time different messengers to Lord Cornwallis with information of his danger. These messengers being intercepted on their way, no movement was made to favor his retreat.

These several corps of American volunteers, amounting to near one thousand men, met at Gilbert Town, and the officers unanimously chose Colonel Campbell to the command. About seven hundred choice riflemen mounted their horses for the purpose of following the retreating army. The balance being chiefly footmen, were left to follow on and come up as soon as they could. The pursuit was too rapid to render an escape practicable. Ferguson, finding that he must inevitably be over-taken, chose his ground, and waited for the attack on King's Mountain. On the 7th of October, in the afternoon, after a forced march of forty-five miles on that day and the night before, the volunteers came up with him. The forenoon of the day was wet, but they were fortunate enough to come on him undiscovered, and took his pickets, they not having it in their power to give an alarm. They were soon formed in such order as to attack the enemy on all sides. The Washington and Sullivan regiments were formed in the front and on the right flank; the North and South Carolina troops, under Cols. Williams, Sevier, Cleveland, Lacey, and Brandon, on the left. The two armies being in full view, the center of the one nearly opposite the center of the other—the British main guard posted nearly half way down the mountain—the commanding officer gave the word of command to raise the Indian war-whoop and charge. In a moment, King's Mountain resounded with their shouts, and on the first fire the guard retreated, leaving some of their men to crimson the earth. The British beat to arms, and immediately formed on the top of the mountain, behind a chain of rocks that appeared impregnable, and had their wagons drawn up on their flank across the end of the mountain, by which they made a strong breast-work.

Thus concealed, the American army advanced to the charge. In ten or fifteen minutes the wings came round, and the action became general. The enemy annoyed our troops very much from their advantageous position. Col. Shelby, being previously ordered to reconnoitre their position, observing their situation, and what a destructive fire was kept up from behind those rocks, ordered Robert Campbell, one of the officers of the Virginia Line, to move to the right with a small company to endeavor to dislodge them, and lead them on nearly to the ground to which he had ordered them, under fire of the enemy's lines and within forty steps of the same; but discovering that our men were repulsed on the other side of the mountain, he gave orders to advance, and post themselves opposite to the rocks, and near to the enemy, and then returned to assist in bringing up the men in order, who had been charged with the bayonet. These orders were punctually obeyed, and they kept up such a galling fire as to compel Ferguson to order a company of regulars to face them, with a view to cover his men that were posted behind the rocks. At this time, a considerable fire was drawn to this side of the mountain by the repulse of those on the other, and the Loyalists not being permitted to leave their posts. This scene was not of long duration, for it was the brave Virginia volunteers, and those under Col. Shelby, on their attempting rapidly to ascend the mountain, that were charged with the bayonet. They obstinately stood until some of them were thrust through the body, and having nothing but their rifles by which to defend themselves, they were forced to retreat. They were soon rallied by their gallant commanders, Campbell, Shelby and other brave officers, and by a constant and well-directed fire of their rifles, drove them back in their turn, strewing the face of the mountain with their assailants, and kept advancing until they drove them from some of their posts.

Ferguson being heavily pressed on all sides, ordered Capt. DePeyster to reinforce some of the extreme posts with a full company of British regulars. He marched, but to his astonishment when he arrived at the place of destination, he had almost no men, being exposed in that short distance to the constant fire of their rifles. He then ordered his cavalry to mount, but to no purpose. As quick as they were mounted, they were taken down by some bold marksmen. Being driven to desperation by such a scene of misfortune, Col. Ferguson endeavored to make his escape, and, with two Colonels of the Loyalists, mounted his horse, and charged on that part of the line which was defended by the party who had been ordered round the mountain by Col. Shelby, it appearing too weak to resist them. But as soon as he got to the line he fell, and the other two officers, attempting to retreat, soon shared the same fate. It was about this time that Col. Campbell advanced in front of his men, and climbed over a steep rock close by the enemy's lines, to get a view of their situation, and saw they were retreating from behind the rocks that were near to him. As soon as Capt. DePeyster observed that Col. Ferguson was killed, he raised a flag and called for quarters. It was soon taken out of his hand by one of the officers on horseback, and raised so high that it could be seen by our line, and the firing immediately ceased. The Loyalists, at the time of their surrender, were driven into a crowd, and being closely surrounded, they could not have made any further resistance.

In this sharp action, one hundred and fifty of Col. Ferguson's party were killed, and something over that number were wounded. Eight hundred and ten, of whom one hundred were British regulars, surrendered themselves prisoners, and one thousand five hundred stand of arms were taken. The loss of the American army on this occasion amounted to thirty killed, and something over fifty wounded, among whom were a number of brave officers. Col. Williams, who has been so much lamented, was shot through the body, near the close of the action, in making an attempt to charge upon Ferguson. He lived long enough to hear of the surrender of the British army. He then said, " I die contented, since we have gained the victory," and expired.

The third night after the action, the officers of the Carolinas complained to Col. Campbell, that there were among the prisoners a number who had, previous to the action on King's Mountain, committed cool and deliberate murder, and other enormities alike atrocious, and requested him to order a court-martial to examine into the matter. They stated that if they should escape, they were exasperated, and they feared they would commit other enormities worse than they had formerly done. Col. Campbell complied, and ordered a court-martial immediately to sit, composed of the Field Officers and Captains, who were ordered to inquire into the complaints which had been made. The court was conducted orderly, and witnesses were called and examined in each case. The consequence was that there were thirty-two condemned. Out of these, nine who were thought the most dangerous, and who had committed the most atrocious crimes, were executed. The others were pardoned by the commanding officer. One of the crimes proven against a Captain that was executed was, that he had called at the house of a Whig, and inquired if he was at home, and being informed by his son, a small boy, that he was not, he immediately drew out his pistol and shot him. The officers on the occasion acted from an honorable motive to do the greatest good in their power for the public service, and to check those enormities so frequently committed in the States of North and South Carolina at that time, their distress being almost unequaled in the annals of the American Revolution.

KING'S MOUNTAIN—BY COL. ISAAC SHELBY.

In 1815, and again in 1819, Gen. Martin D. Hardin, of Kentucky, had conversations with Governor Shelby with special reference to the battles of Musgrove's Mill, and King's Mountain, which he carefully noted down at the time; and which his son, the late Hon. John J. Hardin, of Illinois, communicated to the *American Review*, for December, 1848. That part relative to King's Mountain is as follows:

In the early part of the year 1780, Col. Shelby was appointed Colonel of Sullivan County in North Carolina, with the authority of County Lieutenant. Col. Sevier held the same command in Washington County, North Carolina. These Counties are situated west of the Alleghany mountains, and now constitute a part of Tennessee. Col. William Campbell, at the same time, commanded a regiment in Washington County, Virginia, but was not the County Lieutenant. After the defeat of Gen. Gates, at Camden, on the 16th of August, 1780, the patriots were very much dispirited. Many who resided in the eastern portions of North and South Carolina, sought safety and liberty in the mountains of North Carolina and Virginia, amidst the hardy, patriotic mountaineers of those districts.

In September, 1780, Maj. Ferguson, who was one of the best and most enterprising of the British officers in America, had succeeded in raising a large body of Tories, who, with his own corps of regulars, constituted an effective force of eleven hundred and twenty-five men. With a view of cutting off Col. Clarke, of Georgia, who had recently made a demonstration against Augusta, which was then in the hands of the British, Ferguson had marched near the Blue Ridge, and had taken post at Gilbert Town, which is situated but a few miles from the mountains. Whilst there he discharged a patriot, who had been taken prisoner, on his parole, and directed him to tell Col. Shelby, (who had become obnoxious to the British and Tories from the affair at Musgrove's Mill,) that if Shelby did not surrender, he (Ferguson) would come over the mountains, and put him to death, and burn his whole County.

It required no further taunt to rouse the patriotic indignation of Col. Shelby. He determined to make an effort to raise a force, in connection with other officers which should surprise and defeat Ferguson. With this object in view, he went to a horse-race near where Jonesborough has since been built, to see Sevier and others. Shelby and Sevier there resolved, that if Col. Campbell would join them, they would raise all the force they could, and attack Ferguson ; and if this was not practicable they would co-operate with any corps of the army of the United States with which they might meet. If they failed, and the country was over-run and subdued by the British, they would then take water, and go down to the Spaniards in Louisiana.

Col. Campbell was notified of their determination, and a place of rendezvous appointed in the mountains, east of Jonesborough. At the time appointed, September 25th, Campbell joined them, and their united force numbered about one thousand mounted riflemen. They crossed the mountains on the 27th, in a ravine ; and fell in, accidentally, with Col. Cleveland, of North Carolina, who had under his command about four hundred men.

The force having been raised by officers of equal rank, and being without any higher officer entitled to command the whole corps, there was a general want of arrangement and organization. It was then determined, that a board of officers should convene each night, and decide on the plan of operations for the next day ; and further, that one of the officers should see those orders executed as *officer of the day*, until they should otherwise conclude. Shelby proposed that Col. Campbell should act as officer of the day. Campbell took him aside, and requested Shelby to withdraw his name, and consent to serve himself. Shelby replied that he was himself the youngest Colonel present from his State, that he had served during that year under several of the officers who were present, and who might take offence if he commanded ; that Gen. McDowell, who was with them, was too slow an officer for his views of the enterprise in which they were engaged, and added that as he ranked Campbell, yet as Campbell was the only officer from Virginia, if he (Shelby) pressed his appointment, no one would object. Col. Campbell felt the force of this reasoning, and consented to serve, and was appointed to the command as officer of the day.

The force of the detachment was still considered insufficient to attack Ferguson, as his strength was not known. It was agreed that an express be sent to invite Gen. Morgan or Gen. Davidson to take the command. Gen. McDowell tendered his services for this purpose, and started on his mission. Before proceeding far, he fell in with Col. Williams, of South Carolina, who was at the head of from two to three hundred refugees. Gen. McDowell advised them where the patriot force was encamped. They joined the army, and thus made a muster-roll of about sixteen hundred men.

The board of officers determined to march upon Ferguson. In the meantime, two or three of their men had deserted after their first rendezvous, and had gone to Ferguson, and advised him of the intended attack. The army marched to Gilbert Town, and found that Ferguson had left it several days before, having taken the route towards Fort Ninety Six.

Finding that Ferguson was retreating, and learning what was his real strength, it was determined on Thursday night, the 5th of October, to make a desperate effort to overtake him before he should reach any British post, or receive any further reinforcements. Accordingly they selected all who had good horses, who numbered about nine hundred and ten, and started the next morning in pursuit of Ferguson, as soon as they could see.

Ferguson, after marching a short distance towards Ninety Six, had filed off to the left towards Lord Cornwallis. His pursuers never stopped until late in the afternoon, when they reached the Cowpens. They there halted, shot down some beeves, ate their suppers, and fed their horses. This done, the line of march was resumed, and continued through the whole night, amidst an excessively hard rain. In the morning, Shelby ascertained that Campbell had taken a wrong road in the night, and had separated from him. Men were posted off in all directions, and Campbell's corps found, and put in the right road. They then crossed Broad river, and continued their pursuit until twelve o'clock of the 7th of October. The rain continued to fall so heavily that Campbell, Sevier and Cleveland concluded to halt, and rode up to Shelby to inform him of their determination. Shelby replied, "By ——, I will not stop until night, if I follow Ferguson into Cornwallis' lines." Without replying, the other Colonels turned off to their respective commands, and continued the march. They had proceeded but a mile, when they learned that Ferguson was only seven miles from them at King's Mountain.

Ferguson, finding he could not elude the rapid pursuit of the mounted mountaineers, had marched to King's Mountain, which he considered a strong post, and which he had reached the night previous. The mountain or ridge, was a quarter of a mile long, and so confident was Ferguson in the strength of his position, that he declared, "the Almighty could not drive him from it."

When the patriots came near the mountain they halted, tied all their loose baggage to their saddles, fastened their horses, and left them under charge of a few men, and then prepared for an immediate attack. About three o'clock the patriot force was led to the attack in four columns— Col. Campbell commanded the right centre column, Col. Shelby the left centre, Col. Sevier the right flank column, and Col. Cleveland the left flank. As they came to the foot of the mountain, the right centre and right flank columns deployed to the right, and the left centre and left flank columns to the left, and thus surrounding the mountain they marched up, commencing the action on all sides.

Ferguson did all that an officer could do under the circumstances. His men too fought bravely. But his position, which he thought impregnable against any force the patriots could raise, was really a disadvantage to him. The summit was bare, whilst the sides of the mountain were covered with trees. Ferguson's men were drawn up in close column on the summit, and thus presented fair marks for the mountaineers, who approached them under cover of the trees. As either column would approach the summit, Ferguson would order a charge with fixed bayonet, which was always successful, for the riflemen retreated before the charging column slowly, still firing as they retired. When Ferguson's men returned to regain their position on the mountain, the patriots would again rally and pursue them. In one of these charges, Shelby's column was considerably broken ; he rode back and rallied his men, and when the enemy retired to the summit, he pressed on his men and reached the summit whilst Ferguson was directing a charge against Cleveland.

Col. Sevier reached the summit about the same time with Shelby. They united and drove back the enemy to one end of the ridge. Cleveland's and Campbell's columns were still pressing forward, and firing as they came up. The slaughter of the enemy was great, and it was evident that further resistance would be unavailing ; still Ferguson's proud heart could not think of surrender. He swore "he never would yield to such a d—d banditti," and rushed out from his men, sword in hand, and cut away until he broke his sword, and was shot down. His men, seeing their leader fall, immediately surrendered. The British loss in killed and prisoners was eleven hundred and five. Ferguson's morning report showed a force of eleven hundred and twenty-five. A more total defeat was not practicable. Our loss was about forty killed. Amongst them we had to mourn the death of Col. Williams, a most gallant and efficient officer. The battle lasted one hour.

The victors encamped on the mountain that night, and the next morning took up their line of march for the mountains under a bright sun, the first they had seen for many days. They made the prisoners carry their own arms, as they could not have carried them in any other way. Amongst the prisoners, Shelby found some officers who had fought under him a few weeks previously at Musgrove's Mill. They said they had been compelled to join Ferguson, and when they had been examined, and their account found to be correct, they were well treated.

Owing to the number of wounded, and the destitution of the army of all conveyances, they traveled slowly, and in one week had only marched about forty miles. When they reached Gilbert Town, a week after the battle, they were informed by a paroled officer, that he had seen eleven patriots hung at Ninety Six a few days before, for being Rebels. Similar cruel and unjustifiable acts had been committed before. In the opinion of the patriots, it required retaliatory measures to put a stop to these atrocities. A copy of the law of North Carolina was obtained, which authorized two magistrates to summon a jury, and forthwith to try, and if found guilty, to execute persons who had violated its precepts. Under this law, thirty-six men were tried, and found guilty of breaking open houses, killing the men, and turning the women and children out of doors, and burning the houses. The trial was concluded late at night. The execution of the law was as summary as the trial. Three men were hung at a time, until nine were hung. Three more were tied ready to be swung off. Shelby interfered, and proposed to stop it. The other officers agreed, and the three men who supposed they had seen their last hour, were untied. One of them said to Shelby, "You have saved my life, and I will tell you a secret. Tarleton will be here in the morning. A woman has brought the news."

It was then two o'clock at night, but no time was to be lost; the camp was instantly aroused, everything packed up, the wounded sent into secret hiding places in the mountains, and the line of march taken up.

The next day it rained incessantly, but the army continued its march without stopping, until they crossed the Catawba at two o'clock the succeeding night. The river was breast high when they crossed it. The weary troops bivouacked on its banks, and the next morning it had risen so much as to be past fording. This obstacle being such as to prevent all pursuit, they leisurely retired with their prisoners. As an evidence of the hardships undergone by these brave and hardy patriots, Col. Shelby says, that he ate nothing from Saturday morning until after they encamped Sunday night at two o'clock, A. M.

The information given Shelby by the condemned prisoners, turned out to have been substantially correct. Lord Cornwallis had detached Tarleton to pursue and attack the patriots, and to rescue the prisoners. Soon after Tarleton was dispatched, the former took an old Whig prisoner, and examined him. He told the prisoner he could not learn who had defeated Ferguson. The old man told him. Cornwallis then inquired the force of the patriots. He told him it was three thousand riflemen. Cornwallis asked where they were gone. He replied, they were bearing down on him. Whether this was told under the belief that it was true, or told as a *ruse de guerre*, it answered a very excellent purpose. Lords Cornwallis and Rawdon immediately consulted together, beat to arms, struck their tents, burnt some extra clothing, and retreated to the south side of Broad river in confusion. At the same time, a messenger was sent to recall Tarleton, who was overtaken after he had proceeded eighteen miles, and who immediately returned to Cornwallis' camp.

At the time Shelby and his co-patriots raised their force, Cornwallis, supposing he would meet no further serious resistance in North or South Carolina, had projected the invasion of Virginia in three columns. He was to advance in the centre, a second detachment was to march on his right, and Ferguson was to command the left wing. The time for the invasion was fixed, officers were out through the country collecting the Tories, and a few days more would have made them very strong. The defeat of Ferguson prevented this invasion, and so intimidated the Tories, that most of them declined joining the British, generally preferring to make a profession of faith to King George rather than take up arms in his behalf.

At the time the nine hundred and ten men were selected to pursue Ferguson, they were informed that there were six hundred Tories embodied near them, and it was suggested that they should be attacked. Shelby opposed this, saying that if they turned after any other object they would lose Ferguson.

After the battle at King's Mountain, this force, like all other partisan bodies called out for a particular emergency, was difficult to be kept embodied. The men one after another returned home, so that when they reached the Catawba there were not more men than prisoners.

It is impossible for those who have not lived in its midst, to conceive of the exasperation which prevails in a civil war. The execution, therefore, of the nine Tories at Gilbert Town, will by many persons be considered an act of retaliation unnecessarily cruel. It was believed by those who were on the ground, to be both necessary and proper, for the purpose of putting a stop to the execution of the patriots in the Carolinas by the Tories and British. The event proved the justice of the expectation of the patriots. The execution of the Tories did stop the execution of the Whigs. And it may be remarked of this cruel and lamentable mode of retaliation, that whatever excuses and pretences the Tories may have had for their atrocities, the British officers, who often ordered the execution of Whigs, had none. Their training to arms and military education, should have prevented them from violating the rules of civilized warfare in so essential a point.

35

Those patriots who desired to continue in the service after the battle at King's Mountain, especially the refugees, wished to be formed into a corps and to be under the command of Gen. Morgan. To effect this Col. Shelby went to head-quarters and saw Morgan, who said they were just the men he wanted. Gen. Gates consented, and the Board of War of North Carolina ordered out these militia, who marched up and joined Morgan; most of them were with him the next campaign, and proved the stuff they were made of at the nobly-won battle of the Cowpens.

BATTLE OF KING'S MOUNTAN.—BY GEN. JOSEPH GRAHAM. *

After the defeat of Gen. Gates and the army under his command, on the 16th of August, 1780, and the defeat of Gen. Sumter, two days afterwards, near Rocky Mount, by Col. Tarleton, the South was almost entirely abandoned to the enemy. Most of the troops, both officers and men, who had escaped from Gates' defeat, passed through Charlotte, N. C., where most of the militia of Mecklenburg County, were assembled in consequence of the alarm. The regular troops chiefly passed on to Hillsboro', where Gen. Gates finally established his head-quarters. William L. Davidson, who had served as Lieutenant-Colonel of the regulars in the Northern army, was appointed Brigadier-General of the militia in the Salisbury District, in the place of Gen. Rutherford, who was taken prisoner at Gates' defeat. He formed a brigade, and encamped on McAlpin's creek, about eight miles below Charlotte, and in the course of two or three weeks was reinforced by Gen. Sumner, a Continental officer, but having no regulars to command, he took command of the militia from the counties of Guilford, Caswell, Orange, &c.

After Gates' defeat, the attention of Lord Cornwallis was chiefly occupied with burying the dead, taking care of the wounded, and forwarding, under suitable guards, the great number of prisoners he had taken, to the city of Charleston, and regulating the civil government he was establishing in South Carolina, and examining the state of the posts occupied by his troops on the Congaree, Ninety Six and Augusta. By the 1st of September, he had his arrangements made, and detached Col. Ferguson over the Wateree with only one hundred and ten regulars, under the command of Capt. DePeyster, and about the same number of Tories, but with an ample supply of arms and other military stores. His

---

*Gen. Graham was in the hospital at the time the battle was fought, and gained his knowledge of the action from those who participated in it. He subsequently visited the battle ground with a son of one of the officers. He errs as to the position occupied by Col. Shelby. which, according to his own statement, was on the left center, or north-west side of the mountain. The number executed is over-stated. This paper first appeared in the *Southern Literary Messenger,* for September, 1845, and was afterwards copied into Foote's *Sketches of North Carolina,* and the *North Carolina University Magazine* for April, 1856.

movements were at first rapid, endeavoring to intercept the retreat of a party of mountain men, who were harassing the upper settlement of Tories in South Carolina. Failing in this, he afterwards moved slowly, and frequently halted to collect all the Tories he could persuade to join him. He passed Broad river, and before the last of September encamped at a place called Gilbert Town, within a short distance of where the thriving village of Rutherfordton now stands.

His forces had increased to upwards of one thousand men. On his march to this place, he had furnished arms to such of his new recruits as were without them. The greater part of them had rifles, but to a part of them he had them to fix a large knife they usually carried, made small enough at the butt end for two inches or more of the handle to slip into the muzzle of the rifle, so that it might be occasionally used as a bayonet.

Although Col. Ferguson failed to overtake the detachment of mountain men alluded to, he took two of them prisoners, who had become separated from their comrades. In a day or two, he paroled them, and enjoined them to inform the officers on the western waters, that if they did not desist from their opposition to the British arms, and take protection, under his standard, that he would march his army over the mountains, hang their leaders, and lay the country waste with fire and sword.

Col. Charles McDowell, of Burke County, on the approach of Ferguson with so large a force, had gone over the mountains to obtain assistance, and was in consulation with Col. John Sevier and Col. Isaac Shelby what plan should be pursued, when the two paroled men spoken of arrived, and delivered their message from Col. Ferguson.

It was decided that each of them should use his best efforts to raise all the men that could be enlisted, and that their forces when collected, should meet on the Watauga, on the 25th of September. It was also agreed, that Col. Shelby should give intelligence of their movements to Col. William Campbell of the adjoining County of Washingion, in Virgina, with the hope that he would raise what force he could, and coöperate with them.

They met on the Watauga the day appointed, and passed the mountain on the 30th of Sept., where they were joined by Col. Benjamin Cleveland and Maj. Joseph Winston, from Wilkes and Surry Counties.

On examining their forces, they were found to number as follows:

From Washington County, Virginia, under Col. W. Campbell,	400
From Sullivan County, North Carolina, under Col. Isaac Shelby,	240
From Washington, North Carolina, under Col. John Sevier,	240
From Burke and Rutherford Counties, N. C., under Col. Charles McDowell,	160
From Wilkes and Surry Counties, North Carolina, under Col. Benj. Cleveland and Major Joseph Winston,	350
Total,	1,390

Col. Ferguson having accurate intelligence of the force collecting against him, early on the fourth of October, ordered his men to march, and remained half an hour after they had started writing a dispatch to Lord Cornwallis, no doubt informing him of his situation, and soliciting aid. The letter was committed to the care of the noted Abraham Collins, (since of counterfeit memory,) and another person, by the name of Quin, with injunctions to deliver it as soon as possible. They set out, and attempted to pass the direct road to Charlotte, but having to pass through some Whig settlements, they were suspected and pursued, and being compelled to secrete themselves by day, and travel by night, they did not reach Charlotte until the morning of the 7th of October (the day of the battle). Col. Ferguson encamped the first night at the noted place called the *Cowpens*, about twenty miles from Gilbert Town. On the 5th of October, he crossed Broad River at what is now called Deer's Ferry, sixteen miles. On the 6th he marched up the Ridge Road, between the waters of King's and Buffalo creeks, until he came to the fork turning to the right, across King's creek, and through a gap of the mountain towards Yorkville, about fourteen miles. Then he encamped on the summit of that part of the mountain to the right of the road, where he remained until he was attacked on the 7th.

When the troops from the different Counties met, at the head of the Catawba river, the commanding officers met, and finding that they were all of equal grade, and no general officer to command, it was decided that Col. Charles McDowell should go to Head-Quarters, supposed to be between Charlotte and Salisbury, to obtain Gen. Sumner or Gen. Davidson to take the command. In the meantime, it was agreed that Col. William Campbell, who had the largest regiment, should take the command until the arrival of a general officer, who was to act according to the advice of the Colonels commanding, and that Maj. Joseph McDowell should take the command of the Burke and Rutherford regiment, until the return of Col. McDowell.

Shortly after these measures were adopted, intelligence was received that Col. Ferguson had left Gilbert Town, and it was decided that they would march after him, by that place, and on their way received evidence that it was his design to evade an engagement with them. On the evening of the 6th [4th] of October, the Colonels in council unanimously resolved, that they would select all the men and horses fit for service, and immediately pursue Ferguson until they should overtake him, leaving such as were not able to go, to come after as fast as they could. The next evening the selection was made, and nine hundred and ten men, including officers, were marched before, leaving the others to follow.

They came to the Cowpens, where Ferguson had camped on the night of the 4th, and there met Col. Williams, of South Carolina, with near four hundred men, and about sixty from Lincoln County, who had joined them on their march, under Col. Hambright and Maj. Chronicle After drawing rations of beef, the whole proceeded on, a little before sunset, taking Ferguson's trail towards Deer's Ferry, on Broad river. Night coming on, and being very dark, their pilot got out of the right way, and for some time they were lost; but before daylight they reached near to the ferry, and by direction of the officers, the pilot led them to the Cherokee ford, about a mile and a half below, as it was not known but the enemy might be in possession of the eastern bank of the river. It was on the morning of the 7th before sunrise, when they crossed the river, and marched about two miles to the place where Ferguson had encamped on the night of the 5th.

There they halted a short time, and took such breakfast as their wallets and saddle-bags could afford. The day was showery, and they were obliged to use their blankets, and their great coats, to protect their arms from wet. They passed on a dozen miles without seeing any person; at length, they met a lad, in an old field, by the name of Fonderin, about twelve or fourteen years of age, who had a brother and other relations in Ferguson's camp, and who was directly from it—within less than three miles. A halt was ordered, and the Colonels met in consultation. Several persons knew the ground well on which the enemy was encamped, agreeable to the information given by the boy of their position. The plan of battle was immediately settled, that the force should be nearly equally divided, and one-half would take to the right, cross over and occupy the south-east side of the mountain, and that the other should advance to the north-west side, and that each division would move forward until they formed a junction, when all should face to the front, and press upon the enemy up the sides of the mountain. Orders were given to prepare for battle, by laying aside every incumbrance, examining well their arms, and guarding against alarm. The orders were speedily obeyed, and they moved forward over King's creek, and up a branch and ravine, and between two rocky knobs, which, when they had passed, the top of the mountain and the enemy's camp upon it, were in full view, about one hundred poles in front. Here they halted, and tied their horses, leaving the necessary guard with them. It was now three o'clock in the afternoon.

The enemy's camp was to the right of the road, seventy or eighty poles in length, and on the summit of the mountain, which at this place runs nearly north-east and south-west, the shadow of the timber at half-past one P. M., ranges with it. The troops were led on in the following order:—To the right, Maj. Winston, Col. Sevier, Col. Campbell, Col. Shelby and Major McDowell—To the left, Col. Hambright, Col. Cleveland, and Col. Williams, of South Carolina.

Each division moved off steadily to the place assigned it in the order of battle. Some of the regiments suffered much under the galling fire of the enemy, before they were in a position to engage in the action. Some complaints began to be uttered, *that it would never do to be shot down* without returning the fire. Col. Shelby replied—"press on to your places, and then your fire will not be lost."

The men led by Shelby and McDowell were soon closely engaged, and the contest from the first was very severe. Williams and Cleveland were soon in their places, and with the utmost energy engaged the foe. Ferguson finding that the end of his line was giving away, ordered forward his regulars and riflemen with bayonets, and made a furious charge upon Shelby and McDowell, charging down the mountain some two hundred yards. A united and destructive fire soon compelled him to order his party back to the top of the mountain to ward off the deadly attack from Col. Williams. Ferguson again charged with fury down the mountain. When Shelby's men saw this, they raised the cry, "come on, men, the enemy is retreating." They rallied by the time Ferguson returned from the charge against the South Carolinans, and renewed their fire with great resolution. Ferguson again charged upon Shelby, but not so far as before. Col. Williams' men, in turn, called out, "the enemy is retreating, come on, men !"

At this stage of the action, Hambright and Winston had met, and a brisk fire was poured upon Ferguson's men all around the mountain. As he would advance towards Campbell, Sevier, Winston, and Hambright, he was pursued by Shelby, McDowell, Williams and Cleveland. When he would turn his forces against the latter, the former would press on in pursuit. Thus he struggled on, making charges and retreats, but his left was rapidly losing ground. His men were rapidly falling before the skillful aim, and unbending courage, of the Whigs. Even after being wounded, he fought on with courage. He made every effort that could be done by a brave and skillful officer, according to his position. At length he was shot dead, and his whole command driven up into a group of sixty yards in length, and not forty in width.

The British officer, Capt. DePeyster, who took the command, ordered a white flag to be raised, in token of surrender, but the bearer was instantly shot down. He soon had another raised, and called out for quarter. Col. Shelby demanded, if they surrendered, why they did not throw down their arms ? This was instantly done. But still the firing was continued, until Shelby and Sevier went inside the lines, and ordered the men to cease. Some who kept it up, would call out, "give them Buford's play"—alluding to Col. Buford's defeat by Tarleton, where no quarters were given. A guard was placed over the prisoners, and all remained on the mountain during the night.

The party which led the left wing under Col. Hambright, suffered very much, having to pass very difficult ground to reach their place of destination, and within eighty yards of the enemy's marksmen. Col.

Hambright was wounded, and Maj. Chronicle was killed. Col. Williams, of South Carolina, a brave and efficient officer, was also killed. The loss of the Whigs was not exactly ascertained, but believed to be about thirty killed, and fifty wounded. The enemy had about one hundred and fifty killed, and all the rest taken prisoners. On the morning of the 8th [14th], a court-martial was held, several of the prisoners who were found guilty of murder, and other high crimes, were sentenced to be hanged. About twenty [nine only] were executed.

[From Wheeler's *History of North Carolina.*]

[An account of the *Battle of King's Mountain*, prepared by Gen. William Lenoir for Judge A. D. Murphy's intended *History of North Carolina.*]

Having lately seen in the *State Gazette*, a publication of Mr. Walker's circular letter, in which there is a very imperfect statement of the battle at King's Mountain, brings to my recollection your request for a true account thereof; and having previously observed, that in all the histories of the Revolutionary war that I have seen, the accounts of that battle are very erroneous, induces me to attempt to fulfill your desire on that subject, by giving you as perfect an account of that transaction from my own knowledge, as my memory at so distant a period will enable me to do.

When a report was circulated that a detachment of the British army had advanced through the State of South Carolina, and a part of North Carolina, as far as Cane creek, where a strong party of them were repulsed by the neighboring militia, chiefly of Burke County, under the command of Col. Chas. McDowell, and Maj. J. McDowell, the active Whigs of the western part of North Carolina, and some from the near part of Virginia, like patriots at a moment's notice, without any call from the Government, turned out and concentrated in Burke County, without any aid from public stores, of clothing, arms, ammunition, or any article of camp equipage, not having a single tent or baggage wagon amongst them, and advanced to Green river, near the southern limit of Rutherford County, where they received some further but imperfect information of the progress of the aforesaid detachment of the British army, commanded by the celebrated Col. Ferguson, who was said to be progressing through the country in various directions, committing great ravages and depredations.

A council was held by the principal officers of the Whigs; the result of which was, that, on presumption that, through the medium of the

Tories, Col. Ferguson had daily information of the advancement of the Whigs, and was so on the alert, that men on foot would not be able to overtake him, therefore orders were given for as many as had, or could procure, horses, to go in advance as mounted infantry, there not being a single dragoon in the Whig army. Whereupon, about five or six hundred were prepared and marched off about sunrise on the 6th day of October, 1780, leaving the footmen, about one thousand five hundred in number, encamped on Green river, under the command of Maj. Joseph Herndon. The advance party of mounted infantry being joined by Col. Williams, with a few South Carolina militia, in the evening arrived at a place called the Cowpens, in South Carolina, where two beeves were killed, and orders given for the men to cook and eat as quick as possible; but marching orders were given before those that were indolent had prepared anything to eat; and they marched all night (being dark and rainy), and crossed Broad river the next morning, where an attack was expected. But not finding the enemy, the detachment almost exhausted by fatigue, hunger, cold and wet, and, for want of sleep, pursued their march a few miles, when they met two men from Col. Ferguson's camp, who gave some account of his situation. Then being revived by the hopes of gaining the desired object, the officers held a short consultation—sitting on their horses—in which it was concluded that said detachment should be formed into four columns; two of the columns should march on each side of the road, as silently as they could, and that they should govern their march by the view of each other; Col. Winston was placed at the head of the right hand column; Col. Cleveland at the head of the left; and Cols. Shelby and Sevier at the heads of the two middle columns; and as Col. Campbell had come the greatest distance, and from the State of Virginia, he was complimented with the command of the whole detachment.

When they had marched in that order about a mile, Col. Winston, by a steep hill, had got so far separated from the other columns as to be out of sight or hearing of them, when some men rode in sight and directed him to dismount, and march up the hill, which was immediately done, with an expectation of meeting the enemy on the hill; but before his men had advanced two hundred paces from their horses, they were again hailed, and directed to mount their horses and push on, and that the enemy was a mile ahead. On which they ran with great precipitation down to their horses, mounted them, and rode like fox hunters, as fast as their horses could run, through rough woods, crossing branches and ridges without any person that had any knowledge of the woods to direct or guide them. They happened to fall in upon the left of the enemy, the place of their destination. At this very moment the firing began on the other parts of the lines, when all dismounted under the fire of the enemy, and the right and left hand columns surrounded them as quick as possible. In the meantime, the enemy charged bayonets on the two middle columns, who being armed with rifles, and not a single bayonet amongst them, were twice obliged to retreat a small distance; but they wheeled again with increased vigor, and fought bravely. The enemy being surrounded, their left wing began to retreat, by drawing up in closer order towards their right. At length they hoisted a flag and surrendered themselves prisoners of war; not a single man of them escaped that was in camp at the commencement of the battle.

After the arms and prisoners were secured, some men were appointed to number the dead. They reported two hundred and fifty of the enemy; and thirty-two of the Whigs. There were not near so many of the enemy wounded as were of the Whigs, about forty of whom afterwards died of their wounds. The total number of the Whigs in the battle was between six and seven hundred; and the number of the enemy, agreeable to their daily returns, was eleven hundred and eighty-seven. The Whigs camped on the battle-ground, and marched off with their prisoners the next day; and, having no other way to secure the arms taken, compelled the prisoners to carry them, a great number of them having to carry two guns each. About sunset we met the footmen they had left at Green river, who had provided a plenty of rations, &c. The Whigs who had fought the battle were almost famished.

A few days afterwards, in Rutherford County, the principal officers held a court-martial over some of the most audacious and murderous Tories, and selected thirty-two as victims for destruction; and commenced hanging three at a time until they hung nine, and respited the rest.

Col. Ferguson had placed himself on the top of King's Mountain the morning before the battle; in a boasting manner he had proclaimed that here was King's Mountain, and that he was the King of that Mountain, supposing it to be a very advantageous position for him; but it proved the reverse, from the manner he was attacked and surrounded. His elevated situation secured the Whigs from the danger of their own fire from the opposite side, and he, being surrounded, when his men sheltered themselves on one side, they were exposed to danger on the other. Col. Ferguson had seven or eight bullets shot through him, and fell some time before the battle was over. The number of the Whigs was so inferior, that Col. Ferguson, or his successor in command, might have easily retreated with very inconsiderable loss; if they had known the number and situation of the Whigs, no doubt but they would have retreated instead of surrendering.

It appears that under the auspices of the same Divine Power that so advantageously conducted the right hand column of the Whigs to the battle at King's Mountain, from that period good fortune seemed to preponderate in every direction in favor of the common cause of liberty—except the single instance of Gen. Gates, who was [previously] defeated by his own imprudence; for although the British army kept the battle-ground at Guilford Court-House, it appears to be given up on both sides, that the Americans had the best of that battle, and disabled their enemy. And to contrast the situation of the Whigs after the battle of King's Mountain, with what inevitably would have been their situation in case Ferguson's army had gained as complete a victory over the Whigs, as the Whigs had done over them, it must appear that said battle was the most decisive, the most gloriously fought, and although few in number, was of the greatest importance of any one battle that ever was fought in America.   *   *   *   *

I was Captain of a company of footmen, and left them at Green river, except six of them, who procured horses and went with us. I went as a common soldier, and did not pretend to take command of those that belonged to my company; neither did I join any other company; but fell in immediately behind Col. Winston, in front of the right hand column, which enables me to give a more particular account of the progress of that part of our army than any other.   Before the battle, Adjutant Jesse Franklin, now Governor of North Carolina, Capt. Robt. Cleveland, and myself, agreed to stand together and support each other; but at the commencement of the battle, enthusiastic zeal caused us all to separate.   Each being anxious to effect the grand object, no one appeared to regard his own personal safety.   As to my own part, from where we dismounted, instead of going on to surround, I advanced the nearest way towards the enemy, under a heavy fire, until I got within about thirty paces.   Before they began to give ground, being among strangers, I noticed one particular instance of bravery.   On hearing a man within six feet behind me fall, I looked around, and at that instant another soldier jumped at him saying. "Give me your shot-bag, old fellow!" his own ammunition being exhausted.   The gallant patriot gave him, with his dying, hand his ammunition.   About that time, I received a slight wound in my side, and another in my left arm; and, after that, a bullet went through my hair about where it was tied, and my clothes were cut in several places.   From the account I have given of the battle, it will be understood that it was fought on our side by militia alone.   By that victory, many militia officers procured swords who could not possibly get any before; neither was it possible to procure a good supply of ammunition.

[From the *American Pioneer*, Feb. 1843.]

BATTLE OF KING'S MOUNTAIN.

By Benjamin Sharp.

As well as I can remember, some time in August, in the year 1780,

Col. McDowell, of North Carolina, with three or four hundred men, fled over the mountains to the settlements of Holston and Watauga, to evade the pursuit of a British officer by the name of Ferguson, who had the command of a large detachment of British and Tories. Our militia speedily embodied, all mounted on horses—the Virginians under the command of Col. William Campbell, and the two western counties of North Carolina, now Tennessee, under Cols. Isaac Shelby and John Sevier; and as soon as they joined McDowell, he re-crossed the mountains, and formed a junction with Col. Cleveland, with a fine regiment of North Carolina militia. We were now fifteen or eighteen hundred strong, and considered ourselves equal in numbers, or at least a match for the enemy, and eager to bring them to battle; but Col. McDowell, who had the command, appeared to think otherwise, for although Ferguson had retreated on our crossing the mountains, he kept us marching and counter-marching, for eight or ten days without advancing a step towards our object. At length a council of the field-officers was convened, and it was said in camp, how true I will not pretend to say, that he refused in council to proceed without a general officer to command the army, and to get rid of him, the council deputed him to Gen. Greene, at Head-Quarters, to procure a General. Be this as it may, as soon as the council rose, Col. McDowell left the camp, and we saw no more of him during the expedition.

As soon as he was fairly gone, the council re-assembled, and appointed Col. William Campbell our commander, and within one hour after, we were on our horses and in full pursuit of the enemy. The British still continued to retreat, and after hard marching for some time, we found our progress much retarded by our footmen and weak horses that were not able to sustain the duty. It was then resolved to leave the footmen and weak horses under the command of Capt. William Neil, of Virginia, with instructions to follow as fast as his detachment could bear. Thus disencumbered, we gained fast upon the enemy. I think on the 7th [6th] day of October, in the afternoon, we halted at a place called the Cowpens, in South Carolina, fed our horses, and ate a hasty meal of such provisions as we had procured, and, by dark mounted our horses, and after marching all night, crossed Broad river by the dawn of day; and although it rained considerably in the morning, we never halted to refresh ourselves or horses. About twelve o'clock it cleared off with a fine cool breeze. We were joined that day [really, the night before] by Col. Williams, of South Carolina, with several hundred men; and in the afternoon fell in with three men who informed us that they were just from the British camp, that they were posted on the top of King's Mountain, and that there was a picket-guard on the road not far ahead of us. These men were detained lest they should find means to inform the enemy of our approach, and Col. Shelby, with a select party, undertook to surprise and take the picket; this he accomplished without firing a gun or giving the least alarm, and it was hailed by the army as a good omen.

We then moved on, and as we approached the mountain, the roll of the British drum informed us that we had something to do. No doubt the British commander thought his position a strong one; but our plan of attack was such as to make it the worst for him he could have chosen. The end of the mountain to our left descended gradually to a branch; in front of us the ascent was rather abrupt, and to the right was a low gap through which the road passed. The different regiments were directed by guides to the ground they were to occupy, so as to surround the eminence on which the British were encamped; Campbell's on the right, along the road; Shelby's next, to the left of him; Sevier's next, and so on, till last the left of Cleveland's to join the right of Campbell's, on the other side of the mountain, at the road.

Thus the British Major found himself attacked on all sides at once, and so situated as to receive a galling fire from all parts of our lines without doing any injury to ourselves. From this difficulty, he attempted to relieve himself at the point of the bayonet, but failed in three successive charges. Cleveland, who had the farthest to go, being bothered in some swampy ground, did not occupy his position in the line till late in the engagement. A few men, drawn from the right of Campbell's regiment, occupied this vacancy; this the British commander discovered, and here he made his last powerful effort to force his way through and make his escape; but at that instant Cleveland's regiment came up in gallant style; the Colonel, himself, coming by the very spot I occupied, at which time his horse had received two wounds, and he was obliged to dismount. Although fat and unweildy, he advanced on foot with signal bravery; but was soon re-mounted by one of his officers, who brought him another horse. This threw the British and Tories into complete disorder, and Ferguson seeing that all was lost, determined not to survive the disgrace; he broke his sword, and spurred his horse into the thickest of our ranks, and fell covered with wounds, and shortly after his whole army surrendered at discretion. The action lasted about one hour, and for most of the time was fierce and bloody.

I cannot clearly recollect the statement of our loss, given at the time, but my impression now is that it was two hundred and twenty-five killed, and about as many or a few more wounded; the loss of the enemy must have been much greater. The return of the prisoners taken was eleven hundred and thirty-three, about fifteen hundred stand of arms, several baggage wagons, and all their camp equipage fell into our hands. The battle closed not far from sundown, so that we had to encamp on the ground, with the dead and wounded, and pass the night among groans and lamentations.

The next day, as soon as we could bury our dead, and provide litters to carry our wounded, we marched off to regain the upper country for fear of being intercepted by a detachment from the army of Lord Cornwallis, for we were partly behind his quarters, between him and the British garrison of Ninety Six. A British surgeon, with some assistants, were left to attend their wounded ; but the wounded Tories were unprovided for, and their dead left for their bones to bleach upon the mountain. That afternoon we met Capt. Neil coming on with his detachment, and encamped for the night on a large deserted Tory plantation, where was a sweet potato patch sufficiently large to supply the whole army. This was most fortunate, for not one in fifty of us had tasted food for the last two days and nights, that is, since we left the Cowpens. Here, the next morning, we buried Col. Williams, who had died of his wounds on the march the day before. We still proceeded towards the mountains as fast as our prisoners could bear.

When we had gained a position, where we thought ourselves secure from a pursuit, the army halted for a day, and a court was detailed to inquire into various complaints against certain Tories for murders, robberies, house-burnings, &c. The court found upwards of forty of them guilty of the crimes charged upon them, and sentenced them to hang ; and nine of the most atrocious offenders were executed that night by fire-light, the rest were reprieved by the commanding officer.

We set off early next morning, and shortly after the rain began to fall in torrents, and continued the whole day, but, instead of halting, we rather mended our pace in order to cross the Catawba river before it should rise and intercept us ; this we effected late in the night, and halted by a large plantation, when Major McDowell—brother of the Colonel, and who commanded his brother's regiment the whole route, and was a brave and efficient officer—rode along the lines, and informed us that the plantation belonged to him, and kindly invited us to take rails from his fences, and make fires to warm and dry us. I suppose every one felt grateful for this generous offer, for it was rather cold, being the last of October, and every one, from the Commander-in-Chief to the meanest private, was as wet as if he had just been dragged through the Catawba river. We rested here one day, and then proceeded, by easy marches, to the heads of the Yadkin river, where we were relieved by the militia of the country, and permitted to return home, which those of us who had not fallen in battle or died of wounds, effected some time in November.

During the whole of this expedition, except a few days at the outset, I neither tasted bread nor salt, and this was the case with nearly every man ; when we could get meat, which was but seldom, we had to roast and eat it without either : sometimes we got a few potatoes, but out standing and principal rations were ears of corn, scorched in the fire or eaten raw. Such was the price paid by the men of the Revolution for our Independence.

Here I might conclude, but I cannot forbear offering a small tribute to the memory of our commanding officers. Col. Williams, fell; Cleveland, I have already spoken of; Sevier, I did not see in the battle, but his bravery was well attested; three times my eye fell upon our gallant commander, [Campbell] calm and collected, encouraging the men, and assuring them of victory. At the close of the action, when•the British were loudly calling for quarters, but uncertain whether they would be granted, I saw the intrepid Shelby rush his horse within fifteen paces of their lines, and commanded them to lay down their arms, and they should have quarters. Some would call this an imprudent act, but it showed the daring bravery of the man. I am led to believe that three braver men, and purer patriots, never trod the soil of freedom, than Campbell, Shelby and Sevier.

[*"Narrator"* in *Kentucky Reporter*, July 25th, 1812.]

Col. Shelby, in concert with Col. John Sevier, meditated and carried into execution the expedition against Ferguson, who, thinking himself secure, had permitted some of his Tories to go home. By forced marches, with nine hundred and ten men, they attacked Ferguson on King's Mountain, and killed and took eleven hundred and five men. The honor of the enterprise has been given Col. Campbell most undeservedly. There were six officers along who were entitled to command Col. Campbell by their rank; and Col. Shelby who was one of those six, deserves the nation's thanks for the manner in which he conducted himself at that critical juncture. In the camp, everything was confused for want of a commanding officer. Those who were entitled to command were very unpopular, and I am well informed that had it been left to an election, Shelby would have been elected; but he was not the eldest officer, and he was aware, that should he contend for the command, the jealousy and offended pride of the others might defeat the expedition. He had more at heart the interest of his darling country than the promotion; and to do away all jealousy among equals, he himself proposed a meeting be held for the purpose of an arrangement, that they should jointly every evening provide an order for the government of camp, and that Col. Campbell should be the officer of the day to see that complied with.

This affair being arranged, the army moved on and made a forced march, as it was all important to them to overtake Ferguson before the disbanded Tories could rendezvous and join him. From Friday morning until Saturday evening the little host of soldiers scarcely tarried a moment, and late on that evening coming up with the enemy, the attack was commenced. Col. Campbell was not in this action except in the first onset. To Shelby the enemy surrendered—Shelby was the first man who spoke to them—was the first man among them, and the fire on the opposite side of the mountain did not cease, as they did not know of the surrender, until Shelby, who, was actually among the British, ordered them to sit down. The American fire instantly ceased, and was succeeded by the huzzas of triumph. Campbell, hearing them, came up about twenty minutes afterward, and observed to Shelby, "that he could not account for his own conduct in the latter part of the action."

COL. SHELBY'S LETTERS TO GOV. SEVIER.

July 1st, 1822, Col. G. W. Sevier, caused to be published in the *Nashville Gazette* four letters written by Col. Shelby to his father, Gov. Sevier, three of which, in part, touched upon King's Mountain and Col. Campbell. Those parts follow :

The Legislature of Virginia, shortly after the defeat of Ferguson, upon King's Mountain, in 1780, voted an elegant horse and sword to be presented to Col. William Campbell, as a testimony of approbation which his country bore towards him on account of the part that he had taken in that memorable affair. The horse was delivered to him ; but owing to neglect, or some other cause, the sword was not presented to him before he died. I am lately informed that the friends of Col. Campbell, not long since, have made application to the Legislature of that State for the sword—that they voted the sum of one thousand, five hundred crowns for the purchase of the most elegant sword that .could be procured in France ; and through our Minister in Paris, a most superb sword was obtained, which was presented by the Government of Virginia to young John Preston *, the grandson of Col. Campbell, as an honorable reward due to the memory of his ancestor.

Now, sir, what did Campbell merit more than you or I did ? It is a fact well known, and for which he apologized to me the day after the action, that he was not within less than one quarter of a mile of the enemy at the time they surrendered to you and myself. But I do not mean to detract from the honors of the dead, yet it is a fact I have told to many, both before and since his death.—January 1st, 1810.

At the time I wrote to you on this subject, I had but just heard of the fine sword given by the State of Virginia to a descendant of the late Col. Campbell, and for a moment I felt a degree of indignation and resentment, that my country had attributed the achievement of the victory on King's Mountain to a man who had little share in the action, and it

---

* Wm. C. Preston was probably the person referred to.

determined me to address a letter to you on the occasion. * * * It may be fairly stated, 'that the great body of the men that crossed the mountains on that expedition, were raised and embodied by your and my own united exertions. It was an enterprise undertaken from pure and patriotic motives, without the aid of the Govenment—at a time that tried the souls of men. It was, in its consequences, the salvation of North Carolina, inasmuch as it obliged Lord Cornwallis to retreat out of the State with the whole British army, and he could not advance until he was reinforced from New York. Besides, in the great scale of our national affairs, it was the *very first perceivable event* that gave a favorable turn to the American Revolution.—February 24th, 1810.

I shall be elected Governor by a majority of at least ten thousand votes. Among other falsehoods that were circulated against me, it was said that I was not in the action at King's Mountain ; and by some, that I was only a Lieutenant, or some inferior officer, on that expedition, and this story had gained some credit among better informed people. The object of this letter is, to request you to be so obliging as to state to me, in a letter, as early as convenient, the station in which I commanded on the expedition against Ferguson. You know that the expedition was concerted by you and myself, and that it took some address to induce Campbell and his men to join us. That in the action, I was in the heat of the battle. I well recollect being once very near you as we went up the mountain early in the action ; I saw you animating the men to victory, and feel persuaded you saw me also ; I was on horseback, near you, using the same exertions. And you must also recollect, that I was almost the first—and, I believe, the very first—officer that you met at the surrender of the enemy. Your first words to me at the surrender were—"By G—d, they have burnt off your hair." You must still recollect that circumstance, that my hair on the left side was very much scorched—this happened just before the surrender, when both parties were almost promiscuously mingled together.—August 12th, 1812.

[GOV. SHELBY'S PAMPHLET.]

BATTLE OF KING'S MOUNTAIN.

To the Public.

During the last year, Mr. Wm. C. Preston, a grandson of the late Col. Wm. Campbell, made a publication in the newspapers, under his signature, and headed "Colonel Campbell and Governor Shelby." The professed object of this address, was to claim for his ancestor, as commander of the American forces at the battle of King's Mountain the chief honors of that victory, and to controvert some statements relative to that subject, made in some of my *private letters* to the late Gov. Sevier, of Tennessee, which letters came to the knowledge of the world, and of Mr. Preston, by the inadvertent publication of them by the son of Gov. Sevier, after the death of his father. In the course of his address, Mr. Preston has thought proper to question my veracity,— to deny the statements made in those letters, and to impute to me the most dishonorable motives and purposes.

I paused and hesitated long as to the course I ought to pursue. Conscious of my integrity, I felt a proud confidence, that my reputation could not be affected by the proofs and animadversions of Mr. Preston— that it was placed above the reach of calumny and all attempts to dishonor it. But the labored efforts that have been used, to give the most extensive circulation and the most permanent effect to the publication of Mr. Preston, have determined me to reply to it, least by my silence I might be considered as acquiescing in the justice of his assertions and imputations.

It is with the most sincere and heartfelt regret that I undertake the task ; because in the course of my defence it will be necessary for me to speak of circumstances, which I had rather have seen consigned to oblivion—circumstances calculated, in some degree, to effect the fame of Col. Campbell ; and perhaps to wound the feelings of many of his numerous and most respectable relatives and connections. But the unexpected publication of my private letters to an old friend, and the attack consequently made on me by Mr. Preston, compel me to defend myself; and painful and invidious as the task may be, I owe it to myself, to my posterity and my country, to perform it. I could have wished most earnestly to have been spared this development, but circumstances seem not to permit it.

If, in the course of this investigation, facts should be disclosed, injurious to the fame of Col. Campbell, let it be remembered that I have been forced into it by imperious necessity. Sacred as the memory of Col. Campbell may be, it will be recollected, that I also have a character and reputation which are dear to me, and which it is one of my highest duties to maintain and defend. The history of my life has never before been stained by an imputation of falsehood and dishonor. I am now in my seventy-third year, and almost the only object of wordly ambition that remains between me and the grave, is, that my memory may descend untarnished to my posterity and to my country—that country which has appreciated my services, perhaps too highly, and with a bountiful and generous hand heaped upon me rewards and honors far beyond my poor deserving. But how must she blush at my name, and the recollection of those honors which her mistaken gratitude has confered upon me, if I am guilty of the falsehood and defamation, with which Mr. Preston has charged me ! I am not guilty, my countrymen,

36

and before any other tribunal than yours, I would have scorned to reply to the unworthy accusations with which I am assailed.

To render the subject more intelligible and clear, and to show the grounds upon which I have made the statements contained in my private letters, I shall attempt to give some account of the battle of King's Mountain, and the circumstances which led to it.

Upon the defeat of Gen. Gates and the American army at the battle of Camden, on the 16th of August, 1780, the Southern States were almost entirely abandoned to the enemy. The intelligence of that disastrous affair, and the defeat of Gen. Sumter which soon followed, spread universal consternation and alarm. All the bodies of militia that were in arms through the country, were compelled to fly before the enemy. Some of these detachments (part of which I commanded) fled towards the mountains, and were hotly pursued by Major Ferguson, of the British army, with a strong force. Failing in the attempt to intercept their retreat, he took post at Gilbert Town. At that place he paroled a prisoner, (one Samuel Philips, a distant connection of mine) and instructed him to inform the officers on the Western waters, that if they did not desist from their opposition to the British arms, and take protection under his standard, he would march his army over the mountains, hang their leaders, and lay their country waste with fire and sword. Philips lived near my residence, and came directly to me with this intelligence. I then commanded the militia of Sullivan County, North Carolina. In a few days I went fifty or sixty miles to see Col. Sevier, who was the efficient commander of Washington County, North Carolina, to inform him of the message I had received, and to concert with him measures for our defence. After some consultation, we determined to march with all the men we could raise, and attempt to surprise Ferguson, by attacking him in his camp, or at any rate before he was prepared for us. We accordingly appointed a time and place of rendezvous. It was known to us that some two or three hundred of the militia who had been under the command of Col. McDowell, and were driven by the success of the enemy from the lower country, were then on the Western waters, and mostly in the County of Washington, North Carolina. I saw some of their officers before we parted; Col. Sevier engaged to give notice to these refugees, and to bring them into our measure. On my part, I undertook to procure the aid and co-operation of Col. Wm. Campbell, of Washington County, Virginia, and the men of that County, if practicable.

Having made the arrangements with Sevier, I returned home immediately, and devoted myself to all the necessary operations for our intended enterprise. I wrote to Col. Campbell, informing him what Sevier and I had agreed on, and urged him to join us with all the men he could raise. This letter I sent express to him at his own house, forty miles distant, by my brother, Moses Shelby. Col. Campbell wrote me for answer, that he had determined to raise what men he could, and march down by Flower-Gap, to the Southern borders of Virginia, to oppose Lord Cornwallis when he approached that State;—that he still preferred this course to the one proposed by Sevier and myself, and therefore declined agreeing to meet us. Of this I notified Col. Sevier by an express on the next day, and immediately issued an order calling upon *all* the militia of the County to hold themselves in readiness to march at the time appointed. I felt, however, some disappointment at the reply of Col. Campbell. The Cherokee towns were not more than eighty or one hundred miles from the frontiers of my County, and we had received information that these Indians were preparing a formidable attack upon us in the course of a few weeks; I was, therefore, unwilling that we should take away the whole disposable force of our Counties at such a time; and without the aid of the militia under Col. Campbell's command, I feared that we could not otherwise have a sufficient force to meet Ferguson. I therefore wrote a second letter to Col. Campbell, and sent the same messenger back with it immediately, to whom I communicated at large our view and intentions, and directed him to urge them on Col. Campbell. This letter and messenger produced the desired effect, and Campbell wrote me that he would meet us at the time and place appointed. If Mr. Preston and his relations have been as careful of these letters, as they have been of some others, and will publish them, they will prove the correctness of this statement.

It surely cannot detract from the merits of Col. Campbell, that this expedition was not set on foot by him, but by others. He lived in Virginia, in a state of comparative security, and was preparing to aid his own State when she should be invaded. We lived in North Carolina, a great part of which State was prostrate before the British arms. We were nearer to the enemy, and we were threatened. We, therefore, determined to anticipate the invasion and vengeance meditated against us, and to strike the first blow. To do this effectually, we asked for and received the aid of the nearest County in a neighboring State. This was surely the natural and ordinary course of things. The 25th day of September, 1780, at Watauga, where the time and place appointed for our rendezvous, Col. Sevier had succeeded in engaging in our enterprise, Col. Charles McDowell and many of the refugees before mentioned—and when assembled our forces were as follows: Col. William Campbell with four hundred men from Washington County, Virginia; Col. John Sevier with two hundred and forty men from Washington County, North Carolina; Col. Charles McDowell with one hundred and sixty men from the Counties of Burke and Rutherford, who had fled before the enemy to the Western waters; and two hundred and forty men from Sullivan County, North Carolina, under my command. On the next day, the

26th of the month, we began our march, crossed the mountains, and, on the 30th, were joined by Col. Benjamin Cleveland with three hundred and fifty men from the Counties of Wilkes and Surry, North Carolina.

The little disorders and irregularities which began to prevail among our undisciplined troops, created much uneasiness in the commanding officers—the Colonels commanding regiments. We met in the evening, and consulted about our future operations. It was resolved to send to Head-Quarters for a general officer to command us; and that, in the meantime, we should meet in council every day to determine on the measures to be pursued, and appoint one of our own body to put them in execution. I was not satisfied with this course, as I thought it calculated to produce delay, when expedition and dispatch were all important to us. We were then in sixteen or eighteen miles of Gilbert Town, where we supposed Ferguson to be. I suggested these things to the council, and then observed to the officers, that we were all North Carolinians except Col. Campbell, who was from Virginia; that I knew him to be a man of good sense, and warmly attached to the cause of his country; that he commanded the largest regiment; and that if they concurred with me, we would, until a general officer should arrive from Head-Quarters, appoint him to command us, and march immediately against the enemy. To this proposition some one or two said, "agreed." No written minute or record was made of it. I made the proposition to silence the expectations of Col. McDowell to command us—he being the commanding officer of the district we were then in, and had commanded the armies of militia assembled in that quarter all the summer before against the same enemy. He was a brave and patriotic man, but we considered him too far advanced in life, and too inactive, for the command of such an enterprise as we were then engaged in. I was sure he would not serve under a younger officer from his own State, and hoped that his feelings would in some degree be saved by the appointment of Col. Campbell. In this way, and upon my suggestion, was Col. Campbell raised to the command, *and not on account of any superior military talents or experience he was supposed to possess.* He had no previous acquaintance with any of the Colonels except myself, nor had he at that time acquired any experience or distinction in war, that we knew of. Col. McDowell, who had the good of his country more at heart than any title of command, submitted to what was done; but observed, that as he could not be permitted to command, he would be the messenger to go to Head-Quarters for the general officer. He accordingly started immediately, leaving his men under his brother, Maj. Joseph McDowell, and Col. Campbell assumed the chief command. He was, however, to be regulated and directed by the determinations of the Colonels, who were to meet in council every day.

On the morning after the appointment of Col. Campbell, we proceeded towards Gilbert Town, but found that Ferguson, apprised of our approach, had left there a few days before. On the next night, it was determined, in the council of officers, to pursue him unremittingly, with as many of our troops as could be well armed and well mounted, leaving the weak horses and footmen to follow on as fast as they could. We accordingly started about light the next morning, with nine hundred and ten men, thus selected. Continuing diligently our pursuit all that day, we were joined at the Cowpens, on the 6th, by Col. James Williams, of South Carolina, and several field officers, with about four hundred men. Learning from him the situation and distance of the enemy, we traveled all that night, and the next day, through heavy rains, and came up with them about three o'clock in the afternoon of the 7th of October. They were encamped on an eminence called *King's Mountain,* extending from east to west, which on its summit was about five or six hundred yards long, and sixty or seventy broad. Our men were formed for battle as stated in the report of the action made out and signed by some of the officers, and lately published by Mr. Preston. This report, however, omits to mention, that the men who had belonged to Col. McDowell's command, which had been considerably augmented on the march, formed a part of the right wing under Sevier. Col. Campbell's regiment and my own, composed the centre—his on the right, and mine on the left. The right wing or column, was led by Col. Sevier and Maj. Winston; the left by Cols. Cleveland and Williams; and each of these wings was about as strong as Campbell's regiment and mine united. Our plan was to surround the mountain and attack the enemy on all sides.

In this order, and with this view, we marched immediately to the assault. The attack was commenced by the two centre columns, which attempted to ascend at the eastern end of the mountain. The battle here became furious and bloody, and many that belonged to Sevier's column were drawn into the action at this point, to sustain their comrades. In the course of the battle we were repeatedly repulsed by the enemy, and driven down the mountain. In this succession of repulses and attacks, and in giving succour to the points hardest pressed, much disorder took place in our ranks; the men of my column, of Campbell's column, and great part of Sevier's, were mingled together in the confusion of the battle. Towards the latter part of the action, the enemy made a fierce and gallant charge upon us, from the eastern summit of the mountain, and drove us near to the foot of it. The retreat was so rapid that there was great danger of its becoming a rout. While I was attempting to rally the men, at the distance of about two hundred yards from where the scene of action had been, I looked *down the mountain,* and saw Col. Campbell, sitting on his bald-face black horse, about two hundred yards further off, apparently looking right at me. He was in the same trim—

with his coat off—that he had put himself in to fight the battle. I stopped my horse, and raised myself up in my stirrups, to show him that I saw him. He did not move while I looked at him.

Our men were soon rallied and turned back upon the enemy, who in a few minutes after we again came into close action with them, gave way. We gained the eastern summit of the mountain and drove those who had been opposed to us along the top of it, until they were forced down the *western end* about one hundred yards, in a crowd, to where the other part of their line had been contending with Cleveland and Williams, who were maintaining their ground below them. It was here that Ferguson, the British commander, was killed—and a white flag was soon after hoisted by the enemy, in token of surrender. They were ordered to throw down their arms; which they did, and surrendered themselves prisoners at discretion. It was some time before a complete cessation of the firing, on our part, could be effected. Our men, who had been scattered in the battle, were continually coming up, and continued to fire, without comprehending in the heat of the moment, what had happened; and some, who had heard that at Buford's defeat the British had refused quarters to many who asked it, were willing to follow that bad example. Owing to these causes, the ignorance of some, and the disposition of others to retaliate, it required some time, and some exertion on the part of the officers, to put an entire stop to the firing. After the surrender of the enemy, our men gave spontaneously three loud and long shouts.

It was not till fifteen or twenty minutes after the enemy hoisted the flag of surrender, *nor until some minutes after the shouts of our men had announced the victory,* that I saw Col. Campbell, on the west point of the mountain, *with his light colored coat buttoned around him,* coming down on foot, with three others. (all of whom I knew) to where the prisoners were. He came directly to me, and stood by my side; and after a short space ordered the prisoners to sit down. He then proposed a second cheer, which though joined in by many, was neither so general nor so loud as the first.

Before Col. Campbell came up, the flag of the enemy, and the sword of their commanding officer, DePeyster, had been received, not by me, but by my brother, Maj. Evan Shelby.

About ten o'clock on the day after the battle, I was standing alone, about forty yards south of the spot where Col. Campbell came to me after the surrender, enjoying the warmth of the sun (for I had been very wet the day before, and was exposed to the cold dew of the mountain all night) when I saw Col. Campbell leave the line of guards that surrounded the prisoners, and walked slowly towards me with his sword under his arm, till he came near touching me. He then, in a lower tone of voice than usual, and with a slight smile on his countenance, made the following expression : *"Sir, I can not account for my conduct in the latter part of the action."*

An enterprise so daring, and a victory so complete, were supposed to entitle the officers who had conducted and achieved them, to some testimonials of their country's approbation. The Legislature of Virginia voted to Col. Campbell a horse, sword and pistols ; and the Legislature of North Carolina, at their next session, were pleased to distinguish the services of Col. Sevier, myself and others, by voting to each of us a sword.

Such is the history of the battle of King's Mountain, and of the incidents connected with it, so far as they relate to the present controversy. Of those circumstances which relate to Col. Campbell personally, and which might have a tendency to diminish his reputation, I have seldom spoken, except in confidence, or to those who were previously acquainted with them. I am sure that I may say, with perfect truth, that I have never spoken of them in a spirit of detraction.

I have long ceased to be a citizen of North Carolina. The swords voted by her had never yet been presented, although years had passed away. Of the one which was voted to me, I had for a long time rarely thought, until about the year 1810, when the prospects of approaching hostilities with Great Britain naturally roused in me ancient feelings, and recollections of our Revolutionary war ; and when also I learned from a relation of Mr. Preston, that the State of Virginia had given to him, as the representative of Col. Campbell, the elegant sword which had been voted to the latter for his services at the battle of King's Mountain. These circumstances, and the reflections to which they gave rise, did produce some feelings of emulation and solicitude, and a sense that equal justice had not been done to all who participated in that memorable achievement.

In this state of mind, my letters bearing date in 1810, were addressed to my old friend and fellow soldier, Col. Sevier. The object of them was to concert with him the means of reminding North Carolina of her ancient promise, and of obtaining those swords which thirty years before had been voted to us, as the honorable memorials of our good con-. duct, and our country's approbation. In the course of this correspondence, after mentioning the magnanimous example which Virginia had given to Carolina by the honors conferred on the memory of Col. Campbell, I ventured to make some comparison of the services of Sevier and myself with those of Col. Campbell. I stated in substance that the enterprise which resulted in the battle at King's Mountain, was not set on foot by Col. Campbell, but by Sevier and myself, and that some address was necessary to induce him to unite with us. That the greater part of the men who crossed the mountains on that occasion may be fairly said to have been embodied by Sevier and myself ; that Col. Campbell was not present in the latter part of the action, nor when the enemy surrendered, nor for some minutes after; and that on the next day he apologized to me for his conduct.

These statements are all true within my own knowledge. They are more particularly explained and illustrated in the narrative which I have given above of the battle, and the circumstances which led to it. But Mr. Preston has denied them—has impeached my veracity, and imputed to me the vilest and most dishonorable motives. It is yet in my power to establish the truth of these statements by the most respectable and unquestionable testimony. They are verified by the letters of Col. Sevier, written in reply to mine; by the statements of Gen. Thos. Kennedy, Col. John Sawyers, James Cooper, Henry Blevins, John Long, Major William Delaney, Col. Matthew Willoughby, Col. John Sharp, William King, Esq., Geo. Morrison, Jacob Isely, Jacob Bealer, Joseph Bealer, John Peters, Major Christopher Taylor, Rev. Felix Earnest, William Willoughby, Robert Elder, the affidavit of Col. Moses Shelby, and a multitude of others that might be added. All of whom either participated in the battle of King's Mountain, or speak from long tradition, and the information of those who did, and who are now no more.

In Col. Sevier's letter to me of the 17th of January, 1810, he says, "It is true that Col. Campbell was not within one-quarter of a mile when the enemy surrendered to yourself and me." In another letter of the 27th of August, 1812, when speaking of the battle of King's Mountain, he says, "It is well known you were in the heat of the action. I frequently saw you animating your men to victory; at the surrender, you were the first field officer I recollect to have seen. I have no doubt you must recollect Col. Campbell was some considerable distance from that place, at that time, and that you and myself spoke on that subject the same evening. I perfectly recollect on my seeing you at the close of the action, that I swore by G–d they had burnt off your hair, for it was much burnt on one side. It is well known by some hundreds in Tennessee, that you were Colonel on that campaign, and that we were the only persons who set on foot the expedition, and had considerable trouble to get Campbell to join us."

Gen. Kennedy (who belonged on that day to Sevier's column) states that he was a Captain in the battle of King's Mountain, and fought on the eastwardly quarter of it, where Campbell's regiment was also engaged—that he saw me frequently, but does "not recollect to have seen Col. Campbell during the action," &c. In his statement he further says, "I was within sixty or seventy yards of the enemy when they raised the flag, and was close in with them in a minute or two afterwards, and I well recollect to have seen Col. Shelby there one of the first men I met with. I remember to have heard several persons inquire for Col. Campbell before he came up, which was, I think, about fifteen minutes after the surrender. I also recollect to have heard it talked of in the army, after the action and for many years after when in conversation with men who were in that battle, that Col. Campbell was not at the surrender for some time after the enemy had laid down their arms.

Col. John Sawyers, than whom there is no man more entitled to credit, as certified by the most respectable and distinguished gentlemen of Tennessee—states, that "Isaac Shelby, late Governor of Kentucky, held the command of Colonel at the battle of King's Mountain—that I was a Captain in his regiment, and know that he first planned the expedition with John Sevier," &c. "He (Shelby) was also among the first at the surrender. I saw him and Col. Sevier when the enemy laid down their arms, but did not see Col. Campbell for some time afterwards. I also state, that Maj. Evan Shelby, brother of Isaac, and not Isaac Shelby, Sevier, or Campbell, as I have heard that some now state, received the flag and sword. I also state, that from this circumstance I was led to think of Col. Campbell at the time, looked for him among the officers, and do believe that if he had been there I should have seen him, and that he did not come up for fifteen or twenty minutes after the enemy had laid down their arms, and been placed under guard. I also know, that it was the general talk at the time, and I have frequently since heard it spoken of by men who were in the action, as an indisputable fact, that he was not in the latter part of the action, nor at the surrender. I also recollect distinctly to have heard it said amongst the officers before we left the mountain, as well as on the way home, and since, that Campbell himself admitted it, and in a private conversation with Col. Shelby, on the mountain, had said he could not account for it. I remember to have intended to ask Col. Shelby, if this was so, but it has so happened that I have never mentioned this subject to him, nor he to me."

Maj. William Delaney states, that "I was an Orderly Sergeant in in the action of King's Mountain; that I was with Col. Shelby, and rode with him while placing a guard round the enemy after the surrender— that I did not see Col. Campbell in the latter part of the action, nor at the surrender, for some minutes afterwards, and that I heard this spoken of at the time, as well as since. It is also my belief, from what I understood at the time, (although I did not see it myself) that it was Maj. Evan Shelby, and neither of the four Colonels, that received the sword from the British officer in command."

Col. Moses Shelby states, upon oath, that he was twice wounded in the action on King's Mountain—that he was assisted down to a branch some small distance from the foot of the mountain on the east end, and that he saw Col. Campbell there sitting on his black horse; this was about the middle of the action, and he knows "that Col. Campbell did not leave that place until the battle was over, or until the firing had ceased."

Jacob Bealer states, that he was in Capt. Pemberton's company in the battle of King's Mountain, " and amongst the very first at the place of surrender." The commander asked for our General, and gave his sword first to Maj. Evan Shelby, who kept it until Col. Campbell came up, which was twenty minutes, and I think longer, afterwards. From the discourse which I heard between Col. Shelby and the British officers, I know that Campbell was not there, and that it was that length of time before he came up."

Joseph Bealer certifies, that " I was at the surrender with my brother (Jacob Bealer) at his side, and saw and heard what he has stated in the above certificate, and know them to be true, and have always spoken of them, and heard them spoken of, by those who were there, in this way."

John Peters also states, that he " was in Capt. Pemberton's company with Jacob and Joseph Bealer, and amongst the first at the surrender. That I know of my own knowledge, that what Jacob Bealer has stated in his certificate, is true—that the enemy surrendered, and that there was a ring made round them fifteen or twenty minutes before I looked up and saw Col. Campbell coming with two or three others down the mountain—that is what I have always heard, and never heard it contradicted."

The statements of the other individuals who are above named, tend to confirm the same facts.

With respect to the certificates published by Mr. Preston, I shall leave the public to compare them with the facts I have stated, and form their own judgment. I will only observe, however, that John McCulloch is the only one of those whose statements have been published, that I have had an opportunity of communicating with, and he has certified that he never signed the certificate published as his. The statement which he there makes, 'that he saw Col. Campbell, at the enemy's markee,' &c. is very unimportant and proves nothing. That 'markee' was at the east end of the mountain and five or six hundred yards from where the enemy surrendered.

The testimonials which I have now exhibited will satisfy the world that the statements contained in my letters are true.

I deeply and sincerely regret the necessity that has been cast upon me of discussing, in defence of my own character, a subject so delicate and so invidious. It is a controversy that I have not sought; it is one that I would have avoided, if any alternative had been left me. My letters to Col. Sevier were written in all the confidence of a private correspondence with an old friend. I question not the motives that influenced his son to publish them after the death of his father. But certainly it was an event altogether unexpected by me. The circumstances under which those letters were written, the person to whom addressed, and their private and confidential character must convince the world that I did not write them for the purpose of defaming the memory of Col. Campbell, or with any design of giving an invidious publicity to the unpleasant truths which they contain. And if to have spoken the truth requires an apology—if one be due either to the living or the dead, the circumstances of this case amply furnish it; and ought to have mitigated the violence and injustice with which Mr. Preston has assailed me. I do not say this to deprecate the wrath or censure of any one;—for I am conscious of no impropriety, and I fear no consequences.

Mr. Preston states, that I have charged Col. Campbell with cowardice. I have made no such charge. I have stated facts only, and cowardice is the inference or construction which he chooses to make. The facts stated, I know to be true; but yet I do not believe that Col. Campbell was a coward. I believe that in the commencement, and the first part of the action, he acted bravely, and that his subsequent conduct was the effect of some unaccountable panic, to which the bravest men are subject. Such, at least, are the sentiments which I have indulged and cherished; and these combined with my regard for Col. Campbell, and his relatives and connections, will not only furnish a ready answer to the question so exultingly asked by Mr. Preston, why I did not long ago denounce his ancestor to the world as a coward and paltroon? —but will also account for my long and habitual silence on the subject. They will account, too, when taken in conjunction with Col. Campbell's good conduct during a part of the action, for the expressions which Mr. Preston has quoted as used by me in the autograph letter to which he alludes. I can only say that I have no recollection of that letter. I pretend not, however, to doubt its existence, since it is affirmed by Mr. Preston, and it having ever been my wish to shield the memory of Col. Campbell from reproach.

As to the document of "curious character," (the report of the battle, &c., signed by the officers) to which Mr. Preston so triumphantly refers as furnishing contradictions to the statements contained in my letters; it may be remarked, that it was not drawn up on King's Mountain, nor until some days after we had left it—that it is nothing more than a brief and hurried account, in general terms, of the expedition and the battle, drawn up to authenticate the intelligence of our victory, and give tone to public report. This document, inaccurate and indefinite as it is in some particulars, furnishes none of those contradictions which Mr. Preston has supposed to exist.

To make out one of those supposed contradictions, he quotes that part of it which states, "The troops upon the *right* having gained the summit of the eminence, obliged the enemy to retreat along the top of the ridge to where Col. Cleveland commanded, and were there stopped by his brave men;—a flag was hoisted" &c. Having interpolated, in par-

enthesis, after the word, "right," in the above quotation, the words
"Col. Campbell's division," Mr. Preston, exclaims, "thus it is given
under Col. Shelby's own hand in 1780, that the enemy was routed by
the division commanded by Col. Campbell in person." The document
authorizes no such conclusion, and it is only rendered *plausible* from the
interpolation which *he* has made. The truth is, as I have before stated
it, that a great part of the column commanded by Sevier, owing to the
heavy fire in front of the two centre columns was drawn into the action
on the east end of the mountain, and became mingled and blended with
them during the remainder of the action. This fact is proved by the
certificates of Messrs. Kennedy, Taylor and Earnest, who belonged to
Sevier's column on that day.

"This venerable memoir" is also supposed by Mr. Preston, to furnish
"a contradiction in direct terms" to that part of one of my letters to Col.
Sevier, where I state "that it may be fairly said, that the great body of
the men who crossed the mountains on that expedition, were raised and
embodied by your and my own united exertions." There is in reality no
contradiction. It is true, as stated in that "memoir," that Col. Campbell brought with him four hundred men from Washington County, Va.,
and that Sevier's regiment and mine consisted of only two hundred and
forty men each. But when it shall be recollected, as I have before
related, how this expedition was set on foot, how by the exertions of
Sevier and myself, the refugees were assembled, and brought to unite
with us, and how the co-operation of Col. Campbell was obtained, I
think that I am fully justified in having stated to Sevier, "that it may be
fairly said, that most of the men who crossed the mountains," &c., were
embodied by our exertions ; or, at least, that I shall be relieved from that
direct contradiction which Mr. Preston supposes must entirely destroy
my credibility.

As to the propriety of Mr. Preston's remarks in relation to the newspaper publication of 1812, in which I am represented as being "conspicuous through the thin veil of a fictitious signature," I refer the reader to
a letter addressed to me on that subject by the late Col. Jno. B. Campbell,
and my reply to it, which I am credibly informed was forwarded to Mr.
Preston. I there state, that those circumstances relating to Col. Campbell are true, and that they were known to his immediate relatives and
friends—yet that I had no participation whatever, in giving publicity to
them, but had endeavored to suppress their circulation. Why I was not
then assailed, and why it has been preferred to wait the lapse of so many
years, until I am brought to the very margin of the tomb, and hundreds
of the then living witnesses have been "gathered home" to their fathers,"
the public will judge.

Before I conclude, permit me to ask what reasonable motive or in-
ducement I could have had to fabricate falsehoods for the purpose of

defaming Col. Campbell? Has my reputation been built up by pulling down that of others? Or has it been plundered from the graves of the dead? Let my country answer these questions—that country which has given me all that I have of name or reputation.

I think I have a right to be considered, at least, a witness of fair character, one who has some claims upon the confidence of his countrymen, and who is entitled to be heard without prejudice, although it is his painful duty to speak thus publicly and plainly of the dead. History, however, deals with the dead; and this is a subject of history. And although my reluctance at the task, is certainly increased by the circumstance that Col. Campbell is no more; yet it is very probable that I feel myself more privileged to speak on this subject, than would be consonant with Mr. Preston's ideas of the sanctity and reverence due to his deceased ancestor; for I was a contemporary of that ancestor, and I shall soon lie down beside him in the grave. My career is run. I feel as though I were almost as nearly connected with the dead as the living; and standing thus beside my grave, and between two worlds, I solemnly declare, that the facts I have stated, in relation to the conduct of Col. Campbell in the battle of King's Mountain, are true.

I lament the occasion that has rendered it necessary for me to make this avowal, and to treat of this unpleasant and invidious subject. I now take my final leave of it. I am animated by no spirit of controversy. I have no fears for my reputation, the hardy growth of many years. I can listen undisturbed to the animadversions of Mr. Preston, and nothing shall ever provoke me to engage further in this contest.

April, 1823.   ISAAC SHELBY.

(DOCUMENTS.)

(No. 1.)   [Col. John B. Campbell's Letter.]

" *Hopkinsville, 30th July, 1812.*

SIR:—I have seen in the Reporter of the 25th inst., a publication signed "*Narrator,*" which has treated the character of my deceased uncle, Gen. William Campbell, with great injustice. So far as this publication, and others of the same character, have tended to promote your election to the Chief Magistracy of the State, they have met my hearty concurrence; no man has felt more solicitous than myself for your success; but when the bounds of truth are transcended, and the character of a deceased relative, long since in the silent tomb, basely traduced, and his name unnecessarily lugged into this contest in a manner calculated to dislaurel him, although the scope of the publication may have been intended to promote the cause I approve, I cannot rest patiently without endeavoring to have the ungenerous statements in this publication contradicted. The most prominent of which are, that " Col. Campbell was not in this action except on the first onset;" and that he came up about twenty minutes after the enemy had surrendered, and observed to you, " that he could not account for his own conduct in the latter part of the action ;" thereby insinuating that he had cowardly skulked out of danger after the commencement of the action, and remained in his snug retreat until danger ceased to exist. I cannot for a moment, sir, entertain the belief, that you would give any countenance to a statement calculated to wound the reputation of Gen. Wm. Campbell, and I am persuaded that " *Narrator*," who seems to have undertaken to be your biographer, must have derived his information from some other source, but if from you, must have misunderstood you. That Gen. Campbell acted a conspicuous part in the affair of King's Mountain, all his fellow soldiers with whom I have ever conversed, most unequivocally assert ; and the Legislature of Virginia as an evidence of their approbation of his distinguised gallantry on the occasion, thanked him through the medium of a committee, presented him with a fine horse elegantly caparisoned, a sword and pistols. That youself and Col. Sevier acted your parts with bravery is universally admitted ; but that the whole merit of the affair is to be ascribed to you, to the exclusion of others, is going further than history warrants, or fellow soldiers have asserted.

The great respect I have always entertained for you, from the character my friends gave me of you, and that increased by the small acquaintance I cultivated last summer, forbids my believing that you had any knowledge of this publication previous to its appearance. It will, therefore, give me great pleasure, and no doubt all the friends of Gen. Campbell, if you would correct the misrepresentations of " *Narrator*," and, through the same medium, place my deceased friend's conduct in its proper point of view. I have written to Col. Francis Preston on the subject, and expect from him certificates from persons who served under Gen. Campbell, which I wish not to have occasion to use. I am, Sir, very respectfully,

Your Obedient Servant,

JOHN B. CAMPBELL.

(No. 2.) [Answer to the above letter.]

"*August 14th, 1812.*

"SIR :—By last Saturday's mail I received your favor of the 30th ult. relative to a publication which appeared in the *Reporter* of 25th of last month.

I assure you, Sir, that that publication appeared without my knowledge or approbation, and that I felt as much surprise and regret upon reading it as could have been felt by you or any one else. I knew not, and am still unacquainted with *"Narrator;"* but immediately on seeing that piece I wrote to the two printers in Frankfort, and the editors of the Globe in Danville, expressing my disapprobation of that production, and requesting them not to re-publish it in either of their papers.

Col. William Campbell (for he was not a General at King's Mountain) deserved great credit for the manner in which the action was brought on, and for his conduct through great part of it. He was doubtless a brave man, but the boldest may at some luckless moment be confounded; this, in my opinion, does not detract from his former or subsequent renown. But it is as true as that Heaven and Earth exist, that he was not in the latter part of the action, and that he did apologize to me for it before we left the mountain, and spoke once or twice to me on the subject upon our retreat.

I have rarely mentioned this circumstance, except in confidence, to his friends; among this description was old Col. Preston, and your own father, who had heard something said on the occasion, and conversed with me upon it, about the latter end of the year 1781. I would not for the universe detract from the merits of a brother officer long since in the silent tomb, for whose memory I have ever felt a high respect and esteem, and sincerely regret the appearance of that unguarded production, and would say everything consistent with truth to remove the unpleasant sensations which it may have occasioned. Perhaps you attach more importance to that anonymous publication than it deserves. If, however, you should choose to make any comments upon it, unless they go to impeach my veracity or honor, they shall pass without my notice. But I shall regret it extremely, if you should so notice that unauthorized production, as to compel me to express the foregoing sentiments, or exhibit a document in my hands respecting that delicate subject. I should be glad of an interview with you. Will anything lead you to Frankfort? If, it should, be so good as to drop me a line.

With great respect, I am, Sir, your Obedient Servant,

ISAAC SHELBY.

(No. 3.) [Col. Sevier to Gov. Shelby, Jan. 17th, 1810:]
" It is true, that Col. Campbell was not within one quarter of a mile when the enemy surrendered to yourself and me. Without detracting from the merits of Col. Campbell, there were other officers in the battle of King's Mountain, that merited as much notice from their country as himself.

(No. 4.) [Col. Sevier to Gov. Shelby, Aug. 27th, 1812 :]
" It is well known you were in the heat of the action. I frequently saw you animating your men to victory. At the surrender, you were the first field officer I recollect to have seen. I have no doubt you must

recollect Col. Campbell was some considerable distance from that place, at that time, and that you and myself spoke on that subject the same evening. I perfectly recollect on seeing you at the close of the action, that I swore by —— they had burnt off your hair, for it was much burnt on one side. It is well known by some hundreds in Tennessee, that you were Colonel on that campaign, and that we were the only persons who set on foot the expedition, and had considerable trouble to get Campbell to join us."

————

(No. 5.) [Gen. Thomas Kennedy, of Garrard County, Ky., Nov., 25th, 1822:]

I commanded a company of volunteers in the battle of King's Mountain, on the 7th of October, 1780, and I fought in Maj. McDowell's battalion on the eastwardly quarter of the mountain. I do not recollect seeing Col. Campbell during the action ; he might have been engaged too far off from me. But I well recollect to have seen and heard Col. Shelby, at different times, animating and encouraging the men, before they were compelled to retreat ; and when the enemy charged and drove us rapidly down to the foot of the mountain, I saw Col. Shelby using great exertions to rally the men, and I believe it was owing to his efforts principally, that they were rallied, and turned back upon the enemy, when the firing again commenced most furiously for about ten minutes. The enemy then began to give way in their turn, but continued a scattering fire upon us, until they retreated near to the west end of the mountain, (which was from four to six hundred yards) where they surrendered. I was within sixty to seventy yards of the enemy when they raised the flag, and was close in with them in a minute or two afterwards, and I well recollect to have seen Col. Shelby there one of the first men I met with. I remember to have heard several persons enquire for Col. Campbell before he came up, which was, I think, about 15 minutes after the surrender. I also recollect to have heard it talked of in the army after the action, and for many years after when in conversation with men who were in the battle, that Col. Campbell was not at the surrender for some time after the enemy had laid down their arms."

————

(No. 6.) [Col. John Sawyers, of Knox Co., Tenn., Feb. 16th, 1823, certifies :]

That Isaac Shelby, late Governor of Kentucky, held the command of Colonel at the battle of King's Mountain—that I was a captain in his regiment, and know that he first planned the expedition with John Sevier, who then held a similar commission—that said Shelby went courageously into the action—was the commander who rallied the Sullivan troops when broken—that I saw him, and received directions from him frequently on the mountain, in the heat of the action, and heard him animating his men to victory. He was also amongst the first at the surrender. I saw him and Col. Sevier when the enemy laid down their arms, but did not see Col. Campbell for some minutes afterwards. I also state, that Maj. Evan Shelby, brother of Isaac, and not Isaac Shelby, Sevier, or Campbell, as I have heard that some now state, received the flag and sword. I also state, that from this circumstance I was led to think of Campbell at the time, looked for him amongst the other officers, and do believe that if he had been there I should have seen him ; and that he did not come up for fifteen or twenty minutes after the enemy had laid down their arms, and been placed under guard. I also know, that it was the general talk at the time, and I have frequently since heard it spoken of by men who were in the action, as an indisputable fact, that he was not in the latter part of the action, or at the surrender. I also recollect distinctly to have heard it said amongst the officers before we left the mountain, as well as on the way home, and since, that Campbell himself admitted it, and in a private conversation with Col. Shelby, on the mountain, had said that he could not account for it. I remember to have intended to ask Col. Shelby if this was so, but it has so happened that I have never since named this subject to him, nor he to me.

———

(No. 7.) [James Cooper, of Hawkins Co., Tenn., Feb. 18th, 1823, certifies :]

That in the section of country in which I live, I have heard it generally spoken of by the soldiers who were in the battle of King's Mountain, that Col. Campbell did not act as bravely on that occasion as he did on some others; that it was a well-known fact, that he did not make his appearance at the place of surrender until after the enemy had been taken from their arms, and placed under guard—that this is the way in which I have always heard my neighbors, James Campbell, John Long and several others speak of this matter.

(No. 8.) [The statement of Col. Moses Shelby made upon oath.]

I, Moses Shelby, do state, that I was in the battle against the British and Tories upon King's Mountain, on the 7th day of October, 1780, in Col. Isaac Shelby's regiment. That I received two wounds in that action ; by the last wound, through my thigh near my body, I was rendered unable to walk, or to stand without help, and was assisted down to a branch, some small distance from the foot of the Mountain, at the east end—at which place I saw Col. William Campbell, (our commander) sitting on his black horse. I knew him perfectly, as I was well acquainted with him. This was about the middle of the action, and I do know, that Col. Campbell did not leave that place until the battle was over, or until the firing had ceased. All this is true, and within my own knowledge. Given under my hand at New Madrid, this 2d day of November, A. D. 1822.   MOSES SHELBY.

37

(No. 9.) [Henry Blevins, of Hawkins Co., East Tenn., Feb. 18th, 1823, certifies :]

That I was a private in Capt. Elliott's company, in Shelby's regiment, at King's Mountain—I was not in the action, but in the rear guard with the baggage—I know, however, that it was the general talk in the army on the next day, that Col. Campbell was not in the action, after they were first beaten back down the mountain, and that he himself admitted it, and said that he could not tell how it happened—I recollect to have heard him told of it once, by Gen. Sevier. The way in which this took place was this—there were about thirty Tories condemned to be hanged; nine only were executed. They were executed three at a time, near to Sevier's tent; while it was going on, Campbell came up, and demanded in an angry manner, why they did not hang all these damned rascals at once? Sevier laughed and replied, "Why, Colonel, if we had all been as much in earnest in the action, I think we should have killed more, and had fewer of them to hang." I also heard it thrown up to him by two men who were wounded, William Cox and Moses Shelby. I heard Sevier say, at different times afterwards, that if he had acted as Campbell did in the action, he would not have blamed his men to have killed him. It has been the general talk amongst those whom I have heard speak on this subject at different times since, that Campbell did not act with his usual bravery on that occasion.

(No. 10.) [John Long, of Hawkins Co., Tenn., Feb. 19th, 1823, certifies:]

That I was a soldier in Shelby's regiment at the battle of King's Mountain, that I know that Col. Shelby went bravely into the action, and that it was his influence that rallied our troops when broken —that I saw him at the surrender, and know that he first stopped the firing on the enemy, declaring that as they had surrendered, they ought not to be fired on, which some were disposed to do, who were crying out "*Buford's play,*" wishing to retaliate for their conduct on a former occasion. I also state, that I did not see Col. Campbell either in the latter part of the action nor at the surrender, and that it was the common talk in the army, and among the men coming home, and frequently since, that he was in neither. I also recollect to have heard it laughed about afterwards, that Col. Sevier had told Campbell that if we all had been as brave in the action as about the hanging of the Tories, that we should not have had so many of them to hang. I have heard it said ever since by those who were in the action, that Campbell was not in the latter part of the action, and had not acted as bravely on that day as it is said he had done on other occasions.

(No. 11.) [Maj. William Delaney, of Sullivan Co., Tenn., Feb. 21st, 1823, certifies:]

That I was an Orderly Sergeant in the action of King's Mountain —that I know that Isaac Shelby distinguished himself on that occasion, and that it was generally said by those whom I heard speak of it at the time, that he was entitled to more credit than any other officer at the Mountain—that I was with him, and rode with him, while placing a guard round the enemy after the surrender—that I did not see Col. Campbell in the latter part of the action, nor at the surrender, for some minutes afterwards, and that I heard this spoken of at the time, as well as since. It is also my belief, from what I understood at the time, (though I did not see it myself) that it was Maj. Evan Shelby, and neither of the four Colonels, that received the sword from the British officer in command."   *   *   *   *   *   *

(No. 12.) [Col. John Sharp, of Sullivan Co., Tenn., Feb. 21st, 1823, certifies:]

That I was an Ensign in Capt. Pembertons' company, in the battle of King's Mountain, and that I was in the *front line* when the enemy surrendered—that Col. Shelby was the first man I heard order the enemy to lay down their arms, after they began to cry for quarters; he damned them, if they wanted quarters, why they did not lay down their arms. I also state, that I did not see Col. Campbell until some minutes afterwards, though I never heard him charged with cowardice on that account, and do not pretend to say he did not do his duty. All I can say is, that I did not see him at that time.

(No. 13.) [George Morrison, of Sullivan Co., Tenn., Feb. 20th, 1823, certifies :]

That I have often heard my father, Peter Morrison and my father-in-law Jonathan Wood, who were both in the battle of King's Mountain, but since dead, state, that Col. Campbell was not in the latter part of the action, nor at the surrender for some time after the enemy had laid down their arms.

(No. 14.) [Jacob Isely, of Sullivan Co.,Tenn., Feb. 19th, 1823, certifies :]

That though I was not in the action of King's Mountain, I have ever since lived in the neighborhood of a number of men who were there, and have always heard it said by them, that Col. Campbell was not in the latter part of the battle—that he went bravely into the action, but after the men were beaten back, had staid down at a branch with the wounded men, until the firing had ceased. I also state, that I have often heard old Martin Roler, who was in the action, laugh about what Sevier had said to Campbell, when Campbell wanted all the Tories hung, that if we had all been as brave in the action, there would have been fewer to hang. Moses Shelby and John Fagon, two of the men who were wounded, often stated after their return in my presence, and that of many others, that they saw Col. Campbell at the branch from the middle of the action until after the surrender. I have also heard Thomas Elliott and Martin Roler both say often, that Moses Shelby had stated it to his face.

(No. 14.) [William King, Esq., of Sullivan Co., Tenn., Feb. 21st, 1823, certifies :]

That I have been a resident in this County for about forty years past—that though I was not in the battle of King's Mountain, yet I have very often in early times heard our men who were there, converse on this subject, and state, that Col. Campbell was not in the latter part of the action nor at the surrender to receive the sword from the British Commandant. I also declare that I never heard it either from Col. Shelby or from any of his family connections.

(No. 15.) [Jacob Bealer, of Sullivan Co., Tenn., Feb. 23d, 1823, certifies :]

That I was in Capt. Pemberton's company, and was amongst the very first at the place of surrender—that when the enemy cried out for quarters, I heard Col. Shelby curse them, and ask, if they wanted quarters, why did they not lay down their arms. The commander asked for our general, and gave his sword first to Maj. Evan Shelby, who kept it until Col. Campbell came up, which was twenty minutes, and I think longer, afterwards. From the discourse which I heard between Col. Shelby and the British officer, I know that Campbell was not there, and that it was that length of time before he came up.

(No. 16.) [Joseph Bealer certifies Feb. 23d, 1823 :]

That I was at the surrender with my brother (Jacob Bealer) at his side, and saw and heard what he has stated in the above certificate, and know them to be true, and have always spoken of them, and heard them spoken of by those who were there, in this way.

(No. 17.) [John Peters, of Sullivan Co., Tenn., Feb. 23d, 1823, certifies :]

That I was in Capt. Pemberton's company with Jacob and Joseph Bealer, and amongst the first at the surrender—that I know of my own knowledge, that what Jacob Bealer has stated in his certificate, is true—that the enemy surrendered, and there was a ring made round them fifteen or twenty minutes before I looked up and saw Col. Campbell coming, with two or three others, down the mountain—this is what I have always heard, and never heard it contradicted.

(No. 18.) [Major Christopher Taylor, of Washington Co., Tenn., Feb. 25th, 1823, certifies:]

That I was a Captain in the battle of King's Mountain, and saw Col. Campbell twice in the heat of the action, before we were last beaten down the mountain—but that I did not see him in the latter part of the action, or at the surrender for some minutes afterwards. After the enemy were placed in a ring, and a guard four men deep placed around them, I saw him come up close to the place where I stood, and an opening was made for him to go amongst them—before this, one of the Shelby's, and I think Evan, had received the flag, the first one having heen shot down, and I saw him ride round, or nearly round, the enemy, telling our men that they had given up, and endeavor in that way to stop the firing. I have always believed that Colonels Shelby and Sevier acted with distinguished bravery on that occasion.

————

(No. 19.) [Rev. Felix Earnest, of Green Co., Tenn., Feb. 28th, 1823, certifies:]

That I was in Sevier's regiment, Capt. William's company, at the battle of King's Mountain—that I was at the surrender, and saw the enemy stacking their arms, and a guard placed around them, but that I did not see Col. Campbell at the place of surrender, for some minutes afterwards.

————

(No. 20.) [William Willoughby, of Lincoln Co., Ky., March 17th, 1823, certifies:]

That I was a Lieutenant in Capt. Beattie's company, and Col. Campbell's regiment, in the battle of King's Mountain. It has always been my opinion, that Col. Isaac Shelby and Col. John Sevier deserved as much honor from their country on that occasion as any other officers on the mountain—that I saw Col. Shelby often animating our men during the action. I did not see Col. Campbell after the commencement of the action, nor at the surrender, until the enemy were in the act of stacking their arms. I have always understood, that Col. Shelby received the sword from the British commander; and I also state (although I don't know it of my own knowledge) that it was a report thirty or forty years ago, that Col. Campbell was not present at the surrender, to receive the sword from the British commander.

————

(No. 21.) [Robert Elder, April 2d, 1823, certifies:]

That I was a volunteer of the regiment commanded by Col. William Campbell, in the action, fought upon King's Mountain, on the seventh day of October, in the year 1780, and do hereby declare, that I never saw Col. Campbell on the field of battle after the first onset of the action, until the surrender of the enemy. I also declare, that I often saw Col. Isaac Shelby endeavoring to animate our men, and particularly at the time of the battle when the enemy charged our lines, and drove us down the mountain, from one hundred and fifty to two hundred yards, or upwards. I both saw and heard Col. Shelby make great exertions to rally our men, which he finally effected, and turned them back upon the enemy, and drove them in their turn until they surrendered.

(No. 22.) [John McCulloch, of Washington Co., Va., certifies:]
That though I was applied to by the friends of the late Col. Campbell, to know what I could state in relation to the battle of King's Mountain, I never did subscribe to the certificate which I am told has been published in my name; nor have I ever seen it, either in writing or in print, and cannot therefore say whether it states the truth or not. I saw Col. Campbell at the enemy's markee, how far it was from there to the place of the surrender, or whether the enemy or some of them might not then be surrendering, I cannot state.

(No. 23.)   [Gen'l. James Winchester, of Tennessee, in a letter to
Thomas Smith, Esq., dated February last, says, in relation to
Mr. Preston's, publication:]
"I perfectly recollect in the year 1785, when I first came to this country, that a number of respectable men, among whom were the Bledsoes, well acquainted with the affair of King's Mountain, did not hesitate to say, that Sevier and Shelby had a fair claim to the honors of that day; that Campbell was some distance from the place of action, &c."

REJOINDERS TO GOVERNOR SHELBY.

The papers properly coming under this head are too lengthy for insertion. The first, by Wm. C. Preston, Colonel Campbell's grandson, was addressed, June twentieth, 1813, to the Editor of the *Kentucky Reporter*, in vindication of his ancestor from the charge of cowardice at King's Mountain, made in that paper by "*Narrator.*" Mr. Preston again came forward in defence of Colonel Campbell, repelling the same charge made in Governor Shelby's letters to Governor Sevier, adducing several statements of King's Mountain survivors, disproving the accusation; and citing Governor Shelby's letter of October, 1780, to Colonel Arthur Campbell, and the official report of the battle, signed by Shelby, as conflicting with his recent letters to Governor Sevier, and animadverting upon the motives which could have prompted Governor Shelby to engage in the work of detracting from the merits of the dead.

On the appearance of Governor Shelby's pamphlet publication, in 1823, Wm. C. Preston replied, May tenth, in that year, in the Columbia, S. C. *Telescope*, making a manly defence. His father, General

Francis Preston, at the same time, made a reply in the Abingdon, Va., *Gazette*, bringing forward an explanatory certificate of John McCulloch, stating, in effect, that he had forgotten having made his first certificate when he was induced to give one to Governor Shelby's agent, denying that he had ever made any statement. He also introduced Colonel Matthew Willoughby's affidavit, stating that he was in Campbell's regiment, on the King's Mountain campaign, and he never heard a word uttered at that time derogatory of Colonel Campbell's "great bravery and good conduct" in the battle ; adding that "the statement of Moses Shelby would not, perhaps, be credited, from the character he bore about the time and after the battle, as he, with others, was engaged in plundering, in the Carolinas, both Whigs and Tories, and running the property so plundered to this side of the mountains."

General John Campbell, then a member of the Virginia Council of State, made a vigorous reply to Governor Shelby, in the Richmond *Enquirer*, June twenty-fourth, 1823, discussing the points in controversy, refuting the charge of cowardice, and Shelby's error in supposing he saw Colonel Campbell, during the heat of the battle, two hundred yards away, sitting on his bald-faced black horse—citing the fact *that it was Campbell's servant, John Broddy, who rode the black horse on that occasion.*

The principal certificates adduced by the Messrs. Preston, and General John Campbell, follow in their order :

Col. Wm. Edmondson, the Major of Campbell's regiment, in his certificate, in 1813, states : Campbell was made the chief commander of the King's Mountain Expedition, not by any pre-concert, or as a matter of conciliation towards the older Colonels, but by a caucus of field officers ; and, as well as he could recollect, the whole of the suffrages were given to Colonel Campbell. It was generally understood after the battle, that Colonel Campbell had performed his duty with great judgment and determined bravery. I was acquainted with Colonel Campbell for a number of years, and always found him, and ever believed him, to be a man of dauntless intrepidity.

David Beattie, of Campbell's men, in 1813, states : I saw Col. Campbell, in the hottest of the engagement, riding along the lines, encouraging and exhorting the men, and directly under the enemy's fire. He continually rode along the lines, marshalling and leading on the men until his horse became fatigued, when he dismounted, and commanded on foot until the close of the action. When the flag was raised, the British surviving commander and suite came near to the spot where I and several others were standing, and inquired—"where is your commander ?" Either I, or one of those standing with me, pointed to Col. Campbell, and observed that he was our commander ; when the British officer immediately advanced towards him, holding his sword by the point, and delivered it to him. After the engagement, I heard many of the men express their admiration of the courage of Col. Campbell. I saw him repeatedly during the battle in those places where it raged most violently.

James Crow, of the Virginia regiment, states, in 1813: When charged, we ran down the mountain a small distance, not more than twenty or thirty paces. I saw Col. Campbell not far from us. As the enemy turned we turned.   *   *   *   When the British flag was raised, I was in less than the length of my gun of Col. Campbell, when we closed round the enemy. DePeyster, the British commander, was sitting on a grey beast, and addressed Col. Campbell, referring to the firing after the flag was raised: "Col. Campbell, it was damned unfair," and repeated the words a second time. The Colonel made him no reply, but ordered him to dismount.   *   *   *

Maj. James Snodgrass, of Campbell's men, states: I frequently saw Col. Campbell, during the engagement, in the most dangerous and exposed situations, and am convinced that he could not have left the lines for any length of time. I saw him immediately after the surrender, and before the enemy had entirely ceased firing, coming from amongst the enemy's troops, with several swords in his hands.

Capt. James Keys, of Campbell's regiment, states: When the enemy raised a flag, and called for quarter, I heard a British officer inquire for Col. Campbell, who being pointed out to him, he advanced and tendered his sword, which Col. Campbell declined. The firing had not yet ceased, and I heard the British officer remonstrate with Col. Campbell against the conduct of his soldiers.

John McCulloch, of Campbell's men, in 1813, states: I did not see Col. Campbell at the commencement of the action; but after the regiment had driven the enemy, and had reached the top of the mountain, I recollect perfectly to have seen him, and the spot where he was—I saw him nigh one of the enemy's markees on foot, his horse having given out—he was pressing on with all the speed he could towards the enemy —a few minutes before their surrender.

Gen. George Rutledge, of Shelby's regiment, in 1813, states: I saw Col. Campbell at the commencement of the engagement, and then towards the last of the action, when we had driven the British into small bounds, and surrounded them—when Campbell's and Shelby's regiments had got intermixed. I well recollect to have seen Campbell acting with distinguished bravery. He was on horseback, stripped to his shirt sleeves, and his shirt collar open. He was very hoarse. The enemy raised the flag—it disappeared, when it was instantly raised again. They did not yet cease firing. Campbell rushed through amongst us, calling out—"cease firing" waving his sword downwards—"for God's sake, cease firing!" He met DePeyster with the flag. I saw

DePeyster present the handle of his sword to Campbell, and he received it. I saw several men fall on both sides, after the flag was raised.

Thomas Jefferson writes from Monticello, to Gen. Francis Preston, November tenth, 1822: Your favor gives me the first information I had ever received, that the laurels which Col. Campbell so honorably won in the battle of King's Mountain had ever been brought into question by any one. To him has ever been ascribed so much of the success of that brilliant action as the valor and conduct of an able commander might justly claim. * * * I remember well the deep and grateful impression made on the mind of every one by that memorable victory. It was the joyful annunciation of that turn of the tide of success which terminated the Revolutionary war with the seal of our independence. The slighting expression complained of, as hazarded by the venerable Shelby, might seem inexcusable in a younger man ; but he was then old, and I can assure you, dear sir, from mortifying experience, that the lapses of memory, and the forgetfulness incident to old age, are innocent subjects of compassion more than of blame. The descendents of Col. Campbell may rest their heads quietly on the pillow of his renown. History has consecrated, and will forever preserve it in the faithful annals of a grateful country.*

Henry Dickenson, of Campbell's regiment, May, 1823, states: The enemy charged upon us with their bayonets, and we retreated down the mountain, when I saw Col. Campbell on foot pursuing his men in a quick gait, calling upon them to halt, which they soon did, and came back, and he with them began to fight again. We advanced within thirty or forty yards of the enemy, who made a firm stand for some time ; but after awhile broke and retreated upon the mountain where they halted again a few minutes ; but on our advancing and firing, they continued their retreat to the wagons, and halted behind them, which were on the summit of the mountain, from which we soon drove them down to the end of the mountain, where I suppose they were met by the troops sent around to that quarter, for it was immediately called out by some men just before me, that the enemy had raised the flag. I stepped back a few paces, and called to Col. Campbell, that the enemy had raised the flag. Frequently during the battle I saw him exposed. He directed me to go with him. We went to the line of surrender, where we met the British officers, with their swords in their hands, holding them about the middle, with the hilt down, and Col. Campbell put his hand out to receive them, when the officers drew back, apparently as if they did not intend to deliver the swords to him—supposing, as I presume, from his dress, that he was not the commander, as he had no coat on, and his collar was open. Seeing his countenance alter, I was

---

* The original of this letter is preserved by Robert M. Hughes, Esq., Norfolk, Va.

apprehensive he would use some violence, which they might return. I took my gun from my shoulder, at the same time mentioning that this was our commander. The officers then bowed to Col. Campbell, and delivered their swords to him, which he placed under his arm, as well as I remember, and turned around, directing them to follow him, which they did. I never heard any charge or insinuation of Campbell's want of bravery, or leaving his men during the action, until the unfortunate controversy which I see in the papers, and which I lament, as I do know Campbell was a brave man, having seen him frequently in the battle, rallying his men on the retreat, and encouraging and urging them on the advance, sometimes before them, and sometimes amongst them. I particularly noticed Campbell, as he was our commander, and I was well acquainted with him. Col. Shelby must be mistaken—I hope unintentionably so, in stating that he saw Col. Campbell, when our troops retreated down the mountain, two hundred yards from them, for at that time I saw Col Campbell on foot exerting himself to rally the men. I saw Samuel Newell, a little before we got to the wagons, on horse-back, his thigh very bloody from the wound he had received, encouraging the men to advance—I thought him a brave soldier. He was a man of the strictest veracity, and of very correct deportment. I was not much acquainted with Moses Shelby; he appeared to be a loose, rattling character.*

John Craig, of Campbell's men, states: As we dismounted near the foot of the mountain, I saw Col. Campbell riding along the line, to take the head, and as he passed he said, "Here they are, my brave boys, *shout like hell, and fight like devils!*" He was then in advance of his men. We obeyed his orders, and rushed rapidly up the mountain. We were driven down—rallied, returned, and drove the enemy. They hoisted their flags in token of surrender. Here I saw Col. Campbell on foot, in his shirt sleeves, receive the sword from the surviving and commanding officer of the British army. After the victory was complete, and the sword delivered to Campbell, I remember he being present, as well as sundry other officers and men, they all joined in three loud cheers. I was with Campbell at Whitzell's Mills, where we were much cut to pieces, but he acted with his usual courage.†

Col. John Witherspoon, of Cleveland's regiment, states: When the battle commenced, I saw Col. Campbell engaged bravely animating his men, and watching and defending every point that seemed necessary.

* Judge Peter Johnston certifies to the veracity and integrity of Henry Dickenson, clerk of Russell County court, and has formerly heard him relate the particulars of the action, corresponding precisely with those here detailed.

† Craig's relation of binding up Lieut. Edmonson's wound is omitted. In a subsequent statement, Mr. Craig adds, that the reason the Americans left King's Mountain in such haste was, that a report came that Tarleton was in pursuit, and would rescue the prisoners.

* * When we were driven down the hill, I saw Col. Campbell, with other officers, animating and rallying his men; and I saw him again when the enemy surrendered; he was then attending, with the rest of the officers, to the security of the prisoners.

Col. Benjamin Sharp, of Campbell's men, states: During the heat of the action, I saw Col. Campbell three times, ride backwards and forwards in advance of our lines, in the space between us and the enemy, with his sword in his hand, and, as well as I could understand him, exclaimed, "Boys, remember your liberty!"

William Edmondson, of Campbell's regiment, states: Whilst giving way before the bayonet, Col. Campbell was gallantly rallying the men; at the foot of the mountain he brought them to order, and they again advanced upon the enemy. They were again driven back a small distance, and rallied a second, and then a third time—the last time we succeeded.

Joseph Phillips of Cleveland's men, states: Campbell's regiment acted instantly after the advanced guard flanked off, and was fighting for some considerable time before Cleveland's command could render him any aid. That part of the mountain which Campbell's men were compelled to ascend, was the most craggy, rough, steep and difficult part of it. His men made the attack under a heavy fire of the enemy. Cleveland's command were compelled to ride along the foot of the mountain, three or four hundred yards before they dismounted, and pressed up towards the enemy. The surrender commenced as soon as they reached the top. Encamped that night on the battle ground, marching the next day at ten or twelve o'clock, Col. Campbell remaining behind to bury the dead, joining the army that night.

Col. David Campbell, of the Virginia regiment, states: I saw Col. William Campbell on horseback at the time the battle commenced, riding along the lines, encouraging the men. When driven down the mountain, Major Edmondson endeavored to rally the men; but did not succeed, until Col. Campbell came along the lines, calling to the men to "halt, and return, my brave fellows, and you will drive the enemy immediately;" and, it appeared, as soon as they heard his voice they halted, returned, renewed the attack, and drove the enemy along the mountain, from behind rocks, and their wagons, until Ferguson was slain, and they surrendered. I saw Col. Campbell there, on foot, engaged in securing the prisoners. About this time, I observed Capt. DePeyster inquire for the commanding officer. Col. Campbell, who was but a little distance from him, was pointed out to him; he stepped forward, and delivered his sword. I was not more than twenty feet from DePeyster.

Gen. William Russell, Lieutenant, commanding Neal's company, of Campbell's regiment, states: I saw Col. Campbell go into the action on horse-back. We were forced back, but rallied and engaged again.

About half way between the place where we ascended the mountain and the enemy's wagons, I saw Col. Campbell in his shirt sleeves passing our line, encouraging the men in a loud and animating tone of voice. When the enemy were surrendering, I saw him coming from amongst them with two swords in his hand. I was intimately acquainted with him.

William Snodgrass, of Campbell's men, after giving an account how he and Edward Smith were sent by Col. Campbell, early on the morning after the battle to meet and turn the footmen up Broad river, and how the dead were buried, states : On the top of the mountain, there were but a few steps between us and the enemy in the battle. Capt. DePeyster, the senior British officer, after Ferguson fell, surrendered his sword to Col. Campbell. Our men were sent home as soon as we were out of the reach of Tarleton's Light Horse.

Col. Samuel Newell, of the Virginia men, in April, 1823, states : Was wounded in the attack on the guard—the first of the fighting. As I turned back, after being wounded, Col. Campbell passed me engaged in forming his regiment. I got a horse and rode back to the lines. The regiment advanced—was charged by the British with the bayonet, and broke—retreating farther than was necessary, across the intervening valley, to the top of the next rise, where I met them. I saw Col. Campbell and Maj. Edmondson about half the distance between their own men and the enemy, calling on their men to halt, which they did, and advanced a second time to the charge. They had two partial checks afterwards— only partial, as the men learned not to dread the bayonets as at first. The last charge the regiment made was the longest and warmest—lasting twenty minutes, as stated by the British Surgeon who held his watch. I do not believe the regiment was more than thirty feet* from the British line. In the very midst of this storm, I saw Col. Campbell at the head of his regiment, and so much advanced in front as to be in danger from the fire of his own men. As well as I can recollect, his encouraging words were—"Come on—come on, my brave fellows, another gun— another gun will do it--d--n them, we must have them out of this." This I saw, and this I heard. Col. Campbell was at this time on foot, his horse having given out.

Visited Maj. Lewis, his brothers, and Capt. Smith, all of Cleveland regiment, and all wounded, when billeted in Burke County ; when in a conversation on the battle, Maj. Lewis said : "Boys, I believe you all did your duty, and deserve well for it, but let me tell you, had it not been for Campbell and his Virginians, I'll be d—d if Ferguson would not have been on that mountain yet, had he chosen to stay there."

In May following, Col. Newell further states : I saw Col. Campbell

---

* Gov. Campbell, adds, in explanation, that this is a slip of the pen—it should be yards.

leading his men the moment the British broke; and what infatuation could then induce Col. Campbell to turn his back, and run from his own victorious troops, and a defeated enemy? It is inconceivable—incredible —impossible! I have ever believed that not more than one-half of our regiment, that is two hundred, were in the battle—the rest being left behind. Thirty-five of the killed and wounded were of our regiment, thirteen of whom were commissioned officers; and no regiment or corps gained the summit of the hill until the Virginia regiment opened the way for them. Col. Shelby and his brother state, that they knew Col. Campbell, [whom they thought they saw in the distance, shirking duty and danger] by his black bald-faced horse. The fact is, Col. Campbell *did not ride a black bald-faced horse that day;* but *a pretty large bay horse—not bald-faced,* that was in thin order, and broken down by previous fatigue, giving out early in the action. At the moment alluded to, as the time of Col. Campbell's [supposed] delinquency, he was not on horse-back, but on his feet, encouraging and animating his men to victory, uttering words already stated. *

Maj. James Snodgrass, of Campbell's men, in April, 1823, states: Frequently saw Col. Campbell during the engagement in the most dangerous and exposed situations, part of the time on horse-back, and part of the time on foot. *The horse which Col. Campbell rode, when this affiant saw him, was a bay.* Having seen Col. Campbell frequently during the action, and in different positions, I am convinced that he could not have left the lines for any length of time. I saw him immediately after the surrender, and before the firing had entirely ceased, coming from amongst the enemy, with several swords in his hands, and some of the British officers following him, within a few steps of this affiant. At that time, he never heard any intimation that Col. Campbell did not perform his duty gallantly at King's Mountain, or anywhere else. Instead of being considered cowardly, he was always thought to be too rash. It was the report of the country, after King's Mountain battle, that Moses Shelby was engaged in plundering indiscriminately both Tories and Whigs, and kept very bad company.

Col. Thomas Maxwell, of Shelby's regiment, states: When the attack was made on the main picket guard, *I saw Col. Campbell on a bay horse,* in his shirt sleeves. He had principally rode this horse on the march. I knew both of his horses well. The action commenced at the most eastern end of the spur of the mountain where Campbell commanded. Campbell's and Shelby's men contended with the British regulars directed in person by Ferguson, for some time before Cleveland and Sevier's men got into action. Capt. Shelby's company, to which I

---

* In a third statement, August 4th, 1823, Col. Newell gives an account of the officers of Campbell's regiment, naming the killed and wounded, so far as he could do so—which facts have been incorporated into the text of this work.

belonged, was twice repulsed by the British regulars; were rallied, and renewed the fight, driving the enemy to the top of the mountain, where we were joined by Col. Campbell's main body, and forced our foes along the summit to their wagons and tents. By this time Cleveland's and Sevier's columns were in action. About three minutes after Furguson was killed, I saw Col. Campbell—he was then on foot. The enemy then very quickly hoisted their first flag, and commenced surrendering in every direction.

Andrew Evins, of Campbell's men in May, 1823, states: I saw Col. Campbell at the close of the battle, and at the surrender; for when I went to fire at the enemy, Campbell threw up my gun, and said, "Evins, for God's sake don't shoot—it is murder to kill them now, for they have raised the flag ;" and so passed on round the prisoners, and was on foot. *He rode a bay horse in the battle ; but his horse gave out, and he took it on foot.*

Benjamin White, of the Virginia regiment, in May, 1823, states : *Col. Campbell rode a bay horse.* I saw him receive the sword from the British Captain—I think his name was DePeyster, and heard Col. Campbell order the flag to be received, and I believe it was Evan Shelby that received it. I saw Col. Campbell very frequently during the whole action encouraging his men, and feel confident he was not absent from his men one moment during the whole battle. I was in the battles of Point Pleasant, Princeton, Brandywine, Germantown, and others, and in all these battles I never saw a braver man than Col. Wm. Campbell, according to my judgment.

William Moore, of Campbell's men, in June, 1823, states : Just before the action commenced, *Col. Campbell came riding along the lines, on a bay or sorrel horse*, as well as I remember—*it was not his black horse*, I am confident—and told us to prime our guns afresh, and prepare for action. We commenced the action, and I saw him on *the same horse* in his shirt sleeves, with I think, a handkerchief tied about his head. At the close of the action—when I was just shot down, having my thigh broken—I saw him waving his sword downward, and calling to his men to cease firing, that the enemy had surrendered. He was still in his shirt sleeves. I not only saw him act bravely on that day, but also two or three weeks previously with the Tories on New river.

Israel Hayter, of Campbell's regiment, in November, 1822, and June, 1823, states: From the commencement of the battle until near its close, when he was wounded, and the enemy had hoisted one white flag, he saw Col. Campbell frequently ; and he was during the whole time busily engaged in encouraging his men, and leading them on up the mountain. His regiment twice gave way, and retreated some distance. Col. Campbell rallied them each time, and brought them again into action in the most gallant manner ; and his whole conduct, as far as affiant saw or heard, was that of a brave and good officer. Affiant further well recollects, that *Col. Campbell rode a bay horse in the action, and that his servant rode a black horse or a dark brown.*

Capt. James Keys, of Campbell's men, in June, 1823, states: When the action was about to commence, he saw Col. Campbell give his rifle to his servant man, who, as well as this affiant recollects, *was then on a black horse*; and he well recollects, that *Col. Campbell rode a bay horse in the action.*

William Anderson, of Campbell's regiment; Joseph Phillips, of Cleveland's men; Jacob Norris, James Pearce, and Gideon Harrison, of Sevier's regiment, also furnished statements that it was *his bay horse —not his bald-faced black*—that Col. Campbell rode in the earlier part of the action.

KING'S MOUNTAIN BALLADS.

FERGUSON'S DEFEAT—1780. *

Come all you good people, I pray you draw near,
A tragical story you quickly shall hear
Of Whigs and of Tories, how they bred a great strife,
When they chased old Ferguson out of his life.

Brave Colonel Williams from Hillsboro' came,
The South Carolinians flocked to him amain,
Four hundred and fifty, a jolly brisk crew,
After old Ferguson we then did pursue.

We march'd to the Cowpens—brave Campbell was there,
And Shelby, and Cleveland, and Colonel Sevier,
Taking the lead of their bold mountaineers,
Brave Indian fighters, devoid of all fears.

They were men of renown—like lions so bold,
Like lions undaunted, ne'er to be controll'd,
They were bent on the game they had in their eye,
Determined to take it—to conquer or die.

We march'd from the Cowpens that very same night,
Sometimes we were wrong—sometimes we were right,
Our heart's being run in true Liberty's mold,
We regarded not hunger, wet, weary nor cold.

---

* Snatches of this rude ballad have, from time to time, been published. It has been preserved in its entirety by Dr. J. H. Logan, who found it among the old papers of Robert Long, a Revolutionary soldier, of Laurens County, South Carolina. The writer's name is not known.

Early next morning we came to the ford,
Cherokee was its name—and "*Buford*" * the word,
We march'd thro' the river, with courage so free,
Expecting the foemen we might quickly see.

Like eagles a hungry in search of their prey,
We chas'd the old fox the best part of the day,
At length on King's Mountain the old rogue we found,
And we, like bold heroes, his camp did surround.

The drums they did beat, and the guns they did rattle,
Our enemies stood us a very smart battle,
Like lightning the flashes, like thunder the noise,
Such was the onset of our bold mountain boys.

The battle did last the best part of an hour,
The guns they did roar—the bullets did shower,
With an oath in our hearts to conquer the field,
We rush'd on the Tories—resolv'd they should yield.

We laid old Ferguson dead on the ground,
Four hundred and fifty dead Tories lay round—
Making a large escort, if not quite so wise,
To guide him to his chosen abode in the skies.

Brave Colonel Williams, and twenty-five more
Of our brave heroes lay roll'd in their gore,
With sorrow their bodies we laid in the clay,
In hopes that to heaven their souls took their way.

We shouted the victory that we did obtain,
Our voices were heard seven miles on the plain,
Liberty shall stand—and the Tories shall fall,
Here's an end to my song, so God bless you all !

KING'S MOUNTAIN—1780.†

'Twas on a pleasant mountain the Tory heathens lay,
With a doughty Major at their head, one Ferguson, they say,
Cornwallis had detach'd him a thieving for to go,
And catch the Carolina men, or lay the Rebels low,
The scamp had rang'd the country in search of Royal aid,
And with his owls perch'd on high, he taught them all his trade.

But, ah ! that fatal morning, when Shelby brave drew near,
'Tis certainly a warning that Government should hear,

---

* "Buford" was the countersign that day.

† This ballad, written shortly after the action, was published on a small sheet the following year, and is included in Frank Moore's *Songs and Ballads of the American
Revolution*

And Campbell brave, and Cleveland, and Colonel John Sevier,
Each with a band of gallant men to Ferguson appear.

Just as the sun was setting behind the western hills,
Just then our trusty rifles sent a dose of leaden pills;
Up—up the steep together brave Williams led his troop,
And join'd by Winston, bold and true, disturb'd the Tory coop.

The Royal slaves—the Royal owls, flew high on every hand,
But soon they settled—gave a howl, and quarter'd to Cleveland;
I would not tell the number of Tories slain that day,
But surely it is certain that none did run away.

For all that were a living were happy to give up,
So let us make thanksgiving, and pass the bright tin cup;
To all our brave regiment, let's toast 'em for their health,
And may our glorious country have joy, and peace, and wealth.

SUPPOSED LOYALIST SONG.—By Gen. J. W. DePeyster.

They caught us on a mountain bald, 'twas no place for a stand,
For woods and thickets, dense and close, the summit did command,
But those who led us on that day, of 'Crackers' had no fear,
And when we charg'd the varments ran—did quickly disappear.

But vain was pluck, and vain each charge, for from each tree there
A deadly rifle bullet, and a little spurt of flame;   [came,
The men who fired we could not see—they pick'd us off like game,
To call such work fair fighting seems a misuse of the name.

So ev'ry shot told one by one, till of the reg'lar few,
Most lay stark dead, just where they fell, like beasts in a battue,
Then the militia cried 'enough,' and loud for quarter bawl'd,
And huddled in a bunch, and whipp'd, upon that mountain bald.

Alas! alas! our Gen'ral fell, quite early in the fight,
Eight bullets in him—each enough to kill a man outright,
Our second he got plump'd also, and then the game was up,
When fell the 'Bull-dog' Ferguson, and next the Bull-dog's pup.

D—n 'em, we kill'd as many ' Rebs' as they had kill'd of us.
But then as pris'ners we were bound, some suffer'd ten times worse,
And some had better far been shot than stripp'd, starv'd, and froze,
And see those hung, our comrades dear, a struttin' in their clothes.

Two interesting King's Mountain ballads, written by modern American poets, have appeared in *Harper's Magazine*—one by William Gilmore Simms, in October, 1860; the other by Paul H. Hayne, in November, 1880.

THE END.

.

INDEX.

39